History of the Town of Middleboro, Massachusetts

TOWN HALL, HIGH SCHOOL BUILDING, AND SOLDIERS' MONUMENT

HISTORY OF THE TOWN OF MIDDLEBORO MASSACHUSETTS

BY

THOMAS WESTON, A. M.
OF THE SUFFOLK BAR

BOSTON AND NEW YORK
HOUGHTON, MIFFLIN AND COMPANY
The Riverside Press, Cambridge
1906

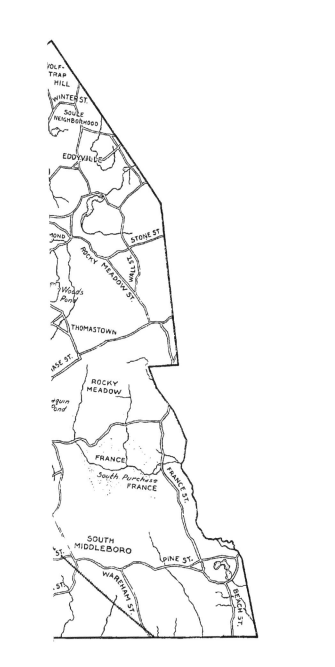

MAP OF MIDDLEBORO IN 1853

HISTORY OF THE
TOWN OF MIDDLEBORO

PREFACE

This volume should have been written fifty years ago, during the lifetime of many men who were familiar with the early history and traditions of the town, which they had learned from older men with whom they had conversed in their younger days, who, in turn, had learned these stories from the early settlers. These men were Wilkes Wood, Zachariah Eddy, his son Samuel Eddy, Colonel Thomas Weston, Alfred Wood, and others. Wilkes Wood delivered an historic address in 1815; Zachariah Eddy wrote the history of the First Church; Samuel Eddy gathered many important facts not before recorded; Colonel Weston was especially familiar with the genealogy and traditions of the settlers, and John Bennett left a number of valuable papers relating to their conveyances of land; but when these men passed away, much of the early history which might have been preserved was lost forever. General Ebenezer W. Peirce, who was interested in the military affairs of the town and the early history of Lakeville, wrote an account of Middleboro and Lakeville for the "History of Plymouth County," a genealogy of the Peirce family, and many articles which were published in the Middleboro "Gazette."

We have transcribed what could be obtained relating to the early history from the records of Plymouth Colony and the Massachusetts Archives; but it is unfortunate that in King Philip's War the records of the town and many ancient documents were burned. There have been kept, however, many of the records of different purchases from the Indians, the original or early copies now being in the possession of the town clerk.

The traditions here given have come down uniformly from father to son through generations, so that they may be regarded as trustworthy and correct statements of facts. Many of the incidents were told to the author in his boyhood by those men before mentioned. For the account of Judge Oliver and the various stories connected with his life, the author is largely indebted to his father, who learned them from Mrs. Mary Norcutt, Judge Oliver's housekeeper. Many years ago, Granville T. Sproat published the same in the Middleboro "Gazette." Family genealogies have given more or less information concerning some of the individuals whose lives are recorded in the following pages.

We desire to make special acknowledgment of the assistance rendered by Joseph E. Beals, chairman of the publication committee, for many valuable suggestions and facts. The author also acknowledges the aid he has received from other members of the committee, from many interested in the preparation of this work, and from his daughter Grace, who examined and transcribed many historical documents, and from her researches added many facts not heretofore published. Most of the illustrations are from photographs taken by Walter L. Beals, and the plates and designs have been made by or under the supervision of Herbert S. Sylvester.

In this volume we have adopted the shorter spelling of Middleboro instead of Middleborough.

This book is submitted with the many imperfections and mistakes which, with the utmost care, a work of this kind must necessarily contain, but the author has endeavored to set forth the story of this ancient town, and something of the lives and character of the men, that they may not be forgotten amid the stirring scenes of the present age and generation.

Thomas Weston

CONTENTS

CHAPTER		PAGE
	INTRODUCTION	xvii
I.	INDIANS	1
II.	PRAYING INDIANS	15
III.	MIDDLEBORO AS FIRST KNOWN TO THE ENGLISH	21
IV.	EARLY SETTLERS BEFORE KING PHILIP'S WAR	29
V.	KING PHILIP'S WAR	68
VI.	THE FRENCH AND INDIAN WARS, 1689-1765	88
VII.	SLAVES IN MIDDLEBORO	101
VIII.	THE REVOLUTION	106
IX.	THE LOYALISTS OF THE REVOLUTION	145
X.	MIDDLEBORO IN THE WAR OF 1812	157
XI.	MIDDLEBORO IN THE WAR OF THE REBELLION	168
XII.	LOCAL MILITIA	193
XIII.	SOCIAL CUSTOMS OF THE EIGHTEENTH CENTURY	206
XIV.	LAWYERS	225
XV.	PHYSICIANS	238
XVI.	EDUCATION, LIBRARIES, NEWSPAPERS, POST-OFFICES	245
XVII.	FOUR CORNERS	272
XVIII.	MAD MARE'S NECK, WAUPAUNUCKET, FALL BROOK	303
XIX.	THE GREEN	309
XX.	THOMASTOWN, ROCK, ROCKY MEADOW, RAYMOND NEIGHBORHOOD, FRANCE, SOUTH MIDDLEBORO	329
XXI.	EDDYVILLE, WATERVILLE, SOULE NEIGHBORHOOD, HALIFAX	342
XXII.	MUTTOCK	355
XXIII.	THOMPSON ROAD, THE LOWLANDS, WARRENTOWN, PURCHADE	386
XXIV.	TITICUT	398
XXV.	LAKEVILLE	419
XXVI.	ECCLESIASTICAL HISTORY	439
XXVII.	TOWN MEETINGS, HERRING FISHERIES, INDIAN PATHS, ROADS AND HIGHWAYS, FIRE DISTRICT	495
XXVIII.	TOWN OFFICERS, PUBLIC OFFICERS	517
XXIX.	CIVIL HISTORY	544
XXX.	EARLY PURCHASES FROM THE INDIANS	582
XXXI.	FRATERNAL ORGANIZATIONS	631
XXXII.	CEMETERIES	634
	DESCRIPTIVE CATALOGUE OF MEMBERS OF THE FIRST CHURCH FROM 1695 TO 1846	639
	INDEX	687

LIST OF ILLUSTRATIONS

Town Hall, High School Building, Soldiers' Monument,	*Frontispiece*
Map of Middleboro in 1853.	vii
Map of Middleboro in 1831	xvii
Proposed Division of the Town of Middleboro to form a New Town with a Portion of Taunton.	xix
View of the Four Corners in 1832 from Barden's Hill	xx
Map of Middleboro in 1855	1
Alexander about to embark on the River.	8
Indian Monument	14
The Beginning of the Lord's Prayer.	16
Samuel Barrows's Autograph	36
Joseph Bumpus's Autograph.	37
The Mayflower.	42
Isaac Howland, Sr.'s Autograph	46
John Miller, Jr.'s Autograph	48
John Morton's Autograph	48
John Morton, Jr.'s Autograph.	49
Samuel Pratt's Autograph	51
Davis Thomas's Autograph.	53
John Tomson's Autograph	55
A Halberd of the Time	58
John Tomson, Jr.'s Autograph	59
George Vaughan's Autograph.	59
Joseph Vaughan's Autograph.	60
Samuel Wood, Sr.'s Autograph.	63
Samuel Wood, Jr.'s Autograph	63
Billington Sea	64
John Cobb's Autograph.	65
The Sturtevant Plough	67
A View of Assawampsett Pond, where the Body of Sassamon was concealed	72
Facsimile of John Sassamon's Letter to Governor Prince, while Secretary of Philip.	72

LIST OF ILLUSTRATIONS

King Philip's Lookout	73
John Tomson's Gun	76
A View of the Rock upon which Isaac Howland shot the Indian at the Beginning of King Philip's War	77
View of Danson Brook, Thompson Street	79
Captain Benjamin Church's Autograph	81
Site of the Encounter at the Bridge, Lakeville	84
Indian Hatchet, Pipe, Mortar, and Pestle	87
A Copy of one of the Stamps under the Stamp Act	106
Ichabod Tupper's Autograph	124
Musket and Powderhorn	144
Doggett House	153
Ransome House	153
Soldiers' Monument	191
Kitchen Fireplace	206
A Family Loom of the Eighteenth Century	214
The Attic of the Backus House	221
Samuel Prince's Autograph	227
Elkanah Leonard's Autograph	228
Wilkes Wood	230
Zachariah Eddy	232
Eliab Ward	234
William H. Wood	235
Everett Robinson	236
Judge Wood's Office	237
Dr. Arad Thompson	240
Dr. Morrill Robinson	241
Dr. Ebenezer W. Drake	242
Dr. William W. Comstock	243
Dr. George W. Snow	244
High School	252
Old Baptist Church, Chapel, and First Academy	253
Baptist Church and Second Academy	255
Professor J. W. P. Jenks	256
Enoch Pratt	259
Pratt Free School	260
Public Library	264
Thomas Sproat Peirce	265
The Silas Wood House	272

THE OLD MORTON HOUSE	273
THE DR. CLARK HOUSE	275
THE OLD BARROWS HOUSE	277
JUDGE WOOD'S HOUSE	278
THE OLD BOURNE HOUSE	278
JOSEPH T. WOOD	279
REV. CHARLES W. WOOD	280
REV. HENRY C. COOMBS	281
EBENEZER PICKENS	282
MAJOR LEVI PEIRCE	283
PEIRCE ACADEMY	284
COLONEL PETER H. PEIRCE	285
HOME OF COLONEL PETER H. PEIRCE	285
COLONEL PETER H. PEIRCE'S STORE	286
BRANCH HARLOW	286
ELISHA TUCKER	290
BANK BLOCK	292
SITE OF BANK BLOCK IN 1875	292
PEIRCE BLOCK	293
SITE OF PEIRCE BLOCK IN 1875	293
ALBERT ALDEN	294
NATHAN KING	295
HORATIO BARROWS	296
THE FOUR CORNERS	297
FOUR CORNERS IN 1850 FROM BARDEN HILLS	298
FOUR CORNERS AT THE PRESENT TIME FROM BARDEN HILLS	299
FOUR CORNERS	300
THE OLD BARDEN HOUSE	302
OLD METHODIST CHURCH OF FALL BROOK	303
COLONEL BENJAMIN P. WOOD	304
SITE OF THE OLD FALL BROOK FURNACE	305
ABISHAI MILLER	306
THE OLD MILLER HOUSE	307
REV. SAMUEL FULLER'S AUTOGRAPH	309
SECOND MEETING-HOUSE	311
REV. PETER THACHER'S AUTOGRAPH	313
REV. SYLVANUS CONANT'S AUTOGRAPH	314
STURTEVANT HOUSE	315
HOUSE OF REV. SYLVANUS CONANT	315

LIST OF ILLUSTRATIONS

John Bennett's Autograph	317
Nehemiah Bennett's Autograph	318
Old Sproat Tavern	319
Signboard of the Old Sproat Tavern	321
Colonel Ebenezer Sproat's Autograph	322
Colonel Ebenezer Sproat	323
Deborah Sampson	330
Deborah Sampson's Home	331
View of the Rock	334
Stillman Benson	340
Samuel Eddy's Autograph	343
Captain Joshua Eddy	344
Residence of Zachariah Eddy	346
Office of Zachariah Eddy	347
Residence of Samuel Eddy and Dr. Powers	347
William S. Eddy	349
John Soule's Autograph	350
Jacob Tomson's Autograph	352
John Morton's Autograph	354
John Tomson's Pistol	354
Oliver's Walk	360
Peter Oliver	363
Peter Oliver's Autograph	363
Plan of Judge Oliver's Estate and Works	365
Peter Oliver's Book-plate	366
Stairs in Sproat House	373
Residence of Peter Oliver, Jr.	374
James Bowdoin	375
James Bowdoin's Autograph	375
William Tupper's Autograph	376
Thomas Weston	380
Abiel Washburn's Residence	381
Ritchie House	382
Backpiece in Fireplace at Oliver Hall	384
Captain Isaac Thomson	386
George Thomson House	387
Shipyard from Woodward's Bridge	388
Cephas Thompson	389
John Weston House	391

COLONEL THOMAS WESTON	392
OLD WESTON TAVERN	393
RESIDENCE OF MRS. TOM THUMB	394
JOHN ALDEN	395
SITE OF THE OLD INDIAN FORT	398
HOUSE OF REV. ISAAC BACKUS	406
HOUSE OF REV. MR. GURNEY	406
ELIJAH E. PERKINS	410
SITE OF SHIPYARD	411
SOLOMON EATON	412
OLIVER EATON	413
FIRST CONGREGATIONAL CHURCH	415
JARED PRATT	416
ISAAC PRATT	417
MAP OF THE PONDS	419
THOMAS NELSON'S AUTOGRAPH	420
CAPTAIN JOB PEIRCE HOUSE	423
SAMPSON'S TAVERN	428
MAJOR PETER HOAR'S RESIDENCE	429
THE WASHBURN HOUSE	430
THE WARD HOUSE	431
GEORGE WARD	432
A BROADSIDE OF THE TIME, BY HANNAH SPROAT	432
SPRAGUE S. STETSON	433
TOWN HOUSE	434
CUDWORTH HOUSE	436
ELKANAH LEONARD HOUSE	438
THOMAS PALMER'S AUTOGRAPH	443
EBENEZER TINKHAM'S AUTOGRAPH	445
PULPIT OF FIRST CHURCH	456
FIRST CONGREGATIONAL CHURCH AT THE GREEN	457
REV. ISRAEL W. PUTNAM, D.D.	458
REV. DAVID GURNEY'S AUTOGRAPH	465
CONGREGATIONAL CHURCH, NORTH MIDDLEBORO	466
CENTRAL CONGREGATIONAL CHURCH	468
REV. I. C. THATCHER	469
OLD BAPTIST CHURCH, NORTH MIDDLEBORO	470
REV. ISAAC BACKUS	470
REV. ISAAC BACKUS'S AUTOGRAPH	471

LIST OF ILLUSTRATIONS

BAPTIST CHURCH, NORTH MIDDLEBORO	473
REV. EBENEZER HINDS	476
BAPTIST CHURCH, ROCK	478
REV. EBENEZER BRIGGS	481
CENTRAL BAPTIST CHURCH	483
REV. HERVEY FITZ	484
REV. EBENEZER NELSON	485
METHODIST EPISCOPAL CHURCH, FOUR CORNERS	488
METHODIST EPISCOPAL CHURCH, SOUTH MIDDLEBORO	489
UNITARIAN CHURCH	491
EPISCOPAL CHURCH	492
ROMAN CATHOLIC CHURCH	493
SQUARE PEWS OF THE OLDEN TIME	494
OLD TOWN HOUSE	497
VIEW OF HERRING-WEIR, MUTTOCK	499
STICK OF HERRING	500
RAILROAD STATION	512
SEAL OF THE TOWN OF MIDDLEBORO	519
MAP OF EARLY PURCHASES OF LANDS FROM INDIANS	582
THE OLD OAK TREE, TITICUT	583
JOHN HOWLAND'S AUTOGRAPH	589
GEORGE SOULE, SR.'S AUTOGRAPH	590
CONSTANT SOUTHWORTH'S AUTOGRAPH	591
THOMAS SOUTHWORTH'S AUTOGRAPH	592
JOHN ALDEN'S AUTOGRAPH	593
THOMAS PRENCE'S AUTOGRAPH	598
THOMAS SAVORY'S AUTOGRAPH	602
GEORGE BONUM'S AUTOGRAPH	604
JOHN CHIPMAN'S AUTOGRAPH	622
ISAAC CUSHMAN'S AUTOGRAPH	623
THOMAS DOGGETT'S AUTOGRAPH	623
ENTRANCE TO HILL CEMETERY	635
GRAVESTONE OF REV. SAMUEL FULLER	637

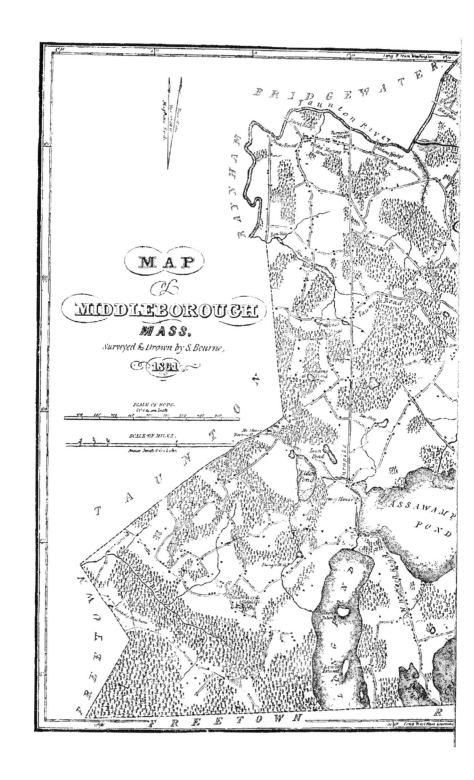

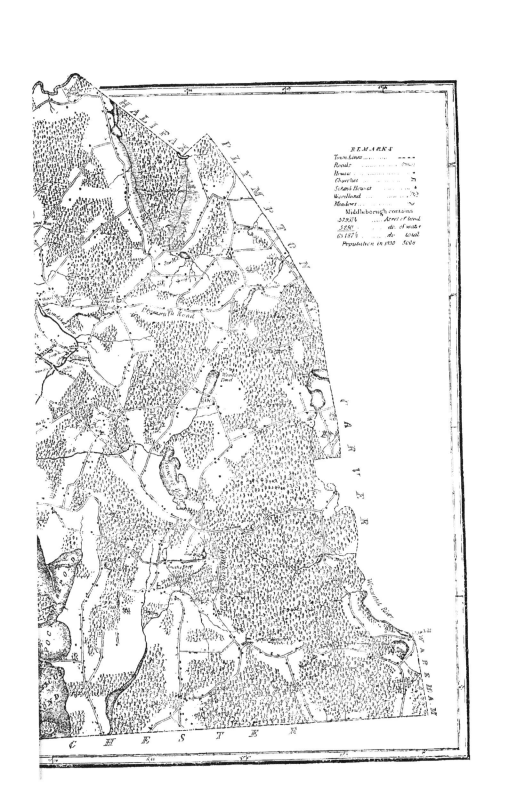

INTRODUCTION

THE history of Middleboro is that of an inland town of the Old Colony, remote from any business centre, a simple story of events, not so stirring as to seriously affect the history of the commonwealth, a story of men, thrifty, intelligent, and able, who have contributed their share to the advancement of the best interests of the country.

By an act of the Colonial Legislature, June 1, 1663,[1] the inhabitants at Nemasket "were accounted to belong to the town of Plymouth," and continued under that jurisdiction until the year 1669, when that portion of Plymouth was incorporated under the name of the Town of Middleberry. This name may have been given on account of its location, midway between Plymouth and the residence of the Pokanoket chief, or it may have come from the town of Middleboro in North Riding of York, England. It included what had been known as Assawampsett, Nemasket, the Titicut land of the Indians, the western portion of the town of Halifax, and the whole of Lakeville. Before the later division, but after that portion of Halifax was set off, it was, excepting Plymouth, the largest town in the state, measuring from north to south over eleven miles, from east to west fourteen miles, and containing an area of more than one hundred square miles.

In 1718 the proprietors of the Sixteen Shilling Purchase, with those who were in possession of much of the land in Taunton formerly owned by Miss Poole and her associates, desired to be incorporated into a separate township. Jacob Tomson drew a map, the original of which is now in the Massachusetts

---

[1] "1663 — 1 June — Prence, Gour.

"It is ordered by the Court that............................those that are sett downe att Namassakett to belonge to the towne of Plymouth vntill the Court shall see reason otherwise to order." *Plymouth Colony Records*, vol. iv, p. 41.

Archives, and a copy on the following page. This project was principally urged by those living within the bounds of Taunton, but as there were few inhabitants at this time in that portion of Middleboro, it was soon after abandoned.

In 1734 the northeasterly part of the town, included in the territory between its present boundary line on the northeast and that on the Winnetuxet River, was set off to form a portion of Halifax.

The setting off of North Middleboro was for a long time the subject of much discussion. At a meeting held December 23, 1741, "The town taking into consideration the petition of Jabez Eddy and others respecting there being set off a separate township; and after the same was fully debated, upon a question being asked the town whether they would grant their request, the vote passed in the negative." In 1743 a petition was presented to the General Court signed by thirty-six subscribers and heads of families, asking that the northern portion of the town be set off from Middleboro to become a new town with part of Bridgewater. This, however, was never acted upon. In 1744 a similar petition was presented to the General Court, which resulted in their separation as a parish distinct from that worshipping at the Green. In 1792 a petition was presented to the General Court, but this was also refused. The last petition was presented in 1821; since then there has been no further attempt at a division of this part of the town.

In 1853 the legislature incorporated as a separate town that part which was substantially included in the Sixteen Shilling Purchase, under the name of Lakeville.

By the act of incorporation, the boundaries of some portions of the town were indefinite; this gave rise to not a little controversy, which extended over many years, and in the case of the adjoining town of Bridgewater, was attended with considerable bitterness. The eastern boundary, which in the early history was the township of Plymouth, as well as the southern boundary, which adjoined Rochester, was settled by agents of that town in 1695. The dividing line between Middleboro and Bridgewater was settled by the agents of the two towns

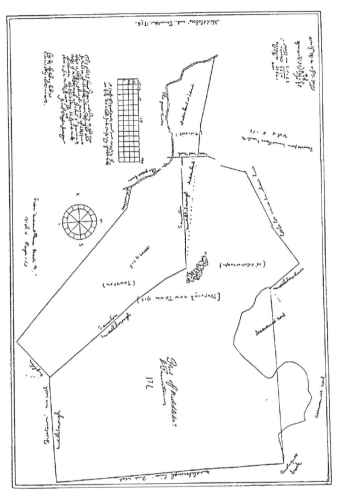

PROPOSED DIVISION OF THE TOWN OF MIDDLEBORO TO FORM A NEW
TOWN WITH A PORTION OF TAUNTON

(Drawn by Jacob Thomson in 1718)

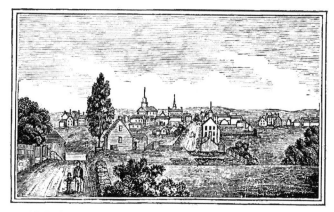

VIEW OF THE FOUR CORNERS IN 1832 FROM BARDEN'S HILL
(From an old picture)

in 1681, and since that time the Taunton River has remained the northern boundary. The line between that portion of Taunton and Middleboro between Baiting Brook and Trout or Poquoy Brook was indefinite, the boundary having been the Indian Reservation, whose western limit was not settled until the year 1686. This has remained as then established, although the older inhabitants of the town claimed that Taunton had acquired a much larger amount of territory than the original act of the legislature authorized. That portion of the western side of Lakeville bordering upon Freetown has been changed; in the year 1718 the boundary was a straight line. It was not until after that time that the indentation as indicated upon the present map of Lakeville was made, but when or by whom authorized, we have been unable to ascertain. On the east a small portion of the town was given to Plympton, and in 1842 a narrow strip of land at the southeastern part of the town was annexed to Carver. The Taunton River has always been the boundary line between Middleboro and Raynham.

Most of the early settlers from Plymouth and the neighboring towns who came to occupy the lands they had previously purchased were farmers, whose prudence and industry soon enabled them to live in comparative independence, their farms, with the rivers, ponds, and forests, supplying them with the necessaries of life.

The Lakeville lands were very productive, yielding large crops of corn and rye; those bordering on the ponds were usually exempt from the early frosts which proved so disastrous in other localities. Flax, at one time raised extensively, is not now cultivated. Fruits were abundant, especially apples. The census of 1781 gives the number of "581 houses, 18 Distill houses, 608 oxen, 1521 cows, 338 horses, 584 coaches, chaises, etc., and 2144 barrels of cider" for that year.

For two generations the only mills were the sawmill, the grist-mill, and the fulling-mill, which have now almost entirely disappeared, and in place of the sawmill there are a few box-board mills. In the early part of the eighteenth century the deposits of iron ore in the larger ponds gave rise to the establishment of six blast furnaces for the making of cast-iron ware. There was a large forge and one slitting-mill, both of which were used for the making of nail-rods, out of which hammered nails were made. In the early part of the last century there were four shovel factories, two cotton mills, and one tack factory, all of which have long since disappeared. In 1837 the two cotton mills had two thousand three hundred and eighty-four spindles, and made about half a million yards of cloth annually. The building of a few ships along the Taunton River entirely ceased after the embargo of Jefferson in 1812. The public houses, or ordinaries, which in early times were scattered throughout the town, are no longer to be seen. Early in the settlement Muttock, Titicut, Eddyville, then connected with Waterville, and Fall Brook were places of business importance for more than a century, but of these villages Titicut alone has retained its population and industrial position, while the Four Corners, which a hundred years ago was sparsely settled, is now one of the largest and most prosperous villages of the country. Social, business, and religious interests have been drawn to this centre. The outlying churches, once so flourishing, have decreased in attendance and importance.

The First Church, which was organized in 1694, was for generations one of the largest and most influential in the colony; in 1800 there were more than fourteen hundred people included within its parish. As the town has grown in size, various societies have been formed, and now the churches are numerous.

Next to the Four Corners, a greater change has occurred in Lakeville in one hundred and twenty-five years than in any other section of the town, there probably being not as many houses and inhabitants there by one third.

Between the years 1772 and 1787, more than fifty families moved from Middleboro to Woodstock, Vt., led, probably, by Dr. Stephen Powers. Among these may be named: —

Dr. Stephen Powers,	1774	Eleazer Wood,	1779
Joseph Darling,	1776	Caleb Wood,	1779
Isaac Tribou,	1776	Nathaniel Wood,	1779
Jabez Bennett,	1776	William Raymond,	1780
Jacob Churchill,	1778	George Sampson,	1783
Joseph Churchill,	1778	David Thomas,	1787

Others moved to various parts of Vermont, and not a few emigrated into that part of the state then known as the district of Maine. It was considered noteworthy that these families should go so far into the wilderness. This tide of emigration seems to have continued up to 1800, so that the descendants of Middleboro men in various pursuits and professions are to be found all over the country, and their records indicate that they have not forgotten the ancestry from which they sprang.

In the early part of the last century the town was noted for the general health of its inhabitants and their remarkable longevity. Dr. Dwight, President of Yale College, in his letters containing an account of the towns in Massachusetts which he visited, has the following table, showing the mortality in the first parish between 1802 and 1812 and their ages, namely: [1]—

---

[1] Dwight's *Travels*, vol. ii, p. 11.

INTRODUCTION   xxiii

Years	Above 90	80	70	50	20	Under 20	Total
1802	1	3	2	2	3	8	19
1803	1	4	2	4	4	16	31
1804		4	1	7	2	6	20
1805			6	3	14	6	29
1806	1		3		1	7	12
1807		5	2	5	6	4	22
1808		2	10	7	4	8	31
1809		2	4	7	4	12	29
1810		2	3	4	5	6	20
1812	4	2	4		5	7	22
Total,	7	24	37	39	48	80	235

From this table it appears that the average number of deaths in this precinct was 23.5. Of the whole number 235, seven, one thirty-third part, lived to be above 90; and twenty-four, a tenth part, above 80; thirty-seven, nearly a sixth part, above 70; and sixty-eight, the whole number that died above 70, was a little less than one third of the total. One hundred and seven died above 50, not far from one half; while those who died under 20 were eighty, a little more than one fourth of the whole.

The population has not materially increased during the past one hundred years as compared with some other towns of the commonwealth. There were not as many inhabitants in 1810 as in 1790. Since 1860 the population has steadily increased.

No official census was taken of any of the towns in the province or in the commonwealth until 1765. The following table gives the population of Middleboro from that time to the present: —

1765	Province	3412	1840	State	5085
1776	"	4119	1850	"	5336
1790	State	4526	1860[1]	"	4565
1800	"	4458	1870	"	4685
1810	"	4400	1880	"	5239
1820	"	4687	1890	"	6065
1830	"	5008	1900	"	6885

[1] The town of Lakeville was set off from Middleboro in 1853, thus reducing its population.

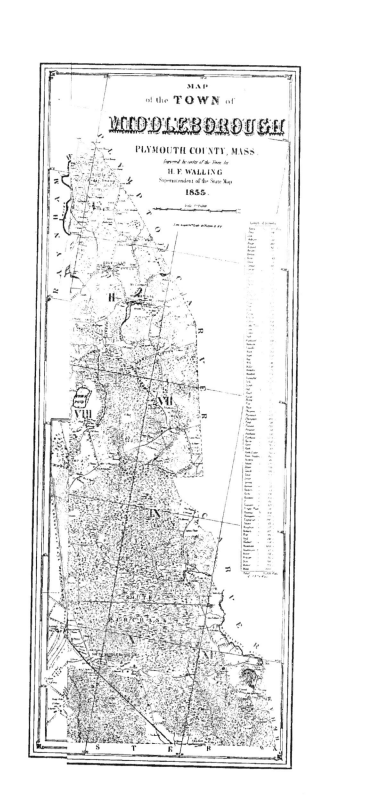

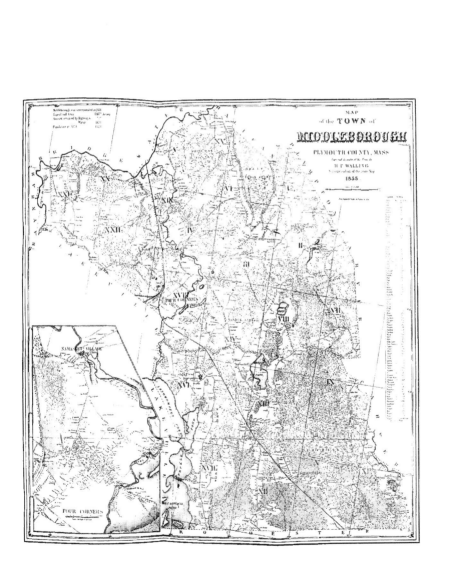

HISTORY OF THE TOWN OF MIDDLEBORO

CHAPTER I

INDIANS

WHEN the pilgrims landed at Plymouth in 1620, Middleboro was occupied by the Nemasket Indians.[1] From them the place took its name until the incorporation of the town in 1669. They were a part of the great nation of Pokanokets,[2] under the sachem Massasoit, whose rule extended over all of the tribes in southeastern Massachusetts; these, with the exception of the Nemaskets, had been greatly decimated by the plague which swept through this region.[3] The principal settlements were at Muttock on the Nemasket

---

[1] The word "Nemasket" is probably derived from two Indian words, "Nemah," meaning "a fish," and its terminal "et," meaning "the place of," and at this place the Indians from time immemorial had a fish weir, and from this the surrounding country was named. In the old records it was spelled Namasket.

[2] The Pokanoket race was composed of the Wampanoags of Bristol County, in Rhode Island, the Pocassets at Rehoboth, Swansea, and Tiverton, the Saconets at Little Compton, the Nemaskets at Middleboro, the Agawams at Wareham, the Manomets at Sandwich, the Sakatuckets at Mashpee, the Mattakees at Barnstable, the Nobsquassets at Yarmouth, the Monamoys at Chatham, and the Nausets at Eastham. The islands at the south were also included.

[3] "The devastation wrought by the disease was horrible . . . and strange to say, the Namaskets, who were in the centre of the path followed by the pestilence, were spared, the deluge of death dividing at that point and depopulating the country on each side of them." Goodwin's *Pilgrim Republic*, p. 136.

See Isaac Backus in vol. iii of the *Mass. Hist. Soc. Coll.* p. 148.

"When Edward Winslow and Stephen Hopkins sent out their two messengers to visit Massasoit at Mount Hope, in July, 1621, they lodged the first night at Namasket, where so many Indians had died a few years before that the living could not bury the dead, but their skulls and bones appeared in many places where their dead had been." Prince's *Chronology*, p. 106.

River, upon the borders of Assawampsett Pond, and Titicut, not far from where the Nemasket empties into the Taunton River.

It was a characteristic of all of the North American Indians to select for their settlements the most sightly and beautiful locations in the country, where there was plenty of water for fishing and a broad outlook over their hunting-grounds. This seems to have been especially true of the Nemasket Indians. Their principal settlement was at Muttock, on the bank of the high hill on the westerly side of the river. There was an abundance of fish in the river below, across which they had erected a fish weir near the site of the present dam. Numerous springs of sweet water were at the base of the hill, and the land adjoining was fruitful and well adapted for their corn gardens.

The settlements at Assawampsett were upon the borders of the beautiful inland lakes and upon the high ground surrounding. At Titicut they extended along the banks of both sides of the river; the site of the wigwam of their sachem was probably upon what is now known as Fort Hill. The Indians living about Middleboro ponds were in the habit of going to New Bedford for the purpose of obtaining shellfish, and their path was the old pond road leading from Assawampsett Pond to New Bedford.

At this time the Indians lived in wigwams, built of poles, which, fastened together at the top, formed a circle from fifteen to twenty feet in diameter. These poles were covered with skins of bear or deer, and a hole was left in the top for the smoke to escape. The ground upon which the wigwam stood was usually hollowed some three or four feet in the centre, and in the middle a fire was built for cooking purposes; the earthen floor was covered with mats or skins, while at the doorway hung a skin which was drawn back during the day, but dropped at night and secured by placing a stick against it. In the centre of the village stood the wigwam of the chief, painted with his totem, and others were placed around it, so near that conversation could be heard from one to another. This continued to be the home of the Indians for almost a century, until they adopted many of the customs of civilized life and it gave place to the cabin, or hut, which formed a much more comfortable shelter from the storm and snow of winter. The site of the chief's wigwam at Muttock may still be seen upon the top of what is known as Oliver's Walk.

The dress of the Indians consisted of moccasins made of the skins of animals caught or killed in their hunting expeditions, breeches made of deerskin, and a kind of blanket made of deer or bear skin, which they threw over their shoulders. They wore nothing upon their heads, and as they gradually adopted the ways of civilized life, they were accustomed to wear whatever clothing could be obtained from the whites.

From the earliest times they secured much of their food by fishing[1] and hunting. Maize or corn,[2] raised in corn gardens,

[1] They used nets made of bark from a species of willow-tree, and of rushes and strong grass.

[2] The following legend of the first growth of corn is interesting: —

"Mon-do-min, an old hunter of the Wampanoag tribe, sat one night alone in his wigwam, on the shores of the Nemasket River. The night was dark and stormy, for Ke-che No-din, the Spirit of the Wind, was very angry, and threatened to tear up the oaks on the banks of the river and scatter them on the ground. Mon-do-min was old and lame; his wigwam stood far apart from all the others; he could no longer hunt the wild deer, or bear; he was very weak, and fainting with hunger, for he had not tasted food for many days. Then he looked up to the Great Spirit for help, and said, 'Oh, Great Spirit! Shah-wain-ne-me-shin! Have pity upon me, and look down out of your window in the southern sky, and send me help from your home in the ish-pe-ming [heavens].' Presently he heard a fluttering among the long poles at the top of his wigwam. He looked, and, lo! a partridge [be-nah-nah] was caught among the poles, and could not escape. Mon-do-min took the partridge in his hand, and said, 'Now has the Great Spirit had pity upon me, and sent me food, that I may not die of hunger.' So he kindled a fire and prepared to dress the partridge for food. Presently, amid the pauses of the storm, Mon-do-min heard cries of distress. It was a woman's voice, crying bitterly; she had lost her way in the forest, and was crouching, for shelter, beneath the cover of the Great Rock, close by the door of his wigwam. Mon-do-min hastened, with all the strength that his old and trembling limbs would permit, and found the woman. He raised her up, brought her into his wigwam, laid her on his own bed of bearskins, and chafed her bruised limbs (for she had fallen from the rock), and tried to restore warmth to her shivering frame. He then took the partridge he had prepared for his own nourishment and said, 'My sister, this is what the Great Spirit had given me to eat, when I was perishing with hunger. Take it; it is thine; there is not enough for thee and for me. Thou wilt live; but I must die. Thus has the Great Spirit spoken. But remember me, when thou

was an important article of diet, and the woods of the country abounded with wild cherries, wild plums, beach-plums, wild gooseberries, strawberries, huckleberries, raspberries, and blackberries. The soil was loosened by a sharp wooden stick; a fish, usually a herring, was buried at a depth of five or six inches, covered by about two inches of soil, then a few kernels of corn were planted, pressed down hard, and this, being fertilized by the decayed fish, produced an abundant crop. When ripened it was shelled and dried, then placed in baskets and stored in pits in the earth, called "caches." It was pounded to meal in the stone mortars with pestles. Their food was often prepared in this way: —

"It is generally boiled maize or Indian corn, mixed with kidney-beans, or sometimes without. Also they frequently boil in this pottage fish and flesh of all sorts, either new taken or dried, as shad, eels, alewives, or a kind of herring, or any other sort of fish. But they dry, mostly, those sorts before mentioned. These they cut in pieces, bones and all, and

seest one alone and perishing, as thou wert, and do to them as I have done to thee. Farewell, I shall not see thee again till we meet in the Country of Souls.'

"Mon-do-min said no more. He laid himself down on the cold earth for his couch, and that night the Great Spirit took him to his dwelling, in the Country of Souls.

"In the morning the woman awoke from her slumbers calm and refreshed, and looked, and saw Mon-do-min dead in the bottom of the wigwam. Then she arose, and went and called the chiefs of the tribe, and they came and buried Mon-do-min on the bank of the river, close by where his wigwam had stood..

"When the Moon of Leaves [June] had come, they went, and behold! the ground around the grave of Mon-do-min was covered with fine, springing shoots, like grass; only the leaves were broader, and more beautiful in the sun. Then they wondered, and said, ' What is this that we see? this that is growing around the grave of Mon-do-min?' And while they wondered, lo! from a bright cloud that stood just above them, the Great Spirit spoke and said, ' My children, listen to what I have to say to you to-day. This that you see shall be food for you to eat, when it shall be ripened into full ears of grain. It shall be called Mon-do-min [corn]. It shall be called by his name, for his kindness to the poor and perishing one, that stormy night, when he brought her into his own wigwam, and gave her of his own food to eat, when he was himself perishing with hunger. And you shall tell it to your children, and your children's children, in all your tribes, when you see the green corn waving by the Lake of White Stones [Assawampsett] and the river of the Nemaskets.' "

boil them in the aforesaid pottage. Also they boil in this fermenty all sorts of flesh they take in hunting, as venison, beaver, bears flesh, moose, otters, raccoons, or any kind that they take in hunting, cutting this flesh in small pieces, and boiling it as aforesaid. Also they mix with the said pottage several sorts of roots, as Jerusalem artichokes, and ground nuts, and other roots, and pompions, and squashes, and also several sorts of nuts or masts, as oak acorns, chestnuts, walnuts; these husked, and dried, and powdered, they thicken their pottage therewith. Also sometimes they beat their maize into meal, and sift it through a basket, made for that purpose. With this meal they make bread, baking it in the ashes, covering the dough with leaves. Sometimes they make of their meal a small sort of cakes, and boil them. They make also a certain sort of meal of parched maize; this meal they call *nokake*. It is so sweet, toothsome, and hearty, that an Indian will travel many days with no other food but this meal, which he eateth as he needs and after it drinketh water. And for this end, when they travel a journey, or go a-hunting, they carry this nokake in a basket or bag, for their use."[1]

"The indians have an art of drying their chestnuts, and so to preserve them in their barnes for a daintie all the yeare. Akornes, also, they drie, and, in case of want of Corne, by much boiling they make a good dish of them; yea, sometimes in plentie of Corne doe they eate thes Acornes for a novelty."[2]

Women were held in great contempt, and were obliged to do all of the hard work. The wife had to skin and dress the deer killed by her husband, prepare the food which he devoured, leaving for her only what he did not care for, and work in the field while he smoked comfortably at home.

The men were brave, courageous, fierce, and revengeful, "much addicted to lying[3] and speaking untruth," with little

---

[1] *New England Historical and Genealogical Register*, vol. iii, p. 216.

[2] Roger Williams's "Key into the Language of America," in *R. I. Hist. Coll.* vol. i, p. 90.

[3] The following is an Indian account of the origin of this trait of character:—

"When the Pale Face came across the Big Waters [Te-che Gah-me], there were straight paths running all through our forests. Our warriors walked in them. They were very narrow. But our warriors' feet went straight forward. It did not hurt them to walk in straight, narrow paths. But the Pale Face could not walk in them. His toes turned out; he was trying to walk two ways at once. He

regard for honor. With few tools, they were yet ingenious and skilful. They kept time by the sun and moon, and were observers of the stars. They were superstitious, submitting to their priests or "powahs" in their worship of many gods, the chief of whom were Kiehtan, the creator and giver of good hereafter, and Alamacho, the evil spirit. They believed that evil spirits always settled where the dark spirit Death, whom they called "Pau-guk," had been. They burned the wigwam to send away these spirits, and if they thought him near, would do their utmost to drive him away, beating drums, throwing hot water into the air, and making unearthly noises. The whip-poor-will was believed to be a messenger from the other world, and on hearing his mournful note they would cry, "Be still! it is the bird from the Spiritland."

Their principal burying-ground was on Muttock Hill. At sunset they would carry the body of the dead, wrapped in furs or mats, to the grave. A basket of meat was placed at his head, a pot of water at his feet, and his moccasins were in his hand. If he were a rich man, his jewels and wampum were buried with him. They then marched around the grave, chanting in solemn words, "Go on thy journey, brother. 'T is late and the sun is set. We will keep the fire for travellers burning to light thee on thy way. We have put food before thee for thy journey and moccasins for thy feet. Fear not, for the dark roaring river thou must cross. Step lightly over and go on thy journey."

After filling the grave, they built a fire at the head and kept it burning four days and nights. They believed his desolate jour-

could not walk straight. His ways were crooked. He taught our people to steal. He came creeping into our wigwams at night. He crept in like a mouse that nibbles the children's corn. He had long fingers — so long that they would reach to the bottom of the sugar mo-ko-ks [birch-bark boxes]. He stole all the women's sugar out of them, made of the juice of the maple-tree. And when our people told him of this, and he opened his mouth to speak, we saw that he had two tongues. One tongue laid very still; the other moved very fast. The lying tongue walked very fast. The Indian no longer walks straight, he has learned to walk two ways at once, like the Pale Face. The tongue that spoke the truth stands still. The lying tongue walks very fast. It is like the brook that runs over the stones. None can stop its babblings."

ney through a prairie, where he was liable to lose his way, was without light save from this fire. If he had been a murderer, he was attacked by snakes, wild beasts, and evil spirits until he reached the banks of the Spirit River. This he crossed on a floating pole, guided by Meno Manito, the Master of Life, to the Happy Hunting-Ground. The wicked spirits could not follow, but the current took them away from him to the prairie.

For half a century after the landing of the pilgrims at Plymouth, the friendly relations which had been established between the whites and the good king Massasoit continued. The two races for the most part lived together in peace and harmony, the white settlers being careful to see that exact justice was done to the Indians, and that all of their rights of person and property should be fairly protected. Whenever a white man offended an Indian he was immediately brought to justice, and compelled by the laws of the colony to make ample and full reparation, or suffer punishment for the offence committed, and the Indians were obliged to submit to the same laws that governed the whites.

Massasoit died of the plague in the year 1660, and was succeeded by his son, Wamsutta. There is a touching incident related by Mr. Hubbard, that not long before the death of Massasoit, the aged chief came to Mr. Brown, who lived not far from Mount Hope in Rhode Island, and brought his two sons, desiring that there might be love and amity between them, as there had been between himself and the whites. It seems, however, that upon the accession of Alexander he failed to obey his father's injunction, and Mr. Hubbard further says that "he had neither affection to the person nor to the religion of the whites."[1]

In the year 1656 his two sons presented themselves before the court at Plymouth and desired that English names might be given them. Wamsutta, the eldest, was afterwards called Alexander, and Pometicon was then given the name of Philip. Some two years after the death of his father, although Alexander had become a party to the league with the whites and

---

[1] Hubbard's *Indian Wars in New England*, Drake's edition, pp. 46, 47.

had received many benefits therefrom, rumors came that he was plotting with the Narragansetts against the English. At length these rumors became so numerous that he was summoned to Plymouth for an explanation. He was said to have been temporarily visiting on the shores of a pond in Halifax, but as he did not immediately respond, Governor Bradford and some others of the colony sought an interview. He had some excuse for not earlier obeying the command, but consented to

ALEXANDER ABOUT TO EMBARK ON THE RIVER
(From *Harper's Monthly Magazine*, vol. 71, p. 815. Copyrighted, 1885, by Harper & Bros.)

return with them. A little later, a satisfactory interview was held in Duxbury, and the party returned to Plymouth, Alexander informing them that he was to go to Boston. A few days after, he stopped at the house of Winslow, in Marshfield, where he was taken sick. From here he was carried by his attendants to Governor Bradford's house in Plymouth. His sickness continuing, his people bore him across the country through Plymouth and Middleboro to the wading-place, then along the Titicut path a little below the weir at Pratt's bridge, where they embarked in canoes, but he died before reaching his home.[1] It was alleged that his death was hastened by ill treatment which he received at the hands of the English while in Marshfield and Plymouth, and that this was one of the causes of King Philip's War, which occurred some years later. There is, however, no proof of this charge.

On the death of Alexander, which occurred in July, 1662, Philip became the chief sachem of all of the Pokanokets, and one of his first acts was to appear before the court at Plymouth and earnestly request a continuance of the amity which had existed between the whites and his father, promising to endeavor in all things to carry himself inoffensively and peaceably toward the English. This compact was witnessed by five of his chiefs. It is said that this was undoubtedly an act of treachery on the part of Philip, but it had the effect of allaying the suspicions which had been for some time excited in the colony. (See chapter on King Philip's War.)

The territory ruled by King Philip was the greater part of southeastern Massachusetts, including a portion of Rhode Island. This was divided among various sub-chiefs, who held sway over the different local tribes. Among these was Pamantaquash, or, as he was familiarly known, the pond sachem, whose domain was the country near the ponds.

About six years after Philip's accession, in 1668, this pond sachem, by an instrument which was recognized as binding by the court at Plymouth, bequeathed his rulership to Tispequin, the black sachem, a chieftain of great power and notoriety, of whom we shall speak hereafter. This will was written by Nathaniel Morton, secretary of the colony, and Samuel Spray. It is as follows: —

"Witneseth these presents, Pamantaquash, the pond Sachem, being weak in body but of perfect disposeing memory, declared it to be his last will and Testament, concerning all his lands at Assawamsett, or elsewhere, that he is now possessed of, that he would after his desease leave them unto his ——, Tuspequin, alius the black Sachem, for his life, and after the sd Tuspequin his decease unto Soquontamouk, alius William, his sone,

[1] Between June 13 and August 26 (N. S.). *Plymouth Colony Records*, vol. iv, pp. 16, 25.

and to his heires forever, and desired severall of his men that were then about him to take notice of it and be witnesses of it if he should not live himself to doe the writing under his owne hande."

This instrument was witnessed by Paempohut, alias Joseph, Sam Harry, alias Matwatacka, Wosako, alias Harry, and Felix, alias Nanauatanate.

The following is an interesting copy from the records in Plymouth: —

"The land that the said Pamantaquash challenges, the names of the places . . . said witnesses have made description . . . followeth Pachamaquast, Wekam, . . . Nekatatacouck, Setnessnett, Anec . . . path that goes from Cushenett to . . . goes through it:

"Wacagasaness: Wacom . . . Quamakeckett, Tokopissett; Maspenn . . . Wampaketatekam: Caskakachesquash Wachpusk, ester side of ye pond: p . . . Pachest; soe or Namassakett riuer Pasamasatuate.

"Harry and his sone Sam, Harry, desiers that neither Tuspaquin nor his sone be prest to sell the said lands . . . by any English or others whatsouer.

"The lands Mentioned which Tuspequin posesseth, Ha . . . Wosako, wch is long as he lives.

"29 October, 1668.

"Witnes,
"WAPETOM, his mark.
"WASNUKESETT, his mark."

Chickataubut was one of the "great sachems" among the Massachusetts Indians. He was styled the " greatest sagamore in the country." "His territory did extend from Nishamagoguanett, near Duxbury mill, to Titicut near Taunton and to Nunckatateset, a pond of considerable size in the southwestern portion of Bridgewater adjoining Raynham and from thence in a straight line to Wanamampuke which is the head of Charles River."[1] Who was his father, or how he obtained this rule, has not come down to us. He was one of the nine sachems who signed the Articles of Submission to King James on the 13th of September, 1621, and Governor Dudley said of him, in 1631,

---

[1] *New England Historical and Genealogical Register*, vol. iii, p. 332.

that "he least favoreth the whites of any of the sagamores that we are acquainted with by reason of the old quarrel in Plymouth wherein he lost seven of his best men." However, the whole intercourse of this chief with the Massachusetts colonies seems to have been friendly. He, with his squaw, visited Boston as the guest of Governor Dudley, and presented the governor with a hogshead of corn. He died of smallpox in the month of November, 1633. His favorite resort was Titicut, and his land comprised three miles on each side of the river, which was granted by his son Wampatuck to the Indians in Titicut before 1644.

Wampatuck, called Josiah Wampatuck, succeeded him in his rule. During his minority, Mr. Gookin says, "he was bred up by his uncle Kuchamakin, a sachem, who resided at Neponset." He is mentioned as one of three sachems who, on the 5th of February, 1643-44, came to the governor of Massachusetts Colony in their own name, and "in the names of all the sachems of Watchusett and all of the Indians from Merrimack to Tecticutt, and tendered themselves" to the Massachusetts governor, and gave him thirty fathoms of wampum and promised to come to the court when it next met. The governor agreed "to accept their presents until the court came in, and if the court and they did agree then to accept them." Upon the coming in of the court, this was approved, it being stated that they desired "to be received upon our protection and government upon the same terms that the other Indians had been." The subsequent conduct of his uncle gave much anxiety to the colony. Under his influence, Josiah Wampatuck seems to have acquired much of the impetuosity and fickleness which characterized his after life. He at one time professed to be one of the praying Indians, but afterwards turned apostate and separated from them, although he seems to have been a faithful friend of the whites, and in 1662 made extensive grants of land in Middleboro. We find him, however, in 1669, joining in the war between the Indians of New England and the Mohawk Indians as the chief sachem. This, however, proved a failure, and the Massachusetts warriors were obliged to retreat, leaving a large number of their slain upon the different battlefields. He was among the dead, and left a son Jeremy, who became a sachem in 1671. He left a son Charles Josiah, who was the last of his race.[1]

Tispequin, the black sachem, who inherited the lands from the pond sachem, made many conveyances in Middleboro to the early settlers of this and adjoining towns. (See chapter on Early Purchases.) He was a fearless and able chieftain, one of the leaders in King Philip's War, upon whom Philip relied more than upon any of the sagamores of the country. He had married a daughter of Massasoit, and was a brother-in-law of Philip. Notwithstanding his numerous dealings with the whites, he never became accustomed to their ways or accepted their religious faith. In the later years of his life his residence was outside of Middleboro, and from his personal relations with King Philip, it is not surprising that he became his confidant and most trusted warrior. It is a little remarkable that, considering his influence and position, he did not succeed in inducing more of the Indians of the town to join Philip in the Indian war for the extermination of the whites in 1675. He had all of the malignity and cruel disposition of the most savage and bloodthirsty of his race, and notwithstanding all of the dealings he had had with the white settlers within his domain, it is not improbable that during the years in which these conveyances of land were so freely given, he was meditating a plot in connection with Philip for the utter extermination of the whites, hoping thus eventually to regain the land conveyed. Upon the breaking out of the war he was the leader of most, if not all, of the savage exploits and terrible massacres in the old colony. (See chapter on King Philip's War.) What became of his son William, who would have been his legal successor as chieftain of the tribes of southeastern Massachusetts, is unknown. His other son, Benjamin, died from the effects of a wound received in battle during this war. One of Benjamin's daughters, it is said, married an Indian by the name of Quam, whose daughter received sufficient education to be at one time a school-teacher among the few remaining children of her tribe.

[1] Drake's *Book of the Indians*, Book II, pp. 44-45; *New England Historical and Genealogical Register*, vol. iii, pp. 339-340.

In a deed dated 1673,[1] wherein he made a gift to John Sassamon of certain land at Assawampsett, he is called Old Tispequin. The descendants from Tispequin were called Squins, a corruption of the great sachem's name.

In 1793 the tribe had so diminished that there were but eight families living in their Indian houses at Betty's Neck. There were in these eight families between thirty and forty Indians, who were poor and improvident, and who became very intemperate, the corn and rye raised on their land being usually sold for liquor. They obtained a meagre subsistence by the sale of brooms and baskets which they manufactured.[2] This tribe is now reduced in numbers to a single family.

Beside the Indian burial ground on Muttock Hill there was undoubtedly an ancient place of burial at the Four Corners, near the site of the house of the late Allen Shaw on Main Street, and a little to the east of the residence of the late Colonel Peter H. Peirce on the other side of the street. In 1826, in making an excavation for the cellar of Mr. Shaw's house, Indian remains were found in a sitting posture. One of the skeletons had a brass kettle over his head, and his body had been profusely decorated with beads and other ornaments. These evidently were of English manufacture, and had probably been procured at Plymouth. Upon the farm of the late Ellis Weston, about half a mile from the Lower Factory, was an Indian settlement, which is indicated by the very rich black soil in circular spots, as though it had been under the wigwams. In ploughing fields in this neighborhood numerous arrowheads, battle-axes, and spears have been found.

Some few years ago the water was drawn off from a pond made by an artificial dam, leaving exposed a large number of tree stumps in a perfect state of preservation; against one of these stumps was found leaning a skeleton of an Indian chief with the remains of various implements of warfare, which had probably been buried with him. The skeleton was given by Mr. Weston to Professor J. W. P. Jenks, and was afterwards

[1] *History of Plymouth Colony*, Lakeville, p. 292.
[2] From notes of Nehemiah Bennett, *Mass. Hist. Soc. Coll.* vol. 35.

moved to the Museum of Brown University. A large number of arrowheads, spears, and stone axes have also been found about the high ground on the east of Assawampsett Pond.

Ben Simonds was the last of the full-blooded Indians who lived at Assawampsett. Upon his death he was buried in a cemetery in the westerly part of Lakeville, and a small granite obelisk was erected by Mr. Levi Reed, which bears this inscription : —

"In Memory of Ben Simonds, the last male of the native Indians of Middleboro. He was a Revolutionary soldier. Died May, 1831, aged eighty years."

INDIAN MONUMENT

CHAPTER II

PRAYING INDIANS

ONE purpose of the early settlers in both Massachusetts and Plymouth Colony in leaving the old country and enduring the hardships of the New World was to teach the gospel to the Indians of America. The Massachusetts charter takes notice of it, and letters from the settlers to their friends frequently refer to this purpose, showing that not a little was done in their endeavors to christianize the Indians in that province. The submission of the five great sachems to the jurisdiction of Massachusetts did much towards preparing for this laudable undertaking. Some of them had expressed the wish "to suffer their children to learn God's Word;" "To worship Him aright and worship Him in their own way." An order was passed November 13, 1644, that the colony should take care that the Indians residing in their several shires should be civilized, and instructed in the knowledge of the Word of God.[1]

In Plymouth Colony we find the same high motive in the reasons set forth by the pilgrims for leaving Holland, the country which had protected them from the persecutions of their native land. "Fifthly and last and which was not the least a great hope and inward zeal they had of laying some good foundation, or at least to make some way thereunto for the propagation and advancement of the Gospel of the Kingdom of Christ, although they should be but as stepping stones unto others for the performance of so great a work."[2]

In order further to carry on this work, Governor Winslow,[3] in July, 1649, was instrumental in forming a society for propa-

---

[1] Barry's *History of Massachusetts*, vol. i, p. 350.
[2] *New England Memorial*, p. 12.
[3] *Ibid.*, Appendix, p. 380.

```
Nꝏskun kesukqur quttianatamunach kꝏwisnonk
Peynmꝏutch kukketassutamꝏk kuttenantameenk
ne n-nach chkeit neane kesukgut
```

THE BEGINNING OF THE LORD'S PRAYER
(From Eliot's Indian Bible)

gating the gospel in New England, while ministers in the mother country stirred up their congregations to contribute liberally for its support. A correspondence was held with the commissioners of the United Colonies as agents, and at one time over seven hundred pounds a year was raised for the use of this society. As a result of these contributions, which were carefully distributed, not only was an attempt made to introduce a change in the customs and dress of the natives, but teachers were appointed to carry out the work of instruction. How well this work was done may be inferred from the fact that in 1674[1] there were in Plymouth Colony four hundred and ninety-seven praying Indians. Of this number, seventy-two could write, one hundred and forty-two could read the Indian language, as it had been reduced to writing by Eliot, and nine could read English. In addition to this number, there were about one hundred children in the Indian schools in the colony, who were being taught not only to speak English, but to read and write.

The Indians who early embraced christianity were from the smaller tribes about Boston, the Cape, and Plymouth Colony, while the larger tribes and the prominent chieftains of New England were never in sympathy with this work. Massasoit, although always friendly with the whites, cared nothing for their religion, and was much opposed to its being introduced among his tribes; when the whites were negotiating for lands in Swansea, he endeavored to have them promise never to convert any of his subjects to christianity. The successful Indian missionary, Eliot, at one time tried to make a convert of Philip,

[1] Winsor's *Duxbury*, p. 75; also Gookin's "Historical Collections," in *Mass. Hist. Soc. Coll.* vol. i, p. 141.

but he, taking hold of a button of his coat, said, "I do not care for your religion more than I care for that button."

Of the Indian teachers and preachers whose names have come down to us, John Sassamon[1] was by far the ablest and best educated. He taught for a while at Natick, under the apostle Eliot, with such success that Eliot advised that his services should be paid for by the London society. He was settled as pastor and teacher over the church at Nemasket, and often taught and preached at Assawampsett and Titicut. His grave is supposed to be in an old Indian burial-ground on the southern shore of Assawampsett Pond.

The membership in the Indian churches shows how earnest and faithful must have been the labors and the exemplary christian character of the descendants of the pilgrims living in Middleboro, who without a pastor themselves, did such effective missionary work. These churches adopted a form of church government; deacons and officers were appointed by the different tribes to adjust and settle matters of dispute and difficulties between them; they had their own schoolmaster, and constables to enforce the orders and the decrees of their officials.[2]

---

[1] For further account, see chapter on King Philip's War.

[2] Whether the attempt to establish a local government by the Indians for their own protection, which was instituted by Eliot for the Indians of Natick and Nonantum in connection with his schools and the establishment of christian churches, ever was adopted in Plymouth Colony may be a matter of doubt, but the employment of the more intelligent christian Indians as teachers and preachers was always acceptable to them and esteemed a great honor. They probably held courts in Barnstable for the adjustment of their rights and the punishment of crimes.

Some amusing anecdotes of Indian justice and its administration have come down to us. The following warrant from an Indian court in Barnstable County was issued by one of the Indian magistrates to an Indian constable, and its conciseness and absence of unnecessary words are quite noticeable.

This was the form of the warrant:—

"I Hihoudi,
You Peter Waterman.
Jeremy Wicket;
Quick you take him,
Fast you hold him,
Straight you bring him,
Before me, Hihoudi."

Davis, ed., *New England Memorial*, p. 415.

There were three churches, one in Nemasket, one in Titicut, and one in Assawampsett, with about thirty members in each; the membership of the church at Assawampsett is said to have numbered thirty-five.[1] They had places of worship of their own, although only the site of that in Titicut on Pleasant Street, near the centre of the parish, can now be identified; the Nemasket meeting-house was burned, with the larger portion of the dwelling-houses, at the time of the war; the Old Pond Church was probably on the site of the Assawampsett meeting-house. Their pastors were devoted christian men, with a good knowledge of the scriptures, whose teaching and influence were so beneficial in promoting friendship between the tribes and the whites that at the outbreak of the war most of them remained loyal to their white friends; many following them to Plymouth and some joining the different companies against King Philip. Without this friendship, the entire colony must have been wiped out, and yet, in spite of this fact, they were distrusted by many.

In 1689 Rev. Grindal Rawson of Mendon and Rev. Samuel Danforth of Taunton were appointed by the society to visit the several Indian settlements in the old colony. They reported "20 houses and 80 persons at Assawampsit and Quittaub [probably Nemasket] John Hiacoomes preacher and constant schoolmaster at Kehtehticut are 40 adults to whom Charles Aham preaches also Jocelyn preacher."[2] After the war and abandonment of their church organization, the praying Indians of Nemasket worshipped with the First Church, where a place was provided for them in the gallery. We have no further records of the church at Assawampsett, although it probably continued for some time. The church at Titicut was apparently well sustained until after the middle of the eighteenth century. Rev. Mr. Treat occasionally visited the Indians of this section, and labored earnestly for their spiritual welfare. Rev. John Cotton, pastor of the church at Plymouth, instructed them from the scriptures of the Old and New

---

[1] Goodwin's *Pilgrim Republic*, p. 536.
[2] *Mass. Hist. Soc. Coll.* vol. x, p. 134.

Testament. Most of the Indians at this time had learned to read the Bible and the books which the apostle Eliot had translated into their language. Some of them could write, and not a few could speak and even write the English language.

Richard Bourne of Sandwich, another minister who often visited them, wrote on the 1st of July, 1674,[1] of the Plymouth Colony Indians: —

"There is good hopes of diverse of them. Some of them being lately dead, having given a good testimony of their being in the faith, and so lifting up their souls to Christ as their Saviour and their All in All, as diverse of the well affected English know, and have been present among some of them that departed this life. I was with one of them, the last summer, that had been sick for a long time, and I staid with him near one whole day, and there came from him very heavenly and savory expressions. One passage I will make bold to insert, the which is this: That he, being very sick, not expecting the continuance of his life, told me that his wife did much solicit him to forsake God and live, forasmuch as many that were not praying Indians were not so afflicted as he was. But he, using those words in Job II: 9, 10, gave her this answer: That he would cleave to God, altho' he died, rather than live and forsake Him."

Governor Hinckley, in a report made by him concerning the praying Indians of the colony, says: —

"Their manner is not to accept any to be praying Indians or Christians, but such as do, before some of their magistrates or civil rulers, renounce their former heathenish manners, and give up themselves to be praying Indians; neither do they choose any other than such to bear any office among them. They keep their courts in several places, living so far distant one from another. Especially the four chief places often desire my help amongst them, at their courts, and often do appeal from the sentence of the Indian Judges, to my determination, in which they quietly rest, whereby I have much trouble and expense of time among them, but if God please to bless my endeavours to bring them to more civility and Christianity, I shall account my time and pains well spent. A great obstruction whereunto is the great appetite many of the young

---

[1] *Mass. Hist. Soc. Coll.* vol. i, p. 198, 1st series.

generation have after strong liquors, and the covetous evil humour of sundry of our English, in furnishing them therewith, notwithstanding all the courts orders and means used to prohibit the same."[1]

In 1746 the praying Indians in Titicut had given lands for the meeting-house, although at that time no action had been taken by the General Court to confirm the grant, which by a law of the colony was necessary, and no title could be confirmed until those steps had been taken.

These three Indians, James Thomas, John Ahanton, and Stephen David, contributed thirty-eight and three quarters acres to the parish in Titicut, and the land included the site of the present meeting-house and parsonage, the public green, and the cemetery.[2] These grants were afterwards duly confirmed by the General Court.

Mr. Joshua Fobes has left on record that one at least of the three Indians was buried in the village cemetery, and he remembered the spot pointed out to him as the grave of James Thomas. Those connected with these churches were desirous of receiving spiritual instruction, and in their deportment showed that they were endeavoring to lead a godly life. They had great respect for the christian men and women living in that community, and seemed to look to them for an example of what their conduct and behavior should be.

When Rev. Isaac Backus came to Titicut as preacher, Nehemiah Abiel, Thomas Felix, and John Simons were pastors there, of whom he writes, "John Simons was the minister of the Indian church and continued for nearly ten years,"[3] at the end of which most of the Indians had disappeared, and their remaining land was sold in 1760.

---

[1] *Mass. Hist. Soc. Coll.* vol. v, p. 134, 4th series.
[2] Emery. *History of North Middleboro Church*, p. 15.
[3] *Ibid.* p. 8.

CHAPTER III

MIDDLEBORO AS FIRST KNOWN TO THE ENGLISH

IN 1619 Sir Ferdinand Gorges sent an expedition to look after certain fishing and fur interests which Captain John Smith had established two years before. Thomas Dermer, one of Smith's captains, was in charge of the expedition, with instructions to join one Rocroft on the Maine coast. On arriving, he found that Rocroft had gone to Virginia. He sent his ship of two hundred tons home, laden with furs and fish; then with a few men and Tisquantum, or Squanto, as guide, proceeded to explore the country in a small boat from the Kennebec to Cape Cod. He went to Tisquantum's native place, Patuxet, and of this he says, "When I arrived at my savage's native country, finding all dead I travelled almost a day's journey westward to a place called Namasket, where finding inhabitants, I despatched a messenger a day's journey west to Pokanoket, which bordereth on the sea, whence came to see me two kings attended with a guard of fifty armed men, who being well satisfied with what my savage and I discoursed unto them, and being desirous of novelty, gave me content in whatsoever I demanded."

On this trip he rescued two Frenchmen, who had been wrecked several years before. They had been subjected to a life of slavery since their capture; a third had lived with them for a time, then had married, but soon after died and was buried with his child.[1] Of the two survivors, one was found in Nemasket, the other at Massachusetts Bay. The natives were hostile to the Englishmen, and later would have killed

[1] "The pilgrims discovered the grave of this man. On opening it, they found a bow between two mats, a painted board shaped like a trident, bowls, trays, dishes, etc., and two bundles which proved to be the bones of a man with fine yellow hair and a child. This caused much interest, as it showed them that white people had been there before them." Goodwin's *Pilgrim Republic*, p. 78.

Dermer had not Tisquantum interfered. After varied adventures he set sail for Virginia with the two Frenchmen, leaving Squanto at "Tawahquatook" Satucket, now Brewster.

Two years later Squanto's services were required as guide by the pilgrims, who sent two of their number to Massasoit, "the greatest commander among the savages." They desired to ascertain where these Indians under the rule of Massasoit were, discover their strength, and make amends for any injuries which had been done. They also wished to continue their league of friendship and peace. Stephen Hopkins and Edward Winslow were chosen for this purpose. With Squanto as interpreter, and a gift consisting of a coat of red cotton and lace to propitiate the chief, they set out at nine o'clock on the morning of July 13, 1621. They planned to spend the night at "Namaschet, a Town under Massasoyt," which they thought but a short distance from Patuxet, but found to be about fifteen miles away. They fell in with several men, women, and children, who insisted on following them, much to their annoyance. At about three o'clock they reached "Namaschet," and were most cordially entertained by the inhabitants. They gave them an abundant repast of spawn of shad, a kind of bread called "maizium," and boiled musty acorns. As their journey's end was still more than a day's travel, Tisquantum advised their going a few miles further that night to a place where they would find a larger store of food. At sunset they reached a camp, where they halted and prepared to spend the night in the open fields, as there was no shelter. They found the Namascheuks (the name given to the people of Namaschet) fishing upon a weir they had made on the river (probably the old Indian weir at Titicut on Taunton River). Winslow wrote of this river,[1] "The head of the river is reported to be not far from the place of our abode. Upon it are and have been many towns, it being a good length. The ground is very good on both sides, it being for the most part cleared. Thousands of men have lived there, which died in a great plague not long since; and pity it was and is to see so many goodly fields and

[1] Young's *Chronicles of the Pilgrims*, pp. 204-206.

so well seated, without men to dress and manure the same. Upon this river dwelleth Massasoit. It cometh into the sea at the Narrobigganset Bay, where the Frenchmen so much use."

The messengers reached Massasoit on July 4, faint and weary. They had given generously of their food to the natives on the way, expecting to find an abundance with the chief. Unfortunately for his guests, he had little or nothing for them, so, worn and hungry, they sought rest with their royal host. Massasoit shared with them his bed, which consisted of a wooden platform a foot from the ground covered with a thin mat; the guests slept at one side, he and his wife at the other, with two of his men close by. In such uncomfortable quarters they passed the night. The Indian custom of singing themselves to sleep was not as conducive to slumber for the whites as for the natives. The next day Massasoit gave them fish to eat, and early in the morning of the day following they set out for home. Winslow writes: "That night we reached to the wear where we lay before; but the Namascheuks were returned, so that we had no hope of anything there. One of the savages had shot a shad in the water, and a small squirrel, as big as a rat, called a neuxis; the one half of either he gave us, and after went to the wear to fish. From hence we wrote to Plymouth and sent Tockamahamon before to Namasket, willing him from thence to send another, that he might meet us with food at Namasket. Two men now only remained with us; and it pleased God to give them good store of fish, so that we were well refreshed. After supper we went to rest, and they to fishing again. More they gat, and fell to eating afresh, and retained sufficient ready roast for all our breakfasts. About two o'clock in the morning, arose a great storm of wind, rain, lightning and thunder, in such violent manner that we could not keep in our fire; and had the savages not roasted fish when we were asleep, we had set forward fasting; for the rain still continued with great violence, even the whole day through, till we came within two miles of home. Being wet and weary, at length we came to Namaschet."[1] On their arrival they were

[1] Young's *Chronicles of the Pilgrims*, p. 212.

urged to spend the night, but in spite of the weather they passed on, and reached home in safety.

A month later startling news came to New Plymouth. Massasoit, their friend and ally, had been driven from the country by the Narragansetts, and one of his sachems, Corbitant, chief of the Pocassets, was in command. He was known to be hostile to the white men, and did all in his power to break the treaty made between Massasoit and the settlers. At this time Nemasket again became the scene of a meeting between the Indians and the English ; for this sachem lived here, and in his chieftain's absence sought by every means to weaken Massasoit's influence, destroy his new allies, and raise himself to power.

As soon as the colonists heard the news, they sent Hobomok and Squanto to ascertain Massasoit's whereabouts, and to observe carefully the plans and actions of Corbitant and his followers. These emissaries proceeded as secretly as possible to "Namaschet," planning to spend the night there, but Corbitant, discovering their hiding-place, attacked the house, seized Squanto and his companion, and threatened them with death on account of their friendship with the white men. He had said that if Squanto were dead, "the English had lost their tongue," and was about to kill them both, when Hobomok, owing to his great strength, escaped from them, and dashed past the guard out of the wigwam. Making his way as rapidly as possible toward Plymouth, he related his experience and the manner of his escape, as well as his fears for Squanto's life.

On hearing this news, realizing the hatred and fury of their enemy, the governor called a council to consider what was best for them to do. They took it for granted that Squanto had been killed, and appointed Miles Standish, with a little company of men, to avenge his death at Nemasket and quell the insurrection against their ally, Massasoit. Standish and his men, with Hobomok as guide, set out for the "kingdom of Namaschet" on the 24th of August. They marched through the woods, in spite of a heavy rain, to within three or four miles of Nemasket. Here they had been ordered to wait until night, that they might approach the town unobserved. While they rested,

Standish called them together to plan their method of attack and to give each man his orders. His instructions had been to surprise the town at night and take all who had been concerned in the seizure of Squanto. If it was found that he had been killed, Corbitant was to be beheaded at once, and his assistant, Nepeof, a sachem, who had joined in the rebellion, was to be held as hostage until Massasoit was heard from.

Midnight seemed the best time for the attack. They had not advanced far on the march when they discovered that the guide had lost his way. They were weary and drenched with the rain, and well-nigh discouraged, but one of the party, who had been to the place before, was able to lead them in the right direction. Before they reached there, they ate what food they had, threw away their knapsacks and baggage, and advanced to the house where they knew Corbitant had been staying. The sound of the wind and rain completely concealed the coming of Standish and his men, the Indians at this time having no thought of the pursuit of one of their chieftains. In the middle of the night they surrounded what was supposed to be the wigwam of Corbitant. It was filled with a large number of his braves, and Standish, with his known courage, suddenly burst open the door and rushed in among them. As they awoke at the sound of his voice and footsteps, they were paralyzed with fear and terror, and some endeavored to conceal themselves by hiding under the skins of the wigwam. Others attempted to escape through the door, but were intercepted. Some of the Indians, having heard that Standish never made war upon their squaws, most piteously cried out, "Don't hurt me, I am a squaw, I am a squaw!" While they were making a fire and searching the wigwam, Hobomok climbed to the roof and called for Squanto and Tockamahamon, who came with many others, some having weapons, which were taken from them, to be returned later, and the object of the journey was explained to them. Standish then released all the savages whom they had seized, after hearing of Corbitant's departure. The next day they took breakfast with Squanto, while all of the friendly Indians gathered near, and again they spoke of their intentions against the hostile

Indians, threatening to destroy Corbitant and his followers if they continued to instigate trouble against them and against their friend and ally, Massasoit, or if he should not return in safety from Narragansett, or if Squanto or any other of Massasoit's subjects should be killed.

After renewing their offers of friendship, even agreeing to take with them those who had been wounded, that Dr. Fuller, their physician, might dress their wounds and care for them, they returned home the next day, accompanied by Squanto and other friendly Indians with the three who were hurt, having so impressed the natives with their bravery that ever afterward Standish was an object of especial terror. This first warlike expedition of the pilgrims in New England thus becomes the first event of importance in Middleboro history.

In January of the next year Governor Bradford found it necessary to buy corn, and an expedition was sent to Manomet and to Nemasket. The Indian women were prevented by sickness from carrying all the corn from Nemasket, and the remainder was taken by the pilgrims to Plymouth.

In March news came to Plymouth that Massasoit was on his death-bed. In accordance with the Indian custom of friends visiting the sick one before his death, the pilgrims decided to send one of their number to the chief's home, and Edward Winslow was chosen. He was accompanied by an Englishman desirous of seeing the country, Hampden by name, and by Hobomok as guide. With numerous medicines and cordials for the chief, they set out, and spent the first night at Nemasket. After visiting Massasoit, they remained a night with Corbitant at "Mattapuyet," and then proceeded to Nemasket, where they again stayed over night.

In the year 1633 Sir Christopher Gardner lived on the banks of the Nemasket, after his departure from England in disgrace. He had sent a petition to the king alleging various charges against the Plymouth and Massachusetts Bay colonies, which were denied by the governors, and the petition was dismissed by the king. In England he had been a gentleman of influence, a knight of the Holy Sepulchre at Jerusalem, and a connection of the Bishop of Winchester, but a zealous papist in disguise. When he came into the colony he was accompanied by one or two servants, and it was understood that he had given up all worldly pursuits and would live a godly life in humble circumstances. He had applied for admission to several churches, but was refused on account of his questionable character. The authorities of Massachusetts Bay had attempted to arrest him, but he had eluded their pursuit, and was living with the Indians at Nemasket. Becoming suspicious, they gave information to the governor, who authorized his seizure, and directed that he be brought uninjured to Boston. The Indians saw him near the river and attempted to capture him, but he escaped in a canoe. Armed with a musket and rapier, he kept them at bay until the canoe was upset upon a rock and his weapons lost. He continued to defend himself with a small dagger, which they finally succeeded in knocking from his hands, and he was made prisoner. He was taken to Governor Winthrop, in Boston, who afterwards sent him to England to meet the criminal charges there pending against him.

The settlers in Plymouth undoubtedly passed through Middleboro on expeditions to Taunton and elsewhere, but until about ten years before the Twenty-six Men's Purchase there were probably no permanent residents.

John Winthrop, Jr., who accompanied an expedition from the Narragansett Bay up the Taunton River in 1636, sailed up the river as far as Titicut, as appears by the following letter to his father: —

SAYBROOK, PASBESHUKE, April 7, 1636.
FROM JOHN WINTHROP, TO THE RIGHT WORSHIPFUL AND MUCH HONORED FATHER, JOHN WINTHROP, WHO DWELLS IN BOSTON.

Sir: — My humble duty remembered to yourself and my mother, with love to my brothers and all of our friends with you. I suppose you have heard of our arrival at Titiquet, an opportune meeting with our vessels. Concerning that place I conceive it is about 22 or 23 miles from Waliston. Very fertile and rich land and so far as we went down it grew wide into Sachems Harbor and a ship of 500 tons may go up to about ten or twelve miles. There is no meadow or salt marsh all the way. The first of the month we set sail from Naraganset and in the evening about six o'clock arrived there. Thus craving your prayers and blessings I commend you to the Almighty and rest,

Your obedient son,

JOHN WINTHROP.

He evidently sailed up the river as far as the wading-place at Pratt's Bridge, as the river is navigable for small ships of not more than five hundred tons up to that point. There is no record, however, that he and his party did more than make a temporary landing at this place.

In 1637 a settlement was made at Titicut, bordering on the westerly side of Middleboro, by Miss Elizabeth Poole and her associates. She was the daughter of Sir William Poole, a knight of Colcombe, in the parish of Coliton, Devon, England. The records of the parish say that she was baptized August 25, 1588. This land was sometimes called the Titicut purchase, not because it was bought of the Indians residing there, but from the fact that it was within the original Indian reservation, which had been conveyed to her and her associates before it had been reserved for the exclusive use of the Indians. Her purchase was between the bounds of Cohanett (the former name of Taunton) and the Titicut weir, and bordered upon what subsequently became the western boundary line of Middleboro between Poquoy Brook and Baiting Brook. Those who settled here about the time of Miss Poole's purchase were her brother, William Poole, Mr. John Gilbert, Sr., Mr. Henry Andrews, John Strong, John Dean, Walter Dean, and Edward Case, who, the next year, were made freemen in Plymouth Colony. The territory which she purchased was known for some time as Littleworth farm and Shute farm, and the records state that it was here Miss Poole lost many cattle. The original purchase of Miss Poole ultimately became a portion of Taunton, and other farms purchased by her and her associates were often referred to in the early records as Meerneed, Bareneed, Cotley, and Pondsbrook, in accordance with the English custom. Bareneed was given to the farm of Edward Case and Pondsbrook to that of John Gilbert.

CHAPTER IV

EARLY SETTLERS BEFORE KING PHILIP'S WAR

ALTHOUGH Middleboro was only fifteen miles from Plymouth and halfway on the Indian Path to the Taunton settlement, it was more than forty years after the landing of the pilgrims before the whites came to dwell there in large numbers. There were from fifteen to twenty thousand Indians within forty miles of Plymouth, and probably more in Middleboro than in any other part of the colony.

For fifteen years after the early settlers came here to live, the territory was a part of Plymouth, and they were described as residents of that town; but after its incorporation in 1669, they were known as "residing in Middleberry." They were mostly the sons or the grandsons of the pilgrims, and united their sturdy virtues and habits of industry with their enterprise and courage. Their fathers had conquered many of the difficulties attending the first coming, and had become accustomed to the new life on these western shores.

Many of them had not only engaged in trading with the Indians in different parts of the country, but had purchased large tracts of land, which were being occupied, and there were not a few among their number who had already acquired a competence. The colony had been settled long enough for the people to begin to be attached to the place where they had been born and reared; this younger generation knew nothing of the luxuries, turmoil, and political distractions of the Old World, except what they had learned from their fathers and grandfathers.

The population was increasing, although not as rapidly as that of Salem and of the Bay. The settlement of Middleboro was unlike that of other places, in that these men supposed that the town was to be occupied in common with the aborigines, who were then the owners of much of the land. We can but note what must have been their heroism in thus choosing homes among the red men of the forest, well knowing, as they did, their characteristics, and the inevitable dangers which would continually confront them.

Their manner of living is of interest. Although many frame houses had been built in Plymouth and the older parts of the colony, all houses in Middleboro prior to the breaking out of King Philip's War were of hewn logs. The doors were made of plank, either sawed by hand or hewn, and logs were hewn upon three sides to form a level floor in the house. The fireplaces were usually built of stone laid in clay, and some of the chimneys were of green oak logs plastered with clay. The latches and hinges of the doors were made of wood; the former were raised by a string extending through the door outside. The windows were usually small and placed high up from the ground. Oiled paper [1] set in a wooden frame admitted light into the windows, although in the better class of houses in Plymouth they had commenced using window-glass in small diamond shapes set in lead.

For generations they obtained from their farms all that was necessary for the support of their families. Most of their clothing was made of flax and of wool from the sheep, the women being skilled in spinning and weaving, and the men often wore trousers made from skins of sheep, deer, or bear, which they tanned.

Their simple food was served from the table, a long, narrow board on standards not unlike sawhorses, called a table board, and the linen covering was called a "board cover," not a table cover till later. Napkins were many and necessary, as they had no forks. The food was frequently "spoon meat," i. e. soups, hashes, etc., which could be easily managed with spoons and knives. The pewter platters usually contained the

---

[1] Edward Winslow in his letter to George Morton, writing from Plymouth under date of December 11, 1621, says, " Bring paper and linseed oil for your windows, with cotton yarn for your lamps." Young's *Chronicle of the Pilgrims*, p. 237.

meat and vegetables, and this metal was used for drinking-cups and porringers. One of the most important articles for the table was a trencher, a block of wood ten or twelve inches square, hollowed out three or four inches. A man and his wife ate from one trencher; an old Connecticut deacon made a trencher for each of his children, but was condemned by his neighbors as extravagant. Myles Standish and others of the "first comers" used trenchers in their homes. In the centre of the table was placed the salt-cellar, and guests were seated "above the salt," near the host, who sat by his wife. No china[1] and but very little silver was used in the colony. The native corn meal became a staple article of food; the morning and evening meals for one hundred and fifty years were commonly of boiled Indian meal, "ye Indian porridge," with milk or molasses. The Indians taught them how to plant and raise the corn, and how to grind it between stones, or with the pestle and mortar. This method gave way to rude hand-mills, called quernes, and grist-mills. Corn was so highly regarded that it was often used for ballots in voting. Suppawn, a coarse porridge of corn and milk, samp, and succotash, an Indian dish, were favorite foods. Roger Williams wrote that "sutsquttahhash was corn seethed like beans."

Squashes and beans were native vegetables. The former was spelled in various ways, "squanter-squashes," "squontor-squashes," "isquonker-squashes." They had not been accustomed to drinking much water, and at first feared it might be dangerous. Home-brewed ale and beer were drunk freely, and liquors and wines were brought to the town from Taunton and Plymouth; later, as the orchards grew, cider became a popular drink, and Middleboro cider was famous. In spite of the free use of all these, a writer from Massachusetts in 1641 said, "Drunkenness and profane swearing are but rare in this country." For coffee they used a substitute, made either from barley or from crusts of brown bread. For sugar they used

[1] "As tea and coffee were unknown to the Forefathers, the many Delft-ware tea and coffee pots and cups preserved as Pilgrim relics are to be regarded as anachronisms." Goodwin's *Pilgrim Republic*, p. 588.

sweet apples and the syrup obtained from beets and pumpkins. Herring, or alewives, were always abundant, and largely took the place of meat at their family meals.

Although there were no schools in town until after the Indian War, the children were taught to "read, write and cipher;" the Bible and a volume of Sternhold and Hopkins's Hymns, with the Bay Psalm Book and a few other books, could be found in almost every family. A study of their old primers well repays one interested in old books. At first the "good King Charles" was referred to, but after the Revolution we find books for children with the statement, "Kings and Queens are gaudy things." The New England Primer and their other books were as severe in binding as was the dress of the colonists, without decoration or ornament.

Nearly all travel was on horseback. Women and children rode seated on a pillion behind a man. If several people were to make a journey, the ride-and-tie system was used. Certain ones would ride a distance, then tie the horse and walk on. The others would then take the horse and ride ahead, again leaving the horse for the two who were afoot.

Many of the settlers brought with them from Plymouth articles of furniture which had either been made there or brought by their fathers from the old country. The bureaus, chests of drawers, etc., were on legs, so no dust could accumulate underneath. Their homes were comfortable, neat, and tidy, although in the forests with savage surroundings.

They often attended church at Plymouth, a distance of sixteen or more miles, going and returning the same day, until Samuel Fuller settled among them as preacher. They were honest, God-fearing men and women, having a clear knowledge of the teachings of the scriptures, and a strong, abiding faith in the religion for which their fathers had suffered, leaving comforts and luxuries of the Old World. (See chapter on Social Customs.)

In our review of these times we are never to forget the hardships which these men and women endured, without murmur or complaint, for more than a generation. The nearest

EARLY SETTLERS BEFORE KING PHILIP'S WAR

settlements were Plymouth, Bridgewater, Taunton, and Dartmouth, reached only by the narrow Indian paths for the most part through dense forests. Their houses were remote from neighbors and distant from friends, the usual communication being only by foot; they were liable at any time to unexpected visits from the savages, who might not be friendly and who were addicted to thieving; they had neither medical skill nor scientific knowledge, when sickness, as a result of hardship and exposure, so often entered their dwellings; they had none of the luxuries, or what we consider to-day comforts, of life; there was also the extreme danger from hostile Indians before King Philip's War, and the constant annoyance and depredations from wolves and bears, which attacked not only their crops, but sometimes the settlers themselves. They were contented and happy in their simple habits and mode of living; honest and industrious, frugal and thoughtful, many of them men of character and enterprise, whom their posterity, remembering their virtues, ever do well to honor.

By the laws of the colony " none shall vote in town meetings but freemen or freeholders of 20 pounds ratable estate and of good conversation, having taken the oath of fidelitie."[1] Those who had taken the oath of fidelity in town up to the uniting of the colonies in 1692 were but few, so that many of the expenditures and public acts were undertaken by the voters in connection with the proprietors of the "liberties of the town," as the owners of land were then called, who were not all of them residents. In 1677, after the return, a meeting was held, at which sixty-five of the proprietors and residents were present.[2]

As the town records were destroyed in the war, it is impossible to give an exact list of men living in Middleboro before 1675. The number has heretofore been variously stated as sixteen, twenty, and twenty-six, but it is hardly probable that the court at Plymouth would have incorporated a town unless there had been a larger number of inhabitants. We give

[1] *Plymouth Colony Records*, Laws, vol. ii, Part III, p. 223.
[2] *Old Middleboro Records*, copy, p. 17. See also chapter on Civil History for list of names.

below a list of forty-one who are known to have lived here, as the names are to be found in Plymouth records, in deeds, as office-holders and freemen, from records of births and deaths, as well as from reliable family note-books, and seven who were here according to generally accepted tradition.

Samuel Barrows	John Nelson o
Edward Bump	William Nelson x
John Bump	Samuel Pratt
Joseph Bump	Andrew Ring
Gershom Cobb o	John Shaw
Francis Coombs x o	David Thomas
William Clark	David Thomas, Jr.
George Dawson	Ephraim Tinkham o
John Dunham x o	Ephraim Tinkham, Jr.
Samuel Eaton x	Ebenezer Tinkham
Zachariah Eddy	John Tomson o
Obadiah Eddy o	John Tomson, Jr.
Samuel Fuller	George Vaughn o
John Haskall	Joseph Vaughn
William Hoskins o	Francis Walker
Isaac Howland o	Adam Wright
John Irish o	Henry Wood x
John Miller	Samuel Wood o
Francis Miller	Jonathan Wood
John Morton o	Joseph Wood
John Morton, Jr. x	

x Freemen in 1670.   o Office-holders before 1675.

Of the seven following, four were in the fort, and are mentioned in the "History of the First Church" in the list of those "who were here when the war broke out and who probably returned after the war:"—

Francis Billington	Jabez Warren
John Cobb	Joseph Warren
John Holmes	David Wood
William Nelson, Jr.	

The following list of men in the fort was obtained from an old Eddy note-book quoted from Mercy Bennett, "whose grandfather was on the list and she had her information from him. This was confirmed from other sources:"—

EARLY SETTLERS BEFORE KING PHILIP'S WAR

John Tomson, Commandant
Isaac Howland
Francis Coombs
Samuel Fuller   } Commandant's Council
John Morton
Nathaniel Southworth [1]
Ephraim Tinkham
Henry Wood [2]
William Nelson
David Thomas
John Cobb
Jabez Warren
Edward Bump
Moses Simmons [1]
Samuel Barrows
—— Eaton (*Samuel?*)
Francis Billington
George Soule [1]
Obadiah Eddy
Samuel Pratt
George Vaughan
John Shaw
Jacob Tomson
Francis Miller
—— Holmes (*John?*)
John Alden [1]

This list differs slightly from that given in the "History of the First Church:" Samuel Eddy [1] is mentioned in place of Obadiah, and John Howland [1] in place of John Holmes.

SAMUEL BARROWS was one of the early settlers of Middleboro, and before the breaking out of the war had built a dam across

---

[1] We find no record that these men were permanent residents of Middleboro. They were extensive land-owners and probably in town at that time. George Soule, Samuel Eddy, and John Howland had children living here, and John Alden had a son in Bridgewater adjoining the Twenty-six Men's Purchase. For a sketch of their lives, see chapter on Early Purchases.

Not a few of the inhabitants of the different towns of the colony lived for a longer or shorter time in other places without changing their legal residence, and this may account for some of the early settlers being in Middleboro before King Philip's War who at that time were citizens of other towns.

[2] As Henry Wood was not living, this probably refers to one of his sons.

the Nemasket River some fifty rods above the present Star Mills, and erected a grist-mill, in which he worked. On the morning of the attack upon the town, after the Indian had been shot, he saw a band approaching the mill and fled to the fort uninjured. The records of the First Church of Middleboro show that he had acquired a share in the Twenty-six Men's Purchase before the breaking out of the war.

The pilgrim ancestor of the Barrows families in this country was John Borowe, or Barrow, from Yarmouth,[1] England, who came to Salem in 1637, at the age of twenty-eight years, with his wife Anne. In 1665 his name appears in the Plymouth records, in which town he resided from that time, and perhaps earlier, until his death in 1692. The Samuel Barrows above referred to was probably his son. Although his name does not appear in any of the published genealogies which we have examined, it has come down in so many ways that there can be no doubt that he resided in Middleboro at this time, and was among those who returned from Plymouth on the re-settlement of the town.

Robert, the oldest son of John, married, in 1666, Ruth Bonum, and later married Lydia, daughter of John Dunham. He had a son Samuel, born in 1672, who about the year 1700 built a garrison house which is still standing and known as the old Barrows house. He was elected deacon of the First Church in 1725. He married first, Mercy Coombs, who died in 1718, and then he married Joanna Smith. He died December 30, 1755, aged eighty-three.[2]

EDWARD BUMPUS. This name was originally spelled Bompasse, now spelled Bumpas or Bump. He arrived at Plymouth in the Fortune, November 10, 1621, and moved to Duxbury, where he bought land of Mr. Palmer at Eagle Nest Creek and

---

[1] *Maine Hist. and Gen. Register*, vol. vii, pp. 136, 199.
[2] *History of the First Church of Middleboro*, p. 53.

EARLY SETTLERS BEFORE KING PHILIP'S WAR

built a house and palisado, which he sold in 1634, and moved to Marshfield. He resided in Middleboro in the latter part of his life, and was in the fort at the breaking out of King Philip's War. He was the father of several of this name who became permanent settlers in Middleboro. He was one of the original owners in the Twenty-six Men's Purchase and in the Purchade Purchase, and was among the proprietors of the liberties of Middleboro in 1677. He died February 3, 1693, and was then called "old Edward Bumpas." He married Hannah —— while living in Duxbury. His children, as far as can now be ascertained, were Faith, born 1631; Sarah ——; John, born 1636; Edward, born 1638; Joseph, born 1639; Jacob, born 1644; Hannah, born 1646; Philip ——; Thomas, born 1660.[1]

JOHN BUMPUS, the oldest son of Edward, was born in 1636. Few facts are given concerning him. In Church's "Entertaining Passages Relating to King Philip's War,"[2] an Indian by this name is mentioned as killing horses with Tispequin, and in a note we find, "There are respectable white people in Middleboro by this name from the ancestors of whom he may have derived his name." His children born in Middleboro were Mary, born 1671; John, born 1673; Samuel, born 1676; James, born 1678. Other children were born in Rochester, where he lived later.

JOSEPH BUMPUS, son of Edward, was born in 1639, and lived in Middleboro later as "a principal settler." His wife Weibra was one of the original members of the First Church in 1694. Their children were Lydia, born 1669; Weibra, born 1672; Joseph, born 1674; Rebecca, born 1677; James, born 1679; Penelope, born 1681; Mary, born 1684; Mehitable, born 1691–92. He died February 10, 1704.[3]

---

[1] *Barnstable Families*, pp. 85, 86.   [2] Page 144.
[3] *Barnstable Families*, p. 86.

WILLIAM CLARK. Few facts are known concerning him. The Eddy note-book says his house,[1] with that of Mr. Coombs, was burned in 1675, and that William Hoskins lived with him as keeper of the records.

There was a William Clark whose name appears on the treasurer's account for Plymouth Colony in 1660 and 1667, and there was a person by that name capable of bearing arms in 1643 in Duxbury and Plymouth; he was on a committee to take the treasurer's account of the colony, June 7, 1674. He died in 1687. In 1655 a William Clark was constable of Duxbury, surveyor of highways in 1659, admitted as a freeman in 1658, and was a constable in Plymouth in 1669. This may have been the Clark who subsequently moved to and lived in Middleboro in 1675, one of those for whom the Five Men's Purchase was made.

GERSHOM COBB, a son of Elder Henry Cobb of Barnstable, was born the 10th of January, 1644-45, and at one time lived in Plymouth. He married Hannah Davis and became a resident of Middleboro, but the date of his settling here is uncertain. He was constable in the year 1671, and a member of the Grand Inquest in 1674. He was one of the settlers for whom the Sixteen Shilling Purchase was made. He was in Swansea at the first attack of the Indians upon that town at the beginning of King Philip's War, where he was killed with eight others, and was buried with them June 24, 1675. His brother John administered his estate, which was divided in equal portions to the children of Mr. Henry Cobb of Barnstable, excepting John, the elder son, who had a double portion.[2]

FRANCIS COOMBS was the son of John Coombs, who was in Plymouth in 1633 with his wife Sarah, a daughter of Cuthbert-

---

[1] In the records of the General Court in 1734, we find a petition of Cornelius Bennett and Lydia Miller, where it is stated "That about the year 1675 the dwelling house of the said Coombs and also the house where the keeper of the records in Middleboro lived was burned and the Indian deed was and is supposed to be burned also." *Massachusetts Archives.*

[2] *Barnstable Families,* p. 171, Cobb Genealogy.

son. They had other children, but probably Francis was the oldest. He was in Middleboro as early as 1670, and was one of the men who took the inventory of the estate of Henry Wood. On July 1, 1674,[1] he exchanged four acres of land on the south of the Indian Path "which goeth from Namasket to Munhutchet Brook at the southerly end of land which he sold to Benjamin Church with Samuel Wood for the 16th lot on the west side of Namasket River, near the wading-place which was formerly Henry Wood's land, deceased."

After the close of the war, he probably did not return for a year or two, but in 1678, when he was in Plymouth, he bought of Edward Gray for thirty-six pounds the 18th, 19th, and 20th lots on the west side of the Nemasket River between the stone weir and the wading-place.

He also owned the 185th and 186th lots in the South Purchase and the 169th lot in the Sixteen Shilling Purchase. His inventory, which was taken January 5, 1682, by Isaac Howland and Samuel Wood, shows that he owned considerable real estate in town.

He was a man of influence in Middleboro, and was a freeman in 1670. He was a selectman of the town in 1674, 1675, and 1680. In 1676 and 1677 he and Isaac Howland were appointed commissioners to distribute charities from Ireland to such as were impoverished during King Philip's War. He was married twice; his first wife was Deborah Morton; his second wife was Mary Barker of Duxbury, who, upon the decease of Francis Coombs, married David Wood of Middleboro, in 1685. She was living in 1711. He died in Middleboro, December 31, 1682, leaving a wife and several children.

The license to Francis Coombs to keep an ordinary or an inn was granted in 1678, and after his death was renewed to his wife, Mrs. Mary Coombs, July 1, 1684. It was probably the same tavern which was kept seventy-five years ago or more by Captain Abner Barrows, and it is said that part of that house was perhaps a portion of the identical building of the Coombs tavern.[2]

[1] *Eddy Note-Book.*   [2] *History of Plymouth County,* p. 947.

June 5, 1666, "liberty is granted by the General Court unto Francis Coombs as by right of his father who was an ancient freeman, to look out for land for his accommodation and to make report thereof to the court that so a competency thereof may be allowed unto him answerable unto other ancient freemen."[1]

His children were Deborah, born 1673; Mercy, born 1674; Lydia, born 1679; Ruth, born 1681; Francis, born 1682.

GEORGE DANSON lived in that part of Middleboro known as Thompson Road, somewhere between Danson Brook and the home of John Tomson.[2]

At one time he was "fined forty shillings[3] for doing servill work on the Lord's Day."

He was one of the original proprietors of the Sixteen Shilling Purchase. There is some uncertainty about his name. Hubbard speaks of him as Robert Dawson or Danson. In Plymouth County Records he is called George Danson of Middleboro.[4] In the Thompson book he is called William Danson. In Middleboro Records he is called George. The references are probably all to the same person.[5]

He was the owner of the 6th lot in the apportionment of the Twenty-six Men's Purchase before the breaking out of the war, as appears in the early records of the town, although his name is not among the owners of this land in the "History of the First Church of Middleboro." His name also appears on the list of proprietors who met, June 28, 1677, to take measures for the resettlement of the town. The clerk of that meeting evidently failed to record his death, and probably no administration had been taken upon his estate.

He was shot by the Indians upon the breaking out of King Philip's War, at the brook which bears his name. He had been urged by John Tomson the night before to go to the garrison, but waited until morning. After starting, he stopped for his horse to drink, when he was shot.

---

[1] *Plymouth Colony Records,* vol. iv, p. 127. [2] *Thompson Genealogy,* p. 7.
[3] *Plymouth Colony Records,* vol. v, p. 156. [4] *Ibid.* vol. vi, p. 70.
[5] Hubbard's *Indian Wars,* vol. ii, p. 41.

JOHN, or JONATHAN, DUNHAM, JR., was a son of Deacon John Dunham (generally spelled Donham) of Plymouth, who was a deputy to the General Court, and served in various offices in the colony [1] of Plymouth; he died March 2, 1669, at the age of eighty. His will bears date January 25, 1668.

The son John, or Jonathan, bought into the Twenty-six Men's Purchase, and was a resident in 1670, his name appearing on the list of freemen of Middleboro for that year; he was one of the Grand Inquest in 1671, and often served as one of the jurors in the trial of causes. He represented the town at the General Court "holden at Plymouth" in the month of September, 1673, and was a constable of the town the same year; he was one of the selectmen in 1674–75. In 1671 he was appointed as an inspector of ordinances in Middleboro "to prevent selling of powder to Indians and extensive drinking and report violence of this to the General Court, and to take notice of any abuse as may arise in reference to the premises or otherwise and make report thereof to the court."

In 1656 he, with John Morton, Richard Wright, Samuel Eddy, and Francis Billington, "desired some portion of land to accommodate them for their posterity, and the court gave liberty unto them for that purpose. If found convenient, it shall be confirmed unto them for the ends aforesaid."

He had a share of thirty acres of land on the western side of Nemasket River assigned to him by order of the court, June 7, 1665. He owned land in different places in the Twelve Men's, Five Men's, Little Lotmen's, and Sixteen Shilling Purchases. In 1671 his lands at Nemasket were laid out by William Nelson and William Crow.

His first wife was Mary, a daughter of Philip Delano, whom he married November 29, 1655.[2] His second wife was Mary, a daughter of Elder Henry Cobb, and a sister of Gershom and John Cobb.

Some time after the resettlement of the town, he probably moved to Plymouth, where he became a minister to the Indians, and afterwards to Edgartown, previous to 1684. He was

---

[1] Savage, vol. ii, p. 81.   [2] *Barnstable Families*, p. 171.

not installed over the church there until October 11, 1694, when,[1] it is said, he came from Plymouth, and the pastor of that town, with a delegate, was present at his installation. His salary was thirty pounds per annum, in addition to which the town made him various grants of land for his cattle, and half share on the common land. He was highly esteemed for his piety and his personal qualities, and died December 17, 1718, at the age of eighty-five years. On his tombstone behind Tower Hill are these quaint lines : —

> " With toil and pains at first he tilled the ground ;
> Called to God's Vineyard, and was faithful found ;
> Full thirty years, the Gospel he did dispense,
> His work being done, Christ Jesus called him hence." [2]

SAMUEL EATON was a son of Francis Eaton, a passenger in the Mayflower, a carpenter by trade, who moved from Plymouth to Duxbury, where he died in 1633, insolvent.

THE MAYFLOWER

Samuel was born in England or Holland in 1620, and was one of the two passengers in the Mayflower who became residents of Middleboro. Governor Bradford, in the appendix of his "History of the Plimoth Plantation," in a note concerning Francis Eaton, thus speaks of Samuel : "His sone Samuell who came over a suckling child is allso maried and hath a child." He was apprenticed for seven years to John Cook the younger. Before moving to Middleboro he resided for some time in Duxbury. He was a resident of the town before the breaking out of King Philip's War, and returned after its close. He was admitted as a freeman in 1670, and was among the purchasers of the town of Dartmouth in 1652, and of Bridgewater. In 1651 "the court admonished Samuel Eaton and Goodwife Hall

---

[1] Barber, *Hist. Coll.* p. 152.
[2] *Historical Discourse*, by Rev. John H. Hall, November 6, 1878 ; Barber, *Hist. Coll.* p. 152.

of Duxbury for mixed dancing."[1] He died at Middleboro in 1684. His estate was appraised at thirty-seven pounds, eleven shillings.[2] He was twice married; his second wife was Martha Billington, a daughter of Francis Billington; his son, Samuel Eaton, was one of the original members of the First Church, and married a daughter of the first pastor, Rev. Samuel Fuller.

ZACHARIAH EDDY[3] was the second son of Samuel, born in 1639. He married Alice Paddock, May 7, 1663, and for his second wife, Abigail Smith. During his boyhood he was apprenticed to Mr. John Brown, a shipwright of Rehoboth, until he was twenty-one years of age. He was propounded for admission as a freeman by the court at Plymouth, June 16, 1681, but there is no record of his ever having been admitted. He was living in Middleboro in 1665. His house stood on the twelve acres granted him by the court near what was known as Eddy's Furnace.[4] This house afterwards came into possession of Dr. Palmer's family. In 1670 his name appears with fifty-four others upon an instrument by which they consented to become inhabitants of Swansea, according to the terms previously agreed upon between the church and Captain Thomas Willett, the original patentee of the land included in the township, and in the allotment of this land under the peculiar plan the settlers there adopted, his name appears under the second rank entitled to receive two acres of land, but when he removed his residence to that town is unknown. He died in Swansea, September 4, 1718, at the age of seventy-eight years.

[1] Goodwin, *Pilgrim Republic*, p. 598.   [2] *Eddy Note-Book*.
[3] *Eddy Genealogy*, p. 115.
[4] " June the 7th, 1665. The Court haue graunted vnto Sachariah Eedey a smale gussett of land lying betwixt his land and the brooke from his house below the path to Namassakett vnto the aforsaid brooke vnto a bridge or way neare vnto Willam Nelsons house ; the said psell of land soe bounded as aforsaid is graunted vnto the said Sachariah Eedey, to him and his heires and assignes for euer, with all the appurtenances belonging thervnto, on condition that the said Sachariah Eedey doe continew a bridge neare his house, in the place where it is needed, for horse and cart, for the vse of the country, for the full tearme of twenty years from the date heerof." *Plymouth Colony Records*, vol. v, p. 128.

OBADIAH EDDY, a son of Samuel Eddy,[1] inherited that portion of his father's land assigned from the Twenty-six Men's Purchase, where he was living at the breaking out of the war. He with his children took refuge in the fort, and when the garrison was abandoned, moved to Plymouth, where he remained for a short time. He was one of the first settlers to return, and rebuilt his house near the site of the first house (in that part of Middleboro now Halifax, near Winnetuxet River, in the field of Nathan Fuller), the cellar of which can be seen. He was admitted a freeman, June 3, 1683; was a constable in 1679, 1681, 1683, and 1689. In 1673, 1679, and 1681 he was a member of the Grand Inquest; in 1692 was a surveyor of highways, and in 1690 one of the selectmen. He was one of the jurors to lay out a road from Middleboro, Bridgewater, and other places toward Boston in 1683.

He died in 1722, aged seventy-seven years, and divided his estate among his seven children.

SAMUEL FULLER. — See chapter on Ecclesiastical History.

JOHN HASKELL was born about 1640, and married Patience, a daughter of George Soule, in January, 1666. In the will of George Soule, bearing date August 11, 1677, it is stated: "I have formerly given to my daughters, Elizabeth and Patience, all of my lands in the township of Middleberry," and in a codicil, bearing date the 20th day of September, he refers to the lands he had given "his daughter Patience at Namasket alies Middleberry." Some portion of the estate of George Soule was evidently owned in common with Francis Walker, who had married his daughter Elizabeth.

He lived in Middleboro before the year 1670, as the town records show birth of children between that time and the year 1684. He was one of twelve who were freemen before the

---

[1] There is a tradition that the name Eddy originated in the fact that a person by the name of John lived near the eddy of a river and was familiarly known as John of the eddy or John by the eddy. The name occurs in the early records of the colony spelled variously, as Edy, Edye, Eddie, Edie, and Eedey.

year 1689, and was a large owner of real estate in the Twenty-six Men's Purchase and other purchases. At one time he owned, with his brother-in-law, Francis Walker, a tract of land bounded by Raven Brook and the Indian Path, which included the pasture land and swamp later owned by Joshua Eddy, Esq.[1]

He died May 15, 1706, aged sixty-six years. His wife, Patience, bought the old meeting-house in 1701. She died March 15, 1705.

WILLIAM HOSKINS came from England about 1633, and was one of the freemen that year. He married Sarah Cushman, and as a second wife, Ann Hynes, or Hinds.

There is but little doubt that upon the incorporation of Middleboro as a town, in 1669, he was chosen town clerk, and continued in that office until 1693, although there is no official record of his election before May 24, 1681.[2] At that time he was unanimously chosen to that office. His first election cannot be verified, as all of the town records were destroyed during the Indian War. He lived in Middleboro before the Indian War, in the house of William Clark, and kept the original deed and records of the Prince and Coombs Purchase, and probably the records of the town. He is one of the soldiers "from Middleboro" who took part in the war, and was promised a grant of land for his services at Narragansett.

His name is on the list of those who, on June 3, 1662, applied to the General Court at Plymouth in reference to a grant to be made to them as being the first-born children of this government, and for disposing of two several tracts of land lately purchased, the one by Major Winslow and the other by Captain Southworth. He was on the jury with John Tomson and Sergeant Ephraim Tinkham to try an Indian for murder in 1674. February 6, 1665, he was appointed administrator of the estate of Nicholas Hodgis, alias Miller, deceased. He had received a grant of land in Lakenham.

[1] *Eddy Note-Book.*
[2] *Eddy Note-Book* says he was town clerk, 1674-75.

He was one of the men in the Twenty-six Men's Purchase and also in the Purchade Purchase, but at the breaking out of the war he does not appear to have been an owner in any portion of that land. His name is among the former proprietors of the liberties of Middleboro, but before 1677 his interest therein passed to George Vaughan, Sr. He lived in Scituate, Plymouth, and Taunton, and in 1680 was "grown old and feeble."

His children were Sarah, born September 16, 1636; William, born November 30, 1647; Samuel, born August 8, 1654.

ISAAC HOWLAND, the youngest son of John Howland of the Mayflower, lived on the western side of the road, opposite the house of the late Thomas Pratt. He was a leader of public affairs, and town meetings were often held at his home. He owned land on which the present town house stands, and also in the Sixteen Shilling and Twenty-six Men's Purchases. When the families moved to the fort, Isaac Howland was ordered by Lieutenant Tomson to shoot the Indian who appeared upon the rock on the other side of the river. He was the first in the commandant's council, probably the man upon whom Lieutenant Tomson chiefly relied for advice when the garrison were in the fort, and he served with great bravery under Captain Church during the war.

He married Elizabeth, daughter of George Vaughan, and in 1684 kept an inn.[1] His name is one of the most prominent in the early history as holding many offices. He was representative in 1689, 1690, and 1691. He died March 9, 1724, aged seventy-four.[2]

His children were Seth, born November 28, 1677; Isaac, born March 6, 1678; Priscilla, born August 22, 1681; Elizabeth, born December 2, 1682; Nathan, born January 17, 1687; Jael, born October 13, 1688; Susanna, born October 14, 1690; Hannah, born October 16, 1694.

[1] Savage, vol. ii, p. 479. [2] *Eddy Memoranda.*

JOHN IRISH, the son of John and Elizabeth Irish, in his youth lived in Duxbury, and was the servant mentioned in the last will of Captain Myles Standish. In 1640 his father had a "mearstead"[1] granted to him, and in 1641 a tract of land at Stony Brook. In the Pequot War he was a volunteer, but was not called into active service. His business seems to have been that of a roper. As one of the proprietors of Bridgewater and an owner in the Sixteen Shilling and Eight Men's Purchases, he was a resident of Middleboro as early as 1671, and constable of the town in 1672. He lived on land now known as the Sturtevant Place, and in the division of the Twenty-six Men's Purchase he was assigned the 11th lot, which was on the north side of Taunton Path. In May, 1708, he married a sister of Captain Church.[2] He passed the later years of his life in Little Compton.

FRANCIS MILLER is mentioned as one of the men who were in town when King Philip's War began, and in the garrison, but we find no trace of his history before or after that, excepting that he was killed by the Indians, probably during the war. There is a monument erected to his memory at the Green Cemetery, on which is written:—

"Francis Miller was one of the householders driven back to Plymouth from Middleborough by the Indians in 1675."

JOHN MILLER was born in England, in 1624, and died May 11, 1720, in the ninety-seventh year of his age. His monument is at the Green Cemetery. He was a member of the Grand Inquest in 1672, and was among the proprietors of the Twenty-six Men's Purchase at their meeting in 1677. He bought a house-lot of Edward Gray previous to April 29, 1678; he owned lot 154 in the South Purchase, and was one of the owners in the Sixteen Shilling Purchase. He lived on Thompson Street, not far from the brook, near the house of the late Elijah Shaw; the site of his house is still pointed out.

[1] Winsor's *History of Duxbury*, p. 273.
[2] Savage, vol. ii, p. 525.

John Miller married[1] Mercy ———. Their son John was born in 1669, in Middleboro, and died in 1727. He married Lydia Coombs.

JOHN MORTON was the second son of George Morton, who lived in Austerfield, Yorkshire, the home of Governor Bradford. George early joined the pilgrims at Leyden, and came to America in the Anne, landing at Plymouth in 1623; he married Juliana Carpenter,[2] a sister-in-law of Governor Bradford, and died in Plymouth, June, 1624. His eldest son, Nathaniel, was a secretary of Plymouth Colony for more than forty years, until his death in 1685. John, his third child and second son, was born at Leyden, 1616-17, and came with his parents in the Anne. He was admitted a freeman of the Colony June 7, 1648, was a constable in Plymouth in 1654, a member of the Grand Inquest in 1660, a deputy of the General Court from Plymouth in 1662, assessor in 1664, selectman in 1666, and a collector of taxes in 1668.[3] He was a freeman of Middleboro in 1670.

He moved from Plymouth to Middleboro a little before 1670, and soon after became a proprietor of the land in the Twenty-six Men's, the Sixteen Shilling, the Little Lotmen's, and the Five Men's Purchases. In 1670 he was the first representative to the General Court from the town, and held that office until his death, October 3, 1673.

He married, in the year 1648, Lettice ———.[4] She afterwards became the second wife of Andrew Ring, and died February 22, 1691. Soon after he moved from Plymouth to Middleboro, he built a house near the river, the site of which is still pointed out, and aside from the large amount of real estate in the vicinity of his house, he held a tract of land of about fifty acres not far from the house of the late Dr. Sturtevant.

[1] *Gen. Register*, 51, p. 192.   [2] *Morton Memoranda*, p. 17.
[3] *Ibid.* p. 25.
[4] She may have been Lettice Hanford, widow of Edward Foster of Scituate. *Ibid.* p. 26.

The inventory of his estate was taken in 1673 by George Vaughan and two other residents of the town. He was a man much esteemed for his intelligence and good judgment, and left numerous descendants prominent in the various walks of life, among whom was the Hon. Marcus Morton, a judge of the Supreme Court and governor of the commonwealth, and his son, Marcus Morton, Jr., chief justice of the Supreme Court.

Volume viii, Plymouth Colony Records, page 35, speaks of him as follows: —

"John Morton, Senir. of Middleberry, died on the third of October, 1673; hee was a godly man, and was much lamented by sundry of the inhabitants of that place. It pleased God, notwithstanding, to put a period to his life, after a longe sicknes and sometimes som . . . hopes of recouery."

Lot 8 in the Sixteen Shilling Purchase was assigned to his wife, Lettice Morton, in the original apportionment of this purchase in 1675.

JOHN MORTON, JR., the oldest son of his father, was born at Plymouth, December 21, 1650, and with his father probably moved to Middleboro not far from the year 1670. He was remarkably well educated for a man of the period, and it is said kept the first public school in America at Plymouth, in 1671, for the education of "children and youth."[1] He lived with his father in the house near the river which was probably burned during the Indian War, and was in the fort, one of the Commandant's Council. There is a tradition that he saw the Indians coming one evening, and fearing to remain in the house, he took a pail as if to get some water, but passed the well and did not stop until he found shelter in the fort.

Soon after the return of the settlers to Middleboro he built the southeastern part of what was known as the old Morton house, additions to which were made at different times by his descendants until it assumed the size which was well remembered by many of the people of the town.

[1] *Eddy Memoranda.*

At the time of his removal from Plymouth he was a member of the church there, and never removed his membership, although in full sympathy with the church in Middleboro. He died in Middleboro in 1717.

JOHN NELSON, a son of William Nelson, was born in 1647.

He, with Samuel Wood, was appointed to administer the estate of Henry Wood, October 29, 1670. By an order dated 1671, with Lieutenant Peregrine White, he laid out one thousand acres of land near the old Indian way, where the Nemasket River runs into Titicut. He was a constable and surveyor of highways in 1669, and laid out land near the old Indian way at Titicut in 1673; he was one of the Grand Inquest in 1675, an owner in the Sixteen Shilling Purchase, constable in 1684, and was one of the selectmen in 1681, 1682, 1683, 1685, and 1686. He was appointed guardian of Isaac Fuller in 1695. He probably lived with his father, William Nelson, until the house was burned by the Indians, but after the town was re-settled he returned, and built a house which he occupied until about the year 1687, when he sold the farm to Deacon John Bennett and moved to Lakeville. His first wife, Sarah Wood, daughter of Henry Wood, he married November 28, 1667, and after her death he married Lydia Bartlett, the widow of James Barnaby.[2] His third wife was Patience Morton, daughter of Ephraim Morton.

WILLIAM NELSON, SR. Several authorities state that William Nelson was a passenger in the Fortune and landed at Plymouth in 1621, but his name does not appear in the list of passengers. He was probably among the first settlers in the town, although it is impossible to state when he first came from Plymouth, or how long he lived in Middleboro. He was married October 27, 1640, to Martha Ford, the first girl born in Plymouth. His name appears in 1643 on the list of those able to bear arms in Plymouth, and he was there admitted as

---

[1] *Plymouth Colony Records*, vol. v, pp. 18-50, 140, etc.
[2] Savage, vol. iii, p. 267, and *Plymouth Colony Records*, vol. v, p. 247.

a freeman in the year 1658 and took the oath of fidelity the next year, and in 1670 he was a freeman of Middleboro. He was one of the original purchasers in the Twenty-six Men's and Purchade Purchases, and an owner in these purchases at the breaking out of King Philip's War. His name is among those in the fort at that time, and in the list of proprietors of Middleboro of June 26, 1677, his name appears as William Nelson, Sr. In the plan showing the allotment of lands to the purchasers in the Twenty-six Men's Purchase, the house of William Nelson is on lot 18, and the only one shown on that plan.

In 1672 he, with Lieutenant Peregrine White, was appointed by the court to lay out or divide certain meadows belonging to Pachague Neck, and the enlargement of upland on the Bridgewater side of the river. In 1669 he and John Tomson were appointed by the proprietors for running the line " between the Namassaketts land, called the Major's Purchase, and the towns of Marshfield, Duxburrow, and Bridgewater."

When he built the house occupied by his son John, he planned an orchard near by. His children, William Nelson, Jr., and John Nelson, were of age, and were both probably residents of the town at the breaking out of the war.

SAMUEL PRATT, one of the earliest of the settlers of Middleboro, came from Scituate about the year 1659, and is mentioned as one of the owners in the Twenty-six Men's Purchase who were in the fort. At the breaking out of the war he " sojourned in Scituate," where he was " pressed " into the service in accordance with an order of court issued early in 1676. He was a member of Captain Michael Pierce's company of soldiers from Scituate, and was in one of the fiercest contests in this war, known as the Pawtucket fight, " where he, with his captain and nearly all his company who had been trepanned into an ambushment of the enemy, was killed on Sunday, March 26, 1676." [1] He married Mary

[1] *Descendants of Phineas Pratt*, pp. 59, 60.

Barker, who after his death married Francis Coombs, and later David Wood.[1]

He had a son Samuel, born November 15, 1670, who died about the year 1745. He is mentioned in Middleboro records, and was a wheelwright by trade. He had two daughters, Susanna Pratt, who married William Thomas of Middleboro, before 1711, often styled "gentleman," and Patience Pratt, who married Ebenezer Lincoln, in October, 1703.

The father of Samuel Pratt was Phineas Pratt, one of the company of about sixty who were sent to Massachusetts to found a colony by Thomas Weston, the London merchant. He sailed from England in the Sparrow, and after touching at several places on the coast, landed at Plymouth in May, 1622. In 1630 he married Mary Priest, and was classed among the old settlers. In 1648 he left Plymouth and moved to Charlestown,[2] where he died April 19, 1680, at the age of eighty-seven years. He was the author of an interesting paper, known as the "Declaration of Affairs of the English People that First Inhabited in New England," which was printed by him in 1662, and published in the fourth volume of the Massachusetts Historical Society, page 476.

ANDREW RING came to Plymouth in 1629, and upon the death of his mother was entrusted to the care of Dr. Samuel Fuller. He was admitted as a freeman in 1646, and was a man of influence in the colony. He was among the first settlers of

---

[1] "His widow afterwards married a Woode, and fearing that her son Samuel might be compelled to serve as a soldier in the French and Indian War, wrote the following remonstrance: —

"These lines may give information that Samuel Pratt's Father, my first husband, was slain by the heathen in Captain Pierce's fight. He was pressed a Souldier when I sojourned att Sittuate. having then noe place of my own, and have brought him up with other small children, and I shall take it very unkindly, Iff he that is the only son of his father that was slain in the former warr should be compelled to go out againe, itt being contrary as I am informed to the law of England and this country, therefore I desire itt may not be.

(No date.)　　　　　　Soe petitions　　MARY WOODE
　　　　　　　　　　　　　　　　from Middlebury [Middleboro]."

[2] *Descendants of Phineas Pratt*, p. 38.

Middleboro,[1] and in King Philip's War his name appears as one who served from Middleboro. He was included among the Twenty-six Men's, Purchade, and Sixteen Shilling purchasers. He married first Deborah, daughter of Stephen Hopkins, in 1646, and in 1674 the widow of John Morton. He died in Middleboro in 1692, in his seventy-fifth year.

JOHN SHAW, whose name appears in Plymouth Colony Records as John Shaw, the Elder, settled in Plymouth before 1627. He had bought into the Twenty-six Men's Purchase prior to the breaking out of the war, and was one of the inhabitants of Middleboro in the fort at that time. He was a freeman of Plymouth in 1636–37, and in 1645 was one of the eight men who went out against the Narragansetts. He had sold his interest in the Twenty-six Men's Purchase before 1677 to Samuel Wood. He was one of the purchasers of Dartmouth in 1665, and one of the original owners of Bridgewater and of the Purchade Purchase. Mr. Savage, in his Genealogical Dictionary, vol. iv, p. 34, says, "he became one of the first settlers in Middleboro in 1662." He brought a complaint against Edward Dotey before the General Court at Plymouth in 1651. He died October 24, 1694, and his wife, Alice, died March 6, 1655.[2]

DAVID THOMAS and his wife came from Salem to Middleboro soon after 1668, the date of his selling his land in Salem. They settled in Thomastown, where their descendants are still living. He bought into the Twenty-six Men's Purchase, and was an original owner of the Eight Men's Purchase. He had several children, David, Joanna, William, Jeremiah, and Edward, the last born February 6, 1669, the first birth in the early records of the town.

DAVID THOMAS, JR., was probably born in 1649, as in the records of the First Church we find that he is spoken of in

---

[1] Savage, vol. iii, p. 542.
[2] *American Ancestors of Alonzo and Sarah W. Kimball*, p. 51.

1710 as being "about sixty." He married Abigail, daughter of Henry Wood, between 1670[1] and 1675.

EPHRAIM TINKHAM. There is a tradition which has come down from the earliest settlers that Ephraim Tinkham and Henry Wood were the first settlers in town, the former having built a house a short distance from Henry Wood, about fifty rods north of the house now occupied by Lorenzo Wood on the other side of the road. He was a man of prominence in the colony, and was known as Sergeant Tinkham.

In 1634 he was a servant of Thomas Hatherly of Plymouth, under an indenture; on the 2d day of August, 1642, this indenture was transferred to John Winslow, when he received for his services thirty-five acres of land, and on the 22d day of April of the same year he had conveyed to him ten acres of upland by Thurston Clark. He married Mary Brown, a daughter of Peter Brown, one of the passengers of the Mayflower, before October 27, 1647, and in that year he, with his wife, sold to Henry Tomson of Duxbury one third part of a lot of land, with the dwelling-house and buildings thereon, which belonged to Peter Brown.

He often served in the trial of cases, and in 1666 he laid out the bounds of land of Zachariah Eddy with Henry Wood, but the instruments assigning these bounds were signed by him with his mark. He was a freeman of Plymouth in 1670, in 1676 a member of the Grand Inquest, and in 1675 one of the selectmen of Middleboro. In 1674, with William Hoskins, he was appointed on a jury to try a murder case, and in 1668 he was a commissioner with William Crowe and Edward Gray to settle the bounds of the governor's land at Plaindealing. He died in Middleboro in 1683. His will bears date January 17, 1683, and was admitted to probate June 5, 1685.

His children[2] were Ephraim, born August 1, 1649; Ebenezer, born September 3, 1651; Peter, born December 25, 1653; Hezekiah, born February 8, 1655; John, born June 7, 1658; Mary, born August 1, 1661, who married John Tomson, a son

[1] *Eddy Memoranda.*   [2] *Eddy Note-Book.*

of Lieutenant Tomson; John, born November 15, 1663; Isaac, born April 11, 1666.

EPHRAIM TINKHAM, JR., and EBENEZER TINKHAM were the eldest sons of Sergeant Ephraim Tinkham, and lived in Middleboro in the house occupied by their father. Whether this house first occupied by them was rebuilt upon the same spot after the resettlement of the town is unknown. They were not married until after the return from Plymouth.

Ephraim Tinkham, Jr.,[1] was born in 1649, and married Esther —— after the resettlement of the town. He was a constable in 1681, and propounded as a freeman in 1682. He died October 13, 1714.

Children: John, born August 22, 1680; Ephraim, born October 7, 1682; Isaac, born June, 1685; Samuel, born March 19, 1687.

His brother, Ebenezer Tinkham, was born September 30, 1651, and married Elizabeth Liscom before 1679. He was one of the original members of the First Church, and one of its first deacons. He died April 8, 1718, aged seventy-three years;[2] his wife died on the same day, and they were buried in the same grave.

Children: Ebenezer, born March 23, 1679; Jeremiah, born August 7, 1681; Peter, born April 20, 1683.[3]

JOHN TOMSON, the most prominent of the first settlers, was a carpenter, and lived on land which was afterwards set off to form a part of Halifax. He was of Dutch origin, and came to Plymouth, a lad of six years, in the month of May, 1622. He, with Richard Church, built the first meeting-house in Plymouth in 1637. Before settling in Middleboro he had purchased land in Sandwich, where he lived for a few years. In common with many early settlers of the country,

---

[1] *Eddy Note-Book* speaks of him as Ephraim of Middleboro.
[2] *History of the First Church of Middleboro*, p. 53.
[3] *Eddy Memoranda.*

he soon desired a larger area of land, and preferred to live in what, at that time, was considered a remote region; he came to occupy a portion of the Twenty-six Men's Purchase, which was assigned to him, and was one of the purchasers of several tracts of land from the Indians, by order of the court at Plymouth. In the expedition against the Narragansetts, August 15, 1645, he was one of the first company, and was away sixteen days. He was a man of great physical strength and unusual stature, being six feet, three inches in height. He married Mary, daughter of Francis Cook.

The log house which he built was situated about twenty rods west of what was then the Plymouth line. There he and his family resided until the house was burned by the Indians, at the breaking out of King Philip's War. This was probably the first house burned in the town. At the time of his settlement he was surrounded by the Indians, and suffered much from their stealing his cattle and the products of his farm. It is related that at one time his wife was cooking fish, when Indians came in and, brandishing a knife over her, attempted to take some of the fish out of the kettle. She repelled them by a vigorous attack with a splinter broom, and such were her courage and bravery that she drove them from the house and they disappeared. When her husband returned, she told him of her adventure, and suspecting treachery among the surrounding Indians, they immediately left the house and retired to the garrison, eight miles distant. At another time a large number of Indian squaws came to the house and manifested unusual interest in her affairs, offering to assist her in gathering vegetables for the next day, and volunteering their services generally about the house. She kindly refused their offers of assistance, and on the return of her husband he remarked: "We must again pack up and go to the garrison," which they did.

Mr. Tomson was in constant peril for his life and property from the savages during these years. It is related that as a matter of protection he, with his nearest neighbor, Jabez Soule, who had settled in that part now included in the town of

Plympton, induced an Indian to come to learn English ways of living and cultivating the soil. He lived and worked with Mr. Tomson and Mr. Soule alternately. They did everything they could to win the confidence and affection of this Indian, who was industrious, and apparently quick to learn the new ways of the settlers. After a little time, although he showed great fondness for them, they noticed that he would absent himself for several days. This looked suspicious, as frequent visits were made by chiefs and others from a distant part of the country, so it seemed more prudent to go to the garrison for the night, the men returning to cultivate the fields in the daytime. Soon after this the war broke out, and they saw but little of their Indian servant. After the close of the war, when asked by one of the neighbors why he never showed any hostility to his employers, Mr. Tomson and Mr. Soule, he replied that many times he had loaded his gun and raised it to fire upon them, but that he loved them so dearly, and they had done so much for him, that he never could make up his mind to shoot.

There is a tradition that one Sunday morning, as the family were about to start to Plymouth to attend church, they noticed a large number of Indians in the vicinity, who seemed to be in an angry mood, and whose bearing was quite different from usual. They continued, however, on their way, but on their return concluded it would be better to go to the garrison house, and after hastily burying their valuables in a secluded place, they left their home. It was none too soon, for they had not gone more than two miles when, looking back, they saw a bright blaze, and realized that their log house was in flames. As they were on their journey, they passed the house of George Danson and urged him to join them and seek shelter, but he refused, thinking there was no danger. The next morning, as they returned to their farm, they found everything destroyed and Mr. Danson killed. He was the first killed during King Philip's War. Mr. Tomson received a commission of lieutenant, and commanded a company of sixteen men, who were in the habit of marching in four columns

A HALBERD OF THE TIME

of four men each, and he was the commandant of the fort and of military operations until the garrison retired to Plymouth and the house was burned by the Indians.

In 1677, after the General Court had granted permission to the colonists to resettle Middleboro, he rebuilt, on the old site, a garrison house, filled in between the posts and beams with brick and mortar; it had several small windows like portholes in the walls for defence from any attack, but as a matter of fact, after the close of the war there was no hostility. This house stood until the year 1838, when it was taken down. It had been occupied by five generations of the descendants of its illustrious builder. Before the Indian War, and until religious services were held in Middleboro, Mr. Tomson's family attended church at Plymouth, a distance of more than twelve miles, starting very early every Sabbath morning and returning late at night. At one time in the winter the family were obliged to start before sunrise. As they were proceeding on their journey, near the swamp not far from the house of the late Isaac Sturtevant, they heard the barking of a pack of wolves, and sought refuge upon a high rock on the side of the road. There they remained until after sunrise, when the wolves retired and they proceeded on their Sabbath day's journey in safety. Mr. Tomson held many important offices in the town and colony during his lifetime. The following epitaph is on his tombstone: —

IN MEMORY OF
LIEUT. JOHN THOMSON, WHO DIED JUNE 16TH, YE 1696,
IN YE 80 YEAR OF HIS AGE.

This is a debt to nature due;
Which I have paid and so must you.

Mary, his wife, died March 21, 1714, in the eighty-eighth year of her age, and was buried with her husband.

He left numerous descendants, who have lived at Middleboro, Halifax, and adjoining towns. The first two generations and sometimes the third spelled the name Tomson or Tompson; the fourth and fifth spelled it Thompson.

JOHN TOMSON, JR., was born November 24, 1648, and married Mary Tinkham, a daughter of Ephraim Tinkham. He was propounded as freeman in 1682. He was a carpenter by trade, and in the early part of his married life lived with his father, Lieutenant John Tomson. He, with his wife and father's family, went into the fort at the time of the attack upon the town by the Indians, and upon the resettlement of the town, he returned and probably lived not far from his father. He was one of the builders of the church in Plymouth.

He inherited much of the land that belonged to his father, and died November 25, 1725, in his seventy-seventh year. His wife died in 1731, in her seventy-sixth year.

GEORGE VAUGHAN was a resident of Scituate in 1653, and was among the first settlers of Middleboro. He married Elizabeth Henchman (or Hincksman), who died June 24, 1693, aged sixty-two. At the General Court of Plymouth, on the 5th of June, 1658, a suit was brought against him by John Sutton for detaining his property, wherein the jury found for the plaintiff and costs, which amounted to one pound, ten shillings, and six pence. He was then living in Marshfield, and, on the 1st of June, he seems to have been fined ten shillings for not attending public worship on the Lord's Day.

He was a resident of Middleboro in 1663, and, for some cause which does not appear, was fined by the court ten shillings. On the 1st of March, 1663, he brought a suit against William

Shurtliff for molesting and taking away an animal for the debt of one Charles Hopkins of Boston. The jury found for the plaintiff, with the charges of court to be paid by the defendant.

June 1, 1669, William Crow and George Vaughan, with John Tomson and William Nelson, were appointed commissioners to lay the line between the "Namasket Men's Land," called the Major's Purchase, and the towns of Marshfield, Duxbury, and Bridgewater. He was the first person granted a license to keep an ordinary for the entertainment of strangers in Middleboro by the General Court in 1669. On the 5th of July, 1670, the General Court conferred twelve acres of land in the Major's Purchase on the south side of Nemasket River, which had not been recorded, and which was ordered at that time to be recorded. In 1671 he and John Morton were appointed by the Court of Commissioners to view damages done to the Indians by the horses and hogs of the English. He was constable of the town in 1675, and at that time bought part of the land in the Twenty-six Men's Purchase, and he was in the garrison at the time of the breaking out of the war.

His daughter married Isaac Howland. He died October 20, 1694, aged seventy-three.[1] His will, dated June 30, 1694, was proved November 10, 1694, and the inventory was taken by Samuel Wood and John Bennett. His property amounted to forty-three pounds, eight shillings, and four pence.

He and most of his descendants for several generations resided in that part of the town known as Wappanucket.

JOSEPH VAUGHAN, son of George Vaughan, was one of the selectmen of Middleboro; he was first elected to that office in 1689, and continued to serve for twenty-five years. At one time he commanded a guard, which embraced all the local militia of the town. He was ensign in 1706, and lieutenant in 1712.

He lived in the house[2] owned at one time by Captain Na-

---

[1] *Eddy Memoranda.*
[2] From Bennett's *Memoranda.* He is spoken of as from Middleboro.

thaniel Wilder, and had much land in Middleboro, being an owner in the Sixteen Shilling Purchase.

He married Joanna Thomas, May 7, 1680, and Mercy, widow of Jabez Fuller, as his second wife, in 1720. He died March 2, 1734, aged eighty-one years.

FRANCIS WALKER married Elizabeth, a daughter of George Soule. He is spoken of as living in Middleboro in 1668, but moved to Duxbury in 1672, returning later to occupy the land left to his wife by her father.[1]

HENRY WOOD. The first mention of Henry Wood is in September 16, 1641, when he, residing in Plymouth, purchased of John Dunham, the younger, his house and land lying in Plymouth for seven pounds, but the time of his arrival and the time of his birth are unknown.

He married Abigail Jenney, a daughter of John Jenney, who at one time owned land in Lakenham, now Carver, April 28, 1644. At or about the time of his marriage, he moved to Yarmouth, where his daughter Sarah and his son Samuel were born. He moved to Plymouth before 1649, where his other children were born, and to Middleboro about 1655.[2]

Tradition has placed the site of his residence as not far from that of the late General Abiel Washburn. He was not among the Twenty-six Purchasers, but received the share that was set out to John Shaw, a portion of which subdivision has always been in the possession of his descendants. He was an original proprietor in the Little Lotmen's Purchase.

He was propounded as a freeman in 1647, and admitted in 1648. Before the incorporation of Middleboro he was a member of the Grand Inquest in 1648, 1656, 1659, and 1668, and often served as a juror in different trials in the colonies. He was a surveyor of highways in Plymouth in 1655 and in 1659, and was one of the complainants to the General Court against the rates which had been established in Plymouth. In 1665 he

---

[1] Savage, p. 392.
[2] Middleboro was not set off from Plymouth until 1669.

had one share of the thirty acres of land on the westerly side of Nemasket River. He was one of the ancient freemen to whom land was granted in Taunton "which should be hereafter purchased, which purchase should not be prejudicial to the Indians." He is mentioned as one of the freemen of Middleboro in 1670, with the mark "deceased" after his name. One of the records of Plymouth Colony refers to him as Henry Wood, alias Atwood. His name occurs as one of the commandant's council for the garrison in Middleboro, and evidently by a mistake, the name was continued on the list of those who took refuge within the fort upon the breaking out of the war. He died in 1670, and John Nelson, his son-in-law, and Samuel Wood, his son, were appointed administrators of his estate, October 29, 1670. His inventory, taken under the oath of Abigail Wood, his widow, by John Morton, Jonathan Dunham, Francis Coombs, and George Vaughan, amounted to sixty-three pounds, three shillings, and three pence, and is recorded in Plymouth Colony Records, vol. vi, p. 142.

March 4, 1673, four of his children, with his wife Abigail, were summoned into court to dispose of his lands that they might contribute to the support of the widow.

His children were: Samuel, John, David, Joseph, Benjamin, Abiel, James, Sarah, Abigail, Susanna, and Mary.

His sons were probably in the garrison house, although no mention is made of them, and they were not married until after the resettlement of the town. Abiel and Samuel were among the original members of the First Church.

JOHN or JONATHAN WOOD, a son of Henry Wood, was born January 1, 1649-50, and died at John Nelson's in 1675. He always lived [1] in Middleboro, but his name is sometimes confounded with Jonathan Wood, alias Atwood, of Plymouth. The Jonathan Wood of the Sixteen Shilling Purchase was undoubtedly the son of Henry, and not the Jonathan Wood of Plymouth. He made a noncupative will in April, 1673, and two or three days after, he gave the town right of way through his land.

[1] *Eddy Memoranda.*

[1670] EARLY SETTLERS BEFORE KING PHILIP'S WAR

JOSEPH WOOD was a son of Henry Wood, who married Hester Walker in Taunton, January 1, 1679. Upon his death his son Josiah was given to Daniel Vaughan and wife to adopt as their child. He was one of the proprietors of the Sixteen Shilling Purchase, and always lived in Middleboro.

SAMUEL WOOD was a son of Henry Wood, born May 21, 1647. He probably moved from Plymouth to Middleboro as a young man with his father, and lived with him as one of the first settlers of the town. He was a surveyor of highways in Middleboro in 1673, and held the office of constable in 1682 and selectman in 1684 and 1689 and at different times for fifteen years, and was one of the original members at the organization of the First Church, December 26, 1694. Upon the death of his father an agreement was made between him, his brother, and mother that he should have thirteen acres of upland, this being the place where his father had lived, and a portion of the Tispequin purchase known as Wood's Purchase. He was an original owner in the Sixteen Shilling Purchase. He died February 3, 1718, aged seventy years. His wife's name was Rebecca Tupper. They were married probably before 1679, and she died February 10, 1718, in the sixty-seventh year of her age. She united with the First Church March 27, 1716.

His children were Ephraim, born in January, 1679,[1] who was one of the deacons of the First Church, ordained July 25, 1725, and who died July 9, 1744, in the sixty-fifth year of his age; Samuel, Jr., who was born in 1684 and died before 1754, who was also chosen a deacon of the First Church January 30, 1735; Rebecca, born 1682; Anne, born 1687, and Jabez, born 1690.

ADAM WRIGHT was a son of Richard, who lived at one time in that part of Plymouth afterwards Plympton. In a record

[1] *Eddy Memoranda.*

of deeds in 1672, we find "George Vaughan of Middleboro sells to Adam Wright of the same place, blacksmith, land in the Major's Purchase at, or near, Namasheesett Ponds." His name occurs in list of the "Proprietors of the Charters of the township of Middlebery," June 12, 1677, as "Francis Cook now Adam Wright." He married Sarah, a daughter of John Soule of Duxbury, and for a second wife, Mehitable Barrows. He died in 1724, aged about eighty years.

FRANCIS BILLINGTON was a son of John Billington, who was a disreputable passenger of the Mayflower, the first settler

BILLINGTON SEA

of Plymouth publicly executed in October, 1630, for lying in wait and shooting a young man named John Newcomb. Francis was about fourteen years old when he landed at Plymouth with his parents, and was one of the two passengers of the Mayflower who settled in Middleboro. He is remembered as the discoverer of Billington Sea in Plymouth, in 1621, although Goodwin thinks his father deserves that credit. While climbing a high tree, the week before, he had seen what appeared to him a great sea, and on that day, with the mate of the Mayflower, set out to examine his discovery. After travelling about three miles, they found two lakes, with a beautiful island in the centre of one, about which the early writers were lavish in their praise. He volunteered in the Pequot War, but was not called into active service. He was one of the twenty-six men who made the purchase of land from the Indians in 1662, as well as the Sixteen Shilling Purchase. He married, July, 1634, Christiana Penn Eaton, the widow of Francis Eaton. "They proved a thriftless pair and were forced to bind out most or all of their eight children."[1]

[1] Goodwin, *Pilgrim Republic*, p. 344.

He died December 3, 1684, aged eighty years. His son, Isaac Billington, was one of the original members of the First Church, and died December 11, 1709, aged sixty-six years.[1]

JOHN COBB, son of Henry, was in the fort at the breaking out of King Philip's War. He was born June 7, 1632. He moved from Barnstable to Plymouth, Taunton, and possibly to Middleboro, then to Scituate. He took the oath of fidelity in 1689. If he was not an actual resident of Middleboro before the war, he probably dwelt here without changing his legal residence, as did a few of the early settlers, living on their lands within the borders of the town but not becoming citizens. The "History of the First Church" gives his name, among others, as being here at that time. He married Martha, a daughter of William Nelson, April 28, 1658.[2]

JOHN HOLMES was one of those in the garrison at the breaking out of the Indian War, but it is impossible to tell at this time which of several who bear that name was one of the first settlers of Middleboro. There was a John Holmes in Plymouth in 1633, a freeman of that year and often a messenger to the General Court, and among the list of men who were able to bear arms in 1643. His son John, who had a grant of land in Duxbury in 1663, married Patience Faunce, November 20, 1661, and died in 1667. Their oldest son was born March 22, 1663, and settled in Middleboro, where he died in 1728, at the age of sixty-eight years. The early records show that he had children born in Middleboro in 1690. He probably lived in that portion of Middleboro which was set off in 1734, to form a portion of the town of Halifax. His son became an inhabitant of the town by the following vote passed on April 19, 1682: —

"At a town meeting held at Isaac Howland's house, the town did jointly agree to receive John Holmes, Jr., to be an inhabitant amongst them."

[1] *Eddy Note-Book.*
[2] *Barnstable Families,* p. 171; *History of the First Church of Middleboro,* p. 4.

WILLIAM NELSON, Jr., lived [1] and died in the house which stood near the old Sproat tavern at the Green, probably built and occupied a few years by his father. But little is known concerning him, and the only record extant [2] is, that on the 5th of July, 1671, he, with Adam Wright, was ordered by the General Court to pay ten shillings, and the Indian William, son of the black sachem, to pay twenty shillings, for the use of the colony, for taking a certain mare and marking and detaining her to the damage of the owner. He was the father of Thomas Nelson, the first settler in Lakeville.

He married Ruth Foxel, daughter of Richard Foxel. The gravestones of William Nelson and Ruth, his wife, were recently found by his descendant, Dr. Abiel Nelson, in the cemetery at the Green, and contain the following inscriptions : " Here lies ye body of William Nelson aged seventy-three years, died March, ye 22nd, 1718 ; " and " Here lies ye body of Ruth Nelson aged eighty-six years, died September, ye 7th, 1723."

JABEZ WARREN was the grandson of Richard Warren of the Mayflower, one of the nineteen signers of the compact who survived the first winter. His son, Nathaniel, the father of Jabez Warren, was at one time the owner of lot number 5 in the Twenty-six Men's Purchase, which was occupied by Jabez and his brother Richard, who some time after the close of King Philip's War removed with his family from Plymouth to Nemasket. Jabez Warren, born in 1647, was probably a resident of the town before the breaking out of the war, and was one of the land-owners who was in the fort at the time Middleboro was threatened by Tispequin's forces.[3] There is no further record concerning his life ; it is said that he was drowned at sea April 17, 1701.

JOSEPH WARREN was one of the proprietors of the Little Lotmen's Purchase, also of the land purchased by Josiah

---

[1] MS. *Genealogy of Descendants of William Nelson, Sr.*
[2] *Plymouth Colony Records*, vol. v, p. 69.
[3] Roebling, *Richard Warren, Descendants*, p. 12.

Winslow and Edward Gray, called by the Indians "Wopanucket." In the apportionment of this land among the different owners he received two hundred acres, which he probably occupied, as at a meeting of the proprietors of the town on the 18th of May, 1675, he was appointed, with others, a committee "to devise measurements for the support of some one to teach the word of God, etc."[1]

He was born at Plymouth in 1627, and died May 4, 1689. He was a prominent citizen of Plymouth and filled many offices, a member of the council of war of the colonies in 1675, and a representative to the General Court of 1681 to 1686. He was a man of enterprise, and an owner of large tracts of land in the different towns in the colony. His lands in Middleboro and Bridgewater were devised to his children, Joseph and Benjamin, and his three daughters. He married, in 1651, Priscilla, the daughter of Thomas Faunce, ruling elder of Plymouth. He was at one time called an "Ancient Freeman of Taunton." While he may have been a resident of Middleboro before the breaking out of the war, there is no record that he returned with the other residents at the time of the resettlement of the town in 1677-78.

DAVID WOOD was born October 17, 1651, and on March 5, 1684, he married Mary, widow of Francis Coombs. Their children were John, born 1686; David, born 1688; Jabez, born 1689.

[1] See note in chapter on Church History.

THE STURTEVANT PLOUGH
(Owned by Moses Sturtevant)

CHAPTER V

KING PHILIP'S WAR

KING Philip's War, which lasted but little more than a year and a half, in 1675 and 1676, was by far the most disastrous event in the early history of New England, and was attended with all of the horrors of savage barbarity. About six hundred of the white settlers perished, and their houses were in ruins. Many towns were utterly destroyed, and it is said that there was scarcely a family in the settlements but had lost one or more of its members. All of the dwelling-houses and outbuildings of Middleboro were burned. Although it was not the scene of many of the bloody atrocities which occurred in not a few of the towns in New England, the murder of an Indian by the name of John Sassamon had much to do with the origin of the war, and here was the home of Philip's most powerful chieftain, Tispequin. A history of the part that Middleboro had in this fearful struggle would be incomplete without entering into some details of the origin of the war, and the more prominent events connected with it.

In 1660 Massasoit died, leaving two sons, Alexander and Philip, who had none of the regard for the English which their father had entertained. They evidently foresaw the results of the white man's civilization in extending their settlements, and that the time would not be far distant when the native rule would be destroyed and their tribes become extinct. Philip, the sachem, had acquired a fame far beyond his deserts. In 1675 his immediate tribe consisted of about three hundred men, women, and children. His cunning and cruelty, his hatred of the whites, inspired in him a sagacity and ability unexpected in so mean a character. He succeeded by his intrigues in stimulating the Indians in the adjacent tribes, but Palfrey says, "The public documents of that time do not indicate a belief on the part of the English of any such comprehensive and far-sighted scheme as in later times has been attributed to Philip. The natural conclusion from their language is that his outbreak was regarded as prompted by the vindictiveness and caprice of an unreasoning and cruel barbarian." On the other hand, we find authorities who speak of his talents as "of the highest order," of him as "a great warrior," etc. Goodwin[1] says, "Philip is not known to have taken part in any one of the fights of the war, nor even to have been in the immediate vicinity of any of them after the initial skirmish at Pocasset Swamp." But his traits of character were such that he always had a very strong influence over the smaller tribes of his territory. They admired his boldness, and not a few sympathized with him in his ambition to expel the English from his borders, and to surpass the great chieftains who in power and authority had ruled over his territory before the coming of the English. He had no sooner commenced his reign than he began his scheming in the most secret manner with all of the sachems whom he could influence. With the characteristics of the savage, he frequently renewed the treaties which his father, the good Massasoit, had made at Plymouth, affecting the strongest friendship for the whites.

He so far ingratiated himself with all of the settlers of the colony that they believed in his sincerity, and doubted the reports of his intrigue which came to them from time to time through friendly Indians. He made complaints that the whites had injured his crops, but these were proved false. There were frequent meetings of Indians; they began to repair their guns and sharpen their hatchets, all tending to arouse the suspicions of the colonists, until it was deemed necessary to call a council at Taunton. The governor and his deputies assembled to examine Philip's conduct. For a long time he would not come to the town as promised. When he came, it was with a large band of his warriors fully armed, but he would not go into the meeting-house where the council was held until it was agreed that his men should be on one side of the house and the men

[1] *Pilgrim Republic*, p. 551.

who accompanied the deputies on the other. It was one of the most dramatic and interesting scenes which ever occurred in the colony. On one side was a large company of the whites, dressed in the garb of the period, with close-shaven heads and solemn countenances, fearless, and confident that their God who had so guided and shielded them in the years past would deliver them from the present dangers. On the other side of the meeting-house were the Indians, with their fierce, savage, angry looks, their tomahawks, bows, and arrows conspicuously displayed under the feathers and war paint with which they were decorated. They had belts of wampum and the skins of the bear or deer ornamented with glowing colors, indicating their readiness for the conflict. On examination, Philip strongly protested against having any designs upon the English, but said that his warriors had been armed to prevent any hostile attacks of the Narragansetts, which had been often threatened. The delegates were enabled from testimony in their possession to deny this statement, and at the same time to show that he had endeavored to induce the Narragansetts to join him in his plans to attack the English. It was also proved that he had meditated an attack upon Taunton, which, at last, he was compelled to confess. The proofs of these charges astonished Philip, and the consequences which he feared might soon be visited upon him induced him again to deny them and to assert his innocence. As a guarantee of this, the delegation insisted that he should deliver up all of the arms in the hands of his warriors as an indemnity and security for the good faith he then professed. To this he consented with great reluctance, and gave up about seventy guns, with a promise that the others should be brought in. He, however, never complied with his promise, but the surrender of this number of guns, then scarce with the Indians, evidently so embarrassed him that he delayed carrying out his plans.

For the next two or three years Philip endeavored to cause other tribes to engage with him in the plot of utterly destroying the English in New England, but when the war finally broke out, in the year 1675, he was evidently not fully prepared for it, which undoubtedly in some measure contributed to his defeat and the complete overthrow of the Indian power. He had secured the Narragansetts and the Pequots, about four thousand warriors, and had fixed upon the spring of 1676 for a united attack upon all of the whites in the colonies. The murder of John Sassamon precipitated the war before his plans were mature.[1]

John Sassamon was a Punkapoag. Mr. Gookin calls him the first martyr of the christian Indians. Increase Mather says he was born in Dorchester, and his parents lived and died there. In his boyhood he was a very bright and intelligent lad, and as a child early became acquainted with John Eliot, the great Indian apostle, who exerted a most benign influence over him and was for many years his instructor. He accepted his religious teachings and was baptized by him, making public profession of his Christian faith, and was one of the most influential and gifted preachers among the Indians. Sassamon was taught to read and write the English language, and aided Mr. Eliot in the work of translating the Bible into the Indian tongue. He was a student at Harvard, and in his early manhood was a teacher of the Indians in Natick.

He had, in 1637, served with the English in the Pequot War. In 1664 Philip desired a teacher of reading, and Eliot sent his son and later Sassamon. His service in this capacity has led to much that is erroneous. Munroe called him Philip's "secretary," and says that as such he was entrusted with all Philip's plan. Goodwin says[2] there is no evidence to support this, nor is there any truth in the statement that Sassamon once abjured christianity and went to live in heathenism with Philip. He says: "He also ignores the fact that Sassamon owed Philip no allegiance, but that he did owe it to New Plymouth, and was by every sense of duty, legal as well as moral, bound to reveal any

---

[1] Bancroft, *History of the United States*, Part II, chap. v, says: "There exists no evidence of a deliberate conspiracy on the part of all the tribes. The commencement of the war was accidental; many of the Indians were in a maze, not knowing what to do and disposed to stand for the English; sure proof of no ripened conspiracy."

[2] *Pilgrim Republic*, p. 538.

plots coming to his knowledge." Whether he was secretary or not, he was authorized to write Philip's letters on public affairs.

After serving as a teacher to Philip, he returned to his Natick home. Later, through Eliot's advice, he moved to Nemasket, and was there settled over the Indian church. He owned twenty-seven acres of land at Assawampsett, and to his daughter Betty the sachem gave fifty-eight and one half acres (called Squawbetty). In 1675 he learned of the great conspiracy against the English, and it seemed to him a christian duty to the whites who had so befriended him to secretly inform the governor at Plymouth of what he suspected were the designs of the chieftain. At the same time he expressed to the governor his danger in giving this information, should it ever come to the knowledge of Philip. Concerning this several other Indians were examined, who denied all knowledge of any such conspiracy and were dismissed, but the court at Plymouth generally believed that there were grounds for the statement that Sassamon had made. A week after this Sassamon disappeared, and general search was made, which resulted in finding his hat and coat upon the ice of Assawampsett Pond, and his body was soon after discovered under the ice. A Titicut Indian by the name of David noticed bruises upon his body, which led to the belief that he had been killed. He was, however, buried by his friends without further investigation into the circumstances of his death. A native by the name of Patuckson was a witness of this murder as he stood on King

A VIEW OF ASSAWAMPSETT POND, WHERE THE BODY OF SASSAMON WAS CONCEALED

KING PHILIP'S LETTER TO GOVERNOR PRINCE, WRITTEN BY HIS SECRETARY, JOHN SASSAMON, IN 1663

philip would intreat that fauer of and axin of the magistrats if aney english or engians spak about aney land he preay you to give them no ansewer at all the last sumer he maid that promis with you that he would not sell no land in 7 years time for tha he would have no english trouble him before that time he has not forgot that you promis him

& just come asune as possible he can to speak with you and so grest your verey loveng frend philip

dewlling at mount hope nek

Philip would intreat that favor of
yow, or of the magistrats if aney english
engians Speak about aney land he pray
you to give them no ansuer at all
this last sumer he maid that promis
with you that he would not sell no
land in 7 years time for that he would
have no english trouble him before
that time he has not forgot that
you promis him

as sune as poseble he can to Speak with you
and Sag reest your ueuery loueng frend philip
dweling at mounthope neck

FACSIMILE OF KING PHILIP'S LETTER TO GOVERNOR PRINCE
(Written by John Sassamon, as secretary; copied from the original in Pilgrim Hall)

KING PHILIP'S LOOKOUT

Philip's Lookout, and in the spring testified to it. An Indian, after meeting Sassamon on the ice as he was fishing in the pond, commenced a friendly conversation with him. He then attacked and killed him by a blow on the head, and with the assistance of two others put the body through a hole in the ice, but with the savage instinct, tried to evade suspicion by leaving his hat and coat to give the appearance of an accidental death.

The three whom he named as the murderers were Tobias and his son, with Mattashinnay, Philip's counsellor. After these three were arrested, a jury of twelve white men and five Indians tried them and heard Patuckson's testimony. All three were convicted, and sentence was passed upon them. Tobias's son then confessed that the other two had committed the murder. Tobias was bailed out by Tispequin for one hundred pounds, with security on land at Nemasket.[1] The two guilty

---

[1] At the General Court, March 1, 1674-75: —

"The Court seeing cause to require the psnall appeerance of an Indian, called Tobias, before the Court, to make further answare to such intergatoryes as shalbe required of him, in reference to the suddaine and violent death of an Indian called John Sassamon, late deceased, the said Tobias and Tuspaquin, the black sachem, (soe called,) of Namassakett, and William, his son, doe all joyntly and seuerally doe heerby bind ouer off theire lands, to the vallue of one hundred pounds, vnto the Court, for the psonall appeerance off the said Tobias att the Court of his matie, to be holden att Plymouth aforesaid the first in June next, in reference to the pmises." *Plymouth Colony Records*, vol. v, p. 159.

men were executed at Plymouth in June, 1675, and young Tobias would probably have been pardoned, had not Philip begun hostilities in the attack on Swansea. The trial and execution of the murderers of Sassamon so enraged Philip that he determined to postpone no longer his threatened attack, and the bloody scenes of that terrible encounter which spread death and devastation throughout the colony soon after began.

The proximity to Plymouth had for some time kept the early settlers here informed of the danger feared by the authorities. In accordance with the requirements of the laws of the colony,[1] the Middleboro men had built a fort[2] for their protection on the western bank of the Nemasket River, not far from the old Indian wading-place, on the land owned in later years by Colonel Peter H. Peirce. No description of this has come down to us. It was evidently something more than a garrison house, and was large enough to accommodate, for more than six weeks, the inhabitants of the town, who, with the men, women, and children, probably numbered seventy-five or more. It was enclosed with a wall strong enough to have deterred the many roving bands of hostile Indians from attempting to attack or to surround it.

There was a general alarm throughout the colony, and many precautions were taken to guard against any unexpected attack. All male inhabitants between sixteen and sixty years of age were ordered to be in readiness to take the field to repel any

[1] Judge Wilkes Wood, Historic Address in 1815.

[2] The fort was probably built by the settlers soon after the incorporation of the town in 1669, in accordance with an act of the General Court holden at Plymouth on the 9th of June, 1653, which was as follows: —

"It is ordered by the Court, That betwixt this present day and the first Tuesday in October next the townesmen of every towne within this government shall make and fully finnish a place or places for defence of theire said towne one or more as reason shall require videlicet, a brest worke with flankers unto every such work as shalbee made; and in case any p.son or p.sons shall refuse to worke att the said worke when the major p^{te} of the townsmen of such townes where they live have agreed for the time and mannor and have given notice thereof; theire names shalbee then returned to the court or counsell of warr; and if any towne shall neglect to performe the worke according to this order they shall forfeite the summe of ten pounds to the use of the country."

assault whenever such should occur, and boys under the age of sixteen years were required to act as watchmen to keep a lookout for the sudden approach of the Indians from any quarter. The court at Plymouth issued the following: —

> "It is ordered that every man that comes to meeting on the Lord's day bring with him his arms, with at least six charges of powder and shot, and that whosoever shall shoot off a gun at any game whatsoever, except at an Indian or a wolf shall forfeit five shillings."

The war began on the 24th day of June, 1675, in the then frontier town of Swansea. The Sunday previous, the Indians had killed many of the cattle belonging to the settlers. Nine men were killed on the highway, and shortly after eight more. Gershom Cobb, a resident of Middleboro, was among the number. It was a butchery attended with all of the horrors of savage warfare. Encouraged by the success of their first encounter, they extended their operations to other parts of the colony, stealthily hiding in woods and swamps, behind fences and bushes, killing the whites as they came upon them, and burning their houses.

Shortly before this, many occurrences had served to confirm the fears of the Middleboro settlers. Some of the Indians were sullen and morose, manifesting unusual boldness and eagerness in procuring firearms and powder at almost any cost. This, in addition to officiousness in many acts of friendliness with the evident design of covering some plot, did not deceive the settlers, who found their cows milked, and occasionally some animal missing. Most of the inhabitants, especially those living far from the centre, thought it unsafe to remain about their farms and came to the garrison, some taking their provision and household furniture, others in such haste that they left everything, on hearing of the attack on Swansea. They were unable to gather any of their crops, and no aid could be sent from Plymouth, as all of the available forces in the colony had been despatched to towns where the danger was even greater than at Middleboro. George Danson had neglected the warning of John Tomson as he was hastening to the fort, and had been shot near Danson Brook.

76 HISTORY OF THE TOWN OF MIDDLEBORO [1675

After the fort had been built, Isaac Howland, Francis Coombs, John Morton, Nathaniel Southworth, Ephraim Tinkham, Samuel Fuller, and Henry Wood were chosen as council,[1] with John Tomson, commander.

John Tomson formed[2] sixteen able-bodied men into a company for their protection. He applied to the governor and council of Plymouth for a commission. They considered the company too small for a captaincy, and gave him a general commission as ensign commander, not only of the garrison, but also of all posts of danger within the town. The company was equipped, beside the ordinary gun,[3] which every settler possessed, with a

[1] The council was selected in accordance with a provision of the law of the colony passed in 1658, which was as follows: —

THE ORDER OF COURT CONCERNING THE COUNCEL OF WARR

In regard of the many appearances of danger towards the Countrey by Enimies and the great nessessitie of Councell and advise in which respect the Court thought meet to make choise of a Counsell of warr consisting of eleven psons whose names are elswhere extant in the Records of the Court which said eleven being orderly called together theire acte to be accounted in force and they to bee continewed in theire places untill others bee elected to bee orderly called together is ment being sumoned by the prsedent or his deputie or in case of theire absence any two majestrates of the Councell of Warr.

The number of these, considering the few in the garrison, was undoubtedly deemed sufficient.

[2] This company does not represent the number of men in town capable of bearing arms. Many were away taking an active part in the war. We have definite record of at least three, and there were probably others.

[3] In addition to the armament of the fort by a provision of the law passed by the General Court for 1636, each male must have provided himself for his own defence in accordance with this provision of the law of the Old Colony, passed November 15, 1636, which was as follows: —

PARTICULAR ARMS

That each person for himselfe &c. according to Jan. 2d 1632 have peece, powder and shott vizt a sufficient

JOHN TOMSON'S GUN

long gun, evidently made for other purposes than hunting. It was seven feet, four and a half inches long; the length of the barrel, six and one half feet; the size of the caliber twelve balls to the pound, and the length of the face of the lock ten inches. This gun, weighing twelve pounds, was probably brought from the old country. Besides these, they had a halberd, a brass pistol, and a sword. The sword was three feet, five inches long; the length of the blade two feet, eleven and three eighths inches.

Early in June a band of warriors was seen from the fort on the opposite bank of the river, near the "hand rock," so called from an impression of a man's hand upon it. Here for several days an Indian came and offered insults in gestures and words to the garrison to provoke an attack. John Tomson deemed it advisable to call his council together, and after careful consid-

A VIEW OF THE ROCK UPON WHICH ISAAC HOWLAND SHOT THE INDIAN AT THE BEGINNING OF KING PHILIP'S WAR

eration it was determined that they should attempt to shoot him. The gun of the commander, especially adapted to a long range, was brought out, and Isaac Howland was selected for his skill as a marksman. He fired, resting the gun upon the shoulder of a comrade, and the Indian fell, mortally wounded. The shot was considered remarkable at the time, as the distance was one hundred and fifty-five rods, much beyond the range of the ordinary musket. The Indians, raising a yell, bore

musket or other serviceable peece for war with bandeleroes sword and other appurtenances for himself and each man servant he keepeth able to beare armes. And that for himselfe & each such person under him he be at all times furnished with two pounds of powder and ten pounds of bullets & for each default to forfeit ten shillings.

the wounded man away to the house of William Nelson, about three miles and a half distant, where he died, and was buried in the field near by with the ceremony for a departed brave. The house was then burned. Immediately after the fall of the Indian, the warriors who were about him sought revenge and attacked the grist-mill of Samuel Barrows. They crept along by a fence to within gunshot, but Mr. Barrows saw them approach and, suspecting their design, ran to shut down the mill, and then fled for his life. The bank of the river between the mill and the fort was lined with alders; through these he ran, holding his coat and hat upon a pole above his head. They fired upon him as he fled, but mistook the coat for the man, and he escaped unharmed to the fort with some bullet-holes in his coat.

After the mill was burned, many of the houses were destroyed by fire;[1] among them the houses of John Tomson, William Nelson, Obadiah Eddy, John Morton, Henry Wood, George Dawson, Francis Coombs, and William Clark.

In July, 1675, a man by the name of J. Marks, while walking through a field of Indian corn in Middleboro, was shot by an Indian, breaking his thigh-bone, and lay in the place where he fell forty-eight hours before he was found. He was yet alive, but his wound was so severe that he died soon after from its effects.[2]

The inhabitants who had found refuge in the fort remained about six weeks; then it was deemed wise to go to Plymouth. With the small amount of provisions, arms, and ammunition, they would have been wholly unable to resist a siege or an attack from as large a band of warriors as had destroyed Swansea and other towns in the colony.

On the 10th of July Ensign Tomson sent a letter to Governor Winslow, asking for an additional guard.

---

[1] In a note to Hubbard's *Narrative*, p. 41, we find that the town's guard was stationed in a mole and was not strong enough to act on the defensive, and thence the Indians swept around and burned most of the houses. Towards night they returned to Tispequin with great triumph and rejoicings.

[2] Hubbard's *Indian Wars*, vol. ii, p. 46.

VIEW OF DANSON BROOK, THOMPSON STREET
(Where George Danson was shot by the Indians at the beginning of King Philip's War)

HONOURED SIR, — My request to you is, that you would be pleased to send sufficient guard, to guard our women and children, with what goods is left, down to Plymouth, for we are every day liable to be a prey to our enemies, neither can we subsist here any longer by reason of want of provision and shot, for we are almost out of them both. And now our rye and other English grain, which is very considerable, is all laid open to creatures to destroy, the rye being almost ripe, which had we some considerable help to preserve, we possibly might have a considerable quantity of it, which might be to the saving of our lives; therefore my earnest request to your honor is, that, if it be possible, with as much brevity as may be, to relieve us. Sir, I conceive this place to be a very convenient place to keep a garrison, by reason the enemy makes Assawamsett and Daniel's Island his place of retreat, as we conceive. Sir, I doubt not, but if God by his providence spare my life till I see you, I shall be able to give a good account of our acting to your satisfaction.

The town's "Court of Guard," as it was termed, stationed at a mole, was overawed by numbers, while scattered parties of the Indians ranged about the settlement and burned most of the houses. "Towards night," says Sergeant Tomson, "they returned to the top of Tispequin's hill with great triumph and rejoicing, with a shout; but we firing our long gun at them, they speedily went away. To such extremity was a settlement, only about twelve or fourteen miles distant from Plymouth, reduced, in a few days after the commencement of hostilities." [1]

After the abandonment of the fort, it was burned by the Indians. The inhabitants remained in Plymouth till after the close of the war, as did also the inhabitants of Dartmouth and Swansea. The town of Scituate was attacked by a company of warriors, probably under the lead of Tispequin, and suffered severely; it was without means of defence, as Captain John Williams, with a company of thirty Scituate men, was absent endeavoring to intercept or waylay the enemy supposed to be somewhere in the woods of Nemasket.

July 19, 1675, a conflict took place at Pocasset, from which Philip escaped, and for several months the fighting continued outside of the old colony. In the most severe battle of the war, which occurred in Rhode Island, in December, 1675, John Raymond, later of Middleboro, took part, and Samuel Pratt, one of the early settlers, was killed.

On March 12, 1676, a massacre took place near Plymouth; eleven men were killed, and Mr. Clarke's house was attacked. This was followed by the destruction of a band of Scituate men at Pawtucket. At this time a body of three hundred additional men was raised, and was ordered to march on the 11th of April. They went through Middleboro, and some refused to march further and returned, it being a time of general insubordination throughout the colonies. On April 20 Scituate was attacked, and nineteen houses were burned.

On the 8th of May, 1676, some three hundred warriors under the leadership of Tispequin made a second attack upon Bridgewater, which was repelled by the inhabitants, and afterwards renewed upon that portion of the town bordering on the Taunton River which included Titicut, where they burned two houses and one barn; but it does not appear that they crossed the river into that portion of Titicut at present included in Middleboro. Philip had given orders that Bridgewater and Taunton should not be destroyed until the last.

[1] *New England's Memorial*, Davis edition, p. 430.

On or about the 11th of May [1] Middleboro was again visited, and the houses which had not been burned in the summer and fall before were totally destroyed.

About this time Captain Benjamin Church had charge of a number of volunteers for the purpose of more vigorously prosecuting the war. *Benjamin Church*
The following was the order from the governor and council of the colony : [2] —

Captain Benjamin Church, you are hereby nominated, ordered, commissioned, and empowered to raise a company of volunteers of about two hundred men, English and Indians; the English not exceeding the number of sixty, of which company, or so many of them as you can obtain, or shall see cause at present to improve, you are to take the command, conduct, and to lead them forth now and hereafter, at such time, and unto such places within this colony, or elsewhere within the confederate colonies, as you shall think fit; to discover, pursue, fight, surprise, destroy, or subdue our Indian enemies, or any part or parties of them, that by the providence of God you may meet with, or them, or any of them, by treaty and composition to receive to mercy, if you see reason, (provided they be not murderous rogues, or such as have been principal actors in those villanies.) And forasmuch as your company may be uncertain, and the persons often changed, you

---

[1] In a letter supposed to be written by Governor Josiah Winslow to Thomas Hinckley and John Freeman, under date of May 23, 1676, referring to Philip's War on the towns of Plymouth Colony, he says : —

"The people in all our towns (Scituate excepted) are very desirous to be ranging after the enemy. Last Saturday, about four, afternoon, a second post came from Bridgewater, informing that they had that morning discovered a party of about two hundred of the enemy at Teeticut, very busy killing cattle and horses, as if they intended some stay there; and that Taunton and Bridgewater had agreed in the night to advance towards them with about sixty men, to fight them in the morning, and requested a few men from us if possible. The warning was very short; yet we obtained from Plymouth, Duxbury, and Marshfield about forty smart lads, and sent to Bridgewater that night, but have not as yet heard of or from them. They knew of your intended march; and, if they miss of those Indians, may very probably meet and join with yours to range towards Dartmouth and Seaconet." The Hinckley Papers, *Mass. Hist. Coll.* vol. v, Fourth Series, p. 9.

[2] Church, *History of Philip's War*, Part I, p. 100.

are also hereby empowered with the advice of your company, to choose and commissionate a Lieutenant, and to establish Sergeants, and Corporals as you see cause. And you herein improving your best judgment and discretion, and utmost ability, faithfully to serve the interest of God, his Majesty's interest, and the interest of the colony; and carefully governing your said company at home and abroad. These shall be unto you full and ample commission, warrant and discharge. Given under the publick seal, this 24th day of July, 1676.

Per Jos. WINSLOW, Governour.

July 25 Captain Church, again on the march with a company of eighteen English and twenty-two Indians, reached Middleboro before daylight in pursuit of a party of Narragansetts.[1]

They were led by Philip's warriors, who for some time had been making depredations in Middleboro and other towns. Friendly Indians had reported their supposed whereabouts, and Captain Church, upon receiving his commission, marched immediately to Middleboro. During the night of the first day he reached Thomastown, where these warriors were encamped not far from the residence of the late Perez Thomas, in a swamp which he surrounded. They were accustomed to hide on an island in the middle of the swamp in the daytime, and to carry on their devastations during the night. Some of his Indian scouts brought the information that they had seen the smoke of their fires. Captain Church immediately ordered his forces to approach the swamp, and to be careful that none should escape. Before the sun rose, tracks were discovered in the dew on the grass on a narrow strip of land that led from the high ground on the edge of the swamp to the island. Seeing that there was no possible means of escape, and that they had been so completely surprised, the whole force of the Indians surrendered,[2] and were conveyed to Plymouth as prisoners of war. Captain Church hastened through the woods back to

---

[1] Baylies's *New Plymouth*, Part III, pp. 152-153.

[2] "Upon examination, they agreed in their stories, that they belonged to Tispaquin, who was gone with John Bump, an Indian, to kill horses." Church, *History of Philip's War*, Part I, p. 176.

Plymouth, where he left them to be dealt with by the governor, with the exception of one Jeffrey, a Narragansett, who had proved a faithful guide, and had been of great assistance to him after the Indians surrendered.

Middleboro men had all moved to Plymouth, and undoubtedly, as this expedition was in part to capture these Indians, not a few of them took part, but of this we have no record. Later, Captain Church's command reached Nemasket in the early morning and discovered another company of the enemy, whom they approached and surprised, capturing sixteen. Upon examination, they informed him that Tispequin was at Assawampsett with a large company. It is to be noted that during this campaign some of the Indians who were taken by Captain Church proved so friendly that they assisted him in capturing the enemy.

Captain Church was in charge of a number of wagons laden with provisions, bound to Taunton, which he had been ordered to protect. He was therefore obliged to lose the opportunity of seizing Tispequin and the warriors with him. Upon reaching Taunton, he was indignant to find Major Bradford, the commander of the forces, idle at the tavern, and asked that the latter's soldiers might be sent over the river to guard the provisions, while he continued on his expedition.[1]

After leaving Taunton, he hastened to Assawampsett Neck, where he proposed to camp that night. As soon as they came to the brook[2] which runs into the great pond through a swamp, the Indians fired, but no one was injured. Those in his command ran into the swamp where the enemy were supposed to be and fired upon them, but it being in the edge of the evening, they escaped.

Captain Church then moved his company to Assawampsett Neck, where, being exceedingly fatigued, he concluded to

---

[1] The route which Captain Church probably took with his train was over what is now known as Summer Street.

[2] This place is probably at the bridge over the stream that connects the two ponds, a little south of the house of Mr. Perry.

encamp and rest for the remainder of the night. He placed a guard about the camp, a part of his men holding his horses while they ate. In the middle of the night, Tispequin's scouts having fired upon them, he stealthily moved away by another route and proceeded to Acushnet, some three miles to the south, where the Indians had previously burned the houses after the inhabitants had fled. Neither party seems to have been willing to risk an encounter, as both were well prepared and acquainted with the country, and, well knowing the strength of each other, they withdrew without further engagement.[1]

On July 30 another force of Indians was reported to the authorities, and the "Governor hastened to Plymouth, raised what men he could by the way, came to Plymouth in the beginning of the forenoon exercise, sent for Captain Church out of the meeting-house, gave him the news. . . . The Captain bestirred himself but found no bread in the storehouse and so was forced to run from house to house to get household bread for their march."[2] They went to Bridgewater, where Philip, with some of his followers, desiring to escape, had cut down a tree to serve as a bridge across the Taunton River. Church, on reaching this temporary bridge, saw an Indian sitting, and was about to fire, but was restrained by one who thought him a friendly Indian. He proved to be Philip, and Church, with Isaac Howland, pursued him to a swamp, where they captured several, but not the wily Philip. On returning to Plymouth, the captain received the governor's thanks for this victory, in which one hundred and seventy-three were killed or captured.

SITE OF THE ENCOUNTER AT THE BRIDGE, LAKEVILLE

---

[1] This encampment was probably upon the farm of Sidney T. Nelson. Pierce, *Indian History*, p. 200; Baylies's *New Plymouth*, Part III, pp. 154-155.

[2] Church, *History of Philip's War*, p. 121.

Again he started in pursuit, and finally, on the 12th of August, surrounded and captured Philip[1] at Mount Hope.

"They let him come fair within shot, and the Englishman's gun missing fire, he bid the Indian fire away and he did so to the purpose; sent one musket bullet through his heart, and another not above two inches from it. He fell upon his face in the mud and water, with his gun under him."

An old Indian executioner was commanded to behead the dead king. Ere he raised his hatchet he said, Philip "had been a very great man and had made many a man afraid of him, but so big as he was, he would now chop him."

Eighteen days later, Church captured another great leader, Annawon, who surrendered, saying, "Great Captain, you have killed Philip and conquered his country: for I believe that I and my company are the last that war against the English, so suppose the war is ended by your means; and therefore these things belong unto you." Then, opening his pack, he pulled out Philip's belt, "curiously wrought with wompom, being nine inches broad, wrought with black and white wompom, in various figures, and pictures of many birds and beasts." This, when hung upon Captain Church's shoulders, "reached his ancles."[2]

Captain Church seems to have been more or less embarrassed by instructions which he had received from the colony, and evidently some jealousy existed concerning him. The insubordination which manifested itself probably grew out of the fact that after the death of Philip it was believed by most of the men that the war would end, and they were desirous of devoting their time to saving what had been lost.

Middleboro, as an outpost of Plymouth, was the nearest town which suffered, as it was visited often by the whites, either in pursuit of the enemy or hastening to the defence of other towns in the colony. The fact that the inhabitants of Middleboro were enabled to reach the fort in safety, and thus escape massacre, which attended other towns of the colony;

---

[1] Church, *History of Philip's War*, Part I. pp. 148, 151.
[2] *Ibid.* pp. 148, 151.

that the fort was not attacked; and that its inmates, so poorly protected, were allowed to escape to Plymouth, are evidences of the way in which the inhabitants of Middleboro were regarded by the Indians.

Tispequin was the commander-in-chief at the various conflicts with Captain Benjamin Church about the great ponds of Middleboro. After Church had taken his wife, children, and attendants upon the promise that if he would surrender he would spare his and their lives, Tispequin went to Plymouth, and gave himself up to the governor and his council. He was soon after tried and publicly executed. This action on the part of the governor and council has led to perhaps more severe criticism than any portion of the public administration at New Plymouth. It may, however, be truthfully said that Captain Church had received no authority from the governor to make this promise to Tispequin, nor did the authorities know of it. He was brought to trial when it was learned that he was the leader of all of the massacres in the colony, and particularly in the burning of the houses of the settlers in Middleboro to whom he had sold land. The exigencies of the times and the perils to which they were still subject did not warrant any other disposition of so treacherous a chief than the death which he received, and which he so justly merited.[1]

In King Philip's War, so far as relates to Plymouth Colony, the decisive battle was the engagement at Scituate. If the Indians had not been defeated at that battle, it was their intention to go down along the coast, burn all of the houses, and destroy the inhabitants. Plymouth was not sufficiently fortified to have escaped the general massacre. The able-bodied men in the western part of the colony had joined the forces of Captain Church to meet the Indians, and their families had gone to

---

[1] "It had always been held by the Indians that Tispequin could not be shot by any bullets from the English, and after the capture of his wife and children, Captain Church sent word to Tispequin that he should be his captain over the Indians if he were found so invulnerable a man, as they said he was shot twice, but the bullets glanced by him, and could not hurt him. He afterwards surrendered and was sent to Plymouth, but upon trial, he was found penetrable to the English gun, for he fell down at the first shot." Hubbard's *Indian Wars* (Drake), vol. i, p. 275.

Plymouth. A defeat at Scituate would probably have rendered the rest of the towns in the colony defenceless, and they would have been destroyed in accordance with the plan of Philip and his warriors. The little fort at Middleboro was the only one on the west, and there was nothing to have prevented the Indians, had they passed Scituate, from continuing their march of destruction to Plymouth.

The war lasted nearly two years. About thirteen towns were destroyed, and many others were attacked; about six hundred whites were killed in battle, beside the many unknown who perished from starvation and in massacre.

HATCHET, PIPE, MORTAR, AND PESTLE

CHAPTER VI

THE FRENCH AND INDIAN WARS, 1689-1765

AT the close of King Philip's War, the old colony was not threatened by attacks of Indians, and suffered nothing from any of the hostilities which were occurring in the remote parts of the country. Middleboro was represented in all of the campaigns fought against the Indians or the French and Indians, in the expeditions organized in defence of the colonies in behalf of the mother country, and in resisting the aggressive attacks of France to obtain possession of the various strongholds; but the names of the soldiers enlisted in these campaigns have most of them been forgotten, about one third of them being Indians.

News of an invasion of England by France reached Boston in the winter of 1688,[1] and on the 10th of January, 1689, a proclamation was issued by Sir Edmund Andros, commanding the officers, civil and military, and all other of his Majesty's loving subjects, to be ready to use their utmost endeavor to hinder any landing or invasion that might be intended; but so bitter was the feeling against Governor Andros that this proclamation was generally disregarded. The colonies of New England had enjoyed a period of peace from the close of King Philip's War until the year 1689, when the Indians on the north and western frontier settlements, instigated by the long and bitter enmity of the French against the English, commenced a series of barbarous attacks.

In August, 1689, the court at Plymouth appointed commissioners to confer with the other colonies as to the course of conduct that they should take in repelling these assaults, and, as a result, there was a general Indian war, in which all of the New England colonies engaged, known as King William's War

[1] Barry's *History of Massachusetts*, First Period, pp. 499, 500.

(1689–97). The troops from Plymouth and Massachusetts colonies were placed under the command of the celebrated Captain Benjamin Church, who had achieved such renown in King Philip's War. Middleboro was required to furnish one soldier and one musket, and to raise the sum of fourteen pounds by taxation towards meeting the expense of this threatened war. The tax was to be paid on or before the 26th day of November, 1689, one third in money, one third in grain, and one third in beef and pork. It is interesting to notice the price at which these articles were then rated; namely, the grain was to be received and credited as follows: corn, two shillings per bushel; rye, two shillings and sixpence per bushel; barley, two shillings per bushel; wheat, four shillings per bushel; beef, ten shillings per hundred, and pork twopence per pound.

Early in May, 1690, a congress of delegates met in New York to consider means of defence. Plymouth[1] and Massachusetts colonies, with Connecticut, were to furnish three hundred and fifty-five men. The militia were to meet at Albany and then proceed to Montreal. Middleboro's quota was one soldier. An expedition had been planned to sail to Quebec, and extensive preparations were made for combined attack on that stronghold of the French. On June 5, 1690, Middleboro was ordered to send three soldiers, and to raise twenty-one pounds, sixteen shillings, and sixpence as her proportionate part of the expenses. Of the three soldiers drafted, Thomas Tomson and James Soule, for reasons which do not appear on record, declined to go, and were sentenced to pay a fine of four pounds each, or be imprisoned until the fines were paid. Benjamin Wood, John Tomson, and John Allen took part in this expedition. Port Royal and Acadia were conquered, but the combined attack on Quebec was a failure, owing to the jealousy and disagreement of the officers in charge of the campaign. Captain Church, in a second expedition into Maine, was to threaten the eastern Indians, but this was also a failure, and a crushing mortification and sorrow ensued to Massachusetts.[2]

[1] Parkman's *Frontenac and New France*, chap. xii, pp. 235, 236.
[2] Palfrey, *History of New England*, Book IV, chap. ii.

The next call for troops in Middleboro was in 1722, for defence against another threatened Indian attack. This war lasted until 1725. A number of men from Middleboro, with friendly Indians, joined this expedition. Of the company raised, William Canedy was an ensign, and was afterwards promoted to the rank of lieutenant. He was placed in command of a small fort at St. George's River, which was attacked on the 25th of December, 1723, by a large force of French and Indians. He so bravely defended this fort until reinforcements arrived, and the enemy[1] was repelled with such great loss, that he was rewarded with a commission as captain.

The following is a list[2] of privates and officers : —

COMMISSIONED OFFICERS

William Canedy, capt.
Benjamin Wright, lieut.

Robert Stanford, ens.

NON-COMMISSIONED OFFICERS

Joseph Bowdin, sergt.
Joseph Studson, sergt.
Joseph Meeds, sergt.
Benjamin Durfee, corp.

Richard Pomeroy, corp.
Joseph Braydon, corp.
John Oliver, corp.

PRIVATES

John Attamon
Thomas Tainor
Daniel Chislen
Joshua Tripp
Benjamin Solomon
Joel Daniel
John Pechue
John Pepeens
Abraham Jones
Joseph Wood
Nehemiah Nahawamah
Abel Obediah
James Queich
Simon Tremmetuck

Henry Pesent
Josiah Crook
Isaac Phillips
Elisha Sachem
Peter Washonks
Joshua Hood
Samuel Copeluck
Ned John
Josiah Popmemanock
Eliakim Quacom
Amos Stanks
Joshua Wicket
David Job
Jacob Paul

[1] *The Peirce Family*, p. 106.
[2] These lists are taken from the *History of Plymouth County*, p. 994.

Thomas Daniel
Abel Tom
Isaac Hassaway
Eben Cushen
Job Mark
Samuel Oliver
John Quoy

John Comshite
Mose Peig
Tom Wily
Abel Blinks
Peter Dogamus
John Boson
Roban Jenney

Another roll bore the following names: —

COMMISSIONED OFFICERS

William Canedy, capt.   Stephen Whitaker, ens.

NON-COMMISSIONED OFFICERS

Daniel Elenthorp, sergt.   Edward Bishop, corp.
Francis Punchard, corp.

PRIVATES

Peter Parrey
Thomas Lawrence
Stephen Morrells
John Norris
Benjamin Speen
John Church
Jeremiah Belcher
Elkanah Topmon
Isaac Chamberlain
John White

Philip Butler
Daniel Ross
John Murphy
Josiah Meeds
Daniel Griffin
Thomas Dan
John Pelkenton
William Thomas
William Kelley

Middleboro men were at the siege of Louisburg, the strongest fortress in the New World, captured and destroyed in 1745. General Shirley had proposed to the General Court an expedition to capture Louisburg, and a circular letter was sent to all the colonies as far south as Pennsylvania. Massachusetts furnished three thousand two hundred and fifty men.[1] The commander-in-chief was William Pepperrell of Maine. On June 17 Louisburg capitulated.[2] A thanksgiving day was appointed on July 18, and Thomas Prince preached a sermon on this at the Old South Meeting-house.

---

[1] Barry, *History of Massachusetts*, Second Period, vol. ii, p. 141.
[2] Hildreth, *History of United States*, vol. ii, chap. xxv, p. 397.

In 1755 occurred the French and Indian War, which lasted eight years, and was by far the most important campaign which up to that time had been carried on by the English against the French, who had succeeded in inducing the Indians in the northwest of the English possessions to join with them. This included most of the Indian troops in New York State, and a few in Vermont and New Hampshire. The English outnumbered the French fifteen to one,[1] but the French controlled the two large rivers. General Braddock, sent over in 1755 by England, was defeated at Fort Duquesne, which was recaptured two years later. In 1759 General Wolfe and General Montcalm were both killed at Quebec, but the fall of this city was the turning-point in the war. From that day France lost her territory in America.

Middleboro furnished one company under command of Captain Benjamin Pratt, and parts of another under command of Captain Samuel Thatcher for this year. The names of the officers and privates in Captain Pratt's company were as follows : —

COMMISSIONED OFFICERS

Benjamin Pratt, capt. David Sears, 2d lieut.
Sylvester Richmond, 1st lieut. Nelson Finney, ens.

NON-COMMISSIONED OFFICERS

Seth Tinkham,[2] sergt. Archippas Cole, corp.
Lemuel Harlow, sergt. Seth Billington, corp.
Silas Wood, sergt. Jesse Snow, corp.
Abiel Cole, sergt. John Miller, corp.

MUSICIANS

Perez Tinkham Jacob Tinkham

PRIVATES

Jacob Allen Joseph Bent
Jesse Bryant Abner Barrows

[1] Montgomery, *History of United States*, p. 134.
[2] Seth Tinkham left a diary of this campaign, which has been published in the *History of Plymouth County*, p. 995.

THE FRENCH AND INDIAN WARS

Abner Barrows, Jr.	Jeremiah Jones
Isaac Bennett	Jeremiah Jones, Jr.
John Bennett	John Knowlton
Samuel Bennett	James Littlejohn
Benjamin Barrows	Robert Makfun
Abraham Barden	Thomas Miller
William Barlow	David Miller
Eliakim Barlow	Noah Morse
John Barker	Jonathan Morse
Perez Cobb	Jacob Muxom
Onesimus Campbell	Isaac Nye
Gideon Cobb	Thomas Peirce
Gershom Cobb	Job Peirce
William Cushman	Paul Pratt
Peter Crapo	Francis Pomeroy
Thomas Caswell	Samuel Pratt
Jesse Curtis	Samuel Pratt, Jr.
Ezekiel Curtis	Henry Richmond
Counselor Chase	Nathan Richmond
Jabez Doggett	Moses Reding
Simeon Doggett	Job Richmond
Ebenezer Dunham	Noah Raymond
Adam David	Barnabas Sampson
Elkanah Elmes	Jabez Sampson
John Elmes	Jacob Sampson
John Ellis	Obadiah Sampson
John Eaton	John Sampson
Asa French	Crispus Shaw
William Fuller	Perez Shaw
Simeon Fuller	Zebedee Sears
Jedediah Holmes	Peleg Standish
John Harlow	Robert Seekel
Zuril Haskell	Benjamin Streeter

The Rev. Ebenezer Hinds, pastor of the Second Baptist Church, was the chaplain of this regiment, and accompanied them during the entire service.

Captain Abiel Peirce,[1] a young man of remarkable courage and enterprise, early noted among the people of the town for his character and devotion to the interests of the mother country, served as a private soldier under General Winslow in the

[1] *The Peirce Family*, p. 102.

expedition to Acadia in the summer and fall of 1755. For his prudence and bravery he was afterwards promoted to the rank of lieutenant, and still later to the rank of captain. He was in the expedition to Canada, and present at the battle of Quebec, "the key of Canada,"[1] September 13, 1759. Before the attack on Quebec he was detailed to serve as a temporary aide-de-camp on the staff of General Wolfe. He saw General Wolfe receive his fatal wound, and heard him say as he fell, "Support me, let not my soldiers see me drop." Then came the shout, "The day is ours!" "They run! They give way everywhere!" A light came into the eyes of the dying hero, who eagerly asked, "Who fly?" and being told it was the French, exclaimed, "Now, God be praised, I die happy."

The company under command of Captain Thatcher probably consisted of many who had served under Captain Pratt, and the following are the names of the officers and privates, most of them Middleboro men :[2] —

"Samuell Thacher Capt.
John Peirce Lieut.
Ignatious Elmes Insign
Abner Barrows
Robert Barrows
Samuel Bobbitt
William Barlow
Ruben Barrows
Joshua Caswell   Sick at Albany
Joseph Drake   Desarted
David Delano   Died the 8 of Septm
Remembrance Donham
Ebnezer Donham
James Fance
Isreal Felix   Sick at Albany

[1] Barry, *History of Massachusetts*, vol. ii, p. 238.
[2] The above names are from the diary of Abner Barrows, a son of Coombs Barrows, now in the possession of Miss Sarah T. Barrows, his great-granddaughter. It is a small book, about $3\frac{3}{4}$ inches wide by $5\frac{3}{4}$ inches long, which was probably carried in his pocket and the entries made from day to day. The list of the officers and privates in this company are in his handwriting at the end of the diary. He was from twenty-three to twenty-five years old at the time he was in this service, and lived afterwards in the old Barrows house.

Samuel Hunter
Peter Hulburt   Desarted
Ebenezer Norcutt   at Albany
John Reed
Barnabas Raymond
William Ransom
Gibbin Sharp
Ephraim Thomas
Oxenbridge Thacher Adj
Perez Tinkham
William Terry   Sick at Albany
William Tupper
Nathan Thomas
Lemuel Wood
Benjamin Washburn   Sick at Albany "

Abner Barrows kept a diary of his service in the French and Indian War from 1756 to 1758. This diary is dated, "Boston, May 11, 1756," the day they left Boston, and contains records of the events during their march, — the places where they encamped, the number of miles travelled each day, with the incidents of their camp life. They reached Albany on the 23d of May, taking twelve days to travel a distance which can now be done by cars in a few hours. After arriving at Albany they proceeded to Saratoga, and to Fort William Henry. The regiment to which this company belonged performed no special service, and the men were discharged and returned to their homes. Mr. Barrows enlisted again in 1757, and served during the campaign of 1758.

The following is a copy of a portion : —

1758, July 2. D Nothing Remarkable hapnd Kept about our Incampment Our army consists of about twenty two thousand.

July 3 this Day thair Was a Generial muster through the Whole Incampment Every Regement mustered by them selves and was Desmised about middle of the after Noon.

July 5 this Day the Whole Incampment by about half way betwext Brake of Day & Son Rise Struk thair tents and marched Down to the Lake thair Shipt in Battoes & in Whail Botes Rowed Down the Lake about Sixteen miles made Something of a halt about three ours or Better then Rowed in our Botes again Sometimes Rowed Sometimes Layd on our ores Till after Day Light by the Son about three hours high then our men Viz Regulars Landed about half a mile above the advanced Guard of our Enemys Major Roggers With his Rangers Went tords them and they perceiving they Was an army they hauled Down thair Tents Ran of With all Speed Left bag and baggage for a prey thay fired a good many Guns which Did no harme Several of the Enemy Wair kild or Taken prisoners

July 6 this morning about Eight o Clock the army Landed our Regulars fired on a few french men and Indians & killed two or three ye french that Wair att the advance Guard Ran off with all Speed all and all thair Things behind allmost behind them Soon after We Landed thair Went out two or three parties of men after thay had bin out an our or two we heard a Very smart Firing which Lasted about an hour & toward Night thay brought the prisoners that thay had taken Which amounted to the Number of about 150 thay had upwards of fifty or 60 Slain this Day we Reckned that our men had upwards of fifteen or 20 Slain Som Wounded & brought In to the C mp our Lord how Was Slain this Day

July 7 this morning Severial Regments marcht from Whair We Landed ours with them then after we had travled three or fore miles thay all Returnd to the Camp then our Regment took meet for two Days & no Bread then about two or three ours after we came in our Regment & a Good many more Regments marcht towards the Enemys fort & made Several Brest works for our own Safegard Whair our Regement Loged in the Night

Saturday July the 8 this morning all the Regements that Lay in their Breast Works travled about a mile then our Regment and one more Viz Colo Bayleys Regment Lay a long two Deep In order for combat the Light Infantry Regment Lay advanced before Us we Lay thair two or three hours Divers Guns Wair Fired in our front Till all In a Sudden thair Was a very Brisk fire in our front We Lay a Short Time Prepared for the Enemy But perceiving thay Did not Come then the Regment that Lay Before Us advanced forward and our Regment marched Briskly the fire Continued in one Continued Volley the Biggest Part of five hours the french that we thus Ingaged wair in thair Brest Work & in thair Intrenchments our Regulars Began the fire With the Enemy thair Was abundance of them Slain Som Conclude thair was two or 3 thousand of them Slain thair Was som Slain of Every Party that Belonged to Every Province Slain and Wounded a great over Sight that We had Not our Cannon two of our Cannon Got allmost to Us but thay wair ordred Back by What Reason I know not O, to See the Slain how thick thay Lay on the Ground when our men Retreated from them We Carred of the Wounded men about a mile to Whair our Brest Work was Made the Night after the Battle was fought the Regement Retreated Back som to the place Whair We Landed Som of the Regments Came No further than the saw mill about two miles they brote thair Wounded men as far as thair Next morning the army Gott Into thair Battoes made What Speed thay Could away I fear a great many Wounded men fell Into the hands of our Enemy & the Slain all Lay on the spoot.

July 9 D this Day the army Returned Back again to the head of the Lake whair We Set out from. We Sett out from the Place Whair We Landed about teen of the Clock in the morning Reacht the head of the Lake about son sett and thairabout

. . . .

July ye 16 this Day the biggest Part of our Regmt marcht from Lake George Down to Fort Edward Severial of our Company Was Very Poorly this Day Capt Pratt Came to us he mett us about 7 miles below Between fort Edward and the old Camp att a place caled the half Way Brook our Camp Campt at fort Edward

July ye 17 this morning Sett out from a Little Below fort EDWARD travled to Saratoga by about two of the Clock in the after Noon thair Drawd Stors in our Company Sett out again Crosed a Little River travled about a mile Down the River thair Picht our tents.

July ye 18 this morning our Company Sett out from Saratoga travled to the half Way house thair made a Small Halt and it began to Rain It Rained and it made the Way Extrodanery bad traveling traveled to the Half Way House Thair Picht our tents and Loged

July ye 19 this morning our Company Sett out from the half Way house travled to the half moon by about Eleven of the Clock thair Picht our tents by the upper Sprowt &c.
this after Noon a Great many of our Regment travled off Crost the River this after Noon Without orders about Soon Sett thair Came a Reagular officer Who Commanded the men back he Struck one man Several blows about thirty men Cockt thar fier Locks on him he past of With Speed

July ye 21 this Day Nothing Remarkable hapned in our

Camp our Company begun to Recrute from thair Illness this afternoon the Whole of the Regt that wair hear wair ordered under armes our Colo made a Speech to us Told us the Danger of Desarting he Said that he had Wrote to the Cort to Know what to Do he said if the Cort sent for us We mought then go hom and not other Wise after the Collo had Walked Round & talked to us then our Chaplain Went to prayer With ye Regiment & We wair Dismissed

July ye 23 this morning about Teen o Clock the Regt Under Colo Thos Dotys Comand being ordered to march about three Score men belonging to the Same Regment Clobed thair fier locks & Was maching off two Sergt headed them the Rest of ye Regt Was Ordered to Load thair fier Locks Emediatly and fix on thair Bayonets then We wair ord to march. We marchd Round them our Colo & adjutant took thair armes from them Putt all under Guard thair they wair kept about two howers then the Ring Leaders of them Wair took and Penioned Six of them wair sent Down to be Putt in the prison at Albany the about fifty or so men that Wair put under guard for the same Crime wair Released by making Good promises for the futur &c

July 31 D this morning sett out from the place Whair We Loged Set Up the falls as Well as We Could about teen oClock our boat Reacht up as far as Whair our Regt Stopt then sett out again Some Times We Rowed then We out Waided halled our botes by hand a grate Way Grate falls bad going Up the River Went by a Grate many Dutch Settlements on both Sides of the River Exceeding Large fealds of all Sorts of Grain

this Night Went off four men belonging to the Batto that I Went in

The different regiments which served in the French and Indian War were probably called out for a single campaign, of short duration, and upon its close were dismissed and afterwards reënlisted as required by the governor of the province. Captain Pratt's company was in the campaign of the summer of 1757 in and about Fort Henry, some of his former men enlisting in other companies as well as in that under the command of Captain Thatcher. The roll of officers and men under Captain Pratt shows the first enlistment, while that under Captain Thatcher is the second enlistment.

In the campaign about Fort Edwards, Ticonderoga, and Crown Point in 1761, Captain Jabez Snow enlisted the following Middleboro men under Colonel Jonathan Hoar's regiment of the Massachusetts Bay forces : —

" Nath[n] Alden
Th[s] Barding
Abraham Barding
Benj[n] Barding
Nath[n] Bennett
Batchelder Bennett
Zebulon Bryant
Nath[l] Covil
John Calloge
Theop[s] Crossman
Richard Dwelly
Isaac Dunham
Lot Eaton

Simeon Fuller
Nath[n] Howland
Jeremiah Jones
Abial Leach
Nath[l] Maybe
Gibens Sharp
Jabez Samson
Reuben Snow
John Thomas
James Willis
Abner Wood
Josiah Wood
Jabez Vaughan "

FRENCH NEUTRALS

In the struggle between France and England for supremacy in the New World, an expedition in 1755 was planned for the conquest of Nova Scotia by General Winslow, a native of Plymouth and a grandson of Edward Winslow. Here dwelt for generations the French Neutrals, better known as the Acadians, who took no part in this conquest, but were suspected on account of their intense attachment for France and their devotion to the Catholic faith. Their priest taught that fidelity to King Louis was inseparable from fidelity to God.[1]

The English Crown issued an order, through the influence of Governor Shirley, that they should be deported to preserve the rights of English subjects. Middleboro furnished a few of the men who took part in this campaign. Abiel Peirce served as a private, and Alexander Canedy accompanied the troops, but was unable to serve on account of illness. The manner in which this order was carried out gave rise to perhaps the severest condemnation of any act of the British government in reference to her dealings with her colonies of America. Fam-

[1] Parkman, *Montcalm and Wolfe*, vol. i, p. 235.

ilies were scattered[1] and separated throughout the English possessions in America. About one thousand were landed in Boston, and distributed among the towns of the province in proportion to the inhabitants. They were usually treated well in the different towns of the state, but were supported as paupers, and were called "cadies." Of this number, Middleboro's quota was nine, but we have no definite trace of their permanent settlement, although the names of some families would indicate that they may be their descendants. All that now remains of their history is the record of three bills for their support, which were sent by the selectmen to the treasurer of the province; the legislature cheerfully attempted to alleviate their sufferings by passing a resolution to pay the different towns for their support.[2]

[1] See Longfellow's *Evangeline*.
[2] The following is a bill copied from the 23d volume of *Mass. Archives*: —

Purfuant to an act of the Grate & General Court of this province, Relating to the Inhabitants of nova Scotia brought to this province, we the Subscribers selectmen of middleborough, by order of the General Courte Committee and had the cear of 9 of Said Inhabitants and have kept an Exact account of the necesary and unavoidable Charge we have been at in Suporting said inhabitants beginning at the 15th day of January to the 4th day of April 1756 Which we humbly submitt; the account is as followeth: —

To 14 1/2 bushels of corn at 2/8 p bushel	£1 — 18 — 8
To — bushels of Ric at 3/4 P bushel	1 — 13 — 4
To 180 pound of good pork	2 — 13 — 0
To 88 pounds of beef	0 — 17 — 7 1/2
To 29 1/2 pounds of hog fat	0 — 10 — 5 1/2
To fier wood & houfe rent	1 — 3 — 0
Paid to Noah Thomas for turnups portators and hogs fat	0 — 10 — 4
Paid to Thomas Fofters Eggs For beens Codfifh and molafes	0 — 11 — 5
To beens portators & Candels	0 — 4 — 10
To five P Shoes	1 — 1 — 5 1/2
To fifh	0 — 6 — 0
To keeping m^r Fofters Teem that carted sd inhabitants	0 — 2 — 2
	11 — 12 — 3 1/2

Dated at Middleborough April 15th. 1756.
about 2/ a week.

ELIAS MILLER } Selectmen
                            of
JOSEPH TINKHAM } Middleborough.

CHAPTER VII

SLAVES IN MIDDLEBORO

PRIOR to the Revolution, a few slaves were held in many of the towns in this commonwealth.[1] There is the record of the sale of but one in Middleboro, and those that were held, upon the death of their owner either passed to some member of the family by will or were given their freedom, and in some cases received a little tract of land with a house in which to live. Upon obtaining their freedom they rarely left their masters, but remained with them, serving in the same capacity as before. Very amusing incidents have come down by way of tradition of the bright sayings of some of them and the innocent pranks they played upon different members of the family.

In 1755 there were at least twelve slaves owned in Middleboro. Rev. Peter Thatcher owned a slave by the name of Sambo, who was imported from Africa, and, not speaking a word of English when he came to live with the good minister,

---

[1] Slaves were never as numerous in Massachusetts as in Rhode Island and Connecticut, and were always treated with great consideration. As early as the "Body of Liberties, printed in 1641, the General Court declared, there shall never be any bond of slaverie, villenage or captivitie unless it be lawful captives taken in just wars and such strangers as willingly sell themselves or are sold to us;" and it seems that all slaves always had the right to come into any public court either by speech or motion for the redress of any wrongs that they may have had.

The slaves of Massachusetts were not held under a rigorous servitude. They were generally instructed in the teachings of the Bible, and were often members of the church and subject to the same rules as their owners. They had their legal rights, which, however, were never enforced against those of their owners.

Among the laws passed by the General Court in 1703, "It was enacted that slaves shall not be absent from the families to which they belong or found abroad in the night after nine o'clock." The early newspapers frequently had advertisements for the sale of slaves.

could be communicated with only by means of signs. It is said that one day, soon after his arrival, Mrs. Thatcher asked him to bring in some wood with which to kindle the fire. Sambo brought it in, but when he saw the flames going up from the mouth of the oven, looked aghast, and darting through the door, was not seen for several days. After a long search by the neighbors, he was found in a swamp and brought home nearly dead from cold and hunger. When he could speak a little English he said, "In my own country, away dar in Af'ica, we hab slaves, we hungry, we kill 'em, we roast 'em, de meat bery good. When I see de fire roarin' in de oben I tink, 'Sambo, you days all ober wid you now, dem white foks roast you in de oben and eat you.' De sweat run down my angles; I lib wid de coons; I cold; I hungry — I go home dey roast me in de oben, which best? I dunno, all de same I tink." One day he came to his mistress bringing a loaf of bread in his hands, his eyes aglare, and his lips extended in a most peculiar manner. "Look, Missy, look haar, de crus' lef' bread and gone up trough de oben; I believe de debil's been here and is tryin' to run away wid de bread." She told him his oven was not hot enough, and therefore his bread fell. "Oben not hot enuf, de bread fall? How could de bread fall, was it not on de bottom ob de oben? Dis nigger no understand," said he, scratching his head. Afterward, his mistress, going into the kitchen, saw loaves of bread around the floor, and Sambo running from one to the other sitting on each one of them. "Look, Missy, is not dis a charmin' way to keep de crus' from risin'?" he said. Sambo became a christian, and joined the First Church in 1742. While Whitefield was in this vicinity, it is said that Sambo walked to Plymouth hoping to hear him preach, but Whitefield did not come, and the people were disappointed, an itinerant minister supplying. During the service Sambo was very much affected, and cried aloud so that one of the deacons went to him and asked him to be still. He said, "I cannot be still; Massa Whitefield preach so, he nearly break my heart." "But," said the deacon, "it is not Whitefield." "Not Massa Whitefield? den I hab made all dis hubbubboo for nothing." Another of Mr. Thatcher's slaves, Callininco, burned the mansion house by his carelessness in placing a wooden vessel filled with coals in an adjoining outhouse. Mr. Thatcher owned two others, named Anna Kolton and Nannie.

Cyrus Wood, a worthy and influential man, who resided at the Four Corners, kept a country store upon the site where stands the house formerly owned by Deacon Abiel Wood. He owned a slave by the name of Elsie, who was industrious, frugal, and neat. She was very fond of display, and wore a great red handkerchief for a headdress. She was a worshipper in the old church, but acquired a taste for strong drink. Her fault reaching the ears of some of the members of the church, she was summoned before them, and with much fear and trembling, she made this confession : " Bredren and sisters, all dat you hab heard about Elsie is true ; it is all true. I did go to de store, I did buy me a bottle of whiskey to cure de rheumatics. A-comin' home trough de woods de bottle was in my hands. I could see de whiskey in de bottle, it looked bery gude. I tink I would take out de stopper and smell of him a little ; maybe, I says, maybe it will do my rheumatics gude, so I takes out de stopper and smell of him a little. It smelled very gude. I just tase him one drop, den de debil, he stan' right at my elbow. He says, ' Elsie, tase him a little more ;' den de debil he pleased, he did not speak to me any more. I did all de res' myself, de debil did not help me. I tase him and tase him and kep' a-tasin' him, till I tase him all up. Now bredren and sisters, if I hab done you any harm, I am much obliged to you." She afterward was restored into the church, and she used to say, when tempted, " Get you 'hind me, debil, you make one big fool ob me once, I will neber tase de whiskey agen, if de debils be as thick as de huckleberries in massa's pasture." After Elsie had been given her freedom, the family built her a little cottage in the pasture land in the rear of the Morton house, where she lived until her death.

Madam Morton had two slaves, Shurper and Aaron ; both

of whom lived to be very old, and remained in the family of their mistress until their death. Shurper in his old age used to spend much time in prayer, in which he was very gifted. One of the members of the family, listening at his chamber door, heard him mention his kind master and mistress and the children, and conclude his prayer by saying, " Lord, bless de white foks, ebery one of dem, but bless de poor nigger in partic'lar."

Aaron was also very devout ; he had all of the superstition of the negro, and he used often to say, " Now, here is de ring wid old Aaron in de middle, de Lord is wid him here ; de debil is on de outside, now keep your distance, Massa debil, and do not dare to come into dis ring." Then with a heavy blow with his cane he would say, " Go your way, Massa debil, and do not come hangin' 'bout here to eat old Aaron up." Some one would banter him by asking how the devil looked, and he would say that he "had a head like a nigger's, only with the horns, and eyes that kep' a-rollin' an' a-rollin' like dis [rolling his own], and a mouth dat would eat you up in a minute. He go about to ketch wicked niggers ; he ketch white foks too, some o' dem," casting a significant eye on those who were taunting him. "Mistress read about him in de Bible, and Aaron has seen him hisself."

All of the negroes at this time seem to have been brought from Africa, and as a part of the old fetish worship the devil was prominent in the theology of the devout old negro. He used to say, " When I die, bury me near de house, dat I may hear de little chillun's voices when dey be playin'."

The Morton family had one other slave, by the name of Prince, of whom there is no record except that, like the others, he was pious, and united with the church in 1742.

Judge Oliver had a slave by the name of Quassia, full of fun and drollery, who always made sport for the guests at Oliver Hall. After Judge Oliver left the country, Quassia lived in the family of Colonel Watson of Plymouth, and not a few anecdotes have come down of his genial wit. Judge Oliver had one servant, Cato, who was probably a slave.

SLAVES IN MIDDLEBORO

Governor Hutchinson, while he lived in Middleboro, had a slave by the name of Phyllis.

Dr. Stephen Powers had a young slave named Cato Boston, purchased in Middleboro for twenty pounds, before 1772. He was very mischievous, and was thought to have set one or two fires in the neighborhood.

Elkanah Leonard had a slave named Tom.

Captain Job Peirce owned two slaves, a man and woman.[1] At the time slavery ceased in Massachusetts, one of these, though free, continued to live with him as his servant until his death.

Isaac Peirce, Jr., of Lakeville, in his will dated 1756, provided for the emancipation of his negro slave, Jack.[2]

John Montgomery, in January, 1769, freed, his negro manservant, Prince, certain parties giving bonds that he should not become a charge to the town.

July 18, 1764, Ebedmelech, a negro servant to Madam Mary Thatcher, published an intention of marriage with Betty Conant, an Indian woman of Plymouth.[3]

In the house built by Judge Oliver for his son, Peter Oliver, Jr., now known as the old Sproat house at Muttock, apartments were fitted in the attic for the slaves of the family, traces of which are still noticeable.

John Alden, a grandson of the pilgrim, settled in Titicut, and brought with him the first slave ever owned in town. Her name was Margaret,[4] and she united with the First Church January 22, 1710. In his will[5] he bequeaths to his wife "my negro man to be at her own disposing."

Before the Revolutionary War, many of the well-to-do citizens of the town had slaves in their families, of whom no record has come down to us. After it, without any legislative act, but from a sense of moral wrong in the holding of human beings in bondage, slavery practically disappeared from the town.

---

[1] *The Peirce Family*, p. 277. [2] *Ibid.* p. 43.
[3] Davis's *Landmarks of Plymouth*, p. 109.
[4] *History of the First Church of Middleboro*, p. 82.
[5] *Alden Genealogy*, p. 14.

CHAPTER VIII

THE REVOLUTION

FOR many years the people of America had lived in peace, with growing prosperity and a closer union of the thirteen colonies. With the accession of George III, a change occurred; their profitable commerce in fish and furs was interfered with, and Parliament began to consider unjust legislation for the oppression of the colonies. In 1765 the Stamp Act was passed, requiring them to use stamps on law and business papers as well as on pamphlets and newspapers. These stamps cost from a half-penny (one cent) up to fifty dollars. Upon the enactment of this statute the indignation of the people blazed out in an unmistakable manner. James Otis had already declared, "Taxation without representation is tyranny."

The people of Middleboro were well informed of the arbitrary measures of the British Parliament, and in various ways expressed their sentiment in regard to the unwarranted action against the rights and privileges of the American colonies and the inalienable rights which belonged to them as loyal subjects of George III. The following letter of instructions to Daniel Oliver,[1] their representative in the General Court at Boston, indicates their attitude: —

A COPY OF ONE OF THE STAMPS UNDER THE STAMP ACT

INSTRUCTIONS TO THEIR REPRESENTATIVE, OCTOBER 21, 1765

At a Town meeting Held by adjournment at the Proprietors meeting House within the first Precinct in Middleborough on Monday the 21 Day of October 1765 at said meeting voted the following Instructions to Daniel Oliver Esq. there Representative.

[1] Daniel Oliver was a son of Judge Oliver.

To DANIEL OLIVER ESQ Representative of the Town of Middleborough. Sr. Every Person of Observation must be Sensible How Extreemly Disagreeable the Late act of Parliment whereby Certain Stamp Duties are Laid on the Several Colonies on this Continent Has been : and Still is to the People of this Province. we Do acknowledge ourselves To be True and Loyal Subjects to our King, and to Have the Highest Esteam and Regard for both Houses of Parliment. Notwithstanding which we Look upon the aforementioned act to be a Grevious and Intollirable Burden upon us, and an Infringment on our Charter Rights and Priveledges, Granted to our fore Forefathers & continued To us there Posterity and as we Humbly Conceive Has not been Forfited nither by them nor us. and fearing the Daingerious Consequences that may follow To this Province if the General Assembly Should by an act of there own Bring upon us a Burden So Insuportable as the operation of the Stamp Act will be. we the free Holders and Other Inhabitants In Town Meeting assembled do Earnistely Recommend and give it as our Instructions To you Sr. not to Comply with any measures That may be Proposed For the Court to take. In order to make way for a Compliance with the above mentioned act, and that by all Lawfull means Consistent with Loyalty To the King you oppose Its Taking Place Till we Can Know what will be the answer To the Prayers, Tears, Petitions of this whole Continent for Relief. and we further Recommend To you not to Consent To any measures for the countenanceing or Pertecting Stamp officers or Stampd Papers.

The Laws of the Land if Duly Executed we Immagine Sufficient to Suppress any Tumultuous & Disorderly Practices.

And in Consideration of the Scarcety of money and the Difficulty most People are put to pay there Tax we must Enjoine it upon you Sr. Not to Consent to any Extroydinary Grants. being made (or any Draughts on the Publick Treasurer of this Province) Except it Be for Defraying the Necessary Charges.

The Sons of Liberty in Boston had destroyed the building where stamps were to be sold, and riotous demonstrations took place all over the country, so that the following year Parliament deemed it wise to repeal this act, but soon after (1767) imposed a tax on glass, paint, paper, and tea. The colonists pledged themselves "to eat nothing, drink nothing, wear nothing" imported from England, although the price of tea was placed so low that even with the tax it cost less than that smuggled from Holland.

A larger number of troops were sent to Boston from England, and this menace aroused the people to call a convention of delegates from more than a hundred towns in the province. The following vote shows Middleboro's action : —

"At a town meeting held Sept. 20-1768 — in Middleboro Capt. Ebenezer Sprout & Capt. Benjamin White were chosen a Committee to join in a convention to be held at Faneul Hall Boston, on Thursday Sept. 22 at 10 o'clock before noon. Said Convention to be held on account of the divisions in the Provinces & other difficulties as being destitute of a General Court & the daily expectation of two or three regiments of Kings Troops to be kept at the Castle & in Boston & the said consequences thereof & the Town unanimously voted that the selectmen be a committee to wait on the several Ministers of the Gospel of the Town defining that the next Tuesday may be kept as a day of solemn fasting & prayer for the above mentioned ocation."

The governor refused to receive the petition drawn up by these delegates, and declared their convention treasonable. This was the first of those popular conventions, destined within a few years to assume the whole political authority of the colonies.

Middleboro men believed that ere long the oppressive measures would be repealed, and that the British government would yield to the wise counsels of Chatham and Burke and other strong men who sympathized with the rights of the American colonists. They loved the mother country; many of them had cheerfully rendered great services for the defence of the Crown in resisting encroachments of the French power; they had served as officers in the French and Indian War; they had volunteered to be led by British officers in maintaining the power and authority of the Crown; they were brave, intelligent men, proud of the names on the pages of English history so illustrious in statesmanship, in war, and in literature; very many of them had friends in the old country, and had received special favors from the government. The second officer under the Crown, chief justice of the highest court in the colonies, had been an honored and revered citizen for almost a generation. The most brilliant governor was a frequent visitor in town, and it is not surprising that, with regret, all but a few citizens sooner or later abandoned their allegiance to the mother country and cast their lot with the patriot cause. The struggle was severe, but the step once taken, no braver nor better soldiers in the Continental army were found than those who had enlisted from the town of Middleboro. Her citizens were found on almost every important battlefield of the Revolutionary struggle.

Probably few of the colonists, at the beginning of the

trouble with Great Britain, contemplated that this opposition would terminate in armed resistance, with the ultimate independence of the colonies. Governor Hutchinson,[1] as early as 1773, said that from his personal knowledge he had no apprehension that the people of the province desired a separation from the Crown, and at this time, when the colonists were sincere in their opposition to the wrongful acts of Parliament, he made appointments with his usual sagacity. Their turbulent spirit began to manifest itself in the House of Representatives and in many of the leading men. He very shrewdly chose for the various officers, both civil and military, those who were supposed, in the event of a conflict, to side with the Crown. The only surprising thing is that among all of his appointments so few followed the wishes of the English government.

Long before the battle of Lexington, the leading citizens were alarmed at the recommendations of the governor and the course of Parliament, fearing serious difficulties in their political rights and privileges. Meetings were held in the different neighborhoods, at which the acts of the loyal officers in Boston were discussed pro and con.

In 1770 occurred the Boston Massacre, and in 1773 the famous Tea Party.

"At a Town Meeting held in Middleborough Jan. 17-1774, It was put to vote whether the Town would take action upon the articles contained in the warrant for said meeting which is to see if said Town would act anything relative to the Teas lately destroyed in the Town of Boston, which was sent by the East India Company and it passed in the negative."[2]

In 1774 the port of Boston was closed, and the colony was placed under the control of General Gage.

The following records, under date of June 20, 1774, show the first decisive action taken in Middleboro. Other towns had appointed a Committee of Correspondence with the officials of Boston and other parts of the colony, and letters had repeatedly passed between them, but it was not until this time that the town cast its first vote in reference to the matter.

[1] Hutchinson, *History of Massachusetts*, vol. iii, p. 390.
[2] Book III, p. 23.

June 20, 1774. Town voted and made choice of Capt. Ebenezer Sproutt, Capt. Benjamin White, Mr. Nathaniel Harlow, Mr. Nathaniel Samson and Mr. George Leonard, their selectmen to be a com. of correspondence for said Town, to correspond with the town of Boston's correspondence Com. and Committees of other Towns relative to the late acts of the British Parliament which bare so hard against our Charter rights and privileges. Also Voted and made choice of Messrs. Ebenezer Wood, Samuel Clarke, John Miller, Abner Kingman, Zachariah Eddy and John Weston as an addition to the above Com. and to have the same power with them, and that the aforesaid Committee shall on the adjournment of this meeting lay their transactions before the Town for the Towns approbation or disapprobation of the aforesaid Committees proceeding on the aforesaid mentioned affair. *Memorandum* The aforesaid last mentioned Committee men personally appeared in Town meeting and declared that they would serve the Town in the afore mentioned affair of correspondence free and clear of any cost or charge to the Town as also the first chosen five selectmen of said Town and then said meeting was adjourned until the third Monday of October next at one of the o'clock in the afternoon.

Sept. 28, 1774. Town voted and made choice of Messrs. Elder Mark Haskol, George Leonard, Ebenezer Wood, Jonah Washburn and Abner Kingman as a Com. to draw up instructions for Capt. Ebenezer Sproutt, their Representative, relative to these times of trouble, which instructions are as followeth and the Town by vote accepted the same.

MASSACHUSETTS BAY

MIDDLEBORO, Sept. 28, 1774.

This Town having made choice of Capt. Ebenezer Sproutt to represent them at the Great and General Court or Assembly of this Province which is appointed to meet at Salem the 5th day of October next, do give him the following instructions to guide his general conduct in that assembly.

SIR — Reposing confidence in you as a friend to our Country and the Charter Government and Constitution of this Province, we commit to you the important trust of representing us as above named and we advise you and direct you in the first place,

To observe a just allegiance to our Sovereign Lord the King agreeable to the compact made with our venerable progenitors.

To exert your self for the recovery of Union good affection between Great Britain and these Colonies on a Constitutional basis.

To fall in with every measure that tends to promote and establish harmony, friendship and good agreement among all the English Colonies on the Continent.

To have a particular regard in all your consultations and actions to the due interest and salvation of this injured province and of its distressed Metropolis.

To avoid joining or acting in conjunction with those enemies of our Charter Government, the Mandamus Councellors unto their assembly be not thou united, guard also against everything that tends to carry into execution any part of the late acts of Parliament for regulating the Government of this Province.

To use your utmost endeavors that the money and other public properties of the Province be lodged in safe and faithful hands.

To use every lawful and reasonable method in conjunction with the honorable house for preventing the late act of Parliament formed against this Province, from taking place and for restoring the Charter Government of this Province in its first and full latitude.

Forthermore by these instructions we impower and authorize you to join with the rest of the Deputies from the several Towns in the Province, who are or shall be appointed to form a Provincial Congress and there to conduct and act those things which have the best tendency to serve and promote the benefit of this Province and to recover and confirm the Charter Rights of this Province, that so the Courts and course of public justice may be open and operate freely and that we may live in peace and safety under the extensive influence of a righteous and good government.

Also to acknowledge the Hon. Board of Councillors elected by General Court at their session in May last as the only rightful and Constitutional Council of this Province.

In the last place we direct and caution you not to act anything rashly or hastily, neither come to any final determination in public matters until the result of the great Congress of the Colonies be made known, from which result we do hope to receive light and direction in this day of darkness and perplexity, touching our future conduct in civil and commercial and governmential affairs.

And we devoutly wish that the wonderful Councillor may preside in the Assembly of the Province and guide and direct their Consultations and measures unto a good and happy end.

MARK HASKOL, GEORGE LEONARD, EBENEZER WOOD, JONAH WASHBURN, ABNER KINGMAN } Committee

and then the meeting was dismissed.

Subsequently Mr. John Weston was made clerk of this committee. The following correspondence has come down to us:[1]—

Oct. 18, 1774.

GENTLEMEN & FELLOW CITIZENS, — Deeply impressed with a sense of your uncommon sufferings from the operation of an Act of the British Parliament, which for cruelty and injustice is unparalleled in history, we have the honor of receiving your resolves, and the Towns contiguous to Boston, respecting the supply of the troops. We are well pleased with the contents, and cheerfully co-operate with you in that and every other rational measure, to the last penny of our fortunes, and the last drop of our blood. We have sent by the bearer about eighty bushels of grain for the use of the industrious poor, with the

[1] *Mass. Hist. Coll.* vol. iv, p. 120, 4th series.

Resolves of the Town, in which, if anything amiss, please to correct, in order for the press.

The painful sensations that constantly afflict us for the losses of your merchants, shop keepers, and mechanics, and all your inhabitants, in stopping your port, induces us to desire you to take an exact estimate of your estates as you conveniently can, and we make no doubt of the generosity of your American brethren, on your receiving an ample indemnification. We regret the decay of God's image in man, when we behold the inhabitants of the other continent, so entirely sunk in luxury and despotism. The eyes of all the friends of liberty are now fixed on America and chiefly on your illustrious Town. Stand firm in the glorious cause of liberty, which is the principal thing that can make life desirable here, and promises to her pious votaries a glorious immortality hereafter.

Gentlemen, we subscribe ourselves your affectionate friends and fellow sufferers.

Per order of the Committee of Correspondence,

JOHN WESTON, Clerk.

TO THE COMMITTEE OF CORRESPONDENCE IN BOSTON

BOSTON, Oct. 25th, 1774.

SIR: Last week Mr. William Cooper, the Town Clerk, handed to the Committee of Donations, your acceptable favor of the 18th inst. Our good friend, Mr. Billington, of Middleborough, has delivered us fifty-one bushels of rye and thirty bushels of corn; a generous present from the worthy inhabitants of that patriotic Town. The . . . of the industrious pen, suffering by means of that oppresive and cruel Act, the Boston Port Bill, commonly called, will doubtless be greatly refreshed, and many thanksgivings go up to God on account thereof. May the Lord reward our kind benefactors a thousand fold into their own bosoms. Please to present the thankful acknowledgments of this Committee, in behalf of the Town, for this instance of their Christian sympathy and affection.

It affords much satisfaction that the conduct of this Town, hitherto, has met with the approbation of our brethren at Middleborough as well as elsewhere. We have great difficulties and dangers to encounter, and they seem to be increasing, but we may set up an "Ebenezer" and say "Hitherto hath God helped us." In all our darkness, we are not without some rays of light; but what is in the womb of Providence, we cannot say. "It is not for us to know the times or the seasons, which the Father has put in his own power." Duty is ours, events are God's. To him let us look for all that wisdom, meekness, firmness and resolution which our peculiar circumstances call for; and may we be enabled to pray and faint not.

Your letter breathes a glorious spirit, and becoming zeal and ardor in the glorious cause of American freedom, both civil and religious. It serves to encourage and animate us to persevere, in a manly steady opposition to all tyrants, their abettors, and iniquitous measures. We may not boast of our own strength, but we may and ought to hope and trust in God. None were ever ashamed who put their trust in him. If he be for us, no matter who or how many are against us. By his help, and that only, we shall be enabled to persevere.

The generosity manifested in your proposal for taking an exact estimate of our estates, is very striking, and endearing, and is a superadded instance of the benevolence of your hearts. It would be matter of no small difficulty, especially as many of this Town are from day to day so engaged in affairs which concern *the general interest* in this day of trial, as that all our attention and time is required, and all little enough. We would hope we should never be reduced to such a necessity; if we should, we must do the best we can.

However this may happen, our obligations and gratitude to our brethren are not a little increased, by so kind and charitable a proposal. It is not easy, and we do not know that it is possible, to determine with any degree of precision what loss and damage this Province and Town have sustained, by the almost annihilation of their trade and commerce. Some doubt whether two hundred thousand pounds sterling would be a compensation even to the Town.

But when we take into consideration the anxiety and distress of mind the inhabitants have endured, we question whether even the wealth of Great Britain could countervail the damage. And for what? What has the Province, what has Boston done to deserve the carrying into execution measures, so unjust, so oppressing, so cruel, so destructive? It greatly stands in hand the promoters and favorers of such a pernicious plan, instead, to have a satisfactory answer ready, when it shall at another, an infinitely more important day, be inquired of them, "What have the Bostonians done to merit such cruel treatment?" But we forbear.

Inclosed is a printed half sheet, giving an account of the

proceedings of this Committee relative to the charitable donations committed to their trust. If it shall be satisfactory to our kind benefactors, our end will in a good measure be answered; but we cannot expect, in this corrupt state of things, to escape the censure of our foes. We hope our brethren will not place undue confidence in the inhabitants of this much abused and distressed Town, nor raise their expectations too high concerning us; but if our gracious God shall afford us strength equal to the day, we trust our brethren will not be disappointed.

We are with great esteem and much affection, Gentlemen, your much obliged friends and fellow countrymen.

DAVID JEFFRIES { Per order of the Committee of Donations.

To the Town Clerk and Committee of Correspondence at Middleborough.

A few months after these objectionable measures, a Continental or General Congress was called to meet in Philadelphia to consider what action the colonies should take. They demanded among other privileges the right to levy all taxes and make laws in their own colonial assemblies.

Massachusetts set up an independent government with John Hancock at its head to aid the cause of the liberties of the people. Twelve thousand volunteers were enrolled, of whom one third were "minute men."[1] Among this number were many men from Middleboro, where the tide of patriotic feeling was strong. The news of the battle of Lexington, April 19, 1775, spread like wild fire through the country, and the patriots began to arm and organize their forces, as it was generally believed that the time for a peaceful adjustment of the difficulties had passed.

The news of the battle was brought to Thomas Ellis by Caleb Bryant, who came riding in great haste[2] over fences and

---

[1] "The Provincial Congress . . . on the 26th of October adopted a plan for organizing the militia. . . . It provided that one quarter of the number enrolled should be held in readiness to muster at the shortest notice, who were called by the popular name of minute men." Frothingham, *History of the Siege of Boston*, p. 41. These were later reorganized, so that one out of every three were minute men.

[2] From *Eddy Note-Book*.

fields, there being no direct road between their houses. Upon hearing of this battle, Mr. Ellis took down his gun to repair it, put a long handle to his hatchet, and made preparations to go immediately to engage in the fight. He did not go, however, but sent his son soon after. A number of other men in the neighborhood started with him. The lieutenant of the company in which he enlisted, during the first engagement, saw some of his neighbors dodging and exclaimed, " Don't! don't! I will tell you when to dodge."

In May Ticonderoga and Crown Point were captured, followed soon after by the battle of Bunker Hill, and in July Washington took command of the army. The following year was a memorable one: the country realized that the time for independence had come. We find the following from the town records showing Middleboro's attitude: —

May 20, 1776 said town did then give their vote and signify their mind whether if the honorable congress should for the safety of the united colonies declare them independent of the kingdom of Great Britain, they the said inhabitants will solemnly engage with their lives and fortunes to support the measure. Voted and allowed by the town to support the above said measure, and then the moderator declared the meeting to be dissolved.[1]

MASSACHUSETTS BAY

MIDDLEBOROUGH 24th June 1776

At a Legal Meeting of this town it was agreed and Voted to Send the Following Instructions to Dea^n Benj^m Thomas our Representative at Court

SIR the Alarming Situation of affairs Between Great Britain and the United american Colonies Renders it In our opinion highly Necessary for all the People towns and Societies of Said Colonies to be as Explicit and particular In Declaring their Sentiments on Som Important Points Especialy of Independancy as Possable

It is with Surprise and Deep Concern we have observed the Unrightous Cruel and Destructive Sistem and Measures of Administration adopted and Prossecuted by the British Ministry Monarch and Parliment against these Colonies and for no other Cause that we can Discern but to gratify Their Enormous Pride and avarice and to feed a Swarm of Idle useless and hungry Pensioners His majesty has Rejected with Disdain all the Remonstrances and humble Petitions Sent him from the Colonies both Jointly and Seperatly we have Prayed for Peace but he has sent us a Sword; we have asked for the Restorations of Charter Priviledges

[1] Book III, p. 52.

but he has sent us Fleets and armies to crush and Ruin us and to Crown the whole he has sent for Large Numbers of foreign Troops to aid in Executing his tyranical Purposes These things Considered we have no alternative left us but Abject Submission to Arbitrary Power and Slavery or Vigorous Self-Defence We Deliberately Choose the Latter and therefore Relying on the Mercy and Providence of God to Pity our Miseries & to Plead our Cause we Direct you to make open Declaration for us and on our Behalf That in Case the Continental Congress in whose Wisdom and fidelity we firmly Confide Shall think it for the Safty and welfare of the United Colonies to Declare them free and Independent of the Power Government & Authority of the King and Parliment of Great Britain and thereby open the way for a Republican or free State Reserving to Each Coloney the Power and Proviledige of Governing themselves by Laws of their own Making Consistantly with the good of the Whole we Seriously Declare we will Support them in so Doeing With our Lives and Fortunes

Furthermore we Direct you to do all in your Power in Conjunition with the Rest of the Hon-ble Members of Court For the Defence and Protection of our Sea Coast also to Use your Best Endeavours that Person or Persons Who have High and Lucrative Places in the Executive Part of Government Should have a Seat in the Legislative Part thereof and further if any measures are or Shall be Proposed in Court for Better Regulating the Prices of things in General and of the Necessaries of Life in Particular the high Prices of Which affect the Poor and for keeping up the Just Credit of the Paper Currency we Direct you to Join with and Promote Such motion as to What further Concerns the Internal and Civil Reglation of the Coloney we Advise you to Prudance moderation and frugality always Resarving in ourselves a free Representation

         Nath^{ll} Wood Chearman
 Attest   Abner Barrows Town Clerk

At the commencement of the Revolution, the militia of the province had been apportioned by an act of the General Court among the various counties. It included all men between the ages of sixteen and sixty, divided into regiments, the governor, appointed by the Crown, being the commander-in-chief. The town was set apart into four military districts, with a company in each district. The commissioned officers were Ebenezer Sproat, major; Nathaniel Wood, captain of the first company; Nathaniel Smith, of the second company; Benjamin White, of the third company; William Canedy, of the fourth company. The officers of these four companies held their commissions from the king, to whom they had sworn faithful allegiance; therefore it was not thought prudent to ask them to join in the forces which were being raised. More than that, at least one of the captains was known to be in strong sympathy with the Crown, and many of the rank and file were in doubt at this time what course they ought to pursue. We have no record of the attempt on the part of these companies to engage in any active service, or even to hold any meeting, after the alarm at Lexington; the organization was undoubtedly lost after that time.

On April 19, 1775, at the famous Lexington Alarm, a company was formed by reorganizing the four companies of the regular militia. Nathaniel Wood, who had been captain of the first company, was its commander.

First Company of Local Militia [1]

Commissioned Officers

Nathaniel Wood, capt.
Amos Washburn, lieut.
Joseph Smith (2d), ens.

Non-commissioned Officers

Zebedee Sproutt, sergt.
Jesse Vaughan, sergt.
Ebenezer Thomas, sergt.
Barney Cobb, sergt.
John Pickens, corp.
Amos Wood, corp.
Joseph Ellis, corp.
Solomon Dunham, corp.

Musicians

Zebedee Pratt, drummer
William Clapp, fifer

Privates

Caleb Thompson
William Bennett
Nathan Wood
Seth Miller
Ephraim Thomas, Jr.
William Armstrong
Isaac Bryant
Israel Rickard
Elisha Cox
William Raymond
Joseph Redding
John Darling
Ebenezer Smith
Zurashada Palmer
George Richmond
George Leonard
Eleazer Thomas
Samuel Pickens, Jr.
Joseph Vaughan, Jr.
Benjamin Leonard
Nathan Leonard
Jacob Miller
Nathaniel Thompson
Jonathan Sampson
Jonathan Ryder
Samuel Raymond

[1] These lists are taken from the *History of Plymouth County*, p. 1000.

James Thomas	Solomon Thomas
Perez Thomas	Seth Peirce
Andrew Cushman	Caleb Tinkham
Micah Leach	Joseph Richmond, Jr.
William Wood	Samuel Rickard
David Shaw	David Vaughan
John Hackett	Edmund Wood

As no one seemed willing to raise another company, Captain Abiel Peirce, who had served with distinction in the old French and Indian War, realizing the need, enlisted the following men: —

Second Company of Local Militia

Commissioned Officers

Abiel Peirce, capt.	Benjamin Darling, ensign
Joseph Macomber, lieut.	

Non-Commissioned Officers

Josiah Smith, sergt.	Bachellor Bennett, corp.
Richard Peirce, sergt.	Jeddediah Lyon, corp.
Elias Miller, Jr., sergt.	Samuel Eddy, corp.
Job Macomber, sergt.	John Bly, corp.

Musicians

Caleb Simmons, drummer	Nathaniel Foster, fifer

Privates

Job Peirce	John Fry
Samuel Hoar	John Douglas, Jr.
David Thomas (2d)	Ebenezer L. Bennett
Michael Mosher	Samuel Miller
Jesse Pratt	Isaac Canedy
Jacob Hayford	Daniel Reynolds
Job Hunt	Rufus Weston
Henry Bishop	Ziba Eaton
Consider Howland	Isaac Miller
Noah Clark	Nehemiah Peirce
Cornelius Hoskins	Samuel Bennett
John Rogers	Joshua Thomas
Lebbeus Simmons	Calvin Johnson

Caleb Wood
John Boothe
Ithamer Haskins
John Reynolds
Nathaniel Macomber
Levi Jones
Josiah Smith, Jr.
Malachi Howland, Jr.
Zachariah Paddock, Jr.
Rufus Howland
Sylvanus Perrington

Joshua Read
Cryspus Shaw
James Willis
Sylvanus Churchill
Samuel Macomber
Richard Omey
Israel Thomas
Ichabod Read
Samuel Ransom
Daniel Jucket

Three companies were organized as "minute men," consisting of a few of the members of the regular militia, but mostly of the young men of the town. They were apparently enlisted but for a short term of service, and held themselves in readiness to respond to any orders which might be issued from the Committee of Safety in Boston. Their names were as follows: —

FIRST COMPANY OF MINUTE MEN

COMMISSIONED OFFICERS

William Shaw, capt.
Joshua Benson, Jr., lieut.
Wm. Thompson, ensign

NON-COMMISSIONED OFFICERS

David Thomas
Ebenezer Cobb (2d)
James Smith, sergt.
Caleb Bryant, sergt.

Job Randall, corp.
John Soule, corp.
Peter Bates, corp.
James Cobb, corp.

MUSICIANS

Sylv. Raymond, drummer
Samuel Torrey, fifer

PRIVATES

Elisha Thomas
Nelson Finney
Lemuel Harlow
Isaac Thompson
Edmund Wood, Jr.

Samuel Raymond (2d)
Eliphalet Thomas
Sylvanus Bennett (3d)
Joseph Thomas
William Le Baron

Zenas Cushman
Joseph Pratt
Phineas Thomas
Caleb Thompson, Jr.
Elisha Paddock
Nathan Bennett
John Soule, 2d
Gideon Cobb
Eliakim Barlow
Ephraim Cushman
Barnabas Cushman
Ichabod Benson
Ebenezer Raymond
Solomon Raymond
Thomas Bates
Asa Benson

John Perkins
Joseph Shaw
Joshua Eddy
Seth Eddy
Joseph Chamberlain
Ebenezer Bennett
Ebenezer Briggs (3d)
Asa Barrows
Benjamin Barden
Jacob Thomas
Nathan Darling
John Sampson
Thomas Shaw
Japheth Le Baron
Abiezer Le Baron
Joseph Bennett

Second Company of Minute Men

Commissioned Officers

Isaac Wood, capt.
Cornelius Tinkham, lieut.
Abram Townsend, ens.

Non-Commissioned Officers

Abner Bourne, sergt.
Joseph Holmes, sergt.
John Benson, sergt.
William Harlow, sergt.

Samuel Wood, corp.
Foxel Thomas, corp.
Abner Nelson, corp.
Joseph Churchill, corp.

Musicians

Peregrine White, drummer   Seth Fuller, fifer

Privates

Robert Sproutt
George Sampson
Josiah Harlow
Gershom Foster
Ebenezer Elms
Consider Barden
Consider Fuller
John Barrows
John Townsend, Jr.

Samuel Ransom
James Peirce
Job Smith
Seth Sampson
Levi Peirce
George Williamson
Abiel Chase
John Tinkham, Jr.
Nathaniel Holmes (3d)

Gideon Southworth
John Smith (3d)
Samuel Wood, Jr.
Elisha Clark
Abraham Parris
Noah Holmes (2d)
Ebenezer Barrows, Jr.
Elisha Peirce
Abishai Sampson
Samuel Barrows
Peter Miller
George Thomas
Thomas Wood (2d)
Eb. Howland
Moses Sampson
Daniel Tinkham
Elisha Rider
Isaac Cushman
Abraham Shaw
Samuel Muxum
James Shaw
Peleg Hathaway
Peter Hoar
Andrew Cole
Aaron Cary
Bartlett Handy
Arodi Peirce
John Holloway
James Ashley
Levi Jones
Jotham Caswell
William Read (3d)
Ephraim Reynolds
Jonathan Hall
Joseph Hathaway
Samuel Parris
Ebenezer Hinds
Philip Hathaway
Isaac Hathaway
John Townsend
Henry Peirce

Third Company of Minute Men

Commissioned Officers

Amos Wade, capt.
Archipus Cole, lieut.
Lemuel Wood, ensign

Non-Commissioned Officers

Isaac Perkins, sergt.
Ichabod Churchill, sergt.
Isaac Shaw, sergt.
Joseph Tupper, sergt.
Isaiah Keith, corp.
Lot Eaton, corp.

Musicians

John Shaw, drummer
Daniel White, fifer

Privates

Zebulon Vaughn
Abner Pratt
Nathan Pratt
Joseph Leonard (5th)
Elnathan Wood
Joseph Hathaway
John Drake
Levi Hathaway
Moses Leonard
Solomon Howard
Nathaniel Richmond
Jonathan Washburn

Michael Leonard	Thomas Cobb
David Weston	Edmund Richmond
Samuel Pratt	Seth Richmond
William Fuller	Asa Richmond
James Keith	Joseph Leonard (3d)
Silas Leonard	Solomon Beals
Stephen Robinson	Jonathan Richmond
Daniels Hills	Zephaniah Shaw
Stephen Richmond	Elijah Alden
Lazarus Hathaway	Joseph Clark
Peter Tinkham	Benjamin Hafferd
Thomas Harlow	

The term of service for the five military companies was not long, and they were not included in the regular Continental Army, but probably served for a short time in and about Boston. The first company of militia and the second and third company of minute men marched to Marshfield in consequence of the Lexington Alarm to suppress what was feared might be a rising of the tories, to whom Governor Gage had sent one hundred stand of arms. After two days' service, they returned to their homes. Nathaniel Wood, who had been captain of the first local militia, enlisted another company for Colonel Simeon Cary's regiment, which was included in the patriot army then upon duty in Roxbury. This company was sent to Roxbury some time in the month of April, 1776, for eight months' service. Its officers and privates were as follows: —

COMMISSIONED OFFICERS

Nathaniel Wood, capt.	Job Pierce, 2d lieut.
Joseph Tupper, 1st lieut.	Jesse Vaughan, ensign

NON-COMMISSIONED OFFICERS

Caleb Bryant, sergt.	Benjamin Reed, corp.
Andrew McCully, sergt.	Josiah Jones, corp.
William Bennett, sergt.	John Sampson, corp.
Joseph Holmes, sergt.	Nathaniel Sampson, corp.

MUSICIANS

Sylvanus Raymond, drummer	Daniel White, fifer

PRIVATES

Joseph Aldrich
Philip Austin
Isaac Bryant
Stephen Bryant
Ebenezer Bennett
Ebenezer Barden
David Bates
Benjamin Cobb
Gideon Cushman
Robert Cushman
Abel Cole
Abel Cole, Jr.
James Cobb
George Caswell
Jonathan Caswell
Zeb. Caswell
George Clemens
Nathan Darling
Paul Dean
Ephraim Dunham
Sylvanus Eaton
Zibe Eaton
Thomas Ellis
Ephraim Eddy
Andrew Fuller
Thomas Foster
Edward Gibsby
John Holmes
George ———
Joshua Howland
John Jones
Consider Jones
Thomas Johnson
Jonathan Morse

John Macomber
William Pecker
John Raymond
Samuel Raymond
Isaac Rider
Nathan Richmond
Daniel Shaw
Nathaniel Shaw
Aaron Simmons
Josiah Smith
Ezra Smith
James Soule
Barnabas Sampson
John Strowbridge
George Strowbridge
Samuel Thatcher
Samuel Thatcher, Jr.
Eliph. Thomas
Eleazer Thomas
David Thomas
Benjamin Thomas
Silas Townsend
John Thomas
Amos Wood
Peter Wood
Abner Vaughan
Ephraim Wood
Robert Wood
Jacob Wood
Samuel Wood
David Shaw
Thomas Shaw
Andrew Warren

Captain Abiel Peirce, who had been the captain of the second company of the militia, soon after raised a company for Colonel Nicholas Dike's regiment on duty near Boston. This was composed of men from Middleboro, Bridgewater, Wareham, and Abington, and served for one year.

The names of men enlisted from Middleboro were as follows: —

COMMISSIONED OFFICER
Abiel Peirce, capt.

NON-COMMISSIONED OFFICERS

Josiah Harlow, sergt.   James Peirce, corp.

PRIVATES

Joseph Booth   Nathan Peirce
William Bryant   John Redding
Ebenezer Borden   Joseph Richmond
James Bump   Benjamin Reynolds
Isaac Ballinton   Samuel Snow
Ichabod Cushman   Jacob Sherman
John Fry   Ichabod Wood
Nathan Hoskins   Andrew Warren
Jonathan Leonard   Abner Washburn
Timothy Leonard   Solomon Thomas
John Harlow   Japhet Le Baron

Although news travelled very slowly in those days, the signing of the Declaration of Independence on the 4th of July, 1776, seemed to spread throughout the country almost by magic. As soon as the report reached Boston, the bells were rung, and as the news was conveyed from town to town, it was received with joyful exultation.

Ichabod, a son of William Tupper, living several miles away, hearing what had taken place, got up in the middle of the night and hurried to his father's house. On reaching the house, he rapped at the window and shouted, "Father, all the bells are ringing between here and Boston, and we are free! we are free!" The old man jumped out of his bed, rushed to the window, and, throwing it open, shouted at the top of his voice, "The angels will sing for joy!" This is but one instance of the great gratification with which this news was received by the patriots of Middleboro.

The moral gain of this position of independence was followed by military disaster. The colonists were defeated at Long Island, August 27, White Plains, October 28, but in December, after crossing the Delaware, Washington won the battles of Trenton and Princeton. In the summer and fall the Americans won the battles of Bennington and Stillwater, leading to the surrender of Burgoyne, October 17, 1777.

In the south events were less fortunate; the defeats at Brandywine and Germantown were followed by a winter of suffering for the army at Valley Forge; after the battles of Monmouth and Stony Point occurred three years filled with victories and disaster.

In the early part of the Revolutionary struggle Rhode Island [1] was a theatre of activity on the part of the patriot army against the British forces. Although no great battle was fought, there were continual skirmishes between the opposing parties, and the whole surrounding country was menaced by the forces of the enemy. This lasted for about three years after the commencement of the struggle. The minute men and the reorganized militia of Plymouth and Boston were often sent there for short terms of service, and these calls were known as the " Rhode Island Alarms." As Middleboro men took part in these frequent expeditions, it is necessary to follow this local aspect of the war more in detail.

Among these troops there were four companies from Middleboro, which were enlisted some time during the year 1776. They were as follows: —

First Company of Infantry

COMMISSIONED OFFICERS

Jonah Washburn, 1st lieut.   James Smith, 2d lieut.

NON-COMMISSIONED OFFICERS

Joseph Smith, sergt.   Ebenezer Pratt, corp.
Francis Thompson, sergt.   Benjamin Cobb, corp.
Caleb Bryant, sergt.   Ebenezer Vaughan, corp.

[1] Arnold, *History of Rhode Island*, vol. ii, p. 390.

Isaac Thomas, sergt.   Nathaniel Wood, corp.
Jacob Thomas, sergt.

MUSICIANS

Sylvanus Raymond, drummer   Francis Bent, fifer

PRIVATES

Samuel Smith	Robert Cushman
Ebenezer Cobb	Samuel Torrey
Jacob Thompson	Jonathan Porter
Silas Tinkham	Thomas Foster
William Thompson	Jesse Vaughan
John McFarlin	Sylvanus Harlow
Isaac Soule	Thomas Ellis
Nathan Darling	Charles Ellis, Jr.
Jacob Soule	Samuel Eddy, Jr.
Abiel Leach	Ebenezer Briggs
Ebenezer Bennett	Joseph Briggs
John Cobb	Daniel Ellis
Zenas Cushman	Willard Thomas
Luther Redding	Samuel Snow
Nathaniel Billington	John Redding
Samuel Raymond	James Tinkham
John Raymond	James Soule
John Soule	Elkanah Bennett
Ephraim Thomas	Solomon Thomas
Jacob Miller	Noah Thomas
Daniel Thomas	Ephraim Wood
Joseph Cushman	Benjamin Thomas
Job Thomas	Elisha Thomas
John Perkins	Cyrus Keith
Joseph Holmes	Thomas Bates
Edward Wood, Jr.	William Soule
Gideon Cobb	Charles Ellis
Nathan Cobb	Zachariah Paddock
Elisha Freeman	Isaac Thompson
Job Randall	Apollos Paddock
Elisha Cox	Joseph Ellis
Ichabod Cushman	

THIRD COMPANY OF INFANTRY

COMMISSIONED OFFICERS

William Tupper, capt.   John Murdock, lieut.

NON-COMMISSIONED OFFICERS

Samuel Eaton, sergt.
Nathaniel Wilder, sergt.
Benjamin Leonard, sergt.
Sylvanus Warren, sergt.
Abner Pratt, corp.
Joseph Leonard, corp.
Peter Tinkham, corp.

PRIVATES

Theophilus Crocker
David Watson
Joseph Bumpus
Perez Leonard
Elnathan Wood
Ziba Eaton
Jabez Cushman
Zephaniah Morton
Micah Bryant
Lemuel Wood
Benjamin Darling
Benjamin White
Cornelius Ellis
Jepthah Ripley
Isaiah Washburn
Archipas Cole
Jesse Bryant
Ebenezer Williams, Jr.
Zebedee Pratt
Joseph Burden
Ebenezer Wood
Joseph Leonard
Joseph Bumpus
Samuel Reed
Joseph Bates
William Cobb
William Cushman
Philip Leonard
Phineas Pratt
Ezra Tupper
Elisha Tinkham

FOURTH COMPANY OF INFANTRY

COMMISSIONED OFFICERS

Job Peirce, capt.
Josiah Smith, 1st lieut.
Samuel Hoar, 2d lieut.

NON-COMMISSIONED OFFICERS

Ebenezer Hinds, sergt.
Abraham Peirce, sergt.
Ezra Clark, sergt.
Enos Raymond, sergt.
Seth Ramsdell, corp.

MUSICIAN

Roger Clark, drummer

PRIVATES

Henry Peirce
Isaac Howland
John Allen
Samuel Parris

Enos Peirce
James Peirce
Isaac Parris
Stephen Hathaway
Moses Parris
John Hinds
Braddock Hoar
Abiel Chase
Zebedee Boothe
Eseck Howland
Seth Keen

John Haskins
Joshua Caswell
William Canedy
Noble Canedy
George Peirce
Benjamin Reynolds
Ephraim Reynolds
Lebbeus Simmons
John Boothe, Jr.
John Douglas

FIFTH COMPANY OF INFANTRY

COMMISSIONED OFFICERS

Consider Benson, 1st lieut.   Sylvanus Cobb, 2d lieut.

NON-COMMISSIONED OFFICERS

George Shaw, sergt.   Benona Lucas, corp.
Phineas Thomas, sergt.

PRIVATES

Roland Benson
Asa Benson
David Bates
Josiah Bryant
John Clark
Japhet Le Baron
Elijah Le Baron
Joseph Lovell
Thomas Shaw
Eleazer Thomas

Seth Thomas
Sylvanus Thomas
James Raymond
Stephen Russell
Stephen Washburn
John Bennett
Ebenezer Cobb
Samuel Hackett
William Raymond
Mark Shaw

These last made eight military companies which had been formed in Middleboro in the latter part of the year 1776. They were organized into a regiment, of which Ebenezer Sproat was the colonel, Ebenezer White of Rochester, lieutenant-colonel, Israel Fearing of Wareham, senior major, and John Nelson of Middleboro, junior major. This regiment was, in December, 1776, ordered to assist in the temporary defence of Rhode Island. They were mostly young men, who had seen no service, were without military discipline and uniforms, and dressed in their ordinary citizen's clothes. They were armed with the king's arm, — one of which was found in almost every house in town, hung, as was the custom for years, over the fireplace in the kitchen, — a powder-horn, and a few bullets which had been moulded from the family bullet mould. They had no tents, but were obliged to find shelter at night in outbuildings or dwelling-houses on the line of march, or near their place of rendezvous. No provision was made for their supplies; they depended largely on what they took with them, or what could be gathered from the country through which they marched. It was a matter of doubt whether they would receive anything for their services, but their patriotic spirit induced large numbers of them to enlist for what had been demanded of them in and about Boston. Many of them were unwilling to take up arms for the defence of Rhode Island, and there was great reluctance on the part of many of the Middleboro men to respond to this order, as appears from the letter of Major Fearing to Colonel Ebenezer Sproat, the commander of the regiment, of which the following is a copy: —

HEADQUARTERS FOURTH REGIMENT,
FOGLAND FERRY, 15th. of Dec., 1776.

SIR, — In consequence of your orders the Towns of Rochester and Wareham have mustered the whole of their military and marched them accordingly to the place required by you.

Being actuated by the most generous and noble motives, the said Towns are generally turned out to the assistance of their Sister State.

But to my surprise I find the several Companies from your Town officered in part, but almost entirely destitute of Soldiers.

One whole company have quitted their post without paying any regard to the orders of Col. Cook, the commander here.

But what is still more surprising to me, I found myself obliged to take the command of the Regiment, which, considering my abilities is arduous and disagreeable, and which I determine to avail of if you or Col. White do not appear to take the command of.

We are amazingly in want of men to guard this coast, therefore most seriously desire you to send your whole military force from Middleborough immediately.

I have wrote to Col. White to send the other part of the Regiment.

If any person hereafter return home without a furlow, I hope you will send them back to their duty.

Your humble Servant, etc.,
ISRAEL FEARING,
Major.

Their term of service, however, was short, and the Middleboro companies soon after returned home.

The calls for troops for the defence of Rhode Island seem to have been very frequent during the years 1776 and 1777. Captain Levi Rounseville of Freetown raised a company for the Ninth Regiment, which was designated as a part of the Massachusetts army, and the following officers and men were enlisted from Middleboro: —

COMMISSIONED OFFICER

Henry Peirce, lieut.

NON-COMMISSIONED OFFICERS

Joseph Macomber, sergt.   Hilkiah Peirce, corp.
Job Hunt, sergt.   Richard Peirce, corp.
David Trowant, sergt.

MUSICIAN

Leonard Hinds, drummer

PRIVATES

William Armstrong   Anthony Fry
Joseph Boothe   Levi Simmons
Ephraim Douglas   Nathan Trowant
Henry Evans

The General Court had passed several laws[1] affecting the

---

[1] The General Court ordered a tax of £100,000 in February, 1777, and of £240,000 in November. Bradford's *History of Massachusetts, 1775-89*, pp. 134, 152.

people of the state, and an act for raising a sufficient sum for carrying on the expenses of the war. Middleboro and some of the other towns sent in petitions and requests calling for the repeal of these acts. They in no way objected to providing for the necessary expenses of the war, and urged that everything should be done by the legislature for that purpose, but doubted the expediency of this measure. As a result of these petitions, the act was so changed and modified that its objectionable features no longer remained upon the statute books.

Following the capture of Burgoyne's army in New York in 1777, it was determined to drive the enemy from Rhode Island, and what was known as the secret expedition [1] was organized in September of that year. This expedition, attended with great expense in the colonies, was in charge of General Spencer. A force of some nine thousand men was collected in Tiverton near the stone bridge (which at that time had not been built), and boats had been provided for ferrying the troops across the river. There were many hindrances which prevented the advance, and the men became so disaffected by what appeared to them the unnecessary delay and shiftlessness on the part of the commander, that nearly one half of them withdrew and returned home. The plan of attack was again changed, and the remaining troops finally embarked in boats to cross the river and make attack upon the island. But no sooner had the troops boarded the transports than General Spencer countermanded the order.[2] He suspected from the delay in the attack that the British had been apprised of his intentions, and seeing no opposition to his landing, he feared that if they allowed his troops to march into the country, they would then capture his whole army after having cut off their retreat and destroyed their boats. This afterwards proved true; but great was the indignation of the patriot army because of the failure of this expedition, and General Spencer was summoned before a court of inquiry. He was afterwards acquitted, but was so offended

[1] Bradford's *History of Massachusetts, 1775–89*, p. 143.
[2] Lossing, *Field-Book of the Revolution*, vol. ii, p. 80.

that he resigned the command, and General Sullivan was appointed in his place. Thus ended the expedition which upon its organization had promised so much.[1]

There were two companies from Middleboro represented in this expedition. The one from Lakeville, enlisted December 9, 1776, by and under command of Captain Job Peirce, was as follows: —

COMMISSIONED OFFICERS[2]

Job Peirce, capt.
Josiah Smith, 1st lieut.
Samuel Hoar, 2d lieut.

NON-COMMISSIONED OFFICERS

Ebenezer Hinds, sergt.
Ezra Clark, sergt.
Abraham Peirce, sergt.
Enos Raymond, sergt.
Seth Ramsdell, corp.

MUSICIAN

Roger Clark, drummer

PRIVATES

Henry Peirce
Isaac Howland
Stephen Hatheway
Enos Peirce
James Peirce
Isaac Parris
Abiel Chace
Braddock Hoar
Moses Parris
Zebedee Boothe
Eseck Howland
Seth Keen
John Allen

Samuel Parris
John Hinds
John Haskins
Joshua Caswell
William Canedy
Noble Canedy
Benjamin Reynolds
George Peirce
Libeus Simmons
Ephraim Reynolds
Joseph Booth, Jr.
John Douglas

Captain William Tupper had a company, which had enlisted for six months' service in Rhode Island in May and June (1777). Their names were as follows: —

[1] Arnold's *History of Rhode Island*, vol. ii, p. 408; Lossing's *Field-Book of the Revolution*, vol. ii, p. 80.
[2] *History of Plymouth County*, Lakeville, p. 310.

Joshua Wood
Francis Wood
Ezra Thomas
James Cobb
Sylvanus Raymond
Ephraim Wood (3d)
William Wood
Peter Tinkham

James Barrows
Robert Cushman
Homes Cushman
Zenas Leach
Perez Cushman
Elisha Thomas
Thomas Bates

Captain Henry Peirce had a company enlisted from Lakeville which served in Rhode Island in the campaign of 1777.

COMMISSIONED OFFICERS

Henry Peirce, capt.
Peter Hoar, lieut.

George Shaw, ensign.

NON-COMMISSIONED OFFICERS

Amasa Wood
Daniel Ellis
Joseph Wood
Roland Leonard
George Hackett

William Halt
James Le Baron
Nathaniel Cole
Israel Eaton
Hazael Purrinton

PRIVATES

Churchill Thomas
Jeremiah Thomas
Andrew Cobb
Samuel Sampson
James Palmer
Elijah Shaw
David Fish
Jacob Soule
Hazael Tinkham
Jabez Vaughan
Samuel Barrows
Joseph Bennett
John Morton
John Morton (2d)
Roland Smith
Rounseville Peirce
Peter Thomas
Edmund Weston
Joseph Tupper
Lemuel Lyon

Ebenezer Howland
Josiah Kingman
Jacob Perkins
Luther Pratt
Seth Wade
Noah Haskell
Lemuel Raymond
Manasseh Wood
Francis Le Baron
Asaph Churchill
Samuel Thomas
Nathaniel Thomas
Edward Washburn
William Bly
Joseph Macumber
Lemuel Briggs
Jonathan Westcott
Ephraim Dunham
Isaac Harlow
Nathaniel Cobb

William Littlejohn
Daniel Cox
Thomas Pratt
David Pratt
Abiel Bothe

Andrew Ricket
Jonathan Porter
James Porter
James Sprout
John Thresher

A large number of British remained [1] at Newport through the spring and summer of 1778. In addition to the troops already in the field, special calls were issued for the militia to assist in driving them out.[2]

To meet this emergency, Captain Perez Churchill enlisted a company whose service commenced August 25, 1778: —

COMMISSIONED OFFICERS

Perez Churchill, capt.
James Shaw, 1st lieut.

James Weston, 2d lieut.

NON-COMMISSIONED OFFICERS

Samuel Smith, sergt.
Samuel Nelson, sergt.
Amos Wood, sergt.
Nathaniel Thompson, sergt.

Stephen Clark, corp.
Luther Redding, corp.
John Holmes, corp.

PRIVATES

Eliab Alden
Abner Barrows
Isaac Bumpus
Robert Barrows
Ebenezer Burdin
Ichabod Burdin
Joseph Briggs
Barnabas Clark
Elijah Dunham
John Ellis
John Ellis, Jr.
Eliphalet Elms
Benona Lucas
John McFarlin
John McCully
Nathaniel Macomber

John Phinney
John Pratt
Jesse Nichols
James Raymond
John Raymond
Electious Reynolds
Jepthah Ripley
James Soule
Joseph Richmond
Ebenezer Thomas
Caleb Thompson
David Weston
Perry Wood
Ephraim Wood
Robert Sturtevant
Micah Bryant

---

[1] Bradford's *History of Massachusetts, 1775-89*, p. 160.
[2] Arnold, *History of Rhode Island*, vol. ii, p. 421.

THE REVOLUTION

In September, 1778, a British force landed in what is now New Bedford[1] and Fairhaven, burned buildings and ships, and threatened the destruction of the place, when among other forces sent to their relief from Lakeville was a company enlisted by Captain Amos Washburn: —

COMMISSIONED OFFICERS

Amos Washburn, capt.
Elisha Haskell, 1st lieut.
Andrew McCully, 2d lieut

NON-COMMISSIONED OFFICERS

Samuel Nelson, sergt.
Job Townsend, sergt.
Robert Strobridge, sergt.
Abraham Shaw, sergt.
James Pickens, corp.
Josiah Jones, corp.

PRIVATES

John Townsend
Job Howland
John Peirce
John Blye
Andrew Perkins
Henry Strobridge
Ebenezer Briggs
Thomas Nelson
Roger Haskell
Zebulon Haskell
David Lewis
Silas Peirce
Jonathan Phinney
Benjamin Smith
Zephaniah Briggs
Darling Shaw
Andrew Cole
Noah Clark
Nathan Peirce
John Blye, Jr.
William Blye
Cryspus Shaw
Thomas Wood
Thomas Pickens
Alexander Pickens
John Pickens
William Pickens
Andrew Pickens, Jr.
William Strobridge
Hugh Montgomery
Solomon Dunham
John Jones
George Hackett
Nathaniel Thompson
John Sampson
Samuel Pickens
Joseph Macomber
John Macomber
Samuel Macomber
Abner Townsend
Nathaniel Shaw

In 1778 there were seven Middleboro men enlisted for eight months' service in Colonel Jacobs's regiment. Their names were: —

[1] Arnold, *History of Rhode Island*, vol. ii, p. 431.

Robert Cushman Isaac Billington
Perez Cushman Timothy Cox
Homes Cushman Jonah Washburn, Jr.
Ezra Leach

In August, 1780, great was the alarm over a British fleet of sixteen ships laden with troops which appeared off Newport. The militia of the entire state of Rhode Island was called out to repel the threatened invasion. At the urgent request of General Heath, the militia from Connecticut and Massachusetts came to the rescue. After this force had assembled, the hostile squadron suddenly disappeared, and the troops were dismissed to their homes. They had no sooner reached home than they were recalled by the unexpected reappearance of the enemy. Another week of the most intense excitement followed, and then again the English withdrew, and the troops so hastily gathered were finally dismissed. In this expedition Middleboro furnished four companies. The second company was commanded by Captain Abner Bourne.

THIRD COMPANY

COMMISSIONED OFFICERS

William Tupper, capt. James Weston, 2d lieut.
John Murdock, 1st lieut.

NON-COMMISSIONED OFFICERS

Samuel Eaton, sergt. Peter Tinkham, corp.
Benjamin Leonard, sergt. Joseph Leonard, corp.
Abner Pratt, sergt. David Weston, corp.
Nathaniel Wilder, sergt. Silas White, corp.

MUSICIANS

Joseph Barden, drummer. Lemuel Bryant, fifer

PRIVATES

Joseph Bumpus (2d) Robert Cushman
Joseph Bumpus William Cushman
Jesse Bryant Zebadee Cushman
Archipus Cole Joseph Darling

Eliphalet Elms
Israel Eaton
Robert Green
Jabez Green
John Heyford
Joseph Jackson
Archipas Leonard
Perez Leonard
George Leonard
Samuel Leonard
Joseph Leonard
Roland Leonard
Ichabod Leonard
Lemuel Lyon
James Littlejohn
Andrew Murdock
John Norcutt
Ephraim Norcutt
Samuel Pratt
Zebadee Pratt
Ebenezer Richmond
George P. Richmond
Joseph Richmond
Ezra Richmond
Joshua Reed
Jepthah Ripley
Hushai Thomas
Elisha Tinkham
Joseph Tupper, Jr.
Israel Thomas
Levi Thomas
Jabez Thomas
Edward Thomas
Enoch Thomas
Daniel Tucker
Seth Tinkham
David Turner
David Wilson
Elnathan Wood
Lemuel Wood
Ephraim Wood
Ebenezer White
Edmund Weston

FOURTH COMPANY

COMMISSIONED OFFICERS

Henry Peirce, capt.
Peter Hoar, 1st lieut.
Ezra Clark, 2d lieut.

NON-COMMISSIONED OFFICERS

Ebenezer Hinds, sergt.
Robert Hoar, sergt.
Nathaniel Macomber, sergt.
Joseph Boothe, sergt.
Ebenezer Heyford, sergt.
Benjamin Boothe, corp.
Henry Edminster, corp.

PRIVATES

Daniel Collins
Roger Clark
John Church
Ebenezer Howland
Samuel Howland
John Howland
Joshua Howland
Eseck Howland
John Hoar
John Holloway
Josiah Holloway
Samuel Parris
Richard Parris
George Peirce
Uriah Peirce
Ezra Reynolds

Electious Reynolds
Benjamin Reynolds
John Reynolds
Enos Reynolds
Isaac Reynolds
Earl Sears
Seth Simmons
Lebbeus Simmons
Isaac Sherman
Nathan Trowant

FIFTH COMPANY

COMMISSIONED OFFICERS

Perez Churchill, capt.
Consider Benson, 1st lieut.
George Shaw, 2d lieut.

NON-COMMISSIONED OFFICERS

Daniel Smith, sergt.
Benona Lucas, sergt.
Joseph Thomas, sergt.
Perez Churchill, sergt.
Ezra Harris, corp.
Japhet Le Baron, corp.
William Shaw, corp.
Eleazer Thomas, Jr., corp.

MUSICIAN

Josiah Thomas, drummer

PRIVATES

Benjamin Thomas
Ichabod Benson
James Le Baron, Jr.
James Raymond
William Churchill
Mark Shaw
Barnabas Shurtliff
Joseph Bessie
David Bates
Seth Thomas
Zephaniah Thomas
Joseph Lovell
Nathaniel Shaw
Abel Tinkham
Samuel Hackett
John Raymond
John Le Baron, Jr.
Robert Sturtevant
Caleb Atwood
Stephen Washburn
Solomon Thomas
Hosea Washburn
Zeb Thomas
Nathan Muxom
William Holmes
Sylvanus Thomas
Isaac Morse
Asa Barrows
Isaac Benson
Samuel Thomas, Jr.
George Howland
Caleb Benson, Jr.
James Raymond, Jr.
Isaac Shaw
Nathan Burden
Ichabod Atwood
Samuel Thomas
Nathan Thomas
David Thomas

In addition to these companies of local militia which were enlisted for a comparatively short term of service in and about Boston, New Bedford, and in Rhode Island, there were many others who were in the continental army for a much longer term than the militia, many for the entire war, whose names it is now impossible to give. We learn of them in following the various family genealogies. In 1777 there were one hundred and seven men from Middleboro in the continental army for three years or during the war, some of whom have been mentioned in other chapters. At one time there were over sixty-four from the First Church absent in active service.

Captain Joshua Eddy [1] raised a company for three years from the adjoining towns for the regiment of which Gamaliel Bradford was colonel; their first service was on the Hudson to resist the progress of Burgoyne.

The final victory at Yorktown and Cornwallis's surrender brought the war to a close, and the final treaty of peace was signed at Paris, in 1783. Then followed the struggle for a union. The nation had no President, no money, a congress destitute of power. Well did Fiske call this the "Critical Period of American History." But the soldiers returned to their farms, and Middleboro soon settled into its regular routine of life.

The following memoranda are taken from the Eddy Note-Book : —

1777 Jan. 31

        Gamaliel Bradford Esq. Colonel
        Baracciat Bassett Esq. Lt. Col.
        Samuel Tubbo Esq. Major

Joshua Eddy Capt.   Cushman 1st. Lt ; David Peterson 2d. Lt
        Jonathan Haskell, Ensign
    Barnabas Bates of Wareham afterwards Lt.

J. Eddy Capt.   Amt. of wages from Jan. 1777 to   258 lbs.
Paid by the Continent 95 — 5 — 0 ; by the state 162 — 15 — 0

COMPANY

Enlisted between Feb. and April 177– in obedience to an order of Council of Nov. 7, 1777 for the Continental service for 3 years or during the war (Bradford's Regt.)

[1] For further service of Captain Eddy, see chapter on Eddyville.

140   HISTORY OF THE TOWN OF MIDDLEBORO   [1780

Samuel Thacher   of and for M——h. — ag. 19, — April 1, 1778
Ebenezer Raymond   "   "   3 yrs.
Simeon Prouty   "   Scituate   ag. 30 — Feb. 23 "
Joseph Chamberlain   Plimpton   ag. 34 Feb. 21.   3 ys.
James Sampson   Kingston Jan. 7, 1780 service to end
William Maxwell of Tisbury for Rochester 17, Feb. 19. 3 yrs. or
                                                          during war
Thomas Hackman of and for Plymouth —— 21   3 yrs. or
                                                          during war
Isaac Wilson   "   "   23   pd cost bounty
John Clark   Rochester   50 Jan. 15. 3 yrs. or
                                                          during war
John Hyller   "   24   3 yrs. or
                                                          during war
Joseph Hatch   16
Samuel Green   "   Jan. 15
Emanuel Doggett ("Doged")   "   20   "
William Conant   Wareham   ag. 31 May 9, 1777
Joseph Samdin   "   " 27   "
Jonathan Sanders   "   " 30   "
Samuel Bates   "   " 22   "
Salisbury Hichmond   "
David Burges   "   " 16   "
Benjamin Swift 2d   "   " 19   "
Lt. Sturtevant   "   " 17   "
Nathaniel Sturtevant   "   " 17   "
Abel Suspason   Plymouth   Feb. 21
Warren   Middleborough   April 28
Abner Morton   Plymouth ag. 18 Feb. 21, pd. cost bounty
John Tolman jr.   "   "   17 enlist Feb. 21 ⎫
John Hosea   "   "   21   "   ⎬ from Nath'l Goodwin's Co.
James Morris   "   "   ⎭
Charles Anthony   Rochester 35 (of John Cottle's Co.) 3 yrs.
                            for Pembroke?
Samuel Green   "   18 ⎫
Samuel Eddy   of Middleboro   ⎬ By Isa Hatch from
                            for Bridgewater 17 ⎭ June 10 to July 9 1777
Nehemiah Curtis   "   16
Moses Standish   Plympton   40   pd. the cost bounty
Joshua Prouty   Scituate   27   "
Pollipus Hammond   Rochester   16   "
Rowel Foot   "   19   "
Able Suppossen   "   36
                            for Pembroke   Feb. 78.
James Newport   Kingston   20   "
Nathan Cobb   Middleborough 48 (for N. Wood's Co.)
                                              3 yrs. or during war
Elisha Paddock   " (for N. W.) 23   "

1777] THE REVOLUTION

Stephen Cobb	Middleborough (for N. W.)	ag. 19	3 yrs. or during war
Zachariah Eddy	"	" 25	"
Thomas Eddy	"	" 20	"
Nicholas Wood	"	" 18	"
Thomas Cushman	Plimpton	18	
Joseph Bump	Washburn	"enlisted," not draught, May 26, 1777 to serve till Jan. 10, '78	
Isaac Willison	Bridgewater	for 3 yrs. to end in 1780 Alden's reg't.	
Thomas Cole	Middleborough	Feb. 19, 78 from Capt. White's Co. in Col. Sprout's reg't. Cont'l. Army.	
Benjamin Simmons jr.	"		
Benjamin Hacket	"		
Lewis Harlow	"	during war	
Moses Sturtevant	Wareham	ag. 19	
Nathan Faunce	Middleborough	" 33 (from N. Wood's Co.) (Jonah Washburn 1st. Lt.) 3 yrs. or during war	
Seth Cobb	"		
Zebedee Caswell	"	ag. 22	"
Benjamin Raymond (a noted drummer)		20	"
Carver Bates	Middleborough	17	"
Stephen Bryant	"		"
Jona or Joshua Eatton	"		"
Leach	"		"
Ephraim Eddy	"		
Ebenezer Smith	"		
William Ellis	"		
Leach	"		
William Paddy	Rochester		
William Randall	"	ag. 21	
Barzillai Nicholson	"	" 29 (or 20)	
Cuff Perry	"	" 28	
Solomon Doty	Middleborough		
Sampson David			
Andrew Warren		FROM Capt. Wm. Tupper's Co.	
John Billington			
Francis Billington			
Pelham Wood	Wareham		
Shubael Bump	"	ag. 18 Feb. 19	
Samuel Philips	"	" 19 Jan. 13	
Joseph Bump 3d	"		8 months
John Mefrick Cary (a Indian)	Middleborough	" 22	
John Morris	Plimpton	" 29	

Perez Simmons	Middleborough	ag. 16	3 yrs.
Gideon Cobb			till Jan. 10, 1778
Simeon Cotton Rathem	"	17	
Micah Leach	"	21	
Thomas Gannet	"	39	

A. Fuller, an officer afterwards a capt.

Prior to 1778 the maintenance of the soldiers who were serving in the different campaigns had been left to their families and neighbors. While the men were absent in service, the work on the farm was done by the old men, by the women, or by those too young to enlist. The long continuance of the war resulted in great hardship to many of those who were in the field. Accordingly we find that from time to time the town provided for their necessities by votes: —

At a town meeting held January 5, 1778, it was voted that " the town treasurer hire the sum of $200. for the use of the committee to enable them to procure necessaries for the families of the soldiers in the continental service."

And on the 9th of March, 1778, at a town meeting it was voted " to choose a committee of 7 persons to take care of the families of the soldiers that are in the Continental army, and that said committee deal out provisions to the families of the soldiers agreeable to a former act of the town.

" Committee is as follows : —

> " Edmund Wood
> Edward Shairmin
> Zaddock Leonard
> Francis Thompson
> George Leonard
> Isaac Peirce
> Ichabod Wood."

At a town meeting held May 5, 1778, it was voted that " the selectmen hire the sum of 626£ and 13 shillings in order to purchase clothing for the soldiers in the Continental army.

" *Voted* to choose a committee of 5 persons to set a price to said clothing.

" *Voted* that the select men and company of inspection assist the above said committee relating to the price of said clothing."

May 5, 1778, committee reported on the price of clothing as follows : —

"Shoes . . . . 1 pound, 16 shillings a pair.
Shirts . . . . 1 " 7 " a piece,
one shirt to contain 3 yards of one yard wide of linen and tow cloth.
Stockens . . . . 1 pound a pair."

The town voted to accept said report.

May 18, 1778: —

"*Voted* to pay the 26 Continental men now raising for Gen. Washington's army the sum of 30 pounds to be paid to each man," and also voted that "the town treasurer give his note for 30 pounds payable to each man in behalf of the town, said note to be paid in nine months from that date without interest."

"*Voted* to deal stores to the families of soldiers of the Continental service to one fourth part of their wages, the committee to deal out said stores."

7th of July: —

"*Voted* that the town treasurer give his note for 14 pounds in behalf of the town to each of the 19 men now raising for the service of the state of Rhode Island, said notes to be on interest to be paid on the first day of Jan. next."

January 1st, 1779: —

"*Voted* that those soldiers that continue at home, with or without furlow, have no supply from the committee while absent from the army."

"An Order sent out by the Great and General Court of the state of Massachusetts Bay, dated June 8, 1779.

"That the Town of Middleboro have 10 men to raise for the Rhode Island Service, to serve until the 1st. day of Jan. next, and said men are to be paid 30 lbs. each out of Treasury of said Town of Middleboro. *Voted* that the Town Treasurer give his note of 30 lbs. to each of said 10 men with interest till paid."

June 14, 1780: —

"*Voted* to raise men to reinforce the army, 55 the number assigned to this town for the term of six months.

"*Voted* that the town treasurer give his security to the men that engage in said service or that were held in said service, the securities, if any are demanded to be given, are to be given in farming produce or silver money or lumber or paper currency."

On June 14, 1780, at a town meeting it was voted that the town treasurer hire money for the help of raising the men if wanted.

"*Voted* that there be paid to each man that engages in the service as a soldier 200.$\frac{1}{2}$ of bloomery bar iron per month or farming produce in proportion to said iron.

"*Voted* that 400 Continental dollars be paid to the men that engage in said service instead of 100 of iron, the said sum to be paid to him that demands it and cannot do without the same."

July 3, 1780, it was voted according to an order sent out by the Great and General Court of this state to raise 65 men for the term of 3 months for the present service of war.

By resolve of the General Court December 4, 1780, the town of Middleboro was required to furnish 49,733 pounds of beef for the use of the army or money sufficient to purchase the same. The town remonstrated to the General Court that they were unable to meet such requisition for several reasons: that they had recently complied with a similar requisition with great difficulty; that the lumber in town which furnished money for inhabitants had failed; that the men engaged in farming had been absent during the season for planting crops; that a large number had been in service and had not had the pay which was promised them, and that the town was not as fertile as many other towns, so that they were unable to realize either the money or the beef to meet with that requisition.

What action was taken by the General Court upon this requisition does not appear.

March 14, 1791 : —

"*Voted* to loan all the old Continental paper money now in the Town Treasury to the United States and that the Town Treasurer be the person to put said money on loan in the Town's behalf."

MUSKET AND POWDERHORN

CHAPTER IX

THE LOYALISTS OF THE REVOLUTION

AT the commencement of and during the struggle for independence, Sabin, in his "American Loyalists," estimates that there were in the province of Massachusetts Bay more than two thousand loyalists, for the most part wealthy influential and professional men of the colony.[1] Many of them had held commissions under the Crown, and had served with distinction in the army of George III, during the French and Indian and other wars. Others had held various civil appointments, which were then regarded as positions of honor. They were familiar with the history and the traditions of the mother country, and had the love and enthusiasm for England of loyal British subjects. While mindful of the wrongs and injustice that the colonies had suffered, the claims of the Crown were so strong that they could not readily throw them off.

Many of the inhabitants of Middleboro had a great struggle in choosing the side of the patriots and taking up arms against the mother country. In the neighboring towns, many of the prominent families of Plymouth, Halifax, Freetown, Marshfield, Rochester, and Taunton early espoused the cause of the king. The loyalists[2] all over the country were banished

---

[1] John Adams was inclined to believe that in the colonies at large not more than two thirds were against the Crown at the breaking out of the Revolution. The last vote that showed the strength of the loyalists in the town of Boston was in 1775, when the vote stood five against two. Of the three hundred and ten persons who were banished from the country and their estates confiscated, over sixty were graduates of Harvard College. *Memorial History of Boston*, vol. iii, p. 175.

[2] "Upwards of eleven hundred retired in a body with the royal army at the evacuation of Boston. This number includes, of course, women and children. Among the men, however, were many persons of distinguished rank and consideration. Of members of the council, commissioners, officers of the customs, and other officials, there were one hundred and two; of clergymen, eighteen; of in-

and went to England, Canada, New Brunswick, and Nova Scotia, and their estates were confiscated under the statutes of 1778 and 1779. The English government paid fifteen million dollars for their relief. Popular feeling early in the struggle was intense against them; Washington was most severe in his expression of contempt. The term "tory" was applied to them as the most opprobrious epithet that could be used, and the position which many of them had held in the colony seemed to be no bar against the treatment they received.

The following instances show to what lengths the popular feeling went in neighboring towns: Daniel Leonard of Taunton, an attorney and barrister of wide reputation, a graduate of Harvard College, and a member of the General Court, had been appointed a mandamus councillor; against him the feeling was so strong that bullets were fired into his house by a mob, and he was obliged to take refuge in Boston. In 1776 he, with his family of eight, left for Halifax and England, and was appointed chief justice for the Bermudas. Daniel Dunbar was an officer in the militia when in 1774 a mob demanded of him that he surrender the colors of his company, which bore the insignia of the British Crown. When he refused to do this, they carried him from his house, put him upon a rail, and held him there until he was exhausted. He was then beaten until he was forced to give up the standard to save his life. Jesse Dunbar bought some cattle of a mandamus councillor in 1774, and drove them to Plymouth for sale. So great was the indignation of the patriots that, on learning that Dunbar had presumed to have business relations with such a hated officer, they commenced punishing him for his offence (after the animals had been slaughtered). He suffered great indignities at their hands. He was carried to Kingston and there delivered to a mob, which carted him into the town of Duxbury. Here another mob seized him, and after beating him severely and

habitants of country towns, one hundred and five; of merchants and other persons who resided in Boston, two hundred and thirteen; of farmers, mechanics, and traders, three hundred and eighty-two." Sabine's *Loyalists of American Revolution*, vol. i, p. 25.

offering him many gross insults, they took him to a house and compelled him to give up the money he had received; then he was left in the road with the remains of his slaughtered animals, to recover and return home as best he could.

At the breaking out of the Revolution, Middleboro was one of the largest towns in the commonwealth, and contained many persons of influence who were well known throughout the colony. It was hoped that Judge Oliver, by reason of his long residence and the universal respect in which he was held, would induce the town not only to resist the tide of patriotism which was sweeping over the country, but to join the loyalists of Marshfield.[1] There a company of one hundred men had been formed, and arms were sent to them to defend the rights of the Crown. Judge Oliver labored faithfully to induce prominent men of his acquaintance to side with him and to resist the growing sentiment against the English nation, but in vain. At one of these interviews Zachariah Eddy asked the judge if the king had done right. The judge replied, "As to that I cannot say, but he has the power."

The people of Middleboro, however strong in sentiment and sympathy with the patriot cause, refrained from many outbreaks of violence toward the tories. A committee had been appointed to confer with them in the early stages of the war, but the most that could be obtained was a promise not to assist the enemy. The only indignity that was offered was burning the house of Judge Oliver at Muttock, in 1778. Judge Oliver, however, had left the colony with his family, with the avowed intention of never returning until the rebellious spirit of the British subjects in America should be subdued and the power of the British throne again reëstablished.

There were but two citizens of Middleboro who were banished by acts of the legislature; these were Judge Oliver[2] and his son, Peter Oliver, Jr. Ebenezer Spooner, a former citizen, was not then a resident of the town. Judge Oliver's son Daniel was a graduate of Harvard University in 1762, and

---

[1] See account of minute men in the Revolution.
[2] For life of Judge Oliver, see chapter on Muttock.

studied law. In 1765 he had been a representative to the General Court from Middleboro. Later he settled in Worcester County and went to England with his father. He died in the year 1826 at the age of eighty-two.

Peter Oliver, Jr., a graduate of Harvard University, was a physician, although he did not practise long in Middleboro. He was one of the eighteen country gentlemen who were driven into Boston in 1775 to address General Gage. In the act proscribing him, he was called "the Middleboro physician." After leaving the country, he resided in Shrewsbury, England, where he died at the age of eighty-one years. He had none of the regard towards his native land which his father showed in his later years, but was very bitter towards everything which reminded him of his former home. In his father's library was the only perfect manuscript of Hubbard's "History of New England." In 1814 the Massachusetts Historical Society desired to publish that work, and applied to Dr. Oliver to give or loan them this copy for that purpose, or to permit a transcript of such parts of the manuscript as were missing in the American copy which we now have. His spirit of animosity against the country was shown in the very curt and surly answer which he sent, refusing to comply with either request, and in consequence, Hubbard's "History of New England," one of the earliest and most authoritative histories we have, is incomplete at the beginning and at the end.

Portions of his diary may be of interest : —

DIARY OF PETER OLIVER, JR., 1757

Abt. the 1st. week in Oct. I got home to Middleborough.

In Novr., about the second week, I went to Boston with my father & mother, lodged at Milton at G. Hutchinson's, who was then only Mr. Hutchinson, or, perhaps Lieutenant-Govr. I remember it was of a Saturday evg. & the 1st. time I ever saw his eldest daughter, Sally, who was afterwards my wife. I went to meeting the next day with the family.

In this month I was examined at Harvard College, Cambridge, & was admitted into the Freshmen's class under Mr. Handcock, the tutor, my elder brother, Daniel, being then a Senior Sophister.

In July my brother took his degree of B. A. and went home. Nothing very particular while at College, only I spent most of my time very agreeably, became much acquainted with Mr. Hutchinson's family (Elisha and I living together the greater part of my last two years), & especially with Sally. She had a very agreeable way in her behavior which I remember pleased me beyond any other of my female acquaint^s, though I had not the least thought of any connection with her.

While I was at college I lost a favorite uncle, Clarke, who was a physician in Boston, & likewise some cousins.

In July, 1761, I took my deg^e of B. A.

In Augt 21, follow^g, I went to live at Scituate with Dr. Stockbridge as an apprentice. Here I enjoyed a many happy & more happier Hour than I ever experienced in my life before. I had no care or trouble on my mind, lived easy, & became acquainted with an agreeable young lady in the neighborhood but only on a friendly footing.

In March 21, 1764, I left Dr. Stockbridge's and went to Boston to reside at the Castle, to understand the nature of the smallpox under Dr. Gelston. I staid there till the last of Ap^l follow^g, when I cleared out, as they term it; went to Middleborough in May; and in June set up for myself in the practice of physic amidst many difficulties & obstructions. My father built me a small shop near his house. I gradually got a little business but poor pay.

In June, 1765, first pay'^{d} my addresses to Miss S. H., and obtained leave of her father in Augt follow^g, being just before his House was tore down, he losing everything he had in his House; his Daughters & rest of the family likewise shared the same fate.

I went down in a few days after to see the family; found Miss S. H. most terribly worried and distrest.

I found that courtship was the most pleasant part of my life hitherto; the family were very agreeable.[1]

At a later date, we find these entries in his diary: —

June 1st 1774. — The Govr, Elisha, and Peggy, sailed for England, just as the Mandamus Counsellors were ordered to take their oaths by G. Gage, who succeeded the Govr H. — Nothing but mobs and riots all this summer. Wednesday the 14 of Sepr I was mobbed.

Aug. 23. — Well Col. Watson is sworn in to be one of His

[1] An account of his wedding reception is given in the chapter on Muttock.

Majesties Council; he has got home; they left the Meeting to the number of 40. The first Sunday they passed him in the street without noticing him which occasions him to, to be very uneasy. Some of our pupies in town are coming to wait on the judge [Peter Oliver, Sen.] You will hear more of it by the time you finish this letter.

Sept. 2. — 3 men deputed from 40 Middlebg. brutes came to the Judges house the 24th to know ab^t these difficulties, and they went away as dissatisfied as they came.

Col. Ruggles, Murry, Willard and some others are obliged to retire to Boston to get rid of the mob. The Judge is now in Boston. We have been threatened and whether we shan't be mobbed is uncertain. I dread to think of the consequences that must follow our behavior here whether ever so mild matters are struck upon by the ministry. If the ministry give way to us we are an undone people; and if they set out to punish us according as we deserve it there will be bloodshed enough before they can reduce us. The Middleborough people and indeed the Province in general, declare solemnly never to submit to this new plan of government. I wish I was safe with my family out of the reach of threats and insults. I never knew what mobbing was before. I am sick enough of confusion and uproar. I long for an asylum, — some blessed place of refuge.

Sept. 10. — The Judge is in Boston yet for safety, and will be this one while. You have no idea of the confusion we are in ab^t the Counsell and new mode of government.

Sept. 14. — To-day I was visited by about 30 Middleborough Puppies, who obliged me to sign their Articles. They proceeded and increased their number to 80, and attack'd Mr. Silas Wood, carried him off, and threatened his life if he would not sign their paper to stand by the Old Charter, and give up the Protest he had then in his pocket. He finally yielded. The next day they visited ab^t 10 or 12 people who are called Tories, and made them resign to their unwarrantable demands. M. R. Spooner among the rest.[1]

The following letters refer to this period: —

MIDDLEBOROUGH, Aug. 11, 1774.

SIR, — We have just heard of the arrival of the Acts of Parliament by a Man-of-War, last Saturday or Sunday. Tuesday the General sent an express to the Judge, Col. Watson,

[1] *Diary and Letters of Thomas Hutchinson*, pp. 246, 459.

Daniel Leonard, Col. Eden [doubtless should have been Edson], N. Ray, Thomas [Hutchinson], and a number of others in the Province, as we imagine as His Majesty's Council, upon the new Establishment. Col. Watson says he bids farewell to all peace and comfort in this world. I never see him so uneasy in my life. He will refuse, and if he does he will do the Tories more dishonor than ever he did them good. There are numbers in the Province that swear they will never consent to this new plan. By next fall, the last of October, the whole matter will be decided."

To his brother-in-law, Elisha Hutchinson : —

BOSTON, June 1st, 1775.

DEAR BROTHER, —

. . . .

We are besieged this moment with 10 or 15000 men, from Roxbury to Cambridge ; their rebell sentrys within call of the troops' sentrys on the Neck. We are every hour expecting an attack by land or water. All marketing from the country stopt ever since the Battle. Fire and slaughter hourly threatened, and not out of danger from some of the inhabitants within, of setting the town of [on] fire. All the interest the Judge and I ound [owned] in Middleborough exposed to the ravage of a set of robbers, Mr Conant at the head of them. Poor Jenny and Phœbe, and children, we can't hear of, or get any word to, whether they are all living or not, or whether the works and buildings are left standing is rather a doubt with me, for we have heard since the Battle, that a number set out to destroy and burn our interest, but that the Selectmen interposed and saved them.

. . . .

James Bowdoin, Esq., is very ill in health, and has desir'd leave of the Judge to live in his house, and improve his land till he shall want it himself. *What consummate impudence!* It is more than I would consent to, but the Judge will consent to it.

10th Instant. — Yesterday I heard from Plymouth : all well at present : can't send your letters.

The rebells, I hear, have put out our Farm, to take the profits themselves : they have serv'd every friend to government in that way.

O *tempora!* O *mores!*   Y^{rs} as usual,

PETER OLIVER, Junr.

BOSTON, Decr 7, 1775.

SIR, — This by Nathl Coffin Junr. I determine to write you by all the opportunities for the future, when I have anything to relate.

. . . .

This once happy country must for the future be miserable. Most of the Governments, especially these 4 Governments of N. England, are inevitably forfeited to His Majesty. All we poor Refugees must be made good our losses and damages. Hanging people won't pay me for what I have suffered. Nothing short of forfeited estates will answer: and after damages are sufficiently compensated, then hang all the Massachusetts Rebels by dozens, if you will.

You may remember our Wilder, the Blacksmith: he has turn'd Rebell. Neighbour Tupper, on the hill as you turn to the Meeting House, or Boston Road: in fine, but a very few in Middleborough but what are Rebells or Devils. The Parson stands foremost in the list: he must be looked up one of the first. The rest of this matter in my next.

Sally [his wife, the Governor's daughter] sends her love to you. — I am   Y^{rs} Affectionately

PETER OLIVER, Junr.

In a letter from Thomas Hutchinson, Jr., to his brother Elisha under date of September 22, 1774, he writes: —

"It is become mighty fashionable here for the people to wait on any person who has done anything that they are pleased to look upon as unfriendly to the cause of liberty, and oblige them to confess, and promise reformation. Dr Oliver was visited last week by about five hundred, who assembled at some distance from his house, and sent a Committee to confess him for having promoted some Address or Protest some time agoe, which penance he readily underwent, to get rid of his unwelcome guests, and I suppose may now remain at Middleborough without molestation."

Others who were put under surveillance by the town authorities were also men of property and of the highest respectability. Such was the confidence in the integrity of these men that although they were known to be in full sympathy with the British cause, they were not proscribed, or banished, neither were their estates confiscated as were those of other tories of the province.

DOGGETT HOUSE   RANSOME HOUSE

The house in which Simeon Doggett lived is still standing on South Main Street, Lakeville. He came from Marshfield in 1742, and was with his brother in the French and Indian War in the company of Captain Benjamin Pratt. He was a skilful cabinet maker, living upon the farm which he cultivated. He was generally known as "the tory farmer," and as a staunch Episcopalian he differed from most of the townspeople in his religious opinions. He was conscientious in his belief that it was wrong for the colonies to rebel against the mother country, and he took no pains to conceal this. Although no treasonable acts were ever proved against him for his opinions freely expressed, he was imprisoned in the New Bedford jail, but was afterwards released upon a promise that he would not leave his farm without permission. One of his contemporaries said that he and his tory neighbor, Lemuel Ransome, while under the injunction of the town, obeyed it carefully, but availed themselves of the privilege of walking daily to the bounds of their adjoining farms, discussing the turbulent state of the times and freely expressing their sympathy for the king they loved so well. When the war was over they regained the esteem and confidence of their fellow citizens. Mr. Doggett was the father of Rev. Simeon Doggett, a clergyman of reputation, at one time principal of the Taunton Academy. His daughter, Abigail, married Judge Weston. He was the grandfather of the Rev. Thomas Doggett and William E. Doggett, an eminent business man of Chicago.

John Doggett, a minor and resident of Middleboro, sympathized with his relative, Simeon Doggett, in the latter's political opinion, and left the country soon after coming of age. He moved to New Brunswick and settled on the Isle of Grand Menan, in the Bay of Fundy, where he died in 1830 at the age of seventy years.

Lemuel Ransome lived upon the farm recently occupied by Clark Bump. He was one of the few men in town against whose character no one was ever known to speak, and his influence was very great until it was known that he espoused the cause of the Crown. Although the feeling was so intense, the community never lost confidence in Mr. Ransome, and regarded him as one of the most upright and honest of citizens. He was known throughout the country as "the honest farmer," receiving that name from the following incident: At one season there was a great frost and heavy drought in some portion of the state, so that almost the entire crop of corn[1] was ruined and yielded but little more than had been originally planted. Mr. Ransome (probably on account of the peculiarity of the soil and the nearness of his farm to the neighboring ponds) was able to gather a large crop during that year. Speculators came to him, offering the highest prices for his corn, two or three dollars per bushel, but he would not sell. "This corn," he used to say, "belongs to the poor people of the town, and they shall have it at the ordinary price of fifty cents a bushel." Such unusual generosity won for him the love and respect of all. Elkanah Leonard said of him, "I have seen an honest man." This trait of character made him conscientious in his loyalty to England. This was his argument: "We must honor the king. Does not the Bible say we must honor him? I cannot go contrary to the Bible." Part of a conversation has come down to us, in which he said to Mr. Doggett, "Does it not make you feel sad to see all our people rising against their king?" "I know not how it will end, but I tremble lest some great calamity should come

[1] It was at this time that part of Scituate received the name Egypt, as corn could be obtained there, and men went long distances, as of old, "to buy corn in Egypt."

upon the colonies for their treason against the royal Crown of England." He, as well as his neighbor, had been indicted for his public utterances, yet on September 2, 1779, the Committee of Inspection petitioned the General Court that

> The indictment against Lemuel Ransome, an inhabitant of Middleboro be stayed for the reason therein given, and that all proceedings in said indictment be and hereby are stayed until the further order of the court, and the Superior Court of Judicature be ordered to stay proceedings.
> (Signed by) JOHN HANCOCK, Speaker.

Mr. Ransome lived to a good old age, and died respected by all. The attendance at his funeral was the largest Middleboro had ever seen.

At the commencement of the Revolutionary War, Captain William Canedy, an influential man in that part of the town now Lakeville, had served with distinction in the French and Indian War. When questioned concerning his loyalty, he replied that he had fought for his king, had held a commission as captain from his Majesty's governor of the province, and he could not be a traitor in his old age.

Stephen Richmond lived on Vernon Street, in the house now occupied by Daniel Aldrich. His temperament and disposition were such that he had nothing of the position and esteem which the other loyalists received. He was known as the "d—d old tory." He died of smallpox in 1777, and was buried on the other side of a stone wall, opposite the grave of Mr. Paddock, the owner of the field positively refusing to allow such a man to be buried on his land.

One George Gye was committed to jail by the committee of safety of Middleboro, January 14, 1777. He was brought before the committee and fairly examined, and

> "Found to have been secretly moving about for several months past among the worst of our Tories who, we find, are all acquainted with him, and have received repeated visits from him, and that no other person but Tories have had the pleasure to be acquainted with him and further we find him firmly

engaged in his mind for government against our liberties and many other things that might be proved against him."

Upon a petition, the legislature paid the expenses of his being kept in jail. Soon after the battle of Lexington, the town took decisive action in its endeavor to suppress any influence which the loyalists might seek to exert in favor of the Crown.

At a town meeting held July 3, 1775, "Com. of Inspection reported that Silas Wood, William Strowbridge 2nd., Simeon Doggett, Josiah Vaughan, Thomas Paddock, Zebulon Leonard, Lemuel Ransom, Joseph Bates Jr., Jacob Bennett and Peter Vaughan, have not given satisfaction to them that they are friends to the Country.

"A Committee of five men were appointed to see what measures should be taken relative to these persons; Adjourned for an hour and reported that said persons be confined to their own homes from the date hereof until such time as they shall make satisfaction to the town or Committee of Inspection excepting that on the Lord's Day they shall be allowed to attend public worship."

At a town meeting held July 17, 1775, the following vote was passed: "Voted that the Committee of Inspection go and inquire into the conduct of William Canedy and John Montgomery Jr. and if they don't give satisfaction to the said Committee of Inspection, that the town have ordered that the captains of each of the military companies are ordered to keep on the homestead farm and not go off until such time as they give the said committee satisfaction, unless it be to attend public worship at the society to which they belong, on the penalty of being carried to the camps at Roxbury and delivered up to some military officer."

At a town meeting held June 17, 1777, "the Selectmen reported the following persons as being enimically disposed toward the United States, Zebulon Leonard, William Strobridge, Lemuel Ransom, Simeon Doggett and Stephen Richmond.

"Each person being called on, the vote put whether they were enimically disposed passed in the affirmative at said meeting. Moved by Isaac Perkins and seconded by Joseph Leonard. Voted and seconded that Stephen Richmond is enimically disposed towards the United American States, the vote being called passed in the affirmative and his name was entered upon the selectmen list."

At a town meeting held July 28, 1777, "the following warned persons were reported as being enimically disposed toward the United States — Capt. William Canady, John Howland, John Montgomery Jr., Josiah Vaughan, James Keith, Thomas Paddock 2nd., and John Clark. Town examined and acquitted by vote John Howland, Josiah Vaughan, James Keith, Thomas Paddock 2nd, and Capt. William Canady and that the others be brought to trial by a court for that purpose."

At a town meeting held December 29, 1777, "Article in the Warrant, To see if the Town will approve or disapprove of measures taken in carrying Simeon Doggett & Lemuel Ransom out of Town.

"Voted not to act anything relative to this article."

CHAPTER X

MIDDLEBORO IN THE WAR OF 1812

THE War of 1812 was not generally popular with the people of Massachusetts. They believed the causes which led to it might have been adjusted by diplomacy, and the declaration of war was too hasty, the long extended coast of the state not being sufficiently prepared for defence.[1] The non-intercourse law came to an end in 1810 without having produced any effect. France's attitude was such under Napoleon's deception that this law was revived against Great Britain. Her vessels watched the whole eastern coast of the United States, and captured many American merchantmen. A conflict seemed unavoidable. With the new Congress, "submission men," who wished to avoid a struggle, were defeated, and "war men" elected, so that on June 18, 1812, war was declared. The British navy numbered one thousand vessels, the American twelve, inferior in tonnage and armament; the army was poorly equipped and disciplined; money was scarce, most of it being in New England. The government endeavored to raise money by loans, but with such poor success that at the end of the war there was hardly enough to arm, feed, and clothe the soldiers.

The principal theatre of the war was in the wilderness near Canada. In 1812 Detroit surrendered, and Canada was invaded with great loss. In the mean time the navy, which had not been expected to take a prominent part, won important victories, causing intense excitement. For twenty years Great Britain had been at war with almost every nation of Europe, and out of hundreds of battles between ships of equal force had lost but five. In six months the little American navy had

[1] Bradford, *History of Massachusetts*, vol. ii, p. 174.

captured five vessels, and had not lost a battle.[1] The warfare was carried on on the lakes, where both sides bought and built, to add to the power of their respective navies there. The Americans held their own on Lake Ontario, and won complete success on Lake Champlain, and in Perry's famous victory on Lake Erie, when he sent the official despatch, "We have met the enemy and they are ours, two ships, two tugs, one schooner and one sloop." The blockade of the Atlantic coast was enforced by British vessels from the beginning of 1813. Early that year they took possession of the mouth of Chesapeake Bay as a naval station, and the government then ordered all lights to be extinguished in neighboring lighthouses. At first they were inclined to spare New England, which was supposed to be friendly to Great Britain, but it too suffered with the other places on the shore. The entire coast was kept in a state of alarm, as British boats landed at exposed points to burn and plunder the towns, and private property was seized everywhere in the general pillage. The coast of Massachusetts was especially exposed to the ravages of the ships of the enemy, and the people justly complained to the general government that it was left without protection. This war destroyed the fishing industries of the state. Its extensive commerce was paralyzed, and all business was at a standstill.

While Middleboro had no shipping interests, the entire business of the town suffered. When war was declared, the people acquiesced in the action of the administration, and responded to the call for troops to defend the commonwealth. A general order[2] was issued by the governor on the 3d of July, 1812, requiring that all officers and soldiers enrolled in the militia of the commonwealth should hold themselves in readiness to march at the shortest notice, wherever their services might be needed; but few of the militia were called into active service at that time. The town early made suitable provision for her soldiers.

[1] Johnston's *History of United States*, p. 182.
[2] *History of Plymouth County*, p. 1006.

At the town meeting held July 27, 1812, it was voted that "the detached soldiers of the town of Middleboro be allowed by said town in addition to their pay allowed by the government an amount sufficient to amount to the whole $13, a month whenever they are called by government into active service of the country."

Also voted that "the non-commissioned officers have an additional sum in addition to their army pay allowed by said town which shall be in proportion to the soldier."

Also voted that "the select men be directed to furnish a set of equipments for one soldier and if Rodolphus Barden, one of the detached soldiers be called into service of the country that the town turn out to him said equipments."

Many of the ship-owners of New England, upon the declaration of war, manned their ships and fitted them out as privateers. These were active and troublesome to the enemy; numerous battles were fought on both sides. Middleboro's part in the war was in the coast defence of neighboring towns. In the summer of 1814 the English ships, Superb and Nimrod, were hovering about the eastern shores of Massachusetts. They had sent detachments of soldiers, who had inflicted great damage at Scituate and Wareham [1] and were threatening an attack at Plymouth. A fort had been erected upon the Gurnet for the defence of Plymouth, Kingston, and Duxbury. Men from Middleboro were in Wareham at the time of the attack by the British soldiers in June, 1814, but only the name of Joseph Le Baron has come down to us.

During this war the militia of Plymouth County were under one brigade, which was composed of four regiments of infantry, a battalion of artillery, and a battalion of cavalry, which were under the command of Major-General Goodwin. On the 27th day of May, 1814, General Nathaniel Goodwin issued the following order : —

"It is absolutely and indespensably necessary at this time when our shores are daily invaded by the enemy that every man should do his duty and all concerned will be responsible for any neglect. Upon any alarm being made at the approach of the enemy on or near our shore Towns or Villages within the limits of the 5th Division, the officers and soldiers of the militia of said Towns and Villages will immediately repair to their respective alarm posts completely equipt for actual ser-

[1] Lossing, *Pictorial Field-Book of War of 1812*, p. 889.

vice, and there wait for their orders from their superior officers, if timely to be obtained, but should the necessity of the case be such that it would not admit of delay in the opinion of the commanding officer present, he will march immediately with the troops to the place or places in danger; and afford all the aid and assistance in his power and repel by force and arms all such hostile invaders. When so marched the commanding officer will give information thereof to the nearest superior officer."

There is no record that any of the troops from Middleboro were in any engagement with the enemy during the war, but in response to this order from General Goodwin the companies were held in readiness. Three companies were sent to New Bedford under Major Levi Peirce.

At this time (June, 1814) New Bedford was blockaded by the Nimrod and La Hogue,[1] which continually threatened to land troops for the devastation of the city and the surrounding country. There was gathered in compliance with this order for the defence of New Bedford and Fair Haven about one thousand men. The people of New Bedford were strong federalists and opposed the war[2] from the beginning, while those of Fair Haven were democrats and heartily endorsed the administration in its declaration of war and preparation for a vigorous assault on the enemy. They were glad to shelter the privateers and all other enemies of the British, and had built a fort on a strip of land at the entrance to their harbor. It was well fortified and guarded by Lieutenant Selleck Osborne. The enemy had planned an attack on the fort and the destruction of the village; everything was ready for the

---

[1] Lossing, *Pictorial Field-Book of War of 1812*, p. 889.

[2] "On July 21, 1814, the town of New Bedford voted unanimously as the expressions of the feelings of the inhabitants of the town that we have considered it our duty to abstain and have scrupulously abstained from all interest and concern in sending out private armed vessels to harass the enemy and which have appeared to us an encouragement to prosecute and increase the ravages of the unprofitable contest; that we have seen with disapprobation several private armed vessels belonging to other ports taking shelter in our peaceful waters and regret that we have not the authority of law wholly to exclude them from our harbor where they serve to increase our danger, where they incite disorder and confusion." *New Bedford Records*.

Nimrod to commence the attack before daybreak. Just before that time the tin horn of a mail-carrier and the galloping of his horse across the Acushnet bridge and causeway were heard. This was mistaken for the advance of a large number of American forces. The Nimrod hastened to withdraw to a safe distance from the fort, and New Bedford and Fair Haven were spared what might have been a bloody battle. The known friendliness of New Bedford to the British cause did not save the inhabitants from the general alarm.

The names of the officers and soldiers of the three companies which Middleboro furnished were as follows : [1] —

CAPTAIN WILDER'S COMPANY

COMMISSIONED OFFICERS

Nath'l Wilder, Jr., capt.
Linus Washburn, lieut.
Calvin Shaw, ensign

NON-COMMISSIONED OFFICERS

Joseph Haskell, sergt.
Isaac Stevens, sergt.
Sylvanus Warren, sergt.
Benjamin White, sergt.
George Leonard, corp.
Abner Leonard, corp.
Abner Leach, corp.
Stephen Burgess, corp.

MUSICIANS

Isaac Tinkham, drummer
Joshua Haskins, fifer

PRIVATES

Benjamin Hayford
Israel Keith
John Perkins
Daniel Snow
Daniel Warren
Jacob Bennett
Jacob Stevens
Andrew Warren
Nathan Reed
Benjamin Tinkham
Calvin Dunham
Ziba Eaton
Willis Sherman
Sylvanus S. Wood
Ira Tinkham, Jr.
Peter Winslow, Jr.
Ichabod Wood (2d)
Joseph Paddock
Alby Wood
John Barden
Cushman Vaughan
Rodolphus Barden
Lemuel Southworth
William Southworth

[1] For the list of men in these companies, see *History of Plymouth Colony*, p. 1008.

Hosea Aldrich
Thomas Washburn
Fran. K. Alden
Alfred Eaton
Silas Hathaway
Solomon Reed
Elisha Shaw

Israel Eaton, Jr.
Cyrus Nelson
George Caswell
John Shaw, Jr.
George Vaughan
Samuel Leonard
Joshua Cushman

CAPTAIN CUSHMAN'S COMPANY

COMMISSIONED OFFICERS

Joseph Cushman, capt.
Pelham Atwood, lieut.

Ebenezer Vaughan, ensign

NON-COMMISSIONED OFFICERS

Zenas Cushman, sergt.
Nathan Barney, sergt.
Ezra Thomas, sergt.
Joseph Barker, Jr., sergt.

Levi Tinkham, corp.
—— Soule, Jr., corp.
Cyrus Tinkham, corp.
S. Fuller, corp.

MUSICIANS

Geo. Thompson, drummer
Samuel Bent, fifer

PRIVATES

Jacob Covington
Caleb Tinkham
Cyrus Ellis
James Thomas, Jr.
Joshua Sherman (2d)
T. Wood
Samuel Shaw
Obed King (3d)
Consider Fuller
George Cushman
Isaac Bryant (2d)
Levi Bryant
Darius Darling
Zebadee Pratt
Timothy ——
Thomas ——
Joshua Swift
Ezra Eddy

Joseph Farmer
Isaac Briggs
Enoch Tinkham (2d)
—— Bosworth
Josiah Robertson
Joshua Shaw
Merchant Shaw
Cyrus Thrasher
—— Standish
Luther Washburn
Edmund Hinds
Leonard Hinds
Thomas Sampson
Amos Washburn
Lemuel Robbins
Abram Skiff
George Peirce
Bennett Briggs

Captain Shaw's Company

COMMISSIONED OFFICERS

Gaius Shaw, capt.
Alden Miller, lieut.
Abiatha Briggs, ens.

NON-COMMISSIONED OFFICERS

Warren Clark, sergt.
Jonathan Cobb, sergt.
Abiel P. Booth, sergt.
Japhet Le Baron, sergt.
Earl Alden, corp.
Caleb Washburn, Jr., corp.
James Sturtevant, corp.
Zenas Raymond, corp.

MUSICIANS

Joshua A. Bent, drummer   Martin Keith, Jr., fifer

PRIVATES

Clothier Allen
Stephen Atwood
William Barrows
Judson Briggs
Malbone Briggs
—— Bumpus
Samuel Cole
Elnathan Coombs
Isaac Cushman (2d.)
Daniel Gifford
Nathaniel G. Hathaway
Eliphalet Hathaway
Samuel Hall
Branch Harlow
Aberdeen Keith
Samuel Lovell
Ziba Lebaron
Elijah Lewis
Eli Peirce
Eliphalet Peirce, Jr.
Elisha Peirce
Enos Parris
Enos Peirce
Henry Pickens
William Nelson
Robert Rider, Jr.
Henry Strobridge
Silas Shaw
Andrew Swift
Winslow Thomas
Thomas Wood
Lemuel Wood
Jonathan Westgate
Jonathan Westgate, Jr.
Joshua Lebaron

The company under command of Captain Shaw served until July 8, 1814; the companies under Captain Wilder and Captain Cushman, until July 10, 1814. Captain Cushman received a ten days' leave of absence, which had not expired when the following order was issued:—

NEW BEDFORD, July, 1814.

CAPT. NATHL. WILDER:

Sir, — You will consider yourself discharged from the present detachment, together with the officers and soldiers recently under your command, and those officers and soldiers recently under the command of Capt. Joseph Cushman, whose absence from service had caused his officers and soldiers to do duty under your command.

You will accept my thanks and also those of Major Levi Peirce, and through you to the Officers and Soldiers under your command, for your and their good conduct and prompt attention to orders.

BENJN. LINCOLN, Col.

Another order had been issued that regiments and battalions should be in readiness to march at the shortest notice to any point within the district. On the 17th day of September, 1814, a battalion of two companies was sent from Middleboro to reenforce the coast guard, stationed at Plymouth. This battalion was under the command of Major Ephraim Ward, who afterwards became a brigadier-general, with Captain Peter H. Peirce in command of one company, and Captain Greenleaf Pratt the commander of the other.

The names of the officers and soldiers in Captain Peter H. Peirce's company are as follows: —

COMMISSIONED OFFICERS

Peter H. Peirce, capt.
Luther Murdock, lieut.
Orrin Tinkham, ensign

NON-COMMISSIONED OFFICERS

Thomas Bump, sergt.
Hercules Richmond, sergt.
George Shaw, sergt.
Ezra Wood, sergt.
Ichabod Wood, sergt.

Daniel Hathaway, corp.
Abner Leonard, corp.
Daniel Thomas, corp.
Andrew Warren, corp.

MUSICIANS

Oliver Sharp
Paddock Tinkham

PRIVATES

Jeremiah Wood
Levi Wood
Cyrenus Tinkham
Gideon Leonard
Peter Vaughan

Thomas C. Ames
Unite Kinsley
Levi Haskins
George Ellis
Cornelius Tinkham

Joseph Clark
Edmund Ellis
Eliphalet Doggett
Oliver L. Sears
Nathan Perkins
Josiah D. Burgess
Joseph Waterman
Isaac Thomas, Jr.
Joshua Atwood, Jr.
Andrew McCully
Daniel Norcutt
Seth Weston
Abel Howard
Benjamin Leonard
Cyrus White
Benijah Wilder
Levi Thomas (2d)
Calvin Dunham
Caleb Tinkham
Abraham Thomas, Jr.
Rufus Alden, Jr.
Daniel Weston
Joseph Paddock
Nathaniel Macomber
William Ramsdell
John C. Perkins
Edward Winslow, Jr.
Isaac Cole
Samuel Cole
Thomas Southworth
Daniel Vaughan
Cushman Vaughan
Sylvanus T. Wood
Cyrus Nelson
Augustus Bosworth
Lorenzo Wood
Jacob Bennett (2d)
Andrew Bump
Josephus Bump
Nathan Reed
Benijah Peirce
William Littlejohn, Jr.
Warren Bump, Jr.
Francis Billington
Joseph Standish
Earl Bourne
George Caswell, Jr.
Israel Keith
Sylvanus Vaughan
Leonard Southworth
James Bump
Elijah Shaw
James Cole
Rodolphus Barden
Sylvanus Barrows

The regiment containing the Middleboro companies was under command of Colonel Lazelle, and troops from different sections of southeastern Massachusetts were hastening to the defence of Plymouth with all possible speed. The battalion in which were companies from this town was under command of Major Ward, but as they had not arrived or sent any word at the time they were expected, Colonel Hector Orr, one of the officers under Major-General Goodwin, was detailed to go out and ascertain the cause of the delay and hasten their approach to Plymouth. Colonel Orr met them in what was called the Bump neighborhood, which, at this time, did not have a good reputation, and found that they were marching in broken ranks without military order. The morning was wet and the roads muddy, and their guns and accoutrements had been taken into the baggage wagons accompanying the regiment. He noticed that the men had no guns, and, approaching Major Ward, asked, "Where are your men's guns?" He replied, "In the baggage wagon." The colonel exclaimed, "What have you got them in the baggage wagon for? You are in more danger from the Bumps in this neighborhood than from any British that you will meet."

The names of the officers and soldiers under command of Captain Greenleaf Pratt are not known. The muster roll is not among the archives of the State House in Boston, and no copy of that roll is known to exist.

No attempt was made by the enemy to pass the fort at the Gurnet or to land their troops, and after several months the men were dismissed and returned to their homes.

On the 5th day of December, 1814, it was voted to make an addition to the pay allowed by the government to the soldiers who were called out by Major-General Goodwin for the defence of Plymouth : —

> Voted " to allow the non-commissioned officers and private soldiers who were detached from the town of Middleboro for the town of Plymouth in September last an addition of wages together with what is allowed by the government of this commonwealth which will raise their wages to $15. per month."

It was many years before the town recovered from the great blow its business enterprises received during 1812 and 1814. Many of the inhabitants were employed in other towns, where they enlisted and served in the war, but their names can be ascertained only from tradition or genealogical records of various families.

A company was organized, a portion of which was from Middleboro and did service on the frontier of New York, but the names of the Middleboro men in that company are not known.

During the entire war the New England states were dissatisfied. At first the army commanders had not been wisely chosen and suffered defeat, the coast defences were neglected, and the government seemed unable to protect them. Late in

1814 they sent delegates to Hartford[1] to consider the difficulties. The meetings of this Hartford Convention — held in secret — alarmed the government, which feared it might be a plan of the federalists to break up the Union. They made a public report recommending that New England be allowed to protect her coast without waiting for the federal government. Peace was, however, soon declared, and no further steps were taken in this matter. The battle of New Orleans, January 8, 1815, resulted in so complete a victory that in twenty-five minutes the whole British line was in retreat, having lost the commander and two thousand five hundred men, while of the Americans eight were killed and thirteen wounded. Peace negotiations had been going forward,[2] and a treaty was ratified at Ghent in Belgium on December 24, 1814, but the word did not reach America in time to prevent the last disastrous battle. One result of the war was the growth of power of the United States. The accurate aim of the American gunners had done much to win the victory. While the gunboats built in such large numbers for the coast defence proved a failure, the naval successes won for the country the respect of other nations, and never again did Great Britain attempt to enforce her "orders in council" or the impressment of seamen, which had caused the war.

[1] Bradford, *History of Massachusetts*, vol. ii, chap. 13.
[2] Montgomery, *History of United States*, p. 219.

CHAPTER XI

MIDDLEBORO IN THE WAR OF THE REBELLION

"LIBERTY and Union, now and forever, one and inseparable," were the closing words of that "most remarkable speech ever made in the American Congress," when Daniel Webster replied to Hayne. Later, in his reply to Calhoun, "There can be no secession without revolution," his words found an echo in the sentiment so widespread over the North. Middleboro was too close a neighbor to Marshfield, Webster's home, too close a neighbor to Plymouth, the home of liberty, too deeply imbued with the spirit of patriotism and loyalty to that Union for which her fathers had fought, not to be stirred to her depths as the murmurs of a great struggle began to be heard. Thirty years after Webster's famous speech, when the Civil War threatened to destroy the Union, thousands all over the land were willing to die to save it.

It is beyond our province to trace the history of those thrilling times, how with the new discoveries, new inventions, new territories, came new problems, or old ones under a new guise. The Compromise of 1850, the Fugitive Slave Law, the struggle between North and South for the possession of Kansas, the Dred Scott Decision, the John Brown raid, the election of Lincoln as President, all led the way to the secession of the southern states from the Union (1861). On March 4, 1861, at his inauguration, Lincoln said, "I have no purpose directly, or indirectly, to interfere with the institution of slavery in the states where it exists. I believe I have no lawful right to do so, and I have no inclination to do so." At the same time he felt it his duty to "preserve, protect, and defend" the Union. On April 12, 1861, the first gun was fired at Fort Sumter. No longer was it possible to settle the slave question by a peaceful arrangement; war had begun, and the next day the President called for seventy-five thousand volunteers.

Middleboro furnished readily her full quota of men, and contributed most liberally to supply the varied necessities occasioned by this great national struggle. Few of the northern statesmen were more active or energetic than John A. Andrew,[1] the illustrious war governor, by whose foresight and alacrity Massachusetts was perhaps better prepared to meet the exigencies of the war than any of the northern states, and was the first to send her troops to the front.[2] Middleboro's patriotism is shown by the promptness with which she responded to the first call. The order from the governor reached the town at six o'clock at night, requiring the company to report for duty on Boston Common at nine o'clock the next morning. Captain Harlow lived eight miles from the station, and the members of the company were scattered through Middleboro and the adjoining towns, covering an area of about fifteen miles, and yet such was the readiness with which the men responded, that when the morning train at twenty minutes past seven left the station in Middleboro, more than three quarters of the company were present.

Of the seventy-five thousand men called to serve three months, Massachusetts,[3] on the 15th day of April, received an order for two regiments, and later for four, and so the Third, Fourth, Sixth, and Eighth were sent. The state system of organization of these regiments required but eight companies, while the United States standard demanded ten, hence a reorganization was necessary where it was possible. The departure of these regiments for three months' service aroused the people to form recruiting companies, so that the call on May 3 for regiments to volunteer for three years met with a ready response. On August 4, 1862, the President called

---

[1] Lossing, *Field-Book of the Civil War*, vol. i, p. 203.

[2] "Before the lapse of forty-eight hours a Massachusetts regiment, armed and equipped, was on its way to Washington." Nicolay and Hay, *Abraham Lincoln*, vol. iv, p. 85.

[3] Bowen, *Massachusetts in the War, 1861-1865*.

for three hundred thousand additional men to serve for nine months. These were organized on the plan of the Massachusetts militia. Other regiments were sent to the field later.

Before we sketch the history of these regiments in which men from Middleboro served, let us take a brief glance at the events of these four years, that we may be better able to follow our men in their brave struggle to defend the Union.

The first great battle at Bull Run resulted in the defeat of the Union forces (July 21, 1861). In February, 1862, Fort Henry and Fort Donelson were captured by the Union forces; in March occurred the famous battle between the Monitor and the Merrimac; in April the victory at Pittsburg Landing and Island Number Ten. The greatest military achievement of that year was the capture of New Orleans (April 25), when Farragut passed the forts and destroyed the Confederate fleet; the second battle of Bull Run, in August, was shortly followed by the battle of Antietam (September 17). From the Proclamation of Emancipation on New Year's Day, 1863, the North strove to make the nation free — to restore the Union — without slavery. In the spring General Hooker met Lee and Jackson at Chancellorsville (May, 1863), where a fierce battle raged for two days, resulting in a dearly bought Confederate victory, and in the fall of their brilliant general, Stonewall Jackson. A month later Lee again attempted to pass to the North and was defeated at Gettysburg (July), while another great battle of almost equal importance was being fought at Vicksburg, followed by the surrender of Port Hudson. In the southwest the Union forces had been successful after severe battles at Chickamauga (September), Missionary Ridge, and Lookout Mountain (November). In May, 1864, occurred the battles of the Wilderness and Spottsylvania; in June the Confederate victory at Cold Harbor and the siege of Petersburg, followed in August by Sheridan's raid in the Shenandoah Valley. At the same time Sherman was marching through Georgia, finally taking Atlanta (September 2), whence he marched to the sea. Meanwhile, Admiral Farragut's last great battle resulted in closing Mobile to Confederate supplies. Then Sheridan cut off Richmond on the west and south. Grant captured Petersburg (April 2, 1865), and on the 9th of April Lee surrendered to Grant at Appomattox Court House.

In order to give an adequate conception of the service which our men rendered in this great rebellion, we have found it necessary briefly to outline the history of the different regiments in which the companies from Middleboro served. In the various engagements, it often happened that some of the companies were detailed to perform other duties than those in which the regiment was engaged, and in many cases it has been impossible to trace their movements in detail.[1]

SECOND REGIMENT

The Second Regiment was the first volunteer organization in the state to begin to form after the order for Massachusetts militia, in April, 1861.

Only one Middleboro man was in this regiment.

SECOND REGIMENT OF INFANTRY (3 YEARS' SERVICE)

COMPANY I

Alfred S. Thayer

THIRD REGIMENT

The Third, for the three months' service, like so many other Massachusetts regiments, was ready almost immediately after the call. It left Boston harbor on the 18th of April, 1861, and its first work was at the Gosport Navy Yard. The order had been given that the navy yard should be evacuated, and against the protest of Colonel Wardrop, the measure was carried out with the assistance of this regiment. It soon after arrived at Fortress Monroe, where it was made a part of the garrison, and engaged in some scouting duty in the vicinity of Yorktown, with a little skirmishing, but the regiment's main duty was to strengthen the fortress. It returned to Boston, and was mustered out on July 23.

[1] For a complete sketch of all these regiments, see Bowen, *Massachusetts in the War, 1861–1865*.

In the summer of 1862 Middleboro's men were again called out, and the nine months' troops responded. Company B of this regiment was composed in part of Middleboro men. It was encamped for a while in Camp Joe Hooker, at Lakeville, and started on the 22d of October for Newbern. The regiment was not well equipped, the Austrian rifle musket being a poor weapon. The first expedition in which it took part was toward Goldsboro (December, 1862), where it assisted in tearing up the railroad track under fire of the enemy, and supported the artillery during the repulse of the Confederate attack. It had before this taken a slight share in the engagements at Kinston and Whitehall. In January, 1863, it moved to Camp Jourdan, near Fort Totten. On the 6th of March it went on a five days' expedition into Jones and Onslow counties, where it won the thanks of the commanding officers for the faithful discharge of duties. It then returned to camp near Newbern, and later joined General Prince's Division in the reconnoissance at Pollocksville; it took part in the skirmish at Blount's Creek and later at Core Creek, and was engaged with other troops in raising the siege at Washington, but was not in any of the decisive battles of the war. After some picket duty, it was mustered out on June 26.

THIRD REGIMENT OF INFANTRY (3 MONTHS' SERVICE)[1]

COMPANY A

Joseph S. Harlow, capt.
Oreb F. Mitchell, sergt.
James W. Bryant, corp.

Opher D. Mitchell
William M. Tinkham

COMPANY H

S. Loring, 2d lieut.
William C. Alden
Lorenzo L. Brown
Seth E. Hartwell

Thomas Morton, Jr.
Robert Parris
Lucius S. Raymond
Francis S. Thomas

[1] For the names of men from Middleboro enlisted in all regiments in this war, I have used the lists published in the *History of Plymouth County*, pp. 1009–1012.

COMPANY K

Asa Shaw, 1st sergt.
Elbridge A. Maxim, corp.
Eben A. Shaw, corp.
Eli Atwood, Jr.
John S. Atwood
George N. Gammons
Martin F. Jefferson
Henry L. McFarlin
Leven S. Morse
Thomas W. Sampson

THIRD REGIMENT OF INFANTRY (9 MONTHS' SERVICE)[1]

COMPANY B

William S. Briggs, 2d lieut.
Asa Shaw, 1st sergt.
Gideon Shurtliff, corp.
James Briggs
Allen Cobb
George Darling
Adoniram B. Lucas
Cornelius Ramsdell
Ezra Shaw
Benjamin Shurtliff, Jr.
Marcus M. Willis
Henry Wrightinton

COMPANY K

Samuel Jones

FOURTH REGIMENT

The Fourth Regiment was the first organization to leave Boston (on April 17, 1861) for three months' service. It was ordered for duty at Fortress Monroe, where it remained until its dismissal, July 22.

Company C of the nine months' troops of the Fourth Regiment was mustered into service on the 17th of September, 1862 (the day of the battle of Antietam), was ordered to Camp Joe Hooker, at Lakeville, and started for the front on the 30th of December of the same year. It joined General Banks's corps in New Orleans, and was for a short time in camp at Carrollton. It was attached to the First Brigade, Third Division, and on March 7 was sent to Baton Rouge, where it encamped for two or three weeks, taking part in skirmishes near Fort Bisland and in the assault at Port Hudson. The company was engaged in one or two skirmishes at Indian Bend, but no Middleboro men were killed or wounded. After-

---

[1] The following men were killed: Company B: Asa Shaw, 1st sergeant. Company K: Samuel Jones, May 26, 1863.

wards it was ordered back, and with the army went up Red River, and returned to Port Hudson in May, 1863. During the siege at this place it was for the most part engaged in skirmishing, the plan being to make a demonstration to aid Admiral Farragut, in order that his fleet might come up the river. On the 14th of June a fierce battle took place, in which the company lost most of its men. A large number left in charge of supplies were taken prisoners and sent to Texas.

Among them were the following Middleboro men:[1] —

William W. Abbott	Joshua M. Jenney
Andrew Alden	Andrew Osborne
Isaac Alger	Morton Robbins
William Barney	Horatio N. Sampson
George W. Barrows	James M. Sampson
Earle Bennett	Dennis Shaw
Grover Bennett	E. Howard Shaw
Augustus N. J. Buchel	Winslow B. Sherman
Edwin M. Cole	Alfred O. Standish
William H. Cole	Henry Swift
William A. Coombs	Sergeant S. Swett
Erastus E. Gay	Sylvester R. Swift
Jonathan L. Hall	Winslow Thomas
Daniel Handy	James H. Waterman
Reuben Harlow	Thomas E. Waterman
George H. Hermann	Dura T. Weston

These men were paroled soon after; some of them reënlisted, joining other companies. During service the regiment suffered severely, one hundred and eighteen of its number dying from disease. It was mustered out at Lakeville on the 28th of August, 1865.

Fourth Regiment of Infantry (3 months' service)

COMPANY E

Thomas Taylor

COMPANY G

Daniel F. Wood   Isaac S. Clark

[1] These names were furnished by Mr. John Sullivan, Register of Probate.

FOURTH REGIMENT OF INFANTRY (9 MONTHS' SERVICE)[1]

COMPANY C

Seneca Thomas, capt.
Daniel F. Wood, 1st lieut.
Sargeant S. Sweet, sergt.
Frederick E. Wood, sergt.
Orlando H. Shaw, sergt.
J. Horace Soule, sergt.
Davis S. Weston, sergt.
Erastus E. Gay, corp.
Sylvanus Mendall, corp.
Dennis Shaw, corp.
Isaac E. Macomber, corp.
David A. Tucker, corp.
George W. Barrows, corp.
Francis S. Thomas, corp.
W. W. Atwood, musician
J. M. Jenney, musician
Asa B. Adams
Andrew Alden
Isaac Alger
Miron E. Alger
Elisha Benson
Earle E. Bennett
Grover Bennett
Sylvanus Bisbee
William B. Bart
Augustus N. J. Buchel
David H. Burgess
Daniel Handy
Reuben Harlow
Reuben A. Harlow
Levi Hathaway
Conrad J. Herman
George H. Herman
Charles H. Holmes
William N. Keith
William Mitchell
Harvey C. Pratt
Cornelius Redding
Morton Robbins
Andrew P. Rogers
William H. Rogers
Howard E. Shaw
Henry L. Shaw
Joseph B. Shaw
Ephraim Simmons
Stillman S. Smith
Rodney E. Southworth
Alfred O. Standish
John C. Sullivan
Henry A. Swift
Andrew E. Thomas
Joseph Thomas
Stephen F. Thomas
Winslow Thomas

---

[1] The following were killed in battle or died from wounds received: —

Corporal Francis S. Thomas, d. at Carrollton Hospital, March 9, 1863.
Miron E. Alger, d. at Brashear City, Louisiana. July 10, 1863.
David H. Burgess, d. August 28, 1863.
Daniel Handy, d. at Centralia, Illinois, September 10, 1863.
Levi Hathaway, d. at Indianapolis, Indiana, August 20, 1863.
Henry L. Shaw, d. (from wounds received at Port Hudson) October, 1863.
Ephraim Simmons, d. at Brashear City, May 24, 1863.
Andrew E. Thomas, d. at Brashear City, June 27, 1863.
Joseph Thomas, d. at Port Hudson, Louisiana, August 1, 1863.
Stephen F. Thomas, d. at hospital in New Orleans, May 1, 1863.
Williams S. Eaton, Jr., d. (from wounds received at Port Hudson) at New Orleans, June 21, 1863.
Alva C. Tinkham, d. at Brashear City, July 15, 1863.

Edwin M. Cole
William A. Coombs
Richard Cox
Williams S. Eaton, Jr.
Thomas W. Finney
Asa M. Franklin
Jonathan L. Hall

Alva C. Tinkham
James H. Waterman
Thomas E. Waterman
Dura Weston, Jr.
Charles M. Wilbur
Edward W. Wood
Jacob Wood

NINTH REGIMENT

The Ninth Regiment was mustered in on June 11, 1861. In the Peninsular Campaign of 1862 it was part of the Second Brigade in the Army of the Potomac.

NINTH REGIMENT OF INFANTRY (3 YEARS' SERVICE)
Thomas B. Burt

ELEVENTH REGIMENT

The Eleventh Regiment was the third in the state to be mustered in for three years' service. It was ordered to Fort Warren, and left for the front on the 29th of June, 1861, its destination being Washington. As it passed through Baltimore, the regiment was ordered to load with ball cartridges, remembering the reception which the Sixth[1] had met the April before. However, its passage through the city was without molestation, and it reached Washington on July 3, where it remained ten days, marching on the 14th to Alexandria, where, with the Massachusetts Fifth and others, it formed the First Brigade, Third Division, McDowell's army, under Colonel Franklin, and on the 21st took part in the battle at the first Bull Run engagement. It suffered severely in this disastrous battle, sustaining a loss of eighty-eight in killed, wounded, or missing.

Later, it joined General Hooker's Brigade, taking part in the siege before Yorktown (April 12), and was one of the first to engage in the battle at Williamsburg. In this engagement it sustained a loss of sixty-seven men, and for gallant conduct received a new standard from Governor Andrew. Although

---

[1] Lossing, *Field-Book of the Civil War*, vol. i. p. 413; Comte de Paris, *Civil War in America*, vol. 1, Book II, chap. 4.

not taking part at Fair Oaks, it did skirmish duty at Oak Grove, with a loss of eighteen, and took part in the reconnoissance and skirmish at Malvern Hill. On August 27, as it was leaving Catlett's Station, it came under fire of the enemy; and on the 29th it was engaged in the second battle of Bull Run. In this terrific fight the loss was very severe; the regiment had been so depleted that there were but two hundred and eighty-three men taken into action, and within twenty minutes, one hundred and twelve were either killed, wounded, or missing.

On May 2, 1863, it reported to General Hancock and was directed to reconnoitre, and at once engaged in repulsing the enemy at Chancellorsville, receiving the thanks of the general for gallantry. Here it lost seventy-nine in killed, wounded, and missing. It arrived on the night of July 1 for the battle of Gettysburg. In the terrible struggle of July 2 this regiment again lost more than half of the number taken into action, a total of one hundred and twenty-nine. It was in the Mine Run campaign (November), and suffered a loss of twenty-nine men. In the battle of the Wilderness it lost seventy-five, and at Spottsylvania, forty-three. It took part in the various skirmishes at Cold Harbor, and on the 12th of June, the term of enlistment having expired, the regiment returned to Massachusetts. Eight of the officers and three hundred and thirty-six of the men reënlisted, forming a battalion of five companies under the original name; these were in active service until the close of the war.

ELEVENTH REGIMENT OF INFANTRY (3 YEARS' SERVICE)

COMPANY B

Albert Dubois

COMPANY C

Jackson Donahue

COMPANY E

Robert King   James Thompson

John Pilkerton

COMPANY G

John Foley   Robert J. Jennings

COMPANY K

John Cunningham   John Flanery

TWELFTH REGIMENT

The Twelfth, or Webster Regiment, took its name from its colonel, Fletcher Webster. It left Fort Warren on July 23, 1861, and was attached to Abercrombie's Brigade under General Banks; then became a part of General Pope's Army of Virginia, and later was under McClellan and Hooker. At the battle of Manassas it met with the heavy loss of one hundred and thirty-eight. At Antietam, for four hours, a terrible conflict took place, in which, of the three hundred and forty taken into action, only thirty-four accompanied the colors to the rear. In the march south McClellan was succeeded by Burnside. In the battle of Fredericksburg the regiment suffered severely, as well as at Gettysburg, and later in the Wilderness.

TWELFTH REGIMENT OF INFANTRY (3 YEARS' SERVICE)

COMPANY A

C. G. Tinkham, 1st sergt.[1]   Andrew B. Morton

SIXTEENTH REGIMENT

The Sixteenth Regiment left Boston August 17, 1861, and joined the Army of the Potomac, Grover's Brigade, Hooker's Division, Heintzelman's Corps, with the First and Eleventh.

The first test of valor was in a reconnoissance at Gosport Navy Yard. At Oak Grove, Malvern Hill, and Centreville it did valiant duty, engaging in various campaigns and marches during the rest of the year. At Gettysburg it lost one third of the men taken into action. It took part at Chancellorsville, Spottsylvania, and Petersburg, and after various movements in skirmishing and fortifying weak places, it was mustered out July 27, 1864.

[1] Died October 1, 1862, from wounds received at Antietam.

SIXTEENTH REGIMENT OF INFANTRY (3 YEARS' SERVICE)

COMPANY D
Benjamin McLaughlin

COMPANY I
Thomas Murphy

EIGHTEENTH REGIMENT

More Middleboro men served in this regiment than in any other. It joined the First Brigade, Porter's Division, and was a part of the Army of the Potomac. At the siege of Yorktown it was on picket duty, but was in no general engagement. After the evacuation it went to Hanover Court House, assisted in burying the dead, and on the 29th of May returned to the camp at Gaines's Mills. After this, it was in the reconnoissance at the Chickahominy, and took an important part in the second battle of Bull Run, where Company D was detailed to support Burdan's sharpshooters. Captain Thomas was in command of the regiment, and under him it won high praise for gallantry. It lost most severely, — forty killed, one hundred and one wounded, and twenty-eight missing. The morning this battle commenced, Company D was cut off from the Seven Days' Fight, and was obliged to fall back at White House Landing. During the battle of Antietam it supported the battery on the west side of the creek, and was afterwards sent to relieve Burnside. At this battle word came that Burnside was out of ammunition, and everything had been taken to reenforce different parts of the army. Mr. Howes, a member of this company, was close by McClellan and General Porter when McClellan said, "What have you in reserve, Porter?" Porter answered, "I have the Eighteenth Massachusetts Regiment, but that regiment is a brigade." "Would to God," said McClellan, "it was a division; send it to relieve Burnside." It was in the fight from four o'clock in the afternoon until morning, and the next day was engaged in burying the dead slain in this battle. It was in the skirmish at Shepherdstown, which was a short but sharp fight, meeting with a loss of three killed, eleven wounded, and one missing. After various experiences it arrived opposite Fredericksburg. In this battle Company D was in two charges which Burnside ordered, and was in the fight for three days. The loss to the regiment was thirteen killed and one hundred and twenty-one wounded. So severe was this fight that every member of the color guard was wounded. These companies took an important part at the battle of Chancellorsville, were active through the whole of General Grant's campaign, and under fire in several battles. They were in the battle of Gettysburg, but did not suffer severely; they occupied a position near Little Round Top; at another time they supported the heavy artillery; on the first day's fight they were on the extreme left; the first night they lay back in the woods, and the next morning started farther on toward the left of the line down a ravine. Several men in this company were wounded. The regiment was regarded as one of the best in the service, and was held as a reserve force for emergencies. It was at Laurel Hill and near Spottsylvania, in an engagement not far from Pamunkey River, and was in the fearful battles before Petersburg until the explosion of the mine. Major Weston, who had been promoted from captain to major, was in command of the regiment the latter part of the service.

The term of enlistment of the men in Middleboro companies expired just before the battle of Petersburg, when some twenty-four of them reënlisted in the Thirty-second Regiment, and were in most of the battles with the Army of the Potomac until the final surrender of General Lee and the close of the war.

Eighteenth Regiment of Infantry (3 years' service)

S. Thomas, lieut.-col.
Thomas Weston, major
Charles F. Edson, capt.
R. H. Holmes, sergt.-major
C. M. Vaughan, drum major
R. F. Barrows, musician

COMPANY B
George F. Atwood, sergt.

COMPANY C[1]

Eli Atwood, sergt.
John S. Atwood, corp.
George H. Swift, corp.
Frederick E. Atwood
William M. Atwood
Francis B. Cushman
Josiah W. Dean
William M. Dexter
Isaac Harlow
Simeon Harlow
John K. Maxim
Charles A. Paul

John S. Raymond
Marcus M. Raymond
Martin V. Raymond
Thomas F. Shaw
Earl T. Smith
Watson N. Smith
Adoniram Thomas
Arad Thomas, Jr.
Nelson Thomas
Edwin J. Wrightinton
George W. Paul

COMPANY D[2]

Solomon F. Beals, sergt.
William H. Carle, sergt.

Edgar Harrison, sergt.
John T. Haskell, sergt.

---

[1] COMPANY C

Corporal George H. Swift, d. in 1863 from wounds received at Chancellorsville.
Frederick E. Atwood, killed in battle, August 26, 1862.
William M. Atwood, killed at Bull Run, August 30, 1862.
Francis B. Cushman, d. May 13, 1862.
Isaac Harlow, d. in camp, March 1, 1862.
John K. Maxim, d. in hospital, January 27, 1865.
Charles A. Paul, d. May 31, 1862.
Martin V. Raymond, killed at Bull Run, August 30, 1862.
Adoniram Thomas, d. from wounds received at Bull Run, September 29, 1862.

[2] COMPANY D

Corporal Darius B. Clark, killed at Fredericksburg, December 13, 1862.
Corporal Henry M. Warren, d. December 20, 1862, from wounds received at Fredericksburg.
Peleg F. Benson, d. November 17, 1862.
William H. Brightman, d. in Libby Prison, September 28, 1862.
Cyrus Hall, d. in hospital at Washington, October 19, 1862.
Charles E. Hunt, killed at Cold Harbor, June 1, 1864.
Samuel Mellen, d. at Hall's Hill, January 10, 1862.
Cyrus Perkins, d. January 1, 1863.
Morrell Perkins, d. December 20, 1862, from wounds received at Fredericksburg.
James C. Record, d. in hospital at Alexandria, November 25, 1864.
Samuel M. Ryder, d. December, 1862, from wounds received at Fredericksburg.
James H. Wade, d. in hospital at Philadelphia, August 7, 1862.
Charles W. Wilmarth, d. in Andersonville Prison, July 18, 1864.

George N. Johnson, sergt.
George W. Jones, sergt.
John W. King, Jr., sergt.
George B. Thomas, sergt.
Charles I. Brown, corp.
Darius B. Clark, corp.
Nehemiah D. Davis, corp.
Charles A. Howes, corp.
James W. King, corp.
Albert H. Pratt, corp.
William B. Shaw, corp.
Charles H. Smith, corp.
Harrison O. Thomas, corp.
Henry M. Warren, corp.

MUSICIAN

James S. Shaw

WAGONER

Erastus M. Lincoln

PRIVATES

Daniel W. Atwood
John S. Baker
Peleg F. Benson
William Benson
William H. Brightman
Phineas Burt
Ezra S. Clark
Ezra S. Chase
Charles A. Churchill
Meletiah R. Clark
James E. Cushman
Timothy M. Davis
Ichabod S. Dean
Lysander W. Field
George L. Finney
Gilmore Fish
Benjamin Gammons
James Gammons
Bernard Glancy
Edward P. Gore
Cyrus Hall
Theodore P. Holmes
Charles E. Hunt
Ephraim A. Hunt
Henry E. Johnson
Ira O. Littlejohn
Henry H. P. Lovell
William H. Marshall
James E. McMann
Charles C. Mellen
Samuel Mellen
John R. Merrick
Emerson P. Morse
Henry S. Murray
Robert Parris
Francis J. Peirce
Cyrus Perkins
Edwin Peirce
Morrell Perkins
Nathan A. Perkins
Thompson Perkins
Thomas B. Pratt
James H. Ramsdell
Christopher C. Reading
Milton Reed
James C. Record
Samuel M. Ryder
Stephen C. Ryder
Albert Shaw
Charles D. Shaw
Henry Shaw
Charles H. Smith
Cornelius Sullivan
Elbron F. Taylor
Benjamin L. Thompson
William F. Thompson

Charles T. Tillson
Charles Tinkham
George B. Tinkham
Charles R. Tripp
James H. Wade
Calvin B. Ward

Henry F. Whitcomb
William R. Whitcomb
Charles W. Wilmarth
William T. Withington
John Young

COMPANY E

Orien E. Caswell
William H. Dunham
Charles L. Morse
Levin S. Morse
Hercules Smith

Marcus Soule
Erastus Wallen
William Walley
Thomas P. Weatherby

COMPANY F

Albert F. Mellen

John T. Whitcomb

COMPANY H [1]

Marcus Bumpus

Cyrus White

COMPANY I [2]

Preston Soule, sergt.

Thomas P. Young,
unassigned recruit

NINETEENTH REGIMENT

This regiment was sent August 28, 1861, for three years' service.

MUSICIAN IN REGIMENTAL BAND
Charles H. Gibbs

TWENTIETH REGIMENT

Early in July, 1861, this regiment was sent to the front. Many of the men were captured; fifty died in Confederate prisons. It has an unusual record for the number of general

---

[1] COMPANY H
Cyrus White, d. November 19, 1862.

[2] COMPANY I
Sergeant Preston Soule, d. May 14, 1862.

officers which it gave to the service; eleven became brigadier-generals.

TWENTIETH REGIMENT OF INFANTRY (3 YEARS' SERVICE)

Henry H. Mathewson, corp.

TWENTY-SECOND REGIMENT

This regiment was raised and first commanded by Hon. Henry Wilson, the senator from Massachusetts. Company C was mustered in in September, 1861. After reaching Washington, it joined Martindale's Brigade of Fitz-John Porter's Division with the Eighteenth.

TWENTY-SECOND REGIMENT OF INFANTRY (3 YEARS' SERVICE)

COMPANY C

Alexis C. Dean, corp.	Peter Fagan
Vanzandt E. Smith, corp.	Joseph E. Tinkham
Charles W. Clark	

TWENTY-THIRD REGIMENT

This regiment, mustered in December 5, was part of the First Brigade with the Twenty-fourth under General Foster and later under Burnside, and took an active part with other Massachusetts regiments. It suffered loss at Roanoke Island in February, 1862, but pursued the Confederates through a swamp which had been considered impenetrable. In April this regiment formed part of the First Brigade, First Division, doing picket duty at Batchelder's Creek, and engaging in battle at Newbern and at Goldsboro. At Arrowfield Church it was called into more active service, and met with loss at Drewry's Bluff and at Cold Harbor. Yellow fever decimated the ranks while in camp, and after serving at Kinston it was sent back to Newbern, and on June 5 was mustered out.

TWENTY-THIRD REGIMENT OF INFANTRY (3 YEARS' SERVICE)

COMPANY D

Leonard B. Haskins	Benjamin O. Tillson

MIDDLEBORO IN THE WAR OF THE REBELLION

COMPANY E

Warren Chubbuck Marcus F. Maxim
Elbridge A. Maxim [1]

TWENTY-FOURTH REGIMENT

The Twenty-fourth, known as the New England Guards, joined the First Brigade.

COMPANY D
Sergeant George N. Gammon [2]

TWENTY-EIGHTH REGIMENT

This regiment was mustered in in December, 1862, for three years' service.

COMPANY B
John Bergen

THIRTIETH REGIMENT (3 YEARS' SERVICE)

This was one of the regiments raised by General Butler, first known as the Eastern Bay State.

COMPANY F
John Grady

THIRTY-SECOND REGIMENT

This was the outgrowth of the First Battalion of Infantry at Fort Warren. In November, 1862, it went south and joined the brigade with the Ninth. After guard duty and loss from fever, it moved toward Manassas, where, as part of the Army of the Potomac, it was in the second battle of Bull Run. It took part in the battles of Fredericksburg, Chancellorsville, Gettysburg, the Wilderness, Spottsylvania, Cold Harbor, Preble's Farm, and Hatcher's Run, besides many skirmishes and encounters; it marched to Sheridan's assistance near Appomattox Court House, and later was in the grand review at Washington. During its three years of service this regiment engaged

---

[1] Died July 25, 1864.   [2] Died March 8, 1862.

in thirty battles. Its history has been so often told that it need not be repeated here.

THIRTY-SECOND REGIMENT OF INFANTRY (3 YEARS' SERVICE)

COMPANY A

Charles H. Smith, corp.   Thomas Morton, Jr.

COMPANY B

Nehemiah D. Davis, sergt.

COMPANY C

Orrin E. Caswell   Meletiah R. Clark
Ezra S. Chase

COMPANY D

Charles I. Brown, corp.   George L. Finney
Josiah W. Dean

COMPANY E

Jennison Morse   Joseph Westgate
Edward S. Westgate   William Westgate
Ezra T. Westgate [1]

COMPANY H

Francis J. Peirce

COMPANY I

James C. Record

COMPANY K

Marcus Soule   William F. Thompson
Elbron F. Taylor

COMPANY L

Henry F. Whitcomb

UNASSIGNED RECRUITS

John T. Haskell, sergt.   George B. Thomas, corp.
Solomon F. Beals, sergt.   Charles W. Wilmarth

[1] Killed at Cold Harbor, June 4, 1864.

Fortieth Regiment

The Fortieth Regiment was stationed for some time in Virginia. It was at Alexandria, at Williamsburg, at White House Landing, and at Baltimore Cross Roads, where it had a lively skirmish, in which this regiment won all the credit of the attack. On the 7th of August, 1863, the regiment embarked for Charleston Harbor, and served in the trenches at Fort Wagner until that stronghold was evacuated by the Confederates. In February it took possession of Jacksonville without opposition, and after some skirmishing captured Gainesville, where there was a large quantity of stores, and gained distinction by repelling a force three times its own number, killing and wounding several without any loss to itself. Olustee Station was the scene of a severe fight of two or three hours. Retreating to Jacksonville, it was stationed at the Three Mile Run, then ordered back to Virginia. Upon joining the Army of the Potomac, it was in the expedition against Richmond and Petersburg, and was engaged in the battle of Arrowfield Church. In the advance on Richmond this regiment led the right wing, and was skirmishing for most of the first day's fight. At Drewry's Bluff it suffered a loss of ten killed, forty-two wounded, and twenty-two missing. The killed and wounded were left in the hands of the Confederates. At the battle of Cold Harbor the regiment suffered severely, and on the 27th of August, so great had been the loss by exposure, sickness, and fire of the enemy that but two officers and forty-five enlisted men in the whole regiment were able to report for duty. They were sent to Bermuda Landing for rest, where they remained until the sick and wounded had recovered.

In the engagement soon after at Fort Harrison, Lieutenant J. Arthur Fitch of Middleboro was killed. On March 6, 1865, the regiment performed provost-guard duty for the city of Fredericksburg, while others who were on this expedition destroyed the railroad at Hamilton Crossing. After this the regiment was before Petersburg, where it remained until its fall and the evacuation of Richmond. Its last service was holding the lines near Signal Hill while the rest of the army were operating upon the left of the city.

FORTIETH REGIMENT OF INFANTRY (3 YEARS' SERVICE) [1]

James W. Bryant, capt.
Oreb F. Mitchell, capt.
J. Arthur Fitch, lieut.
Southworth Loring, lieut.
Edwin P. Holmes

COMPANY A

William E. White, sergt.
Henry A. Eaton
J. Addison Shaw, Jr.

COMPANY E

W. H. Harlow, sergt.
H. L. McFarlin, sergt.
A. M. Perkins, sergt.
William E. Bryant, corp.
F. O. Burgess, corp.
Albert F. Finney, corp.
Francis M. Hodges, corp.
Sidney B. Wilbur, corp.
Benjamin W. Bump
James Carter
Oramel H. Churchill
Ansel A. Cobb
Robert V. Cole
James C. Fessenden
Hazen K. Godfrey
Harrison Haskins
George Hinckley
Edward Jennings
Henry F. Maxim
Benjamin S. McLaughlin
Silas H. Murdock
Darius M. Nichols
John J. Perkins
Albert G. Pratt
John Scanlin
William N. Shaw
Christopher C. Smith
Timothy J. Sullivan
Charles G. Tinkham
Thomas E. Wilmot
Asaph Writington

FIFTY-EIGHTH REGIMENT

This, called Third Veteran Regiment, was ordered to the

---

[1] Lieutenant J. Arthur Fitch, killed at Fort Harrison, September 30, 1864.
Corporal Francis M. Hodges, d. at Beaufort, October 27, 1863.
Corporal Sidney B. Wilbur, d. June 2, 1864, from wounds received at Cold Harbor.
Oramel H. Churchill, d. September 11, 1863.
George Hinckley, d. February 24, 1863, from wounds received at Olustee.
Edward Jennings, died.
Timothy J. Sullivan, d. August 22, 1864, from wounds received at Petersburg.

front in April, 1864, was assigned to the First Brigade, and was engaged in the battles at Chancellorsville, Cold Harbor, Petersburg, "Battle of the Crater," and at Poplar Spring Church. It took part in the grand review at Washington, May 23, 1865, and on July 26 was mustered out.

FIFTY-EIGHTH REGIMENT OF INFANTRY

COMPANY B

David W. Deane, corp.   Richard Cox [1]

COMPANY C

John L. Cobb [2]

COMPANY E

David S. Pason

COMPANY K

Henry Fitsimons

FIFTY-NINTH REGIMENT

This regiment left the state earlier than the Fifty-eighth for three years' service.

COMPANY G

Benjamin Chamberlain [3]

CAVALRY REGIMENTS

Middleboro was represented in several regiments of cavalry: the First, mustered in during the autumn of 1861; the Third, which was organized from troops actually in the field (Mass. Forty-first), travelled fifteen thousand miles, and engaged in more than thirty battles; and the Fourth, which, not organized till 1864, was almost annihilated in the several battles in which it took part. In a company of unattached cavalry, several Middleboro men were enlisted, but it is impos-

---

[1] Killed June 3, 1864.   [2] Died August 12, 1864.
[3] Died December 10, 1864.

sible to trace in detail the varied and brave services of these regiments.

FIRST REGIMENT OF CAVALRY (3 YEARS' SERVICE)

COMPANY I

R. S. Capen, sergt. William A. Smith
Francis O. Harlow

COMPANY K

Thomas Doran Washington I. Caswell[1]
John E. Smith

THIRD REGIMENT OF CAVALRY (3 YEARS' SERVICE)

COMPANY H
George Cummings[2]

COMPANY L
T. P. Benthuysen, sergt.

COMPANY M
John Grant Charles F. Smith

READ'S COMPANY (SO CALLED)
James E. Nichols

FOURTH REGIMENT OF CAVALRY (3 YEARS' SERVICE)
Robert S. Capen, sergt.-maj.

COMPANY A
Horace S. Flagg

COMPANY B
Andrew P. Rogers, sergt.

COMPANY D

Albert Eddy, sergt.[3] Thomas S. Ellis
Jeremiah Callihan, corp.

---

[1] Died August 29, 1863.   [2] Died at New Orleans, July 28, 1864.   [3] Died.

COMPANY B, UNATTACHED CAVALRY (KNOWN AS BUTLER'S BODYGUARD)

James G. Nichols	Thomas P. Vanbenthuysen
Thomas Ellis	Sanford Weston
Louis Phinney	

During the war Middleboro furnished about four hundred and sixty-five men, thirteen of whom were commissioned officers, and had a surplus of twenty-one after filling its quota upon every call made by the President. The town expended, exclusive of state aid, $31,915.57. $6633 was also raised by private subscription, $7821 was raised by a club, and $5000 by persons liable to draft to procure substitutes, making the total amount raised by and in the town, $51,326.90. Of this amount there was repaid by the commonwealth for state aid which had been purchased, $36,962.40.

Great sacrifices for the defence of the Union were made by the men of Middleboro, and in no instance was there ever reported any lack of bravery or want of discretion on the part of the officers or privates who went out from our town. Not a few of

SOLDIERS' MONUMENT

the inhabitants enlisted in companies in other parts of the state.

SOLDIERS' MONUMENT

This monument, erected by the citizens of Middleboro to perpetuate the memory of her soldiers who fell in the War of the Rebellion, stands on the lawn in front of the town house. It is built of selected Quincy granite, nine feet at the base, rising to the height of forty feet and eleven inches. Action was first taken towards its erection by the E. W. Peirce Post 8 of the Grand Army of the Republic, and those who served in the quota raised by the town. It was completed at a cost of about five thousand dollars, and dedicated May 30, 1896, with appropriate exercises and an address by Ex-Governor John D. Long. The monument is a beautiful structure, and will stand for all time to perpetuate the lives, the valor, and the sacrifices of Middleboro men in the War of the Rebellion.[1]

[1] The town first acted upon matters relating to the war on the 6th of May, 1861, when it was voted to raise a company for three years, and to guarantee each man $26 a month while in service. At the same meeting it was voted to raise $5000 for war purposes, $2000 of which was to be expended in uniforming and equipping the company, and each recruit was to be paid $1.25 a day while drilling, not to exceed three days in a week for four weeks, and when the company was called into service, each volunteer was to receive a month's pay in advance. July 28, 1862, it was voted to pay a bounty of $125 to each volunteer to the number of 56 who should enlist for three years, to be credited to the quota of the town within twenty days.

The 25th of August it was voted to raise a company for nine months' service, and to pay each volunteer for that term a bounty of $150, when mustered in and credited to the quota of the town.

The 21st of September, 1863, the town voted that the selectmen should continue the payment of said aid to the families of soldiers who had been discharged for wounds or sickness the same as they had before received, this to be continued for six months, and to borrow money to pay the same.

CHAPTER XII

LOCAL MILITIA

ILITARY affairs of the towns in the old colony form a very important place in their history. Next to the church and the town meeting, more interest seems to have centred about the militia than any of the organizations of the times. Few persons qualified to serve presumed to neglect that duty, and the most important men were selected to fill the various offices. In the early history of these towns they occupied so important a position in the defence against the attacks from the Indians, and were so efficient an arm of the government in resisting the encroachment of the French against the English sovereignty in the New World, and later performed such heroic service in establishing the liberties of the country, that their power and influence were always felt in all public affairs.

The first account of a military drill was during the struggle of that small but brave band to maintain life on the barren lands of Plymouth. Early in 1622 rumors reached the pilgrims of hostile bands of Indians, and Canonicus, king of the Narragansetts, sent to Tisquantum, the pilgrims' interpreter, some new arrows tied with a rattlesnake's skin. Bradford, filling the skin with powder and bullets, sent it back, but as the messengers feared to carry it, it was passed along from one to another, finally returning to Bradford, having served its purpose of quelling Canonicus's revolt. Immediately, however, they began to fortify the little village, and Standish formed four companies of all those able to bear arms. The captain of each company in turn was to hold the command in his absence. His military skill was such that he realized fully the value of drill and training, and the men received special instruction in the tactics of the soldiers of the Old World, with which he was familiar. The early record is that each company took its place for the defence with a discharge of musketry, then accompanied the captains to their houses, where "again they graced them with their shot and so departed." In a note to Young's "Chronicles of the Pilgrims," we find this was the first general muster in New England, and the embryo of our present militia system. Bradford says:[1]—

"They agreed to inclose their dwelling with a good strong pale, and make flankers in convenient places, with gates to shute, which were every night locked, and a watch kept, and when neede required ther was also warding in ye day time. And ye company was by ye Captain and ye Govr advise, devided into 4 squadrons and every one had ther quarter apoynted unto them which they were to repaire upon any suddane alarme. And if ther should be any crie of fire a company were appointed for a gard, with muskets, whilst others quenchet ye same, to prevent Indian treachery. This was accomplished very cherfully and ye towne impayled round by ye beginning of March."

This little battalion of fifty strong was a garrison sufficient to defend the town, and with Standish's discipline and military tactics may well be called the first volunteer militia.

By the old militia laws the men were required to give six days'[2] duty each year. The companies chose their own captains. After the union of the two colonies the militia of each county was commanded by a lieutenant, and under him was a sergeant-major.[3]

In the Plymouth Laws of 1683[4] we find:—

"This Court doth order that Swansey and Middlebery shall chose some for Officers To lead theire Milletary Companies and Instruct them in Marshall disiplyne and that orders to each of those Townes to send such to the Court as they shall see Cause to choose."

[1] *History of the Plimoth Plantation*, p. 134.
[2] *Plymouth Colony Laws*, p. 36: "That the Inhabits of euery Towne wthin the Gouerment fitt & able to beare armes be trayned (at least) six tymes in the year." September 1, 1640.
[3] Palfrey's *History of New England*, vol. ii, p. 51.
[4] *Plymouth Colony Laws* p. 201.

The first organized regiment of Plymouth Colony militia was commanded by Major William Bradford of Plymouth. At this time there were not men enough in Middleboro capable of bearing arms to form a full company, only sufficient for an ensign's command, and Isaac Howland was then in charge, holding such commission from the governor at Plymouth.

One third of the company was required to be armed with pikes and the remainder with matchlock muskets, called snaphances. The pike had been substituted for the halberd, which at first was brought from England, it being found that the pike was as efficient a weapon and much less difficult to manufacture. In the matchlock musket the powder was placed in a pan similar to that in the flintlock, but exploded by a coal of fire or by a lighted string; the end of this string was placed in the powder by hand, or by a simple device behind the pan. The muskets used in hunting were fired by sparks communicated to the powder from a flint; they were not allowed in military drills, and were not used in war until after King Philip's time. The Indians would use no other, and they became very proficient in aiming and firing, which accounts for the large number of whites killed in King Philip's War. So cumbrous were the match and flintlock muskets of those times that they required as a support, when used, a forked stick about five feet in length, with an iron point at the other end, which was placed in the ground.

For fifty-eight years after the incorporation of Middleboro, there was but one company. In 1727 the population had so increased that this was divided into two, known as the First and Second Foot Companies. The town was divided into two precincts, and this division formed the basis for the companies. The increase in number of inhabitants caused another division to be made soon after, and again in 1754.

While Massachusetts remained a colony of England, all commissions in the militia expired at the death of the reigning sovereign, and were renewed on the accession to the throne of the next monarch.

Governor Hinckley, in 1689, said that besides the commissioned officers there were in the train band five hundred and ninety able, effective men of the colony, and in the town of Middleboro there were forty-four, but their names are not given.[1]

From 1754 until the commencement of the Revolution, there were four companies in Middleboro, and their assembly and parade were matters of considerable importance. These companies and their officers at that time exerted a strong political influence, and to be a captain was regarded as the introduction to any public office. John Adams said in a letter, "The American States have owed their existence to the militia for more than two hundred years. Neither school nor town meetings have been more essential to the formation and character of the nation than the militia." In 1741 the First Cadet Corps grew from the state militia, and until 1777 attended the provincial governor upon all state occasions.

The colonial law was that all from sixteen to sixty should serve in the local militia; the only men exempt were "timorous persons." By act of the Continental Congress, July 18, 1775, it was provided that "all able bodied, effective men between sixteen and fifty in each colony should form themselves into regular companies of militia." It was also suggested that one fourth of these should be "minute men."[2] The whole state was organized under this provision of law into companies called the "train band."[3] Citizens from the age of fifty to sixty-five were included under the "alarm list." These two bodies of train band and alarm list were required to be ready for service upon the call of the governor. All former officers in the militia under sixty-five years of age were included in this alarm list. The equipment required was: a good firearm with steel or iron ramrod and worm, priming-wire and brush, a bayonet fitted to the gun, a cartridge-box holding at least fifteen rounds of ammunition, six flints, one pound of powder, forty leaden bullets, a haversack, blanket, and a canteen which would hold one

---

[1] Hinckley Papers, *Mass. Hist. Coll.* vol. v, p. 11, 4th series.
[2] See chapter on Middleboro in the Revolution.
[3] This term comes from the famous train bands of Cromwell's army.

quart. In 1781, after the stirring events of the Revolution, the local militia of Massachusetts was reorganized. There were in this enrollment, in Middleboro, in 1782, 566 persons liable to perform this duty, of whom 421 were in the train bands and 145 in the alarm list. (There were probably over one hundred more, but the list of one company is lost.) In 1786 a new uniform of white faced with scarlet was adopted for the state.

So important was the military organization of the town that in the year 1717 a training-green was provided near the grounds of the First Church, and for more than a century the Training Day was one of the holidays, and the citizens generally came from all parts of the town to witness the drilling and manœuvring of these companies. This parade ground was given to the town by James Soule, who conveyed about two acres of this land "to the proper use, benefit and behoof of the military company of Middleboro forever successively."[1] With the decline of the military spirit before the middle of the last century, the parades were held in other parts of the town, and were not as largely attended as formerly. One of them was at Muttock, in the field bordering upon the pond and Nemasket Street, adjoining the shovel shop; another, in Warrentown, on grounds opposite the residence of the late James Bump, and another at the Rock.

After the close of the War of 1812 more attention seems to have been paid to the uniform and equipments of the local militia. Each company usually had a fife, drums, and sometimes clarinets and bugles. It consisted of commissioned officers, petty officers, musicians, privates, with some six or more in peculiar uniforms, called pioneers, who preceded the musicians as the company marched through the streets. At the time of their parade, it was often the amusement of the boys and spectators to erect barricades along the highways or at the gates through which the company was supposed to pass from different parts of the town, and then witness with delight the masterly exertions of the pioneers in clearing a way for the troops to enter the training-grounds for their military evolutions.

[1] See chapter containing account of The Green.

One of the most interesting days of the year was the annual muster of the regiment or brigade, which sometimes was held on the level tract of land in Lakeville, not far from the schoolhouse in the Upper Four Corners, and usually lasted one or two days. These annual musters drew together many from the surrounding towns, for the parades, drills, and reviews attracted much attention, and the music from the bands was always entertaining. The grounds were carefully guarded by sentries, and it was impossible to come within the military lines without a pass from the commanding officer. It required not a little tact and many men to keep mischievous intruders from the camp grounds. Upon the outskirts were booths for refreshments and various shows in tents, which never failed to interest the assembled multitude. Confectionery was then rare, and was sold in small quantities at large prices, but sugar gingerbread was the staple article, and was eagerly purchased.

The following is a bill of the expense at "the Militia Muster," 1783, of Colonel John Nelson: —

20½ gallons rum	at 2s 8d per gallon	2—14—8
29 Dinners	at 1s 8d each	2—18—4
23 Bottles Wine	at 2s 5d "	2—15—7
12 Bowls of Punch	at 3s 4d "	2— 3—4
17 Mugs of Punch	at 1s 6d "	1— 5—6
½ Bowl of Punch		0— 0—9
		11—8—3

The earliest record of the first military company of Middleboro,[1] taken January 19, 1710-11, is as follows:

Captain, Jacob Tomson.	Corp. Thomas Darling
Sergt. Jeremiah Thomas	Samuel Pratt, drummer
" Samuel Eddy	James Soule
" Seth Howland	Abiel Wood
" Samuel Barrows	John Miller
Corp. Samuel Eaton	John Soul
" John Tinckom	Elmer Bennet
" John Alden	

[1] From *Eddy Note-Book.*

Josiah Connant
Henery Wood
Joseph Bumpus
Ebenezer Tinkham, Jr.
Ephraim Wood
Jeremiah Tinkcom
Elisha Vaughan
Jonathan Morse
John Raymond
Jonathan Thomas
John Barden
Stephen Barden
Abraham Barden
Joseph Barden
Samuel Warren
James Bumpus
Jabez Vaughan
John Tomson
William Hascol
Samuel Wood
George Vaughan
William Reed
Ebenezer Fuller
Isaac Howland
Jonathan Smith
James Smith
Ephraim Tomson
William Thomas
Benjamin Barden
Samuel Cob
Aaron Simmons
William Barden
Samuel Sampson
Ebenezer Hall
Josiah Hascol
Ebenezer Redding
Isaac Tinkcom
Ebenezer Vaughan
Shubael Tomson
John Wood
Nathaniel Thomas
Nathan Howland
Jonathan Cob
Elnathan Wood
Thomas Raymond
Nathaniel Southworth
Samuel Tinkcom
David Wood
John Fuller
Josiah Thomas
Nathaniel Barden
James Raymond
Thomas Tomson, Sr.
Rodolphus Elms
Thomas Tomson, Jr.
John Cob
Isaac Renolds
Ebenezer Cob
Joseph Thomas
Joseph Vaughan
Jeremiah Thomas, Jr.
John Wood
Experience Bent
Benjamin Eddy
Edward Southworth
Joseph Bennett
Shubael Tinkham
Edward Hacket
Jonathan Fuller
John Vaughan
Joseph Cob
Peter Tomson
Isaac Billington
Abiel Wood, Jr.

The captains of this First Company [1] were: —

Jacob Tompson, —— to 1716.
Joseph Vaughan, March, 1716, to ——.
Peter Bennett.

[1] These lists are from the *History of Plymouth County*.

Ebenezer Sproutt, 1762 to 177-.
Nathaniel Wood,[1] 1776 to July 1, 1781.
William Shaw, July 1, 1781, to ——.

The captains of the Second Company were: —

Ichabod Southworth, 1727 to 17—.
Nathaniel Southworth, 17— to 17—.
Ebenezer Morton, 17— to 1754.
Nathaniel Smith, July 23, 1754, to 1762.
Gideon Southworth, October 27, 1762, to 1772.
Robert Sproat, June 12, 1772, to 1774.
Nathaniel Smith, October 10, 1774, to September 19, 1775.
Nehemiah Allen, May 9, 1776, to 1778.
John Barrows, April 8, 1778, to 1780.
Abner Bourne, June 2, 1780, to July 1, 1781.
Ezra Harlow, July 1, 1781, to 1790.
George Vaughan, April 12, 1790, to 1793.
Peter Hoar, June 6, 1793, to January 4, 1797.
Jabez Thomas, January 25, 1797, to 1799.
John Morton, May 7, 1799, to 1802.
Sylvanus Tillson, May 4, 1802, to 1805.
Nathaniel Cole, May 7, 1805, to 1809.
Abner Barrows, Jr., July 27, 1809, to 1811.
Ephraim Ward, March 18, 1811, to 1814.
Peter H. Peirce, February 18, 1814, to 1816.
Orrin Tinkham, September 10, 1816, to 1817.
Enoch Haskins, April 14, 1817, to February 25, 1818.

This company was disbanded by order of the governor, February 25, 1818.

The captains of the Third Company were: —

Joseph Tinkham, 175- to 17—.
William Tupper, 1776 to July 1, 1781.
Nathaniel Wilder, July 1, 1781, to 17—.
Nathaniel Wilder, Jr., April 6, 1802, to 1817.

The captains of the Fourth Company [2] were: —

Joseph Leonard, 17— to ——.
William Canedy, 177- to September 19, 1775.

[1] At the breaking out of the Revolution the four companies of local militia were reorganized, and Nathaniel Wood was the commander of the first company to respond to the Lexington alarm.

[2] The men in this company were from the part of the town now Lakeville.

Job Peirce, May 9, 1776, to 1778.
Henry Peirce, 1778 to 1787.
James Peirce, July 17, 1787, to 179–.
Abanoam Hinds, August 15, 1796, to 1802.
Elkanah Peirce, May 4, 1802, to 1806.
Elisha Briggs, September 29, 1806, to 1811.
Sylvanus Parris, March 20, 1811, to 1815.
Ethan Peirce, June 6, 1815, to 182–.
Apollos Reed, 182– to 1827.
John Strobridge, May 19, 1827, to 1829.
Samuel Hoar, June 6, 1829, to 1831.
Silas P. Ashley, August 15, 1831, to 18—.

The captain of the Fifth Company was:—

Perez Churchill, 1776 to July 1, 1781.

The captains of the Sixth Company were:—

James Shaw, July 1, 1781, to 1784.
John Miller, June 3, 1784.

The captains of the Seventh Company were:—

Amos Washburn, 177– to 1781.
Abraham Shaw, July 1, 1781, to 1787.
John Smith, July 17, 1787, to 1794.
Ebenezer Briggs, Jr., August 4, 1794, to 1801.
Elias Sampson, August 31, 1801, to 1807.
Daniel Smith, May 5, 1807, to 1810.
Ebenezer Pickens, September 21, 1810, to 1814.
David Sherman, May 2, 1814, to 1820.
Abiel M. Sampson, October 17, 1820, to 1827.
Richard B. Foster, April 28, 1827, to 1828.
Horatio G. Clark, July 19, 1828, to January 28, 1829.
James Pickens, May 29, 1829, to May 30, 1830.

The captain of the Eighth Company was:—

David Vaughan, July 1, 1781.

There was a company of cavalry, consisting of men from Middleboro, Rochester, and Wareham. The captains of this company were:—

William Bourne, May 22, 1797, to September 12, 1803.
Thomas Bennet, 1804 to April 10, 1807.

Seth Southworth, August 2, 1813, to 1815.
Nehemiah Leonard, June 3, 1818, to 1823.

In 1818 the second company of militia was disbanded, and two companies of light infantry were organized in Middleboro, the captains of which were: —

Isaac Stevens, April 3, 1818, to 1823.
Sylvanus Barrows, September 9, 1823, to 1827.
Job Peirce, April 24, 1827, to 1829.
Rufus Alden, June 8, 1829, to 1830.
Josiah Tinkham, April 28, 1830, to 1833.
Abiel Wood, May 7, 1833, to 1835.
Morton Freeman, April 2, 1835, to 1840.
Jacob T. Barrows, April 30, 1841, to 1842.
Amasa J. Thompson, May 12, 1842, to 1844.
Daniel Atwood, 1844 to July 10, 1844.
Andrew J. Pickens, August 3, 1844, to 1846.
Dexter Phillips, March 20, 1846, to 1847.
Arad Bryant, February 20, 1847, to 1849.
Albert Thomas, May 20, 1849, to 1851.
Joseph Sampson, Jr., 1851 to November 28, 1851.

The other company of light infantry was formed a little later, of which the following persons were captains: —

Jonathan Cobb, June 16, 1818, to 1824.
Darius Miller, May 19, 1824, to September 12, 1828.
Jacob Thomas, —— to 1830.
Lothrop S. Thomas, April 24, 1830, to 1834.
Levi Morse, September 27, 1834, to 1837.
Sylvester F. Cobb, September 20, 1837, to 1842.
Ichabod F. Atwood, July 26, 1842, to 1847.
George Ward, March 12, 1847, to May 4, 1850.
Stephen Thomas, May 29, 1850, to April 3, 1852.
Lothrop Thomas, May 26, 1852, to 1853.
Thomas Weston, July 6, 1853, to July 12, 1856.
Robert M. Thomas, August 2, 1856, to August 6, 1857.
Sylvanus Barrows, September 5, 1857, to September 25, 1858.

This company was disbanded September 25, 1858.

The captains of the train bands and alarm lists and the numbers in each company were as follows: —

FIRST COMPANY

William Shaw, Train Band, 68.
—— ——, Alarm List, 13.

SECOND COMPANY

Ezra Harlow, Train Band, 68.
Abner Bourne, Alarm List, 39.

THIRD COMPANY

Nathaniel Wilder, Train Band, 71.
Lemuel Wood, Alarm List, 32.

FOURTH COMPANY

Henry Peirce, Train Band, 45.
—— ——, Alarm List, 8.

SIXTH COMPANY

James Shaw, Train Band, 66.
—— ——, Alarm List, 17.

SEVENTH COMPANY

Abraham Shaw, Train Band, 53.
Amos Washburn, Alarm List, 20.

EIGHTH COMPANY

David Vaughan, Train Band, 50.
Josiah Carver, Alarm List, 16.

The following is a list of officers residing in Middleboro who attained in the service of the local militia a higher rank than that of captain from 1741 : —

GENERAL OFFICERS

Abiel Washburn, brigadier-general, September 4, 1816, to 1824.

Ephraim Ward, brigadier-general, January 27, 1825, to 1831.

Darius Miller, brigadier-general, July 20, 1831, to 1833.

Eliab Ward, brigadier-general, April 8, 1850, to 1855.

Field Officers

First Regiment of Infantry

Elkanah Leonard, major, 1741 to 1745.
Ebenezer Sproutt, major, 17— to 1776.
Benjamin Drew, Jr., February 14, 1835, to April 24, 1840.

Third Regiment of Light Infantry

Eliab Ward, colonel, July 10, 1844, to April 8, 1850.
Elnathan W. Wilbur, colonel, May 4, 1850, to 1853.
Stephen Thomas, colonel, March 12, 1853, to 1858.
Lothrop Thomas, lieutenant-colonel, August 23, 1834, to 1836.
Eliab Ward, lieutenant-colonel, September 15, 1843, to July 10, 1844.
Daniel Atwood, lieutenant-colonel, September, 1845, to 1850.
Ebenezer W. Peirce, lieutenant-colonel, April 3, 1852, to November 7, 1855.
Thomas Weston, lieutenant-colonel, July 12, 1856, to 1858.
Daniel Atwood, major, July 10, 1844, to 1845.
Joseph Sampson, Jr., major, 1845 to 1849.
Elnathan W. Wilbur, major, 1849 to May 4, 1850.
George Ward, major, May 4, 1850, to 1851.
Ebenezer W. Peirce, major, August 2, 1851, to April 3, 1852.
Stephen Thomas, major, April 3, 1852, to March 12, 1853.

Fourth Regiment of Infantry

Ebenezer Sproutt, colonel, February, 1776, to 1781.
John Nelson, colonel, July 1, 1781, to 1787.
Edward Sparrow, colonel, October 29, 1793, to April 1, 1796.
Abiel Washburn, colonel, July 22, 1800, to September 4, 1816.
Ephraim Ward, colonel, April 25, 1817, to January 27, 1825.
Benjamin P. Wood, colonel, September 7, 1826, to 1829.
Darius Miller, colonel, August 31, 1829, to July 20, 1831.
Thomas Weston, Jr., colonel, 1832 to 1834.
Edward G. Perkins, colonel, February 4, 1837, to 1839.
Nathan King, colonel, February 7, 1839, to April 14, 1840.
William Tupper, lieutenant-colonel, July 1, 1781, to 1784.
Edward Sparrow, lieutenant-colonel, July 17, 1787, to October 29, 1793.
Abiel Washburn, lieutenant-colonel, January 4, 1797, to July 22, 1800.

Ephraim Ward, lieutenant-colonel, 181– to April 25, 1817.
Peter H. Peirce, lieutenant-colonel, April 25, 1817, to 1823.
Benjamin P. Wood, lieutenant-colonel, October 10, 1823, to September 7, 1826.
Southworth Ellis, Jr., lieutenant-colonel, September 7, 1826, to 1829.
Thomas Weston, Jr., lieutenant-colonel, August 31, 1829, to 1832.
Oliver Eaton, lieutenant-colonel, 1832 to 1834.
Edward G. Perkins, lieutenant-colonel, May 1834, to February 4, 1837.
Nathan King, lieutenant-colonel, February 4, 1837, to February 8, 1839.
Peter Hoar, senior major, July 22, 1800, to 1807.
Jacob Cushman, senior major, November 27, 1807, to 1809.
Levi Peirce, senior major, 1812 to 1816.
John Nelson, major, May 9, 1776, to July 1, 1781.
Edward Sparrow, major, July 1, 1781, to July 17, 1787.
Abiel Washburn, major, May 1, 1794, to January 4, 1797.
Peter Hoar, major, January 4, 1797, to July 22, 1800.
Levi Peirce, major, June 8, 1809, to 1812.
Ephraim Ward, major, 1814 to 1816.
Peter H. Peirce, major, 1816 to April 25, 1817.
Branch Harlow, major, April 25, 1817, to 1823.
Philo Washburn, major, September 7, 1826, to 1828.
Darius Miller, major, September 12, 1828, to August 31, 1829.
Oliver Eaton, major, August 31, 1829, to 1832.
Isaac Fuller, major, February 8, 1839, to April 24, 1840.

BATTALION OF CAVALRY

William Bourne, major, September 12, 1803, to 1807.
Thomas Bennett, major, April 28, 1807, to November, 1811.
Harry Jackson, major, January 29, 1823, to death, in 1823.

BATTALION OF ARTILLERY

William Thomas, major, August 23, 1834, to 1836.

Since the middle of the last century there have been many changes in the militia law of the commonwealth and the interest in that service seems gradually to have declined, so that at the present time there is no military organization in town.

THE KITCHEN FIREPLACE

CHAPTER XIII

SOCIAL CUSTOMS OF THE EIGHTEENTH CENTURY

THE people of Middleboro, like all of the colonists, were taught to employ every moment of their time. Children knew the value of everything in the house; they knew how each article was made and its use. It was the natural outgrowth of their life that they should be thrifty and economical; they had come to a new country, where much, if not everything, had to be made by hand. With the wealth of primeval forest, it is not to be wondered at that many a farmer's boy worked long and hard to obtain a jack-knife, and then what marvels he could make! Daniel Webster said that these Yankee jack-knives were the direct forerunners of the cotton-gin and thousands of noble American inventions. We have spoken of the trenchers used in early times, cut out of wood; sleds also were of home manufacture, the runners made from saplings bent at the root. Most of the farm implements were of wood,[1] — ploughs, shovels, yokes for the oxen,

---

[1] "The importance of locating near a spring of never-failing water, instead of attempting to dig wells, is apparent when we consider that shovels and spades in those times were made of wood instead of iron; wooden shovels were used by the

cart-wheels, scythes, and flails. The making of these occupied the spare time of the men. No wonder the people developed skill as well as sturdy, independent characters. They were their own masters,[1] dependent on no one; their lives were a training for the test of independence which came in 1775.

The frames of the dwelling-houses and barns of this period were of oak timber hewn with broadaxes, the sills, posts, and beams being often from nine to ten inches in diameter, fastened by tenons fitted into a mortised cavity and held in their place by oak pins. The raising of the frames of these buildings was attended by a large number of friends, whose services were required to lift the heavy timbers into their proper position. It was customary for the owner of a building to furnish an ample supply of New England rum for the refreshment of his guests.[2] There are a few of these houses still standing in different parts of the town, and the massive oak frames have kept them in the same position as when first built.

third and fourth generations from John Tomson. When Ebenezer, a grandson of his, had a wooden shovel pointed or shod with iron, it was considered a very great improvement, and was borrowed by the neighbors far and near. The ancient practice of building dwelling-houses near springs and running water accounts for the very crooked roads in many localities of the old colony." *Descendants of John Thomson*, p. 23.

[1] "It is interesting to observe how little the character of the gentleman and gentlewoman in our New England people is affected by the pursuit, for generations, of humble occupations, which in other countries are deemed degrading. Our ancestors, during nearly two centuries of poverty which followed the first settlement, turned their hands to the humblest ways of getting a livelihood, became shoemakers, or blacksmiths, or tailors, or did the hardest and most menial and rudest work of the farm, shovelled gravel or chopped wood, without any of the effect on their character which would be likely to be felt from the permanent pursuit of such an occupation in England or Germany. It was like a fishing party or a hunting party in the woods. When the necessity was over, and the man or the boy in any generation got a college education, or was called to take part in public affairs, he rose at once and easily to the demands of an exalted station." *Autobiography of Seventy Years*, by George F. Hoar, vol. i, p. 41.

[2] At the raising of the house of Colonel John Nelson, about 1800, "A man stood on his head upon the roof-tree or ridge-pole, rum was drunk by the barrell by the best people, the better the people, the more the rum. With its painted inside walls this fine old house is still occupied by his descendants." *Nelson Genealogy*.

For a few years after the close of King Philip's War, dwelling-houses were sometimes covered with two-inch oak plank to render them bullet-proof against attack. The windows were small and placed high up in the wall, so that the family would not be exposed to the shots of any hostile Indian. The roofs and walls of these houses were covered with shingles, prepared by sawing logs about fourteen or sixteen inches long, which were split with a long iron knife into pieces about half an inch in thickness, and then shaved upon a bench, which every farmer had, to hold the shingles in their place. The shingles so prepared from the original growth of pine and cedar were very durable; some which were put on the old Morton house at the time it was built retained their place when it was taken down, although they were not much thicker than paper.

The kitchen was such an important part of the house that it deserves special mention. The huge fireplaces[1] were often built with seats on the sides. The back bar of green wood was fixed across the chimney, several feet from the floor. On this hung the many pots and kettles needed. Later, this back bar, or "luge-pole," gave place to one more practical of iron, and a hundred years after the first settlement, cranes were in use everywhere. Over the fireplace frequently hung rows of dried apples and pumpkins. The large brick ovens were at one side of the fireplace, and had a smoke "uptake" into the chimney. The door was of iron. Once a week a great fire of dry wood, or "ovenwood," was kindled in the oven and kept burning for several hours until the bricks were thoroughly heated. The coal and ashes were then carefully swept out, the chimney

---

[1] "In the coldest weather the heat did not come out a great way from the hearth, and the whole family gathered close about the fire to keep warm. It was regarded as a great breach of good manners to go between any person and the fire. The fireplace was the centre of the household, and was regarded as the type and symbol of the home. The boys all understood the force of the line:—

'Strike for your altars and your fires!'

"I wonder if any of my readers nowadays would be stirred by an appeal to strike for his furnace or his air-tight stove." *Autobiography of Seventy Years*, by George F. Hoar, vol. i, p. 46.

draught closed, and the oven filled with brown bread, pies, etc. In earliest days, the bread was baked on leaves gathered by the children. Later, Dutch ovens were used; these were kettles on legs and with a curved cover, which were placed on the hot ashes and then covered with ashes.

By the oven hung a long-handled shovel, called a "peel" or "slice," which was used to put dough on the leaves, and, when the bread was baked, to remove it. A "peel" was always given to a bride as a good-luck present. Thanksgiving week, the oven was kept hot in preparation for the greatest day of the year. Christmas day was too closely associated with the frivolity of the Old World to be observed as it is at present.

At first pails were of wood or brass without bails; tin was not used, but utensils were made of latten-ware, a kind of brass; pots, kettles, gridirons, and skillets (made later in the blast furnaces of the town) had legs, as it was necessary to have these raised above the ashes. The first fork brought to America was in 1633 for Governor Winthrop. It was in a leather case with a knife and bodkin. "Probably not one of the Pilgrims ever saw a fork used at table."[1] The spoons were of pewter, and every family of importance owned a spoon mould, in which these could be made from the worn-out platters and porringers. The large platters for holding the meat and vegetables were of pewter, — very little silver was to be seen at first. Later, handsome silver was found in the houses of the wealthy. Cups without handles were used till the early part of the last century.[2]

---

[1] Goodwin. *Pilgrim Republic*, p. 589.

[2] From these old inventories we learn some of the articles in use: —

September: the 5. 1695.
this is a tru inventary of the Estate of m^r Samuell fuller Teacher of the church of Middlebury Lately deaseased prised by us whose names are under written

```
his wearin cloathing woollen and linnen . . . . .  09 — 00 — 00
his books . . . . . . . . . . . . . . . . . . . .  04 — 00 — 00
to beds with bedin . . . . . . . . . . . . . . .  07 — 00 — 00
puter with table linnen . . . . . . . . . . . . .  01 — 04 — 00
a still . . . . . . . . . . . . . . . . . . . . .  01 — 00 — 00
the brase to kittells and a spise mortler . . . .  00 — 14 — 00
A. iron pot and kittell and mortler . . . . . . .  00 — 16 — 00
```

210 HISTORY OF THE TOWN OF MIDDLEBORO

The kitchen served as dining and sitting room, usually being the only comfortable room in the house. The bedrooms

tramells tongs and pot hooks	00—08—00
chests and trays and dishes and chairs	00—15—00
tubs and pails	00—08—00
Earthen ware and glasses	00—02—00
runlets and barells and a churn	00—07—00
a siften trof and a frien pan	00—04—00
a loom and taklin	01—05—00
hors taklin	00—18—00
taklin for a teem and old iron	00—12—00
a pare of oxen	05—00—00
3 Cowes	04—10—00
3 heifer	03—10—00
2 calves	00—12—00
swine	01—15—00
a hors and a mare	03—00—00
3 swarm of bees	00—08—00

at middlebury his dwellin hous and 20 Akers of Land and A full share of his six and twenty mens purshas only twenty-five Akers and twelf Akers of Land near John haskels and a parsell of Land commly called the sixteen shillin purshas and A hous and Land plimouth

more to books and a bibell	00—15—00
tow pare of scalles	00—06—00
three wheells and a pare of cards	00—10—00
A pot and a Spoon	00—07—00
A gun	00—08—00
toue yarn	00—02—00
The widdows Bed not apprised	

JOSEPH VAUGHAN
SAMUELL WOOD

Mrs. Elizabeth ffuller Relict & widdow of mr Saml ffuller above named made oath in plimouth September 25: 1695 that ye above written is a true Inventory of ye goods chattels Rights & credits of ye sd Deceased so far as she knoweth & that if more shall come to her knowledge she will make it known

Before me
WM. BRADFORD Esqr &c.
Attest. SAML SPRAGUE Register

Recorded in Plymouth County Probate Office, vol. i, p. 223.

In the inventory of " Peter Oliver, Esq. late of Middleborough who is fled to our enemies " we find, among other things, "one gold mourning ring, picktor of Charlotte, Two umbrillos, green Camblet Skirt, White firstin Skirt, 12 pr Linnen Stockens, Ironin Blanket, Two Cracket Bowls, Medison Case, Small Chease press, Puter Basons, One Shays Wheel," etc.

In another old inventory a "Brass Platter, a Brass Kettle," "for the use of my daughter," and "Brass Candle sticks, one bell-metal Skillet, two pairs of strong Iron Dogs, a Brass Mortar, a brass basting Ladle, a brass Chafing Dish, a true Looking Glass, a dozen Cane Chairs, Curtains and Vallurs for Bed, Tester and Camlet and Chintz Quilt," etc.

were so cold in winter time that the huge feather-beds were very necessary, and the heating of the sheets by a warming-pan made them more comfortable.

The problem of lighting was solved in the earliest days by the use of pine knots. To avoid smoke in the room, these knots were usually burned on a flat stone in a recess made in the side of the fireplace. Ministers all over New England wrote their sermons by this light, and every family laid in a supply of "light wood" for the winter evenings. Candles at four pence apiece were considered costly luxuries, and the making of them was part of the work of every household. Bayberry was used for the nicer ones; for the others, grease or fat from meat was carefully stored away to be tried out into tallow. The wicks were of loosely spun hemp, tow, or cotton, sometimes of milkweed, the silk down of which was "spun grossly into candle wicke." Two large kettles two feet in diameter, called seventy kettles, were hung over the fire on the hearth, half filled with boiling water and melted tallow, which had two scaldings and two skimmings. The candle-rods with six or eight wicks attached were dipped into the pot of melted tallow, then allowed to cool gradually, then dipped again and again until they were of the required size. Candles were afterwards made by turning the melted tallow into moulds, which were groups of metal cylinders with the wicks in the inside fastened by small wooden rods at the top and small pegs at the bottom. Later, itinerant candle-makers went from house to house, taking charge of the work, each autumn. Wax candles were made by hand by pressing pieces of heated wax about the wicks. Bees were kept for the wax as much as for the honey. Candlesticks, at first rough, grew to elegant metal standards, and later sconces, called candle arms, were an ornamental part of the house furnishings.

For many years the method of striking a light was very primitive. If the fire went out, a small boy of the family was sent to a neighbor's (it might be at some distance) for coals to relight it. The tinder-box, a necessary part of the house furnishings, was usually a small, circular box containing flint, steel, and a tinder of some vegetable matter; scorched linen or cambric was the usual tinder to catch the spark. Another method of starting the fire was by flashing powder in the pan of a gun. It was not until 1827 that friction matches were made in England, and they cost twenty-five cents for eighty-four, a contrast to our time, when seventeen million can be made in a day, and the expense is trifling.

Aside from the making of candles, there was the preparing of apples for winter use. Days were spent in drying apples and peaches, making apple sauce, which was stored away in barrels, and apple butter, which was made from apples boiled down with cider.

An uninteresting, but necessary piece of work was the making of soft soap. All the refuse grease was stored through the winter as well as wood ashes from the fireplaces. Lye was first made from ashes and water in huge barrels (these barrels were frequently made from birch-trees); then the grease and lye were boiled together in a huge seventy kettle over the fire. It took twenty-four pounds of grease and six bushels of ashes to make one barrel of soap. A hard soap was made from bayberry for the toilet, but the soft soap was used for the great monthly washings. For over a century, all the New England housewives allowed the family washing to accumulate for a month, and there was no weekly wash-day till a short time before the Revolution.

We treasure the spinning-wheel as an ornament and an heirloom; it was no ornament two hundred years ago, but a practical necessity. Every spring, as soon as the ground was prepared, flax and hemp were planted as regularly as the corn and beans. In June or July they were carefully dried. To accomplish this, "pulling or spreading," or turning the flax in the sun for several days, was done by the men and boys in the Middleboro fields. Then a heavy wooden or iron comb, called a ripple comb, was fastened on a plank. With this, the flax was "rippled;" it was drawn through the comb, thus pulling off the seeds, which were kept for the next year. The flax was tied up at the seed end in "bates" and stacked, —

the base of the stalks spread out tent-shaped,—and then was well watered, to soften the fibres, for four or five days. It was then broken with a flax brake to separate the fibres; on a dry, sunny day it was "scutched" or "swingled" with a block and knife to get rid of any bark. The clean fibres were made into bundles, "swingled" again, then "beetled" (i. e. pounded) until soft, then "hetcheled" or pulled through a comb or rows of fine, long wire bristles. After this wearying and dusty process, the fibres were spread and drawn to various finenesses of threads. After passing through twenty manipulations, the flax was at last ready for spinning on the small wheels. The spinning of two skeins of linen thread was a good day's work; for it, a spinner was paid eight cents a day and "her keep." Is it to be wondered at that linen sheets, etc., were handed down from one generation to another and treasured with care?

Flaxseed was used extensively. The flax was allowed to remain in the ground until it grew yellow, and the seed was then made into oil. In 1640 the court of Massachusetts passed two orders, for the growth of flax and for the teaching of boys and girls to spin, and a bounty was paid for linen grown, spun, and woven here.

Deborah Sampson was one of the best-known spinners of linen and worsted. She was engaged to do the finest work at many a house, and frequently spun at the Morton, the Bourne, the Clarke, and the Sproat houses. In 1749 the fair spinsters of Boston met on the Common, and spun on a wager from sunrise to sunset. Spinning became very popular; not to be a "spinster" was a disgrace. Neighbors frequently carried their wheels to each other's houses to work together; classes were formed that young and old alike might learn, for each family must contain at least one skilled worker.

Preceding the Revolution, so loyal were the women all over America that homespun goods were in great demand. They agreed to wear no imported linen or woollen. Prizes for spinning and weaving were given. Not only was linen made into garments, but wool goods were also home-made. In "New

England's First Fruits" is written : " Linnen fustian we are making already ; sheep are coming on for woollen cloth ; — deer, seal and moose skins are to be had plentifully which will help this way, especially for servants' clothing." As early as 1664 there were in Massachusetts about three thousand sheep. When Middleboro was resettled, sheep-raising was encouraged, and the wool was much used. The fleeces were opened and cleansed, the coarser parts were spun into yarn, the finer were carefully prepared, tossed, and separated, then tied in bags to be " dyed in the wool." For this, indigo was in great demand, peddlers carrying it from place to place; pokeberry boiled with alum made a crimson dye, and many flowers and vegetables were used in this art of coloring.

After carding, the wool was rolled deftly, ready for spinning. The wool spinning was done on large wheels, the "spinster" standing, stepping a few steps forward and back, gracefully guiding the threads to the motion of the wheel. The spinning of six skeins of yarn was considered a good day's work, and it is estimated that in doing that amount she must have walked backward and forward almost twenty miles, and all that by her wheel in her own room.

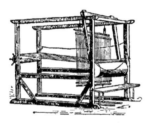

A FAMILY LOOM OF THE EIGHTEENTH CENTURY

The work easily furnished occupation for an entire family by the firelight, one carding the wool into rolls, one spinning it into yarn, one sitting at the clock reel, one filling quills with woollen yarn for the loom, one placing new teeth in a wool card, etc. Weavers (or websters) frequently went from house to house as well as spinsters.

With the hand loom of early days, we must not forget other important industries showing the thrift of our mothers. Nothing was wasted ; old rags were carefully gathered and used to make rag carpets. The warp of these was frequently strong, coarse flax thread, while the filling was of narrow pieces of

SOCIAL CUSTOMS OF THE EIGHTEENTH CENTURY 215

rags cut about half an inch wide; the different colors were sewed together in one long strip and rolled into a ball. A ball weighing a pound and a quarter would make about a yard of carpeting.

Bed coverlids of remarkable and varying design can be found in many an old attic in town. Girls were taught to knit as soon as their fingers could control the needles, — one little girl of four knit a pair of stockings. All stockings, mittens, and scarfs were made at home. As a variety, scarfs were sometimes "pegged" or crocheted. The bead purses and bags now so popular called forth all the ingenuity and skill of our early grandmothers. They had landscapes and figures; memorial bags in black and white with purple beads had "mourning designs" of weeping willows, urns, and gravestones. Sometimes mottoes or initials were wrought in.

Samplers were to be found in every family. Each girl proudly worked her name, age, and some appropriate motto on a strong, loosely woven canvas. With their love of needlework, we must not forget the patchwork quilts of varying design and color. So great was the interest in neatly sewing bits of wool, calico, or silk together that much skill was shown. Neighbors exchanged patterns of different names, such as "log cabin," "rising sun," "blue brigade," "fox and geese," "old maid's ramble," etc. When the patchwork was completed, it had to be quilted, and many a merry-making was held at these quilting-parties. The patchwork was placed on a lining, with layers of wool or cotton wadding between, and stretched on four bars of wood ten feet long, — the quilting-frame. Around this outstretched quilt several would sit, fastening the whole together. At first, woollen pieces only were used; calico was a later luxury, and still later silk. Netting and lace work was another industry, as well as straw braiding for hats. Lace veils were made by mothers and daughters for street wear, and the preparing of the bridal veil was of great interest to all.

The work of the men was largely out of doors on the farms. In the winter they made and mended their utensils by the firelight. The crops had to be gathered and stored for the winter, or prepared for sale and exchange. They had no white bread; the barley, corn, and rye had to be taken to the mill to be ground. Threshing was done by huge hand flails made by the farmers. The apple crop was gathered, part dried for winter use, and part made into cider, for which Middleboro was famous. Roads had to be cleared from one place to another in winter days, and all the farmers in the neighborhood joined in the "breaking out" with ploughs or sleds and oxen. Four-wheeled vehicles were but little used until after the Revolution. Before this, chaises had been used somewhat, but the usual mode of travel was by horseback.

One of the most welcome visitors was the peddler, who made at least one annual tour through the villages of the town with his various wares. As stores were few, his coming was looked for with interest, with the possibility of buying some article necessary for the home work, a jack-knife for the boys, a needle, or a pin (rare in the early days) for the industrious housewife. Another visitor was the tailor, a woman who helped in the dressmaking as well as in the suit-making for men and boys.

In early winter, if they did not raise the cattle and tan their leather, a family would purchase a calfskin, a "side of upper" and a side of sole leather, and a travelling shoemaker went from house to house making shoes. Calvin Dunham's name has come down as one of Middleboro's shoemakers of a few generations ago. He would bring bench and tools with him, the family would have the shoe thread on hand from the yearly spinning, and seated in a warm corner by the kitchen fire, he would make and mend the shoes for the family and neighbors who dropped in for a social evening. Hannah Reed was another shoemaker, noted for her energy and strength,[1] her wit

---

[1] Hannah Reed's great strength can best be illustrated by the fact that she frequently walked to Boston — and back the next day — to purchase leather, etc., for her work. She made "good substantial shoes, well fitting to the feet."

At one time two clerks in the store were talking, and one said, "There comes Hannah Reed. I bet you five dollars you don't dare to kiss her." He took the bet, and stepping up as she was making her purchases, kissed her. The indignant shoemaker turned, seized him by the collar and seat of his trousers, dragged him

and cheery disposition. Another travelling workman was the wheelwright or wagon repairer. Frequently men repaired their carts from the stock of wood kept on hand, but John Paddock was sent for in case of a serious break in axle-tree or other parts of wagons and sleds.

When Franklin spent a few days here,[1] he gave them many practical suggestions in their domestic economy, as he told of his "Franklin stove," of an improved water trough for horses, of the corn broom in place of the stiff old birch broom. His visit was one of the great social events, as life was not filled with the excitement and rush of modern times. Aside from the gay assemblages at Oliver Hall and a few of the larger houses, there was none of the modern so-called social life. Card playing[2] and dancing were frowned upon by some; the old-fashioned games were enjoyed by all; quilting-parties, husking-bees, tea parties, were the occasions of merry-making. The old singing-school should be mentioned as one of the festive gatherings for the young people. At the tea parties, the guests frequently sat in little groups. Small tables were placed near them, and the tea was passed on large trays with gingerbread, cookies, and such dainties as the housewives of Middleboro knew so well how to prepare. Neighborliness was cultivated, — women would carry their work to others' houses for sociability. Frequently they would have what was called "change work:" if two were to make soap, candles, or sew, one would spend a day helping the other. In a few days the visit would be returned. Even house-cleaning days meant social pleasure, for then they usually had a "whang," a gathering of the neighbors, and on the principle that many hands make

---

to the door, and pitched him out. He won his bet, but never tried that trick again.

[1] See chapter containing an account of The Green.

[2] In *Plymouth Colony Laws*, Part III, p. 250, we find: —

"Be it also Enacted, That no person in this Government, shall play at Cards, Dice, Cross and Pile, or any such unlawful Game, wherein there is Lottery, at any private house, or elsewhere in this Government on penalty of ten shillings fine, to be paid by every one that so playes, and twenty shillings by the Master or Head of a Family that shall know of and suffer such Gaming in his House or where he hath Command."

light work, a house was soon cleaned. This sharing of burdens helped much in accomplishing a task quickly.

The dress of the early settlers was of the simplest all through the colony.[1] The court forbade the purchase of woollen or silk garments with silver or gold thread or lace on them. "Cut works imbroid or needle or capps bands & rayles," ruffs and beaver hats, were forbidden. In Plymouth Colony the dress was simpler than at the Bay or at Salem. From some of the old inventories which have come down we can judge of their clothing. Leather was used, — tanned buckskin breeches and jackets for out-of-door work. Before the Revolution dress had become very showy and elegant in some parts of Massachusetts. The gay dresses worn at Oliver Hall were frequently imported, and were equal to court costumes in their elaborate trimmings. In the country places, while silks were used somewhat, there was a marked difference. The pilgrim quietness in dress had not been altogether outgrown. Mrs. Rebecca Scollay Clarke wrote of a visit to the old church at Middleboro : —

"I stood on the steps and saw the men and women come riding up — most of them on horseback ; the women sitting behind the men on pillions. They dismounted at the horse block at the door. The sight was strange to me just from the city where we all walked our short distance to meeting. The women's dresses too looked very queer. They were nearly all dressed in linsey-woolsey of their own weaving. It was very handsome cloth, well pressed and glossy, almost as silk, but very different from what the Boston women wore, of foreign make and manufacture."

At about that time the calash, a curious form of bonnet with a bridle in front to prevent its shutting up, was much worn.

---

[1] One of the early members of the Bennett family was a well-to-do farmer, who, although having more money than many of his townsmen, dressed in a simple suit of homespun made from the undyed wool of his own sheep ; the buttons were of leather cut from the hide and sewed on with a stray piece of home-made cord. In this costume he stopped at one of Boston's old taverns for supper and lodgings. The landlord, fearing he might be a tramp, inquired if he had money to pay for this, at which the farmer drew from his pocket a rough piece of sheepskin, and unrolling it, took out a hundred dollars, with the remark," If this is not enough, I will send out to Middleboro and get more, so I think you will be satisfied."

Long cloaks, or capes, called capuchins or pelisses, beautifully embroidered skirts,[1] and silk petticoats with daintily draped overdresses, thin-soled shoes which necessitated the wearing of overshoes, known as "goloe shoes"[2] and "pattens," mits knit or made of kid, are in the list of women's apparel, as well as "Sad Grey Kersey Wascote, blew Apron, Greene Searge Wascote and Linsey Woolsey petticoats, Whittle that is fringed, Jump, fine Neck Cloath," etc. In the chapter on Muttock there is a description of the gowns of some of the ladies and the elaborate costumes of the men.

When the early colonists came, they wore their hair shaved in contrast to the long hair of the cavaliers. This soon gave place to the wigs, which, uncomfortable as they must have been, lasted in fashion for a century and a half. The old men wore their hair braided in a queue, as shown in many of the old portraits in town.

Jewelry was little worn at first,—a few rings, bracelets, pins, and sleeve-buttons were seen. Watches were rare luxuries, and clumsy at that. Time was frequently kept by sun-dials in front of the houses of the wealthy, but in the simpler homes "noon marks" were the time-keepers. These marks were usually small cuts made in the window frames where the sun rested at high noon.

There was a curious custom of collecting mourning rings, which were given to chief mourners at a funeral, and families of prominence all had them. They were usually of gold enamelled in black or black and white, and ornamented with a death's-head, a coffin, a skull, or a lock of hair. Mottoes were frequently engraved, such as, "Prepare for Death," "Death Parts United Hearts," etc. So universal was this custom that

---

[1] Fine embroidery was a source of great pride to the New England women, and in many of the old attics in Middleboro can be seen embroidered quilts, scarfs, and dresses. Miss Susan Hayes Ward has studied some of these dainty pieces, and revived the quaint stitches and designs from a bride's petticoat found in the Sampson family and from curtains in the Stetson family. These beautiful stitches, of old Persian coloring and pattern, have been restored as an important addition to the modern art work under the name of the New England stitch.

[2] Thoreau calls them "glow-shoes."

many rings can be found among the old colony heirlooms, and such was the expense entailed that a vote was passed in 1767, in Boston, "not to use any mourning rings but what are manufactured here." Other gifts usual at the time were gloves, fans, white linen scarfs, etc.[1] As far back as 1633, in Samuel Fuller's will we find that his sister should have gloves worth twelve shillings; "John Jenny and Job Winslow each a paire of gloves of five shillings."

Funeral "baked meats" and drinks were an important part of the preparation on these occasions. Rum, cider, beverage, and beer were freely dispensed until a change in the customs of drinking brought an end to this phase of hospitality. One old gentleman remarked, "Temperance has done for funerals."

In the earliest times it was the custom to make the coffin from the trunk of a tree. This was hollowed out, and the body placed inside, then pieces of plank were nailed on the ends. John Tomson was buried in the Nemasket cemetery in this manner. Gravestones with inscriptions cut upon them were imported from London until about 1700. Before that, the simple stones without inscriptions were used if the families were unable to meet the expense of imported ones.

It was not the custom in early days to have any religious service at the burial. An address was made when Captain Jonathan Alden was buried, in Duxbury, in 1697, and this was considered a decided innovation. Not until 1720 did the custom become general.

The church bell was tolled, and the mourners walked by the side or followed the body. On the death of any one in Middleboro, the bell at the First Church tolled the number of years of his age. Before tolling it would strike three if a child had died, six if a woman, and nine if a man.

A description of the church and its service has been given elsewhere. The sermons were long, and people frequently stood when they felt tired of sitting on the straight, wooden seats. One minister of the First Church is described as wear-

[1] *New England Historical and Genealogical Register*, vol. iv, p. 33.

ing black gloves with the fingers partly cut off, that he might the more easily turn the leaves of the Bible.

Isaac Backus, writing February 20, 1794, says, speaking of the people in the old colony of Plymouth : —

"There are very few men who are very rich, but the people are more upon a level than in most parts of our country, and the people retain many of the excellent qualities that were possessed by their fathers, and capital crimes are less known here than in many other places."

There was but little money in the inland towns of the colony until some time after the beginning of the last century. Payments for work and other things were usually made in products of the farm, wood, and lumber, the prices of which were fixed by a general understanding in the community ; contracts and promissory notes were often made payable in so many pounds of pig iron. During the Revolutionary War, to supply this want of money, the Continental Congress issued paper bills to pass as a circulating medium, which, however, soon so

THE ATTIC OF THE BACKUS HOUSE

depreciated in value as to become comparatively worthless. This money failed to supply the want of a standard value in currency, and served merely to embarrass people in the payment of taxes which had become burdensome. Under an act of the legislature in 1777, standard prices were fixed by the selectmen of the town, which continued in force for many years.

FOR THE INHABITANTS OF THE TOWN OF MIDDLEBOROUGH

Pursuant to an act of the General Assembly of the State of Massachusetts Bay in the year of our Lord 1777 — to prevent Monopoly and oppression it is hereby Enacted By the Selectmen and Committee of Said Middleborough That from and after the 24th Day of February 1777 — that the Goods Labor and Every Necessary and Convenient Article of Life herein after particularly Enumerated or otherwise included Shall not in said town of Middleborough Exceed the Price hereinafter particularly Enumerated or otherwise Proportioned to Said Goods and articles mentioned or included.

Common Farming Labour in the Summer season From the middle of aprel to the middle of october at 2s 6d a Day Common Labour From the middle of october to the middle of Aprel at 2s a Day mowing and Reaping at 3s 4d a Day Good Indian Corn at 3s 4d a bushel. Good Merchantable Wheat at 6s–4d a Bushel Good Merchantable Rye at 4s–2d a Bushell Good Merchantable Sheeps wool at 2s a Pound Good Merchantable Flax at 1s a Pound Good Beef at 2d¾ a Pound Good Fresh Pork at 4d a lb and Salt pork in proportion according to its Goodness and the price of Salt Raw hides at 3d a lb and Calf Skins at 6d a lb Good Cheese at 6d a lb Good Butter at 10d a lb potatoes at 1s : 4d a Bushal Small Turnips at 1s–8d a bushel mens Best Yarn Stockings at 5s : 4d a pair and so in Proportion for a meaner Quality Mens Shoes made of neats Leather of the Best Common Sort at 8s a pair and so in Proportion for a Lesser or Meaner Quality Salted Beef at 3£–12s–0d a Barrel oats at 1s–8d a Bushel Good tried tallow at 7d½ & Good yard wide tow Cloth at 2s a yard and so on in proportion for other tow or Linen Cloth according to its widths and quality Good yard wide flannel Cloth Striped at 3s : 4d a yard and other flannel or woolen Cloth in proportion according to its width and Quality. good oak Wood Delivered at the Door of the Byer at 7s a Cord tanned hids at 1s : 3d a lb and Currid Leather in usual Proportion according to the Price of oil home Spun yard wide Cotten and Linnen Cloth at 3s : 4d yeard and other widths and Quallities in Proportion

Mutton & Lamb at 3d : ½ a lb Veal at 2d : ¾ a lb

Horse Keeping or one Yoke of oxen one night or 24 hours with English hay 1s : 2d Good English hay from the meadow at 2£ : 0s : 0d a Load and in Winter or Spring at 2£ : 10s : 0d a Load and so on in Proportion for a meaner Quality or Sort of hay Teaming Work one yoke of oxen one Day Equal to a man in Common Labour and a Horse one day Two thirds as much as a yoke of oxen Excepting in plowing alone, and then equal to oxen : Horse hire at 2d ½ a mile for a single man and to Carry Double in proportion Milk in the Winter Season at 2d a quart

Charcole at 10s: a Load or one third Part of a 100 of Good Bloomd Iron: nail Rods at 2f: 5s: 0d a 100 allowing an addition Sufficient for the Extraordinary Price of Sea Coal Common Good White pine or pitch pine Merchantable Bords at 2f: 5s: 0d a 1000 and so in proportion for other Qualities and Sorts: Common Good Board Nails and all other Sorts and Sizes of Nails at a price in Proportion to the price of Nail Rods Now Equal to What nails and nail Rods were in the former Usual proportion Oak Bark for Tanners at 13s: 4d a Cord Delivered the tan yard Hemlock Bark in proportion according to Usual Custom a Good Dinner at a Tavern 1s: 0d and Supper or Breakfast at: 9d: and Lodging at 3d ½ pr Night Good Sider at the press at: 6s: a Barrel and at other times at: 8s: a barrel Drawd off Shoe Making at home at 3s a pair from mans or womans Shoes or Pumps and so on in proportion for Smaller Shoes or Pumps, and Shoe making abroad at two thirds the Price of that at home to be proportioned as above Linen foot Wheals at 13s: 4d a Pair Clover Sead at: 9d: ½ a lb Hards Grass Seed at 1s: 2d a Quart. Shoeing a Horse with plain Shoes all round at 4s: 4d: ½ and so in Like proportion for Steel Corks Consider the Price of Steel and all other Black Smith Work in Proportion to the above Said Shoeing Comparing The Same with former Smith work and the former prices of Plain Shoeing all Round at: 3s: 4d miling & masons work at 4s a day men Tailors Work abroad at 2s: 4d a Day Carpenters Joiners and other trades men not above mentioned at 3s 4d a Day and the Home Labor machaies and Tradesmen such as wheels plows yokes Carts Bedsteads Chairs and all other necessaries for Common Use not above mentioned are set at a price in proportion to farming Labour Comparing the former Price of Each article With the former price of farming Labour and all other Articles of Trade not above mentioned Common or Necessary among us not to be sold at a Greater Price Than in proportion with the present Price of the Articles above Mentioned Compareing the former price of Said articles of Trade with the former price of the Said articles Whereto a Price is now Set

Given at Said Middleborough February ye 20th: 1777
Wishing Love and Unity Peace and Plenty Fortitude Strength and Victory to be Constant Portion of all the Geneuine Friends to America

    attest ZEBEDEE SPROUT   By order of
                                         Said Selectmen and
                                         Committee

attest ABNER BARROWS Town Clerk

Notwithstanding the act of the legislature fixing the prices of all commodities, the depreciation of the currency issued by the Continental Congress deranged every branch of trade. All pecuniary obligations could be met by this depreciated money, which added to the great financial distress throughout the country. Middleboro, being generally a farming community, did not suffer as much as other towns, and to meet this condition, contracts and promissory notes were here often given, payable in so many pounds of pig iron or other articles for which there was a constant demand, instead of money, although all taxes were to be in specie.[1] In 1780 pig iron was worth four dollars a pound in continental money.

[1] The following bill of items and prices shows the value of the continental money in 1781: —

CAPTAIN A. M'LANE,
Bo't of W. NICHOLLS,
January 5th, 1781.

1 pair boots	$600
6 3/4 yds. calico, at 85 ds.	752
6 yds. chintz, at 150 ds.	900
4 1/2 yds. moreen, at 100 ds.	450
4 hdkfs., at 100 ds.	400
8 yds. quality binding, 4 ds.	32
1 skein of silk	10
	$3,144

If paid in specie . . . . £18 10s.

Received payment in full,

For WM. NICHOLLS.

JONA. JONES.

Lossing's *Field-Book of the Revolution*, vol. i, p. 319.

CHAPTER XIV

LAWYERS

AFTER the resettlement of the town, although the purchases of land had included almost the entire township, transfers of the different allotments were very numerous, and questions were continually arising therefrom. There was no one in town who had sufficient knowledge of the necessary forms and requirements of law to enable him to engage in its practice until about the year 1723. While there must have arisen various disputes over the bounds of lands bought and sold and questions of property rights, we have records of only two such controversies between the early settlers.

One of the first cases on record was that of trespass, March 5, 1691, on the cedar swamp owned by the proprietors of the Twenty-six Men's Purchase, and a committee consisting of Lieutenant Tomson, Benjamin Bartlett, John Doggett, Isaac Howland, and Thomas Delano was appointed to prosecute the suit. The trespassers chose John Soule, John Nelson, and Adam Wright to defend them, and the tribunal so constituted decided that the trespassers should pay to the constable for the use of the proprietors: —

The widow Thomas, trespasser by Edward Thomas 4 shillings

William Thomas	3	"	
John Miller	2	"	
Phillip Bumpus	1	"	6 d.
Samuel Eaton	1	"	2 "
James Wood	5	"	
John Holmes	2	"	

The proprietors of the South Purchase held a meeting on the 17th of May, 1698. John Soule and Jacob Tomson were chosen agents by the inhabitants and proprietors to defend their title in Assawampsett Neck, giving them "power to choose one or more attorneys to be helpful to them in the premises."

In January, 1662, Josiah Winslow of Plymouth recovered forty pounds damage in an action of trespass against Nathaniel Warren for felling timber upon lands included in his purchase.[1]

These are the only accounts which appear in the early records of disputes between the inhabitants. Whatever questions might have arisen seem usually to have been amicably settled without the aid of attorneys, or by reference to the selectmen, who had authority by statute to act in a judicial capacity. As the business of the various towns increased and necessarily became more complicated, it was found necessary to obtain professional assistance. Soon after the union of the colonies, the need of men learned in the law was recognized, and by statute of 1701 they were regarded as officers of the court, and an oath of office was required when they were admitted to practice; various enactments were passed regulating their practice, fees, etc. By the province laws of 1708, only two sworn attorneys were allowed to one party in any case.

The distinction between attorneys and barristers recognized by the English courts continued here until after the Revolution.[2] Barristers alone could appear and try cases in the highest

---

[1] *Records of Plymouth Colony*, vol. vii, p. 106.

[2] By rule of the Supreme Court of Judicature for Massachusetts Bay in 1761, no one was admitted as a barrister who had not practised three years in the inferior court, and no one but a barrister could appear before that court either in the trial of causes or arguing questions of law. It was the practice for them to wear the black silk gowns, bands, and wigs used by the barristers of England. This practice seems to have been discontinued for a few years, but was resumed at the close of the Revolution and again given up a few years after. In John Adams's diary, this appears: "The bar has at last introduced a regular progress to the gown and seven years must be the state of probation."

At that time three years' study in the office of a reputed attorney was required for an admission to the office of attorney at law. After the admission as attorney, two years' practice was required before the practitioner became a counsellor at law, and after two years' practice as a counsellor he attained the rank of barrister.

In 1806 the profession was divided into two ranks, attorneys and counsellors; but a few years after, all distinction between attorneys and counsellors was abolished by the revised statutes.

court; the duties of attorneys were to prepare causes for trial, draft the pleadings, advise clients, draw contracts, make deeds and wills, and do other work of lawyers, excepting the trial of cases in the higher courts. The office of barrister was regarded as one of great dignity, and while he might do the work of an attorney, it was rather beneath him. There were no barristers in Middleboro, and only three in the colony. They were James Hovey, Pelham Winslow of Plymouth, and Oakes Angier of Bridgewater. After the Revolution, those who had been known as barristers assumed the title of counsellors, and it was not until the early part of the last century that those admitted to the bar were called attorneys and counsellors at law. Samuel Prince began the practice of the law about the year 1723, but as a counsellor rather than as an advocate. Elkanah Leonard was much employed in the courts until his mental condition forced his retirement.

The following is the list of lawyers who have been, or who are now, in practice in Middleboro: —

George D. Alden	Dennis D. Sullivan
Bert J. Allan	John C. Sullivan
Hercules Cushman	George Fox Tucker,
Zachariah Eddy	Francis M. Vaughan
Elkanah Leonard	Eliab Ward
Samuel Prince	James Washburn
Everett Robinson	Nathan Washburn
George W. Stetson	Wilkes Wood
Isaac Stevens	William H. Wood

SAMUEL PRINCE was the first lawyer who ever lived in the town of Middleboro. Before taking up his residence here, he practised law in Sandwich and in Rochester, and in 1723 he moved to Middleboro, where he resided with his son-in-law, Rev. Peter Thacher. While a resident of Sandwich and Rochester, he successively represented these towns in the General Court. He was one of his Majesty's justices of the peace, and a man of great ability and influence throughout the colony, but no record has come down to us of the extent of his practice. He was probably a man of considerable means, and did much to promote the best interest of the colony in different ways.

He was twice married; the second wife was a daughter of Governor Hinckley of Barnstable. He was the father of the Rev. Thomas Prince, the celebrated' pastor of the Old South Church of Boston, and the author of Prince's "Chronology," a notable book of the time. Mr. Prince had the reputation of being an eminent scholar, well read in literature, a man of excellent judgment, whose advice was always safe and reliable.

He died July 3, 1728, at the age of eighty years. At his funeral, five of the justices of the county and an ancient captain of the town were bearers.

ELKANAH LEONARD, the second practising lawyer in Middleboro, was born in 1703. The house in the "Tack Factory Neighborhood," Lakeville, in which he lived is still standing, and although it has seen many changes, it still retains much of its original appearance. Mr. Leonard was a man of unusual ability, and acquired a reputation as a successful lawyer in southeastern Massachusetts. The Rev. Dr. Forbes, speaking of him, says : " He possessed strong powers of investigation, a sound judgment, and an uncommon brilliancy of wit, and his inventive powers were not surpassed, if equalled, by any of his time. His assistance in the defence of criminal prosecutions was much sought for, and his abilities were never more conspicuous than in these defences."

He represented the town of Middleboro in the years 1735 to 1743, with the exception of 1738, when the office was filled by John Bennett. He held the office of his Majesty's justice of the peace from 1736 until his death, and was one of the selectmen from 1733 to 1742. He was major of the first regiment of Plymouth County militia. In 1740 he was interested in the famous land bank which proved so disastrous to all who had invested. Some thirty years before his death, his mind became so impaired that he was obliged to give up all professional labor. He died July 24, 1777, in the seventy-fourth year of his age, and was buried in the cemetery of the Taunton and Lakeville Congregational Society, a brown stone marking the place. He was a member of the First Church under the half-way covenant.

JAMES WASHBURN, a practising lawyer in that part of Middleboro now Lakeville, was the son of Amos Washburn, and was born about the year 1767. His house stood not far from the town house in Lakeville. He was the first postmaster in Middleboro, being appointed by President Adams in 1804. He continued in that office and in the practice of his profession until the year 1811, when he moved from Middleboro to New Bedford. While living in New Bedford he was chosen to the House of Representatives. He died November 19, 1815, and was buried in his native town.

WILKES WOOD, a descendant of Henry Wood, always lived in the house of the late Joseph T. Wood. He was graduated from Brown University in 1793, and forty years after he was elected a fellow of the corporation. He studied law with Judge Thomas at Plymouth, and was admitted to the bar of that county in 1796. He began the practice of his profession in Middleboro, where he continued until his appointment as judge of probate, and later was elected president of the Bar Association of the county. He was a state senator for two years, and a member of the Electoral College which cast its vote for William H. Harrison. Upon the death of Judge Thomas in 1821, he was appointed his successor as judge of probate for Plymouth County, an office he held at the time of his death.

As a lawyer he was respected throughout the county, having the reputation of adjusting differences between those who should be friends, never resorting to litigation unless the best interests of his clients demanded it. He was an able judge, well read in his profession, a man of sterling integrity, and conscientious in the discharge of all his public duties. He died October 1, 1843, in the seventy-third year of his age.

When he commenced practice, the lawyers were scattered over the country and were sought out by clients, who often made long journeys in order to obtain advice and counsel upon matters of interest to them. The sessions of court were generally attended. It was the custom of lawyers in town to go to Plymouth at the opening of the session and remain there until the court adjourned. With the change which has come over the country, this custom has passed away, and the sessions of court have nothing of the interest, wit, and humor in which both judge and attorneys participated a century ago. Many men [1] commenced their professional studies with Judge Wood while in practice in Middleboro.

WILKES WOOD

ZACHARIAH EDDY, one of the most prominent lawyers in southeastern Massachusetts, was born in 1780. He was graduated from Brown University in 1799 with the second honors

---

[1] Among them were Alexander Wood of Hanover, Thomas and Harry Sturtevant, sons of Dr. Sturtevant, Hercules Cushman, Isaac Stevens, Seth Miller, William R. P. Washburn, Abram G. Randall, and William H. Wood, his son, who afterwards occupied the position held by his father as judge of probate.

of his class, and taught school before he commenced the study of law in the office of Joshua Thomas, one of the leading lawyers in Plymouth. He was admitted to the Plymouth bar in 1806, and as a counsellor in 1810. He was noted for his studious habits, and early showed remarkable powers of memory. Such were his talents that soon after his admission as counsellor he was acknowledged the leader of the bar in southeastern Massachusetts, and in the intricacies of special pleading, he had no equal in the state. He was a personal friend of Daniel Webster, and was often associated with him in different cases. The late Chief Justice Shaw said he was one of the ablest lawyers in the state. Among his intimate friends were John Quincy Adams, Judge Hubbard, Timothy G. Coffin, William Bayles, Marcus Morton, and other prominent men. Not a few of the briefs used by Mr. Choate were prepared by Mr. Eddy. Something of the extent of his practice may be inferred from the fact that more than three hundred cases which he argued in the Supreme Court are given in the Massachusetts Reports. In a letter to a friend in 1833 he casually remarked that he had just returned from Plymouth, where he found that he had seventy-one cases on the docket of the court. His active practice continued for a period of forty years, and such were his ability and reputation that, although his office remained in the small village of Eddyville, clients and lawyers from all parts of the state were frequently there for advice or consultation. It used to be said of him that by his judicious counsel he settled many more cases outside than in court. At the height of his practice he was offered a place in the Supreme Court of Massachusetts, but declined.

He was a lover of literature, a great reader, and owned a well-selected library. His ready memory and knowledge of books supplied him with argument and precedent in illustration which made him a difficult man to defeat. He was authority on the history and polity of the church of the pilgrims of Plymouth, was often consulted by clergymen in ecclesiastical matters, and his opinions were taken without question. In the latter part of his life, he was a frequent contributor to religious and historical journals; his extensive knowledge made the articles of great value, and added not a little to our present knowledge of the early history of Plymouth Colony. The notes to the edition of the "New England Memorial" issued by the Congregational Publishing Society in 1855 were largely from his pen. He was the author of the "History of the First Church of Middleboro," published in 1852. While he was in practice, more than twenty men, who afterwards became prominent lawyers, were students in his office.[1]

ZACHARIAH EDDY

He retired from the practice of law about 1850, and the remainder of his years were spent in the quiet of his country home and in the enjoyment of his large circle of friends. He died February 14, 1860.

HERCULES CUSHMAN was, in the early part of his life, the principal of Peirce Academy. After leaving the academy, he

[1] The following is a list of students who studied law in the office of Zachariah Eddy: —

Samuel Atkinson, Samuel Briggs, Benjamin F. Hallet, Mr. Wright, Boston. Joseph Clark, Charleston, South Carolina. William Miller, Milton. Charles C. Burleigh, Conn. Jacob Atkinson, Amesbury. William A. Latham, David Perkins, Bridgewater. Southard Bryant, William H. Eddy, Samuel Eddy, John Eddy, A. H. Tinkham, Everett Robinson, Windsor Briggs, — all of Middleboro. Russell Hathaway, Ephraim Ward, Lakeville. John S. Holmes, New Bedford. Samuel S. Chase, Thomas F. Anthony, Fall River.

entered the office of the Hon. Wilkes Wood as a student of law, and was admitted to the Plymouth bar. In 1810 and 1811 he was elected as a representative to the General Court. He was appointed justice of the peace in 1811, and from 1811 to 1813 served as clerk of the courts in Plymouth. In 1814 he moved his residence to Assonet Village in Freetown, and while residing there represented the town in the General Court, was a member of the governor's council, and a collector of the customs when Assonet was a place of considerable business activity. He returned to Middleboro about the year 1828, and was elected representative to the General Court in 1830 and 1831. He married Mary, daughter of General Abiel Washburn. At the time of his death in 1832 he was a storekeeper in the building which stood upon the present site of the American Hall.

ISAAC STEVENS was born in Wareham in 1792, and admitted to the bar in 1818. After practising law for a few years in Middleboro, where he built a one-story house,[1] he moved to Athol, Mass. He was captain of one of the companies of light infantry in Middleboro.

ELIAB WARD, the son of General Ephraim Ward, was born in Carver, July 1, 1805, and moved to Middleboro, now Lakeville, in 1806. He entered Amherst College, and soon after his graduation studied in the office of Jacob H. Loud of Plymouth, a well-known lawyer, and was admitted to the county bar in 1836. He at once opened an office in Middleboro, where he commenced practice. He had the confidence of a large clientele, but the active duties of his profession were distasteful to him, and he preferred to serve his clients in matters of advice and counsel rather than to appear often in court. In the local militia he rose from one office to another until he reached that of brigadier-general, which he held from April 8, 1850, to 1855. As a prominent member of the Democratic

[1] This was later raised to two stories, and here Mr. Joseph Jackson recently lived.

party he was representative to the General Court in 1838–42 and 1852, and was elected to the state Senate in 1843. He was trustee of Peirce Academy from 1843 until his death. About 1855 he retired from active practice and from politics, spending his last days with family and friends. He was a gentleman of the old school, was much interested in the early history of the town and Plymouth Colony, and had a large circle of friends in southeastern Massachusetts, where he was widely known and revered. He married, October 17, 1852, Prudence K., daughter of John Holmes of Middleboro. He died May 12, 1885.

ELIAB WARD

WILLIAM H. WOOD was born October 24, 1811, and died March 30, 1883. He was a son of Wilkes Wood, and at the time of his death held the same office that his father had filled for twenty years. He fitted for college at Peirce Academy, and at the age of nineteen years entered Brown University, from which he was graduated with honor. After leaving college, he was principal of the Coffin School at Nantucket for one year, when he resigned for the purpose of entering the Harvard Law School. After pursuing his studies there for three years, he was graduated with honor, and immediately afterward formed a copartnership with John T. Eldridge, who, at that time, was president of the Hartford and Erie Railroad. They commenced practice in Boston, but in 1840 the copartnership was dissolved, and Mr. Wood moved to Middleboro, where he opened an office. He filled many positions of trust in town with great credit. He was one of the original founders and ablest advocates of the Free Soil party, and by his ability and political sagacity maintained a high rank among its leaders; such were his eloquence and popularity that he was much sought after at political gatherings. In 1848 he was a member of the Massachusetts Senate, and served on the judiciary committee in that body. He was an able and effective debater, and most of his speeches were reported in full in the Boston papers. In 1849 he was defeated because of his fearless and unflinching advocacy of the doctrines of his party. In 1850 he was reëlected, and by his influence did much towards securing the election of Charles Sumner to the United States Senate. In 1853 he was a delegate to the Constitutional Convention, and in 1857 was a representative to the General Court, and a year later a member of the executive council. In 1858 he was earnestly solicited to accept the Republican nomination for Congress from this district, but was obliged to decline on account of feeble health. Soon after, he was appointed by Governor Banks judge of probate and insolvency for the county of Plymouth, which position he retained until the time of his death. In 1873, upon promotion of Judge Devens, he was offered a position upon the bench of the Superior Court, but his ill health forced him to de-

WILLIAM H. WOOD

cline the appointment. He was an able judge, and those who applied to him for help without the aid of a professional adviser found him a sympathizing friend, ready to render all assistance in his power. He was remarkable for his conscientiousness, his patient industry in matters connected with his office, he was courteous and affable in his relations to all, ambitious to discharge faithfully all duties placed upon him, a man of unusual literary ability, and a lover of good books.

EVERETT ROBINSON was born in Middleboro, January 22, 1816. His father was Josiah Robinson, a farmer, who lived in the northern part of the town. Mr. Robinson was educated under private teachers, in the public schools, and at Peirce Academy. His legal studies were pursued in the office of Zachariah Eddy, and he was admitted to the Plymouth bar in 1846. He at once opened an office at the Four Corners, and continued practice until the time of his death, August 5, 1897. He was noted for his knowledge of human nature, his shrewdness, good judgment, and remarkable memory, which, with diligent application to his profession, made him one of the most successful lawyers in the county before a jury.

EVERETT ROBINSON

He was a man of simple habits, most scrupulous in his integrity and professional honor, and commanded the confidence and respect of the entire community. Few lawyers at the Plymouth bar were more dreaded by opposing counsel than Mr. Robinson. His wit and sarcasm at times were most severe, and yet he was a man of the kindest heart, generous, and thoughtful for his friends. He filled many offices in town; was town clerk, selectman, assessor, collector of taxes, member of the school committee, member of the House of Representatives for four years, a senator three years, and president of the Middleboro Savings Bank. He married Sarah W. Taylor of Dartmouth.

FRANCIS M. VAUGHAN was a lineal descendant of George Vaughan, one of the first settlers of the town. He was born in Middleboro, March 30, 1836, fitted for college at Peirce Academy, and entered Brown University in 1857, where he remained for two years. On account of ill health, he was obliged to leave the university, and soon after commenced the study of law with Hon. William H. Wood. He was admitted to the Suffolk bar November 8, 1861, and was in practice for a few years in the West, but soon returned to Middleboro. He was elected a representative to the legislature in 1860, and was at that time the youngest member of the House. Upon the dividing of the commonwealth into judicial districts in 1874, he was appointed a justice of the Fourth District Court of Plymouth, the sessions of which were held alternately in Middleboro and Wareham. He held this office until the time of his death in 1891, and was regarded as a most impartial judge, who administered the duties of his office to the general satisfaction of the entire district.

JUDGE WOOD'S OFFICE

CHAPTER XV

PHYSICIANS

IN no profession has there been greater change in methods and practice than in medicine. In olden times doctors were dentists, surgeons, and physicians. If a tooth needed pulling, a rough, powerful instrument with a handle like a gimlet was used, and a strong man had to hold the patient's head. The story is told of Dr. Sturtevant that, when called on to extract a tooth in haste, he got hold of two, pulling out a good one as well as the aching member. When the youth naturally remonstrated, he remarked, "I only intended to pull one, but never mind, the other one will never have to be pulled again." While they could extract teeth, doctors had not the art of supplying artificial ones; once out, they were gone for all time, no false ones were to be had.

Prescriptions to be filled at drugstores were unheard of, but drugs and herbs were used extensively and generously. The usual method of practice was for the doctor to examine the patient's tongue, feel his pulse, let his blood, then dose him with calomel, jalap, senna, etc.

In the discoveries of modern times, probably as much advance has been made in medical science and in the treatment of disease as in any other department of human progress, and we to-day can scarcely appreciate the difference in the care of the sick as compared with that which the early settlers of the country received at the hands of those who were then considered able physicians.

DR. ISAAC FULLER, the son of Rev. Samuel Fuller, was the first physician,[1] and his practice extended into the neigh-

[1] He was called "mountebank," a title which in those days was given to a skilled physician, although to-day the meaning of the word is far different.

boring villages. He lived in that part of the town now Halifax.

REV. THOMAS PALMER became proficient in medicine after he had been deposed from the pastorate of the First Church. He reformed his habits of drink, and practised with success until his death.

DR. PETER OLIVER, JR., was a physician (see chapter on Loyalists), and had an office in a small building at the corner of the lane in front of his home (the Sproat house).

DR. SAMUEL CLARK. (See chapter on Four Corners.)

At the time Dr. Clark was in practice there lived here two "botanical" or herb doctors, named Lunt and Bryant.

DR. JOSEPH CLARK. (See chapter on Four Corners.)

DR. THOMAS STURTEVANT,[1] who lived on the Sturtevant place at the Green, was contemporary with Dr. Joseph Clark. He was born in Halifax in 1749, and died in Middleboro, November 14, 1836. He married Sarah Soule of Halifax. At his death, after sixty years of practice in Middleboro, he left eleven children.

DR. GEORGE STURTEVANT, the youngest son, succeeded his father, residing at the homestead until his death in 1852. He had a large practice in this and adjoining towns.

---

[1] Dr. Thomas Sturtevant was a son of Dr. Josiah Sturtevant, a physician in practice in the town of Halifax before the Revolutionary War. He early espoused the cause of the king, and on account of his pronounced utterances against the patriot cause, was compelled to leave the town and flee to Boston. He was there appointed a surgeon in the British army, but died soon after, and was buried under the Old South Meeting-House, Boston. The following letter illustrates the feeling that existed at the time on the part of the loyalists: —

August 18, 1775.

My dear husband departed this life at Boston in his fifty-fifth year where he was driven by a mad and deluded mob for no other offence but his loyalty to his sovereign. God forgive them and grant that his death may be sanctified to me and our children for our souls everlasting good. LOIS STURTEVANT.

DR. STEPHEN POWERS practised as a physician in Eddyville from 1760 to 1774. During his residence in town he was prominent in its affairs, and for a time was the leader of the choir in the First Church. He was so influenced by the general talk of the better opportunities for enterprising young men in what was then known as "up country," that with many other citizens he moved to Woodstock in 1774. While a resident of Middleboro he lived in the Harrison Clark house, and was then and ever after an earnest supporter of liberty in the stirring events which preceded the Revolution. After the battle of Lexington he came to Boston, and at the battle of Bunker Hill he rendered great assistance in caring for the wounded. He married Lydia Drew in 1760, and died in Woodstock, November 27, 1809, aged seventy-four years. He was the grandfather of Hiram Powers, the sculptor.

DR. ARAD THOMPSON was born December 30, 1786. He was the son of William Thompson, a large land-owner in Middleboro, and a brother of Cephas Thompson, the celebrated portrait painter. He married Mercy, a daughter of Hon. William Bourne, in December, 1816. He served for some thirteen years as adjutant of the Fourth Regiment of the militia of this district. He was representative to the General Court[1] in 1825.

DR. ARAD THOMPSON

He died April 23, 1843, at the age of fifty-six years.

[1] Dr. Arad Thompson was for many years the moderator of the town meetings.

DR. MORRILL ROBINSON was a much-beloved physician, who practised forty-five years in North Middleboro. (See chapter on Titicut.)

DR. GEORGE KING was born in Rochester, July 5, 1822. He received his medical education in New York, and succeeded to the practice of Dr. Hitchcock in Middleboro, in 1849. He practised from 1848 until 1857, when he moved to Franklin. In 1852 he married Lucy Ann Eddy, a daughter of William S. Eddy. August 14, 1862, he was appointed assistant surgeon of the Sixteenth Massachusetts Regiment, and continued to serve in that capacity until March 18, 1864, when he was appointed surgeon of the Twenty-ninth Massachusetts Regiment by the War Department. He was taken prisoner at Fort Stedman and confined for a short time in Libby Prison. He died in May, 1902.

DR. MORRILL ROBINSON

DR. HENRY D. HITCHCOCK was born in Westminster, Vermont, in 1820. He was in practice but a short time, as he was killed in a railroad accident, February 23, 1847.

So sure was he of being chosen to this office, which he always expected, that a wag suggested that it would be appropriate for him to call the town meeting to order and request the voters to bring in their votes for Dr. Arad Thompson as moderator.

DR. EBENEZER W. DRAKE was born in Sharon, Mass., in 1815. He entered Brown University in 1839, remaining there

DR. EBENEZER W. DRAKE

three years, then entered the medical school in Baltimore, Md. After pursuing his studies there for a while, he continued them with Dr. Winslow Lewis of Boston, and was graduated in 1846 from the Harvard Medical School. He married Mary E. Capen, a daughter of the late Dr. Robert Capen of Boston. He practised in town from 1847 to the time of his death in 1887. Dr. Drake was influential in all town affairs, religious, educational, and political. He was a member of the school committee of the town for twenty-five years, and one of the first appointed medical examiners for southeastern Massachusetts, holding the office during his lifetime.

DR. HENRY SUTTON BURGESS SMITH was born in Bridgewater, Maine, July 12, 1838. After graduating from Bowdoin College in 1861, he taught school in Brunswick, and on August 26, 1862, he married Ophelia, daughter of Jason and Mary Cheney Ripley of New Hampshire. His ambition was to become a physician, and in the midst of school duties he studied hard. In April, 1864, he was commissioned as assistant surgeon of the Thirty-second Regiment Maine Volunteers, and started with the regiment for active service in Virginia. He was in battles at the James, Petersburg, Cold Harbor, and the Wilderness, where he rendered valuable service. At the close of the war he attended a course of lectures at Berkshire Medical College, then settled in Bowdoin, Maine, where he had a large practice. On the death of Dr. Comstock he moved to Middleboro, and continued in practice till his death, October 31, 1894.

Dr. WILLIAM W. COMSTOCK was born in Smithfield, R. I., March 23, 1801. In 1826 he married Saba, daughter of Thomas Sturtevant. In 1829 he went to Buckfield, Maine, and at one time was elected as its representative in the state legislature for a year. At the death of George Sturtevant, he settled in Middleboro, where he remained until his death. In the early part of his practice he lived in the Sturtevant house, and afterwards moved to the Four Corners. He was a member of the Massachusetts Medical Society, of the American Medical Society, and of the Bristol South District Medical Society.

DR. WILLIAM W. COMSTOCK

He was a man much respected and esteemed, not only as an eminent and skilful physician, but as a good citizen. Before his death he had the following motto printed for his grandchildren, "Power of thought is the only true measure of intellect, as force of principle is the only true measure of moral greatness." He died October 20, 1878.

DR. GEORGE WALTER SNOW was born in Rochester, September 30, 1800, and was in active practice at the Rock and South Middleboro until his death, May 7, 1867. His parents died when he was young, and he was brought up in Providence in the home of his uncle, Hon. Tristram Burgess, then a member of Congress. He studied medicine with Dr. John Perkins of South Middleboro and surgery at Harvard. He married Jane H. Hines, August 23, 1832, but left no children. He was a member of the Rock Baptist Church and is buried in that cemetery.

DR. GEORGE W. SNOW

The following is a list of physicians who have been in practice recently in Middleboro:—

Joseph C. Baker, William Chamberlain, —— —— Chapin, C. S. Cummings, Benjamin Eldridge, George L. Ellis, Winsor F. Fryer, —— —— Gilman, Edward I. Hall, Thomas S. Hodgson, Daniel S. Holmes, C. S. Jackson, E. C. Knight, Amos B. Paun, John Perkins, J. H. Sherman, James F. Shurtleff of Highlands, A. Vincent Smith, William K. Wells, A. C. Wilbur.

CHAPTER XVI

EDUCATION, LIBRARIES, NEWSPAPERS, POST-OFFICES

WITH the exception of the professional men, there were few, if any, residents of the town who had received a college education up to the year 1750, yet the early settlers appreciated the value of sound learning. As early as 1663 the General Court at Plymouth recommended that the several townships within its jurisdiction should take some course by which every town should have a schoolmaster for the training of the children in reading and writing.

In 1677 it was enacted,[1] —

"That in whatsoever townshipp in this Gov'ment consisting of fifty families or upwards; any meet man shalbe obtained to teach a Gramer Scoole such townshipp shall allow att least twelve pounds in currant merchantable pay to be raised by rate on all the Inhabitants of such Towne and those that have the more emediate benefitt thereof by theire Childrens good and generall good shall make up the resedue nessesarie to maintaine the same and that the profitts ariseing of the Cape Fishing; heertofore ordered to maintaine a Gramer Scoole in this Collonie, be destributed to such Townes as have such Gramer Scooles for the maintainance therof; not exceeding five pounds p anum to any such Towne unless the Court Treasurer or other appointed to manage that affaire see good cause to adde thereunto to any respective Towne not exceeding five pounds more p^r anum, and further this Court orders that every such Towne as consists of seaventy families or upwards and hath not a gramer scoole therein shall allow and pay unto the next towne which hath such Gramer scoole kept up amongst them, the sum of five pounds p annum in currant merchantable pay, to be levied on the Inhabitants of such defective townes by rate and gathered and delivered by the Constables of such Townes as by warrant from any Majestrate of this Jurisdiction shalbe required."

[1] *Plymouth Colony Laws*, p. 185.

In 1706 we find by vote of the town John Bennett[1] was "to keep a free school and he doth engage to teach all to read, write and cast accounts as shall come to him to be taught." His service as schoolmaster could not have been long, as in 1709 the grand jury found a bill against the town for not having, or not being provided with, a schoolmaster according to law. What course they pursued in reference to this action on the part of the grand jury does not appear. A town meeting was held on the 1st of March, 1709, probably as a result of that action, and Ephraim Wood was employed to be the schoolmaster. His salary for such service to be "as the selectmen and he can agree for the year." The next mention we have of a school in town is that recorded on the 1st of March, 1711, when the town agreed with Eleazer Lewis " to teach all that shall come to him to be taught upon the same terms as was agreed with the schoolmaster for the last year." In 1713[2] a committee was appointed to choose a teacher; again, in 1715, we find a Mr. Gardner was employed "to keep school at the meeting house this ensuing quarter of the year." The grand jury, in 1716, found a bill against the town for not being provided with a teacher, and on May 18, 1716, "Mr. John Morton was chosen to answer the town's presentment for want of a

---

[1] John Bennett, who taught school in 1703, made the following entries in his note-book: —

    Scollers com to begin the scole
Elizabeth V̊oge - - -	May 10, 1703
William Ring	May 17
George Barrale 16 weeke	October ye 18 – 1703
Captain Warrens Children	6 weeke October 18
Mr Tomas 2 Children	2 weeke October 18
Mr Shirtlife 3 days weeks	October 18 1 week 3 days
Mr Barnabie 3 days weeks	October 18 1 week 3 days

[2] At the town meeting March 8, 1713-14, the town made choice of Mr. Rodolphus Elms, Mr. Nathaniel Winslow, and Mr. Nathaniel Southworth, "to be a committee in the town's behalf to seek out a schoolmaster to serve the town for this present year, or so much of the year as they shall agree for, and the town voted to pay said schoolmaster what said committee shall agree with him for which schoolmaster shall be removed four times a year for the benefit of the several neighborhoods in the town."

school master." As a result of the action of the grand jury, four schools were appointed to be kept in different parts of the town. These were taught by Thomas Roberts, who spent two or three months in each school.[1] It appears, however, that there were no schoolhouses, but it was the teacher's habit to gather the children in different neighborhoods at some dwelling-house and instruct them for a few weeks during each year.

Among the teachers we find Mr. Foster, a relative of Madam Morton, Nathaniel Morton, the father of Governor Marcus Morton, and Miss Anna Dilley, a quick, self-reliant little woman, who wrote poems, and lived by herself in the schoolhouse surrounded by an orchard near the residence of Deacon Abiel Wood. The low ceilings were covered with unpainted pine boards, and a large open fireplace occupied one corner of the schoolroom; the desks were arranged upon three sides, and the older scholars sat with their backs to the master. Some of the older inhabitants remember the little red schoolhouse in Muttock opposite the house where Asaph Churchill lived. This was probably one of the oldest in town, built before the Revolutionary War through the influence of Judge Oliver. Not long after, others were erected, at least one in Eddyville, and possibly one within the bounds of the present town of Lakeville. Soon after the Revolutionary War there were schoolhouses in many neighborhoods, and before the middle of the last century there were forty, possibly more than within any other town of the size in the commonwealth.

Schools were held in the summer and winter months, the

[1] At a town meeting May 18, 1716, the town voted that Mr. Thomas Roberts "shall be the town schoolmaster for one year next ensuing, and that the town will pay him for the same £20 a year and find his board, and that he shall keep school each quarter of the year at a several quarter of the town, that so the whole town may have the benefit thereof in the year's time, and that the town shall be divided into quarters by a committee appointed by the town, and that each quarter of the town shall have the privilege of keeping the school in such places as they shall find to be most for their general benefit, and also for boarding said schoolmaster at such place as may be most convenient. The men appointed for the aforesaid committee are John Morton, Samuel Eaton, Peter Bennet, and Jacob Thomson, which said committee shall also determine which quarter of the town the school shall first be kept in."

summer schools being taught usually by young women, while the winter schools were invariably taught by men. There were always a number of men and women who were well equipped to teach the rudiments of education as required in the district schools, so that the teachers were usually residents of the town. The winter school commenced on the first Monday after Thanksgiving, and continued from two to four months, as the number of pupils in the different schools warranted. The summer schools commenced about the first Monday in May, and continued during the summer. On the first day of the winter term, the names of pupils were taken, their places in class determined, and a " fire list " made out. This list contained the names of the larger boys, whose duty it was to see to the building of fires each day. After school closed at night, the boy appointed gathered wood, locked the schoolhouse door, and took the key preparatory to early work there in the morning, — that the fire might be in readiness, a bucket of water drawn, and the room swept. Wood was furnished by those living in that district in pieces from eight to ten feet in length. The larger boys would cut it; the smaller ones would pile it neatly, ready for use.

There were various methods of punishing the unruly; the simplest, but effective, was to make a small boy sit with the little girls. The children were not spoiled, if sparing the rod was the cause, for the white birch rod and ferule were used frequently on the larger boys to maintain discipline, and the teacher was usually respected for his strength. The teacher "boarded round" with the parents, a certain number of days for each pupil in part payment of wages. The average pay of the men who taught the winter schools was about the same as that received by skilled mechanics of the time, while the women who taught the summer schools received very much less.

One of the most intelligent and honored men in the early history of the town said, " The only instruction I ever received was the six weeks' schooling during the winter months of the school at Muttock." In considering this seemingly meagre education, it must be remembered that these men read carefully and with thought the few books they had. This gave them a mental discipline and grasp of affairs which enabled them to fill positions with honor and credit.

As the population increased and the business of the different neighborhoods changed from time to time, the boundary lines of the school districts were subject to frequent alterations; in many instances the population so diminished that the district was abolished, the schoolhouse removed, and the children were sent to adjoining neighborhoods for their education. These changes have been frequent, and in the latter years have been radical, so that, by a provision of the legislature of Massachusetts, the towns were authorized to transport scholars from one part of the town to the other to save expense, rather than maintain a school in the respective districts. In each of these, school agents were chosen by the districts and approved by the next town meeting; they were authorized to engage the teachers for the ensuing year and to look after the various interests of the school in connection with the committee. The teachers, before entering upon their duties, had to pass a satisfactory examination.

Before high schools were established, children desiring to fit for college, or to continue their studies in the higher branches of learning, were sent to some of the numerous academies which at this time existed all through New England.

HIGH SCHOOL

The New England academies had for many generations done much to foster a more extended education than could be acquired in the district schools. The advantage to be derived from such a course of study was apparent, and it was felt that the state should furnish means so that all should have the advantages which academies afforded for advanced study. This idea so generally prevailed that the legislature had passed a general law that

"Any town containing five hundred families shall, beside the common schools, maintain a school to be kept by a master of competent ability and good morals, who shall, in addition to the branches of learning already mentioned, give instruction in History of the United States, Book-keeping, Surveying, and Algebra, and such schools must be kept for the advantage of the inhabitants of the town ten months at least in each year."

For many years this law had been a dead letter in our town, until the establishment of the high school, for which we are specially indebted to Mr. Thomas Covington, who for years had been a noted teacher in the district school. He was a man of superior intelligence, appreciating the value of learning, and was desirous that his own children should be further instructed without going to the great expense of sending them to an academy. He had for some time made a strong appeal that the town should establish a high school. His endeavors seem to have been disregarded, until at last he threatened to commence legal proceedings against the town unless they established such a school as the law required. He followed this matter with such persistency that an article was inserted in the warrant for town meeting to be held the 6th of August, 1849, and, after much opposition, the town voted "to establish a high school as the law directs."

In the school committee's report for the years 1849 and 1850, which was the first printed, they make this statement: —

"Your committee have attended to the duty assigned to them by the town in relation to the high school and report as follows: The first term commenced in the vestry of the church at the Green, which was under the instruction of Ephraim Ward, Jr. Number of scholars twenty-one. The results were very satisfactory. The second term was taught in the school house, District Number Twenty, Titicut, with the same teacher, number of pupils fifty-five."

The committee, however, did not regard the establishing of a high school under compulsion with much favor, as appears by another clause in this report wherein they say: —

"Your committee share in the prevalent feeling of the town that the money expended for this school might be more usefully appropriated to the use of the other schools. The probable expense of the school will be about four hundred dollars for the year."

The high school was continued with apparently but little success, and after the year 1853, when Lakeville was set off as an independent town, the requisite number of families had so diminished that they were not obliged by law to maintain such a school. No further action was taken until the year 1865, when the legislature enacted that "every town having four thousand inhabitants should maintain a school for all, having a teacher qualified to teach the higher branches and the languages." The committee recommended that such a school be supported, and urged that it would "raise the standard of the town, as the scholars would be ambitious for the honor of being members of the high school." They further suggested that it would be much the better way to have it located in some place near the centre, as the idea of a movable school was not practicable. This was the first definite action taken towards establishing and maintaining a permanent high school. In the year 1867 the town appropriated one thousand dollars for that purpose, and the committee were instructed to locate such a school in four different sections. For lack of pupils, but two such schools were established, one at the Rock, and later an arrangement was made with the trustees of Peirce Academy that that building should be secured for a high school. In March, 1871, the town voted three hundred dollars for travelling expenses, and one central high school was held in the Academy building, taught by Professor Jenks; he so reorganized the course of study that it was completed in three years. It was not until the building of the new town house in 1873 that suitable accommodations were provided, four rooms being set apart as a high school, with Mr. J. H. Willoughby, a graduate of Dartmouth College, as its principal. Under his management the school was systematized, and at the close of the year, in June, 1876, the first class was graduated. In 1886 the present commodious building was erected. Since Mr. Willoughby withdrew from his position, the principals have been Dr. Charles

HIGH SCHOOL.

S. Ober, A. K. Potter, Jr., and Walter Sampson. Under the latter's management the school has grown, and every year has sent pupils to the various colleges and professional schools of the country. The fondest hopes and expectations of the early founders have been more than realized in the success it has attained.

PEIRCE ACADEMY

The history of Peirce Academy has been interesting, and under the management of Professor J. W. P. Jenks it did much for the cause of education. During the middle of the last century there were more than four hundred students who came from all parts of the United States, and some from foreign lands; its graduates are represented in every profession, and in the various departments of business and industry.

In the early part of the last century many of the influential men of the town felt the need of an academic institution, and Major Levi Peirce, who realized the want of a place for public worship in the village at the Four Corners, decided to erect at his own expense an academy building, the lower part to be used for educational purposes, the second story for religious meetings. This plan was carried into effect, and on the 18th

OLD BAPTIST CHURCH, CHAPEL, AND FIRST ACADEMY

day of August, 1808, the building was raised. The following is taken from the records of the institution : —

"Academy raised August 18, 1808; prayer on the foundation by Rev. Mr. Simeon Coombs. Thanks returned after the raising by the Rev. Mr. Wm. Bentley."

The cost of this building, which was paid by Major Levi Peirce, was about two thousand five hundred dollars. Among the records in his handwriting is the following : —

"The above academy with the lot on which it stands is given to the Trustees of the Baptist Education Fund by deed including all appurtenances thereto belonging, reserving, however, the hall for holding religious meetings when it does not interfere with the school, and also if said Trustees neglect to keep a school in said Academy for twelve months, it shall return back to its original owner." Signed "L. Peirce."

The hall of the Academy building was used by the Baptist Church until its house of worship was built in 1828. At first there were but few pupils in attendance, and the receipts were small. After the institution had been supported for a few years, it was neglected by the trustees of the Baptist Education Fund and so reverted to its original owner. During the first ten years of its existence, part of the building was used for a district school in winter and part for academical teaching. The struggle to maintain this academy may be gathered from the memoranda which have come down in the handwriting of the Hon. Wilkes Wood, under the date of March 20, 1817: —

"The subscribers proposing to institute a school in the academy building at the Four Corners in Middleboro for one year do agree to support the same for said term in proportion to the numbers set against our respective names, provided there shall be twenty shares subscribed for."

These names, with the number of shares taken, are as follows: —

Wilkes Wood	3	Levi Peirce	2
Abiel Washburn	3	William Bourne	1
Levi Briggs	1	P. H. Peirce	2
John Shaw	1	George Leonard	1
James Sproat	1	Arad Thompson	1
Thomas Weston	3	Zachariah Eddy	1
Zachariah Weston	1		

The result of this, with the interest taken by the above gentlemen, was that it was kept alive, and but a small amount of the money subscribed was paid. The next year the same gentlemen agreed to contribute globes for the use of the academy. There seem to be no further records until the time of its incorporation in 1835.

The incorporators and trustees were as follows: John Allen, John O. Choules, Harvey Fitz, Peter H. Peirce, Isaac Stevens, Wilkes Wood, Avery Briggs, Elisha Tucker, and James A. Leonard.

The various principals connected with the school have been as follows: Hercules Cushman, Esq., Rev. Charles Wheeler, Mr. Hezekiah Battelle, Jr., Rev. Isaac Kimball, Rev. B. F. Farnsworth, Abraham G. Randall, Rev. Leonard Tobey, Rev. Avery Briggs, and Professor John W. P. Jenks.

The act of incorporation was the turning-point in the history of the academy. From the first it had fitted students for college, competing without an endowment with other institutions

BAPTIST CHURCH AND SECOND ACADEMY

largely endowed, but it did not obtain great success until the year 1842, when Professor Jenks became its principal. From that time its reputation was not excelled by any academy in Massachusetts.

When Mr. Jenks first took charge, it was entirely destitute of proper equipments, and it was the first duty of the principal to supply this deficiency. By almost Herculean labor, by denying himself his salary and the aid of an assistant male teacher, he was able after a few years to secure suitable apparatus and a cabinet of natural history specimens.[1] In 1850 the reputation of the academy was so extended that more commodious quarters were needed; it had outgrown the old building, which was sold for three hundred and thirty-five dollars. With this as a nucleus, the principal undertook the erection of another building at a cost of ten thousand dollars, one half of which was raised by private individuals through the solicitations of the principal, and the remainder, assumed by him, was not repaid until the summer of 1855.

After this, the first effort of the principal was to establish

[1] In 1879 this museum was presented to the South Jersey Institute in Bridgeton, where it is now known as the Peirce Collection. Guild Memorial address.

an English department of a high order, together with a classical and a mathematical department, which were placed in the hands of separate teachers; music, drawing, painting, and biology were also taught. With this equipment, the institution soon outgrew its second building, and it was found necessary in 1853 to enlarge this to its present size by adding to both front and rear. For ten years it was barely sufficient to accommodate the increasing number of students who desired to avail themselves of its opportunities. With the establishment of high schools in almost every town, affording facilities for an education without charge to pupils, this was given up in common with other unendowed academies in Massachusetts, and after service of about thirty years, Professor Jenks resigned to take charge of the department of Natural History at Brown University.

PROFESSOR J. W. P. JENKS

John Whipple Potter Jenks was born in West Boylston, May 1, 1819, and was the oldest son of Dr. Nicholas Jenks, a physician of that place. When thirteen years old he determined, through the influence of Dr. Messer, to obtain, if possible, a collegiate education. With great self-denial he was fitted for college, and by his own exertions met his expenses and was graduated with credit, having won a reputation for industry and scholarship which followed him all his life. He taught in a small village school in Georgia, and in 1840, having in the mean time prepared himself for the ministry, he accepted a call as a colleague of Dr. Mercer over the Baptist Church in

Washington, Wilkes County, Georgia. Here he labored about a year, occupying the pulpit Sunday morning and conducting the prayer and conference meeting through the week. Among his hearers were Robert Toombs, Alexander H. Stevens, and other noted men of the South. When Dr. Mercer's health failed, he was unanimously invited to become the pastor of that church, although not twenty-one years of age. This he declined, not having as careful a theological training as he deemed necessary, and after remaining for two years in the South as a teacher in a seminary for women and adjunct professor in Mercer University, he accepted the invitation of Major Levi Peirce to become the principal of Peirce Academy.

In 1872 he was appointed Professor of Agricultural Zoölogy and Curator of the Museum of Natural History at Brown University, where he remained until his death on the 26th of September, 1892. At the time of this appointment his large collection was removed from Middleboro and enriched their zoölogical cabinet; to this he added many rare specimens during the latter part of his professorship from his extensive journeys in the South. He was the author of the greater part of Steele's "Fourteen Weeks in Zoölogy," and in 1886 revised and rewrote that book, making it a most acceptable and popular text-book. During the many years that he was principal of Peirce Academy, and later when connected with the university, he exerted a wide and helpful influence over all who came under his instruction. Perhaps there is nothing in past years which has added so much to the reputation of Middleboro and made it so widely known as Peirce Academy and its beloved principal.

During the years following, the academy was taught by Dr. Charles Green, Professor Willard T. Leonard, and George W. Coffin. After it ceased to be used for academic purposes, it reverted, in accordance with the terms of the original founder, to the Central Baptist Society. Since that time it has been used for different purposes, for the Young Men's Christian Association, as a Post of the Grand Army, a lodge of the Sons of Temperance, etc.

TITICUT ACADEMY

In 1856, by an act of the legislature, this academy was incorporated, the expenses of the land and the buildings being secured by contributions of fifty dollars each from various individuals. The late Zebulon Pratt was largely instrumental in obtaining the act of incorporation, securing the necessary funds, and erecting the buildings. It remained as an academy for nine years, supported by the tuitions and contributions from friends. During this time it was taught by the following gentlemen: T. Newton Snow, Roland F. Alger, Arthur Lake, Nathan E. Willis, Lucien D. Fay, John Shaw, Barton F. Blake, and Linus A. Gould.

In 1864 the shareholders voted to convey the property to Enoch Pratt[1] of Baltimore, who had expressed a wish to endow

[1] The following is a copy of the deed of the Titicut Academy building: —

Know all men by these presents that we the undersigned stockholders in the Titicut Academy situated in North Middleboro in the County of Plymouth do hereby sell and convey unto Enoch Pratt of Baltimore all the right, title and interest in the real and personal estate connected therewith and all shares of stock that we hold therein, to have and to hold the same to him his heirs and assigns forever. Nevertheless upon the following trust and conditions, namely, the said Pratt is to establish a Free School in the academy building now owned by said proprietors for the benefit of all the children residing within two and one half miles of said academy who are above the age of eight years, the same to be placed under the control of a board of Trustees to be appointed by said Pratt with the power of filling vacancies, the said board of Trustees to be Incorporated and to hold such estate for the purpose above specified for ever, and upon the further consideration that the said Pratt convey said estate to the said Trustees and endow the said Institution with a fund not less than Ten Thousand Dollars, the income of which is to be expended in keeping said academy building in repair and supporting Teacher or Teachers in said Institution and for the purchase of a library, apparatus, and for other necessary expenses connected therewith.

Witness our hands and Seal
Witness Wm. H. Wood

Ebenezer Shaw	Zebulon Pratt
Daniel L. Hayward	Isaac Pratt Jr. Ex^r will of Isaac Pratt
A. F. Hooper	Elijah E. Perkins
Vassal Keith	Morrill Robinson
Otis W. Hathaway	Albert G. Pratt
Paul Hathaway	Jared Pratt 2^d
Bela Forbes	Abraham Perkins
Edwin Holmes	Solomon White
Holder W. Keith	Job H. Johnson

the school. Other citizens[1] besides the shareholders contributed money for necessary repairs and alterations in the building.

On receiving the deed from the stockholders, Mr. Pratt sent the following letter : —

BALTIMORE, Jan. 20th 1865.

To MESSRS. ZEBULON PRATT, DR. MORRILL ROBINSON, AUGUSTUS PRATT, REV. E. G. LITTLE, N. F. C. PRATT.

I wish to endow a free school for both sexes to be always located near the present meeting house in Titicut, North Middleboro, Mass., for the benefit of all children over eight years of age within the limits of Titicut Parish or a radius of two and one half miles, as my Trustees may determine. I appoint you a board of five Trustees to establish and organize said Free School leaving all the details proper for its government and future management to your judgement and discretion, your number to be always kept up, when a vacancy occurs you and your

ENOCH PRATT

Lysander Richmond	Jonathan Richmond
James M. Alden	Nathan Williams
Samuel Keith	Emory Johnson
Earl H. Cushman	William Shaw
I. Sanford Wilbar	Lucy Shaw
Justin Andrews	Job Hall

PLYMOUTH SS. Dec. 9th 1864

Then personaly appeared Zebulon Pratt and acknowledged the above to be his free act and deed of the Titicut Academy

before me WM. H. WOOD
Justice of the Peace.

[1] Christopher C. K. Pratt, Jeremiah K. Pratt, Augustus Pratt, Hosea Washburn, and Seth Washburn.

successors shall immediately fill such vacancy by a judicious selection from the capable male inhabitants of said Parish. Being informed the owners of the academy building and ground are willing to convey the same in fee simple free of all debt or incumbrance to such School, and that a proper charter free of taxation can be obtained from your Legislature with a capital not exceeding $25,000 in personal and real estate, I therefore propose to transfer after the first of April next Two Hundred Shares of the Stock of the Philadelphia, Wilmington & Baltimore Railroad, the par value of Fifty Dollars each, now worth about Sixty-eight dollars per share. — The income from which to be devoted to the support of suitable teachers to keep said free school open during all the scholastic terms, commencing about the first of September. — Also to keep the building insured, in repair, and the grounds in order, and I hope a moderate amount from said income may be devoted each year to the increase of a circulating library to be attached to the school, and for the free use of all the inhabitants of said Titicut Parish, but under no circumstances is the capital to be at any time expended or diminished. If at any time it produces no income, it is my wish the School to be kept up as far as possible by a moderate charge for tuition. I impose upon you and your successors to guard the capital with care, giving you full authority to invest, and reinvest, the same as

PRATT FREE SCHOOL

in your judgement you deem proper, as I make this endowment solely for the benefit of the constant rising generation of my native place. I hope and trust the present and future generations will take such an interest in this free school as to guard it and its funds in the most sacred manner.

I also authorize you and your successors to enlarge or diminish limits and also the ages for the first admission of children, and also to take scholars from a distance under proper charges, but in no event to deprive the children as above named from having a preference, and a chance for a free education. I wish every youth to have the advantage to acquire a good English education.

Trusting gentlemen without further details you will be able to establish and carry on this free school and to transfer it in a flourishing condition to your successors as time brings them forward, and I shall be pleased to receive notice of your acceptance of this trust, and with best wishes for the success of the school

I am your obt Servant

ENOCH PRATT.

BALTIMORE, Feb. 21st, 1868.

TO THE TRUSTEES OF PRATT FREE SCHOOL.

Enclosed I hand you certificate for $10,000 U. S. 5/20 Stock interest from Nov. last in gold at Boston and worth to-day $11,000, which I add to the fund the income for the support of your School Library & Repairs.

Yours Respectfully

ENOCH PRATT.

In accordance with the offer of Mr. Pratt, in 1865, it was incorporated under the name of the Pratt Free School,[1] with

---

[1] The act of incorporation is as follows: —

COMMONWEALTH OF MASSACHUSETTS

In the year one thousand eight hundred and sixty five

An Act

to incorporate the Trustees of the Pratt Free School.

Be it enacted by the Senate and House of Representatives in General Court assembled and by the authority of the same as follows

SEC. 1. — Zebulon Pratt, Augustus Pratt, Nathan F. C. Pratt, Morrill Robinson, Elbridge C. Little and their successors are hereby incorporated under the name of the Trustees of the Pratt Free School to establish and maintain a school to be located in Titicut Parish in the Town of Middleborough with all the

Zebulon Pratt, Augustus Pratt, Nathan F. C. Pratt, Morrill Robinson, and Elbridge G. Little and their successors as trustees. The act of incorporation provides that the school shall be maintained upon terms and conditions in accordance with the previous communication of Mr. Pratt to the trustees. In addition to the fund originally given, Enoch Pratt from time to time added to it, until now it amounts to fifty thousand dollars.

The following persons have had charge of the school as principals since its organization: Moses C. Mitchell, Earl Ingals, George G. Pratt, E. H. Peabody, H. B. Lawrence, T. W. Tilton, C. S. Jackson, B. J. Allen, H. LeBaron Sampson, and Elmer W. Barstow.

duties, liabilities and restrictions set forth in the general laws which now are or may hereafter be in force relating to such corporations.

SEC. 2. — Said Trustees may hold both real and personal estate to an amount not exceeding Fifty Thousand Dollars to be devoted exclusively to educational purposes according to the intent of Enoch Pratt of Baltimore the founder of said School as set forth in the third section of the Act.

SEC. 3. — Said Trustees shall maintain a free School in said Titicut Parish in the Town of Middleborough for youth of both Sexes during thirty-six weeks at least of each year so long as the income of the fund and estate held by them is sufficient for that purpose. The qualifications of the pupils to be received and the territorial extent of the School district shall be determined by the Trustees.

SEC. 4. — Any vacancies occurring in said board of Trustees may be filled by a majority vote of the remaining Trustees at any meeting so called for that purpose, Provided no person shall serve as a Trustee who is not a resident of said Titicut Parish.

SEC. 5. — The Corporation heretofore established or under the name of the Titicut Academy in said town of Middleborough is hereby authorized to transfer and convey to the Trustees of the Pratt Free School all the real and personal estate which it now holds and upon such transfer said Titicut Academy shall cease to have any further corporate existence.

Provided that all the outstanding liabilities thereof shall be assumed by said Trustees of the Pratt Free School and that the rights of any creditor of said Titicut Academy shall not be affected thereby.

SEC. 6. — This Act shall take effect upon its passage.

House of Representatives, March 13th 1865 passed to be enacted.

ALEXANDER II. BULLOCK, Speaker.

In Senate, March 15th 1865 passed to be enacted March 16th 1865.

I. E. FIELD President.

Approved, JOHN A. ANDREW, April 18th 1865.

A true Copy, OLIVER WARNER, Secretary of the Commonwealth.

In 1850 the Rev. Mr. Roberts, an English clergyman of ability, purchased an estate on the shores of Great Quittacus, the grounds of which he laid out with care and expense after the style of the English parks. At the same time he established a Young Ladies' School, which was quite generally patronized for several years. At the time of his death in 1864 the school was given up, and the building afterwards became the residence of his son, A. J. Roberts.

Mr. S. W. Marston established a boarding-school for boys on Grove Street about the year 1854. Some few years after that, about 1859, he was succeeded by the Rev. Perez Lincoln Cushing, whose school was attended by pupils from different parts of the state. Mr. Cushing was assisted by his wife, who was formerly Miss Lavinia M. Parker, a preceptress of Peirce Academy for many years. Upon the death of Mr. Cushing it was conducted by Amos H. Eaton, under the name of the Eaton Family School, until 1898.

LIBRARIES

In the early part of the century an organization known as the Philological Society was formed for the purpose of reading, obtaining information, and diffusing knowledge in the community. The membership included the clergymen and prominent men of the town. Public meetings were often held in the First Church, at which there was either a debate upon some question of interest or an address upon historical or literary subjects. These meetings were largely attended, and were regarded as among the important gatherings of the town. After this society had been in existence some twenty-five years, it seems to have been given up, and its books were purchased by the Middleboro Social Library, an association organized in June, 1832. The funds for its support were raised by subscription in sums from five to twenty dollars; the library was owned by shareholders, and contained several hundred volumes, some of them of great value. This was maintained with more or less interest for some twenty years, when

PUBLIC LIBRARY

most of the books had disappeared and the organization was virtually extinct. Some time after 1870 the question of having a town library began to be discussed, and at a town meeting held on the 19th of September, 1874, it was voted to establish the Middleboro Public Library, and to choose a board of nine trustees, who were to serve without compensation. Their duties were to select books and properly organize such a library as would be of service to the inhabitants of the town. About a year was spent by the trustees in obtaining books from different sources, in making a catalogue, and in properly arranging them for the convenience of the public. The library was formally opened September 27, 1875. The trustees succeeded in collecting many of the volumes which had formerly belonged to the old Social Library, as well as a few books from the Middleboro Agricultural Library, organized in 1860. They also received books from Peirce Academy and from the Young Men's Christian Association, which at that time had been abandoned. Many of the citizens of Middleboro contributed liberally either in books or in funds for this purpose.

Upon its opening, there were about two thousand volumes, some of them of rare value. It was first located in the north corner room of the town hall. After the erection of the high school building in 1886 and 1887, the library was moved to the rooms formerly occupied by the school, and in March, 1904, to the new building. During the first year of its organization, in addition to the appropriations of the town, money was raised by contribution, public lectures, and other means.

THOMAS SPROAT PEIRCE

In 1899 the sum of $10,000 was received as a bequest from the will of the late Enoch Pratt of Baltimore, the income of which is used for its support. By the generous provision in the will of the late Thomas S. Peirce, a large and commodious building has been erected upon North Main Street upon the site of the old garden of its liberal benefactor, who bequeathed the sum of $50,000 for that purpose. It is of brick and stone, with a large reading-room, a young people's room, and rooms for the trustees, besides the delivery and stack rooms for books. There are about twelve thousand volumes in the main library, and the stack-room is planned to contain sixty thousand. Another legacy by the same donor gives $50,000 for the purchase of books and periodicals.

The officers of the library have been as follows: —

Presidents: William H. Wood, 1874–75; William R. Peirce, 1875–95; Calvin D. Kingman, 1896 to present time.

Secretary and Treasurer: Joseph E. Beals, 1874 to present time.

Librarians: N. Josephine Bullard, 1875–83; Charles M. Thatcher, 1883–84; Adelaide K. Thatcher, 1884 to present time.[1]

NEWSPAPERS

We have spoken of the taverns as news centres, where the gossip of the town was learned, and where tidings from the outside world were brought as travellers stopped to rest. In the olden time this social intercourse was the usual method of disseminating news.

The printing of newspapers belongs to the nineteenth century. The first one in America, "Publick Occurrences," which appeared September 25, 1690, was discontinued shortly after its publication. Soon a paper was issued weekly in Philadelphia, but in Boston the first daily, "The Boston News-Letter," was published April 20, 1704. This was printed on two pages of large folio sheets, the other two pages being blank so that letters could be written on that side; a bit

---

[1] The following have been trustees: —
William H. Wood, 1874–82.
William R. Peirce, 1874–96.
George Brayton, 1874–97, and 1898 to present time.
Abner L. Westgate, 1874–86.
Joseph E. Beals, 1874 to present time.
James M. Coombs, 1874–1900.
W. Clarkson Ryder, 1874–77.
Willard T. Leonard, 1874–75.
N. F. C. Pratt, 1874.
Noah C. Perkins, 1875–80.
Edward S. Hathaway, 1876 to present time.
Everett Robinson, 1877–97.
Warren H. Southworth, 1881 to present time.
James H. Willoughby, 1883–86.
Amos H. Eaton, 1886–88.
Calvin D. Kingman, 1887 to present time.
Andrew M. Wood, 1889 to present time.
Nathan Washburn, 1896 to present time.
Millard F. Johnson, 1897 and 1898.
David G. Pratt, 1899 to present time.
Warren B. Stetson, 1900–03.
Kenelm Winslow, 1903 to present time.

of economy and convenience much appreciated by merchants and business men, who could thus send public news with private messages. Soon other papers were printed, so that there were one thousand two hundred and fifty-eight published in this country by 1835, the year in which Middleboro's first paper appeared.

Although there had been a printing-office in East Middleboro before the Revolution, from which almanacs, hand-bills, and small pamphlets had been issued, there seems to have been no newspaper in town until about the year 1835, when the "Old Colony Democrat," which had been published by Benjamin Drew, Jr., in Plymouth, was moved from that place to Middleboro Four Corners. Mr. Drew was an able editor, and a business man of sagacity, but for some reason the paper was not a success and was discontinued. About this time Benjamin Crandon began the publication of a small weekly paper, called the "Essay and Literary Journal," which was not long-lived.

In 1852 Mr. Samuel P. Brown edited the "Namasket Gazette," a small weekly printed on a sheet seventeen by twenty-four inches. For a country paper devoted especially to local news, it obtained quite a circulation, when in 1854 it was sold to Rev. Stillman Pratt, who changed its name to the "Middleboro Gazette and Old Colony Advertiser." Mr Pratt was a retired clergyman of literary taste and culture. Under his charge the paper gained a wide reputation for the number of historical communications relating to the early history of Plymouth Colony, and particularly relating to historic matters of the town. These communications were from Granville T. Sproat, General Ebenezer W. Peirce, Benjamin Wilder, and others. Mr. Pratt continued as editor and proprietor for about ten years, and at his death the paper passed into the hands of his son, Stillman B. Pratt. In 1869 he sold it to Mr. James M. Coombs, who enlarged it and changed the name to "Middleboro Gazette." In August, 1894, the paper was purchased by Lorenzo Wood and Wallace Tinkham, who, in connection with this, publish the "Wareham Times."

In 1881 the growth of the town had become such that it was thought two newspapers could be well supported, and Mr. H. H. Sylvester published the "Middleboro News," which in 1901 was enlarged and issued semi-weekly. As an organ of the Republican party it has an extensive circulation, and is now owned and edited by Marcus M. Copeland.

POST-OFFICES

The early method of sending and delivering letters was rather precarious. In the colonial days before regular post-riders were appointed, letters were carried by chance travellers on horseback. In 1673 the first regular mounted post started from New York to Boston, but it was many years before the smaller towns had any service. In 1773 one Hugh Finlay was appointed postal surveyor from Quebec to St. Augustine. He reported carelessness as to mails and delivery; letters were often left in tavern tap-rooms to be pulled over by any and all loungers who frequented these places, and were thus lost. The early post-riders and stage-coaches plying between Boston and New Bedford and Plymouth, later by way of Taunton, would leave letters and chance papers and parcels at Weston's, Sproat's, or Foster's (Sampson's Tavern).

A law was passed forbidding the carrying of letters by private messenger, as the postmaster's salary was paid according to the number of letters he carried. But these post-riders were chief offenders, carefully pocketing any money paid for postage, and carrying all way-letters at their own profit. No one would complain, lest he offend these petty officials; it was part of the revolt of the colonies against the oppression of England. Bundles could be carried free by private persons, and to avoid any possible government detection letters were bound up in bundles. The stage-coach between Boston and New Bedford, driven by Rufus Godfrey, passed and stopped at the various taverns along the road: in Dorchester, at one kept by Mr. Eaton, next at Quincy, at Newcomb's Tavern, then through Weymouth, where there were two taverns, to

Abington which boasted three, and on to the two taverns at Bridgewater. The last stop, before reaching New Bedford, was at Sampson's in Lakeville. The advertised route was: —

"New Bedford stage sets off from Waltons and Gales Broomfield Lane [Bromfield St., Boston] Mondays, Wednesdays & Fridays at 4 a. m. and arrives at New Bedford at 4 p. m. leaves New Bedford, Tuesday, Thursday & Saturday at 5 a. m. and arrives in Boston at 4 p. m."

In winter and stormy weather the journey took a longer time.

The first post-office of Middleboro was established about the year 1804, the office being not far from the present town house in Lakeville. It was a distributing office, and mails were left to be sent to the adjacent towns; the mail was usually carried on horseback. The rules of the post-office give the following as the rates of postage: —

For a single letter,	40 miles	. . . .	8 c
	90 "	. . . .	10 c
	150 "	. . . .	12½ c
	300 "	. . . .	17 c
	500 "	. . . .	20 c
and over 500	"	. . . .	25 c

Magazines and pamphlets, not over 50 miles, 1 cent per sheet; over 50 miles and not exceeding 100, 1½ cent; over 100 miles, 2 cents.

Letters were enclosed in a bag, called a "post mantle," which could be carried on horseback or in the coach. They were usually written upon one sheet, folded without an envelope, and addressed on the outside; for a letter of two sheets, the postage was double these rates.

In 1816 this tariff was changed by Congress, — a single letter carried not over thirty miles cost six and one-quarter cents, etc. Newspapers under one hundred miles or within the state where published, one cent, etc. A new tariff rate was adopted in 1845, another in 1855, and another in 1872.

The first postmaster was James Washburn, a lawyer, who was then in practice in that part of Middleboro. The post-office continued at this place until 1811, when it was moved to the Four Corners.

In 1893 the system of appointing the postmaster's assistants by civil service examination was inaugurated, as was the free delivery of mails. In 1902 the rural districts were included in the delivery.

POSTMASTERS

James Washburn, Cyrus Keith, John Smith, Levi Peirce, Allen Shaw, Levi Peirce (second term), Allen Shaw, Jacob B. Shaw, Sidney Tucker, Andrew L. Tinkham, Charles W. Turner, Augustus M. Bearse, Thacher B. Lucas, and Augustus M. Bearse (second term)

In 1824 an office was reëstablished in that part of Middleboro now Lakeville, under the name of the Assawampsett post-office. Captain Daniel Smith was the first postmaster, and was succeeded by Elias Sampson, Jr. In 1831 the name was changed to the West Middleboro post-office, and the office was discontinued about the year 1846.

In 1833 a post-office was established at Eddyville known as the East Middleboro post-office. The first postmaster was W. F. H. Weld. He was succeeded by Andrew B. Cobb, Nathaniel Eddy, Joshua M. Eddy, Anna C. Eddy, and William Pratt.

In 1821 a post-office was established in Titicut, officially known as the North Middleboro post-office. Jared Pratt was first appointed postmaster, but was soon succeeded by Isaac Pratt, February 1, 1821. He was succeeded by George Pickens, Jr., Rev. Philip Colby, Dr. Morrill Robinson, Solomon White, Nathan W. Pratt, Percy W. Keith, and Lucy H. Pratt.

In 1846 an office was established in the southern part of the town, known as South Middleboro post-office. C. LeBaron was appointed postmaster in 1846. He was succeeded by Chandler R. Smith, Nathaniel Sears, Simeon D. Wilbur, John S. Benson, James M. Clark, and E. H. Gammons.

In 1849 the Rock post-office was established. Israel Smith was appointed the first postmaster, and served until October, 1889. He was succeeded by John Q. Morton, Harvey N. Atwood, Herbert L. Cushman, Clarence L. Cushman, and Joseph L. Turner.

CHAPTER XVII

FOUR CORNERS

IN the diary of Miss Rebecca Scollay we find many entertaining pictures of Middleboro life, and the places with which she was familiar. A quotation from this may help us to imagine the Four Corners of long ago.

"I remember my first visit to where is now the village of the Four Corners. There was not a house there then. There were several farms scattered on the way between there and Muttock village. Morton town was quite a neighborhood with a goodly number of houses. There was a tavern there, kept by Mr. Levi Wood and called Wood's Tavern. There was also a hall at the Morton house where the young people used to assemble and have their dances and winter pastimes."

This in 1775! It is hard to realize that the enterprising and flourishing centre of the town was then a densely wooded tract with a few houses at Court End. The tavern kept by Mr. Levi Wood stood on the site of the residence of the late Charles F. Peirce, and bore the usual sign of the king's coat of arms, which hung over the entrance door. After the close of the Revolution this sign was removed and some appropriate words substituted, indicating that it was a place of resort for the patriots.

THE SILAS WOOD HOUSE

The old Silas Wood house, now standing, was built shortly

THE OLD MORTON HOUSE

before the war, the date being on a tile in the chimney; later it was occupied by Deacon Abiel Wood. A little to the south was the store kept by Mr. Silas Wood; this, and that of Mr. Leach in Muttock, were the only stores in town. Mr. Wood was a wealthy and influential citizen, a man well known throughout the colony for his integrity and ability, and his opinions were sought after and respected in all matters relating to public affairs.

Of the houses built at the close of King Philip's War none, perhaps, attained so much celebrity as the Morton house, which at the time of its removal in 1868 was undoubtedly the oldest house in town. There was no monument so closely connected with the early history as this old Morton house, which stood directly in front of the spot where the house of the late Albert G. Pickens now stands, and it was with great regret to many that this venerable pile, associated with so many interesting events, and the home of so many prominent men and women, should have been taken down in order to straighten Main Street at this point. Mr. Pickens decided that the house was too old to be moved, so he sold the timber, and it is now in one of the Crossman houses on Crossman Avenue. He built a new house near the old site, but farther back from the road, on the land owned by a descendant of the Morton family until within a few years. There is a tradition that this house was built before King Philip's War, and was spared in the general destruction of houses on account of the friendship existing between King Philip and John Morton, but this is undoubtedly erroneous, as it lacks confirmation, and there are many facts which prove the contrary, so that we may say that the old Morton house was built soon after the resettlement of the town, by John Morton, Jr. The first house, built by John, Senior, was near the river, the site of which can still be identified. There John, Jr., probably lived as a boy, and on returning after the war he erected this house. At the time of its removal it was about sixty feet in length, twenty feet in width, of two stories, with a gambrel roof, and stood upon an open green, without fence, trees, or shrubbery about it, with an end toward the street. When it was first built, the street was probably at some little distance; it was considerably enlarged, additions having been made at two different times. The southern part was the original building, and upon the walls were shingles made of the first growth of pine, put on when the house was built, but worn so thin by exposure to the weather that they were not much thicker than ordinary brown paper. Portions of the garret were known as the "Guinea rooms," from the fact that they were occupied by the slaves.

Ebenezer Morton inherited the place from his father. His wife, Madam Morton, a lady of remarkable intelligence and social influence, was an intimate friend of many in the colony, who often enjoyed the generous hospitality of her house. She was a devout christian woman, a member of the church, of strong will and energy, and a leader of the sect called the "New Lights." Their daughter Mary married Ebenezer Spooner in 1743, and their daughter Phœbe was the wife of Andrew Oliver. She did not choose to return to England with her father-in-law and family, but shortly after their banishment she came with her son and daughter to this house, where she lived until her death in 1831. Before the Revolution the many guests at Oliver Hall in Muttock were in the habit of visiting at the old

Morton house and enjoying the cheer and hospitality which the family and their friends so bountifully dispensed.

Another of the old houses in Morton Town was the Clark house, built about 1710 by Seth Morton, from whom it was called the Morton house until purchased by Dr. Clark. This nomenclature causes some confusion in the early history. Built of solid oak timber, with high pitched roof and steep gable ends, it was moved with difficulty to its present situation (the house now occupied by E. B. Dorrance) on rollers propelled by men with handspikes, a work of much interest to the townspeople. In the hurricane of 1815 much damage was done all through the village; the roof of this house was so wrecked that a new one was necessary.

THE DR. CLARK HOUSE

Dr. Samuel Clark, a descendant from Thomas Clark, for whom Clark's Island was named, was born in Plymouth in 1732. He settled in Middleboro about the year 1752, and soon after married the daughter of Ebenezer Morton. He was not only a skilful physician, but a man of good judgment, commanding the universal respect of the people of the colony, scholarly in his tastes, and well informed on all matters of colonial history. He kept a journal, in which he recorded the incidents of interest connected with the early history, particularly what had come to him from the first settlers relating to the Indian War and the struggles and hardships of those trying years. He was a friend of Dr. Franklin, and his journal contained an account of conversations, anecdotes, and interviews with him; also, a minute description of Oliver Hall, of its distinguished guests, and of the reception which Dr. Peter Oliver gave to Dr. Franklin. It is a matter of the most profound regret that this journal was lost, as its evidence would be invaluable upon matters relating to this history.

Another occupant of this house was Dr. Joseph Clark, son of Samuel Clark, who, upon the death of his father, succeeded to his practice of medicine in Middleboro and surrounding towns. He built what is known as the Briggs house soon after his marriage to Rebecca Scollay, an adopted daughter and niece of John Scollay.[1] She, with her brilliant aunt of the same name, had come to Middleboro during the siege of Boston. They stayed at the Peter Oliver, Jr. House (Dr. Oliver had gone to England), and here it was that Dr. Clark met his future wife. The aunt, Miss Rebecca Scollay,[2] lived with her niece after the marriage. She was a woman of culture and of unusual intellectual gifts, a follower of Jonathan Edwards, and a friend of Dr. Hopkins and of Phillis Wheatley, the African poet. Dr. Clark, in addition to his extensive practice as a physician, was especially interested in matters of local history. He served as surgeon with General Cobb in the Revolution. He had a very retentive memory, and used to tell of thrilling scenes and experiences during the struggle for independence, and the interviews which he had with General Washington and other patriot leaders. He died in 1837, at the advanced age of eighty-seven.

Among the houses of interest before the Revolution was that of Ebenezer Spooner, which stood upon what was then called Spooner Hill, probably on the site of the house owned by the late Alpha Crossman. Although not a resident of Middleboro at the breaking out of the war, he with the other loyalists espoused the cause of the English Crown, and left with Governor Gage and his troops in 1776, never to return.[3]

From Morton Town there was a cow-path leading to the garrison house of Thomas Barrows on Main Street. This

---

[1] A well-known merchant of Boston, for whom Scollay Square was named.

[2] Mr. Pemberton (from whose family Pemberton Square in Boston was named) was an ardent admirer, but she declined his offer of marriage. At his death he left her furniture, money, and his coat of arms, which was hung in the Clark house.

[3] Sabine, *American Loyalists*, vol. ii, p. 580.

is perhaps one of the oldest houses now standing, having been built in 1700 near the site of the house of Samuel Barrows. After the resettlement of the town, so many Indians lived in Titicut and Lakeville that for many years most of the houses built were garrison houses, framed, covered with oak plank from two to two and one half inches thick instead of boards, to be bullet-proof in case of attack. This house was built with small windows, very high from the ground, lest any shot should reach the family. There is still a port-hole to be seen in the corner of the house.

THE OLD BARROWS HOUSE

The fort, or garrison house, built before King Philip's War and burned in 1675, stood on the brow of the hill not far from the Barrows house, some two or three hundred feet from Main Street where it turns to descend to the Star Mills. But slight description of this has come down to us. It was a large palisado, enclosed by logs set firmly in the ground, standing some eight or ten feet above the level, and there must have been a well inside. Tradition says that Miles Standish's encounter with Corbitant in 1621 took place near here.

The Briggs house formerly stood near the old town house. Dr. Joseph Clark sold this in 1812 to James Sproat, who sold it to Joseph Clark, Jr., for a public house; from his hands it passed to Lemuel Briggs, from whom it takes its name. Next the Briggs house was the home of Judge Wood, built by John Morton and occupied by Judge Wood during his lifetime, and later by his sons. Between the Judge Wood place and the place known as the Thomas house stood the old town house, where Grove Street now crosses Main Street. Beyond the Thomas house, on the same side of the road, was the Major

JUDGE WOOD'S HOUSE   THE OLD BOURNE HOUSE

Bourne mansion, now known as the Charles F. Peirce place, by far the most pretentious of all the houses then standing at Court End. A schoolhouse on the corner of this land was the only building from here to the Silas Wood place. The old Bourne house was built by Dr. Samuel Clarke about 1752, and was afterwards sold to Captain Abner Bourne. Near the site of the present high school building stood the old Washburn place, which was moved to Webster Street in 1887, to give place to the high school building.

In 1815 Judge Wilkes Wood[1] gave an historical address before

---

[1] In memoranda left by Judge Wood, 1838, he gives his recollection of the houses from the town house on the road to Plymouth as follows: —

"The owners of dwelling-houses at my earliest memory standing N. E. of the Town House in Middleborough on road to Plymouth.

"The house now owned and occupied by Maj. William Bourne, was owned, that is the back part of it, by Leon Wood. Sd. Bourne's house on the S. E. of the highway by Elias Miller. Sd. Bournes 3d. house formerly owned by his father Dea. Abner Bourne by Doct. Samuel Clark. The next house on the N. W. now owned by Abiel Wood by his Grandfather Silas Wood. On the S. E. near the present widow Miller's house, a small house by Abraham Miller. Next N. W. a small old house on the spot where I. Stevens since built a house. Next the house now owned by Abiel Washburn, by Isaac Cushman. Next on the N. W. a house since removed, standing where Elisha Tucker's house stands, by David Thomas. Next N. W. a house where Capt. Silvanus Barrows' house now stands, by Isaac Miller, with whom his father and mother lived. Next N. E. the house where Capt. Abner Barrows has since enlarged and now lives in by Abner Barrows now deceased. Next following old road, the house now owned by Albert Thomas, standing N. W. out of the road by Jabez Thomas and his son Jabez Thomas. Next a house long since removed, by Tilson Ripley. Next a house S. side near the river bridge by Widow Ruth Bennett and his sons William and

the citizens of Middleboro, and at this time the company visited the site of the old fort, where appropriate exercises were observed.

In Judge Wood's house lived his son, JOSEPH T. WOOD, who died February 6, 1890, at the age of seventy-one. In later years but few men have been more respected than Deacon Wood. He was educated in the public schools of the town, and worked upon his father's farm during his early manhood. In 1854 he was first elected representative to the General Court, and the same

JOSEPH T. WOOD

Sylvanus. Next after passing the bridge on the S. of road, on the hill out of the road by widow Sarah Elmes.

"Next a two story house in front and one back near the brook, now owned by Jacob Barrows, by Ichabod Churchill, N. W. of road. Next Ebenezer Wood's house same side of the road, opposite Thomas Pratt's house. Mr. Pratt's house was built by Nehemiah Allen, and the first I recollect was after the frame was raised and before it was boarded when a mason was underpinning it. Next on the E. a house near the brook owned by N. Allen. Next N. W. upon the hill by widow Purrington and James Little — John her tenant.

"Next N. W. a house long since gone down by Doct. Thomas Sturtevant. Next same side, where John Morey's house now is, a house by Lemuel Bryant, a tenant of John Morey. Next same side Capt. Thacher's house where Mr. Pool now lives. All the other dwelling houses between the Town house and the Easterly P. Meeting House have been built since my memory.

"On the New Bedford road from Town house —

"The great Morton house on the S. E. by Thomas & John Morton and widow Oliver. Next N. W. the old part of the house now occupied by Doct. Joseph Clarke family by Seth Morton. Next where Alpha Crossman lives. Next N. W. Dea. Ichabod Morton lately owned by Nathaniel Thompson. Next Thomas Doggett his Grandfather Simeon Doggett then N. Macumber then the Job Peirce house, then Seth Thacher, next N. Smith widow Howe by *Job Peirce*."

year was chosen selectman, to which office he was elected again in 1855 and 1863, and afterwards each successive year up to the time of his death, excepting the year 1876, when he failed of an election, but was reëlected at the April meeting following. He was one of the first water commissioners of the town, and held the office of a county commissioner for about ten years. He was one of the trustees of Peirce Academy, and at an early age was elected deacon of the Central Baptist Church.

On Oak Avenue leading from Grove Street, a little distance from the home of his father and brother, REV. CHARLES W. WOOD resided during the latter part of his life. He was born June 20, 1814, and after studying at Peirce Academy entered Brown University, from which he was graduated at the age of twenty, in the class distinguished in later years for the number of able men in business and professional life. After graduating, he spent four years in teaching at Rochester, Wareham, and Peirce Academy. He was first installed as pastor of the Congregational Church in Ashby, Mass., but on account of poor health he resigned, and was for some years an agent of the American Sunday School Union. Later, he accepted a call to the Congregational Church in Campello. For two years after that he occupied the position of superintendent of the schools in Brockton, and preached in Lakeville, and in Scotland, Bridgewater. He was a clergyman of ability, universally respected for his genial nature and his kind, sympathetic manner, and

REV. CHARLES W. WOOD

had a wide influence for good as a friend of all with whom he came in contact. He was much interested in the early history of the town and of Plymouth Colony, and did much to perpetuate events of interest within his knowledge. He died March 3, 1895.

Rev. Henry C. Coombs was born in Beech Woods, September 3, 1810, and at the time of his death, April 5, 1904, he was the oldest ordained Baptist clergyman in the state. He was educated at Peirce Academy, and ordained by the Rev. Hervey Fitz, in December, 1834. In his active life he was settled as a pastor in many places in this and other states, but for the last twenty years he made Middleboro his home. He continued his ministerial services when past the age of ninety years, and was always a strong advocate of

REV. HENRY C. COOMBS

temperance and an active worker in that cause. He was known as the "grand old man," and in his ninety-fourth year was often seen sturdily walking the streets, vigorous mentally and bodily, and was frequently called to supply neighboring pulpits.

One of the well-known men who lived at the Four Corners was EBENEZER PICKENS, son of Samuel and Matilda Briggs Pickens. He was born in that part of Middleboro now Lakeville, not far from the Bell schoolhouse, October 6, 1787, and was the youngest of three brothers. He married, October 5, 1813, Mary Bourne Thompson, a descendant of Francis Cooke. They had three children, Caroline Matilda, and Andrew Jackson and James Madison, twins. They lived near his birthplace until the year 1832, when he removed his house to its

EBENEZER PICKENS

present site near the corner of Main and Courtland streets. He resided there for twenty years, and in 1852 purchased land on the southerly side of Main Street and erected a large house with a room on the east side for an office and court-room for his use as trial justice. He was appointed a justice of the peace in 1822, and trial justice June 18, 1850, which office he held until his death. He was elected a county commissioner in 1847, and served nine years. When he lived in Lakeville, and later, he attended church at the Green with his family, and, though it was eight miles distant, they were seldom absent from the services through the summer's heat or the winter's cold.

On the formation of the Central Congregational Church, he was one of the deacons, an office he held until his death at the age of eighty years, May 8, 1868.

Perhaps the selection of a proper place for the future business and development of the town was due more to MAJOR LEVI PEIRCE than to any other person. He was the son of Captain Job Peirce, and was born in that part of Middleboro now Lakeville, October 1, 1773. His sister Elizabeth had married General Abiel Washburn, with whom he remained, serving as a clerk, until he attained his majority. He opened a store on the lower floor of the first addition to the old Morton house, while his family occupied a tenement on the floor above. After remaining here for a few years, he moved his place of business to a house which he had purchased near the town house. He became a partner of General Washburn and Major William Bourne, and carried on business for a number of years in what was known as the "old store," which was burned about forty years ago, and on its site the present bank building was erected. Upon the dissolution of this firm he commenced business with his brother, Peter H. Peirce. He was prominent in all the affairs of the town, was a delegate to the Constitutional Convention in 1820, and postmaster for thirty-two years. He served upon the staff of his brother-in-law, General Washburn, and was afterwards promoted to the office of major in June, 1809, which office he held for many years. He was largely instrumental in the formation of the Baptist Church in Middleboro, and in the foundation of Peirce Academy, which was named for him, as it was largely through his benefaction that the academy and the Central Baptist church were built.

MAJOR LEVI PEIRCE

About the same time his younger brother, PETER H. PEIRCE, who was born March 25, 1788, commenced his business career at this place. After the death of his parents, he was brought up in the family of Peter Hoar, a prominent citizen of Lakeville, for whom he was named. He had few advantages, but early developed unusual business ability, and by his energy and persistent endeavor he became the leading business

PEIRCE ACADEMY

man of the town. He began as a storekeeper in the two-story house now standing at the Upper Four Corners, but moved into the Four Corners, realizing that that would in future be the business centre, and that there he could enlarge his business and use the water power on the Nemasket River for manufacturing, which was then coming into prominence in the business interests of New England. He early formed a copartnership with Horatio G. Wood, under the firm name of Peirce & Wood, and erected the factory at the Lower Works. When there came a decline in the cotton industry of New England near the middle of the last century, he erected a large shovel manufactory, and in connection with this, carried on a general retail store, which has stood in its present position for nearly one hundred years. Aside from his connection with the various manufacturing interests in the Upper Works, he became a large owner of real estate, and at the time of his death, was by far the wealthiest man in town. In addition to his ability as a business man, no one in southeastern Massachusetts had more political influence than he; at great sacrifice, he served several terms in the state senate. At the breaking out of the War of 1812, he was in command of a company which did coast-guard duty at Plymouth and elsewhere. He was afterwards promoted to the office of lieutenant-colonel of the Fourth Regiment of Infantry of the Plymouth County Brigade, from which he received the title of Colonel Peirce. It was due to his influence that the railroad was laid near the Four Corners rather than in Titicut. He left a large family of children, his sons Job, Thomas, and James succeeding him in business. At one time his son Charles was in business in the West. William superintended the large farm and real estate interest, and gave his attention largely to literary pursuits. Thomas, who survived his brothers and inherited much of their wealth, gave at his death over half a million dollars to the town of Middleboro and a hundred thousand to the public library, after liberally providing for more than twenty-five of his relatives.

COLONEL PETER H. PEIRCE

HOME OF COLONEL PETER H. PEIRCE

Colonel Peirce's partner, HORATIO G. WOOD, was a descendant in the fourth generation from Henry, one of the first settlers. He was in the store of Hon. Thomas Weston as a clerk until the

COLONEL PETER H. PEIRCE'S STORE

age of twenty-one, when he moved to Titicut to do business for two years. Later he became interested in the "Lower Factory" as one of the incorporators of the Middleboro Manufacturing Company, and was associated with Colonel Peirce until his death, September 9, 1861, at the age of seventy-two years and eight months. He originally built and lived in the house on the corner of Main and North streets, now occupied by George Brayton. He married Mary, a daughter of Abner Weston of Vermont, for his first wife, and for his second wife Abigail, a daughter of Thomas Weston. He was deacon of the First Congregational Church, and a leader of the large choir for many years.

BRANCH HARLOW

Major Branch Harlow was born in Halifax, September 18, 1792, and died in Middleboro in 1861. In the early part of his life he was a successful teacher in the public schools in Middleboro, and afterwards was engaged in the iron business at Fall Brook, Pocasset, and Sandwich. During the latter part of his life he lived in the "old Briggs house."

He held various offices in the militia of the county up to that of major, and served as high sheriff from 1845 to 1854, an office he filled with satisfaction to the court and the county.

Joseph Jackson, Milton Alden, and James Cole were appointed successively as deputy sheriffs. They were favorably known as faithful and efficient officers of the law.

STAR MILLS

One of the manufacturing sections of the town has been known at different periods as the Bennett Mills, the Lower Dam, the Lower Factory, and more recently as the Star Mills. Upon a dam about three hundred feet above the present one was the first grist-mill, which, after the resettlement of the town in 1679, was rebuilt, probably by Mr. Barrows. It passed into the hands of Francis Coombs, as has been mentioned, and upon his death was owned and carried on by his daughter. This dam was capable of holding only water enough to run a grist-mill of that time, and at low water some rocks can still be seen which were used in its construction. It was abandoned probably in the early part of the last century, and the present dam built as more convenient and nearer the principal road from the Indian path, at the wading-place, to Plymouth. In the latter part of the eighteenth century Jacob Bennett became the owner of this privilege and erected, or carried on, a grist-mill.

When the cotton industry was started in New England in the form of small, three-story factories, a corporation was formed, known as the Middleboro Manufacturing Company, in 1815, for the purpose of making cotton yarn and cloth. The incorporators were Benjamin Shepard, Jr., Thomas Weston, Horatio G. Wood, Nancy Nelson, Sarah W. Shepard, and Alanson Witherbee. They were empowered to hold real estate not exceeding $50,000, and personal property not exceeding $100,000. About the time of their incorporation, a small factory was built, which afterwards passed into the hands of Peirce & Wood, on the site of the old fulling-mill, so essential in finishing the woollen cloth woven by the hand-looms. The grist-mill, however, continued here in operation. The shovel manufactory, before mentioned, of Peirce & Wood, furnished employment to a large number of operatives.

These industries were succeeded by the Star Mills, incorporated August 5, 1863. The mill was built that year on the old dam for the manufacture of fancy cassimeres, with eight sets of machinery. Its capital of $100,000 was furnished principally by New Bedford parties. President, Loum Snow; Treasurer, George Brayton; Superintendent, Timothy L. Dunlap.

In 1887 its name was changed to Star Mills Corporation, and new machinery was introduced for the manufacture of ladies' dress goods. President, Loum Snow, Jr.; Treasurer, George Brayton; Superintendent, Charles H. Tobey.

On November 15, 1899, Frank S. Farwell of Valley Falls, R. I., became its manager, and it is now known as Farwell Worsted Mill No. 2.

THE UPPER FACTORY

A dam was built across the Nemasket River about the year 1762, and soon after a forge, which was owned by Silas Wood, Elias Miller, and others until the year 1785, when the forge was partially destroyed by fire but was rebuilt. This "New Forge" changed hands in 1796, when Benjamin Leonard, Abiel Washburn, George Leonard, and Abner Bourne became the owners. After other changes in 1801, we find that in 1809 it was owned by George Leonard and Levi Peirce. The forge continued in operation for about seventy years.

By an act of the legislature of Massachusetts in 1813, Abiel Washburn, George Leonard, Levi Peirce, Peter H. Peirce, William Bourne, Joseph Brown, John Barden, Jr., John Tinkham, Ephraim Leonard, Edward Sparrow, Jr., Wilkes Wood, James Sproat, Abraham Wilson, and their successors were incorporated under the name of the "New Market"

Manufacturing Company, for the purpose of manufacturing iron, cotton and woollen cloth, and yarn, with power to hold real estate not exceeding $50,000, and personal estate not exceeding $150,000. This corporation erected a cotton factory at the upper dam, and for a while manufactured cotton cloth, until the depression of that industry throughout New England obliged them to abandon it. Afterward the corporation passed into a copartnership, which, in 1864, was known as the Nemasket Manufacturing Company.

Here were a store and a grist-mill for many years. Among the leading business men connected with this company were Major Levi Peirce, Colonel Peter H. Peirce, Elisha Tucker, Allen C. Thatcher, and Major William Bourne.

The HON. WILLIAM BOURNE, a tall, portly man, was a son of Captain Abner Bourne. He once met some natives from the South Sea Islands, one of whom on observing his commanding figure said, "You in our country, you be king." He was active in the militia, and was major of the Plymouth County Brigade from September 12, 1803, to 1807. He held many offices of trust in the county, and was a member of a court-martial which tried Captain Albert Smith of the Hanover Artillery. Major Bourne was a man of wealth, a prominent federalist, and a member of the state senate in 1820. He married a sister of General Abiel Washburn, and entered into partnership with him and Peter H. Peirce. Afterward, General Washburn moved his business to Muttock, and the firm was conducted under the name of Bourne & Peirce. During the later years of his life he lived in the house now occupied by Mrs. Charles F. Peirce, where he died December 10, 1845.

ALLEN C. THATCHER was a quarter owner in the Nemasket Manufacturing Company, and at one time interested in what was known as the corner store with Major Tucker and Major Levi Peirce. He was born in Rochester, June 17, 1793, and as a young man left his native town and entered upon a clerkship in a wholesale house in Boston, where he resided until his removal to Middleboro in 1831. He retired from business in 1860, and died May 13, 1885, at the advanced age of ninety-one years and eleven months. He lived in the house on Main Street adjoining the block recently erected by the Middleboro National Bank, and was a prominent member of the Baptist Church.

MAJOR ELISHA TUCKER, who died June 22, 1878, at the age of eighty-one years, became by his faithful industry and economy another of the prominent merchants and manufacturers of Middleboro. He lived in the house now occupied by Elisha T. Jenks. In addition to his business interests, he was active in the militia of the county, and for many years served as major in one of the regiments. He was for more than forty years treasurer of Peirce Academy, and in connection with his son-in-law, Professor J. W. P. Jenks, did as much as any of the trustees toward securing the erection of the new academy and its subsequent enlargement. He was always interested, from the time he first came to town, in the Central Baptist Church, and was its clerk and treasurer for many years, a regular contributor in making up the expenses of the church, and also gave largely to the various organizations connected with the denomination.

ELISHA TUCKER

In 1867 the company sold out to William L. Brown, Nathaniel B. Sherman, and Peter Washburn. Later the factory was burned, but a sawmill and grist-mill continued in operation for a few years. Quite recently an electric plant has been established upon this dam, which furnishes power for lighting the streets.

Prior to the building of the Fall River Railroad through the town in 1842, the manufacturing interests of the Four Corners had been confined exclusively to the Upper and Lower Works, as they were called. There were then at the Corners a general retail store belonging to Peter H. Peirce & Co., and a confectionery store adjoining the site of the present Jones Brothers' block, carried on by Amos Thomas, always known as "Uncle Amos," and later by his son, Deacon Ira Thomas, as a general grocery store; he was succeeded by his son, Ira M. Thomas. At the corner of Main and Center streets was what was known as the old store for dry goods and groceries, owned at first by Major Levi Peirce and afterwards by Allen C. Thatcher, by George Vaughan, and by George Waterman. Enoch Tinkham had a store on Center Street, which is still standing. There was also an apothecary shop and post-office kept by Levi Peirce on the site of the Peirce building. Allen Shaw kept an apothecary shop, and was succeeded by his nephews, Jacob B. and John Shaw.

About the time that manufacturing commenced at the Upper Factory, the HON. PHILANDER WASHBURN opened his store, in connection with his father's business. Upon the death of his father he sold his interest in this store, which was purchased by Sampson & King, and in 1854 it was doubled in width and a story added above, called American Hall. Mr. Washburn was state senator in 1848; he died September 6, 1882, at the age of eighty-four. His son, the Rev. George Washburn, D. D., has been for many years the successful president of Robert College, Constantinople.

The manufacture of straw hats and bonnets was begun at the village about the year 1828, by Ebenezer Briggs, who had been in this business in Lakeville before he moved to the Four Corners. At this time hats were made from prepared straw, braided by women at home and taken to the factory. The braid was sent out and sewed by women in the neighborhood into hats and bonnets, which were returned to the factory, properly sized, pressed, and finished ready for the market. At first only native straw was used, but this gave place to

BANK BLOCK

imported straw, which took away the occupation of many women, who had braided it by hand. About the year 1844 Mr. Briggs sold out to Andrew J. Pickens, James M. Pickens, and William A. King, who formed a copartnership under the firm name of Pickens, King & Co. At the end of two years Mr. King retired, and the factory was conducted by the firm of Pickens Brothers. Andrew J. and James M. Pickens were men of great industry and enterprise, influential in church affairs and successful in their business, which, in a few years, had so increased that the few rooms occupied at first were insufficient, and in 1855 they erected the main building of the straw factory on Courtland Street. In 1858 Andrew J.

SITE OF BANK BLOCK IN 1875

PEIRCE BLOCK

Pickens sold the factory and business to Albert Alden. Between 1858 and 1861 William A. King was associated with Mr. Alden under the firm name of Alden, King & Co. They were succeeded by Plummer, King & Co. In 1862 Mr. Alden purchased the property, and for several years carried on the business under the names of A. Alden and A. Alden & Co., and the general name of Bay State Straw Works. He was succeeded by his son, Arthur B. Alden, who died in 1895. From that time the business was not reëstablished, and the buildings have since been taken down or removed and made into dwelling-houses, and a street has been cut through where the main building stood. When Mr. Alden took the business,

SITE OF PEIRCE BLOCK IN 1875

it did not amount to more than $10,000 a year, but under his management it was increased to one quarter of a million invested capital, and gave employment to about four hundred operatives during the busy season. When much of the sewing on braid was done by hand outside the factory, as many as fifteen hundred in the families within a radius of twenty miles found work.

MR. ALBERT ALDEN, of the seventh generation from his ancestor, John Alden, was born in 1817. He was a man of great energy and sagacity, and engaged in different enterprises in this and adjoining towns.

ALBERT ALDEN

Soon after the establishment of the straw factory, the manufacturing of boots and shoes was commenced in town. This was at first carried on in shops, where the upper and sole leather were cut by the manufacturers. The upper leather was sent out, and the necessary sewing and stitching done in families in town; then these "uppers" were taken to the manufacturer, who cut the soles into proper shapes, prepared the heels and other leather for the filling, and in turn handed them over to the different shoemakers, who completed the work in small shops, some of which may still be seen standing in different parts of the town. The shoemakers would take stock enough to make from one to ten dozen pairs of shoes at a time, returning them when finished. The manufacturer then packed these shoes and sent them to the different customers. About the year 1855 this method of making boots and shoes by hand gave place to machinery, which has since been improved, until now substantially the whole work is done in that way.

The first shoe manufacturer was Stephen B. Pickens, whose business was very small, as compared with the large amount of capital and number of hands employed to-day. He was succeeded by Eaton & Leonard, who occupied a small wooden building on the site of Wells Block on Main Street. Later, B. Sumner Washburn joined the firm.

The firm of Ward & Doggett in Wells Block consisted of George Ward, who then lived in Lakeville, and William E. Doggett. In a few years they sold out to Bassett & Dunbar, who soon after sold their interest in Middleboro to Major Joseph Sampson, Jr., and Colonel Nathan King, and moved to Chicago, where they became large and successful shoe manufacturers. Sampson & King's place of business was in the American Building.

COLONEL NATHAN KING, who lived for many years at Court End, died December 7, 1901, at the advanced age of eighty-six years. In early life he was engaged in different mercantile pursuits. He was elected registrar of the court of insolvency in 1856, which office he held for the years 1857 and 1858, when the jurisdiction of the court was united with that of the probate court. He was prominent in the militia, and was elected lieutenant-colonel from February 4, 1837, to February 8, 1839, and colonel until April 24, 1840. For many years he served as the moderator in all general

NATHAN KING

meetings of the town, and he was a member of the Massachusetts senate during the years 1856 and 1857.

James Allen Leonard and his son manufactured boots and shoes until the death of Mr. Leonard in 1870, doing business in a building adjoining Mr. Leonard's residence on Center Street, now owned by Dr. G. L. Ellis. In 1853 Noah C. Perkins, Charles E. Leonard, and Horatio Barrows occupied the building now known as T. W. Peirce's store. In 1860 this firm was dissolved, and Leonard & Barrows formed a partnership in Wells Block. In 1862 C. D. Kingman joined the firm for a short time. In 1883 Mr. Barrows died, and since then the business has been carried on by Mr. Leonard with his sons, C. M. Leonard and A. H. Leonard, under the same firm name of Leonard & Barrows.

HORATIO BARROWS

They employ about six hundred operatives, and have a branch factory in Belfast, Maine.

NOAH C. PERKINS, who was first connected with the firm, was prominent in the public affairs of the town, being a representative to the General Court, and a member of the Constitutional Convention to revise the constitution of Massachusetts, in 1853.

After leaving the firm of Leonard & Barrows in 1867 or 1868, C. D. Kingman built a factory on the corner of Oak and Center streets, where he carried on a large business for some time, subsequently taking in his sons, C. W. and P. E. Kingman,

THE FOUR CORNERS

as partners, and employing about two hundred and fifty men. In 1888 C. D. Kingman retired and left the management to his sons, who closed out the business in 1891.

The firm of Leonard, Shaw & Dean, consisting of Cornelius H. Leonard, Samuel Shaw, and W. H. Dean of Quincy, began business in 1895, and erected a factory on Peirce Street, employing about one hundred men.

William O. Penniman and Josiah F. Penniman commenced business in 1890, under the firm name of Penniman Bros. Soon after, they admitted Elmer E. Phinney into copartnership under the firm name of Penniman & Phinney; this was followed by another change, and Phinney, Penniman & Lightford manufactured ladies' shoes till Mr. Lightford left the firm.

In 1881 Andrew Alden, C. H. Leonard, George A. Hammond, and E. W. Richmond manufactured shoes under the firm name of Alden, Leonard & Hammond in North Middleboro; but in 1886 they moved to Cambridge Street, and in 1887 they were succeeded by Savory C. Hathaway, Rufus A. Soule, and Herbert A. Harrington, who had a large business, with factories in New Bedford and Campello.

Arthur H. Alden, George A. Walker, William H. Wilde, and Frederick L. Alden commenced the shoe business under

FOUR CORNERS IN 1850 FROM BARDEN HILLS

the firm name of Alden, Walker & Wilde, in 1900, occupying at first the old needle factory on Clifford Street, which, proving inadequate for their business, was greatly enlarged. In 1904 their building was destroyed by fire, and they have removed from town.

The varied business of the old blast furnaces of early history was revived in 1855, when John B. Le Baron and Samuel Tinkham of Taunton, under the firm name of Tinkham & Le Baron, built a foundry at the Four Corners, and carried on business until the fall of 1864, when Mr. Le Baron purchased the interest of Mr. Tinkham for the casting of stoves. In 1884 he was succeeded by his sons, J. Baylies and Eugene P. Le Baron, and later by E. Leonard and Frederick N. Le Baron.

In 1888 Clark & Cole began the manufacture of boxes on Water Street, but as the building was not large enough, they moved to their present site on Cambridge Street near the railroad, where from seven to ten million feet of lumber are used yearly in this industry.

In 1885 the Murdock Parlor Grate Co., now known as the

FOUR CORNERS AT THE PRESENT TIME FROM BARDEN HILLS

Murdock Corporation, bought the building on Cambridge Street which was built for the George Woods Co., manufacturers of organs and pianos.

In 1901 the New England Rug Co. was started by J. A. White and W. Osgood Eddy for the making over of old carpets into rugs. The office and factory are at 5 Clifford Street.

About 1888 Carlton W. Maxim commenced the manufacture of woodwork for furniture and for the finish of stores and houses. From a small shop near the railroad station this has so increased as to occupy nearly the whole of the Hathaway, Soule & Harrington Factory on Cambridge Street.

Elisha T. Jenks carries on a successful business on Wareham Street, in the manufacture of museum locks and bolts.

A. H. Alger & Co., manufacturers of paper boxes, occupy one of the buildings of the old straw works.

BANKS

The Middleboro National Bank was organized in April, 1889, with a capital of $50,000.

FOUR CORNERS

The first President, Calvin D. Kingman
Vice-President, George E. Doane
Cashier, William R. Mitchell

BOARD OF DIRECTORS

Charles F. Alden   Dr. George W. Copeland
Charles E. Leonard   Charles M. Leonard
George E. Doane   Arthur B. Alden
Matthew H. Cushing   Calvin D. Kingman
          Herbert A. Harrington

In the year 1900 William R. Mitchell became the president, upon the resignation of C. D. Kingman, with A. A. Thomas as cashier. In 1902 Mr. Mitchell resigned to enter other business, and Granville E. Tillson became president.

For several years the bank conducted business in the town house, and in 1896 moved to the savings bank building. The officers at present are, —

President, Granville E. Tillson
Cashier, A. A. Thomas
Book-keeper, Harriet B. Sylvester

PRESENT BOARD OF DIRECTORS

Arthur H. Leonard	George E. Doane
C. D. Kingman	Matthew H. Cushing
C. W. Kingman	H. P. Sparrow.
Charles M. Leonard	George R. Sampson

The Middleboro Savings Bank was incorporated on March 15, 1873.

> The first President, Everett Robinson
> Vice-President, Noah C. Perkins
> Treasurer, Cornelius B. Wood

The Savings Bank occupied rooms in the town house until 1895, and then moved to the present building.

James H. Harlow became the president after the death of Everett Robinson, and Andrew M. Wood succeeded Cornelius B. Wood as treasurer. James H. Harlow resigned in 1904, and David G. Pratt was elected in his place.

```
Total number of open accounts at present  .   4440
Total number of books issued  .  .  .  .  .  11,045
Total deposit in 1904  .  .  .  .  .  $1,499,154.35
```

Mr. Robinson died August 5, 1897.
Mr. Cornelius B. Wood died March 23, 1885.
Mr. Matthew H. Cushing is present Vice-President.

The Middleboro Loan & Fund Association was organized in 1854 under the same principle as building and loan associations of other states.

The first president was Nathan King, the second and last president, Everett Robinson.

Jacob B. Shaw was its secretary and treasurer during its existence. The monthly meetings were held in Jacob B. Shaw's store.

The shares were two dollars a month and reached maturity of $500. They matured in 1867, when the Association was closed.

The Middleboro Coöperative Bank, on somewhat similar

lines, was organized in May, 1889, and is still in existence. Shares one dollar a month and maturity $200.

It has now assets of about $250,000.

The first President, S. S. Bourne
The present President, W. H. Southworth
Secretary and Treasurer, Joseph E. Beals
The Board of Directors composed of fifteen men
Office of secretary, No. 1 Town Hall Building

BARDEN HILLS

Across the river, east of the Four Corners, is the neighborhood long known as Barden Hills. The old Barden house and lands have been in the family for a little more than two centuries.

THE OLD BARDEN HOUSE

Probably all of the Bardens (or Burdens) in this country, and some of the Bordens, have descended from William Barden, who came over in the year 1638, and was apprenticed for seven years to Thomas Boardman to learn the trade of a carpenter. After about seven months of service, his apprenticeship for the remainder of the time was transferred to John Barker of Marshfield, for him to become a bricklayer. After completing his service, he lived in different places until about 1660, when he married Deborah Barker, his master's daughter, and settled in Barnstable, and in 1684 they moved to Middleboro. She was one of the original members of the First Church. He became an owner in nearly all of the purchases made from the Indians in town, and twenty years after his death, which occurred in 1692, his estate was divided among thirteen children.

CHAPTER XVIII

MAD MARE'S NECK, WAUPAUNUCKET, FALL BROOK

ABOUT the eastern shore of Great Quittacus and Pocksha ponds, in the early days, a wild horse roamed, injuring the crops of the farmers, and from this the place takes its name. On the opposite shore lies Betty's Neck. Mad Mare's Neck is beautifully situated on the high land which commands an extensive view of the ponds in Middleboro and Lakeville, including the whole of the Twelve Men's Purchase and portions of the Sixteen Shilling and Snippituet Purchases. Marion Road and Miller Street are the principal highways; the latter leads from Great Quittacus to Fall Brook. On Pond Street stands the schoolhouse. In the early part of the last century the Miller family owned large tracts of land; one of the lots on Miller Street being known as the Thousand Acre Lot. This farming region, noted for the fertility of the soil, has perhaps kept the number of inhabitants during the last hundred years better than any of the outlying districts of the town. All the land bordering on the pond has been bought by the city of New Bedford in connection with its water supply, and many summer residences are being erected in this vicinity.

OLD METHODIST CHURCH OF FALL BROOK

One of the best-known citizens of a hundred years ago was

Abishai T. Clark. He served for many years on the school committee, and was often employed in the winter in teaching the district schools. The house in which he lived, probably the oldest one here, built not far from the year 1750, is at present occupied by Clement Barrows.

WAUPAUNUCKET

Waupaunucket, known as Walnut Plain, was often spelled in the early history of the town Wappahnucket. The name is found among the various Algonquin tribes, and is probably derived from two words, "wap-pah," meaning a "village," and "kook-ah," meaning "among the hills," which well describes its beautiful hill and dale. The land lying between the shores of Assawampsett Pond, the Nemasket River, and the Cape Cod Railroad was first occupied by George Vaughan, whose descendants have resided there, as well as some of the descendants of Elder Thomas Cushman. The inhabitants have for the most part been farmers, and, with the exception of one or two small mills, there never has been any manufacturing.

BENJAMIN P. WOOD, a prominent citizen during the middle of the last century, lived on Wood Street. He held many important offices, and was greatly respected for his good judgment, integrity, and kindness of heart. He was colonel in the Fourth Regiment of Infantry from 1826 to 1829, and was

COLONEL BENJAMIN P. WOOD

chairman of the selectmen for five years, an assessor, and overseer of the poor for many years. He came, as a young man, from Woodstock, or Hartland, Vt., and was a descendant from one of the many Middleboro families who had years before moved there.

FALL BROOK

About 1692 Captain Peter Bennett, a son of John Bennett, from England, settled in that part of Middleboro known as Fall Brook, so called from the brook which connects Tispequin Pond with Nemasket River. Here he bought a farm of John Nelson, which included what has since been known as the Miller farm,[1] and married Priscilla, daughter of Isaac Howland, and granddaughter of John Howland of the Mayflower. He was a man of enterprise and business ability; he owned a water privilege on Fall Brook, and had a grist-mill near what is now Grove Street, then known as Rochester Lane. About the year 1735 he and Francis Miller petitioned the town for liberty to build a dam across the brook on which to erect a furnace. The petition was granted, and one of the first blast furnaces, subsequently known as the Fall Brook Furnace, was erected. It was for a time owned by John Miller, a son-in-law of Captain Peter Bennett, was afterwards enlarged, and in 1792 was used for the manufacture of hollow-ware under the superintendence of James and Zachariah Porter, who married into the Miller family, and still later was owned in part by Peter H. Peirce. There was a

SITE OF THE OLD FALL BROOK FURNACE

[1] *Eddy Note-Book.*

grist-mill a little farther up on this stream. Near the present Wareham Street was a grist-mill and a sawmill, owned by Captain Bennett and operated at one time by Abishai Miller.

In the early part of the last century Seth Miller resided here, the father of Darius and Seth Miller, the latter a lawyer in Wareham. The Miller family were large owners of real estate, their ancestors having acquired much land from the different Indian purchases. John Miller, one of the first settlers, married a daughter of Francis Coombs, and lived halfway between the homes in later years of Seth and Abishai Miller.

ABISHAI MILLER was born June 22, 1809, and was the youngest child of John and Susanna Miller. As a child he attended school in Middleboro, and on the death of his father was sent to Taunton, to learn the trade of a machinist. In 1837 he went to Boston, and was employed in the machine shop of Otis Tufts on Bromfield Street. In 1853, with others, he organized the Atlantic Works in East Boston, and obtained a charter from the legislature. As superintendent of construction, by hard work, energy, perseverance, and economy, he built up a large business, from which he retired in 1859 to his home in Fall Brook. At the outbreak of the Civil War he was again drawn into active business life at the urgent request of his former associates, and undertook the position of superintendent, to fill the government or-

ABISHAI MILLER

ders, which for four years demanded all his time and strength. He superintended the building of the monitors Casca and Nantucket, the turrets for the four monitors Monadnock, Shackamaxon, Passaconaway, and Agamenticus, as well as machinery for four gunboats, Osceola, Sassacus, Sagamore, and Canandaigua, and the man-of-war Nyphon. At their completion he again retired from business, and was a director of the company until 1876, when he was elected president of the board, an office which he held until his death. Early in his career he had a reputation as one of New England's best machinists, and the success of the Atlantic Works is due largely to his management. His active business life gave him little leisure to attend to town affairs, although at one time he served as selectman. He attended the Congregational Church when in Middleboro, and helped in its support. He died in East Boston, January 30, 1883, and was buried at the Green Cemetery.

THE OLD MILLER HOUSE

The shores about the two ponds were frequented by Indians before the coming of the colonists, and many relics have been found. Here for many years Feb Wicket, one of the last of the Nemasket tribe and the last of her generation, lived, supplied by the neighbors with food and clothing. She died in the early part of the last century, and was buried in the corner of the Miller farm.

Upon the borders of Wood's Pond, Ephraim Wood is said to have lived. Tispequin Pond, named from the noted Indian sachem, is about a mile in length, and with the other ponds furnished quantities of bog ore, which was carted to the furnace above mentioned, to Waterville, and to Muttock. In many deeds of land abutting on this pond, the proprietors reserved the right to take ore therefrom. The reddish color of the water is probably due to the presence of iron.

In the early part of the last century, with the general decline of the iron industry in the country, the business of Fall Brook terminated. For a few years there was a store opposite the house of Squire Seth Miller, and another on Wareham Street near the brook, where the farmers found a market for the linen and woollen cloth woven from their hand-looms. This neighborhood, on the old stage road, was one of the important villages for several generations. The land was formerly owned by the Millers, Sparrows, Porters, Vaughans, Tinkhams, and Westons.

CHAPTER XIX

THE GREEN

THE location of the first meeting-house and the subsequent church edifices erected on or near the Green have made it from the earliest times a place of more than ordinary interest.[1] The parish originally connected with the First Church included the whole town as originally incorporated. This continued until July, 1719, when it was divided into two parishes:[2] the one embracing nearly the whole of the present area of the town, having the First Church as its place of worship, and the other including the western part of the town, now Lakeville, and a portion of Taunton. There were three meeting-houses on or near the Green before the present one. The majority of the congregation went from three to five miles, and some even a distance of eight miles, to attend service.

The first minister was SAMUEL FULLER, a son of Dr. Fuller, the skilful physician who came over in the Mayflower. He married Elizabeth Brewster. Before his removal to Middleboro he was one of the deacons of the church in Plymouth. When he first

---

[1] In the initial is shown a measuring-post which stood near the liberty pole by the Sproat Tavern, used to ascertain the height of soldiers who volunteered in the patriot army.

[2] *History of Plymouth County*, p. 969. Deed recorded in Plymouth. Book 23, folios 203, 204. Later we find the following in the Middleboro records: —

"A meeting of 'the proprietors and owners of the land called the new burying place in Mid near the old meeting house,' was held tuesday Sept. 24, 1734 — agreable to a warrant issued from a justice to John Bennet who notified it the 21st previous. Adjourned to the last tuesday the 29th of Oct. next, when they met again in the old meeting house and chose Deac. Wood and Ebnr. Redding to see that no intensions were made by proprietors one upon another in burying the dead." The same committee were instructed to notify the owners of the schoolhouse to remove it from "said burying place."

came to town it is impossible to state, but he was here before the Indian War of 1675, and from the statement in Rev. Mr. Barker's sermon, he returned shortly after the resettlement. He preached to the people for sixteen years before he was ordained, and died a few months after his ordination, August 17, 1695, at the age of seventy-one. The following is the inscription on the stone marking his grave: —

> [HER]E LYES BURIED YE
> [BOD]Y OF YE REVD MR
> [SA]MUEL FULLER WHO
> [D]EPATED THS LIFE
> AUGST YE 17TH 1 6 9 5
> IN YE 71ST YEAR
> OF HIS AGE   HE
> WAS YE 1ST MINISTER
> OF YE 1ST CHURCH OF
> CHRIST IN MIDDLEGH

The town voted to pay[1] Mr. Fuller a "salarie" in 1680, of £20 a year; at one time "$\frac{1}{3}$ was to be paid in silver, and the $\frac{2}{3}$ in Wheat at 7/6, Rie at 3s, Corn at 2/6;" this was later changed to "$\frac{1}{4}$ in silver money, $\frac{3}{4}$ in current pay as passeth between man and man." He was one of the few to have the title of Mr. prefixed to his name. There is no record of his holding office, although he served as magistrate in writing wills and preparing other legal papers for the people. He was not a college graduate, as were many ministers, but was none the less regarded as a learned man. It was doubtless through his influence and labors that there were so many praying Indians in the town, and that their churches before the breaking out of the Indian War were so prosperous. As one of the original owners in the Twenty-six Men's Purchase, his allotment was set off in 1664, and was not included in what was given as the "ministers lot." In 1679 the town by vote gave to Mr. Samuel Fuller a tract of land[2] upon which he then lived, embracing about twelve acres, a little to the east of the Sturtevant place. The town also voted "to turn out and fence his fields, and every one who did not was to pay a bushel of corn."

The first meeting-house stood on the northerly side of

[1] Voted February 7, 1680.   [2] Voted August, 1679.

Plymouth Street, opposite the Sturtevant house. It was sold at auction[1] in August, 1701, for the sum of five pounds and two shillings.

In accordance with a vote passed in November, 1690, the town built a second meeting-house, which stood on the Lower Green opposite the present schoolhouse, " 36 foot in length 30 foot in breadth and sixteen foot the stud." It is not known of whom the land on which it stood was purchased, nor do we know the price paid. The records state, May 29, 1700, "the meeting house in Midlebery was Raised."

SECOND MEETING-HOUSE
(Reproduced from a very old pencil drawing)

It was sold and taken down in the year 1754 or 1755, and the materials used in building a dwelling-house which stood on the site of the present parsonage.

On June 20, 1717, the two acres of land west of the cemetery, known as the Lower Green, were conveyed by James Soule "unto military officers and military companies in Middleboro for the only proper use, benefit and behoof of the Military Company in Middleboro, successively, forever, lying near the meeting-house in Middleboro." The consideration of this deed was " The good will which I bear unto the military officers and company in Middleboro." For many years it was used for a training-green, and has since remained open for the public.

Adjoining this at the east is the parish burying-ground, which was purchased of James Soule March 30, 1717, for forty shillings, by " Peter Thacher, Jacob Thomson, Isaac Howland, John Morton, John Thomson, Thomas Thomson, Jeremiah Thomas, William Thomas, Jonathan Cobb, Sen'r., Jonathan Cobb, Jr., John Cobb, Sen'r., John Cobb, Jr., Rodulphus Elms, Ichabod King, Shubael Thomson, William Nelson, Daniel Vaughan, Ephraim Wood, John Soul, Aaron Simmins, John Fuller, Edward Thomas, Elisha Vaughan, Jabez Vaughan,

[1] See *History of the First Church of Middleboro*, p. 5.

George Vaughan, John Vaughan, John Hascol, William Hascol, Henry Wood, Samuel Barrows, Benjamin Eddy, Samuel Eddy, Jonathan Morse, Jr., Isaac Fuller, Ebenezer Redding, Jonathan Smith, Joseph Barden, John Miller, Jr., Jonathan Fuller, Samuel Tinkham, Seth Howland, Joseph Bennet, Samuel Cobb, Peter Bennet, Joel Ellis, Samuel Sampson, Benjamin Stuart, Thomas Bicknell, Josiah Conant, John Tinkham, Isaac Tinkham, Joseph Cobb, Ebenezer Fuller, John Bennett, Samuel Bennett, John Raymond, Jr., Samuel Bennet, Jr., Samuel Parlour, and Nemiah Holmes, said Soul reserving one share: to be used for a burying-ground for the persons above named, their heirs and assigns." It consisted of about two acres of land, lying in the Twenty-six Men's Purchase, and "is a part of my fifty acre lot, lying near the land I formerly gave for a training Green." "The first person buried in this cemetery" was Lydia Thomas, in July, 1717.

February 17, 1745, the following named persons, residents of the town, agreed to build a new meeting-house: "Jabez Vaughan, Jonathan Smith, James Smith, Gersham Cobb, Seth Tinkham, Ebenezer Finney, Noah Thomas, William Cushman, Benjamin Tucker, Edward Thomas, Samuel Eddy, Jr., Zachariah Eddy, John Cox, John Cobb, Ezra Clapp, William Thomas, Jas. Tinkham, John Smith, Edmund Weston, John Soule, Henry Thomas, Jeremiah Tinkham, Oxenbridge Thacher, Joseph Bates, Jr., Thomas Darling, Jonathan Smith, Jr., Joseph Thomas, Samuel Thomas, Samuel Smith, Benjamin Thomas, William Short, Hezekiah Purrington, John Thompson, Samuel Wood, Eph'm. Wood, Enen'r. Wood, and Caleb Thompson."

On June 9, 1745, the deed was recorded for two acres of land purchased of Ebenezer Sproat, "for 35 pounds in bills of credit of the old tenor." The land so purchased had been previously owned by James Soule.

The third meeting-house was built on the Upper Green in 1745, and remained until 1829.[1] The present meeting-house was built in 1827.

---

[1] A portion of the foundation is still to be seen a little east of the present edifice.

In early times, one of the most notable buildings in the neighborhood of the Green was the first parsonage, known as the "mansion house," on the site of the dwelling now occupied by William W. Wood. It was probably built about the time of the organization of the church, and remained until 1780, when it was destroyed by fire. With the exception of Oliver Hall, it was considered one of the finest houses in the town ; built with four gable ends, its rooms were spacious and high studded, and its front door opened into an enclosed yard.

PETER THACHER,[1] the first minister to live here, was born October 6, 1688, and was graduated from Harvard in 1706. He had an excellent library, was a diligent student, and one of the most learned men of his time. He married, January 25, 1711, Mary, daughter of Samuel Prince. She was known as "Madame Thacher," and was a woman of intelligence, of great help to the church, and noted for her benevolence.

Peter Thacher

The mansion house was used as a place of worship by Mr. Conant while the third meeting-house was being built, and it was here that he entertained Whitefield on his memorable visit to Middleboro in 1746. In this house also lived Samuel Prince,[2] one of the most prominent men in the colony. He died in 1728, and was buried with distinguished honor between the two large trees now standing at the west end of the burying-ground. His body was afterwards removed to the family tomb. Nathan Prince, his son, was a member of the First Church, and after graduating from Harvard, became an Episcopal missionary. "He was the author of a book on the Resurrection of our Lord, and of another on the government of the College, both of which were in great estimation."[3] Mrs. Prince was a daughter of Governor Hinckley of Plymouth Colony.

[1] See *History of the First Church of Middleboro*, p. 36.
[2] *Ibid.* p. 56. He came to Middleboro in 1723.
[3] Allen's *American Biographical Dictionary*, p. 683.

The Rev. SYLVANUS CONANT,[1] the fourth pastor of the church, lived in the house formerly owned by James P. Sparrow; the house, built in 1752, is now standing on Plympton Street, and the garden adjoins the land known as the "Upper Green." It was supposed that Middleboro would remain loyal to the Crown on account of the influence of Judge Oliver, but this was nullified by the ardent patriotism of Rev. Sylvanus Conant and Zachariah Eddy. From the beginning of the oppressive legislation, Mr. Conant was bold and fearless in his utterance in the pulpit and elsewhere against the injustice of the mother country. He not only went as a chaplain in one of the regiments, but, owing to his earnest words, thirty-five of the members of his church enlisted, and Captain Joshua Eddy raised a company for service during the war. The following anecdote is told of him at the time of the general alarm throughout the town and country on the entry of the British into New Bedford: "It was on Sunday, and a messenger came in breathless haste into the meeting-house where Mr. Conant was preaching, and standing in the broad aisle cried, 'There is an alarum!' There was no answer nor any stir; the announcement was repeated; the congregation were still unmoved; again he cried in a loud voice, 'There is an alarum!' Mr. Conant, bending towards him, replied with great mildness and simplicity, *We know it!*' The messenger retired. Many of the men went out, but Mr. Conant resumed his discourse, most of his hearers being less disposed to be grave at the dreadful portent of the alarum than to smile at the manner in which the minister disposed of it."[2]

Mr. Conant was a graduate of Harvard College, and delivered an oration in 1775, in commemoration of the landing of the pilgrims at Plymouth. This, with a volume of sermons published during his lifetime, shows his patriotism, scholar-

[1] *History of the First Church of Middleboro*, p. 37.
[2] *Eddy Note-Book.*

STURTEVANT HOUSE HOUSE OF REV. SYLVANUS CONANT

ship, and profound knowledge of the great doctrines of the New Testament. It is said that upon his death there was weeping in every house in town, at the loss of one of their best and dearest friends. Some years after, Samuel Joseph May, one of the earliest anti-slavery men, said in a public utterance, " He was a strong man, he was a sound man whom many loved, his disposition was fortunate, for it was full of disposition for others. He seemed more than most men to be at home in the world. He found ways of doing good wherever he went, and thus made for himself of all places a heaven; such glad interest for others beamed forth in his eyes that he seemed to have forgotten himself for others' welfare and their interest became his own. He was full of sunshine, radiant with hope, trusting in his God, and believing in man." He died of smallpox in the height of his usefulness as a minister of the gospel, a patriotic citizen, and a devout lover of his country, inspired with the belief that she would yet become a free, great, and mighty nation of the world. Eight of his parishioners, who died[1] between December 5 and 18, 1777, were buried with him in the field then owned by one of them, John Smith, near the house of the late Otis Soule. They were Zachariah Eddy, Widow Rhoda Smith, Joseph Smith, Bethia Smith, John Smith, William Soule, Sarah Reading, and Hannah Love. The following is the inscription on the stone at his grave : —

[1] *History of the First Church of Middleboro*, p. 37.

Memento Mori.
IN MEMORY OF
REV. SYLVANUS CONANT,
MINISTER OF THE FIRST CHURCH IN MIDDLEBOROUGH,
WHO DIED OF SMALLPOX, DEC. 8, 1777,
IN THE 58TH YEAR OF HIS AGE,
AND 33D OF HIS MINISTRY.

So sleep the souls, and leave to groan,
When sin and death have done their worst,
Christ hath a glory like his own,
Which waits to clothe their wasting dust.

Rev. Joseph Barker[1] lived in the Conant house during his ministry. He was a profound student, an able preacher, and a man of large influence throughout the town and county. At the one hundredth anniversary of the organization of the church, he preached a commemorative sermon. A volume of his sermons, published at the time, is still extant, which indicates his scholarship and ability. While faithful in the dis-

---

[1] Among his papers was the following letter to his daughter, which gives a picture of one phase of his life: —

WASHINGTON, Jan. 5th, 1809.

MY DEAR ELIZABETH: — Last Sabbath being new year's day, I preached for the first time for Mr. Bolch, to a respectible and attentive audience from Eph. 2:7.

On Monday we had clear cold weather. This day attended levee at the President's. A very large collection was there; English, Scotch, Irish, French, Spanish, Italian, German, Indian, Whigs, Tories, Federalists, Republicans; men, women, old ladies and young ladies. We all stood about and walked about to see and speak to one another. I had considerable talk with one of our red sisters, she is the lady of Cherokee Sachem who is here; she can talk some English though her husband cannot. She is dressed well in English habit with silk gown, &c. She appears to be a sensible woman and intelligent. She tells me that they spin and weave, make their own clothes, keep cows, make butter and cheese and attend to agriculture and all the employments of civilized life; that they have schools for their children and the gospel preached among them sometimes by missionaries.

Now, this great change in their habits has been effected by divine blessing attending the means used by Mr. Jefferson. All the missionaries ever sent there by the French and English have never done so much good as Jefferson has done since he has been President of the United States, and yet he is called an enemy to religion. I heartily wish all enemies of religion had as much humanity, benevolence, wisdom, moderation and firmness as that one man whom Federalists and Tories are wishing to destroy; but his character will shine upon the page of history, while those of his vile calumniators will not.

I am your affectionate Father,

JOSEPH BARKER.

charge of his duties as a minister of this church, he was, from the beginning, deeply interested in the public events of the day, and was elected, in 1805 and 1808, by a large majority to represent southeastern Massachusetts in the Ninth and Tenth Congress. While a member of the national House of Representatives, he was highly esteemed for his learning and his broad, statesmanlike views upon the great questions then before the nation. He served upon prominent committees, and took an important part in the debate upon the resolution prohibiting the importation of slaves into the country.

Rev. William Eaton lived in the house formerly occupied by Ira Bryant. The other clergymen settled over this church have resided at the Upper or Lower Green.

About one mile to the east of the church on Plympton Road was the farm of John Nelson, one of the first settlers of the town.[1] When Mr. Nelson went to Lakeville, he sold this farm to John Bennett. In 1824 Major Thomas Bennett, then the owner, while ploughing the ground where this first log house stood, came upon an Indian grave, in which were a knife, tomahawk, pipe, and other implements. There is no doubt that these belonged to the Indian who was shot from the fort and taken to Mr. Nelson's house, where he died.

JOHN BENNETT was the son of Peter Bennett of Bristol, England, from which place he emigrated in 1665. He was a weaver by trade, and on account of some domestic trouble, at the death of his mother he moved to this country, at the age of twenty-three. He settled at Jamestown, Va., then went to Beverly, Mass., where he became a landholder. From there he moved at the time of the Salem witchcraft, probably to escape annoyance from that delusion, and after spending a year in Weymouth, he came to Middleboro in 1687. He lived near the Cox sawmill, then built a house between that formerly occupied by Elijah Shaw

[1] See chapter on Early Settlers.

and the sawmill, and afterwards purchased[1] a farm owned by John Nelson, where he built a house on the site of the one which had been burned by the Indians after the death of their comrade. He took the oath of fidelity in 1689, and was selectman of Middleboro in 1692, 1693, 1695, 1697, and 1698. He was elected town clerk, March 28, 1693, which office he held for about thirteen years. He was a proprietor in the Twenty-six Men's Purchase at the running of the bounds in 1696, and owned lots in the Sixteen Shilling Purchase, and four lots in the South Purchase, of which he was clerk in 1689.[2] He married Deborah Grover of Beverly, in 1671. She died March 22, 1718, aged seventy, and was buried in the grave with her husband.

The house was built with a single room in front, and a porch projecting from one end, facing the highway. It was low in the ceiling, with large oak beams crossing overhead; the sills and sleepers rested on the ground. The door was filled with large-headed nails for protection against the Indians. This house, famous as the birthplace of several generations of Middleboro's citizens, was taken down in the early part of the last century. It had been visited by Peregrine White, the first child born to the pilgrims in this country, and was the home of Nehemiah Bennett and his wife Mercy. From him many facts relating to the early history of the town were obtained by the Massachusetts Historical Society, and published among their collections, and it is to him and his wife that we are indebted for much which would probably have been lost had it not been for their interest in local affairs.

Mercy Bennett was born in 1699, and died in 1799. She was a woman of unusual intelligence, and retained her mental faculties until the time of her death. In the great snowstorm of 1717, she with two other girls walked to Plymouth and back the same day to attend public service.

Upon the eastern corner of the Lower Green and facing

---

[1] There is a discrepancy as to the date of this purchase. General E. W. Peirce says 1687; *Eddy Note-Book*, 1691.
[2] *Early Records of Middleboro*, p. 114.

OLD SPROAT TAVERN

Plymouth Street stood the famous Sproat Tavern, taken down in the year 1898. For many years it was the only inn in this part of the town, and for more than two centuries was justly celebrated for its generous hospitality.

One writer of New England history says, " Religion was an ever present thought and influence in their lives, but they possessed another trait — with them neighborliness was as ever present, as sincere as their godliness — hence the establishment of the ordinary for the entertainment of travellers, the mutual comfort of the settlers." All through the country, licenses to keep taverns were granted on the condition that they be near the meeting-house, and inn-keepers were obliged to clear their houses during the church service. Orderly conduct was required and drunkenness was frowned upon, yet liquor was freely used by minister and layman alike. As early as 1646 the General Court passed a law by which landlords were forbidden " to suffer anyone to be druncken or to stay drinking in his house above an hour at one tyme "[1] under penalty of five shillings. The use of tobacco was considered much more degrading than indulgence in intoxicating drinks. Newspapers were not common, but at the tavern one could usually be found, and here men and women gathered to read and discuss the news of the day and all items of interest. The tavern was so situated that the arrival of the stage-coach was an

[1] *Laws of Plymouth Colony*, p. 50.

event of daily interest, — bringing visitors, or travellers on the way from Plymouth to Taunton and New Bedford. In the French and Indian War, the men of the town came here to enlist. In the Revolutionary War, it was the rendezvous for military men, and here the patriots of the town assembled to discuss the stirring events of the times. From this tavern, after the drill upon the Green, the companies, of Middleboro men marched to join the army in the different parts of the country. The spot is still pointed out where stood the famous liberty pole,[1] with the scale, showing the required height of the soldier. The prominent men of the colony, as well as distinguished noblemen from England, on their way to visit Oliver Hall, have stopped here. Probably at few inns in the colony were more illustrious men entertained than in this noted hostelry. It was the rendezvous of the men who marched to Plymouth in the War of 1812, and for a generation after, training day was observed on this "Green" each year.

This famous old house was built by James Soule in the year 1700, and soon after was occupied by the well-known family of Littles. Originally, it was only one half as large as when taken down, the northeastern part having been built first. From the second story was hung the sign, which is still preserved, and which is said to have been the first on any tavern to publicly express the sentiments of liberty, then creating so much excitement throughout the country. It was particularly daring on the part of Colonel Sproat, the proprietor of this old inn, to thus advocate the cause of independence in oppo-

[1] In a letter of Dr. Peter Oliver, Jr., under date of October 27. 1774, he writes:
"The week before last our Sons of Lyberty here, put up a Lyberty Pole on the Green. Our Minister grac'd the solemnity with his presence, and made a prayer under the Pole, and an harangue upon Lyberty. It was a day sat apart for the Officers of the Company to resign their offices. Mr. Conant took the pikes, and gave them to the new Officers: he has rendered himself very ridiculous to many of his friends.

"Ere this reaches, you will receive the News-Papers, which will give you an insight of our present troubles and difficulties. The Judge (Chief Justice Peter Oliver,) has been in Boston these 8 or 10 weeks. to save his life; and Madam has been there these 3 weeks, and are both going to winter there." *Diary and Letters of Thomas Hutchinson*, vol. i, p. 264.

sition to the views of so influential a man as Judge Oliver. The house retained much of its original furnishing in the wainscot, the great fireplace, the deep-seated square windows, and latticed panes of glass. In the room which formerly led to the tap-room were to be seen a shelf and panel, relics of the past; the tap-room continued for generations with the same furnishing. The kitchen showed the large oak beams as first placed over the ceiling, with the Dutch brick and panel work of English make about the large fireplace. In the early part of the last century it was enlarged to accommodate the many patrons of the inn. Here many of the congregation who worshipped in the adjoining old meeting-house used to assemble every Sabbath noon during the intermission.

SIGNBOARD OF THE OLD SPROAT TAVERN

There was a roaring fire in the large open fireplace, and near by was the well, still to be seen, with its long well-sweep. There are those now living who remember the gilded ball which hung on a post near the well.

During the "noonings" the large room was crowded, and the conversation there carried on was interesting and instructive. Some of the best thinkers of the town were there, discussing the current news of the day, as well as the sermon from its theological, argumentative, and scriptural point of view. Captain Joshua Eddy in Revolutionary times, and later his son, Zachariah Eddy, were often the chief speakers on these occasions. It was at one of these noonings that Franklin met them and spoke concerning their crops and the best way of enriching and draining their land. He gave them a few copies of "Poor Richard's Almanac," which were afterward eagerly sought after, and were usually hung over the fireplace under the king's arm. The old were never tired of repeating the sayings of that Sabbath afternoon, and taught them to their children and their children's children, so that the name of Franklin was one of the most honored in the old parish. In after years, the men of Middleboro appreciated what George III had said to his ministers during the early days of the Revolution, "Beware of that crafty rebel, Benjamin Franklin, he has more brains than all the rest put together, and will outwit you all."

Ebenezer Sproat was an influential man, of large and commanding figure, and held the office of treasurer and selectman for some years. He was the proprietor of the Sproat Tavern, and under his management the house acquired much of its reputation. He died January 23, 1786,[1] aged sixty-nine. His son, COLONEL EBENEZER, was born in the year 1752, and inherited the virtues of his father, and in addition to this, he was

noted for his boldness and energy, tempered by prudence and sagacity. When quite young he became interested in public affairs of the colony, and before he reached his majority, saw the inevitable consequences of the tyrannical acts of the Crown. He was one of the first to enlist in the Revolutionary army, and was with the troops to oppose the British possession of Newport at the time of its first invasion. He entered the army as captain, and such was his ability that he was promoted to the rank of major in the Tenth Massachusetts Regiment, commanded by Colonel Shepard. In 1778 he was with John Glover's Brigade of four regiments in Providence, as lieutenant-colonel. It was said at that time that he was the tallest man in his regiment, being six feet four inches in height, and of perfect proportions. He had winning ways, and yet the sternness of an able military commander. He was a strict disciplinarian, but his agreeable manner, his intelligence and cheerful disposition, made him a universal favorite with his officers and men. His knowledge of the art of war and the thorough discipline that he maintained attracted the attention of Baron Steuben, who

[1] *History of the First Church of Middleboro*, p. 240.

appointed him inspector of the brigade, an office he filled to the satisfaction of his superior officers. He was a friend of General Washington, and was frequently admitted to his confidence. Dr. Thacher, in his journal of military events, thus speaks of Colonel Sproat: —

"In the mutiny which broke out in January, 1781, in the New Jersey line, stationed at Pompton, in New Jersey, a detachment of five hundred men was ordered out to suppress it. In this detachment Col. Sproat was second in command, and Maj. Oliver was one of the field-officers. The distance from the main encampment was thirty or forty miles, and the snow two feet deep; it took nearly four days to accomplish the march. When they came in sight of the insurgents, Gen. Robert Howe, the commander, ordered his men to load their arms ; and as some of the officers distrusted the faithfulness of their own men, so prevalent was disaffection in the army, that, before making the attack, he harangued the troops on the heinousness of the crime of mutiny, and the absolute necessity of military subordination ; that the mutineers must be brought to an unconditional submission. The men entered fully into the patriotic spirit of their officers, and marching with the greatest alacrity, surrounded the huts so as to admit of no escape. Gen. Howe ordered his aide-de-camp to command the mutineers to parade in front of their huts, unarmed, in five minutes. Observing them to hesitate, a second message was sent, when they instantly obeyed, and paraded in a line, unarmed, two or three hundred in number. The general then ordered three of the ringleaders to be selected for condign punishment. These

COLONEL EBENEZER SPROAT

unfortunate men were tried on the spot, Col. Sproat being president of the court martial, standing on the snow, and they were sentenced to be shot immediately. Twelve of the most active mutineers were selected for their executioners. This was a most painful task, and some of them, when ordered to load their guns, shed tears. Two of them suffered death on the spot; the third one was pardoned, as being less guilty, on the representation of their officers. Never were men more completely humbled and penitent. Tears of sorrow and of joy streamed from their eyes, and each one seemed to congratulate himself that his forfeited life had been spared. The general then addressed the men in a very pathetic and impressive manner: showing the enormity of their crime, and the inevitable ruin to the cause of the country, to which it would lead. They remained true and faithful soldiers to the end of the war."

That service, Colonel Sproat often said, was the most painful ever imposed upon him, but such was the position of the continental army at this time that the insubordination manifested in the New Jersey troops called for most severe measures, and after that lesson there was no further mutiny on the part of any of the troops.[1] It is to the credit of the men from the New England colonies that no revolt ever occurred among them, and Washington said at one time in view of this, "God bless the New England troops."

In the early part of the war Colonel Sproat was at home on a furlough, when his fondness for a joke was seen in the following incident: Three soldiers, passing through Middleboro, stopped at the tavern, where his mother placed what he considered a rather scanty meal before them. When they inquired the price, he called to his mother, "How much is it worth to pick those bones?" "About a shilling, I suppose," was the answer. He returned to the room, took three shillings from the drawer, and handed one to each of the men, who went on their way much pleased at their treatment. Later, when his mother asked for the money, he exclaimed as if in surprise, "Money! did I not ask you what it was worth to pick those

[1] Hildreth, *Lives of the Early Settlers of Ohio.*

bones; and you replied a shilling? I thought it little enough for such a job and handed them the money from the till, and they are gone."

After the war he lived in Providence, where he married Catherine, daughter of Abraham Whipple. In 1786 he was appointed surveyor for Rhode Island of the lands west of the Ohio, and later settled upon the banks of the Marietta River. His fearless character, as well as his fairness in dealing with the Indians, soon won their respect. The Indians called him Hetuck, or Big Buckeye, from his eagle eye and stately bearing. He rose to be a prominent man in the state, and from the name the Indians gave to him, Ohio took the name of the Buckeye state. At the recent celebration of the city of Marietta, Colonel Sproat was duly honored as the founder of a number of institutions which have rendered Ohio the Massachusetts of the West. He was an original member of the Society of the Cincinnati. He died in February, 1805.

Colonel Sproat had a brother Thomas, who, upon the death of his father, succeeded to the paternal estate and successfully carried on the old tavern. It is much to be regretted that a building so connected with the historic events of the town, county, and state could not have been preserved as a memorial of former times.

Dr. Thomas Sturtevant, a physician of skill, and widely known throughout this and adjoining towns, commenced his practice on the old Sturtevant farm, and died in 1836, leaving several children. George became a well-known physician, and succeeded to his father's estate and practice. Another son was Thomas, whose genial good-nature, ready wit, and remarkable fluency of language gave promise of much which was, unfortunately, never realized. There was scarcely an event in town which was not made a subject of his ready rhyme in longer or shorter poems, epitaphs, or sonnets. While a prisoner in Canada, in the War of 1812, he wrote at one sitting, apparently without thought or preparation, the following acrostic on the Lord's Prayer: —

1 Hildreth, *Lives of the Early Settlers of Ohio*, p. 240.

"Our Lord and King, who reign'st enthroned on high,
Father of light! mysterious Deity!
Who art the great I AM, the last, the first,
Art righteous, holy, merciful and just.
In realms of glory, scenes where angels sing,
Heaven is the dwelling place of God our King,
Hallowed thy name, which dost all names transcend.
Be thou adored, our great Almighty Friend,
Thy glory shines beyond creation's space,
Named in the book of justice and of grace.
Thy kingdom towers beyond thy starry skies;
Kingdom satanic falls, but thine shall rise.
Come let thine empire, O thou Holy one,
Thy great and everlasting will be done!
Will God make known his will, his power display?
Be it the work of mortals to obey.
Done is the great, the wondrous work of love,
On Calvary's cross he died, but reigns above,
Earth bears the record in thy holy word,
As Heaven adores thy love, let earth, O Lord;
It shines transcendent in th' eternal skies,
Is praised in Heaven, — for man the Savior dies.
In songs immortal angels laud his name,
Heaven shouts with joy, and saints his love proclaim.
Give us, O Lord, our food, nor cease to give
Us that food on which our souls may live!
This be our boon to-day. and days to come,
Day without end in our eternal home :
Our needy souls supply from day to day.
Daily assist and aid us when we pray.
Bread though we ask, yet Lord thy blessing lend,
And make us grateful when our gifts descend.
Forgive our sins, which in destruction place
Us the vile rebels of a rebel race ;
Our follies, faults, and trespasses forgive,
Debts which we ne'er can pay, or thou receive ;
As we, O Lord, our neighbor's faults o'erlook,
We beg thou'dst blot ours from thy memory book.
Forgive our enemies, extend thy grace
Our souls to save, e'en Adam's guilty race.
Debtors to thee in gratitude and love,
And in that duty paid by saints above.
Lead us from sin and in thy mercy raise
Us from the tempter and his hellish ways.
Not in our own, but in his name who bled,
Into thine ear we pour our every need.

> Temptation's fatal charms help us to shun,
> But may we conquer through thy conquering Son!
> Deliver us from all which can annoy
> Us in this world, and may our souls destroy.
> From all calamities which men betide,
> Evil and death, O turn our feet aside;
> For we are mortal worms, and cleave to clay;
> Thine 't is to rule and mortals to obey.
> Is not thy mercy, Lord, forever free?
> The whole creation knows no God but thee.
> Kingdom and empire in thy presence fall!
> The King eternal reigns the King of all.
> Power is with thee, to thee be glory given,
> And be thy name adored by earth and Heaven,
> The praise of saints and angels is thine own;
> Glory to thee, the everlasting One,
> Forever be thy triune name adored;
> Amen! Hosanna! blessed be the Lord!"

A little beyond the house of Dr. Sturtevant, southwest of the Deacon Tilson place, were the house and lands of Luke Short, who died at the age of one hundred and sixteen, having lived during the reign of eight British sovereigns. He was born in Dartmouth, England, where he spent the first sixteen years of his life. He had seen Oliver Cromwell ride through the streets, of whom he spoke as "a rough, burly, soldierly looking man and a good soldier," and was present at the execution of Charles I. After leaving England, he pursued a seafaring life in Marblehead, then settled in Middleboro and there reared a family of children. At one hundred years of age he used to work on his farm, and his mental faculties were but little impaired. He was hoeing corn one day, and stopping to rest at a rock near by, recalled a sermon preached ninety years before by John Flavel, the great London preacher, who at the close of his sermon had said: "How can I bless whom the Lord hath not blessed!" He had paused and all was silence; no one moved, or spoke; an English baronet who was present fell to the floor in a swoon. The recollection of this scene was so vivid that Mr. Short became a changed man, a devout christian, uniting with the church, of which he remained a loyal member until his death in 1746.

Rev. Thomas Palmer,[1] the second pastor of the church, lived in one of the garrison houses built soon after the resettlement, later known as the Morey place, on the northern side of Plymouth Street, west of the house of Ira Bryant. The house had four gable-ends and two ridge-poles, after the style of the old meeting-house. He died June 17, 1743, aged seventy years.[2] A stone which has this inscription marks his grave in the parish burial-ground : —

> " All ye that pass along this way,
> Remember still your dying day,
> Here 's human bodies out of sight,
> Whose souls to —— have took their flight,
> And shall again united be
> In their doomed eternity."

His wife Elizabeth died April 17, 1740, aged sixty-four. He had a numerous family, most of whom died young. His estate descended to a daughter, who married a Mr. Cheney, and from her to Mrs. Morey and her children, Jack and Hannah, well known for their marked peculiarities, which made them the subject of constant jest and joke.

Until recently there has been no business here save a blacksmith shop opposite the mansion house, and later one on the Green.

[1] See chapter on Ecclesiastical History.
[2] *History of the First Church of Middleboro*, p. 36, gives his age as seventy; p. 82 as seventy-eight.

CHAPTER XX

THOMASTOWN, ROCK, ROCKY MEADOW, RAYMOND NEIGHBORHOOD, FRANCE, SOUTH MIDDLEBORO

HISTORY associates the name of Thomastown with that of David Thomas and his descendants, but Deacon Benjamin Thomas, whose residence is still standing, was, in the century before the last, perhaps the most prominent man of the place. He was not liberally educated, but was a man of strong common sense, of sturdy principle, well versed in the scriptures, conscientious in the performance of every duty, and was well known throughout the county. He was chosen deacon of the First Church May 23, 1776, and filled many important positions in the town.

"In 1782, he was a representative, and in 1788, a member of the convention which adopted the Federal Constitution. When a bill was under discussion for repealing the law of primogeniture, the deacon declared his doubts, as the Scriptures showed special favors for the first born. A Boston gentleman said, the deacon mistook the Scriptures, for they said that Jacob, though the younger brother, inherited the birthright. The deacon said, the gentleman had forgotten to tell us how he obtained it, how Esau sold his birthright for a mess of pottage, and how Jacob deceived his father, pretending to be Esau, and how his mother helped on the deception — he had forgotten all that. The laugh was at first against the deacon, but at last turned against the gentleman from Boston."[1]

He died January 18, 1800, in the seventy-eighth year of his age.

Deborah Sampson, a young woman widely known for her patriotism in enlisting as a young man in the Revolutionary

[1] *History of the First Church of Middleboro*, p. 61.

army, lived in this neighborhood in the early part of her life. She was born in the adjoining town of Plympton, December 17, 1760, and was a descendant of William Bradford. Her father, Jonathan Sampson, Jr., was deprived of the portion of the property which should have descended to him, and is said to have fallen into habits of intemperance; this finally led to the separation of his children, and the family were scattered. At the age of ten years Deborah was received into the home of Jeremiah Thomas, where she lived for ten years and more, until the time of her enlistment. Mr. Thomas, as an earnest patriot, did much towards shaping the political opinions of the young woman in his charge, who early developed talent and a strong desire for knowledge. Her perceptions were quick and her imagination lively; she soon became absorbed in the stirring questions of the day. For a few years before she lived with Mr. Thomas, she was in the home of the Rev. Peter Thacher, the third minister of the First Church.

DEBORAH SAMPSON

It is said that early in life she kept a journal, recording her good deeds on one page and her bad deeds on the opposite page. The events during the early years of the war for independence made a deep impression upon her mind, and without informing her closest friend of her intention, she had probably determined to see something of the world beyond her neighborhood and to help in some way the patriot cause. Such was her ability that before she was nineteen, in 1779, she was employed to teach six months in a public school in Middleboro. She had been bound out to service, but after this term expired, she was at liberty to choose for herself. The house in which her school was kept stood on the spot where Elisha Jenks now resides, but the building was afterwards moved to Water Street and occupied as a dwelling-house. She then boarded in the house of Abner Bourne, and such was her success as teacher that she was engaged for the next season. She was accustomed to attend church at the meeting-house in the Upper Green, but afterwards became interested in the preaching of Rev. Asa Hunt, a Baptist minister at the Rock, and joined that church. While she was with Deacon Thomas, she grew very skilful in spinning linen and worsted, and during the winter months was employed by many of the residents of the town to do their nicest spinning. She was often in the old Morton house, the Bourne house, and at the Sproat Tavern, engaged in her work. The hope that she might in some way serve her country had been cherished for months before she determined to assume male attire and enlist as a soldier in the Continental army. She had purchased from Mr. Leach's store in Muttock cloth which she secretly took home and made into a suit, working after her day's spinning was finished and at odd hours that her secret might not be discovered. It is said that after she had completed these clothes she walked to Taunton in the night for fear of meeting some of her old acquaintances on the road, and remained there until she became accustomed to her new attire. Early in the year 1782, as a recruiting officer was in Middleboro, she enlisted under the name of Timothy Thayer. When the supposed Timothy Thayer was signing the articles of agreement, an old lady who sat near the fire carding wool remarked that Thayer held his pen just as "Deb" Sampson did. Feeling that this circumstance would excite suspicion, she absented herself from that neighborhood. Her disappearance and the suspicions excited created no little talk thereabout, but her courage and determination were undaunted. It is said that from Middleboro she walked

DEBORAH SAMPSON'S HOME

to Taunton, and from Taunton to New Bedford, where she offered to enlist on an American cruiser, but withdrew upon learning that the commander treated his men badly. From that place she walked to Boston, Wrentham, Worcester, Roxbury, Dedham, and finally enlisted in May, 1782, in Medfield, with fifty others. She marched with her company to West Point under the name of Robert Shurtleff, and followed the fortunes of the army until the close of the war. She was in many of the skirmishes and battles of the Revolution, and belonged to Captain Webb's company of Light Infantry in Colonel Shepherd's regiment. In the first battle of the regiment she was wounded in the left breast by a musket-ball, and never recovered from its effect. She hastily staunched the blood, and by the light of the camp-fire took out the bullet with a soldier's sharp knife, and dressed and took care of her wound without any assistance. She said afterwards that the pain made her faint, but that was of small account compared with the danger of having her sex discovered, as it would have been had she submitted to the examination of a surgeon. After the first battle she met Colonel Ebenezer Sproat, but fortunately he did not know her, although she had often been employed as spinster in his father's house. By her skill and adroitness she was not recognized as a woman by the army, although one day, while waiting on a poor wounded soldier, she spoke to him in such tones of kindness that he exclaimed in amazement, "Bob Shurtleff, you are a woman, no man ever spoke in a tone like that;" then seeing, no doubt, the distress his remark had caused, he said quickly, "but never mind, Bob, your secret is safe and I will never betray you."

On one occasion her duty called her near General Washington, and she used often to relate incidents and sayings which she had heard from the great father of his country. She served with Lafayette and worked in the trenches at the siege of Yorktown, where she was again severely wounded, but her sex seemed to escape the notice of the surgeon, and before the wound had healed she rejoined the army and continued to do most valiant service.¹ In the spring of 1783 she was appointed aide-de-camp to General Patterson and taken into his family. At the close of the war she remained but little in Middleboro, and the church with which she had been connected commenced proceedings against her, and excluded her for unseemly conduct in assuming the dress and manner of a man. This did not affect her standing in the estimation of all who had known her, and some of the ladies of Middleboro, after the war was over, used to say that they wished they had taken some part in the war as "Debbie" did. In the early part of 1784 she resumed the apparel of a woman and her old employment of spinning, and on the 7th day of April, 1784, she married Benjamin Gannet, a respectable and industrious farmer, who resided in Sharon. She was placed on the pension list in 1805, and by a special act of Congress, her heirs were granted the same pension as was allowed to widows or orphans whose husbands or fathers had died from wounds received in the army. She was placed on the pension roll of invalid pensions by the commonwealth of Massachusetts, where she received $48 per year, which was afterwards increased to $76.80 per year. This she relinquished in 1818 for the benefit of the act of May 18, under which she received $8 per month, which was continued until her death.

She died April 29, 1827, aged sixty-eight years. It is worthy of remark that while she served in the army and all through her subsequent life, no word of suspicion was ever raised against her character. She seems to have been a worthy, upright woman, respected and revered by all who knew her.²

---

[1] She used to relate that at one time she felt the wind from a cannon-ball, which passed over her head and killed four men behind her. She was with a detachment under General Lincoln opening trenches within a short distance of the enemy's lines. The labor and exposure were such that she contracted a severe cold, blistered her hands, and showed signs of extreme exhaustion. When General Lincoln noticed her condition, he said, "You have too great a measure of fatigue upon you, my fine lad, retire to your tent and pleasantly dream an hour or two." Then followed several days when she was in the thickest of the fight. She witnessed the surrender of Cornwallis. *Sampson Genealogy*, p. 60.

[2] For many of these facts, see the *Life of Deborah Sampson, the Female Soldier of the War of the Revolution.*

ROCK

A large ledge running for half a mile from one road to another has given the name to this thriving little village, which was before this called Beaver Dam. The post-office was established here in 1849. On this rock the early settlers worshipped, and after the church was established it was called Rock Meeting-house, but this has now been changed to Rock. Since the erection of the Atwood Lumber Mill and the box factory, and the establishing of a post-office and the stores of Turner and Atwood, it has grown to its present size.

In early days there was a training-green on the common, which was used until the land was sold, about 1845, and set apart as an addition to the Rock Cemetery.

ROCKY MEADOW

Rocky Meadow is sometimes known as Mahuchet, probably from an Indian chief by that name, and like many other parts of the town, was formerly much more thickly settled than at present. In this neighborhood is a hill called Robin's Hill, said to be the highest point of land in the county, and to the northwest is a remarkable tract of land, known as Rocky

VIEW OF THE ROCK

Meadow Pond. It has an area of about forty acres entirely turfed over with grass, and is sometimes called Mahuchet Pond, and from it a brook by that name flows to the south. The roots are so woven together that when people walk upon them the surface waves like that of the ocean, but they are strong enough to bear up a man without difficulty. Under this depth of grass and roots there seems to be water to the depth of from twenty to thirty feet. Nearby there was a sawmill dating back for more than one hundred years, owned by Captain Joshua Eddy; on its site has been erected a house for the storing of cranberries, which are gathered in large quantities from the extensive bogs.

RAYMOND NEIGHBORHOOD

In the change of population, this place has, within the past fifty years, lost much of its significance. It is situated between Waterville and Thomastown, and although in the early settlement its soil was productive, it is now one of the poorest and most uninviting parts of the town. A hundred years ago its population was quite numerous. They were the descendants of John Raymond, who came from Salem during the witchcraft excitement. While a resident of Salem, he early enlisted in King Philip's War in the company commanded by Captain Joseph Gardner, and was one of the bravest and most efficient men in his command. He was in the great battle at the taking of the Indian fort in the Narragansett country on the afternoon of Sunday, December 19, 1675, and is said to have been the first soldier who[1] entered the fortification. After this campaign, he continued in various commands until the close of the war. He united with the First Church, April 29, 1722, and was a worthy, devoted christian, a man of much influence, commanding the respect of all. He died July 5, 1725, in the seventy-seventh year of his age. Some of his descendants, with other residents of Middleboro, moved to Woodstock, Vermont.

[1] *History of Plymouth County*, p. 949.

FRANCE

France takes its name from Dr. Francis Lebaron,[1] a native of France, who bought a large tract of country in the early part of the eighteenth century, some two miles in extent, on the south side of the Weweantitt River.[2] His son James and others of his descendants settled there shortly after. About the middle of the last century the numerous families of that name moved to other parts of the country, and only a few now reside here.

Dr. Lebaron was a surgeon of a French ship of war which was wrecked in Buzzard's Bay in 1694, when England was at war with France. He, with the officers and crew of the ves-

---

[1] The modern spelling is Le Baron.

[2] The real estate purchased by Dr. Francis Lebaron in the South Purchase was as follows: —

From Philip and Thomas Delano of Duxburrow, November 16, 1701, lots 145 and 146, containing 90 acres, more or less.

From Abram Jackson of Plymouth, April 13, 1702, lot number 193 in the seventh division and lot number 215 in the eighth division, with other rights in the land belonging to the said Jackson.

From Francis Curtis of Plymouth, May 6, 1702, lots 112 and 124.

From John and Samuel Dogget of Marshfield, August 17, 1702, lots 142 in the fifth division and lot 176 in the sixth division.

From John Jones of Marshfield, March 31, 1703, all of his share in lot 121 in the South division one half mile in length, and lot 143 in the fifth division.

From John Benson, Jr., of Rochester, April 17, 1703, lot 23 and lot 24.

From Joseph Vaughan, June 16, 1703, lot 144 in the fifth division and one other lot bounded but not numbered in the deed.

From David Thomas of Middleboro, July 5, 1703, two acres of meadow.

From Jeremiah Thomas of Middleboro, August 31, 1703, one third of the meadow bought with his two brothers as appears in the town records of Middleboro.

From Nathaniel Jackson of Plymouth, October 19, 1703, one share of upland which was Major Winslow's in the 130th lot in the fourth division and lot 211 in the eighth division. One share which was John Winslow's in the 14th lot in the first division and in the 122d lot in the fifth division. One share which was John Alden's, the 109th lot in the fourth division and the 58th lot in the second division.

From William Thomas of Middleboro, November 9, 1703, one half share of the lot 217.

sel, was made a prisoner of war and sent to Boston. As they stopped at Plymouth for the night, they were lodged in the house of William Bacon near the Plymouth Green, where Dr. Lebaron learned that a lady residing in the town had suffered a compound fracture of the leg. The doctors were about to amputate it, but Dr. Lebaron, by his skilful treatment, prevented the operation. The war ended soon after the prisoners reached Boston, and such had been his success, and so winning were his manners, that at the request of the selectmen of Plymouth, with the consent of Lieutenant-Governor George Stoughton, he settled permanently in Plymouth. He married Mary Wilder, a daughter of Edward Wilder of Hingham, and died in Plymouth in 1704, and was buried on Burial Hill. He left three sons, James, Lazarus, and Francis.

At the time of his capture he was called by his brother officers "Le Baron," and refused to give his rank or name even to his wife and family. He was a cultivated gentleman, of courtly bearing, far better educated in his profession than the physicians of the colony, and was always reported to be a nobleman in disguise. The leading events in his life at Plymouth, with his romantic marriage, are the subject of an interesting romance by Mrs. Jane G. Austin. He was a Roman Catholic, wearing a cross upon his breast, and although he had no sympathy with the religion of the colony, he remained silent in reference to his faith.

His oldest son, James, inherited his father's ability, and in the early part of his life was a surveyor. There is a well-authenticated tradition that he came to Middleboro to survey the lands which his father had purchased, and while there was overtaken by a severe storm which made the roads impassable for some time. He stopped in the house of John Benson, and while there became engaged to his daughter Martha. His proud-spirited father did not approve of this marriage, and threatened to disown him, but he afterwards became reconciled, and the son settled upon the land which had been purchased by his father. At his death he was a man of wealth, as shown by his inventory,[1] and prominent in the affairs of the colony.

Captain Joseph Lebaron, who served in the volunteer militia in the War of 1812, and with his company went to the defence of Warcham, was a descendant of "the nameless nobleman."

Among other men who lived in this neighborhood was Lieutenant Josiah Smith, and the cellar of his house can still be pointed out. He served in the army throughout the Revo-

---

[1] A true Inventory of all & singular the Goods Chattels & Real Estate of Mr. James Lebaron prized at Middleboro Oct. 2nd. 1744 by John Shaw, Benjamin Churchill and Neh. Bennet as followeth, to the value of bills of the old tenor.

Impremis.

His apparel, silver spoons & silver buttons & silver pieces	£29. 4
Item His armes & Ammunition His Razor and hone	10. 6
Item his books of all sorts	3.19
Item his Beds & all yᵉ furniture belonging to him	33. 8
Item his puter Brass Glass & Leather ware	6.18
Item his holler Iron ware & Chimney brass	7.
Item his chests chairs & wooden ware	16. 4
Item his Carpenter tools Blacksmiths tools	12. 3
Item his tools for husbandry, saddle & bridle	19.
	£136.12
Item his cattle sheep, Goats, Swine & horse	244.10
	£382.12
Item his 142 and 143 with the improvement that is on them with his House, Barns Corn House & Orchard	600
Item his 112 lot part cedar swamp	86
Item his 121 lot with some improvement	60
Item his half of the 123 lot	20
Item his 144 and 145 lot	80
Item his 146 lot	50
Item his uppermost lot of meadow on South meadow river with half what is called the coast	140
Item his Meadow that lyeth below the double brook	100
Item his salt meadow by estimation two acres	100
Item his land that lyeth on the East side of South Meadow River by estimation twenty nine acres	25
Item his Indian Corn Rye & hay	42
Amounting to	£1679.12

PLY. ss. Dec. 19, 1744. Martha Lebaron Adm. sd estate made oath that the inventory contains all his estate so far as she knows, and when she shall know of more shall give it in yᵉ sd. appraisers being also under oath

Before me

J. CUSHING

Judge of Probate.

lutionary War; he was with Ethan Allen at the capture of Fort Ticonderoga, and followed him, the second man to enter the fort; he was at Valley Forge, crossed the Delaware with Washington, and for a time was a member of his body-guard. He used to say with pride that he had taken a glass of wine from the hand of Lady Washington. Soon after the Revolutionary War he moved to Wareham, and lived on Indian Neck.

During the century preceding the last there were many large farms here, which, with the houses, were usually away from public roads, and connected by private paths from one farm to another.

This place has now become an almost unbroken woodland, with scarcely any trace of its former prosperity, excepting the well-built stone walls which here and there are still to be seen marking boundaries of farms or extensive cultivated fields. The growth of pine lumber has been remarkable; there is in this vicinity one lumber mill, known as Cushing's Mill, which with those at the Rock and South Middleboro saw not less than three thousand cords of white pine lumber a year, and have been doing so for a generation.

SOUTH MIDDLEBORO

South Middleboro was not settled until some time after the close of King Philip's War. In the latter part of the eighteenth century the Stillwater Furnace furnished employment for about forty men in the manufacture of hollow-ware from the iron ore obtained from the neighboring ponds, which was landed at the wharf on the eastern shore of Great Quittacus and carted from there to this furnace. This business was successfully carried on by Captain Zenas Wood, one of the best-known citizens, who also owned a retail store, to which Mr. Hooper succeeded on the death of Captain Wood. Mr. Hooper, a man much respected here, was often called to settle estates, advise with his neighbors, and adjust difficulties. Near the site of the furnace was a box-board and shingle mill.

In the middle of the last century Stillman Benson built

and carried on the Benson Lumber Mill. He was elected to different offices in town, and was largely instrumental in securing the location of the Cape Cod railroad and in establishing a station here.

Here are the most extensive pine woods of the town; their rapid growth has been remarkable, and they have not been materially diminished, notwithstanding the large amount of timber used in the lumber mills. Twenty-five years ago Middleboro was one of the largest lumber-producing towns of the state. There are now three mills in this neighborhood, known as the Witham, Benson, and Gammons mills.

STILLMAN BENSON

Here lived Samuel Smith, whose eventful life is entitled to something more than a passing notice. He was born in Rhode Island in 1757, and after the battle of Lexington enlisted in the Continental army. He was stationed in the Highlands on the Hudson where Major André was brought into camp, and remained until he was hanged. At Red Bank he was engaged in a severe battle with the Hessians, and in November, 1776, he marched with others to Valley Forge, suffering great hardships from cold and hunger, with the army, during that terrible winter. He acted as attendant to the army physician, who became one of his warm friends. During all the years of success and defeat he continued with the patriot army, until it disbanded in 1783. He had various adventures at the close of the war in many parts of the world: he was a baggage driver from Providence to Boston; a whaler to the coast of Brazil; later, he shipped for the West Indies, and after several voyages, he lived in Middleboro until his death. In 1853 an account of his life was published by the Middleboro "Gazette," which yielded him a small income during his old age. He lived in the house later owned by Frank Wallen.

Captain Abiel Peirce, whose services in the French and Indian War have been mentioned, lived about two and a half miles southwest fróm the Rock meeting-house, on Miller Street. The farm he owned is now in the possession of Joseph Sherman, Esq. ; the house he occupied was taken down a few years ago and a new one erected on its site.

CHAPTER XXI

EDDYVILLE, WATERVILLE, SOULE NEIGHBORHOOD, HALIFAX

EDDYVILLE takes its name from Samuel Eddy and his descendants, who from the first settlement of the town have owned and occupied much of the land. They were men of character and influence, noted for their enterprise and public spirit, and have done not a little in aiding the various enterprises of the town; some of them were widely known throughout the colony and the commonwealth. The history of this locality necessarily includes much of the lives of the various members of this family. A sketch of the life of Samuel Eddy has been given in the chapter on Early Purchasers. The name of his wife is unknown. She came from Kent, and probably had not been educated to observe all of the religious tenets of her neighbors in the pilgrim church, especially as to the observance of the Lord's day. Among the records of the court in Plymouth, we find that at one time she presumed to hang out clothes washed just before the going down of the sun on a certain Lord's day, for which she was brought before the governor and council and fined ten shillings, but for reasons the records do not show, it was remitted. Again, she was brought before the council "upon a most grievous offense," in walking from Plymouth to Boston upon a Lord's day, but her answer was that she had taken this walk for charity for a sick friend, Mistress Saffin, whom she had known in the old country. The court excused this as an act of mercy, but admonished her to do so no more.

Samuel Eddy's name occurs in the records of the colony in many transactions until about the year 1662. He possessed several hundred acres in the eastern part of the town, extending over a portion of Halifax, and including all of the land now known as Eddyville. In 1685 he was described as of Plymouth, living in Swansea. Part of the time before his death, in 1688, he lived with his son Obadiah,[1] who inherited his father's estate in Middleboro and Halifax, and after the war rebuilt his house, the site of which can still be pointed out in Halifax.

His son Samuel built a house in Eddyville near the great pear-trees, which was destroyed by fire in 1720, and the next year he built and occupied a house, now owned by C. F. Eddy, his descendant. This, probably one of the oldest houses standing, was inherited by Samuel's son Zachariah, and after his death was moved across the street, where it now stands. He was an ardent patriot, and four of his sons served in the Revolutionary War.

On the northerly side of Plympton Street, nearly opposite the house of the late Andros Eddy, stood a printing-office, owned and carried on by John, the eldest son of Zachariah Eddy. This was the first printing-office in town, and probably the only one in the old colony at that time. In 1759, at the age of twenty, he prepared and published an almanac from this office. It was printed in good type, and was quite similar in appearance to the Old Farmer's Almanac. The late Professor West said, "It was the best almanac that had ever been made up to that time." In the preface John Eddy writes : —

"These calculations I believe, and do not doubt that my readers will find and agree that they are very near the truth. Some may condemn what is here wrote perhaps for nonsense and folly, but I shall have this for my consolation that the world is a scene of folly and strange if an almanack maker shall not have his part therein."

The second almanac was written bearing this date, "Middleboro, Sept. 1759." He was a brilliant man, a mathematician,

[1] See chapter on Early Settlers.

and an astronomer. He was killed during the French and Indian War, at Crown Point, New York, when twenty-four years old.

Upon the Green, opposite the house of Samuel Eddy, stood the house of Captain Joshua Eddy, which was burned in 1820, rebuilt by him, and occupied a few years before his death. This is now owned by William C. Eddy.

Joshua Eddy joined the army in 1775, as a private in Colonel Cotton's regiment. He was present at the siege of Boston. In 1776 he was appointed lieutenant, and in 1777 he was offered a captain's commission in Colonel Gamaliel Bradford's regiment, on the usual condition of furnishing a certain number of men for three years.[1] Before leading on his recruits, he complied with a general order to go down to the hospital at Braintree and have the smallpox. He then started immediately, and took a large quantity of clothing, provisions, and equipments. He did not reach Ticonderoga, but fell in with the American forces at Hubbardstown on the retreat. His company suffered severely in that disastrous affair. The baggage was put on board boats to go to Skenesborough (Whitehall),

CAPTAIN JOSHUA EDDY

but was taken or destroyed by the British. He remained at Albany with the army till they rallied, marched back to meet Burgoyne, and was present at the two battles by which he was compelled to surrender. In the second (October 7) they were reënforced by several brigades, and fought with courage. He

[1] See chapter on the Revolution.

used to speak of the ruin and the booty of Burgoyne's camp, after his retreat, as prodigious. The evening after the surrender of Burgoyne they had orders to proceed down the river to Æsopus to meet General Vaughan. They pursued him to King's Bridge; he retired into the city of New York, and they then passed over into New Jersey. They went into winter quarters with the rest of the army under General Washington in December. Captain Eddy did not remain there long; but on hearing of the death of his father, he applied to General Heath for a discharge. His request being refused, he applied to the commander-in-chief, but on account of the scarcity of officers, he was allowed only an indefinite furlough. He immediately returned, and spent the winter in settling the affairs of his father. On April 10, 1778, he was married to Lydia Paddock, daughter of Zachariah Paddock of Middleboro.

The next May he returned to the army, and was at the battle of Monmouth, June 28. His regiment was not called into action, but was employed in scouting and foraging. At the close of the battle he heard General Washington, in great excitement and pale with rage, accuse General Lee of disobedience of orders, saying with an oath, "Had you taken the position with your command as I directed, you would have captured the whole British army." Great was his surprise at Washington's profane language, but the consequences of this disobedience were so serious, and the disasters so great to the struggling patriot army, that it would have required more self-control than man possesses to have refrained from such an outburst.

The summer of that year he spent with the Continental army in the vicinity of New York and Philadelphia. In the fall he again applied for his discharge; but all he could obtain was, as before, an indefinite furlough, leaving him still liable at any time to be called. For his services he received an annual pension of £20 a month, commencing April 4, 1818.[1]

At the close of the Revolutionary War he settled upon his large farm, which he cultivated with care, kept a store on the

[1] *Eddy Family*, p. 249.

RESIDENCE OF ZACHARIAH EDDY

Green, and built and carried on a large blast furnace at Waterville, known as Eddy's Furnace. During this time he built a schooner on the southerly side of Taunton River at Woodward's Bridge, which was launched and floated into Narragansett Bay. He is said to have been a man of deep religious feeling, and nothing better illustrates his christian character than the fact that, after his five sons were settled with their families about or near the Green, they were accustomed to meet for family prayers at his house every Sabbath afternoon and one evening in the week. He was a devoted, earnest member of the First Church, and was for some years one of its deacons. The only time his family ever saw him in tears was upon his return from the war on a furlough, when he found the state of religion so low that many had left the old church; and it was mainly by his exertions that it was saved from going over to another faith with so many of the Old Colony churches.

His son Zachariah, one of the prominent lawyers of the state, lived on the east side of the Green, Joshua lived next to his father, Nathaniel opposite, Ebenezer a half a mile away, and William S. in Waterville; Morton and John, his other sons, did not live in town. Nathaniel occupied the store formerly owned by his father and next to that owned by his brother Joshua. The business reputation of the sons of Captain Joshua brought a large circle of men to the neighborhood, and the office of Zachariah Eddy was usually full of clients. His house is still standing on the eastern side of the Green, and the office, a little south of the house, remains as he left it.

On Plympton Street, opposite Mr. Eddy's office, was the blacksmith shop of Captain William Ellis, a skilled workman, who had served in the Revolution, and who occupied the house built by Samuel Eddy in 1721.

Later, in the store formerly occupied by Nathaniel, shoes were manufactured for a number of years by Mr. George M. Leach and Joshua M. Eddy, a grandson of Captain Joshua. West of Eddyville, on Raven Brook, there was for many years a lumber mill, recently used as a box factory by Isaac Bryant.

OFFICE OF ZACHARIAH EDDY

On Plympton Street, a short distance from Eddyville as you approach the village from the west, stands the Clark place, built and occupied by Samuel Eddy, Jr., about 1725. He was born in 1710, and died November 8, 1746. He was a man of note, and filled many important positions. During the troubles in the First Church which followed Mr. Thacher's death, his judgment and opinion were relied on. When the committee from the General Court were considering the matters which had been brought before them, they are said to have stated that they could not understand the difficulties of the church until Samuel Eddy, Jr., came before them. It was a general remark at the time of his death that there was no member of the First Church who had so much intelligence, firm and consistent piety, and sound discretion as Samuel Eddy, Jr.[1]

RESIDENCE OF SAMUEL EDDY AND DR. POWERS

[1] *History of the First Church of Middleboro*, p. 58; *Eddy Genealogy*, p. 247.

At one time this house was owned and occupied by Dr. Stephen Powers, the grandfather of Hiram Powers, the celebrated sculptor, who, the latter part of his life, resided in Rome. Here Isaac McClellan, one of the poets of New England, often spent his summers. The house was later owned by Major Clark, and upon his death, by Harrison Clark, a well-known wit of the town, whose sayings have not been forgotten.

Rev. Francis Greenleaf Pratt, a son-in-law of Zachariah Eddy, made this village his home, after retiring from the ministry.

About the middle of the last century Eddyville was a place of much business activity as well as one of the social centres of the town. In 1833 a post-office was established there under the name of East Middleboro.

WATERVILLE

This village, formerly included as a portion of Eddyville, known as the Furnace, has within the past fifty years taken the name of Waterville. Eddy's Furnace, located on Whetstone Brook and built by Captain Joshua Eddy, was carried on for a few years after his death by his sons. William S. Eddy commenced business in Plympton in one of the first cotton factories of the country, where he lost all of his money. It took him ten years to pay the amount lost. With his brother Nathaniel as partner, he took charge of the furnace. The hollow-ware, or iron utensils, pots, kettles, and andirons, were not only sold here, but were shipped in large quantities to supply the market in other sections of the country. The iron used for these castings was obtained from the ponds, and when the supply gave out, it was brought from New Jersey to New Bedford by ships and carted from there; old iron was collected and brought to the furnace to be recast. This business furnished employment for about twenty-five men during the active season. When this furnace was in operation, one or two blasts were made during the year, which, when commenced, were worked night and day for a month or two. On the other side of the street and on the westerly side of the pond stood what was known as the cook house, where the workmen boarded during the continuance of the blast.

About the year 1840 the casting of hollow-ware was given up, and shovels were manufactured here, and still later, tacks. After Nathaniel retired from the firm, the business was carried on by William S. Eddy and his son, William C., who also kept a large store opposite his residence. Upon the death of William S. Eddy, the privilege was bought by Albert T. Savery, who successfully carried on a lumber mill for many years. A little below, but upon the same stream, is a sawmill at one time owned by Joshua M. Eddy, but since his death it has been carried on by Mr. Savery as a box-board mill. In early times there was a hat factory here. The dam and privilege are now unused.

WILLIAM S. EDDY

A little to the west of the residence of Mr. Eddy was the house occupied by Mr. Ichabod Tilson, familiarly known as "Skipper" Tilson, a title given to the foreman of a blast furnace, who had charge of melting the ore, preparing moulds, and superintending the castings. It was a position of responsibility, as the work of the furnace depended largely upon his oversight and skill.

A ridge of hills on the northerly side of the road has been known for many generations as Mount Carmel. The Plymouth railroad passes through this neighborhood, and has a station of this name.

SOULE NEIGHBORHOOD

In the will of George Soule, the thirty-fifth signer of the compact in the Mayflower, he leaves his "Middleberry land" to his daughters. Elizabeth married John Haskell, and Patience, Francis Walker, both of whom became residents of the town. Later, there was some fear lest his son John should endeavor to dispossess his sisters of this portion of the estate, and steps were taken to guard against this.

James moved from Duxbury to Middleboro in 1690, with his brother John, then a small boy. He married Lydia Tomson, a daughter of John Tomson, and built his first house about the year 1700 (near the site of the late Isaac Soule's house), which was soon after burned. It was a cold, wintry day, and the flames soon destroyed the wooden house, and with it all of his possessions. He and his young brother, who were alone in the house, barely escaped with their lives. In their distress he placed his small brother under a haystack while he went over the river Winnetuxet to his friends to obtain clothing for both of them.

At the time of the running of the bounds of the Twenty-six Men's Purchase, he and John were extensive land-owners. James was fined, October 2, 1690, five shillings for refusing to go on the expedition to Canada.

John Soule was born in 1632, and died in 1707. In his father's will he is referred to thus: "And forasmuch as my eldest son John Soule and his family hath in my extreme old age and weakness bin tender and careful of mee and very healpfull to mee and is likely for to be while it shall please God to continew my life heer therefore I given and bequeath unto the said John Soule, all the remainder of my housing and lands whatsoever."[1] He and John Tomson settled the dispute of the bounds of the town, June 24, 1681.

In this neighborhood Rev. Sylvanus Conant and eight of his parishioners, who died in 1777, were buried.

The name of Wolftrap Hill is associated with these two

[1] Windsor's *Duxbury*, p. 310.

brothers' early experiences. One of them was troubled by a wolf, which caught his poultry and otherwise injured the farm. He set a trap, digging a long trench in the ground,[1] and covering it with boughs and bushes so that it was entirely concealed. One morning he found in one part of the trench a wolf, and in the other part an Indian. He soon killed the wolf, and after an examination he found the Indian was on his way from Nemasket to Plymouth upon legitimate business, so he was released and allowed to continue on his journey.

Isaac Soule, a grandson of James, born about the year 1732, was an astrologer, or as then called, a conjurer, telling future events by the stars. His predictions were quite remarkable, and gave him an extended reputation; he was visited by many people from a distance, who came to inquire into their future.

One of the prominent men a century ago was William Soule, a great-grandson of the pioneer James. He was a man of stern principles, active in his religious duties. In different sections of the country there are many who claim James and John as their ancestors, but there are few of that name now living in Soule neighborhood.

Aside from the farming here, there are now some shingle and box-board mills; formerly there were two blacksmith shops, a brick kiln, and a tannery.

HALIFAX

"At a town meeting September 17, 1733, the town by vote so far granted the petition and request of Mr. Thomas Thompson, John Drew, John Drew, Jr., Ebenezer Fuller, John Fuller, John Thompson, Ephraim Thompson, Jacob Thompson, Francis Thompson, Ichabod Standish, Isaac Tinkham, Ebenezer Cobb, Timothy Wood, and Barnabas Thompson as to set off all the said petitioners and inhabitants that lie on the northeasterly side of Winnetuxet River in said town with their estates lying on the said side of the river to join with the adjacent parts of the towns of Plympton and Pembroke into a separate township, also the town chose Captain Ichabod Southworth,

---

[1] This was the usual method of catching the wolves which caused the early settlers so much trouble.

Benjamin Wood, Esq., and Mr. Thomas Nelson a committee to enquire into the circumstances of those of the said petitioners that lie on the southwesterly side of the said Winnetuxet River respecting their joining with those on the north side of said river with the adjacent parts of Plimpton and Pembroke as aforesaid and the said committee to view the land by them requested to be set off on said southwest side of said river as aforesaid and to run and stake such lines and bounds as they shall think proper for setting off them or any part of them with their estates if the committee think reasonable, Jacob Thompson as surveyor to assist said committee in running the lines, the said committee or any two of them to make report of their doings and concur therewith if they think reasonable."

As a result of this petition, in 1734 a small portion of the northerly part of what was formerly known as Middleberry was incorporated to form a part of the town of Halifax. Before this the boundary of the town extended to the Winnetuxet River. It was almost an unbroken wilderness,[1] but well adapted for agricultural purposes, as the soil was naturally rich. As the early settlers of the country depended entirely upon their farms for support, this portion of the town was considered most desirable. From the earliest time there have been large and valuable tracts of timber land, and the sawmills were among the first erected in this section. In the early part of the last century a large amount of ship timber was taken from here for the construction of vessels built in Kingston by the late Joseph Holmes.

JACOB TOMSON was the son of John Tomson, and lived near his father. He was born April 24, 1662, and died September 1, 1726, aged sixty-four. He was one of the original members of the First Church, and selectman from 1697 to 1701 and again from 1706 to 1726, except in 1710, and representative to the General Court, 1716 and 1719.

In the local militia he was ensign in 1700, and in 1708

---

[1] Much of this territory was included in the purchase made by Lieutenant John Tomson of William Wetis-pa-quin, sachem of the Neponsets, and included, with other purchases, about six thousand acres of land. Upon this land stood the log house built by John Tomson.

became captain. From 1720 he held a commission as justice of the peace, and was town clerk from 1706 for several years. His son Jacob, born in 1695, was town treasurer for several years and held various offices in town. His name is sometimes confused with that of his father in the early records.

In 1703, at the time of the dissension on account of Rev. Mr. Palmer, he became dissatisfied and left the church for some time, desiring a recommendation to join the church in Plymouth.[1] It occasioned much sorrow and hard feeling, and, as a result of a council, he and his family asked the forgiveness of the church and were dismissed with great regret. He seems to have taken the lead in the deposition of Mr. Palmer and the conduct of the church in relation thereto.

He was distinguished throughout the old colony as a surveyor, and as a most excellent and upright magistrate. He bought into the Twenty-six Men's Purchase before the war, and surveyed and divided it among the proprietors in lots; he also surveyed many of the other purchases from the Indians and settled many estates in this and adjoining towns. He was a man who had the respect, not only of the town but of the colony.

Upon the death of Lieutenant John Tomson, in the division of his estate, his homestead with about seven hundred acres of

---

[1] "1703. The Church of Christ in Middleboro having laid Leut. Jacob Tomson & his wife (who upon some scruples & dissatisfaction withdrew from ye communion of ye church & desired a dismission to ye church in ye New Society in plimouth that being nearer to y^r dwelling &c) und^r publique censure for y^t s^d withdrawing & refusing to grant y^m s^d dismission he & his wife sent to this church to send ye pastors & messengers to Joyn in Councill wth ye Elders & messengers of ye churches of weymouth bridgewater & Taunton (whom he had sent to) to be attended on ye 26 Oct. 1703, ye church made choice of our brother William Shertleff & our Brother Nathaniel Morton to Go wth ye pastor & Eld^r to ye service. It must also be observed y^t ye Sabbath before ye Councill was to meet ye church in Middleboro also sent Letters to us to be wth y^m (they Joyning wth Leut. Tomson in Councill) & sent also to ye chchs of Barstable and Sandwilch — ye s^d Councill was attended on ye time abovs^d & Came to a result y^t Leutenant Tompson & his wife should make an acknowledgment for y^t Irregular withdrawing from ye Communion of ye church and upon y^t ye church should give y^m a dismission to ye church in ye New Society in plimouth wch were both Complyed wth and attended."

land fell to his son Thomas, who was born October 19, 1664. Among his intimate friends was John Morton. There is a tradition that Mr. Morton often urged him to marry, saying that he had arrived at a proper age, then being twenty-five years old. He replied, "I will marry that daughter of yours" (pointing to his infant child Mary, then lying in a cradle) "when she is old enough." He evidently waited, for we find the record of his marriage to Mary Morton when she attained the age of twenty-five years. Thomas Tomson was a farmer and glazier, setting the diamond-shaped panes of glass in lead,[1] and after the glass had been so prepared, adjusting it to the sash and window frames. At the time of his death, which occurred October 26, 1742, he was reputed one of the wealthy men in town, and was noted for his piety, large generosity, and wisdom in adjusting the various difficulties which arose among his neighbors. John Cotton said of him, "He was the wealthiest man in town, but what was more to his honor, he was rich toward God."[2]

Among the other early settlers was Isaac Fuller, a son of the first pastor and a distinguished physician.

In October, 1734, nineteen members of the First Church were dismissed to form a church in Halifax. (See chapter on Ecclesiastical History.)

[1] Brown paper saturated in oil was at first used for windows. (See chapter on Early Settlers.) Afterwards small panes of glass set in lead took its place for about one hundred years until the wooden sash was introduced.

[2] *Descendants of John Thomson*, p. 30.

JOHN TOMSON'S PISTOL
(From the original in Pilgrim Hall, Plymouth)

CHAPTER XXII

MUTTOCK

INDIAN names and traditions still linger about this place and give it a peculiar charm in its association with the past. The first comers gave it the name of Muttock, from Chesemuttock, one of the last of the Nemasket tribe of Indians, who resided upon the brow of the hill, now known as Oliver's Walk. The Indian name of Muttock was Pau-wá-ting, meaning "a swift river running between hills."

This was one of the favorite resorts of King Philip before the Indian War, the residence of Wettamoo, the queen of Wamsutta, from which, towards the close of the war, she fled. Her body was found near Mattapoisett, stripped of regal attire. Near this place Mary Rowlandson first met King Philip in her captivity after the destruction of her house and family, and here the Indian chief received her kindly and took good care of her. It was here, in all probability, that the deputation sent out in 1621 from Plymouth Colony to meet the great sachem Massasoit first stopped on their journey.

On Muttock Hill, a few rods northwest of the house recently owned by Cornelius B. Wood, was the burial-place of the tribe, reserved in the Little Lotmen's Purchase. In this immediate neighborhood, west of the site of the wigwam of Chesemuttock, was probably the meeting-place for the forty praying Indians in 1660.

In 1734 the Indians then living upon this reservation petitioned the General Court for leave to sell their land, which they alleged had become unprofitable by reason of long cultivation, while game in the immediate vicinity had become scarce. The petition was granted, and the Indians, after selling the land here, moved to Titicut.

The following is their petition with the action of the General Court : —

To His Excelency Jonathan Belcher Esqr Capt Genll and Commander in Chief In and over his majesties Province of the Mafsechusetts In New England &c — To the honourable his majesties Council and house of Representatives In Genll Court afsembled Boston may 1730 The Humble Petition of Samuel Thomas of middleborough In the County of Plymouth & Province aforsaid Indian Planter humbly Sheweth That Petitioner (haith in his own Right) for many years last past lived on & improved a Certain Tract of land, lying in middleborough aforsaid upon an hill Called Chassemuttuck which Tract of land Contains fourteen or fifteen acres and is now worn out by long Improvement & no firewood or fenceing Stuff on the same and it lyes four miles or more Distant from any other Indian plantation and your Petitioner being old & feble and in no wise able to gett a livelihood off of the abovesaid land & and there being good Land enough att Tetticutt in middleborough aforsaid where your Petitioner Belongeth and haith good Right to take up and Improve what land he haith occession for Therefore your Petitioner humbly prayeth that your Excelency & honr would be pleased to take these things Into your wise Concideration and Grant to your Petitioner Liberty to Sell his land att Chassemuttuck aforsaid unto Mr. Samuel Thacher of middleborough aforsaid (who haith Relieved me In my Necessity) to whome I am Indebted and to whom it Lyy very Conveniently att the value to be apprised by Such meet Persons as your Excelencey & honr. Shall appoint That therby your Petitioner may be enabled to pay his just Debts to Settle himself and to Settle his said lands att Tetticutt where he may be neer the meeting and have many other Conveniencey which he is now Destitute off and your Petitioner as In Duty bound Shall Ever pray.

we the Subscribers having been appointed
By the Great and Genll Court Trustees of the Judiary
att Tetticutt and being desired by Mr. Samuel Thacher the Petitioner abovsd to view the Circumstances of the abovsaid Lands and we having viewed the same, we find it almost Destitute of fence & fenceing Stuff and firewood wherefore we are Humbly of opinion That it may be best for the Petitioner if he may Sell the land abovesaid for the Value Thereof.

BENJAMIN WHITE.
ESRA CLAP.

In the House of Representatives June 30th. 1739 Read and Ordered That John Allden and Elkanah Leonard Esqr. Be a Committee to Inquire into the Subject matter of this Petition That they Duly Consider the Same and Report Their Opinion att the next Setting of the Court what may be proper to be Done Thereon.
    A Copy from Files
    E. E. C.   JOHN WANRIGHT CLERK Repr.

In the house of Representatives Sept. 1739 Ordered that Ira Little Esq. (In the Room of John Allden Esq. Deceas[d]) be added to the Committee to Conscider & Report upon the Petition above Refer[d] & Report Thereon

MUTTOCK

To all People To whom These Presents . . . Greeting Know yee That I Samuel Thomas of middleborough in the County of Plymouth in New England Indian man Planter For and In Conscideration of the sum of one hundred and fourteen pound to me In hand before the ensealing hereof well and Truely paid by Samuel Thacher of middleborough aforsaid merchant The Receipt whereof I do hereby acknowledge and my self Therewith fully Satisfied & Contented and Thereof and of every part and parcel Thereof, do exonerate acquitt and Discharge him the Said Samuel Thacher his heirs executors & administrators forever by These Presents: Have given, esranted, Bargained, Sold, alien^d Conveyed and Confirmed and by These Presents, Do freely fully and absolutely Give, Grant, bargain, sell, aliene, convey and confirm, unto him the said Samuel Thacher his heirs and assigns forever, all that my Orchard Tract and parcell of land and meadow lyeing att a place, Called Chassemuttuck in middleborough aforsaid Supposed to Contain Fourteen or fifteen acres be the Same more or less Bounded Northeasterly by the mane Stream of Namaskett River North westerly by the Indian land Sold to the owners of the Slitting mill and South westerly by a highway That leads from the County Rhod by Deacon Barrows to Pochade Southeasterly by the Land now or late belonging to Ensigne William Thomas or however otherwise the Same is bounded or Reported to be bounded with all the fences and appurtenances to the same belonging, I being enabled by the Genl Court held in December and January last To Sell and Convey the Same   TO HAVE & *to* HOLD the said Granted and bargained Premises with all the appurtenances, Priviledges, Commodities To the Same belonging, or in any wise Appurtaining To him The said Samuel Thacher his heirs & assigns forever To his & their only use Bennefit & behoof forever, and I the Said Samuel Thomas for my Self my heirs, executors, administrators do Covenant, Promise & Grant to and with him the said Samuel Thacher his heirs and assigns, That before the ensealing hereof I am the True Sole & lawfull owner of the above Bargained Premises and am lawfully seized & possessed of the same in my own Proper Right as a good Perfect and absolute Estate of Inheritance in fee simple and have in myself good right full power and lawfull authority to grant Bargain sell convey and confirm said Bargained Premises in manner as aforsaid and that the Said Samuel Thacher his heirs and assigns Shall & may from time to time and att all Times forever hereafter by force and virtue of these Presents, lawfully peaceably and Quietly, Have, hold, use, occupy, Possess & enjoye the Said demised and bargained Premises, with the appurtenances Free and Clear & freely & Clearly acquitted exonerated & Discharged off from all and all manner of Former or other gifts, grants, Bargains, Sales, Leases, mortgages, wills, entails, joyntures, dower, judgements, executions or Incumberances of what Name or Nature soever that might in any measure or Degree obstruct or make void This Present Deed — Furthermore, I The Said Samuel Thomas for my Self my heirs Executors & administrators Do Covenant & engage the above Demissed Premisses To him the Said Samuel Thacher his heirs and assigns against the lawfull claims or Demands of any Person or Persons whatsoever forever hereafter to warrant Secure & Defend by These Presents — Furthermore Elizabeth The wife of the Said Samuel Thomas is Consenting to the Bargain & Sale of the Premisses and hereby Surrenders and yeild up her Right of Dower or Power of Third in The Premises to the Said Samuel Thacher his heirs and assigns forever. In wittnes whereof The Said Samuel Thomas and his wife have hereuntoo Sett Their hands and Seals The fifth Day of April Anno Domini one Thousand Seven hundred and forty Anno que R R Georgei Secundi Decimo Tertio

Signed, Sealed & Delivered by Saml Thomas
In Presence of us
BENJAMIN WHITE
EBENEZER BARROWS

SAMUEL × THOMAS (Seal)
his mark
her
ELIZABETH × THOMAS
mark

The committee appointed on the petition of Samuel Thomas of Middleboro Indian planter, having examined into the subject matter of said petition are of opinion it is best for the petitioner to be entitled to sell lands mentioned in the said petition, the lands being much worn and the fences almost gone, there being not timber or fencing stuff on the land sufficient to repair the fences and the lands being hemmed in by English land chiefly under improvements, and it fully appears to us that the petitioner can't improve his land to advantage; then we are also of the opinion that the land petitioned to be sold lieth more conveniently for Mr. Samuel Thacher, it being partly in his mill yard and adjoined to his land and mill and we are further of opinion that the said Indian lands are worth about £100 — and that the same be sold and the produce arriving of thereby be applied according to the prayer of the petitions and agreeable to the order and direction of this court, all which is humbly submitted Dec. 21, 1739

ELKANAH LEONARD.

In the House of Representatives Dec. 27, 1739, read again and ordered that the prayer of the petition be so far granted and the petition is hereby allowed and empowered to make sale of the land mentioned in the petition for the most the same will fetch for proceeding herein — To observe the direction in the act of the province of the 6th. year of the Reign of his late Majesty King George Chapter 3d. relating to real estates and Elkanah Leonard Esq. with such as shall be joined by the Honorable Board are hereby desired and empowered to be aiding and assisting the petitioner and see justice done him in the premises, the produce thereof to be applied according to the prayer of the petition, they to render an account of their proceedings herein to this Court.
Sent up for concurrence

J. QUINCEY Speaker.

In Council January 2nd., 1739, read and concurred and John Cushing Esq. is joined in the affair Simon Frost Deputy Secretary Jan. 4th.
Consented to J. BELCHER.

We The Subscribers Being appointed by the Genll Court to see Justice Done the Said Samuel Thomas In the Sale of the within Land and we accordingly

Pursued the Order of the Gen! Court and attended the Sale and took Care that Justice was Done And In our Judgment the Land was Sold for the full worth of it witnes our hand April 5, 1740

                                          JNO CUSHING
                                          ELKANAH LEONARD

Rec^d march 3. 1740 and Recorded with the Records of Deed for the County of Plymouth Book 34, Folio 37-38

                                          JOSIAH COTTON Reg

Recording
    15/   A True Copy Compared with the
                    original by me
                        SAMUEL THACHER

Here the first two settlers, Henry Wood and Ephraim Tinkham, lived.[1] In 1734 Moses Sturtevant and Peter Brown built a dam across the river in place of the old Indian weir.

In March, 1734,[2] Benjamin White, Samuel Eddy, Joseph Bumpas, Shubael Tinkham, and Mrs. Thomas petitioned the court for their "free consent to build a slitting-mill on Nemasket River on land of Moses Sturtevant." They had already agreed to erect the building, and had procured timber for the mill and dam. Objections were made by many to enlarging the dam and putting up such a mill, because it would interfere with the catching of herring, would spoil several Indian weirs, and so destroy multitudes of the young fish. Notwithstanding the opposition, the petition was granted, though the dam was not built until later. There had been before on this dam a grist-mill and sawmill, among the first erected after the resettlement of the town. This dam then, as now, had a sufficient opening for the passing of herring up to the great ponds, and very careful provision was made that the herring fishery should in no way be obstructed by it or by subsequent enlargements and improvements.

In 1744 Peter Oliver, a son of Daniel Oliver, one of the wealthy business men in the town of Boston and a brother of Andrew Oliver, who in after years became lieutenant-governor of the province, moved from Boston to Muttock and made it his permanent home. He was undoubtedly attracted by the

---

[1] See chapter on Early Settlers.   [2] See chapter on Civil History.

OLIVER'S WALK

beauty of the place, and probably also by the notoriety it had attained from the petition of the remaining Indians dwelling at Muttock to sell their land and move to Titicut. Mr. Oliver was a graduate of Harvard College in the class of 1737, became a very prominent citizen in the colony, and perhaps did more for the town than any other individual. He early bought much of the land about Muttock, including the dam and water privilege, and at once proceeded to erect a forge and slitting-mill on the dam, and an iron foundry, known as Oliver's Furnace, a little below upon a point of land extending into the middle of the river. The dam was considerably enlarged and strengthened for these new works. While it was being constructed, the bed of the river was changed by digging a canal above the pond, which extended near the stable of the late Earl Sproat, and ran into the river a little below. Afterward the ditch was carefully filled, although it can be traced at the present time in places.

A blast furnace at this period was heated entirely by wood, and the walls of the wood house, with which it was connected by a bridge over the river, can still be seen. Judge Oliver was enabled to secure large contracts from the Crown, so that in addition to hollow-ware, heavy ordnance, consisting of cannon, mortar, howitzers, shot, and shell, were here manufactured. Some letters relating to this are still extant.[1]

There is a tradition, which the subsequent owners regarded as true, that when Judge Oliver came to Middleboro there was but one other slitting-mill of the kind, and that in a town near Boston. So carefully was it guarded that it was impossible for any one to ascertain the kind of machinery used, or its method of operation. Judge Oliver agreed to give Hushai Thomas, a young man of remarkable mechanical skill, a certain sum of money if he would build him a slitting-mill which should produce nail-rods equal in kind and quality to those

---

[1] MIDDLEBORO', March 21, 1756.

GENTLEMEN, — Your Favour of 27th Febr. relating to supplying you with two Howbitzers I received on Saturday Night, & now send a Messinger to acquaint you that had I known of your having occasion for them 10 Days ago, I could have supplied you, but I finished my Blast 3 or 4 Days since; which I am sorry for, as I had been at a great Deal of Trouble & Charge to procure Mountain Ore to make warlike Stores, of which ore is of a far better Quality than any we have in these Parts, especially for Guns and Mortars. I have sent for more Mountain Ore, & expect to blow again this month, & if you should then want any Stores, I believe I can supply you with those of as good a Quality as can be made, for I am sensible of the Risque of making guns and Mortars from Bog Ore that I shall not attempt them again with that.

I am, Gentlemen, your very humble Servant,

PETER OLIVER.

MIDDLEBORO', May 21, 1756.

GENTLEMEN, — I received your Letter 19th instant this Day. I had already given my reasons for not writing. w^{ch}, whether they are sufficient or not, I must leave to you gentlemen to judge of.

The Carcasses are shipped, & I hope will be with you by the Time this Letter arrives, which I suppose are not engaged. As to the Granadoe Shells & Mortars, I have quitted them, & have lent Mr. Barker my Pattern for the mortars, who no doubt will send them soon, & had it been in my power to have forwarded the matter I should not have been wanting, but I have sent vessel after vessel, at great Expense, and have been daily expecting one after another with one proper to have a Furnace in order for stores of such Consequence, which, had they arrived, a few Days would have conveyed to New York sooner than they could be any other Way, unless they are made to Hand, for I had procured a Vessell to carry them.

I am, gentlemen, with great esteem y^r very hum^l Servant,

PETER OLIVER.

To the Honble Committee of War.

made near Boston. Mr. Thomas suddenly disappeared from the town, and some apprehension was manifested lest evil had befallen him, although it was noticed that his wife and family did not share the anxiety of the neighbors. A few days after, an unkempt person was seen in the vicinity of Boston, apparently a foolish, demented fellow. After lounging about, sleeping in barns and wherever he could find accommodation, he became friendly with the boys as they came and went from school, often playing with them about the mill. One day, he noticed that the door was open, and with the boys following, innocently ran in. He was there but a few moments, and the next day left the place, taking with him the secret of the mechanism of the mill. The long-absent Hushai Thomas returned. The foundation of the slitting-mill was immediately laid, and when in running order it was found that his journey had not been in vain. The single glance at the machinery by "this foolish, unkempt fellow" was all that was necessary; the nail-rods of Muttock could now rank with any in the province. This, with the business of the foundry, made Muttock the largest and most enterprising village of the town. In addition to these interests, Peter Oliver was a large owner of real estate and one of the most prudent and successful farmers of the country.

In 1747 he was appointed judge of the Court of Common Pleas, and while occupying that position planned and superintended the erection of the court house in Plymouth. In 1756 he was appointed judge of the Superior Court of Judicature, the highest court in the province, and in 1762 was appointed chief justice. Later on, he presided at the trial of the British soldiers for the massacre on King's Street just before the breaking out of the Revolution, and his charge to the jury was regarded as a clear and impartial exposition of the law. His rank as chief justice made him the second man in the colony, no one but the governor being his superior. He rode from Boston to Middleboro in his coach, with outriders dressed in scarlet, maintaining the dignity and elegance of the judges of the highest court in Westminster, London.

Soon after coming to Middleboro, he built Oliver Hall, one

of the finest country residences outside of Boston. It stood upon the level tract of land between the two hills at Muttock, about two hundred feet back of the residence of the late Mr. Edmund Deane and a little west of the wall on the brow of Muttock Hill. He enclosed as a part of his grounds and park all of the land between Nemasket Street and the river. This was laid out after the manner of an English park and garden. Indications of the driveway around the base of the hill from the bridge to the end of Oak Street may still be seen. The principal entrance was through an avenue of trees from North Street opposite the former residence of I. D. Bump, following the road on the northerly side of the triangular common, at the top of Muttock Hill; then turning, it passed in front of the residence of Edward Tinkham, and following the line of the road nearly to the house of the late Edmund Deane, turned again through an orchard until it came to the Hall. The other entrance was near the junction of Oak and North streets, at present indicated by a lane leading toward the pond. At the end of the lane the driveway divided, one part bordering upon the edge of the pond at the foot of the hill and the other passing over the brow and winding into the garden in front, and so connecting with the main driveway above referred to.

Oliver Hall was built after the style of an old English mansion, with steep roof and deep, jutting eaves, with walls of white plaster and portico of oak, over which grew a rose not only celebrated for its beauty, but valued as a present to Madam Oliver from England. The doors and much of the inside furnishings were sent from London. The house contained the usual drawing-room of that period, the entrance-hall, the dining-room, a large and valuable library, and other apartments, with kitchen and extensive quarters for servants. The large hall opened on the river; the lower part of the wall was wainscoted with English oak, and the upper part was decorated with rich hangings of birds and flowers. When the house was on fire, some of the townspeople tore these off and preserved them as mementos of the days when "George was king, and Oliver was judge." The oaken floor was polished daily by the servants until it fairly shone, and was so slippery that it is said one of the maids slipped and fell, spilling the hot tea and cream over the beautiful gown of one of the ladies and staining her white satin slipper, whereupon the enraged guest from Boston "drew off the slipper and spanked her soundly, in high dudgeon." The furnishings of the hall were elegant and costly; there were high crownback tapestry-cushioned chairs, with a Turkish carpet on the floor. The library was built separate, facing the north and connected with the hall by a lattice

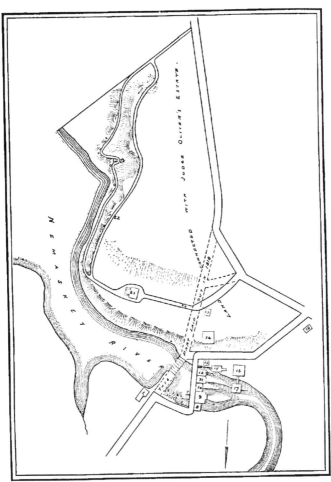

PLAN OF JUDGE OLIVER'S ESTATE AND WORKS

1. Shovel Shop. 2. Blacksmith Shop. 3. Finishing Shop. 4. Finishing Shop. 5. Fishing-Weir. 6. Fishing Place. 7. Coal House. 8. Coal House. 9. Hammer Shop. 10. Grist-Mill. 11. Slitting-Mill. 12. Forge. 13. Iron House for Forge. 14. Coal House for Forge. 15. Sawmill. 16. Site of old Wood House for Judge Oliver's Furnace. 17. Site of Judge Oliver's Furnace before the Revolution. 18. Andrew Leach's Store. 19. Residence of Andrew Oliver. 20. Entrance to Oliver Hall. 21. Oliver Hall. 22. Site of Sachem's Wigwam. 23. Summer Pavilion.

gallery; in it were portraits of the family, the celebrated coat of arms, and a bust of George III with the banner of England over it in loyal tory style.

The dining-room was spacious, with a large, heavy, claw-foot table of English oak in the centre, with high straight-back chairs of the same wood, the royal arms carved at the top. It is said that in 1762, when news was brought of an heir to the Crown, a notable company gathered there, the sound of rejoicing rang high, and many were overcome with the excitement and revelry. Within this dining-room companies, including distinguished men from abroad as well as the most prominent men of the colony, often partook of the sumptuous entertainment provided.

PETER OLIVER'S BOOK-PLATE

In the hollow between two of the highest hills on Oliver's Walk, and overlooking the pond, was a small house, called by the family the banqueting-house, the site of which may still be seen. Guests at the hall often wandered about the grounds to this place, where they were not infrequently served with such refreshment as the generous hospitality of the judge never failed to provide. The spring adjoining this banqueting-house was reached by a flight of steps a few feet from the entrance, and was used to cool the wine during the long and hot summer days. Many years ago bottles were found bearing Oliver's initials printed on the side.

At the Hall was held the wedding reception of Peter Oliver, Jr., and Sarah, daughter of Governor Hutchinson. The marriage took place in Boston,[1] and later the party, distinguished by guests from home and abroad, were here entertained. The display of magnificent costumes was most brilliant. Ladies wore rich silks and satins with long trains, and their hair, puffed and powdered, was rolled high on their heads. This required so much care that it is said one of them sat up all night that the work of her hairdresser might not be disarranged, and another slept with her hands and arms tied over her head that they might appear white for the approaching reception. Gentlemen were there in gay colored suits of velvet with dainty satin vests, knee breeches, silk stockings with silver knee and shoe buckles, their coats decorated with old lace ruffles at the neck and sleeves, others in full military and court dress; but the ladies and gentlemen from the town, although not attired in the brilliant dress then worn by the fashionable people of Boston, received the same consideration and attention from the judge and his wife as were shown to the titled personages from England. The hall was profusely decorated with plants and flowers taken from the gardens and grounds. Tables in the dining-room and banqueting-hall were laden with every variety of meats, pastry, fruits, and flowers, and wines and cider flowed freely. The guests from abroad remained four days, enjoying their lavish entertainment. The reception was regarded as one of the most brilliant affairs which had ever occurred outside of Boston.

The estate contained a large variety of fruit, ornamental, and forest trees, which grew luxuriantly over the hills, but

---

[1] In the diary of Dr. Oliver we find this amusing note of the "end of the happiest time:" —

"Feb. 1, 1770. I was married by Dr. Pemberton to Mrs. [abbreviation for Mistress] S. Hutchinson; exceedingly private, of a Thursday Evg., according to the Old Charter. Thus ended the happiest time of my life, as it was freest from cares and solicitudes, which now hastened apace. I was at this time in the latter part of my 29th year, and Mrs. Hutchinson in the 26th year of her age."

only a few large oaks at the side of the hill, and the pear-tree near the edge of the pond not far from the bridge, are now standing. There were numerous walks about the grounds and the garden, celebrated for its choice flowers. In their diaries Judge Sewall and John Adams speak of the beauty of the place and the pleasure they had in visiting the Hall.

On the breaking out of the Revolution, Judge Oliver conscientiously adhered to his sovereign, and his great wealth, his official position and influence, made him extremely obnoxious to the patriots, and in the troublesome time following the battle of Lexington, notwithstanding his high character and the universal respect in which he was held, he was impeached for receiving a salary from the Crown, and compelled to leave the country, with many other tories. After the mob had attacked the house of his brother in Boston and destroyed its contents, he rode on horseback, unattended, from Boston to Middleboro, and arrived there in the edge of the evening, travel-stained and weary. He immediately entered the Hall, where he had spent so many happy years, went to a secret drawer, took out a box of valuables, cast a longing glance about, bade the faithful housekeeper good-by, and mounting his horse, galloped out into the night. The next day, with his family, he embarked with Governor Gage for London, never again to return to the home which he had enjoyed so much and where he had received such honor [1] and distinction. The last years of his life were

[1] Judge Oliver's Diary from the time he left Boston until the time of his death was published in the second volume of the *Diary and Letters of His Excellency Thomas Hutchinson, Esq.* The following are extracts of the same, under date of 1776: —

After having retired to Boston, under the protection of the King's troops, for the security of my person against the fury of the most unnatural, ungratefull, wanton, and cruel rebellion that ever existed, and after having been confined to the limits of that town for eighteen months, the rebels, who had for many months surrounded the town with strong intrenchments, began to bombard and cannonade it on the 2d of March 1776, which held for three nights successively, but with very little damage.

General Howe, the Commander-in-Chief, thought proper to abandon the town, and gave publick notice to the inhabitants, that such of them who inclined to quit the place, should have transports provided for them.

spent in England in literary pursuits and in the society of his friends. He received an honorary degree from Oxford, and died in 1782, beloved by all who knew him.

March 10th. — Accordingly, on the tenth day of March I embarked on board the Pacific, Indiaman, Capt James Dun, which lay in King Road, it being a very commodious vessell, which General Howe was so polite as to appropriate to the accommodation of my friends and me.

11th. — There was an hot cannonading to and from Boston and Dorchester Neck, and also to and from Castle William and Dorchester Neck, which continued from 8 o'clock at night untill the next morning.

12th. — Some firing at Boston in the night.

16th. — A hot firing at Boston ab^t 11 o'clock at night, till 9 o'clock next morning.

17th. — The troops at Boston embarked, and about 20 sail fell down into King Road by 11 o'clock this morning.

18th. — The King's troops began to blow up the Castle William.

19th. — I dined on board the Chatham with Admiral Shuldham. The south Blockhouse of the Castle was burnt at night, and some of the walls of it blown up.

20th. — The blowing up of the Castle Walls continued: and at night all the combustible part of the Castle was fired. The conflagration was the most pleasingly dreadful that I ever beheld: sometimes it appeared like the eruption of Mount Etna; and then a deluge of fire opened to the view; that nothing could reconcile the horror to the mind, but the prevention of such a fortress falling into the hands of rebels, who had already spread such a conflagration of diabolical fury throughout America, which scarce anything can quench but the — metu tremefacit Olympum.

21st. — The fleet fell down from King Road into Nantasket Harbour, which afforded a grand prospect, there being at least 150 sail of vessells at anchor.

22d. — A high N. W. wind.

23d. — D^o.

24th. — A high N. W. and very cold at night, so that the vessell's bows and cables were loaded with ice.

25th. — The first Division sailed from Nantasket to Hallifax, as also the Lord Hyde Packet, Cap^n Jeffries for London, with Mr Thomas Hutchinson and my son Peter, and their families, as passengers.

26th. — I dined on board the Renown, Commodore Banks.

27th. — I sailed from Nantasket, ab^t 70 sail, for Hallifax, under convoy of the Chatham, Admiral Shuldham, and of the Centurion, Cap^n Braithwaite.

here I took my leave of that once happy country, where peace and plenty reigned uncontrouled, till that infernal Hydra Rebellion, with its hundred Heads, had devoured its happiness, spread desolation over its fertile fields, and ravaged the peacefull mansions of its inhabitants, to whom late, very late if ever, will return that security and repose which once surrounded them; and if in part restored, will be attended with the disagreeable recollection of the savage barbari-

On November 4, 1778, after reports had reached the colony of the disasters to the patriot army, an unusual number of people gathered in Muttock. In the night, flames were seen issuing from one portion of the house; no attempt was made to extinguish them. The neighbors rushed in, took away the remaining furniture and hangings and many of the doors,[1] and in a few hours nothing was left of the beauty and splendor of Oliver Hall. Some of these doors were afterwards carried to the old Ward house in Lakeville, where they were placed to form the walls and ceiling of one of the chambers. The shrubbery, trees, and outbuildings were destroyed in the next generation, so that the grounds, once so beautiful, were desolate.

Mrs. Mary Norcutt, when a young woman, was the housekeeper at Oliver Hall, and later in life she lived in the family of Judge Weston. She was very fond of giving a description

ties, and diabolical cruelties which had been perpetrated to support rebellion, and which were instigated by ambition and malice, and infernal in their dictates. Here I drop the filial tear into the Urn of my Country.

"O fortunatos nimium, sua si bona norint —
Nov-Anglicanos."

And here I bid A Dieu to that shore, which I never wish to tread again till that greatest of social blessings, a firm established British Government, precedes or accompanies me thither.

The Diary gives a detailed account of the events of his voyage, and upon his arrival a detailed account of how his time was occupied. It seems to have been largely in travel, with calls made and received from the prominent public men in England at that time. He mentions his visit at Lord Edgcumbe's seat as follows: —

7th.— This morning visited Lord Edgcumbe's seat. . . . We then descended the walks around the sea shore, which were varied with taste, and yet seemed formed on the plan of nature, with seats to rest on, and with hermitages; promontories on one side, and the sea opening through trees on the other, — filled the mind with pleasure. But I was in one walk deprived of pleasure for a moment, it being so like a serpentine walk of mine on the banks of the river Namasket, which so lately had been wrenched from me by the Harpy claws of Rebellion, that I was snatched from where I now was to the loss of where I had so late been in the arms of contentment. . . .

[1] Most of the personal property of Judge Oliver had been removed and an inventory made which is now in the Probate Court, Plymouth.

of the place, the parties, incidents, and prominent men who were accustomed to visit there. These incidents were often told to the father of the writer, and an account of the burning of the hall as she used to relate it was written by the late Granville T. Sproat and published in the "Middleboro Gazette," a copy of which is here inserted.

"We had long expected that the Hall would be burned — the people were so enraged; especially after we heard how they had sacked Governor Hutchinson's house in Boston, and had brought out and burned all his fine library of books in the street. We never went to bed at night without thinking that we should be aroused before morning by the Hall being on fire. And it was so. One night, a little past midnight, we were awakened by a loud knocking at the door, and a cry, 'Get up! get up! the Hall is on fire!' We sprang up; we could see the Hall from our windows; the main building was not then on fire; it was the library which was connected with the Hall by a latticed gallery, that was all in a blaze. We ran out to the Hall; a good many people had got there; they had broken in the doors and were running through the building with the hopes of finding something to lay their hands on. But there was nothing there; everything had been carried off months before. I ran up into the servants' room above the great guest parlor. This parlor was very high in its walls — higher than the other rooms of the house; and the servants' chambers were above it — quite low, under the roof. There was nothing there; everything had been carried off. I then ran into the great parlor, to the money closet. It stood open. I put my hand in on one corner of a shelf; there was a piece of money about the size of a dollar. I took it home with me and kept it for years afterwards. I kept it as a keepsake, for it always reminded me of Judge Oliver and that last visit of his, and his looks — so pale and careworn — when he came into the house, the last time he ever entered it.

"The Hall was a long time burning. It was covered with plaster of some kind on the outside, and did not burn very fast. The roof kept falling in, one part after another. It was a long time before the great guest parlor was burnt out. That was the most famous room in the house. It was wainscoted with oak below the windows; above, it was hung with gorgeous paper hangings, all gilt and velvet. The women who were there tore off the paper and took it home with them.

They used to wear the sprigs of gold leaf in their hair, when they went to a dance in the town, for years afterward. I could not bear to see it, for I felt bad when I thought of the fate of the old Hall.

"I tried to save the rose-bush — a present to Madam Oliver from London, which trailed over the east end of the house, but I could not do it. The fire was too hot and drove me away. All the elms and locusts around the Hall were burned. Nothing was left. Oh! what a sight it presented the next morning! I sat down and cried as if my heart would break; for I never expected to see Oliver's Hall brought to a pile of ruins like that.

"After the Hall was burned everything went to ruin. The walk, so famous in the old times, and where the ladies of the Hall used to walk so much, grew up to bushes; the benches on the sides rotted down, and the way to the summer house was all choked up. The summer house stood a good many years; the tables grew black and mouldy, but they did not fall away very fast; and the spring, close by, where they used to store their wine to keep it cool, was kept open for a long time afterward. I used to go and sit there and think of the merry times they used to have there. Well do I remember the day when an heir was born to his Majesty, George the Third, and Queen Charlotte — how a messenger came riding all the way from Boston to bring the news — how he rode up the hill, swinging his hat and shouting 'Long live the King! A prince has been born to the royal family of England!' There was feasting that night at the Hall; and a great party assembled to drink wine and give toasts in honor of the occasion. Governor Hutchinson was there at the time; and, that day, Lieutenant-Governor Oliver, with some ladies, came out from Boston. He wore a suit of scarlet silk velvet, with gilt or gold buttons, and lace ruffles for the sleeves and bosom. He wore short breeches, as was the fashion at that day. White silk long stockings, with gold shoe and knee buckles, made up his suit. Governor Hutchinson was dressed in nearly the same way; only his suit of velvet was blue trimmed with gold lace. They had a dance at the Hall that night, and there was music and wine in abundance.

"After about ten years there was but little left to mark the spot where Oliver's Hall had once stood. The seats of the walk were all gone; the roof of the summer house had fallen in; the tables had rotted down and lay scattered on the ground; only the spring remained, and the spot where the summer house stood. After that the trees were cut down or gradually decayed with age, and it was hard to tell where the walk once was. It was the same with the spot where the Hall once stood. The trees around it had all been destroyed by the fire, and only the cellar remained to mark the spot. That, too, gradually filled up, so that I hardly knew the place where we used to store our winter supplies at the Hall; and now the stranger can with difficulty find the place where the great Hall once stood. Oh, the change that a few short years have made in one of the loveliest spots that my eyes have ever beheld! I remember, one day, hearing Governor Hutchinson say to Judge Oliver, as they were walking in the garden together, 'Judge Oliver, you have here one of the loveliest spots in all his Majesty's colony;' and I think he told the truth."

Judge Oliver's son William married a sister of Captain John Fuller, and lived in the Haskins neighborhood near his wife's father. Andrew Oliver, another son, is said to have been remarkably fine looking; he married Phœbe, a daughter of Ebenezer Spooner. She died at an advanced age in the old Morton house, and was known the latter years of her life as Madam Oliver.[1] Her husband, who died before the war, was of intemperate habits. At the time of the marriage, Mr. Spooner was much opposed to it and disinherited his daughter, but the judge provided for her, and is said to have built a house for them in Muttock. This was afterwards occupied by Jesse Bryant, Judge Oliver's foreman in the forge and slitting-mill, and was taken down by the late Henry Arnold. An account of his other sons, Daniel and Dr. Peter Oliver, is given in the chapter on Loyalists.

STAIRS IN SPROAT HOUSE

Dr. Oliver lived in the house which his father built for him in 1762, now known as the Sproat house. In 1794 this was

---

[1] June 29, 1776, Phœbe Oliver, wife of Andrew Oliver, and daughter-in-law of Judge Oliver, petitioned the General Court for relief, as the selectmen of the town had taken the house which she had occupied for seven years, rent free, and two cows and firewood from her, and petitioned to the court that she would be destitute unless the court granted her relief. The petition was referred to a committee, but it is not reported what action was taken upon it.

purchased by Judge Weston, and was his home for nearly forty years until his death. During Dr. Oliver's time the slaves occupied the attic, but these rooms have long since been removed. This house is famous for the men whose lives are associated with its hospitable halls. Governor Hutchinson was accustomed to spend part of the summer here, and one of the chambers was afterwards known as the Hutchinson chamber.

RESIDENCE OF PETER OLIVER, JR.

James Bowdoin, also a frequent guest of the house,[1] spent parts of two years here, while governor. He was a large land-owner[2] in Middleboro, although

[1] Peter Orlando Hutchinson, in his *Diary and Letters of His Excellency Thomas Hutchinson, Esq.*, vol. i, p. 463, says: "James Bowdoin had better have had Judge Oliver's house as that might have protected it from being burnt, a fate to which it soon arrived."

[2] The following parcels of land were owned by Governor Bowdoin, in Middleboro: —

April 17, 1777, he received a conveyance of 80 acres of land in the Twenty-six Men's Purchase and 3¼ acres of meadow land which was formerly owned by John Adams, one of the original purchasers.

June 17, 1729, Lemuel Bosworth conveyed a tract of land in the 5 Men's Purchase.

In October 7, 1729, Benjamin Durfey conveyed to him 40 acres of land in the West Precinct.

In 1740 Thomas Crode conveyed to him ½ of the 29th lot in the first allotment of the Sixteen Shilling Purchase, containing 44 acres.

July 12, 1742, Elkanah Leonard conveyed to him 185 acres of land in the Sixteen Shilling Purchase.

August 20, 1744, Peter Thacher's estate conveyed to him four and one-half sixteenth part of the slitting-mill utensils, forge, grist-mill on the dam across the Namasket River and 5 acres of land on the south side of the river and 1 acre of land on the north of the river, also a dwelling-house.

In 1757 Robert Brown conveyed to him 72 acres of land.

Another tract from Deacon Shaw containing 16 acres and another from Ichabod Sampson containing 6 acres which was the 11th lot in the first allotment of the Twenty-six Men's Purchase.

The works and land at Muttock were conveyed to Peter Oliver and Jeremiah Gridley June 12, 1745.

never a voter, and some of his official papers bear the mark and date from here. He was born August 8, 1727, died in Boston November 6, 1790, and was buried in the Bowdoin vault in the Old Granary Burying-ground. In 1779 he was president of the convention to frame a constitution for Massachusetts, was governor 1785–86, and in 1788 a member of the State Convention to ratify the Constitution of the United States. His estate on Beacon Street, Boston, extended back as far as Ashburton Place, and contained one of the finest gardens in town. At the beginning of the insurrection, when in Cambridge to review the troops (he was then about fifty-eight years old), he is described as wearing a gray wig, a cocked hat, white broadcloth coat and waistcoat, red small-clothes, and black silk stockings.[1]

As a public man he was firm and courageous, moderate in his opinions, and although an earnest friend of the patriot cause from the beginning, he was more conservative than many of his companions, an attitude which led some of the more zealous supporters to question his sincerity. During his administration the famous Shays's Rebellion occurred, and it was largely owing to his firmness and decision that it did not assume greater proportions. After it had been suppressed, he was defeated in his third term, mainly by the voters from the western part of the state, who were in sympathy with the insurgents, and John Hancock was chosen in his place.

[1] *Memorial History of Boston*, vol. iii, p. 194.

He was the founder of the college which bears his name, an accomplished scholar, with an extended reputation for scientific studies and love of literature.

Mrs. Bowdoin, while a resident of the town, presented the First Church with a large silver cup, which at one time was used upon the communion table, but is now preserved by the church as a relic.

Dr. Benjamin Franklin was a guest of Dr. Oliver in 1773, attended the First Church, and at a reception given to him met many Middleboro people.

Opposite the end of Nemasket Street, which has been discontinued, stood the house of Asaph Churchill, and upon the other side of the street was the old red schoolhouse. For years the house was the residence of William Tupper, whose name and family have now become extinct in this part of the state. He was a well-to-do farmer and a staunch patriot, and is said to have been the only man in town who did not stand in awe of Judge Oliver, and who never hesitated to cross him in his endeavors to carry any particular matter either in town or in church. He and Captain Joshua Eddy were more outspoken against his political views than any of the citizens. At one time, in the presence of a large number of people standing near the rock on the side of the pond between the two roads, he said to them in derision: "If Judge Oliver told you that that rock had been moved during the night, you are all d—— fools enough to believe it." At the close of the war, upon the reorganization of the militia of the county, he was appointed lieutenant-colonel.

In the year 1778, by an act of the legislature, many of the tories of the province were banished and their estates confiscated, including that of Peter Oliver. In 1786 Nahum Mitchell and Edward Winslow, appointed to dispose of the confiscated land of the tories, sold a portion of the Peter Oliver estate to Jesse Bryant and Abner Weston. This afterwards came into the possession of Andrew Leach, who had opened the first store here about 1745. He was a Scotchman, keen and quick in manner and blunt of speech. Opposite the store was his house, which was burned many years ago. Soon after his death he was succeeded by Gamaliel Rounseville, a man of ability holding many offices in town, who also lived there. He carried on business for more than fifty years, and upon his death his stock of goods was sold at public auction; this created unusual interest from the fact that many articles had been in the store for more than forty years.

In the beginning of the last century there were in this village four stores: Mr. Rounseville's at the corner of the road; one at the top of the hill belonging to E. T. Soule, which was later moved to another part of the town; one owned by General Abiel Washburn, opposite his house, which was afterwards taken down and a new store, now standing, built and occupied by him; and next to this, on the site of Dr. Oliver's office, the store of Judge Weston, since moved to a position near the herring-weir. A new store was erected on Muttock Hill and occupied by Colonel Thomas Weston. This also was moved away and used as a dwelling-house.

The making of hammered nails is now one of the abandoned industries, to which it is interesting to give a passing note. Iron was collected from different parts of the county, together with what could be obtained from the blast furnaces, and was brought to the forge, where it was made into bars about six feet long, three inches wide, and half an inch thick. These bars were then taken to the slitting-mill, cut up, and rolled into nail-rods about six feet in length and about a quarter of an inch square, or according to the thickness of the nail desired; these were bound up in bundles of fifty and taken by the farmers and others to their shops in this and surrounding towns and made into hammered nails, which were then taken to Mr. Weston's store, put into kegs, and shipped over the country. In addition to those at the forge and slitting-mill, there were over fifty men thus given employment when not at work upon their farms. The shops where these nails were made were from twelve to twenty feet square, and at the present day, as one rides through the town, many of them may still be seen as reminders of an occupation which was superseded by the invention of the nail machine.

Here shovels were manufactured by General Washburn and his son, Philander, and found a ready market all over the country, the men employed being known as "shovel busters."

After the confiscation and sale of Judge Oliver's property at Muttock, the works there were managed for short periods by different men, but in the latter part of the eighteenth century, when they came into the possession of General Abiel Washburn and Thomas Weston, a large and successful business was carried on for more than a generation. One can scarcely realize, in passing over the bridge, that a hundred years ago it was a place of so much business activity. At that time the following manufacturing establishments were built upon the dam: a large sawmill, the iron house for the forge, opposite on the other side a large coal house, the ruins of which can still be seen, the forge, the slitting-mill, a grist-mill, the hammer and finishing shop, a large coal house on the other side of the dam, two finishing shops for shovels, a large blacksmith's shop, and on the other side of the street the shovel factory. Below the dam were the ruins of the old Oliver furnace and the wood house connected with it.

The men employed here and the clerks in these stores were many of them among the brightest young men of the town. Some of the leading spirits were Louis Weston, Thomas Sturtevant, Harry Hubbard, Joseph H. Bisbee, William E. Doggett, and Alpha Crossman. The stories of their witticisms, their fun, their genial good-fellowship, and the pranks which were played upon customers and countrymen who came to the village, have been repeated in the neighborhood with the zest of former times. Strange purchases were made: one desiring material for a suit of clothes was induced to buy several yards of furniture covering of a gay pattern as "the latest style." At the commencement of the great temperance movement in the early part of the last century, the stores in Muttock were among the first to discontinue the selling of rum, the favored intoxicant among the common people. Afterward many of the topers, Jube, an old colored man, among the number, would come and earnestly beg for a dram, and some strange mixtures were prepared by these clerks, compounded of almost everything in the store which would mix with water, with a large portion of cayenne pepper to give flavor to the drink. These practical jokes were not always confined to the village. A maiden lady, who by some of her remarks had provoked the enmity of these young men, had met with an accident which was made the subject of another joke of a little more serious character. For generations it had been the custom of those attending the First Church to send requests for prayers for the sick or bereaved. These were usually carried to the clergyman by the sexton after he had taken his seat in the pulpit. One Sabbath morning a man noted for his absent-mindedness occupied the pulpit, and as he was about to read the requests for prayers, a stranger walked hastily up and gave him an additional notice. Without glancing at it he opened it and commenced to read : —

> "Desire Morse desires prayers
> For falling down Deacon Nathan's stairs."

The good man's thoughts were evidently elsewhere and he did not notice what he had read, but continued : —

> "She broke no bones but bruised her meat,
> Which was not fit for dogs to eat."

Great was the consternation of the assembly, but the poor man was so absorbed in the duties before him that he did not comprehend the situation. While it was not known who was the author, it was not difficult to trace this to these fun-loving clerks. Many another tale could be told did time and space permit.

The prominent business men in Muttock were Judge Thomas Weston and General Abiel Washburn. They were men well known for their business ability, their sterling integrity, and the esteem in which they were held throughout southeastern Massachusetts.

Thomas Weston was born March 20, 1770. In the early part of his life he was engaged in business at Pope's Point furnace in Carver; in 1798 he moved from Carver and made Muttock his home, having purchased a large tract of real estate there, including the Peter Oliver house and a portion of the works upon the dam. He held many public offices, was a member of the house and senate, and for four years a member of the governor's council. He was nominated as representative for Congress when nomination of his party made election sure, but declined to serve. In the latter part of his life he was appointed chairman of the Court of Sessions, a position which at that time gave him the title of Judge. He died June 17, 1834, in the sixty-fourth year of his age. Upon his death his son, Colonel Thomas Weston, succeeded him in business until the year 1844, when he moved to Warrentown.

THOMAS WESTON

General Abiel Washburn had previously been in business at the Four Corners with Major Levi Peirce and Major William Bourne, under the firm name of Washburn, Bourne & Peirce. This partnership was dissolved a little before Judge Weston came to Muttock, General Washburn having purchased an interest in the dam and water privilege there, and a large farm, now occupied by his grandson, Charles E. Grinnell, a member of the Boston bar. He commenced manufacturing shovels, and built the hammer shop upon the dam. He was also interested in the sawmill and grist-mill. This business was continued until his death, and was afterwards carried on by his son, Philander Washburn, who had been in partnership with him for several years. General Washburn was the son of Edward Washburn, a patriot soldier in the Revolution, and from him he inherited what in those days was considered a large property. This was afterwards lost in business, but by his sagacity and enterprise he later became the wealthiest man and the largest tax-payer in town. He was for many years the acknowledged leader of the Federal party, which at that time was hopelessly in the minority, yet upon all important town matters he was consulted, and his suggestions were usually adopted. He was interested in the local militia of the state, and held commissions for thirty-six years through the different grades of office to that of Brigadier-General of Plymouth County Brigade, from 1816 to 1824. General Washburn was a gentleman of the old school, of large and commanding stature; he died June 17, 1843, in the eightieth year of his age, leaving a large family of children.

ABIEL WASHBURN'S RESIDENCE

Until the early part of the last century the highway from Muttock Hill to the Green was over the old dam upon which Oliver's works were located. On July 27, 1818, the town voted, "that an agent be appointed to petition the court to locate a highway across the mill pond at Oliver's works." Judge Wilkes Wood was chosen, and was authorized to contract for the building of this bridge. The records do not show any further action, although by that contract the bridge was built and the road over Muttock Hill was made. The bridge was of wood, and the road over the hill was so steep that it was considered unsafe. This gave rise to so much complaint that a town meeting was held May 12, 1856, when it was voted, "that the selectmen be a committee to cause to be rebuilt the bridge over Nemasket River at Oliver's works." May 9, 1859, a committee was appointed to replace the bridge by a stone structure and to raise the grade several feet; at the same time the top of the hill was cut down some eight or ten feet, leaving the road as at present.

In this neighborhood lived Ephraim Norcutt (the husband of Mary Norcutt before mentioned), who had taken part in the French and Indian War, and was afterwards in Judge Oliver's employ, working on his estate as "skipper" of the furnace.

In the latter part of the eighteenth century John Ritchie, a Boston merchant, bought an interest in the confiscated Oliver's works, and built the house opposite the entrance to the cemetery which was recently burned. There is a tradition that very soon after Mr. Ritchie left, two ladies of apparent means and education came and lived in the place for a number of years.

RITCHIE HOUSE

They refused to give their names, or to have any intercourse with the people of the town. They were very fond of flowers, and had a large garden on the southerly side of the house. After residing there a few years, one of them died and was buried quietly in the cemetery opposite; the other went away, leaving no trace of their names or previous history.

In the early part of the last century Benaiah Wilder lived in the house occupied by the late Captain Leonard Driggs, and opposite this house he had anchor works until the embargo of Jefferson's administration destroyed that industry; now a few cinders are all that mark the place. He was one of those whom Judge Oliver hoped to influence, but who disappointed him by joining the patriots early in the Revolution. He was a brother of Ebenezer Wilder of North Street, who for a long time was a deacon and prominent member of the First Congregational Church.

Henry Weston, whose home was with Captain Earl Sproat, served with distinction in the navy during the War of the Rebellion. Before he reached his majority he was a master's mate in Farragut's squadron, and was in many of the battles in the famous Red River expedition, where he was promoted for bravery in several engagements. He was in command of the gunboat Diana in one of the battles on the Atchafalaya River. After a most desperate fight, in which all of his officers were either killed or wounded and not men enough were left to fire a single gun, he was obliged to surrender his ship. He was then taken to the rebel prison in Texas, known as Camp Ford, where he remained until the close of the war.

Beautiful for situation, between Plymouth Street and the Nemasket River, lying on its eastern bank, is the Nemasket Hill Cemetery, known as the Old Burial Hill, or simply The Hill. March 24, 1885, it was incorporated as the Nemasket Hill Cemetery Association, and is the oldest and by far the largest in town.

Soon after Peter Oliver came to Middleboro, he bought the following parcels of real estate : —

Jan. 15, 1742, From Joseph Haskall one half of a certain piece of land containing eight acres lying in Wareham near Wankinco River, with a mill dam and stream.

Jan. 25, 1744, From Ebenezer Morton fourteen acres and a quarter of land in the 17th. lot of land in the 3rd. allotment of the little Lot Purchase in Middleboro.

Jan. 29, 1744, From Joseph Bumpas one half of the saw-mill on south side of Namaskett River in Middleboro near the slitting mill.

March, 1744, From Nathaniel Bumpas one fourth part of a saw-mill on Namasket River in Middleboro, with utensils etc.

Dec. 26, 1744, From Peter Thacher, with Jeremiah Gridley, six sixteenth shares of the slitting mill on Namasket River in Middleboro; also six sixteenth shares in the dam on sd river and tools & instruments of the mill; also Thacher's remaining right in five acres of land lying on south side of river and some interest in a saw-mill.

Mar. 30, 1745, From Samuel Thacher certain tract of land in Little Lot Purchase, 17th. lot in number about $16\frac{3}{4}$ acres.

April 6, 1745, From Thomas Hubbard, with J. Gridley, tract of land lying in

Middleboro upon Chusamuttock Hill containing fifteen acres and the lands that Samuel Thacher purchased of one Thomas, an Indian; also one eighth and one quarter of an eighth share in an Iron mill or forge, slitting mill, and grist mill, all near Namasket River.

April 24, 1745, From Lemuel Donham, with J. Gridley, certain lot of land which sd. Lemuel bought of Simeon Totman, together with dwelling house thereon.

May 1, 1745, From Ichabod Tupper, with J. Gridley, one acre of land in Middleboro butted on the country road adjoining lot of Moses Sturtevant, also adjoining Namasket River.

May 13, 1745, From James Bumpas one fourth part of a saw-mill on Namasket River in Middleboro.

June 12, 1745, From James Bowdoin, with J. Gridley, $4\frac{1}{2}$ sixteenth parts of a slitting mill, of a forge and of a Grist mill standing on a dam erected across Namasket River in Middleboro, also of five acres of land adjoining sd. works on south side of river, and of one acre adjoining sd. works on north side of river; also of a Way through lands of Ichabod Tupper to the highway, and of buildings — Coal House, Store House etc.

BACKPIECE IN FIREPLACE
AT OLIVER HALL

March 26, 1746, From Moses Sturtevant, with J. Gridley, certain tract of land in Middleboro on the purchase commonly called the Twenty-six Men's Purchase near Namasket River, containing about twelve and a quarter acres bounded by land bought by Gridley & Oliver from Tupper and by lands of Joseph Bumpas & Joseph Leonard.

Sept. 4, 1747, From Benjamin White, with Jeremiah Gridley, one sixteenth part of a Grist mill on Namasket River in Middleboro, with tools and implements.

Sept. 10, 1747, From Jeremiah Gridley his one, two & thirtieth share in Slitting mill, tools etc., Mill dam, one acre of land on northeast side of river, five acres on southwest side of river, with buildings Forge, Coal House, & Store House.

Nov. 1747, From Simeon Totman, with J. Gridley, westerly half of a lot of land bought from Samuel Thacher in 1741, together with buildings thereon.

Mar. 28, 1748, From Andrew Oliver, with J. Gridley, one hundred and seventy-three acres of land in Middleboro being part of the Great Lot in the Eight Men's Purchase of the whole 240 acres being the part lying on the southwest of the division line. Also, a 20 acre lot laid out in the right of John Blackwell in the second allotment in Eight Men's Purchase.

Aug. 15, 1748, From Moses Sturtevant, a certain lot containing about 78 acres, being a part of the 10th. lot of the land called the Twenty-six Men's Purchase. Also, a 10 acre tract in the Twenty-six Men's Purchase, being a part of the 4th. lot in the last allotment of sd. purchase.

Sept. 6, 1748, From Andrew Oliver, with J. Gridley, two lots in Eight Men's Purchase, one, the 3rd. lot in the 1st. allotment in John Blackwell's right, containing 60 acres; the other, the 4th. lot in the 1st. allotment in Francis Walker's right, containing 80 acres.

Oct. 11, 1748, From Amos Ahanton lot of land in Middleboro, containing four acres commonly known by the name of Indian Burying Ground, near Oliver's other lands.

Nov. 14, 1749, From Nathan Thomas, one eight part of slitting mill, forge, and grist mill on a dam across the Namasket River in Middleboro: five acres of land on south side of river; one acre of land on north side of river; tools etc.; Coal House; Store House and dwelling house, right in an Iron ore lot; dwelling house, barn and land adjoining any of forementioned premises.

Sept. 1, 1758, From Jeremiah Gridley one half of: Slitting mill, forge, gristmill, saw-mill, store house, dam, 5 acres of land on south side of Namasket River, one acre on north side, way through land of Thomas Tupper. 2 lots of land bought from Andrew Oliver, 1 lot bought from Sturtevant, 1 lot from Thomas Hubbard.

Jan. 27, 1759, From Joseph Leonard, tract of land adjoining at lower corner the land Oliver bought of Sturtevant, on easterly side of Namasket River, containing seven acres.

July 3, 1759, From William & Mary Sherman, homestead in Rochester containing $60\frac{1}{4}$ acres of land where Joseph Oliver (Peter Oliver's father) lived — adjoining Arthur Savorey's land. Also 17 acres laid out to W. Sherman in 1755 by Hiller, Briggs & Barlow.

Sept. 3, 1767. From William Oliver (one of his sons to whom he had given or sold these mills etc.) one sixth part of: Slitting mill, forge, grist-mill, saw-mill, boulting mill, cider mill, axe house, all near dam across Namasket River, the dam, stream of sd. river. 5 acres south of river; 1 acre north of river, way through Tupper's land, four lots in Eight Men's Purchase (total 335 acres), tract of land in Twenty-six Men's Purchase ($107\frac{1}{2}$ acres) four acres purchased Ahanton, building etc.

July 11, 1771, From Nathl. Perkins & Ezekl. Lewis, all Jeremiah Gridley's right in lands in Middleboro, all his interest in one-half of 500 acres of land, 5 dwelling houses, saw-mill, forge etc.

April 5, 1774. From Oxenbridge Thacher, one-half of the Tomb which is in the Burial Place in the East Precinct in Middleboro, near the East meeting house in sd. precinct.

CHAPTER XXIII

THOMPSON ROAD, THE LOWLANDS. WARRENTOWN, PURCHADE

THE Thompson Road district extends for two miles and a half on Thompson Street on the western side of Bartlett's Brook and the great cedar swamp. Thompson Street was among the first roads in town, extending from the meeting-house toward Boston, substantially as at present. At one time many descendants of John Tomson lived here. What is known as Danson Brook crosses the street, running into Bartlett Brook between the houses occupied by the late Reuel and Venus Thompson. Here George Danson, neglecting the warning of John Tomson, was shot by the Indians in King Philip's War. The residents have been for the most part well-to-do farmers. Perhaps the most prominent man, next to the first settler, was Isaac Thomson, a descendant of John Tomson, familiarly known as "Squire Isaac." He married Lucy Sturtevant[1] in 1775, and died December 21, 1819, in the

CAPTAIN ISAAC THOMSON

---

[1] Sturtevant is probably the same as Stuyvesant. *Thompson Genealogy.*

seventy-fourth year of his age. He served the town in different capacities for more than twenty-five years. He was selectman for seventeen years, one of the representatives to the General Court for five years, and state senator for nine years. He was for thirty-three years a prominent member of the First Church, and was widely known throughout the county as a man of more than usual intelligence, thrifty, and faithful in the discharge of every duty. The house in which he lived is still standing on the western side of Thompson Road. Mr. George Thompson, who occupied this house from his early manhood until his death in 1875, was a worker in marble, and not a few of the gravestones in the different cemeteries of the town were of his workmanship.

Upon the western side of this neighborhood lay the great swamps known as White Oak Island, Beaver Dam Swamp, and Meeting House Swamp, which cover a tract of land almost entirely destitute of houses or cultivated land, measuring nearly four miles in length and a mile and a half in width.

GEORGE THOMPSON HOUSE

A familiar spot in the early history of the town was Bear Spring, opposite the junction of Plain and Thompson streets. It is often mentioned in bounds of land connected with the great swamps in this immediate vicinity.

Upon Bartlett Brook, which flows a little to the east of Thompson Street along its entire length, was in 1715 erected the first sawmill of which we have any record in the town of Middleboro. It was built by Edward Thomas, Jacob Thomson, Henry Wood, and John Tinkham. They were owners in equal shares of the mill and the meadows lying near it.

September 10, 1725, Jacob Thomson, John Tinkham, and Isaac Tinkham, the owners, agreed that "the price for sawing boards should be twenty-five shillings a thousand, of two inch oak plank and oak slit work forty-five; of two inch spruce plank thirty-five; spruce and pitch pine slit work to be measured by board measure twenty-two shillings and six pence, and to have half the slabs, the owners of said mill to saw by turn." In 1744 Isaac Tinkham, Jacob Thomson, and Caleb Thomson rebuilt this mill.

THE LOWLANDS

This place in the extreme northeastern portion of the town bordering upon Taunton River, including River Street and the northern portion of Thompson Street, was never thickly settled. It was the home of Thomas Darling, one of the early settlers, and for many generations his descendants have been found here as well as some of the descendants of John Tomson. Soon after the close of the Revolution, Captain Joshua Eddy built a small vessel at Woodward's Bridge. There was a shipyard from which small ships were built and launched in the river back of the house occupied many years ago by Thomas Covington. Upon the south of this neighborhood lies White Oak Island, partly included in the Thompson neighborhood, through which no street or road has ever been built.

SHIPYARD FROM WOODWARD'S BRIDGE

On River Street was the home of Captain William Thomson, called "Squire Bill," a great-grandson of John Tomson, born February 15, 1748. He married Deborah Sturtevant, a lineal descendant of Peter Sturtevant, the celebrated governor of New York under the Dutch rule. Her portrait, painted by her son Cephas, is described as that of "a most beautiful woman." "Squire Bill," a captain of a company of militia in the Revolution, was at the battle of Bunker Hill, and was known as a most fearless advocate of the patriot cause. He was a large land-owner, and a man of great energy, who held many positions of trust until his death, March 14, 1816. His house, later occupied by his son, Cephas Thompson, was of solid oak boards and timber, and was probably the last of the blockhouses built after King Philip's War to resist any attacks of the Indians. It would probably have stood for generations, had it not been destroyed by fire about the year 1860. It was a one-story house, with the old-fashioned gambrel roof. In the front rooms were the "beaufats," placed there when the house was first built; one of the chambers was hung with ancient tapestry of a beautifully wrought biblical scene, made by nuns at a convent in Paris.

CEPHAS THOMPSON

Cephas Thompson was born July 1, 1775, and from his earliest boyhood could readily, with pencil and paper, draw excellent likenesses of his school friends. His great love for portrait painting made him a successful artist, and he attained great celebrity in the South, where he had a wide circle of acquaintances. He was a friend of Parke Custis, Jefferson, and Chief Justice Marshall, whose portrait he painted, and of whom he used to relate many interesting anecdotes. Once when in Richmond, having occasion to go into the court house where the chief justice was presiding, he was invited to take a seat with him on the bench, and he remained there during the session of the day.

Mr. Thompson had a select library, in which were some valuable books. In his parlor used to hang a number of pictures of tropical scenery which had been presented to him by his southern friends. The latter years of his life he spent in quiet in the enjoyment of his library and attractive studio, a two-story building on the opposite side of the street. Here his friends used to gather; and during the summer days one could rarely visit his home without finding men and women of note who came to spend a short time in his genial society. In most of the well-to-do homes in town of three generations ago could be found portraits from Mr. Thompson's brush.

Cephas G. Thompson and Jerome B. Thompson, his sons, artists, and Marietta T. Thompson, his daughter, a miniature painter, settled in New York. His brother, Dr. Arad Thompson, was for years a physician in practice at the Four Corners.

WARRENTOWN

This village is situated on the road to Bridgewater, about two and a half miles from the centre of the town. It takes its name from Jabez Warren, an early settler, and from his numerous descendants, who, until the past twenty-five years, lived upon lands formerly owned by their ancestor. Mr. John Warren, his great-grandson, built and maintained a grist-mill, a shingle mill, and a sawmill on Murdock Street, across the Nemasket River. Business was done here for many years, but upon the death of Mr. Warren it was given up, and later the buildings and the dam were destroyed. The house of John F. Alden was the home of John Warren, and in the latter part of stage-coach days was a tavern.

This is one of the old houses in town, and was probably built in 1734 by Edmund Weston for his son, soon after he moved here from Plympton. At the time, he had purchased a large tract of land, which, upon his death, was divided between his sons, John taking this house and land, and Edmund taking the house and land near Plain Street.

Nathan Warren, a descendant of John Warren, was born in Middleboro in 1757, and died there May 28, 1807. He was a Revolutionary soldier, serving as private in several companies, and as sergeant in Captain Edward Sparrow's company from the 23d of July, 1777, to October 27, 1780.

JOHN WESTON HOUSE
(Afterwards the home of John Warren)

Another descendant of John Warren was Captain Sylvanus Warren, who lived on the Bridgewater road for many years. He was a day laborer, working on the farm of Judge Weston, and afterwards upon that of his son, Colonel Thomas Weston. Before that he had worked for President John Quincy Adams. In accordance with the custom throughout New England, the workmen were introduced to all guests, with whom they talked freely as they sat at table together. He was fond of relating that he had often dined with President Adams, and sometimes members of his cabinet and foreign ministers were at the table.

Opposite the junction of Plain Street and the road to Bridgewater stood the shovel shop of Benjamin F. Warren. The hammer shop connected with this was on a brook which crossed the Bridgewater road a little to the north; here a dam had been erected, and a pond of six or eight acres furnished the water power. In the field stands the dwelling-house for many years occupied by Captain George Hartwell, where Abner Weston lived in the early part of the century, and here Edmund Weston was born; in his boyhood he moved to

Vermont, and afterwards became a distinguished judge of the probate court in that state.

In the year 1824 the town authorized the laying out and construction of Plain Street, running from the Bridgewater road to the lowlands. This was built as a substitute for a very crooked way which branched off from the Bridgewater road near the blacksmith shop of the late Eber Beals. It led to the pasture lands formerly owned by Colonel Thomas Weston; crossing the brook at that place, it ran in an irregular direction for about two miles to Thompson Street. A hundred years ago there were eight houses upon this street, all of which long ago disappeared. They were owned or occupied by a Mr. Nims, Josiah Dunham, who was nicknamed "Governor Dunham," Edmund Weston, a Mr. Leach, and Livy Morton, the grandfather of Levi P. Morton, ex-Vice-President of the United States. In the latter part of the eighteenth century many descendants of the first Edmund Weston lived near here. His house, which in 1772 had become so old as not to be habitable, was taken down, and the materials were used to erect the present one located on Summer Street, later occupied by Colonel Thomas Weston. This was a tavern during the Revolutionary War.

COLONEL THOMAS WESTON

A short time before the battle of Lexington, several British officers, on their way to Boston, stopped here for dinner. As they left, they saw a good horse fastened in the yard, and took it, leaving a poor one in its place. When the exchange was discovered, the angry owner started in pursuit, and overtaking them, was so forceful in his demands that the officers returned his horse. This incident tended to increase the bitter hostility which was beginning to permeate the whole country.

OLD WESTON TAVERN

Colonel Thomas Weston was born February 27, 1804, and died February 12, 1888. In the early part of his life he was engaged with his father in general mercantile business and in the manufacture of wrought nails. In 1844 he moved to the old Weston house, where he resided until shortly before his death. After retiring from active business, " he was especially interested in agriculture, and at the time of his decease was the oldest member of the Plymouth County Agricultural Society, and for many years one of its trustees. In his early life he was active in the militia of his county, and held the office of colonel for some years in the Fourth Regiment of the First Brigade of Massachusetts Volunteer Militia. He was a member of the First Congregational Church of Middleboro for more than sixty years, and was always active in promoting its temporal and spiritual interests. He was an unassuming man, of great strength of character, of positive convictions, of sterling integrity, of great industry, and an earnest and devout christian." [1]

The descendants of Edward Bump have always resided in this neighborhood. In the latter part of the eighteenth century there were three named Joseph, called respectively Chin Joe, Thumb Joe, and Jockey Joe, the latter being widely known for his great strength; he is said to have been able to lift and carry more than three ordinary men.

Captain Nathaniel Bump lived on the road to Titicut, just

[1] *Doggett Genealogy.*

across the Nemasket River. He was a man of great energy, and was in command of the company from Middleboro in the War of 1812. James S. Bump, the father of Lavinia Bump and Minnie Warren, lived in this vicinity. In 1863 Lavinia married Charles S. Stratton, known as Tom Thumb; her second husband was an Italian, Count Magri.

RESIDENCE OF MRS. TOM THUMB

In 1864 Mrs. Stratton erected a summer residence upon the grounds near one of the old training-greens. Minnie Warren married Major Newell, but died soon afterwards.

In the early part of the century there were here three wheelwright shops, owned and occupied by Reuel Atwood, Edward H. Waterman, and Venus Snow, and the three blacksmith shops of Thomas S. Harlow, John Warren, and William E. Bump.

PURCHADE

Purchade, formerly known as School District Number 19, takes its name from the purchase made from the Indians in the year 1662. It is principally on Purchade, Everett, and Plymouth streets, and includes a large tract of meadows known as the Purchade Meadows, through which flows a brook by the same name, which empties into the Nemasket River. The descendants of Francis Eaton have always lived here.

John Alden, a grandson of the pilgrim John Alden, inherited his father's homestead in West Bridgewater, but he conveyed this to Isaac Johnson and moved to Middleboro in 1700. Here his descendants have lived, very many of them residing in this neighborhood. His son, John Alden,[1] was

[1] *History of the First Church of Middleboro*, p. 61.

born October 8, 1718, and lived to the great age of one hundred and two years, five months, and ten days. He was a member of the First Church of Middleboro for nearly seventy-eight years, and always lived upon his homestead. On the completion of his one hundredth year, a sermon was preached in his house by the Rev. Isaac Tompkins, pastor of the church in Haverhill. This was printed and is still extant. At the time of his death[1] he had two hundred and nineteen descendants: nineteen children, sixty-two grandchildren, and one hundred and thirty-four great-grandchildren, and four of the fifth generation. This family seems to have been noted for the longevity of its members.

JOHN ALDEN

Elijah Alden, a grandson of the last-named John Alden, was born on Purchade Street, June 10, 1780, and lived to the age of ninety-eight. In the War of 1812 he marched with the company from Middleboro to defend Plymouth, Wareham, and New Bedford against threatened attacks of the British, and for many years received a pension for his services in the war. When hammered nails were manufactured at Muttock, he was employed in fall and winter, and was considered an expert, boasting that he made three thousand in one week.

Upon Everett Street stands the house built and occupied by Samuel Sampson, a Revolutionary soldier, who entered the army when he was seventeen years of age, and was one of

[1] *Alden Memorial*, p. 18.

the forty men enlisted by the town of Middleboro for three years' service or during the war. He was chosen deacon of the First Church June 30, 1826, and served until his death, July 30, 1850, at the age of eighty-six years. The community had great confidence in his judgment in settling disputes, so that for years he bore not only the title of deacon, but that of peacemaker.[1]

On the other side of Everett Street, some little distance to the south of his house, stood the residence of Archippus Leonard and his son, Seth. Archippus Leonard worked in the furnace of Judge Oliver at Muttock. In the War of 1812 Seth Leonard was captain of a schooner which sailed from Wareham to Stonington, Conn. Upon his arrival he was informed that the place was threatened by a British man-of-war, which arrived the next morning opposite the town. The inhabitants were wholly unprepared for defence, and most of them had fled into the country. Captain Leonard, a man of great courage, determined to defend the town, and finding a seven-pound cannon with sufficient ammunition, had it placed at a point which would bear upon the ship. The few remaining women brought their dresses for wadding. The man-of-war was too far off to have its shell effective, and owing to the shallowness of the harbor, was unable to come to the wharf, so the commander proceeded to land men in boats. Captain Leonard and his crew fired with such precision, as the boats approached, that several were destroyed and the others retreated to the vessel. The man-of-war soon after sailed away.

Several generations ago bricks were manufactured by Calvin and Levi Murdock in the lowland in the northern part of this neighborhood, and within a few years George R. Sampson has carried on a large brick business upon the land which he inherited from his grandfather, Deacon Sampson. Opposite the residence of Mr. Sampson was a cartway, in the early part of the last century, leading to a settlement of some five or six dwelling-houses known as "the city." These houses were one after another removed, and the place they occupied is a dense

---

[1] *Sampson Genealogy*, p. 77.

wood, with nothing to indicate the secluded village of former times.

Some sixty years ago the neighborhood on the hill south of Warrentown was known as "Tribou's," from Melzar Tribou, an old-time shoemaker. His son, Nahum M. Tribou, was a large farmer, and had a sales stable connected with his farm. His son, Nahum M. Tribou, Jr., who died in 1871, was a well-known physician in practice in Norwich, Conn. In the open yard adjoining the residence of Melzar Tribou were the carpenter shop of Horatio N. Wilbur and the shoe shop of Richard Carter. On the other side of the road was the blacksmith shop of Eber Beals, a skilful and reliable mechanic; he was a citizen of strong character. The house owned by the late James Snow on the hill was formerly the residence of his father, Aaron Snow, who bought the place in 1794 and had a wheelwright shop near his house. This house, although its exterior has been much changed, is known to have been standing before 1740, and probably contains the only fireplace in town of a style in use when the house was erected. It is about six feet high, ten feet long, and six feet deep, with a large, brick oven in one corner.

Lysander Richmond, a well-known citizen of this neighborhood, commenced the manufacture of shoes in 1848. This so increased that he erected a large building on Plymouth Street upon what is known as the Elisha Richmond farm. His business was largely with the South, and upon the breaking out of the War of the Rebellion he lost so heavily that he was obliged to give up this enterprise, which was never afterwards resumed.

CHAPTER XXIV

TITICUT

THE northern part of the town still retains its Indian name of Titicut.[1] This included the southern part of Bridgewater on this side of the Taunton River, and from the earliest time was noted for its productive soil and natural beauty. It was first known to the English settlers through the journey of Stephen Hopkins and Edward Winslow under the guidance of the friendly Indian Tisquantum, who started from Plymouth July 13, 1621, to seek an interview with the great Indian sachem, Massasoit. Of this visit Governor Winslow gives an account, to which we refer elsewhere. Here was one of the three settlements of the Namascheuks.

SITE OF THE OLD INDIAN FORT

It was on the high ground on both sides of the river, southwest of the Congregational meeting-house. The hill on the easterly side of the river, southwest of the church, is known as the Indian Fort,[2] and there Winslow and Hopkins probably spent the night.

[1] Kehtehticut, Cututicut, Tetiquid, which often occur in the early deeds and records, are different spellings of Titicut.

[2] "The Nemasket Indians and neighboring tribes built this fort for their own protection. They had two doors to the fort: one next to the river, the other on the opposite side. One day they were surprised by a formidable force of the Narragansett Indians with whom they were at war, at which time, unfortunately, there were only eight men in the fort; the remaining part were hunting and

After the death of Chickataubut in 1633, the Titicut Indians seem to have been divided into two bands, separated from each other by the Taunton River. On the river was the old weir where they caught herring.

Here was the old Indian reservation,[1] the southern corner of which was at that point where the present bounds of Middleboro, Lakeville, and Taunton meet.[2] From there the line ran easterly, or northeasterly, to an oak-tree on the brow of a hill; thence easterly by a black oak-tree to what was known as the old English line; thence to the river. The oak-tree, still

fishing. What therefore now to do they could not tell, but something must be done and that immediately. Therefore, every Indian bound on his blanket and arrows and took their bows and rushed out of the back door through the bushes down the bank to the river, then by the river in an opposite direction from their enemy a small distance, then ascended the bank in sight of their enemy, then rushing in and through the fort and down the bank again, then up the bank and through the fort as before. This round of deception they continued till their enemy, being surprised that their fort consisted of so formidable a number, left the ground precipitately and retired, fearing an attack from the vast number in the fort." Memorandum in the Bennett Family.

[1] It was through the influence of the court that Josias Wampatuck, the son of Chickataubut, was induced to give a deed without consideration:—

PRENCE G^{ovr}
A deed appointed to bee Recorded

THES p^rsents witnesseth that I Josias allies Chickatabutt doe promise by these p^rsents to giue vnto the Indians liueing vpon Catuhtkut Riuer (viz) Pompanohoo Waweens and the other Indians liueing there: that is three miles upon each side of the Riuer excepting the lands that are alreddy sold to the English either Taunton Bridgwater or to the Major and doe promise by these p^rsents not to sell or giue to any any P^te or P^cell of land; but that the aforsaid Indians shall peacably enjoy the same without any Interuption from mee or by my meanes in any respect: the which I doe engage and promise by these p^rsents: witnes my hand this 9th of June in the yeare 1664

CHICKATABUTT allies JOSIAS + β
his marke

WUTTANAUMATUKE ⟨⟩
his marke

Witnes
Richard Bourne
John Low ⟨⟩
his marke

Book of Indian Records, Plymouth Colony Records (1620–51), vol. xii, p. 238.
[2] See map of Indian Purchases.

standing, is mentioned in several of the early deeds.[1] This reservation was carefully guarded by the General Court for more than two generations; the whites settling in this region were instructed not to encroach on the territory of the Indians, or in any way molest them; they retained exclusive possession long after other portions of the town had been settled.

Among the early settlers was a Mr. Richmond,[2] who was here before King Philip's War; a man of gigantic stature, bold and fearless. He was much dreaded by the Indians, with whom he had many contests, and as he was usually victorious, they were constantly planning to capture him. He served as one of Captain Church's scouts, and in the latter part of the war was attacked by a number of Indians when there was a great freshet in the Taunton River. He was driven to a spot where the Poquoy brook enters the river, and as escape was impossible, he was killed. He lived near the house of the late Jonathan Richmond by the bend of the river, a few rods this side of the Richmond town bridge.

A few years ago, when the highway was straightened and repaired, his remains were found, and he was re-interred. Afterwards, his body was exhumed in presence of Dr. Morrill Robinson and others to test the truth of the tradition as to his gigantic size and strength. When his skeleton was measured, it was found that his thigh-bone was four inches longer than that bone in an ordinary man, and that he had a double row of teeth in each jaw. His height must have been at least seven feet and eight inches. There is a tradition that he was the brother of Jonathan Richmond, who, four years after his brother's death, occupied the land which he had formerly cultivated.

Here was situated one of the three churches of the praying Indians. Probably its site was near the present centre of the parish, on Pleasant Street, not far from the shoe factory of Keith & Pratt.

This church continued until after 1755; it was then dis-

---

[1] See picture of this tree in chapter on Early Purchases.

[2] A sketch of the life of this man appeared some years ago in a pamphlet which is now lost.

banded, and the few remaining Indians united with the Congregational Church. From the first visit by Hopkins and Winslow down to their complete extinction, they seem to have lived quietly and peacefully. Their territory was not disturbed during King Philip's War, and one after another they passed away until, at the time of the Revolution, none of them remained. During the French and Indian War many of them enlisted with their white brethren to defend the rights and honor of the English Crown.

In the early history of the town, efforts were often made to incorporate Titicut as a separate town, either alone or by joining with a portion of Bridgewater. Both the town and the legislature declined to grant these various petitions.[1] In 1744 a petition was sent to the legislature "that if your Excellency and Honors do not see meet to set off a township that you will establish a distinct precinct so that we may enjoy the gospel privileges by ourselves." This was granted that year, and plans were immediately made for erecting a place of worship.

Although they had occasional preaching, the religious controversy between the New Lights and the Old Lights prevented the organization of a church until the year 1747, when the first meeting-house was erected. It was built near the cemetery on Plymouth Street, on land given by three of the praying Indians, in what was then a pine forest, beautifully shaded in the heat of summer and protected from the blasts of winter. Soon after this, the sixteen persons who had signed a covenant for a new church extended a call to the Rev. Isaac Backus, minister from Norwich, Conn., to become their pastor. Later he espoused the faith of the Baptist denomination. A separation of his congregation resulted. Those adhering to the old faith built a church on the site of the present Congregational Church, and services were held in both of these edifices. The church occupied by Mr. Backus's congregation was known as the Old English or Indian Church, and was situated opposite Keith & Pratt's shoe factory. Owing to its insufficient size, it was subsequently abandoned, and a new one was built on the same

[1] See Introduction.

site about 1757. This they occupied until 1806, when they built a new house of worship on Bedford Street near the present Baptist Church. On fast day of that year the Rev. Isaac Backus preached his last sermon, the first one in the new building. The old building on Pleasant Street was afterwards sold and moved to a lumber yard in Taunton. Great was the lamentation over the removal of this first place of worship, and it is said that a number of those who were in the habit of attending service there followed the house as it was being removed, and such was their sorrow that many were moved to tears.

Few men in Plymouth Colony during the middle of the eighteenth century attracted more attention or exerted greater influence than Rev. Isaac Backus. He was the son of Samuel and Elizabeth (Tracey) Backus, and was born in Norwich, Conn., January 9, 1724. His mother was a descendant of Edward Winslow, of pilgrim fame. He is said to have received his first religious impression from the preaching of Whitefield during the Great Awakening. He early had misgivings as to the laxity in the admission of members to the Congregational Church, and espoused the views of the New Lights. He did not receive a collegiate education, but felt it his duty to become a preacher of the gospel, and his first sermon was delivered on the 28th of September, 1746. In 1747 he was called to the Congregational Church in Titicut, where he served until 1756; he then became pastor of the Baptist Church[1] formed there at that time, and continued in this office until the close of his life. He was the leading pastor of his denomination in this part of the state. His ability was early recognized, and in 1772 he was chosen agent for the Baptist churches in Massachusetts.

In 1774 he was sent to the Continental Congress in Philadelphia, and it is said, travelled on horseback there and back. There he urged that greater religious liberty and privileges of worship be granted to christian people. Upon his return, there were rumors that his mission was to interfere in some way with the union of the colonies, which gave rise to a

[1] For further account, see chapter on Ecclesiastical History.

memorial to the Provincial Congress of Massachusetts, which was so patriotic in its sentiment and so able in its argument that he was at once relieved of all suspicion. He was one of the members of the convention to adopt the Constitution of the United States, and was probably the leading spirit in most vigorously and earnestly insisting that there should be no connection between church and state. It was during this critical period following the Revolution, when the country was debating that most important question, the ratification of the Constitution, that this convention was called to meet in Boston on January 9, 1788. There were three hundred and fifty-five delegates present, a much larger number than took part in any other state convention, and among these were twenty-four clergymen. In the discussion over various clauses in the Constitution, a complaint was made that it did not recognize the existence of God, in that it had no religious tests for candidates for federal offices. This objection was not raised by the ministers present, but by members from the country.

"The Rev. Isaac Backus of Middleboro said, 'In reason and in the Holy Scripture, religion is ever a matter between God and the individual; the imposing of religious tests hath been the engine of tyranny in the world.' With this liberal stand firmly taken by the ministers, the religious objection was speedily overruled."[1]

In 1789, at the earnest request of his denomination, he took a journey into Virginia and North Carolina, and was absent from his people some six months, preaching one hundred and seventeen sermons during that time.

In those days, every one in the commonwealth was taxed to maintain the preaching of the Congregational Church. As he was a Baptist, he refused to pay the assessment, which he considered unjust, and was taken by the authorities as far as Bridgewater. Here a woman saw him and paid the tax herself; the officers then took him from their horse and left him in the road to walk back to his home.

In 1797, in appreciation of his intellectual vigor and patri-

[1] Fiske, *Critical Period of American History*, p. 322.

otic service, Brown University conferred upon him the honorary degree of Master of Arts. He died November 20, 1806, in the eighty-third year of his age.

The Hon. Zachariah Eddy, in a letter [1] concerning him, says:

"All New England is indebted to Mr. Backus more, I think, than to any other man, for his researches in relation to our early ecclesiastical history. Mr. Bancroft bears the most honourable testimony to his fidelity, and considers his History, as to its facts, more to be depended on than any other of the early Histories of New England. And there is good reason why it should be so; for he sought the truth, like the old philosophers, who said 'it was in a well, and long and persevering labour only could bring it up.' He went to the fountain head. All our early Records at Plymouth, Taunton, Boston, Essex, Providence, Newport, Hartford, New Haven, — the Records of Courts, Towns, Churches, Ecclesiastical Councils, were thoroughly searched, and he has fully and accurately presented the results of these researches, and brought to light and remembrance many important facts and events, which, probably, would never have gone into our history but for him. His diligence, patience, and perseverance, in this department of labour, are above all praise.

"And what renders this the more remarkable is that it was done in the midst of domestic cares, pastoral duties, and, I might almost say, 'the care of all the churches.' He was often called upon to preach at ordinations, and on other special occasions, and he wrote numerous tracts on the Order of the Churches, and in defence of True Liberty of Conscience. He was also an efficient representative of those who were seeking to enjoy this liberty, before Legislative Bodies and Civil Tribunals, Councils, and Associations. Let any man open his History, and observe the numerous extracts from documents contained in the depositories of towns and churches, in public offices, and printed books of authority, and bear in mind the extent and variety of his other engagements, and he will not doubt that he was one of the most industrious and useful men of his time. In his own day, his labours were certainly appreciated. It is truly wonderful that, amidst the poverty and privations incident to the War of the Revolution, there could have been awakened interest enough to defray the expense of publishing large volumes of History, at the high price which

[1] *Annals of the American Pulpit*, vol. vi, p. 57.

was then demanded for such works. The effect was a rapid increase of light and knowledge, and a rapid increase of churches and communicants."

The Rev. S. H. Emery, the pastor of the Congregational Church, and the author of the history of that church, says of Mr. Backus : —

" He was a man of remarkable [1] vigor of mind, true to his convictions of truth and duty. There is hardly another of the whole range of the denomination of Baptists who has in his day and generation wrought a greater work in their service as well as of the common Master." [2]

His grave is in the old burying-ground near the Congregational Church. In 1872 the Old Colony Baptist Association held its jubilee anniversary in this village, and a movement was set on foot to erect a monument worthy of this distinguished man. It was not, however, completed until 1893, when it was dedicated by a large memorial gathering.

[1] The following is a list of Mr. Backus's Publications: A Discourse on the Internal Call to preach the Gospel, 1754. A Sermon on Galatians iv, 31, 1756. A Sermon on Acts xiii, 27, 1763. A Letter to Mr. Lord, 1764. A Sermon on Prayer, 1766. A Discourse on Faith, 1767. An Answer to Mr. Fish, 1768. A Sermon on his Mother's Death, 1769. A Second Edition of his Sermon on Galatians iv, 31, with an Answer to Mr. Frothingham, 1770. A Plea for Liberty of Conscience, 1770. Sovereign Grace Vindicated, 1771. A Letter concerning Taxes to support Religious Worship, 1771. A Sermon at the Ordination of Mr. Hunt, 1772. A Reply to Mr. Holly, 1777. A Reply to Mr. Fish, 1773. An Appeal to the Public, in Defence of Religious Liberty, 1773. A Letter on the Decrees, 1773. A History of the Baptists, vol. i, 1777. Government and Liberty described, 1778. A Discourse on Baptism, 1779. True Policy requires Equal Religious Liberty, 1779. An Appeal to the People of Massachusetts against Arbitrary Power, 1780. Truth is Great and will Prevail, 1781. The Doctrine of Universal Salvation examined and refuted, 1782. A Door opened for Christian Liberty, 1783. A History of the Baptists, vol. ii, 1784. Godliness excludes Slavery, in Answer to John Cleaveland, 1785. The Testimony of the Two Witnesses, 1786. An Address to New England, 1787. An Answer to Remmele on the Atonement, 1787. An Essay on Discipline, 1787. An Answer to Wesley on Election and Perseverance, 1789. On the Support of Gospel Ministers, 1790. An Essay on the Kingdom of God, 1792. A History of the Baptists, vol. iii, 1796. A Second Edition of his Sermon on the Death of his Mother; to which was added a short account of his Wife, who died in 1800. Published in 1803.

[2] S. H. Emery, *History of North Middleboro Church*, p. 23.

The house in which Dr. Backus lived still stands. It is a low, old-fashioned building, full of relics of the past, and

HOUSE OF REV. ISAAC BACKUS

was occupied for many years by his grandson, Joseph A. Backus. Many valuable records and important documents were given by J. A. Backus to his nephew, Isaac F. Perkins, the present owner of the house, who has loaned them to the Backus Historical Society of Newton, on certain conditions.

Rev. David Gurney, one of the early ministers, was much respected and loved throughout this community; he was a man of unusual intelligence, fond of children and youth. This love for young men caused him to open a school in his own house, which was well patronized, students coming from many parts of the town to enjoy his influence. Many prominent men were fitted for college under his instruction, and others for the ministry. He published an English Grammar, which was used extensively at the

HOUSE OF REV. MR. GURNEY
(Now occupied by Augustus Pratt)

time. His salary was not far from two hundred dollars per annum, the parish by sale of ministerial land and other sources having a fund which yielded an income for this purpose.

Mr. Gurney was on intimate terms with Mr. Backus, the pastor of the neighboring Baptist Church. He died on the 30th of July, 1815.[1]

[1] See chapter on Ecclesiastical History.

In the early history of the country, there was a foundry perhaps fifty rods west of Titicut bridge on the Bridgewater side, where during the French and Indian and Revolutionary Wars cannon balls and cannon[1] were made. There is a tradition that the first cannon cast solid in the United States were here made, and taken elsewhere to be bored. The owners of this foundry endeavored to cast four cannon which were six or seven feet long, to be used in the Revolutionary War; an undertaking attended with great expense. The cannon were made, but upon being tested, exploded, and the owners lost all of their property in this venture. The Rev. Philip Colby tried to obtain a pension for the widow of one of these men, but it was not granted because he was not in active service, although the department acknowledged the work. During the early part of the last century, fire frames were manufactured here by Albert Pratt.

At Pratt's bridge, David Charles, Isaac Wanno, and other Indians, in 1707, owned the land with the old mill privilege. It was used for some years until, in 1725, iron works were there established, and a company was then formed for the manufacture of hollow ware. In the early part of the last century there were here a grist-mill, a sawmill, a tolling mill and a gun shop. In 1730 Ebenezer Robinson had a sawmill and a furnace on the south side of the river. The dam for these mills was placed below Pratt's bridge, not far from the house of Mr. Hunt; the water was taken from canals on each side

---

[1] The following letter refers to this industry

WAR OFFICE

10th, Feb., 1779.

Sir, You are required to proceed to Titicut to prepare the metal from the common ore for casting twenty twelve pounders for the ship Protector, which are to be bored completed and finished by the first of May next. You are also to direct the boring of the twenty four pound cannon that they may be finished without loss of time. Col. Orr will give you every assistance that you may want and should anything farther be necessary, the board will furnish it.

Wishing you a pleasant jour, and are with much regard your friend and very humble servant,

JOHN BROWN PPS

Col. Marbquelle.

of the river, both of which can be seen at low water. Some years later, when the large iron works were built at Squawbetty, it was found necessary to construct another dam across the river at East Taunton. The company had the right of flowage, but their dam so interfered with the privilege above it that they were obliged to buy out the owners, and there has been no manufacturing at this place since.

The Titicut bridge, at first a rude structure, stood a little further up the stream than the present one. There was much discussion in reference to its reconstruction, and as a result the General Court of the province, on the 10th of June, 1755, authorized the money for building this bridge to be raised by lottery, as appears by the following statute enacted by the General Court at that time: —

Chap. 3. " June 3d 1755. A Petition of Ephraim Keith, Agent for the Precinct of Tetticut in the Town of Middleboro, setting forth the Necessity of erecting a Bridge over the River there, and the Difficulty of getting the Charge thereof defrayed, & praying that the same may be done by a Lottery, to be allowed by the Authority of this Court. In the House of Representatives; *Whereas* it appears *to this House* to this House that a Bridge over the River in Tetticut is necessary not only for the great Advantage of the Towns of Bridgwater & Middleboro, but also for several other Towns in the Counties of Bristol & Plymouth, as also for the great Advantage of the Southern Inhabitants travelling Westward; Therefore, Ordered that the Prayer of the Petition be so far granted as that the Petitioner have Liberty to bring in a Bill for the Purposes in the Petition mentioned; — In Council, Read & Concur'd." [1]

"April 14, 1756. A Petition of Ephraim Keith for himself, and the other Managers of the Lottery for raising a Sum for Building a Bridge at Tetticut, shewing that they have proceeded therein in preparing for drawing the said Lottery so far as to dispose of near half the Tickets, but have been hindered by Sickness; and whereas the time for Drawing is at hand, Praying that this Court would consider & determine upon some proper way for their Relief —

" In Council; Read & Ordered that George Leonard Esq. with such as the Hon[ble] House shall join be a Committee to consider of this Petition & report what they judge proper for this Court to do thereon.

"In the House of Representatives; Read & Concur'd; And Mr. Moorey & Capt. Howard are joined in the Affair."[2]

"April 15, 1756. Report upon the Petition of Ephraim Keith, Entered yesterday — vizt —

"The Committee appointed to take under Consideration the Petition Of

---

[1] *Council Records*, vol. xx, p. 460.   [2] *Ibid.* vol. xxi, p. 162.

Ephraim Keith in behalf of the Managers of a Lottery for the Building of a Bridge over Tetticut River, so called, having met the said Managers & Considered of the Difficulties they labour under respecting the Disposal of the Tickets for said Lottery, report that the Scheme of said Lottery be altered in the following Manner in Order to finish & Compleat the same — vizt.

"That there be,

"One Prize of £125 — £125. — Three ditto of £40 each £120.

"Three ditto of £25 each 75. — Seven ditto of £20 each £140.

"Eleven ditto of £10 each 110. — Twenty ditto of £5 — each £100.

"Fifty ditto of £3 each 150. — Six Hundred & Thirty of £1 each £630. — In all £1450. — And that the Number of Blanks be proportioned to the said Prizes as in the Scheme, published by said Managers, and the Deduction of Ten per Cent only be made from the above Prizes for the Charge of Building said Bridge: which is humbly Submitted — By Order of the Committee —

GEORGE LEONARD —

"In Council; Read & Accepted, and Ordered that the said Scheme be and hereby is altered accordingly — In the House of Representatives; Read & Concur'd — Consented to by the Governour."[1]

The act authorizing the building of this bridge was passed on the 10th of June, 1755:[2] —

"Whereas the precinct of Teticut have represented to this court the necessity of building a bridge over Teticut River, and prayed this court would enable them to raise a sum, by way of lottery, for that purpose, —

"*Be it therefore enacted by the Governour, Council and House of Representatives,*

"That Samuel White, Esq., of Taunton, Israel Washburn of Raynham, Ephraim Keith and James Keith, both of Bridgewater, and David Alden of Middleborough, or any three of them, be and hereby are impowered to set up and carry on a lottery, amounting to such a sum, as by drawing ten percent out of each prize, may raise a sum of two hundred and ninety pounds lawful money, and no more; and that the said sum be by them, or any three of them, applied to the building a good, sufficient bridge over the said river, and paying the charges of said lottery; and that the said Samuel White, Israel Washburn, Ephraim Keith, James Keith and David Alden, or any three of them, be the managers of said lottery, and impowered to make all necessary rules for managing thereof, and shall be sworn to the faithful discharge of their said trust; and as well the said managers as the said precinct shall be and are hereby declared answerable to the owners of the tickets, in case of any deficiency or misconduct; and if the sum raised thereby shall be more than sufficient, after paying the charges of the lottery, to build the said bridge, the surplusage shall be lodged in the hands of the treasurer of the said precinct, to be put at interest, and the interest applied towards the repairs of said bridge.

"*Passed and published June 10.*"[2]

[1] *Province Laws*, vol. iii. pp. 939, 940: *Council Records*, vol. xxi, p. 163.

[2] *Province Laws*, vol. iii, p. 861.

About the middle of the last century this bridge was rebuilt by Mr. George W. Wood.

A store was kept by Jared Pratt and his uncle Isaac near the Congregational Church; they were afterwards succeeded by Seth Fuller.

Another store on the turnpike near the Baptist Church was kept by Mrs. Goodwin. In 1812 Mr. Charles Goodwin was drafted into the service and went to Plymouth with the Middleboro companies. His mother was so distressed that she travelled all the way to Plymouth to obtain his discharge. When this was granted, there was general rejoicing among his comrades.

ELIJAH E. PERKINS

The first store on the hill was kept by Amos and Robert Clark. Afterwards, Mr. Hooper was admitted as a copartner, and in 1861 the store was moved near the present post-office.

The shoe business of this portion of the town since the middle of the last century has been an important industry. Mr. Amos Clark was the first to put out shoes to be made, from 1838 to 1848, the year of his death. About this time Mr. Hosea Kingman commenced this business, which he carried on successfully, selling his product generally in New Bedford. In 1848 Nahum Keith and Elijah E. Perkins also commenced manufacturing shoes. The former was in the business until 1849, and again from 1856 to 1860. The latter admitted his son, D. Sumner Perkins, as partner in 1865. They continued until 1881, when Sumner died and his father retired, and was succeeded by the firm of Stetson, Hammond & Holmes.

Nahum Keith will always be known among shoe manufacturers as the inventor of a jack for holding shoes.

Mr. Jared Keith commenced business on the turnpike just north of the Baptist Church about 1847, and continued until about 1854.

Stetson, Hammond & Holmes, who succeeded E. E. Perkins & Son, were in business a few years, and were succeeded by Alden, Leonard & Hammond, who moved to the Four Corners.

N. Williams Keith started manufacturing shoes in 1869. Herbert A. Pratt was admitted as partner in 1879, under the firm name of Keith & Pratt. Mr. Keith retired in 1905, and was succeeded by Mr. Pratt's son, Alton G. Pratt, the firm name continuing as before.

C. H. Alden and Enoch Pratt started in business about 1886. After a few years Mr. Pratt withdrew from the firm, and soon after Mr. Alden moved the business to Abington.

One of the most ingenious men who lived in this part of the town was Mr. Heffords, who was famous for clocks of superior quality, which he invented and manufactured, as well as for many other delicate pieces of machinery. His place of business was on the corner opposite the Baptist Church.

About a quarter of a mile below Pratt's Bridge was formerly a shipyard, and one ship was built there by Deacon Holmes of Kingston in the early part of 1800, called the Two Brothers. A little later, Captain Benjamin Pratt built several ships of forty or fifty

SITE OF SHIPYARD

tons burden, which were used in the coast trade which he and his sons carried on with the South.

There was formerly a furnace on land of Mr. Stafford on the southeast portion of Center and Pleasant streets, where kitchen ware was cast, which was carted to Taunton and there sold. This business was carried on by a Mr. Shaw, who at one time left with a load of goods to sell and was never heard from afterwards.

SOLOMON EATON

The first iron ploughs made in Massachusetts were brought into this neighborhood in 1835 and put together by Mr. Nahum Keith, who endeavored to introduce them among the farmers. There was, however, a great prejudice against them, and in order to do away with this feeling, he would allow neighboring farmers to use them, who tried in every possible way to break them, to convince people of the folly of "new-fangled ploughs." It is said that one man broke three.

About forty rods east of the Congregational Church stood a two-story shop, where Williams Eaton and Otis Pratt manufactured hubs, the only industry of the kind in eastern Massachusetts.

The turnpike, of which we have spoken in the account of Lakeville, was laid out in 1804, and was three years in construction. This corporation, with little stock held in town, was not a pecuniary success, and was assumed by the town after the Fall River railroad was built. There was a toll-gate in the Haskins neighborhood and another near S. Eaton's Inn.

The rates of toll were very high for those days, twelve cents for every ten miles. There used to be two stages a day, one from Boston and one from New Bedford, and about seven baggage wagons every week.

There were three taverns well known between 1810 and 1812, when the turnpike was in full operation. One of the houses, known as the old Solomon Eaton house, is now standing. It was a hostelry of the olden time, and over its door swung the customary sign of the proprietor, which in this case bore the name S. Eaton's Inn. It is related that two Irishmen passing by desired accommodation, but when they read the sign over the door, one said, "It's Satan's Inn, begorra! We don't want to be afther stoppin' here."

Mrs. Goodwin kept another hotel on the turnpike not far from the Baptist Church.

OLIVER EATON

The Jonathan Leonard house is probably the oldest in this part of the town, and is now owned by E. G. Shaw. In 1777, during the prevalence of the smallpox, it was used as a pest-house.

There are many prominent business men of past generations who have lived in Titicut; among whom may be named COLONEL OLIVER EATON, an architect and master-builder. A great many of the churches in the old colony were planned and built by him. His first work is said to have been the Raynham meetinghouse. His brother, Solomon K. Eaton, was also well known. He drew plans for the town house, but died before it was completed. Captain William Pratt was an extensive land-owner, holding at one time a large portion of the real estate in this neighborhood.

Among the Revolutionary soldiers who lived here, we have the name of Captain Zadock Leonard, in whose honor his grandson has erected a stone, which now stands near the Green.

IN MEMORY
OF THE
REVOLUTIONARY CAPTAIN ZADOCK LEONARD
DIED DEC. 27 — 1795
AGED 57 YEARS

Erected by his Grandson
Geo W. Hayward of Providence, R. I.

A Mr. Redding, who married a daughter of Daniel Leonard, lived just over the line in the Dunbar place. He went to the war, but never returned. Captain William Pratt, son of Captain Benjamin Pratt, noted for his bravery and sagacity, rendered most efficient service in the Revolutionary War.

HARRISON GRAY OTIS COLBY, the son of Rev. Philip Colby, the pastor of the First Congregational Church, was graduated with honor at Brown University, and commenced the practice of law some time after 1847; he was appointed one of the justices of the court of common pleas, which office he held until the time of his death.

Among the prominent clergymen may be mentioned Rev. W. H. H. Alden, who filled many pastorates with success.

REV. DAVID WESTON, D. D., after fitting for college at Peirce Academy, graduating at Brown University, and completing his theological course in Newton Seminary, served as a pastor in several churches. He afterwards filled the chair of theology in the Seminary, where he acquired unusual reputation not only as a profound thinker, but as one of the most eminent theologians of his denomination. He was the author of a number of volumes, among them being the life of the Rev. Isaac Backus. He died in 1872.

DR. MORRILL ROBINSON was born in South Raynham (now known as Judson), August 15, 1803. In 1827 he was graduated from the Medical Department of Brown University, and

FIRST CONGREGATIONAL CHURCH

in the same year he settled in North Middleboro, where he spent more than forty-five years in the practice of his profession. He was a member of the state legislature in 1842-43, where he served on important committees. He was postmaster at North Middleboro from 1836 to 1865, retaining his office through many changes of administration. On February 12, 1828, Dr. Robinson was married to Mary Shaw, daughter of Calvin Shaw of Abington. He died March 16, 1873, aged sixty-nine years and seven months.

Among the successful farmers in the middle of the last century was Paul Hathaway. He lived on Pleasant Street and owned a large tract of land near the schoolhouse, and in the early part of his life was engaged in making sewed shoes. His son, Dr. Joseph Hathaway, lived for a while on Bedford Street, and with Cephas Thompson painted many of the portraits which are to be found in town. In addition to his ability as a portrait painter, he was a skilful chemist, and discovered the refining of petroleum for use as a burning fluid. After leaving Middleboro, he settled in New Bedford and Boston.

In the middle of the last century Jacob Perkins, a blacksmith, acquired a fortune of from seventy-five to eighty thousand dollars by careful savings and wise investments. He died in 1846 at the age of eighty years.

Abraham Perkins, brother of Elijah E. Perkins, was an able business man and a prosperous farmer.

Solomon White and his son, Solomon White, Jr., were respectively clerks of the Congregational Church from 1834 to 1894. Calvin, Ebenezer, and Zephaniah Shaw were among the early carpenters of this neighborhood, and lived on the westerly side of Pleasant Street.

The Pratt Free School, founded by Enoch Pratt, is near the Green.[1]

Jared Pratt was born in Bridgewater, July 27, 1792. His parents were Josiah Pratt, a farmer, and Bethiah Keith Pratt. After receiving a good education in the public as well as in private schools, he taught in Taunton when he was nineteen, and then went into business there. He was at first clerk in the nail factory of Crocker & Richmond, but later worked with other manufacturers. On January 1, 1818, he was married to Jemima Williams, daughter of Job King of Taunton. They made their home in North Middleboro, where he began business as proprietor of a general country store in partnership with Isaac Pratt. In 1819 this firm, I. & J. Pratt, carried on business

JARED PRATT

[1] See chapter on Education.

in different lines at Wareham, where they owned a forge, a
"bloomery." The business gradually outgrew its modest proportions, and became the large manufacturing establishment
known as the Wareham Iron Company. The growth and extent of this industry were due largely to the financial ability
and shrewd business management of Mr. Pratt, who, as treasurer, conducted the monetary affairs with great skill. In 1824
it was necessary for him to move to Wareham ; and in 1836 he
went to Harrisburg, Pa., and established extensive iron works,
where nails, bar-iron, plates, etc., were made. In 1842 his
son Christopher was associated with him under the name of J.
Pratt & Son.

In 1859 he retired from business and settled in his North
Middleboro home. Aside from his remarkable business ability, Mr. Pratt was a valued citizen of Middleboro, doing much
to assist in the growth
and improvement of
the town. From his
wide experience his
advice on all mat-
ters was much sought
after. He served as
sergeant in Captain
Keith's Company of
East Bridgewater in
the War of 1812, and
later held a commis-
sion as captain of the
militia, by which title
he was well known.
He died July 4, 1864.

ISAAC PRATT

Isaac Pratt was
born March 6, 1776.
His father, the sixth
generation from Phineas Pratt, was a farmer of Titicut, who
married Mary King of Wareham.

He was educated in the schools of Middleboro at a time

when the schooling did not exceed two or three months in the year. He married Naomi Keith of Bridgewater, May 19, 1804. He early became interested in the manufacture of nails, and with his nephew, Jared Pratt, before mentioned, he carried on an extensive business. When the Reed nail machine was perfected, this firm purchased the right to its use, gave up the store in Titicut, and moved to Wareham. Here they erected a mill, which was known as the "Parker Mills," for rolling iron into nail plates and then cutting the plates into nails. This firm was among the first in the United States to manufacture cut nails upon a large scale. In 1829 their establishment was incorporated under the name of the Wareham Iron Company, with a capital of $100,000. Although this was a corporation, it continued under the name of the firm until 1834, when the partnership was dissolved and Mr. Pratt returned to his farm in North Middleboro. He died December 3, 1864, at the age of eighty-nine years.

The Boston "Evening Traveller," at the time of his death, said: —

"He was industrious, frugal, and unostentatious; benevolent and hospitable; a patron of educational interests, a kind neighbor, a devout Christian, and a public-spirited citizen. For more than seventy years he was an exemplary member of the Congregational Church. Although he adhered to the tenets of his faith with steadfastness characteristic of his Puritan ancestry, he was neither bigoted, dogmatical, nor ascetic. He was conservative, but liberal in his views. He will be remembered as a fine type of a class now rapidly passing away, — the sturdy, honest, liberty-loving farmers of the early days of the Republic."

CHAPTER XXV

LAKEVILLE

LAKEVILLE, incorporated as a separate town in 1853, comprised originally about one third of the western portion of Middleboro; it took its name from the number of ponds in this vicinity: Assawampsett, the largest body of fresh water in Massachusetts, Long Pond, Great Quittacus, Little Quittacus, Pocksha, Elder's, Loon, Clear, and Dunham. This region has always been noted for the natural beauty of meadow and forests, hills and valleys, about these inland lakes. Here was one of the settlements of the Indians, and here a few continued to live long after their lands in other parts of the colony had been purchased or occupied by the whites; the last full-blooded Indian died in 1852.

We are, however, concerned only with its history before its separation from the town of Middleboro. As before stated, this was included in King Philip's domain, and was under the rule of a sub-chief, Pamantaquash, or as he was

MAP OF THE PONDS

known to the whites, the pond sachem. His rule extended over all of the neighboring tribes, his seat being probably at King Philip's Lookout, Shockley Hill. At the close of King Philip's War, the General Court at Plymouth, in 1679, passed an act "that all lands formerly belonging to John Sassamon in our Collonie shalbe settled on Felix, his son-in-law." This land so conveyed has ever since been owned by Indians, and at the present time is occupied by two half-breed women, the last of the once powerful and numerous tribe which for so many centuries have had their homes about these picturesque ponds. It was not until other parts of Middleboro had been settled for more than a generation that the whites found their way to these Indian lands.

Thomas Nelson, son of John, perhaps the first white settler in Lakeville, purchased what is known as the Thomas Nelson homestead on Assawampsett Neck, and moved there in 1717. He was born June 6,[1] 1675, and when an infant was taken by his mother from his father's house (the Bennett place) to Plymouth to escape the horrors of the Indian War.

After he became dissatisfied with the conduct and preaching of the Rev. Mr. Palmer, pastor of the church at Middleboro, and moved to Assawampsett, he joined the Swansea Baptist Church. Every Saturday he travelled the twenty miles with his family, and returned on Monday morning; while there he occupied a small house which he had built for this purpose. He is said to have been the first member of a Baptist Church in Middleboro. His farm, portions of which have always been held by his descendants, was between Long Pond and Assawampsett, the land on the other two sides being owned and occupied by Indians. His house stood near an apple-tree, opposite that now owned by Sydney T. Nelson, near the Perry place.

Mr. Nelson married Hope Huckins, or Hutchins, of Barn-

---

[1] The date is taken from the *History of Plymouth Colony*, but in the manuscript of descendants of William Nelson we find that he was born May 17.

stable, about the year 1698. She was a woman of strong character and great courage. There is a tradition that while they were living far distant from any white settlers, she heard a noise in the cellar one night when no man was about her premises. Suspecting that an Indian had entered to steal, she went into the cellar in the dark and suddenly attacked him, so fiercely that he was surprised and made frantic efforts to release himself from her grasp, succeeding only by the tearing of some of his garments.

She became a member of the Baptist Church in Swansea August 5, 1723, and with her husband continued her membership there until the formation of the Second Baptist Church in Middleboro. She attended the communion service of that church after she was one hundred years old. Mrs. Nelson died December 7, 1782, at the age of one hundred and four years. The Rev. Isaac Backus, in an account which he gives in the Massachusetts Historical Collections, states that at her death three hundred and thirty-seven descendants had been born (of whom three were Baptist ministers), and that two hundred and fifty-seven were living. Thomas Nelson died March 28, 1755.

Captain John Nelson, a grandson of the first settler, was born October 25, 1737, and died September 11, 1803. He lived upon a farm, which is still owned by his descendants, about two miles south, adjoining the Washburn farm. In the year 1800 he built a new house, which is still standing. He was major and colonel in the Revolutionary War, and was on duty in Rhode Island and New Bedford. He was a man of wealth and influence, justice of the peace, and for several years selectman of Middleboro.

The following is a copy of a letter addressed to him by his former commander: —

MIDDLEBORO, 17th Nov. 1781.

DEAR COL.: Last Thursdays Paper gives an Account from his Excellency Gen. G. Washington and Congress of the Compleat surrender of Cornwallis; and the Troops under his Command, a long wished for period; now we have no reason to

Doubt or suspect it. In Consequence of which this is to Desire you to come next Monday afternoon and see us ; that we may join our generous hearts in festivals of triumph and joy ; while we Usher on the scene with the Crack of thirteen Guns to the honour of the States and give a toast to our worthy Brethren who have with such a becoming Ardor pressed forward with undaunted bravery till they have Compleated the Glorious work whereby Peace may not only be restored to us but extended from Pole to Pole. (Monroe Doctrine) At the same time let all the Glory be given to That omnipotent being who Crowns our Arms with such signal success. Be kind enough to take Doct. Montgomery and Capt. Shaw or any other you shall Please to nominate with you. . . .

I am in haste with Sentiments of Esteem,
Yours Obsequiously
[Signed] JAMES SPROUT.

The Spooner place, which borders on Elder's Pond, takes its name from Benjamin Spooner, Jr.,[1] a soldier in the English army who served in the French and Indian War.

Isaac Peirce, Sr., was probably the first settler in Beech Woods. He was born about 1661, and died at an advanced age. He enlisted as a soldier in the Narragansett War at about the age of sixteen, and was in the fight near Warwick, R. I., which resulted in the capture of the Indian fort.

Mention of the services of Captain Job Peirce has been made previously in the chapter on the French and Indian War. As a boy, he was apprenticed to William Strobridge to learn the trade of blacksmith. As he was very desirous of going to war, he purchased his time, was enrolled as " ward of William Strobridge," and served for three campaigns in the French and Indian War. At the close of his second term of service, he embarked from Halifax with others in a transport for Boston, which, encountering a severe storm, became unmanageable and with great difficulty was kept afloat. It drifted for several weeks, the crew suffering great hardships from their scanty supply of food, until finally they came in sight of one of the West Indian Islands. Here they landed and remained during the winter, until they were discovered by a homeward bound

[1] *Peirce's Genealogy*, p. 69.

vessel and brought into the port of New Bedford. The crew and returning regiment of soldiers had been given up for lost, and much sorrow was manifested throughout the colony. Funeral exercises were held, and a monument was erected in memory of the services of Captain Peirce. In the early spring, after his landing in New Bedford, he hastened to his home, and arrived there one Sabbath morning to find the family at church. As he entered, great was the consternation of the congregation, who had not heard of his rescue, and Rev. Mr. Hinds, who was about to commence his sermon, changed his text and preached from the verse, "For this my son was dead and is alive again; he was lost and is found."

Two years after, he enlisted in his Majesty's service in the company of Ephraim Holmes, and after his honorable discharge he spent the remainder of his life upon the farm, honored and revered by all. His house stood on the site of the house recently occupied by Elbridge Cushman, but the time of its erection is unknown. Captain Peirce became the owner of it in the year 1767, when he added the porches and a portion of the main body of the house. It was taken down in 1870.

CAPTAIN JOB PEIRCE HOUSE

A generation after its settlement Lakeville increased in population much more rapidly than other portions of Middleboro, and before the Revolutionary War there were more people of wealth who occupied substantial houses of the colonial type than in any other section of the town.

Assawampsett is the largest pond, and the surrounding country was known to the Indians under the name Assawampsett, from two Indian words, "assah," meaning a "stone," and "wamsah," meaning "white," with the termination "et," meaning "the place of," the whole word meaning "the place of the white stone." The Indian name was probably suggested by the white sands and pebbles about the shore. This pond seems to have attracted the attention of the General Court at Plymouth long before any whites had settled here.

The early settlers learned from the Indians that formerly there were two islands in Assawampsett Pond, one on the west side about half a mile from the Indian shore, where there are now three large rocks in water not more than knee-deep, occupying a space about three rods wide and ten or twelve rods long; the other one on the opposite side of the lake and about the same depth under the surface of the water. These islands were probably washed away by some severe storm, and the sites are considered dangerous on account of the rocks and the shallowness of the water. The following is an Indian legend of the enchanted island (Man-i-to Me-nis):—

On the first day of the Moon of Flowers (May), there was joy and hilarity in the village on the shores of the Assawampsett. The chief of the tribe had, that morning, sent forth a crier throughout all the village, saying, "To-morrow is the great feast of Me-ta-wa" (a festival, or dance of worship before the Great Spirit). "Come ye. all of you, to the feast!"

All that day, women might be seen coming in from the forest, bearing loads of evergreen on their shoulders, to build the Sacred Lodge for Worship. It was long and narrow, and open at the top; for they said, "The Great Spirit will want to look right down into the hearts of his children. He wants no covering to their Lodge of Worship."

Hunters were scattered, that day, through all the woods in the neighborhood of the lake, to procure game for the feast; and fishers plied their canoes on the waters, in search of fish. The children were out, gathering wild flowers to deck the Sacred Lodge, among all the hills that overlook the beautiful sheet of water on which the village was situated.

Among the fishers on the lake were two brothers, named Kwah-sind (The Strong Man) and O-skin-a-wa (The Youthful). They were fishing by themselves in a distant part of the lake. O-skin-a-wa was successful in fishing, and soon had the bottom of his canoe covered with them, fluttering and shimmering in the sun. Kwah-sind, on the contrary, had not a single fish in the bottom of his canoe. He had offended the Nee-ba-naw-baigs (Water Spirits), and they had frightened away all the fishes that came near his canoe.

He was very angry. He said, "Here I have been fishing for hours, and have not had a single bite. It is the work of these hateful Nee-ba-naw-baigs. They are determined to be revenged. But.I will be revenged. I will find out some way to repay them for all this injury."

Then, seeing that his brother's canoe was half filled with fishes, he said, "Give me a share of your own, that I may not return to the village empty-handed." But his brother said, "Not so. If you have offended the Water Spirits, it is no fault of mine. You, alone, must suffer the consequences. I must return and present my canoe load of fish to the chief, to be used for the festival."

On hearing this, Kwah-sind was pale with rage. He raised his paddle, and struck O-skin-a-wa across his head. The blood flowed down into the canoe. He reeled over and fell into the waters of the lake.

Then Kwah-sind, when he saw what he had done, was in a great strait, and set himself down in the bottom of his canoe, thinking of some way to escape the consequences of his crime. He said, "I must not return to the village with my brother's blood upon my head. Therefore, I will go and hide myself in that little island yonder, until nightfall; then I will escape to the country of the Pequods."

So he steered his canoe for the island, laid himself down on its shores, and, overcome with care and anxiety, was soon fast asleep.

Now the island was inhabited by a race of little people, called Puk-wudjees. They were smaller than the red men, and were, like them, subject to the rule of Ke-che Mani-to, the Great Spirit. They were sitting down to their simple feast of strawberries (O-da-me-non), which grew in abundance on the island; also the wild gooseberries (Shah-bo-min). It was evening, and all was still. Soon they heard the plaintive cry of the Wah-won-a-sah (whip-poor-will) on a tree, directly overhead. They started up in alarm. They said, "What can this mean? Never before was the voice of the Wah-won-a-sah heard on the island of the Puk-wudjees. He has come to us with a message from the Land of Souls. Some one has suddenly entered it. He must have been murdered, and the murderer must be concealed somewhere on our shores." So they started to search the island for the murderer. Soon they discovered Kwah-sind asleep in the shade of a willow. They said among themselves, "What shall we do with this man of blood? He is not of our race; but the Great Spirit will hold us guilty if we suffer him to escape. We will send for Wah-ba-no (magician), and he shall try his arts and incantations upon him. Perhaps he will put him into a deep sleep, that he will never awake again."

So they summoned Wah-ba-no. He tried his skill on the murderer. He cast him into a long and deep sleep, and left him there, sleeping in the shade of the willow.

When the villagers found that the two brothers did not return, they went, with their canoes, in search of them. They found the canoe of O-skin-a-wa half filled with fishes and covered with blood. They then searched the islands, far and near, for the murderer. Presently they approached the little island of the Puk-wudjees. They found Kwah-sind asleep on its shores. They tried to awaken him, but could not. They bore him home to the village, and many days he lay before them, in that deep and dreamless sleep. Then his spirit departed from him, and they buried him in the burial-place for murderers.

From that day the Indians would never approach the little island after nightfall, or lie down to rest on its shores; for they said, "Although we have done no murder, who knows but that Wah-ba-no may also put us into a deep sleep, that knows no waking, as he did the murderer of his brother, the strong man, Kwah-sind."[1]

In the latter part of the eighteenth century abundant iron ore, much better than bog iron, was discovered in the bottom of these ponds; that in Assawampsett was by far the best, and as much as five hundred tons a year was taken from this one pond. From a mine about one third of a mile from the shore, opposite the house now owned by Mr. Parkhurst or directly east of the old Pond meeting-house, a large quantity of ore was taken for many years; the dredging and carting to the many furnaces in this and in the surrounding towns was a great source of income. It was taken from the bed of the pond with tongs, such as are used for oysters, lifted into boats, and carried ashore. For many years a man could easily procure two tons in a day, but it was worked so extensively

[1] *Middleboro Gazette.*

that the amount was reduced to half a ton; ere long, even this became exhausted, and the mine ceased to be worked. There was plenty of ore in the adjoining ponds, but it was raised to the surface with some difficulty, as the water was about twenty feet deep. Stephen Nelson, a lineal descendant of William Nelson, a man of note in his time, mentions in his diary the work done by himself and neighbors in taking out ore from the pond and carting it to the different furnaces. This industry was attended with not a little danger, and one or two men lost their lives while engaged in it.

It was in this pond in Sampson's Cove, about opposite where the Pond meeting-house stood, that the murderers of John Sassamon concealed his body under the ice.

From the top of Philip's Lookout is one of the most beautiful prospects to be found in the whole region. On the eastern side of this pond, at Betty's Neck, there are two rocks, on which are the imprint of a man's hand and a number of other marks supposed to be the work of the Indians. It is said that the impression of the foot is that of Betty, the wife of Felix and daughter of Sassamon. The date of this is 1747, and the name "Felix" is cut into the rock, but these are probably more recent than the marks.

In 1816 "Abiel Washburn, Thomas Weston, Levi Peirce, and Horatio G. Wood, their associates and successors, were incorporated under the name of the Middleboro Canal Company, to operate, maintain, and manage a canal from the northerly part of Assawampsett Pond to unite with Nemasket River between said pond and Vaughan's Bridge." It was their purpose to supply a larger body of water for their cotton mill and other manufacturing establishments recently built at the new works at Middleboro. A large amount of money was expended, but it was not a success, and was soon after abandoned. The river now runs through a portion of this canal, and its site can still be traced through the remaining distance.

In recent years a large number of summer cottages have been built on the shore of this delightful and historic lake.

One of the hostelries for many generations was Sampson's

Tavern, now a private house owned by Arthur E. Perry of New Bedford. The house was built and first occupied by a Mr. Foster, who was succeeded by Mr. Sampson. From Revolutionary times to within the memory of many now living, it was celebrated for its good cheer and for the number of guests who were entertained at all seasons of the year. The stages to and from Boston and New Bedford stopped here. Some time during the latter part of the eighteenth century a very serious accident occurred in the vicinity of this tavern, on account of the great drifts of snow. The stage passed for some distance on the ice on the edge of the pond. Unexpectedly the ice had worn away, and it fell through. The driver was drowned and one of the passengers; the others were more or less injured by the great fright and exposure. At this tavern some of Hezekiah Butterworth's best stories were written.

SAMPSON'S TAVERN

Just beyond where the stream connects Assawampsett with Long Pond, on the western side of the road, occurred the battle in the Indian War, the details of which are given in the chapter relating to King Philip's War.

A little further on the eastern side of the road, at Betty's Neck, Captain Church with his men pursued the Indians, and fearing an ambush, retreated in the night to Dartmouth.

Long Pond is the next in size in this group, the southern portion of which extends a little way into Freetown. There are here two picturesque islands, known as Nelson's Island and Lewis Island. The water is considerably deeper than that of Assawampsett Pond, and at the bottom iron ore has been found, but the water is too deep to make the mining of it profitable. Upon the eastern shore, on the road leading to

Rochester, stands the house in which Governor Marcus Morton was born and spent his early childhood days. The shores of this pond are exceedingly picturesque, and in recent years it has been a summer resort.

Great Quittacus, which takes its name from an Indian chief, has three rocky islands covered with pine-trees in its deep water. It was formerly noted for the variety and excellence of its fish. Upon the western shore, on the New Bedford turnpike, stood the house of Rev. Mr. Roberts. Later, the house passed into the hands of Mr. Jewett of New Bedford, and more recently was moved to where it now stands, on the Long Point road. In the early part of the last century it was used as a tavern.

Elder's Pond, much smaller but deeper than the others mentioned, takes its name from John Montgomery, an elder in the First Baptist Church.

At the beginning of the last century Upper Four Corners had more inhabitants than the present Four Corners, and promised to be the industrial centre of the town. A store was kept by Colonel Levi Peirce, who afterwards moved to the Four Corners. That store forms the southern portion of the two-story house now standing.

A little to the north of this stands the residence of Major Peter Hoar, a well-known and influential man, whose house is a fine sample of the colonial mansions of those days. He served in the company of militia commanded by Captain Isaac Wood at the battle of Lexington, and later was in several of the expeditions into Rhode

MAJOR PETER HOAR'S RESIDENCE

Island. He was major in the Fourth Regiment of militia of Massachusetts, and was afterwards promoted to the office of lieutenant-colonel, but retained the title of major instead of that of lieutenant-colonel. He was one of the selectmen of Middleboro for more than fifty years, and representative of the town in the legislature during the years 1809, 1810, and 1811. During his life he was an active member of the Second Baptist Church in Middleboro, and at his death he made provision in his will for the church which worshipped in the Pond meeting-house.

Upon Main Street, toward the Four Corners, stands the house of Simeon Doggett, and a little to the westward, on the Rhode Island road, the house of Lemuel Ransome; a sketch of their lives has been given with the loyalists of Middleboro.

Gamaliel Rounseville, the proprietor of one of the stores at Muttock, had before his removal a store a little this side of the present house of John H. Nelson.

James Washburn, the first postmaster of Middleboro, built his house on the site of the present town house of Lakeville. He was unmarried, and after holding the office a few years, resigned in favor of Major Levi Peirce and afterwards moved to New Bedford.

THE WASHBURN HOUSE

Upon the road leading from Main Street to the Ward place was formerly a mill for making cotton batting; this was in successful operation until the breaking out of the War of 1812, which caused such financial disaster to many of the industries of New England. A little later, a successful tannery was established in place of the cotton mill, and the business was carried on for a number of years by General Ephraim Ward and Mr. Barrows.

A little distance to the west, at the corner of the road which leads to the station, stands the Ward house, probably the oldest house in town, but the exact age is unknown.

James Sproat,[1] of Scituate in 1711, was the owner of a tract of land upon which this house stands, and in the next year was a resident of Middleboro. This estate was conveyed in 1737 to his son Robert, and in 1778 to Zebedee Sproat; later to William and Ebenezer Nelson, who in 1806 sold the property to General Ephraim Ward, from whom the place takes its name.

THE WARD HOUSE

At first it seems to have been a single house, with a doorway and room on the front; a most interesting relic of the past, which has been enlarged from time to time by successive additions. Several years ago its late owner, Sprague S. Stetson, in making some repairs on the ancient part of this house, found that it was boarded by two and one-half inch oak planks, which were spiked on to the sills and beams to form a garrison house against attacks from the Indians.

Over the chimney-piece in one of the chambers was the portrait of King George, but upon the breaking out of the Revolutionary War, so intense was the patriotism of the owner, Mr. Robert Sproat, that a floral design was painted in its place, which can still be seen. This room was ceiled with panel work after the manner of ancient houses, and draperies were painted upon the walls. Before the house was much altered, there was a secret chamber, which it would have been almost impossible for a stranger to find. Upon the burning of Oliver Hall, some fifteen of the doors were taken out by Mr. Sproat and used for panels and ceilings in two of the chambers and upper entry way.

[1] James and Ebenezer Sproat were sons of Robert, who came to America and settled in Scituate. His sons moved to Middleboro.

Mr. Zebedee Sproat was a man who showed much taste in beautifying this place; he planted many trees about the house, and laid out a terrace garden with choice trees and shrubs, which remained until a late day. Tradition has come down that he was a very unpopular man. After the Revolutionary War, he committed many offences against the public and his family, and later was drummed out of town as a slight punishment for the many wrongs which he had done. It is said that a daughter-in-law of Judge Oliver joined in the procession which followed him as he left town. The story of the wrongs he inflicted upon his wife, Hannah Sproat, was published as a broadside in accordance with the custom of the time.

From 1806 until his death in 1856, this house was the residence of General Ephraim Ward. General Ward was a prominent man, extensively engaged in many business affairs, and represented the town in the General Court for several years. He served as aide-de-camp on the staff of General Lazell upon the threatened invasion of Plymouth in the War of 1812, and for a series of years after was connected with the local militia of the state; he was the father of General Eliab Ward, George, Rev. Ephraim, Mrs. Priscilla Stetson, the wife of Captain Peleg Stetson, and Mrs. Holmes, the wife of Horace Holmes. George Ward was born September 16, 1814. He was one of the first to manufacture shoes, in partnership

GEORGE WARD

The FAITHFUL and LOVING WIFE's
GARLAND:

Being a Serious and Solemn Warning and Caution to all those and such HUSBANDS, who are often led astray from their Families, by the delusive and false Arts of designing Women.

[Sung to a Mournful Tune.]

"The Siren's sweet melodious voice
"May cause the Sailor to rejoice;
"But should he hoist his ——
"His ruin is as sure as late.

1. FORTY-FIVE years of fleeting time
Hath swiftly roll'd away,
Since this immortal part of mine
Put on a form of clay.

2. The dupe of fortune I have been,
Her weight upon me lies,
All her vicissitudes I've seen,
Display'd before mine eyes.

3. I've had a share of peace and joy
Of happiness and wealth,
Yea happiness without alloy,
In joy and perfect health.

4. Alas! a share of woe and grief,
Which rends my bleeding heart,
No mortal hand can give relief,
Or comfort can impart.

5. Cast from the pinnacle of peace,
On misery and woe,
Nothing on earth can give me ease,
Nor none my sorrows know.

6. My Father di'd and left me here,
A Mother yet I know,
Who brought me up with tender care,
To them my thanks I owe.

7. When I arriv'd to proper age,
Myself for to look out,
I had an offer of marriage,
Made me by Mr. S——T.

Whose kind proposals won my heart,
I gave to him my hand;
He play'd so fair, so kind a part,
He seem'd a pleasant man.

9. In peace and joy our days we past,
For nearly twenty years,
He seemed wholly to be bent
To keep my eyes from tears.

10. I was by him almost ador'd,
And call'd his Angel bright,
For many years could not afford
To have me out of sight.

11. But now alas! the scene is turn'd,
And gloomy aspects rise,

His looks which like flame hath turn'd
his very thoughts do ——

12. From ——— in toil ——more stern
With frowns upon his brow,
But nev'r from him could I learn
What did disturb him now.

13. And then my company he slights,
More strange and churlish grows,
At length he leaves my bed a nights,
And after others goes.

14. Heavy reproaches then he throws
With many a bitter curse,
And every day more angry grows,
Treating me worse and worse.

15. His malice now is grown to great,
He treats me so absurd,
That in his presence now of late,
I must not speak a word:

16. Not to relations ne'er so near,
But ——— must keep,
Neither unto my children dear,
One single word can speak.

17. Altho' to please him I have strove,
No pity can I have;
But from his table I am drove,
Just like a negro slave.

18. My character he strove to stain,
By lying and deceit,
But hitherto it is in vain,
And fell on his own pate.

19. So drunk with passion in a rage,
His hatred to display,
Now in the decline of my age,
Hath drove me quite away.

20. From Friend and Neighbors dismiss'd,
And from my children dear,
And all my hopes are vanished,
Of being happy here.

21. He drove me out with wretched spite,
In a most cruel form,
And would not shelter me one night
From a most tedious storm.

22. With cruelty beyond account,
My youngest child he sent
Out of the State up to Vermont,
What heart would not relent.

23. In ——— to my friends, who take
my part,
And to my Neighbors dear,
You ever shall be near my heart,
While I continue here.

24. My Father and my Mother too,
I bid you both farewell,
Since I am banished from you,
No more with you to dwell.

25. Farewell my SAM——LUCINDA
Farewell my little KATE; (too
Since I can't longer live with you,
No more to hear you prate

26. PETER and SALLY farewell too,
I pray you may he bless'd;
I leave you all though drove from you
And JUDITH with the rest.

27. Farewell my Friends and Neighbors too,
It puts me into pain,
To think I cannot live with you,
But love doth still remain.

28. And now thou false and treacherous man,
O think of what you've done!
And justify it if you can,
Your glass is almost run.

29. When that is out you must appear,
Whenever death doth call,
To answer for your conduct here
Before the Judge of all.

30. And can you hope then to be found,
Among ———————
When risen from the dust.

31. I hope repentance you will have
Before that awful day,
And be not sent down to the grave
In such a shocking way.

32. These lines which I to you do send
Don't entertain a doubt,
But that they were compos'd and pen'd
By injur'd HANNAH SPROUT.

Sold by the Travelling-Traders.
(Price Five Pence.)

with William E. Doggett. He built the house opposite the Ward place, which was occupied by his widow.

Upon the death of Captain Peleg Stetson, the old Ward place came into possession of his son, Sprague S. Stetson. He was born February 12, 1841, and died January 12, 1899. He was a successful farmer, and held many positions of public trust. He was a member of the legislature representing Middleboro and Lakeville in 1883, and was appointed by Governor Greenhalge a member of the Board of Agriculture, upon which board he served for several years. He was a member of the Plymouth County Agricultural Society. He was prudent yet enterprising, conscientious in the performance of every duty, always courteous and unassuming, and the cordiality of his manners and his thoughtful regard of others won the respect of the entire community.

SPRAGUE S. STETSON

On the road leading from the Ward place past the residence of the late Josiah C. Bump, there was at one time a forge, the dam connected with it flooding the meadow land to the west of the road.

In the early part of the last century, perhaps the most notable improvement in the western part of the town was the turnpike, constructed by private enterprise, running from the site of the present town house in Lakeville northerly in a straight course about six and one half miles to the Bridgewater line, and southerly, after winding about the western shore of Assawampsett Pond, in substantially a straight direction to the Rochester line. The traffic between Boston and New Bedford made it desirable to have such a direct route as was being constructed in different parts of the state. It became the thoroughfare for the transportation of passengers in the stage-coaches and private conveyances, as well as the principal route for the baggage wagons with various kinds of merchandise. Tolls were charged between the town house and Bridgewater. There were several toll-gates,[1] one of which was opposite the site of the present town house. After the construction of this turnpike many houses were built, and it continued to be one of the great highways until the building of the Fall River and New Bedford railroads. In the year 1846 the town acquired possession of this road and kept it in excellent repair, but since the abandonment of the stage-coach and the baggage wagon there has been comparatively little travel, excepting from the town house to New Bedford. That portion from the town house to Rochester was not included in the turnpike.

TOWN HOUSE

Among the prominent families in the last century were the Canedys, the Montgomerys, the McCullys, the Pickenses, the Strobridges, and the McCumbers.[2] There is a tradition, which has always been regarded as true, that these families were of Scotch-Irish descent, and that, as protestants in the north of Ireland, they joined with William in the heroic resistance at the siege of Londonderry and the Battle of the Boyne in 1690.[3]

[1] See chapter on Titicut.

[2] Land first acquired in Middleboro by William Canedy (or Kanedy), December 2, 1717, from Nathan Rowland. *Plymouth Registry of Deeds*, vol. xiv, p. 25. William Strowbridge, December 3, 1728, from Thomas Tomson and Samuel Barrows. *Ibid*. vol. xxviii, p. 28. Thomas Pickens, December 26, 1732, from Barnabas Eaton. *Ibid*. vol. xxviii, p. 111. John Montgomery, May 19, 1735, from Elkanah Leonard. *Ibid*. vol. xxx, p. 92. John McCully, January 23, 1735, from Elkanah Leonard. *Ibid*, vol. xxxiii, p. 141.

[3] Sullivan, *Two Centuries of Irish History*, Part I, chap. i.

For their services they were rewarded by the British Crown with various tracts of land in the New England colonies, and nearly a generation after, those residing in and about Londonderry determined to leave the land for which they had fought and seek a home where they would be free from the persecutions to which they had been so long subjected. These families were probably among those who in 1718 despatched Rev. William Bodye with an address to Governor Shute of Massachusetts, signed by two hundred and seventeen of their number. Such was their intelligence that of these, two hundred and ten wrote their names very plainly and applied to be allowed to emigrate to Massachusetts; the governor's reply was such that they concluded to embark for Boston. It is said that some of these emigrants, after wandering about seeking in vain for a suitable home, finally came and settled in Lakeville, taking tracts of land, portions of which are still held by their descendants. They brought with them their sterling integrity and love for the English Crown and for the protestant faith.

Alexander Canedy, the first of the Canedy family, was the father of William Canedy, one of the eminent men in Middleboro in the early part of the eighteenth century. He served as lieutenant against the Indians in Maine. Isaac Winslow, the commander of that expedition, sent a letter to Governor Drummond showing his appreciation: —

May it please your Hon^r
this comes by Ensign Canada who I percieve has had some hope of your Honors favoring him with a Leuit Commission which if it be acceptible to all that are concerned he being very deserving of it in my opinion having acquitted himself very well ever since he hath been out. thus beging your favor for him I am your most obedient servant,
                                                    ISAAC WINSLOW.
Scituate January
the 17 : 1723

In the troublous times preceding the Revolution, he could never forget the love he bore to his sovereign and to the home of his ancestors. He and Judge Oliver were among the first citizens of Middleboro to espouse the cause of the Crown, and were included in the list of loyalists, but he was not banished nor was his estate confiscated. He lived in that portion of Lakeville known as Beech Woods, in a two-story double house, of colonial style. This was taken down a few years since, but the site is still pointed out.

William Strobridge, a descendant of the family whose name he bears, was also a tory in the time of the Revolution. The land which was acquired by the Strobridges is in one of the most beautiful parts of the town, and the site of his house is still to be seen.

The numerous descendants of the Pickens family have always occupied a prominent position in the affairs of the town and county.

Among the men who came about 1720 from the north of Ireland and settled in this locality was Nicholas Roach. He was a devout christian, holding with great tenacity the religious faith of the protestants of Ireland, and was one of the founders of the Precinct Church, contributing largely to its support. He is buried in the Thompson Hill burying-ground.

CUDWORTH HOUSE

The tract of land originally owned by the Montgomery family was near Elder's Pond. From this family descended Hugh Montgomery, a lawyer in Boston of the last generation, a man of learning, who added materially to the fortune inherited from his father.

The old Cudworth house is another example of the substantial dwelling of a hundred years ago. The building, commenced by Samuel Nelson and finished by his son William, was bought in 1806 by General Ephraim Ward, and afterwards reconveyed to Mr. Nelson in exchange for the Ward place. At the beginning of the last century there was a store kept not far from the present town house; there has always been a store near the Precinct Church.

Before Lakeville was set off as a distinct township, there were a large number of school districts, known as the Upper Four Corners, the Haskins', Miller, Canedy, McCully, and Howland neighborhoods, the Tack Factory, the Bell schoolhouse, and Beech Woods. The Bell schoolhouse is so called by reason of the bell placed upon it when it was used as a place of worship.

That portion of the town known as Beech Woods in the early part of the last century had the unenviable reputation of being the home of Malborne Briggs, the thief, one of the most notorious criminals in Plymouth County. He would never commit any depredations in his immediate neighborhood, his operations being confined to other parts of the town and county. He had a large family of seven sons, who inherited the criminal tastes of their father, and in 1823, when the committee of the governor's council visited the state prison at Charlestown, he and his seven sons were there imprisoned.

The village known as the Tack Factory was early noted as a place of business activity in this part of the town. Upon the stream which flows through that neighborhood, there was a forge built by Major Thomas Leonard early in the century before the last, which was in operation for about eighty years. Later, there was a sawmill upon the same site, and afterwards a tack factory, from which this neighborhood takes its name, built by Albert Mason and three associates from Bridgewater. This enterprise was not a financial success, and was soon after abandoned, but is now in operation again. Albert T. Mason, whose house stood on Taunton Street, was the father of the chief justice of the Superior Court of the commonwealth, who was born here and educated in the public schools and Peirce Academy, and admitted to the bar at Plymouth in 1860. He served with distinction as captain in the War of the Rebellion, and on returning to practice rose rapidly in his profession. While a resident of Plymouth he held the office of selectman, and was afterwards appointed chairman of the River and Harbor Commission of the commonwealth. In 1882 he was appointed by Governor Long one of the justices of the Superior Court, and afterwards, upon the promotion of Marcus Morton, was made its chief justice. He was recognized by the bar as one of the ablest of the judges of that court. On January 2, 1905, he died at his home in Brookline.

ELKANAH LEONARD HOUSE

This neighborhood was also the home of Elkanah Leonard, an account of whose life has been given in the chapter on Lawyers.

CHAPTER XXVI

ECCLESIASTICAL HISTORY

WITH the early settlers of Middleboro, in common with those in the other towns of the Old Colony, the religious life entered so largely into their thoughts, duties, and activities that any account of those times would be incomplete which did not consider with more or less detail their church history.

Their church organization and those who worshipped with its members included almost the entire population, and aside from the family, the church, its order, its care, and its teachings seems ever to have been foremost in their minds. It was here that they were strengthened in the faith and doctrines to which they adhered with such tenacity; here they were encouraged to meet manfully not only the duties but the perils and hardships attendant upon their frontier life; it was here at the weekly service on the Sabbath that they met their fellow citizens and learned the news of the day. The church meeting was the great social cord which bound them together. For more than one hundred years, the meeting-house of the First Church was generally the place for the transaction of all public business of the town.

In 1675 the General Court at Plymouth, by an ordinance, enacted that every township within the colony should have a house of worship and a church duly organized, with proper provision for the support of an ordained minister, who officiated over such church. So few were the families, and so far removed were they from each other, that no church was organized until December 26, 1694. Provision was made in 1675 for the support of the gospel, although the war prevented any action being taken until after the resettlement.[1] Mr. Fuller had, how-

---

[1] "Whereas a committee was appointed and chosen by the proprietors of Middlebery the 18th. of May in Anno 1675 vis. — Mr. Constant Southworth, Left.

ever, preached here before that time. Indian churches had been organized at Assawampsett, Nemasket, and Titicut. These were prosperous until the war, but afterwards seem to have been disbanded, and the members worshipped with other churches. Probably the majority of the early settlers were members of the church in Plymouth or in some of the neighboring towns from which they had come, and not a few of them were in the habit of attending public worship at Plymouth, taking their families with them.

In 1678 the inhabitants called Mr. Samuel Fuller to become their pastor, and the question of his accepting the call came before the church at Plymouth, of which he was a member, on the 19th of December.[1] On the 16th of January, 1679, the church unanimously recommended that he should preach to

Morton, John Thompson, Joseph Warren and Isack Howland, who were impowered to meet together for some orders in reference to the prosecuting and supportation of some help to teach . . . of God att Middlebery and to settle some course to procure means for the erecting of a meeting house there, and for building of bridges and setteling high ways in that town, they the said proprietors did at this meeting reëstablish and confirm the said order and did ratify the said power and settle it on the forenamed persons to act as aforesaid." *Early Records of Middleboro*, p. 18.

[1] "1678. December 19: Our brother, Mr. Samuel Fuller being called to preach at Midlebury did aske counsell of the chh, which motion they tooke into serious consideration till the next chh-meeting, which was on Jan. 16: & then the chh. did unanimously advise & encourage him to attend preaching to them as oft as he could, but not yet to remove his family but waite awhile to see what further encouragement God might give for his more setled attendance upon that service there.

"1694. November 28: Divers of our brethren at Midlebury sent letters to us to desire our Counsell about their gathering a chh & calling a Teaching officer with them, the chh tooke it into consideration & after some-time manifested to them our consent to & approbation of their motion. Then those brethren & those of other ches & some others who offered to joyne with them sent letters to desire our Pastor with other brethren to helpe them in carrying on that worke on Dec. 26: the chh chose Deac; Faunce, Deac; George Morton, Bro: Eliezer Churchel & Bro: Ephraim Morton to accompany the Pastor thither on that occasion, & voted, that if God carryed on the worke, that wee dismisse our members, namely, five brethren & 4 sisters to be of that chh; that Pastor & those chh-messengers went at the time appointed, the chh was gathered, & then Mr. Samuel Fuller was chosen & ordained to be their Teacher." *Records of First Church, Plymouth*, vol. i, deposited in Pilgrim Hall.

the inhabitants of Middleboro as often as convenient, but that he should not move his family there, but wait to see what further encouragement might be given him for a permanent settlement. This service on the part of Mr. Fuller probably continued until the organization of the church. In 1680 he became a permanent resident of Middleboro, the town having provided a house-lot and twelve acres of land.

The first meeting-house stood on Plymouth Street, north of the Sturtevant house. It was probably built soon after the resettlement of the town, but its size and capacity are not known. It had no pews, and the congregation were seated on rude benches without backs. The records of the organization of the church were lost, but an authentic copy has come down to us : —

Middleborough, March 8, 1734. — A copy of the record of the First Church of Christ in Middleborough, which was written by Mr. Samuel Fuller, first pastor of that church.

THE COPY OF EBENEZER FULLER, IN 1734

I. Thou shalt remember all the way which the Lord thy God hath led thee these forty years. Deut. 8 : 2.

December 26, 1694 (O. S.). — A church of Christ was gathered at Middleborough, formerly called by the heathen Namassacut, a fishing place. as some say.

The persons and their names that entered into church fellowship, some of them members of Plymouth church before, being dismissed from Plymouth for that intent; some of them members of other churches dwelling here then, and some that were never in church fellowship before that time, whose names are as followeth : —

Samuel Fuller and his wife,
Jonathan Morse and his wife,
Samuel Wood, Isaac Billington,
Samuel Eaton, Samuel Cutburt,
Jacob Tomson and his wife, John Cob, Jun.,
Hester Tinkham, The Widow Deborah Barden,
Weibrah Bumpas, Ebenezer Tinkham, — his wife,
John Bennet and his wife,
Abiel Wood and his wife,

Not being present by reason of sickness in their family, yet after owning the covenant of the rest, being in the esteem of the rest, it is as well as if she were present at that assembly.

Ebenezer Tinkham, Isaac Billington, Jacob Tomson; these then baptized.

Soon after were baptized the children of John Cob in their infancy: John, Martha, Patience. Also Lidia Bumpas, the daughter of Weibra Bumpas.

II. In order to the gathering to a church, it pleased God, who hath the hearts of all men in his hands, to move upon the hearts of sundry of those to desire a church may be gathered in this place, — to desire and seek it of God; and Divine Providence made way for it.

Letters were sent for ministers and brethren to assist in the work, namely: to Plymouth, Sandwich and Barnstable: and the Elders sent Mr. John Cotton, Mr. Rouland Cotton, Mr. Jonathan Russell, and brethren to assist them. Mr. Samuel Fuller, then ordained to be a Teacher to that church; who had lived there and preached the word amongst them, whose preaching God had made beneficial to divers of them, and made choice of by mutual consent. God can, and oft doth, out of the mouth of babes and sucklings ordain praise.

John Bennet, Sen., our brother, ordained Deacon, — Deacon in the church of Middleborough, March 10, being the second Sabbath in that month, and chosen by a full consent to that office some considerable time before; who formerly dwelt at Beverly; whom God in the way of his providence sent to dwell in Middleborough to be serviceable there in church and town.

The articles of christian faith and covenant,[1] similar to those of the church at Plymouth, were first printed in 1722, and reprinted in 1771, with some changes. They were in accord with the teachings of the venerable John Robinson, pastor of the Pilgrim Church in Leyden.

As this was for many years the only church in town, and was so prominent in the thought of the people, it may be of interest to cite some of the features of its polity. Any number of christian believers could organize themselves into a church for

---

[1] These articles of faith and covenant are published in the *History of the First Church of Christ, in Middleborough*.

What is known as the "half-way covenant" was in force for more than fifty years after the organization of this church, and has made it difficult to determine the question of full membership in most of the old churches of the Old Colony. It is very probable that the records of the church, coming to us in the way that has been noted, do not give the membership of all who, during the first thirteen years of its organization, were members. *Ibid.* p. 79.

There were later about one hundred admitted under this covenant.

Those who entered into the half-way covenant had the privilege of baptism for their children without being members of the church. The phraseology, although in different churches slightly changed, was in substance as follows: —

"I take God the Father to be my chiefest good and highest end. I take God the Son to be my only Lord and Savior. I take God the Holy Spirit to be my Sanctifier, Teacher, Guide and Lawgiver. I take the people of God to be my people in all conditions. I likewise devote and dedicate unto the Lord my whole self, all I am, all I have and all I can do. And in all this I do deliberately, promptly, successfully and forever."

worship and for discipline, although they held that no church ought to consist of more members than could conveniently meet together for worship. They had the power of self-government, independence, open communion, and free toleration; the majority ruled in all matters. They had a right to choose their pastor and church officers, and to maintain discipline by vote of the church, but in all of these matters the advice of neighboring churches was asked in council. All of the officers and members were equal in respect to their rights and privileges; no pastor or elder could control or embarrass the action of the church over which he ministered. They communed with churches of other denominations in good standing, and dismissed their members to the other churches when desired. The doctrine and polity of this church was the same authoritatively embodied in what is called the Cambridge Platform, and in a later period in the Saybrook Platform.

MINISTRY OF REV. SAMUEL FULLER, 1694-95

Mr. Fuller was born in 1624, and died August 17, 1695; he was called to preach in 1678, and was ordained December, 26, 1694.[1]

MINISTRY OF REV. THOMAS PALMER, 1702-08

Upon the death of Rev. Samuel Fuller, after a ministry of a little more than seven months, Mr. Isaac Cushman[2] of Plymouth received a unanimous call to the pastorate, which was not accepted, and he afterwards became the minister of the church at Plympton. Mr. Clapp and Mr. Cutting were invited to supply the pulpit, but for different reasons declined. In August, 1696, Mr. Thomas Palmer was engaged to preach one quarter of a year, for which he was paid a salary of thirteen pounds. This was the beginning of the most unfortunate ministry in the history of this church. In October the town voted him a yearly salary

[1] For a sketch of the life of Mr. Fuller, see chapter on The Green.
[2] See chapter on Early Purchases.

of thirty-five pounds. He continued his services as minister of the church from that time until his dismissal. In November, 1698, the town voted "that his goods should be brought from Plymouth at the town's charge." There was much opposition by some of the neighboring clergymen and members of the church to his becoming a settled pastor. After his ordination, May 2, 1702, the opposition increased, and the unfitness of Mr. Palmer for his position became more and more evident.

Soon after his settlement, committees were chosen by the town and by the church to devise some means for the peaceful adjustment of the difficulties which were increasing. In addition to these, Mr. Palmer was charged with misbehavior and with intemperance. A council was convened by the church *ex parte*, which condemned him and advised his removal. He and some of his friends felt aggrieved by the action of the council, and they, with the town and church, called a second council, "as the town earnestly desired both old and young to enjoy his ministry, and that he should continue his ministry until the council should meet more fully;" finally, "twelve churches were convened, which were unanimous in sustaining the action of the former council." The church records under date of June 2, 1708, are as follows: —

"Voted, by the church of Middleborough, that, in pursuance of the advice of twelve churches, in council here convened, which have declared that Mr. Thomas Palmer, the former minister and pastor, ought to be removed from the work of the Gospel ministry, and suspended from communion at the Lord's table for his scandalous immoralities, — therefore, in conformity to said advice of said council, as also upon the advice of a convention of reverend ministers at Boston, the church doth now declare that they now look on Mr. Thomas Palmer as no longer their pastor, but as deposed from the work of the ministry, and also suspended from the table of the Lord; and we withdraw from the said Mr. Palmer, and unite in our endeavors to settle the ordinances of the Gospel among us."

In 1705 his salary had been voted at forty pounds, and the next year the town voted the same salary, "provided he continued in the work of the ministry the whole year, and if removed, to pay him proportionately;" in November, 1706, some time before the final action of the council, such was the opposition that they "voted to seek out a man for the supply of the ministry." He did not preach through the whole of that year, but sued the parish for his salary, and recovered a judgment to the amount of fifty-two pounds up to the time when the council advised his dismissal. Upon final settlement this amount was somewhat reduced. After the action of the council, Mr. Palmer preached some time in his own house, where he had a few hearers, and then commenced the practice of medicine. He became sincerely repentant for his former course, and on November 13, 1737, the censure of the church was taken off and he was restored to his communion by unanimous vote of the church, after full confession of his error.

During his pastorate fourteen members were added to the church.[1]

John Bennett, chosen deacon at the organization of the church, was ordained in 1695, and died March 21, 1718.[2] *Ebenezer Bonfeon*
Ebenezer Tinkham was one of the first deacons, but there is no record to show when he was chosen.

In August, 1701, the first meeting-house in which the church worshipped was sold at auction for five pounds and two shillings, the town having the year before built a new house of worship on the Lower Green. It was thirty-six feet long and thirty feet wide, with the walls sixteen feet high, and had two ridgepoles and four gable-ends. This edifice, like all other meeting-houses of that time, had at first no pews. The congregation were seated upon benches, without any support for the back. Rev. Mr. Thacher, after much opposition, obtained consent to erect a square pew with seats on three sides, for the use of his family and his distinguished father-in-law, Samuel Prince. Afterwards, this privilege was granted to nineteen others. But slight description of the second meeting-house has come down to us. In 1745 the old roof was taken off and a "pitched roof"

---

[1] See Appendix.

[2] In the *History of the First Church* we find the statement that "these first deacons and their wives died in March, 1738, and were buried in one grave." There seems to be a misprint, as they died in 1718.

put in its place. This building was occupied as a place of worship for more than fifty years. In the town records for 1723, we read that the "hind seat in the meeting-house and the hind seat in each of the men's galleries shall be for the boys."

MINISTRY OF REV. PETER THACHER, 1709-44

Rev. Peter Thacher began his ministry over this church some few months before the action of the council in suspending Mr. Palmer. He commenced preaching before the church in September, 1707, but was not chosen pastor until the next June, and was ordained on the 2d of November, 1709. This was his first pastorate, and was begun when he was a little over twenty-one years of age. He commenced his services under very adverse circumstances, as the prejudice in favor of and against Mr. Palmer was still strong. In the course of a few months Mr. Thacher's ability was such, and his manner and bearing were so conciliatory, that he won the hearts and affection of the entire church and congregation. At one time in his long pastorate, it is said that he seriously thought of preaching his farewell sermon and leaving the church, and he declared to his biographer that he would have done so, had he not been "embarrassed in finding a suitable text."

In 1740 there was a revival, called the "Great Awakening," which lasted two years. During this time about one hundred and twenty-five persons were admitted to the church, and during his entire ministry four hundred and thirty, among them Samuel Prince, Nathan Prince, Madam Morton, Mercy Bennett, Dr. Isaac Fuller, Luke Short, John Alden, and Barzillai Thomas, a sketch of whose lives has been given elsewhere in this volume.

During his ministry Samuel Barrows and Ephraim Wood were ordained deacons, July 25, 1725. Samuel Wood and Ebenezer Finney were chosen deacons January 30, 1735, and ordained March 5, 1737.

Various members of the church were dismissed to form other societies. For about fifty years the whole town by law was constituted one parish, with this church as the place of worship. July 16, 1719, the West Precinct was incorporated as a parish, and a church was organized October 12, 1725, by a number of the members who went from this church. In 1734 the town of Halifax was incorporated, which included a part of Middleboro, and nineteen members were dismissed to join the newly organized church and parish. February 4, 1743, a parish was incorporated in Titicut, where preaching service had been held regularly since 1741. At South Middleboro a church was afterwards organized. These various removals to form other churches materially diminished the attendance for a while, but the numerous accessions under Mr. Thacher more than made up for this decrease.

MINISTRY OF REV. SYLVANUS CONANT, 1745–77

After the death of the Rev. Mr. Thacher, serious troubles sprang up within the church, a reaction after the religious revival called the Great Awakening. Some of its resident members desired to settle a man who was in full sympathy with the former pastor, while others, with Deacon Barrows and a small number of the members of the church, desired a man of different religious teachings. This division gave rise to much feeling and discussion. The church extended a call to their former pastor's son, but probably as this was not acceptable to the parish, the call was withdrawn, and the Rev. Sylvanus Conant was asked, in September, 1744, to become their pastor. Notwithstanding conciliatory actions of the church, the parish invited the Rev. Thomas Weld to preach for them as a candidate, the one preaching in the forenoon and the other in the afternoon; but the feeling so increased that the parish refused to permit Mr. Conant to preach in the meeting-house, and he held his service in the "mansion house," then occupied by Madam Thacher. He continued preaching for several months. A council was called to consider the difficulties then existing, and as a result he was ordained in March, 1745, in front of Madam Thacher's house. Immediately after this, his friends commenced a new meeting-house on the Upper Green, which represented about three quarters of the members of the church and one quarter of the members of the parish. During this time about three quarters of the parish with its standing committee and sixteen of the members of the church, with Deacon Barrows as their leader, called Rev. Mr. Weld to be their minister. He was a resident of Boston, and a graduate of Harvard College in the class of 1723.

The church chose a committee, consisting of Edward Clapp, Edmund Weston, and Samuel Eddy, to attend the council and protest against any action which looked to his ordination. This, however, was without avail; he was ordained in the old meeting-house October 3 of the same year, and commenced his pastorate, which continued for about four years, the church peremptorily refusing to concur in his call or in his ordination. This resulted in a more bitter feeling than had ever been witnessed, the different parties taking the name of the Old Lights and the New Lights, and sometimes that of the Church and the Standing Party. The old church edifice was much out of repair, a new meeting-house had been built, and there were two ministers and two churches to be supported. Those who had united in the call of the Rev. Thomas Weld held the old meeting-house, the ministerial land and parsonage, and were the legal representatives of the parish, while the church members who worshipped at the "mansion house," under the law as it then existed, were taxed to support Rev. Mr. Weld, and the parish were also obliged to pay the expenses of their own church services. Litigation had been commenced in regard to the custody of the records and other parish matters. These difficulties were finally adjusted, and April 22, 1746, the church chose a committee, consisting of Ebenezer Clapp, Seth Tinkham, and Samuel Eddy, to present a petition to the legislature for relief. A law was passed by the General Court, by which every member of the society should have liberty to choose the Old Lights or the New Lights by filing his name with the society of which he desired to become a member. It is stated that more than two hundred members of the old parish were recorded in the year 1748. Religion was at a very low ebb in both churches. In a short time the church and society representing the New Lights became dissatisfied with the Rev. Mr. Weld, and after some dissension among themselves, he was obliged to leave. He afterwards commenced suit for his salary, which he failed to recover. Under the winning spirit of the Rev. Mr. Conant, the pastor of the old church, the societies were united; this action was afterwards confirmed by the legislature, and no further dissension prevailed in this old church and society. It is said that Mr. Conant, before the enactment of this statute, had petitioned that "no presentment might be made against this society for being destitute of a minister until the precinct is in a better condition to settle one."

He continued as minister until his death [1] in 1777. Seventy-six joined the church during his ministry.

In November, 1745, Benjamin Tucker and Gershom Cobb were chosen deacons. Benjamin Tucker joined the church March 24, 1729, and died July 9, 1781, in his seventy-sixth year. He had held the office of selectman of Middleboro for the years 1748, 1749, 1750, 1751, and 1752. He was town treasurer in 1744, and representative to the General Court in 1746. He was a coroner for the county in 1754, 1755, and 1762.

Gershom Cobb was born in 1714, and was admitted to the church July 1, 1739.

Benjamin Thomas was chosen deacon May 23, 1776.[2]

Before the final action of the council dismissing Mr. Weld, Elijah Packard was called as his successor in the old church.

After the settlement of this difficulty, the old meeting-house, which had been sadly neglected, was sold to David Simmons for the sum of thirteen pounds, six shillings, and eight pence, exclusive of the pews and the pulpit, and the materials were used for building a dwelling-house where the present parsonage now stands. It had not been considered large enough to accommodate the church and parish, and in the early part of 1744, at the close of Dr. Thacher's ministry, measures had

[1] For a further sketch of his life, see chapter on The Green.
[2] For a further sketch of his life, see chapter on Thomastown.

been taken for building a larger place of worship.[1] Up to the year 1745, four hundred and eighty were enrolled as members.

This, the third meeting-house, was by far the largest and most imposing structure at the time in town, and was situated a little to the east of the present building.[2] It was built in

[1] We the Subscribers Inhabitants of the Easterly Precinct within The Township of Middleborough under Consideration of the Decay of our Old meeting house which we apprehend is not worth Repairing. Not Only By Reason of its Being old and much Decayed But also its Being So Small that there is not Sufficient Roome therein to accommodate Said Precinct wherefore we do Now by mutual Agreement Bind and Oblidge Our Selves to Buld a new meeting house (at or near the Same place where Our Old meeting house now Stands) of the following Demention (viz) 55 feet Long 45 feet wide & 25 feet in the walls and to proceed to Cut Timber There for and Provid Sutable matterials as Soon as may be (viz) now while the Season will permit Dated middleborough East precinct February The 14th 1744 —

Nathan Thomas	Jonathan Smith
Thomas Darling	James Smith
Benjamin Thomas	Ebenezer Finney
John Soul	Seth Tinkham
Samuel Smith	John Cox
John Tomson	William Cushman
Edmand Wood	John Cobb
John Canedy	Gershom Cobb
Joseph Thomas	Samuel Wood Junr
Joseph Bates Jn^r	Daniel Vaughan
John Smith	Mary Thacher
Edmand Weston	William Thomas
Jonathan Smith Jn.	Henery Thomas
Samuel Thomas Jn.	Joseph Tinkham
Benjamin Tucker	Nathaniel Bumpas

Memorandon That on the 16th & 17th Days of July A. D. 1745 we begun and finished Raising our meeting house and on the next Day which was the 18th of July we met in the meeting house Frame Both fore and after noon : it Being the Day of General Thanks Giving Through ont this Province on account of the Success of the English Armes against Cape Breton

[2] The meeting-house was paid for by cash and materials furnished by members of the congregation, and afterwards the pews were assigned at the following prices : —

		£.	s.	d.
Pew No. 49 to Ebenezer Cox . . . . for	17	6.	8
" " 48 to Jabez Cushman . . . . "	22.	13.	4
" " 35 to Ichabod Morton . . . . "	22.	16.	0
" " 32 to Simeon Dogget . . . . "	14.	10.	8
" " 2 to Peter Oliver, Jr. . . . . "	26.	13.	8
" " 8 to Charles Ellis . . . . "	17.	9.	4

1745,[1] and remained until 1829. It had upon its sides two rows of windows, in which were small panes of glass. It faced toward the east, where there was a large porch extending across the end, the main entrance of the church; upon this was a steeple,

		£. s. d.
Pew No. 46 to John Alden	for	8. 13. 4
" " 40 to Jacob Soul	"	20. 0. 0
" " 41 to Ephraim Tinkham	"	23. 12. 0
" " 34 to William Harlow	"	22. 16. 0
" " 43 to John Miller	"	27. 1. 4
" " 52 to Elias Miller	"	23. 9. 4
" " 39 to Hushai Thomas	"	5. 6. 8
" " — was taken by Elias Millin in "Roome of His old one."	"	2. 2. 8
" " 22 to Isaac Cushman	"	22. 5. 4
" " 36 to John Bennet	"	22. 13. 4
" " 45 to Ichabod Wood	"	26. 80. 0
" " 13 to Andrew Oliver	"	25. 12. 0
" " 54 to Francis Tomson	"	13. 17. 4
"The Ground where the Woming Slaves were Taken up was Sold to Jeremiah Thomas"	"	14. 5. 4
Gallery Pew No 25 to Silas Wood	"	13. 12. 0
" " " 26 to Amos Tinkham	"	13. 6. 8
" " " 27 to Nathaniel Bumpas	"	12. 5. 4
" " " 28 to Shubael Tinkham	"	9. 6. 8
" " " 29 to Elkanah Elmes	"	8. 2. 8
" " " 34 to Isaac Soul	"	13. 9. 4
" " " 33 to Thomas Ellis	"	11. 6. 8
" " " 32 to Zechariah Weston	"	11. 6. 8
" " " 31 to Benjamin Thomas	"	10. 2. 8
" " " 30 to Isaac Tomson	"	9. 9. 4
Pew next forward and gives the precinct, taken by Capt. Prat	"	1. 17. 4
Pew next forward taken by Ichabod Cushman and gives the Precinct	"	1. 17. 4
Gallery Pew No. — to John Smith	"	5. 12. 0
" " " — to Archipas Cole	"	14. 18. 8
Little Pew between Madam Thacher's and Lut. Smith to Shubael Tinkham	"	13. 9. 4
Little Pew No. 35 to Noah Cushman	"	5. 14. 8
The Hon. Peter Oliver Esq. To have for the Addition to His Pew	"	2. 0. 0

Soon after completion, the remaining pews in the body of the house and galleries were sold to various persons who had been admitted by vote to be proprietors of the meeting-house.

At a meeting of the proprietors held on the 7th of April, 1760, Peter Oliver, Esq., was admitted "to be a proprietor of said meeting house and to be entitled to all of the privileges thereto belonging and also that he have liberty to take up the two fore seats on the woman's side in said meeting house and in their place build two pews of his own cost and charge and to have one of the pews for his own and to give 13£ 6s. 8d. to the proprietors for the privilege."

[1] For deed of land, see chapter on The Green.

with a place for a bell. Large doors opened from the porch into the body of the church, and from either side of the house were folding-doors opening directly into the audience-room. In this vestibule were posted notices of marriage intentions, town meetings, sales, and any other matters relating to the church and town. On the west side was a large window, in front of which was the high pulpit; the inside of the church was surrounded with deep galleries upon three sides, while opposite the pulpit was a second higher gallery, occupied by the Indians and slaves. It is said that these galleries were always well filled. They were supported by pillars painted in rough imitation of marble sculpture by Cephas Thompson, the celebrated portrait painter of the town. The pulpit was ascended by a flight of steps, and the minister's desk was hung with velvet tapestry, while above the pulpit was hung the large sounding-board of panel work, circular in shape, supported by a rod from the roof.[1] The pews (sometimes spelled pues) were square, about five feet high, the upper part lattice work, through which the occupants could look into adjoining pews. They were on the sides of the house, with narrow, uncomfortable seats on three sides. These seats were hung on hinges, and were raised during the time of prayer, when the congregation stood. Oftentimes, at the close of the prayer, they were let down with a noise to be heard all over the house, and in some towns there was an ordinance to prevent unnecessary noise in the slamming of the seats in the pews. The space in the centre was filled with benches without backs for people who could not afford to own pews, and was so irregular that it was difficult sometimes to find one's way to the seats desired. In front of the pulpit was a large inclosure called the "deef" seats, where sat[2] members of the

[1] The old sounding-board over the pulpit was to the children a most marvellous piece of work, as the supporting rods were out of sight. They were one day wondering what held it up, when one boy said, "Why, don't you know? God holds it up, just as He does the world; and that is why it does not fall down and break the minister's head."

[2] Mr. Wood in an address gives the following amusing incident: In the meeting-house, it was no uncommon thing for the snow to drift in at the pulpit win-

congregation who were hard of hearing. Next came an elevated seat for the deacons, and before this was the communion table, the leaves of which were raised on hinges whenever that service was observed in church.

Judge Oliver owned one of the pews, which his family always occupied; with him frequently came the distinguished guests who, during the summer, were constantly at Oliver Hall. He was known to give up the head of his pew but once, and then to Governor Hutchinson, his guest, who came to church with his scarlet coat and sword. There was also the minister's pew, occupied by his family and such guests as were stopping with him. It was customary for members of the congregation to rise during the sermon when fatigued, and stand until they were rested, when they would resume their seats. In the gallery a seat was reserved for the tithing-man, always an important officer in every church.

This was one of the churches where the great Whitefield preached during his visit to America. The church was then so crowded that his only way of reaching the pulpit was by a ladder to the window in the rear. Governor Bowdoin, while living in town, worshipped here, as well as Samuel Prince, father of the pastor of the Old South Church in Boston, and Benjamin Franklin on his visit to Middleboro.[1] It was customary to have a morning service, and then an intermission of an hour and a half or two hours. All of the families brought their lunches, and lingered in the meeting-house, at the tavern, or about the sheds in the rear of the church for conversation and the gossip of the day.

As there were no means of heating the old meeting-house, the worshippers were obliged to sit during the long services wrapped in their overcoats and shawls. Some of them carried

dow. One Sunday, the minister found the pulpit desk covered. He stood up, and with his right hand brushed off a portion of the snow, not noticing where it went till he observed that his congregation smiled. He looked over, and saw that he had sent a cold shower on the head of the solitary individual occupying the deaf seats. He then brushed the remainder off in the other direction with his left hand, only to find that the poor man, who had moved after the first fall of snow, was again a victim.

[1] See chapter concerning Social Customs.

foot-stoves, — small, square tin boxes filled with live coals, the heat of which served to keep the feet warm. During the nooning, those fortunate enough to possess a foot-stove were accustomed to repair to the Sproat Tavern to replenish the coals for the afternoon service.[1]

The introduction of musical instruments met with great opposition on the part of many of the older members of the church and society. Several animated church meetings were held to consider the matter.[2] The violin was admitted if it could be played upside down as a viol, not as a "fiddle." As early as 1732 we find a vote, in regard to singing, that the pastor, Mr. Thacher, should "set the tunes of the psalms in the time of public worship as long as he could find it for the peace and satisfaction of the church and congregation." Another innovation, which did not meet with approval, was the singing by a choir in the old meeting-house.[3]

This, as well as the former churches, was used for the town meetings until the erection of the town house, which was raised in 1796, and soon after completed.

MINISTRY OF REV. JOSEPH BARKER, 1781–1815

Upon the death of the Rev. Mr. Conant, Mr. Abram Camp, a graduate of Yale in 1773, was invited to supply the pulpit during the winter of 1778, and later, in December of the same year, the church voted to give him a call on probation, and in the February following, unanimously invited him to become

---

[1] There was much opposition to the introduction of stoves. One woman was carried out fainting from "the effects of the heat," but when assured that the stove had not been lighted, she was somewhat surprised.

[2] Among the most zealous opponents of the innovation was one who had been accused by his neighbor of trespassing upon his wood-lot and cutting and selling large quantities of wood for the market. In one of the discussions this gentleman said that " if such an innovation as introducing musical instruments into the church is permitted, I will never again attend the church meeting." His neighbor replied, "I wish those musical instruments could be carried up into my wood-lot."

[3] One of the venerable dames, in expressing her disapprobation of the whole proceeding, wrote to a friend. " Even the judge of the land was in the gallery bawling with the boys."

their pastor. In his reply to the invitation, he requested that the vote of the sisters might be taken, a decided innovation in church action. In November, 1780, there were five votes against him, due to his request; he afterwards declined the call on account of this opposition. Upon the suggestion of that very eminent man in the denomination, `Rev. Dr. Emmons, Mr. Barker was recommended as a suitable pastor for the church. He was a graduate of Yale in 1771, and on the 9th of August, 1781, the church unanimously invited him to the pastorate; he was ordained on the 5th of December of that year. His ministry, although strongly contrasted in many respects with that of Mr. Conant, was acceptable. He was of the Hopkinson school of theology, then prominent in most of the Congregational churches of the state, and it was undoubtedly through his influence that this church was kept from changing its faith to that of the Unitarian denomination, as did the church of the pilgrims in Plymouth and a large majority of the churches in the Old Colony. How successful his ministry was may be judged from the fact that two hundred and forty-seven were admitted to the church during his pastorate. In 1807 and 1808 there seems to have been a general revival in town, during which over eighty persons united with the church. In 1794, at the one hundredth anniversary of the founding of the church, Mr. Barker preached an anniversary sermon, which was published at the time, and from which we learn much relating to its history. He died July 25, 1815, deeply lamented, not only by his parish and congregation, but by the whole town.[1]

During his absence in Congress, 1805-08, his pulpit was supplied by the Rev. Azel Washburn, Rev. Simeon Doggett, afterwards the principal of Bristol Academy in Taunton, Rev. Mr. Robinson of Westboro, and Rev. James Davis.

MINISTRY OF REV. EMERSON PAINE, 1816-22

Mr. Paine, a graduate of Brown University, 1813, was settled over this church with some opposition, which so in-

[1] For a further sketch of his life, see chapter on The Green.

creased that, at his own request, he was dismissed by a council. Notwithstanding the embarrassment under which he labored, fifteen people united with the church.

During the two years the pulpit was vacant, seventy-two joined the church.

MINISTRY OF REV. WILLIAM EATON, 1824-34

Rev. William Eaton, a graduate of Williams College and Andover Theological Seminary, was installed March 10, 1824. Some laxity in reference to intemperance and Sabbath-breaking, with un-christian conduct on the part of a few members, made it necessary for Mr. Eaton, during his pastorate, to make them the subject of discipline, which occasioned much adverse criticism. He, however, was conscientious in what he did, and his course seems to have been generally approved by the church. He was dismissed by council, at his own request, March 3, 1834. During his ministry sixty-three persons were added to the church.

PULPIT OF FIRST CHURCH[1]

The most important event at this time was the erection of the present meeting-house of the First Church in 1828, at a

---

[1] The curtain back of the pulpit was placed there immediately after the edifice was completed. It was the occasion of much opposition on the part of the older members of the church and society. The leader of this opposition was Captain Joshua Eddy, then one of the deacons of the church. On the Sabbath after it was put up he was in church, but said nothing about it until he returned home, when he called his oldest son, Zachariah, to his house, and said, "Zach, how about that curtain?" He replied, "It is for glory and beauty, like Aaron's robe." There was a moment's silence, then the conversation turned upon other subjects, and no further opposition was heard in regard to the curtain.

FIRST CONGREGATIONAL CHURCH AT THE GREEN

cost of from twelve to thirteen thousand dollars, which was paid by the sale of the pews. The vestry connected with the church was built the following year. Four acres of land were purchased of Zenas Cushman for the site of the new meeting-house and common in 1827. The parsonage was built in the year 1832, upon land purchased of Hercules Cushman. The architect of the church was James Sproat. The dedication sermon was preached January 1, 1829, by the most celebrated clergyman of his day, the Rev. Lyman Beecher, the father of Henry Ward Beecher. Daniel Webster, seeing it soon after its dedication, remarked that it was one of the finest church edifices in the country.

For more than twenty years after its erection every pew was occupied. The early prejudice against musical instruments had so far abated that, in addition to the choir, there were for many years two double bass viols, two 'cellos, three violins, and two bassoons. The choir was led by Deacon Horatio G. Wood, and the double bass viols were played by Colonel Southworth Ellis and James M. Pickens.

MINISTRY OF REV. ISRAEL W. PUTNAM, D. D., 1835-65

Rev. Dr. Putnam was born in Danvers, Mass., on the 24th of November, 1786. He spent two years at Harvard College, and was graduated at Dartmouth in 1809. After reading law two and a half years in the office of Judge Samuel Putnam in Salem, Mass., he became impressed with the idea that it was his duty to become a minister of the gospel. He entered Andover Theological Seminary, and was graduated in September, 1814. After a settlement as pastor in the North Church in Portsmouth, N. H., for twenty years, he was installed pastor over this church October 28, 1835. He received a degree of D. D. from Dartmouth in 1853.

REV. ISRAEL W. PUTNAM, D. D.

Dr. Putnam was an accomplished scholar, always dignified in his bearing, a gentleman of the old school, courteous and large-hearted, the warm personal friend of every member of his church and society. He was sound in his denominational belief, yet charitable to those who differed from him. It was during his ministry that the First Church had its largest membership. Among the congregation might be numbered twelve merchants, two or three physicians, and a number of lawyers; a notable congregation. Worshippers would come from distant parts of the town, many of them travelling from three to five miles. The row of sheds bordered the parish common, and at the close of the afternoon service it was interesting to see the line of carriages which left the church to wend their way along the five different roads radiating from the Green.

The parish extended almost ten miles, and it was the custom of the pastor, in addition to the Sabbath service, to have evening meetings in the different neighborhoods alternately. This, in addition to the pastoral work, made the duties of Dr. Putnam very laborious.

The most important event which occurred during his ministry was the colonization of the Central Congregational Church at the Four Corners. In 1847 thirty-three of the members of the church were dismissed to form the new congregation, which was increased by most of the worshippers who lived at the Four Corners. This materially diminished the former large attendance. No pastor was ever more honored and beloved than Dr. Putnam. In 1865 he resigned, on account of the weight of years and failing health, and died May 3, 1868, at the age of eighty-one years. Two hundred and thirteen united with the church during his ministry.

The parish at one time had a fund of nine thousand dollars. The house formerly owned by James Sparrow was built by the Rev. Sylvanus Conant, whose heirs sold it to the parish; afterwards Mr. Barker bought it, and the proceeds were given as a fund for the support of the church. Samuel Tinkham, a member of this church, who died March 28, 1796, left his farm in the little precinct to the parish, and the incomes of these two estates were used in part payment of the minister's salary until after the dismissal of the Rev. Mr. Eaton. During the ministry of the Rev. Dr. Putnam some of this fund was lost, so that there is but a small portion of it left, the income of which continues to be appropriated for its original purpose.

The pastors of this church since 1866 have been: Rufus M. Sawyer, 1866-69. Ephraim M. Hidden, 1869-74. Theophilus Parsons Sawin, 1875-78. Nathan Tirrell Dyer, 1878-85. Howard Alcott Hanaford, 1885-88. Josiah Weare Kingsbury, 1889-91. George Warren Stearns, 1891-1905.

CONGREGATIONAL CHURCH AND SOCIETY OF LAKEVILLE

Up to the 19th of July, 1719, Lakeville was included in the parish of the First Church. At that time the town was divided into two precincts, known as the East and West; the dividing line was from a point near the mouth of Fall Brook and running westerly by the trout brook to the line of Taunton. The East contained the meeting-house of the First Church, and was by far the larger part of the town; with the West was included a portion of Taunton. There was no stated preaching until July, 1723, and the next year the first meeting-house was erected a short distance to the east of the present house of worship.

October 12, 1725, the church was first formed, partly from the First Church in Middleboro and partly from the adjoining towns. The early records were lost, as is the case with so many other churches. The number of women who first joined is unknown; the number of men, so far as can be ascertained, was twelve: John Thrasher, Ebenezer Richmond, James Reed, Richard Waste, Samuel Hoar, Thomas Pickens, William Hoskins, John Hackett, James Sproat, Electious Reynolds, Edward Richmond, and William Strowbridge.

MINISTRY OF BENJAMIN RUGGLES, 1725-53

Rev. Benjamin Ruggles, the first pastor, was ordained November 17, 1725, and continued his ministrations there until his dismissal, December, 1753. He was graduated from Yale College in 1721.

Soon after the ordination of Mr. Ruggles, Edward Richmond and John Hackett were chosen deacons of the church.

From the death of Mr. Ruggles, for nearly eight years, the pulpit was supplied by seven different clergymen, in the absence of any settled pastor. Notwithstanding this, the old meeting-house was abandoned in 1759, and a large, and for those days an expensive church was erected. This was built in the usual form of the times, with galleries upon its three sides, a high pulpit, and a sounding-board. There seems to have been no steeple upon the church, and the outside was never painted.

MINISTRY OF CALEB TURNER, 1761–1801

Rev. Caleb Turner was ordained April 16, 1761. He was a graduate of Yale College, and continued as pastor of the church until 1801, when he was dismissed upon his own request at an advanced age.

During this period John Macomber, Seth Richmond, John Leonard, Benjamin Deane, and George Staples served as deacons.

MINISTRY OF THOMAS CRAFTS, 1801–19

November 18, 1801, Rev. Thomas Crafts, a graduate of Harvard College, was installed as the third pastor, and remained eighteen years, until his death at the age of sixty-one. At the commencement of his labors the church numbered only twelve, but at its close had increased to forty resident members.

MINISTRY OF JOHN SHAW, 1819–34

The fourth pastor was Rev. John Shaw, a graduate of Brown University, who was installed July 21, 1819, and continued as pastor until 1834.

After his dismissal, the church was without a pastor for two years. In 1835 they erected their present house of worship.

MINISTRY OF HOMER BARROWS, 1836–42

The fifth pastor was Homer Barrows, who was ordained in 1836. He was a graduate of Amherst College, and continued as pastor of the church until June 1, 1842, when he was dismissed.

MINISTRY OF JESSE K. BRAGG, 1842–51

The Rev. Jesse K. Bragg was ordained the sixth pastor October 19, 1842. He was a graduate of Amherst College, and his pastorate continued until June 30, 1851. At that time the church numbered one hundred and fifty resident members.

MINISTRY OF CALVIN CHAPMAN, 1851-57[1]

Calvin Chapman was ordained October 22, 1851. In 1808 the church and society received from Nicholas Roach a fund of $4000, and later from Hugh Montgomery $3000, the income of which is appropriated for the support of the church.

MIDDLEBORO AND HALIFAX

Halifax was incorporated in 1734, and on October 13 the following were dismissed from the First Church to form a church there: Hannah Fuller, Phœbe Standish, Ichabod Standish, Abigail Tinkham, Elizabeth Fuller, Mary Wood, Elizabeth Thompson, Mary Thompson, Sr., Mary Thompson, Lidea Cobb, Sarah Drew, Elizabeth Drew, Isaac Tinkham, Ebenezer Fuller, John Fuller, Timothy Wood, Thomas Thompson, Ebenezer Cobb, and John Drew, Jr.

The first pastor was John Cotton, who attained eminence in the colony and church.

TITICUT CHURCH AND PARISH

For more than three fourths of a century after the first settlement of the town, the residents of Titicut were in the habit of attending worship at the First Church, a distance of more than five miles. After the Great Awakening of 1740, Mr. Byram commenced preaching in this neighborhood, and in 1744 it was made a distinct parish. This extended to the West Precinct line on the Purchade Brook, with the exception of certain estates which continued to belong to the old parish. It included a part of Bridgewater to the Four Mile line.

The first parish meeting under this law was held at the house of Nehemiah Washburn on the 21st of March, 1744. The Indians gave land for a meeting-house.[2] The citizens of

---

[1] The subsequent history of this church does not belong in this volume.

[2] See chapter on Praying Indians.

the place had been collecting materials, and had voted, as early as January 25, 1744, "to raise fifteen pounds old tenor for the support of their minister," but it was not until March 29, 1747, at a parish meeting held in the house of James Keith, that they voted "to provide materials to enclose and cover the meeting-house." This was a plain structure, with doors on three sides and the high pulpit on the north. The windows were small, with diamond-shaped glass set in lead; it had no spire or bell upon it. It was situated in a pine forest, and was afterwards moved to a position near the site of the present Congregational Church. During these years a dissension existed, and for nearly four years after the incorporation of the parish there was no church organization. At this time, however, the Rev. Joseph Snow, pastor of a "New Light" Church in Providence, R. I., and Isaac Backus, a young man from Norwich, Conn., were preaching here. Both of these men were in sympathy with the Great Awakening, and the Rev. Mr. Backus was invited to remain with them for some time.

The meeting-house, which had been raised and covered in 1747, was not completed, and in 1748 a tax was levied upon the whole parish for that purpose, which gave great offence to those who styled themselves "New Lights," and who had not worshipped there.

February 16, 1748, the Congregational Church was formed, with the articles of faith and covenant similar to those of the First Church, which were signed and entered into by sixteen persons: Jonathan Woods, Joseph Harvey, William Hooper, Ephraim Leach, Onesimus Campbell, Samuel Alden, Joseph Phinney, Israel Washburn, James Hooper, Joseph Harvey, Jr., Leah Washburn, Ruth Leach, Sarah Leach, Esther Fobes, Abigail Fobes, and Abigail Fobes, Jr. During this year the membership was increased to forty-four; then followed in the succeeding years dissensions upon the subject of baptism, so that the church was much divided, and five ecclesiastical councils were held.

Mr. Backus, having preached in the new house for a short time, turned it over to the "New Lights," and was taxed and restrained for it, which he declares was all that he got for his preaching. Owing to the differences of opinion concerning baptism, Mr. Backus left this church on January 16, 1756, and organized a church in accordance with his views. Although the building had been partially completed in 1749, measures were taken to finish it, as seen in the account of the precinct meeting June 4, 1756, when it was voted "to sell the pew ground and appropriate the money toward finishing the meeting-house." Ephraim Keith, David Alden, and Abiezer Edson were appointed a committee to sell "pew spotts." The bids were made October 21, 1756, "in furnace credit, to be paid the next blast, and security given."

"No 1 on ye west side of the pulpit, being 7 feet long and $5\frac{1}{2}$ feet deep was sold to Mr. James Keith, at 110 old tenor, furnace credit;" "No. 5" was "under the men's stairs," No. 8 was "under the women's stairs." The men and women were separated; the records mention the men's side and the women's side. On the same day, Rev. Solomon Reed was called as pastor at an annual salary of "sixty pounds lawful money."

MINISTRY OF REV. SOLOMON REED, 1756–85

Mr. Reed, a graduate of Harvard College in 1739, lived on Pleasant Street, nearly opposite the old Hathaway place, in a house which was characteristic of that age, the roof coming nearly to the ground in the rear. During the term of his ministry thirty persons were received into the church, and three of its members were dismissed to other churches.

The first deacons were a Mr. Fobes, whose full name is not given, Samuel Keith, Zephaniah Wills, and Daniel Leach. Among other votes passed by the church, we learn that they should sing Dr. Watts's version of the psalms for the present, and Isaac Perkins was "to take care of the young people on Sabbath days."

To show how Continental money had depreciated at this time, in 1779 there was voted to Rev. Solomon Reed "one thousand pounds for his salary for the year passed, the one thousand pounds being considered equal to the sixty pounds heretofore" given him. Another vote on the 6th of September, 1784, was the petition "to the Great and General Court for a lottery to raise a fund in order to support a minister in this parish." There are in the library of the Pilgrim Society a few of his manuscript sermons. Mr. Reed died May 7, 1785.

MINISTRY OF REV. DAVID GURNEY, 1787–1815

Mr. Gurney was called to this church September 27, 1787, was ordained December 5, the same year, and served until his death, July 30, 1815. Seventy persons were admitted to the church during his pastorate. In 1808 the parish built a new meeting-house, the second in its history. This had a tower and bell, and its location was the subject of much discussion at the time. In 1812 permission was granted to erect sheds on the common near the meeting-house, under the direction of the parish committee.

MINISTRY OF REV. PHILIP COLBY, 1816–51

Rev. Philip Colby was born July 30, 1779, and was ordained January 1,[1] 1817. He continued as minister here until his death, February 27, 1851. In the year 1817, certain individuals having agreed to build a house for the use of their minister, land was leased to them by the parish for the term of nine hundred and ninety-nine years, and here the parsonage was erected.

During his ministry one hundred and seventy-eight persons were admitted to the church. The church edifice was burned February 28, 1852, but with great sacrifice the parish erected another house, which was also burned in 1898, and the present house of worship was then built.

---

[1] In the records we find the following, showing the temperance movement had not arisen: "Voted to allow for spirits for ordination, $8.90," and again, "for spirits, $2.39," and next year, "for spirits not bro't into former bills, $2.50."

CONGREGATIONAL CHURCH, NORTH MIDDLEBORO

The pastors of this church since 1850 have been: Thomas E. Bliss, 1852–55. Charles Packard, 1855–57. E. G. Little, 1859–67. Henry L. Edwards, 1868–73. Samuel Hopkins Emery, 1874–76. Ephraim W. Allen, 1877–83. Dwight W. Prentice, 1884–86. Clarence Eddy, 1886–90. Herbert Keightley Job, 1891–98. Charles L. Tomblen, 1899–.

In 1808 Nicholas Roach left a legacy of $2000 to the church, Deacon and Mrs. Elijah E. Perkins gave $3000, Mrs. Seth Fuller $500, and Enoch Pratt $5000. The interest of this fund is used for the support of the gospel here.

NORTH ROCHESTER PARISH

In 1793 part of Middleboro was set off to form the town of North Rochester. A church had been formed there, probably during the ministry of Mr. Weld. The records have been lost, but from the diary of Mr. Bennett, one of the members, it is learned that Rev. Calvin Chaddock was the first pastor.

BEECH WOODS

A Separatist Church was formed in Beech Woods as a result of Whitefield's preaching, but it was never in a flourishing condition. James Mead was ordained its pastor October 3, 1751. He died in 1756, and its members joined the church over which Ebenezer Hinds presided. Their church edifice was purchased and removed by them from East Freetown, and, upon the dissolution of the church, was occupied by the Second Baptist Church. It was destroyed by fire, May 19, 1798.

INDEPENDENT CONGREGATIONALIST CHURCH

In 1879 about twenty persons at the Rock covenanted together under the name of the Independent Congregational Church, one of the chief objects being to teach the doctrine of holiness or entire sanctification. A commodious chapel was erected in 1880, and dedicated in June. This church was organized in 1882 and incorporated in 1901. W. Clarkson Ryder, who was ordained in 1886, died in 1905. The present membership is thirty-nine. An annual camp-meeting has been held under the auspices of this church in a beautiful oak grove about a mile from the Rock station.

THE CENTRAL CONGREGATIONAL CHURCH

Towards the middle of the last century the village at the Four Corners had so increased in population that it was by far the largest in town, and more than one hundred were in the habit of worshipping every Sabbath with the First Church at the Green, a distance of more than two miles. They had built a chapel for the purpose of holding evening and mid-week services, which were usually conducted by the pastor of the First Church, and here, on the 25th day of March, 1847, the Central Congregational Church was formed. An ecclesiastical council had been called, in which the organization of the church was heartily approved. The society then formed was not like the

CENTRAL CONGREGATIONAL CHURCH

First Church by metes and bounds, but formed under the provisions of the statutes as existing at the time, the members who lived in this immediate vicinity being taken from the bounds of the old society. The First Church cheerfully, but not without regret, dismissed thirty-three of their members, recommending them to join the new church. Their names were as follows: Cornelius Burgess, Mrs. Melissa Burgess, Mrs. Betsey T. Burgess, Horatio G. Wood, Consider Robbins, Mrs. Ruth Reed, James D. Wilder, Mrs. Bathsheba Wilder, James Warren, Mrs. Margaret Warren, Nathan Perkins, Jr., John Perkins, Mrs. Ann S. Perkins, Ebenezer Pickens, Mrs. Mary B. Pickens, Mrs. Abigail S. Pickens, Miss Caroline M. Pickens, Mrs. Abigail W. Wood, Miss Emily T. Wood, Adoniram J. Cushman,

Mrs. Ann S. Cushman, Nathan King, Mrs. Elizabeth H. Washburn, Mrs. Olivia A. Hitchcock, Mrs. Freelove P. Rounseville, Mrs. Betsey Thomas, Mrs. Elizabeth Wood, Miss Eleanor B. Wood, Mrs. Almira Goddard, Miss Sarah Jackson, Mrs. Zilpha M. Clark, Miss Hope Writhington, Mrs. Mary Dunham.

In 1849 they built their present house of worship, which was enlarged in 1891.

MINISTRY OF REV. ISAIAH C. THATCHER, 1849–52

After the organization of the church and parish, a unanimous call was extended to the Rev. Isaiah C. Thatcher, a graduate of Union College in 1841. He was installed by council, August 16, 1849.

During his ministry sixty-seven members were added to the church. The pastors of this church since 1854 have been: William C. Dickinson, 1854–56. Isaiah C. Thatcher, 1856–60 (a second pastorate). Harvey M. Stone, 1860–63.

REV. I. C. THATCHER

Stephen G. Dodd, 1866–70. Ellis R. Drake, 1871–76. Henry M. Grant, 1878–88. John B. Lawrence, 1888–93. Richard G. Woodbridge, 1893–1901. Samuel M. Cathcart, 1902–.

FIRST BAPTIST CHURCH

From the scanty materials which we have, and the conflicting statements relating to the two churches in Titicut, it is

470   HISTORY OF THE TOWN OF MIDDLEBORO   [1756

OLD BAPTIST CHURCH, NORTH MIDDLEBORO

difficult to give an accurate account of the early history of either. Mr. Backus, in his unabridged History of the Baptist Church, states that this church was organized in Titicut on the 4th of February, 1749, consisting of sixteen members, and was afterwards dissolved. Mr. Emery, in his history of the Congregational Church, says, " If this be so, we can easily understand how this Baptist Church, organized about a year later than the New Light Church, and with the same number of members, has been confounded with it, and its dissolution been made to apply to the wrong church." Without attempting to reconcile these conflicting and scanty records, it is sufficient to say that the present Baptist Church was organized on the 16th of January, 1756, Mr. Backus acting as pastor and preacher; and at that time the following individuals entered into covenant as a Baptist Church; namely, Isaac Backus, Timothy Bryant, John Heywood, Susanna Backus, Mary Caswell, and Esther Fobes.

The covenant entered into on the formation of the church is still in existence in the handwriting of Mr. Backus. This was one of the first Baptist Churches organized in this part of the country, and attracted widespread attention in the call-

REV. ISAAC BACKUS

ing of various councils and in the discussing of the subject-matter set forth in the teachings of the leader. He says, in reference to his ordination, that a "number of brethren being convinced that thorough freedom towards all men ought to be shown as far as it can be in truth, yet truth limits true communion to believers baptized upon a confession of their faith." He was installed July 23, 1756, assisted by pastors from Boston and Rehoboth.

Notwithstanding the earnest, devout piety of Mr. Backus and his great ability as a scholar and preacher, the church seemed to be small for many years, and it was not until a revival in 1779 and 1780 that it had increased from fifty-nine members to one hundred and thirty-eight. At this time about two thirds of the members of his church were residents of Bridgewater, and the remainder were from Titicut.

Isaac Backus.

He continued his ministry over this church until his death, November 20, 1806.[1] The records, under date of November 3, 1804, contain the following: "As the infirmities of old age have so far overtaken our pastor, Elder Backus, we chose Elder Kendall as our pastor with him." It is said that he never desired to leave Middleboro for another church.

He is buried in the cemetery at North Middleboro, the stone marking his grave bearing this inscription: —

HERE LIE DEPOSITED THE REMAINS
OF THE
REV. ISAAC BACKUS, A. M.,
WHO DEPARTED THIS LIFE NOVEMBER 20, 1806,
AGED 82 YEARS AND 10 MONTHS,
IN THE SIXTY-FIRST YEAR OF HIS MINISTRY.

As a Christian and Minister the character of this man was truly conspicuous. As pastor of a church in this town, for fifty-eight years, he was eminently useful and beloved. His domestic and relative duties, as a husband and parent, were discharged with fidelity, tenderness, and affection. His zeal and persevering industry in the cause of civil and religious liberty, through a long, laborious life is still manifest in his writings as an Historian of the Baptist denomination, and defender of the truths of the doctrine of Christ. Having uniformly borne testimony

---

[1] For further account of Mr. Backus, see chapter on Titicut.

> in his life, conversation, and ministry, of his ardent love to his Divine Master and the doctrine of the Cross, in an advanced age he was called from his beloved charge, and numerous Christian friends and brethren, to sleep in Jesus, and his spirit into the garner of his heavenly Father, as a shock of corn fully ripe.
> God was his portion and his guide through this dark wilderness.
> And now his flesh is laid aside, his soul has endless Rest.

MINISTRY OF REV. EZRA KENDALL, 1804–07

Rev. Mr. Kendall served as an assistant pastor with Mr. Backus until the time of his death. Some dissension having arisen, a little after the death of Dr. Backus, he resigned his ministry in 1807, and was succeeded by Elder Samuel Abbott.

MINISTRY OF SAMUEL ABBOTT, 1807–17

Elder Samuel Abbott was ordained August 29, 1804, and filled the ministry here from July 29, 1807, to March 21, 1817. He had before served as minister in the Fourth Baptist Church at Lakeville.

From 1817 to 1819, there was occasional preaching.

MINISTRY OF SILAS HALL, 1819–26

Rev. Silas Hall was born in Raynham, January 16, 1789, and prepared for Brown University under the Rev. David Gurney of Middleboro. After his graduation in 1809 and theological course, he was pastor in several places. He was settled in North Middleboro at three different periods.

He was a man of intellectual gifts, recognized as a scholar, and was especially proficient in Greek and Latin. After he was seventy-five he preached but little, spending his last years with his son in Whitman. He died December 26, 1876, aged eighty-seven. From 1826 the pulpit was supplied by several men for a short time.

MINISTRY OF SHUBAEL LOVELL, 1826 [1]

Mr. Lovell had been a physician, but gave up that profession

---

[1] It is to be regretted that but few brief facts could be ascertained with regard to these ministers.

BAPTIST CHURCH, NORTH MIDDLEBORO

for the ministry, preaching in Rowley and Taunton before supplying here.

MINISTRY OF JEREMIAH KELLY, 1829–31

After leaving Titicut, Mr. Kelly preached in Hanson, Carver, and Halifax.

MINISTRY OF ASA NILES, 1832–33

Asa Niles was born in North Middleboro, February 10, 1777, and died April 15, 1849. He preached to this church from September 23, 1832, to March 5, 1833.

MINISTRY OF PROFESSOR AVERY BRIGGS, 1834–38

Avery Briggs was born in East Stoughton, July 5, 1795, and was a graduate of Brown. He was for eight years principal of Peirce Academy, and supplied this pulpit for a few years. He died October 26, 1883.

SECOND MINISTRY OF SILAS HALL, 1839–47

MINISTRY OF JAMES ANDEM, 1847-49

Mr. Andem had been a business man before entering the ministry. He preached here from January 1, 1847, to November 18, 1849, when he went to North Bridgewater, and then moved to the West.

The pastors of this church since 1850 have been: Silas Hall, 1850-51. Lorenzo Tandy, 1852-56. Samuel Richardson, 1856-62. Alexander McLearn, 1862-65. Joseph Hutchinson, 1865-75. George L. Ruberg, 1875-79. S. T. Livermore, 1879-80. Henry C. Coombs, 1880-86. Benjamin Francis Turner, 1886-87. (For two years after this, he was a missionary in Burma.) James W. Tingley, 1887-88. Isaac W. Coombs, 1889-90. James W. Tingley, 1890-92. (Second pastorate here.) Douglass Hazard Simpson, 1892-94. Otis Osgood Ordway, 1895-97. George Fletcher Beecher, 1897-1900. Frank S. Cann, 1900-01. Alfred S. Hill, 1901-03. J. R. Lawrence, 1903-.

This church, aside from being prominent in this denomination and from the extended reputation for scholarship and piety of its first pastor, has earned an enviable name as the mother church of its denomination, and as the church from which some seventeen ministers have gone forth.[1]

SECOND BAPTIST CHURCH, LAKEVILLE

Although the records of this church are probably lost, and it has been extinct for more than fifty years, its history is important in the ecclesiastical annals of the town. Its first members were probably among those who were dissatisfied with the teachings of the Congregational Church, and who, owing to the great influence exerted throughout the colony by the preaching of Whitefield, assumed the name of Separatists, New Lights, or Come-Outers, as they were often called. This church was formed through the influence of Thomas Nelson, who had

[1] James Mellen, Asa Hunt, Abner Lewis, Elijah Codding, Job Macomber, Samuel Nelson, Stephen S. Nelson, David Leonard, Zenas L. Leonard, Lewis Leonard, George Leonard, Samuel Tainter, Thomas Conant, Silas Hall, William Harrison Alden, David Weston, Joshua F. Packard.

joined the church at Swansea; but in 1753 he and his sons, with several others who sympathized with him in his religious views, commenced worship in their house in Assawampsett, and secured the services of Ebenezer Hinds to preach for them.

Two years before this, a Separatist Church had been organized four miles southeast of this, with James Mead as the pastor and William Smith as deacon. Mr. Mead had been employed in adjacent towns as a schoolmaster, and we find in the records of Freetown, under date of December 17, 1744, the following quotation: "James Mead was dismissed from serving longer as a schoolmaster." He had previously worshipped at the Congregational Church at North Middleboro, and in 1751, with William Smith, resigned, "to embody together into a church where they lived at Beech Woods in one edge of Middleboro." At his death, in 1756, the majority of the church became Baptists, those who had worshipped in the house of Mr. Nelson uniting with them to form a church in the meeting-house at Beech Woods, November 16, 1757, with the Rev. Ebenezer Hinds as pastor, who was ordained January 26, 1758. On May 19, 1798, the church was accidentally destroyed by fire, together with the parsonage standing near. New buildings were erected a few years later near the site of the old ones; the meeting-house was used until about the year 1843; the parsonage is now occupied by Dennis Tinkham.

In 1840 Elder William Shurtleff, known as a "Christian" Baptist, became pastor, and as a result of his preaching this became a "Christian" Church. Although an extensive revival followed as a result of Mr. Shurtleff's preaching, in 1841 the church was divided, a large part following Elder Shurtleff, while others formed a Free-Will Baptist Church, and the remainder adhered to the Calvinistic faith of that denomination. As a result of this division, three church buildings representing these different denominations were commenced; the Baptist was never completed, and its church organization, with that of the Free-Will, soon became extinct. These churches were located on the County Road, a short distance to the west from Canedy's Corner.

MINISTRY OF REV. EBENEZER HINDS, 1753-93

Ebenezer Hinds was born in Bridgewater, July 29, 1719, and was at one time a member of the Second Baptist Church in Boston. During his ministry a revival of religion occurred, whereby this church was increased to one hundred and four persons. During the French and Indian War he served as chaplain in Captain Benjamin Pratt's company, and was with them in their march to Saratoga, where he often preached. He was a man of unusual ability, and an earnest and devout christian pastor, who did much to build up his church and increase the spirituality of its members during his forty years of service. He was remarkable for his bodily health and activity, and it is stated that at the age of eighty years he would spring upon his horse unaided and take long rides to visit his parishioners. Probably on account of his great age, he gave up his pastorate about the year 1793, and until the year 1805 there seems to have been no regular pastor, Mr. Hinds preaching occasionally as his strength would allow. At his death, April 29, 1812, he conveyed to the church the parsonage which he had built and the land upon which it stands.

REV. EBENEZER HINDS

MINISTRY OF REV. SIMEON COOMBS, 1805-15

The Rev. Mr. Coombs was a member of the Third Baptist Church in Middleboro, and at one time served as pastor of the Calvinistic Baptist Church in Montague, Mass., and in Wardsboro, Vt., from which he moved to Lakeville to accept the pastorate of this church. From 1815 to 1840 there was no regular service, but during this time Elders Loring, Handy, Culver, and Whittemore occasionally preached.

MINISTRY OF ELDER WILLIAM SHURTLEFF, 1840–41

But little is known of Elder William Shurtleff; he was said to be an able preacher, although not in sympathy with the creed of this church. After the close of his ministry, a number of his church and society followed him in the formation of a Christian Church. See Christian Church.

THIRD CALVINISTIC BAPTIST CHURCH

At the close of the Rev. Peter Thacher's ministry in the First Church, the dissension growing out of the New and the Old Lights extended throughout the town, and the families living in South Middleboro and the adjoining towns of Carver, Rochester, and Wareham called a Baptist minister to preach to them from time to time. In 1761 ten persons united in forming a Baptist Church under the name of the Third Calvinistic Church, with Rev. Ebenezer Jones as their pastor. At first the meetings were held in a private dwelling, but afterwards a house of worship was erected on the site of the meeting-house in South Middleboro, now occupied by the Methodists, and known in the last century as the Spruce meeting-house. At the close of the ministry of Rev. Asa Hunt, in 1789, so much dissension was caused by the removal of some of the members to Beaver Dam (now Rock), that it resulted in the church and society being moved there, and later the church edifice came into the hands of the Methodists, as mentioned above.

Services were first held by the Baptist Church near the first parsonage on Miller Street, upon a ledge of rock from which the place took its name. After the removal of this church to Rock, the Rev. Samuel Nelson became the pastor, and from him for many generations the meeting-house, built in

BAPTIST CHURCH, ROCK

1795, was known as "Mr. Nelson's meeting-house." It was a house with sixty-eight pews. It had three alcoves, one at the end and one upon each side, and was built substantially like the meeting-house of the First Church at the Green. Since the removal of the church from South Middleboro to Rock, it has been small but prosperous. It was of this church that Deborah Sampson of Revolutionary fame was a member, and here she was disciplined for "unseemly conduct" in taking male attire and serving as a private soldier. The church edifice was torn down in 1852, and the present one erected.

MINISTRY OF REV. EBENEZER JONES, 1761-69

Ebenezer Jones had preached to them before his ordination, which occurred October 28, 1761. During the first year the church enjoyed a revival, which spread throughout the community, and many united with the church. Mr. Jones died in Albany in 1791.

MINISTRY OF REV. ASA HUNT, 1771–89

Asa Hunt was born in July, 1744, and was ordained pastor here October 30, 1771. During his ministry the meeting-house was built, and in 1780 a great revival began among his people, and one hundred and thirteen were added to the church. In 1782 the church membership consisted of one hundred and ninety-four members. He died in Providence, September 20, 1791.

MINISTRY OF REV. SAMUEL NELSON, 1794–1822

At the close of the ministry of Mr. Hunt the church was without a pastor for some time, and a dissension arose owing to the removal of ten members to Rock. They were fortunate in securing the services of Rev. Samuel Nelson, who was born April 6, 1748; he was a grandson of Thomas Nelson, one of the first settlers of Lakeville. Fifteen of the members still remained at South Middleboro, and for some time he conducted preaching services in both places, but soon the services at South Middleboro were discontinued. It was during his ministry that the first meeting-house was erected at Rock. Mr. Nelson was an able man; during his first year thirty new members were added. He continued as pastor of this church, but on account of the failure of his eyesight and his feebleness in body, in 1818 Mr. Isaac Kimball was chosen his assistant. Mr. Nelson died September 9, 1822, at the age of seventy-seven years, four months. He was a man small in stature, of sandy complexion, and very mild in his disposition.

MINISTRY[1] OF REV. ISAAC KIMBALL, 1822–24

MINISTRY OF REV. WILLIAM HUBBARD, 1825–30

From 1830 to 1833 the church was without a settled pastor, but was supplied most of the time by the Rev. Mr. Ball.

[1] But few facts could be obtained concerning these ministers.

MINISTRY OF E. C. MESSENGER, 1833-37

MINISTRY OF REV. R. B. DICKEY, 1837-40

Thirty-one were added to the church during his pastorate.

MINISTRY OF REV. ALEXANDER MILNE, 1841-43

Rev. Alexander Milne's ministry was marked by an extensive revival, which brought many members into the church.

The pastors of this church since 1844 have been : Mr. —— Holbrook, 1844-45. George Daland, 1846-48. T. M. Symons and H. C. Coombs supplied the pulpit. J. W. Horton, 1852-57. P. R. Russell, 1857-60. A. E. Battell, 1860-63. George Carpenter, 1864. E. S. Hill, 1864-68. J. E. Wood, 1868-71. I. J. Burgess, 1871-75. C. D. Swett, 1876-82. William M. Weeks, 1883-84. J. W. Merrill, 1884-85. Philander Perry, 1886-88. Joseph Barbour, 1888-93. Ward Fisher, 1894-95. Archibald Kerr, 1897-1900. Charles W. Allen, 1900-.

FOURTH BAPTIST CHURCH IN LAKEVILLE — UNITED BRETHREN

This church was commonly known as the Pond Church. A number of members of the Second Baptist Church, probably desiring a nearer place of worship, met on the 30th day of November, 1795, for the purpose of building a meeting-house more convenient than that at Beech Woods. They organized a new society under the name of the United Brethren, and in the records we find the " old meeting-house is now very much decayed and quite out of centre, we find it necessary to build a new one. We therefore severally agree to contribute our assistance upon the following conditions." Here follow various items, and among others they " should have the liberty occasionally to invite ministers of good character of any denomination to preach in said house and that the minister who statedly supplies the pulpit shall be in full fellowship with the Warren Association."

At first it was voted that the church should be built upon

Shockley Hill, but the site was afterwards changed to the narrow strip of land between the highway and Assawampsett Pond. Major Peter Hoar seems to have been a prominent member of the society, and it was largely through his influence that the church edifice was erected and completed in 1797. It is said to have been a very fine structure, and was occupied as a place of worship until about the year 1861, when public worship was discontinued, and it was sold by the proprietors, a portion being made into a public hall, called Sassamon Hall, a portion into a grocery store, and the remaining part used as a tenement. It was burned in the early part of 1870.

The church was not formed until August 19, 1800, when the organization took the name of the United Brethren, worshipping in the house which had been erected three years before. From the completion of the place of worship until the organization of the church, service was conducted by various clergymen of the Baptist denomination. During the first seven years of its organization there were thirty-three com-

REV. EBENEZER BRIGGS

municants. In 1804 the church voted to change the name to the Fourth Baptist Church in Middleboro. The Rev. Samuel Abbott, the first preacher, remained over this church for a short time. Afterwards the pulpit was supplied at intervals by various clergymen, until about 1809 or 1810, when Elder Ebenezer Briggs was chosen. He continued as the pastor of the church until 1846, and was widely known in this and the adjoining towns as an able minister, genial and thoroughly devoted to his work, having the confidence and love of all.

A fund was left to the deacons of this church under the wills of Asa King and Andrew Cole, which upon the dissolution of the church and society was transferred to the deacons of the Central Baptist Church of Middleboro and the Baptist Church of Raynham, to be held by them in trust to carry out the wishes of the donors.

CENTRAL BAPTIST CHURCH

In the early part of the last century Major Levi Peirce, then an influential member of the Pond (Assawampsett) Church, thought it desirable that religious services should be conducted under the auspices of the Baptist denomination at the Four Corners. He made arrangements for the erection of a building, the lower part of which was to be used for educational purposes, the upper part to contain a hall where religious services could be held.[1] On the 26th day of April, 1828, a meeting was held in the Academy Hall to organize a religious society of the Baptist denomination. Proper officers were chosen, a declaration of their faith was drawn up, and a covenant entered into similar to the one now in use in the church. Prominent clergymen and laymen from the adjoining churches were present, and at a council, August 13, unanimously voted to recognize the brethren and sisters so organized as a distinct church, to be designated the Central Baptist Church of Middleboro.

Major Peirce erected at his own expense, at a cost of about four thousand dollars, the meeting-house for the church and society adjoining the academy grounds. He also erected a parsonage and established a fund of one thousand dollars, which he soon after gave to the church. Upon its complete organization the church property was deeded to trustees, to be held by them and their successors for the maintenance of religious worship.

On August 9, 1828, eight persons were received from the

[1] See chapter containing an account of Peirce Academy.

CENTRAL BAPTIST CHURCH

Pond Baptist Church, namely, Levi Peirce, Elisha Tucker, Molly Leonard, Prudence Holmes, Anna Hines, Sally Peirce, Sally B. Tucker, Thankful Miller, with Patience Barden and Priscilla Tinkham from the Rock Church.

After the organization of the church, they called Elder Briggs, September 5, 1828, to become their pastor. This invitation was, however, declined.

MINISTRY OF NICHOLAS MEDBERRY, 1828–32

October 4 of the same year a call was extended to Nicholas Medberry of Seekonk, which was accepted, and he was ordained November 12, 1828. During Mr. Medberry's pastorate more than one hundred united with this church. He resigned July 15, 1832.

MINISTRY OF REV. HERVEY FITZ, 1832-36

Upon the resignation of Mr. Medberry, on the 31st of August, 1832, a call was given to the Rev. Hervey Fitz, who continued as pastor of the church until May 15, 1836, when he resigned. He was born in Charlton, Mass., November 23, 1792, and was graduated at Amherst College in 1826, and Newton Theological Seminary in 1829; in 1843 he was state missionary of the Baptist convention. He was a warm friend of Peirce Academy, and did much for it during his lifetime. During his ministry fifty-seven people were added to the church, and William S. Peirce and Joseph T. Wood were elected deacons. He died in Middleboro June 10, 1878.

REV. HERVEY FITZ

MINISTRY OF REV. EBENEZER NELSON, 1837-51

Ebenezer Nelson was born in Lakeville, November 19, 1787; he completed his theological studies at Waterville, Maine; in 1818 he was approved as a minister of Christ by his church, and two years after accepted a call from the Baptist Church in Lynn. On account of ill health, he soon after resigned his pastorate in that church, and was employed for some time as special agent for the Newton Theological Seminary. Having regained his health, he accepted a call to West Cambridge and remained there a few years, but at the earnest solicitation of the Northern Baptist Education Society, in 1834, he became their secretary. After two years' employment in that capacity, he accepted a call to the Central Baptist Church in Middleboro, where he commenced his work as minister in January, 1837. He continued as pastor of this church for a period of fourteen years. His relation with the venerable Dr. Putnam, pastor of the First Church, was so cordial that they seemed like brothers. During his residence in Middleboro he did much for Peirce Academy, not only as president of its Board of Trustees, but he assisted by every means in his power the able and efficient principal who so long stood at the head of that institution.

In September, 1850, he desired a vacation from his pastoral duties on account of ill health, and again accepted an agency for the Newton Theological Seminary. His health, however, was so poor that he was obliged to give up this employment, and realizing from the nature of his disease that he had not long to live, he desired to pass the closing days of his life in Lynn, among the people of his first settlement. He died on the 6th of April, 1852. One hundred and forty-one were added to the church during his ministry.

REV. EBENEZER NELSON

The pastors of this church since 1852 have been : Jonathan Aldrich, 1852–53. John B. Burke, 1854–55. John F. Bigelow, D. D., 1855–59. Alexander M. Averill, 1859–62. Levi A. Abbott, 1863–68. George G. Fairbanks, 1869–83. William H. Bowen, 1884–88. M. F. Johnson, 1889–98. J. H. Foshay, 1898. Elmer S. Williams, 1898–.

CHRISTIAN CHURCH

Many years ago there was a small church of this denomination in Lakeville, of which Rev. Daniel Hicks was the first pastor, and where afterwards the Rev. George Peirce preached for a little time. Abiel Nelson was the deacon and clerk of the church. It has, however, long since become extinct, and no records of the church organization are known to exist.

THE CHRISTIAN SOCIETY OF MIDDLEBORO, NOW LAKEVILLE

This church was organized February 19, 1842, by sixteen of the members of the Second Baptist Church, who seceded to form this organization under the leadership of Elder William Shurtleff. About the time of its organization it erected a church edifice, which is known as the Mullein Hill meetinghouse. The following are the names of the pastors of this church: William Shurtleff, William M. Bryant, Bartlett Cushman, George Tyler, E. W. Barrows, Theophilus Brown, M. S. Chadwick, and Elijah W. Barrows.

Occasional preaching services are held by neighboring clergymen.

CENTRAL METHODIST CHURCH

A meeting was held on the 15th of September, 1823, to form this church, and the usual Articles of Association of the denomination were entered into by the following persons, who were its original members: Edward Winslow, Deborah Winslow, Martha Thomas, Mercy Barden, Susan S. Clark, Augusta Clark, Nathan Savory, Alanson Gammons, and Nathan Perkins. They obtained permission to worship in the town hall, with Rev. Asa Kent as their first pastor.

In October, 1830, a site was chosen for this society at Fall Brook, as the most central, and it was voted to build a house of worship, which was completed and dedicated early in 1831. Worship was continued in this chapel until the death of Rev.

Israel Washburn in 1861 ; after this, services were held here, with various intermissions, until the latter part of 1889, when the chapel was closed and afterwards sold. During this time the following clergymen officiated : John Q. Adams, Theophilus Brown, Mr. Pierson, William Packard (Baptist preacher), Roland Gammons, and John Hull.

In 1863 regular preaching service was again commenced at the Four Corners, and has been conducted by different clergymen settled over the church a few years, in accordance with the usual custom. A hall was secured over the furniture store of Mr. George Soule, and in 1865 the chapel formerly occupied by the Central Baptist Society was leased for three years, and dedicated in March of that year. From generous contributions the present church, costing $12,500, was completed February 9, 1869. The membership has rapidly increased, and in the years 1876 to 1879 an extensive revival brought the number from one hundred and thirty to two hundred and eighty. Many improvements have been made in the church edifice, and a handsome parsonage on the corner of School and Peirce streets was given to the society by Mr. Abner L. Westgate, one of its most prominent members.[1]

The pastors of this church and their terms of service have been as follows : Asa Kent, 1823-24. Isaac Stoddard, 1825. Lemuel Tompkins, 1826-27. Elias C. Scott, 1828. David Culver, 1829-30. Amos Binney, 1831-32. Lemuel Harlow, 1833-34. Thomas G. Brown, 1835-36. Josiah Litch, 1837-38. Proctor Marsh, 1839-40. Otis Wilder, 1841-42. George H. Winchester, Sr., 1843-44. Elijah Willard, 1845-46. Ebenezer Ewer, 1847-48. William Tamplin, 1849-50. Edmund A. Standish, 1851-52. George Macomber, 1853-54. George H. Winchester, Jr., 1855-56. Philip Crandon, 1857-58. Asa N. Bodfish, 1859-60. Israel Washburn, 1861-62. John Q. Adams, 1863. Jason Gill, 1864. Samuel Whidden, 1864-65. F. C. Newell, 1866-67. Freeman Ryder, 1868-69. S. T. Patterson, 1870-71. J. S. Carroll, 1872-74. Charles A. Mac-

[1] For a further history of this church, see *History of the New England Southern Methodist Conference*, pp. 108-110.

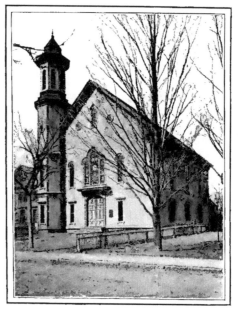

METHODIST EPISCOPAL CHURCH, FOUR CORNERS

reading, 1875. E. D. Towle, 1876–77. A. W. Kingsbury, 1878–79. George W. Hunt, 1882–83. Edward L. Hyde, 1884–86. Samuel McBurney, 1887–88. Thomas J. Everett, 1889–91. William F. Davis, 1892–95. George A. Grant, 1896–1900. Eben Tirrell, 1901–03. Oscar E. Johnson, 1904–.

METHODIST EPISCOPAL CHURCH, SOUTH MIDDLEBORO

The Third Baptist Church had built their first house of worship here, which they occupied from 1761 to 1795. There is no continuous history of any religious organization from 1795 to 1868, although the Reformed Methodist Church occupied this building. Among those who preached during this period were Messrs. Johnson, McLish, Todd, Wallen, Clark, Mayall, and Barrows. Not all of these, however, were Methodists or clergymen. During the preaching of Elder Pliny Brett, in 1827, there was a revival of religion ; Rev. Uriah Minor preached from 1830 to 1835, and Theophilus Brown from 1841 to 1858. The present building was erected in 1841 upon the site of the old meeting-house of the Third Baptist Church, and the

METHODIST EPISCOPAL CHURCH, SOUTH MIDDLEBORO

church was reorganized in 1847, but there seems to be no history of it until 1868.

The following-named pastors have been settled over this church: John G. Gammons, 1868. Isaac B. Forbes, 1869. Benjamin L. Sayer, 1870-74. John W. Price, 1874. Philip Crandon, 1874-76. Charles Stokes, 1876-77. Isaac Sherman, 1878-81. O. R. Higgins, 1881. S. P. Snow, 1882-84. J. Livesey, 1885. E. A. Hunt, 1886-90. J. A. Wood, 1891-92. J. S. Thomas, 1893-95. C. A. Purdy, 1896. Charles N. Hinckley, 1897-98. B. F. Raynor, 1899-1901. J. S. Bell, 1902-03. C. E. Jenney, 1904-.

UNIVERSALIST SOCIETY

The first organization of the Universalists was made in 1842, although twenty years before, several people had filed certificates of membership in the Universalist Society in Halifax and other towns. In this year the Rev. E. H. Lake organized a society, and for a number of years meetings were held fortnightly, alternating between Peirce Hall at the village and the Purchade schoolhouse. Later, meetings were held at the School Street schoolhouse and in Hinckley Hall; regular resident ministers were employed, Rev. E. R. Crocker and Rev. Joseph Hemphill each serving for a term of years.

In 1854 a lot on Oak Street was purchased for a meeting-house and conveyed to the First Universalist Samaritan sewing-circle; a fund of money was accumulated and placed on deposit. The society gradually declined, the meetings ceased, and in 1872 the remaining members of the sewing-circle sold the lot to Jonathan T. Washburn and divided the proceeds.

An effort was made a few years later to revive this society, but the project was finally abandoned, and the members united with the Unitarians.

FIRST UNITARIAN SOCIETY

In September, 1888, largely through the instrumentality of Rev. C. Y. DeNormandie of Kingston, services of this denomination were first held in Middleboro. Rev. C. H. McDougall of Rockland preached here Sunday evenings in connection with his charge as secretary of the Plymouth and Bay Unitarian Conference. During his ministry a permanent organization was made, March 5, 1889, of twenty-two individuals, under the name of the First Unitarian Society. "Its object shall be to provide for public religious worship and instruction and for such charitable and benevolent activities as belong to a religious society." Encouraged by the gift of a lot from Enoch Pratt of Baltimore, and of a thousand dollars from an unknown friend, the society, during the ministry of Rev. William H. Ramsey, built a church on Pearl Street at a cost of ten thousand dollars, which was dedicated September 2, 1891.

At the first meeting of the society Mr. Eugene P. LeBaron was elected president, and held that position until the time of his death, December 1, 1893. He was an able business man

UNITARIAN CHURCH

and an earnest supporter of this church, and perhaps the society owes more to his business and executive ability and generous contributions than to any one else. Since its first organization the church and society have always been in a prosperous condition.

The following have been the pastors of the church: William H. Ramsey, from August, 1889, to May, 1892. William C. Litchfield, from September, 1892, to April, 1895. J. Foster Tucker, from September, 1895, to September, 1896. Frederic C. Brown, from October, 1896, to May, 1898. Fred R. Lewis, from September, 1898, to May, 1902. George E. MacIlwain, from September, 1902–.

EPISCOPAL CHURCH

This church was established in Middleboro in 1889, with an organization of eleven members. In the fall of that year the Rev. Mr. Cressey of Bridgewater assumed charge of the Sabbath evening service, and in November of the same year the first confirmation service was solemnized in the Central

EPISCOPAL CHURCH

Congregational Church, and the Church of Our Saviour was duly formed. For a while they worshipped in the hall of the Academy building, but in 1898 the new church was dedicated. This was built at a cost of about forty thousand dollars, largely through the munificent contribution of James E. Peirce, the treasurer of the parish from its organization to his death.

The rectors of the church have been William Bayard Hale, 1889–99. Gilbert W. Laidlaw, 1899–01. Charles J. Ketchum, 1901–05.

CHURCH OF THE SACRED HEART

In 1850 about thirty members of the Roman Catholic Church had become residents of Middleboro, and for many years they were obliged to go to Taunton to attend mass. As their numbers increased, service was occasionally held at different residences, then at the old town house, until the hall over the store of the late Colonel Peter H. Peirce was engaged as the place of worship, a priest from some of the neighboring towns officiating. This hall was occupied for about ten years, but in 1880 the present church edifice was erected at a cost of nearly five thousand dollars, and dedicated in June, Archbishop Williams officiating, assisted by priests from churches in the neighboring towns. In May, 1885, the society was

ROMAN CATHOLIC CHURCH

made a separate parish, and since that time has had a resident priest. For about eighteen years during the early history of the church, Father Conlin, who was pastor of the church in Bridgewater as well as that of Middleboro, came here monthly.

In 1885 Father Oliver Boucher officiated for a few months, and was succeeded by Father P. J. Sheedy, and in 1890 by Father J. H. O'Neil. During his ministry the present rectory was built, the lot of land on the corner of Center and Oak streets was purchased, and the St. Mary's Cemetery was purchased in 1891. In 1896 he was succeeded by Father Murphy, and in 1900 the present priest, Father D. C. Riordan, took his place.

ADVENT CHURCH

There has been an organization of an Advent Church in this town for many years. They have no church building nor settled pastor, but worship in a hall on Jackson Street.

YOUNG MEN'S CHRISTIAN ASSOCIATION

The Young Men's Christian Association was organized in the early seventies, with Professor J. W. P. Jenks as its president. In 1883 it was reorganized, and continued with varied success until March 19, 1892, when it was incorporated. Since then it has steadily grown in numbers and influence, until it now has a membership of over two hundred and fifty. The work of the association in its various departments is in a prosperous condition, and it has its rooms and gymnasium at present in the Academy building.

SQUARE PEWS OF THE OLDEN TIME

CHAPTER XXVII

TOWN MEETINGS, HERRING FISHERIES, INDIAN PATHS, ROADS AND HIGHWAYS, FIRE DISTRICT

THE provisions of the colonial laws[1] in reference to the government of the towns and the election of officers were very generally observed in Middleboro from its first incorporation until the commencement of King Philip's War. The early settlers then abandoned the town for two or three years, and did not return in sufficient numbers to warrant the reëstablishment of town affairs until about 1678. The town meetings were held in different dwelling-houses, and frequently at the house of Isaac Howland.

There was a provision in the colonial law, as early as 1675, that there should be a "publicke house erected in every Towne" where the people could meet and worship God, "and in case any Town shall apparently neglect or refuse to build the said house it shalbe in the power of the Govr and Majestrate to appoint and authorise a pson or psons to build the said house according to the abillitie and nesessitie of the people and the charge thereof to be defrayed by all the Inhabitants or propriators of the Towne." This provision was reaffirmed with some slight changes in the year 1678. The meeting-houses in the colony were used for the transaction of business of the towns. The records show that the First Church was so used as early as August, 1679, when the town meeting was held at the "town house." On the 18th of May, 1675, a few weeks before the outbreak of King Philip's War, a committee had been appointed to take measures for the erection of a "meeting house," which the war prevented; but plans were made, and the work was begun soon after their return. Mr. Fuller came to preach in the year 1679, and it is generally be-

[1] *Laws of Colony of New Plymouth*, p. 175.

lieved that before he accepted the invitation, the meeting-house in which the First Church worshipped had been built. As early as 1681, the town agreed that if any neglected or refused to attend the town meetings, being legally warned, they should be liable to pay a fine of two shillings, six pence for the town's use. After the settlement of the Rev. Mr. Fuller, the town meetings were usually held in the meeting-house of the First Church, until the latter part of the eighteenth century, when the centre of population had so changed that another location was desirable.

The erection of a town house for the transaction of public business met with much opposition. The first article appeared in the warrant, September 8, 1788, and was voted down; again, on March 1, 1790, the town voted to take no action. The matter came up on March 16, 1795, and a committee was appointed to take into consideration the expediency of building and the location of a new town house. The committee were Captain Joshua Eddy, Isaac Thompson, Esq., Dr. Joseph Clark, David Richmond, Captain Job Peirce, Colonel John Nelson, Captain William Canedy, Nehemiah Bennett, Esq., and Deacon Benjamin Thomas. They were to report at the April meeting. At that time they voted to postpone any action upon the report of the committee until the May meeting; they then voted not to accept the report of the committee, but to build in accordance with the eleventh article of the warrant for the annual meeting, and agreed that a town house should be built on the hill opposite the dwelling-house of Widow Sarah Morton. A committee was appointed to draw a plan and report at an adjourned meeting.

According to the plan which this committee submitted, the building was to be forty feet long, thirty-five feet wide, together with a back room twenty feet in length, fourteen feet in width, and twelve feet in the stud, four windows in front, three in each end, and three at the back, with a hip roof; but at a meeting held February 1, 1796, the town voted "to reconsider all former votes passed in said town heretofore relative to the building of a town house." At the same meeting the question

OLD TOWN HOUSE

was put "whether the town will build a town house or not," to be determined by count, those opposing the measure to pass out of the house ; four were chosen to stand at the doors of the meeting-house and count the number. It was found that a majority of ninety-three opposed the building, but at the annual meeting, March 21, 1796, the measure was carried. The opposition continued, although somewhat weaker, there being one hundred and forty-six votes for and one hundred and six opposed.

In regard to the location there was a division of sentiment, one hundred and forty-eight voting for the site near the dwelling-house of Dr. Joseph Clark as against one hundred and thirty-four opposed to it. They then voted to raise one thousand dollars for the building, and a committee of three were appointed to agree with Levi Wood for the land. This committee consisted of Captain Joshua Eddy, Mr. Simeon Doggett, and Captain Joseph Richmond. At the next meeting in April, the town voted "to omit the building of a selectmen's room in the town house and directed that the building of said house be put up at public vendue and strike the building of the same off to the lowest bidder." The house was completed and accepted by the town January 2, 1798, but there were disputes in reference to various matters connected with the house which were not settled for some time. The house thus built served as the town house until 1872, when it was sold and a new one built, much of the material being used for a dwelling-house next to that of Mr. Job Braley on North Street.

Negotiations for the new town house were made in the early part of 1872. The building committee consisted of Horatio Barrows, Albert Alden, Zebulon Pratt, and I. H. Harlow, who were empowered to transact all necessary business. Solomon K. Eaton of Mattapoisett, the architect and contractor, died before it was completed, and it was finished by Mr. Horatio Barrows, chairman of the building committee. It was dedicated in December, 1873, by a public celebration, at which appropriate remarks were made on the part of the building committee and representatives of the town, and a public address was given to commemorate the event. The cost of the building was $48,984.36.

HERRING FISHERIES

When Governor Winslow stopped at Nemasket upon his visit to Massasoit, Indians were found fishing at a weir built across the river near the present dam. The herring fishery furnished much of their food; they were familiar with smoking and drying the fish for a ready supply during the fall and winter. In the spring they used herring as a fertilizer in their corn gardens, which enabled them with little labor to produce abundant crops of maize or Indian corn. In the early part of the last century, during the fishing season, herring were so abundant that a person wading into the river, with a bushel basket, could in some seasons dip up a basket half full of these fish. Every spring, the last of March sometimes, but usually the first week in April, the herring leave the deep sea and ascend the rivers all along the New England coast, to cast their spawn in the lakes, ponds, or head-waters of the rivers. "All the records of the early settlers, and the traditions of Indian lore, testify to the abundant yield of edible fish." At Titicut

VIEW OF HERRING-WEIR, MUTTOCK

was a fishing-weir built by the Indians, from which they were in the habit of taking herring, and another near the dam a little above the wading-place at the Star Mills. There may have been another fishing-place upon the Nemasket River in the rear of Mr. Lorenzo Wood's house. As long as the Indians lived in town, they continued to take the fish from these weirs, and the town made generous provision for their supply.

The herring and all that pertains to their protection have always been jealously guarded by the town, and probably no subject in the commonwealth has given rise to more enactments than that relating to the protection and the catching of alewives. The alewife takes its name from the Indian word "aloof," meaning a fish.

Since the first introduction of water power as a means of propelling the machinery in the different factories and from the building of dams, great care has been taken to see that these did not in any way interfere with the fish going into the ponds in their season, nor with the catching of them at different weirs. From the earliest times many applications were made by the dwellers upon the river for the privilege of erecting new dams, and of catching fish in other places than at Titicut,

Nemasket, and the New Works, but these petitions were invariably refused by the town.

For more than a century each inhabitant was entitled, upon the payment of a moderate sum, to have two hundred fish. Widows, spinsters, and those who for various reasons were unable to procure this supply had that number given to them. Agents were appointed every year to superintend the catching and the distribution of the fish, to collect the money due, and to see that the fish were properly guarded, and that none were caught except at the weir, by those authorized by the town, and at times appointed. Two days, sometimes three, in the week the herring were allowed to pass up into the ponds, but after sunset, men, as well as boys, had their hiding-places to catch the fish secretly, and boasted of their thefts afterwards and of their escape from the fish wardens. Many a one at night, stealthily fishing below the water-wheels of the different mills, found the gates suddenly open and a body of water rushing upon him sufficient to wash him into the stream, and with great difficulty he would escape drowning. The officers were subjected to great indignities, such as an ingenious and reckless company of enterprising youth could suggest. It was thought the best of sport, and the convictions were so infrequent that these escapades were regarded with special zest by a large number of people who would probably not care to have their names known.

STICK OF HERRING

The records are filled with votes relating to this matter, from which may be cited : —

"At a Town meeting March 29th., 1706, the town hath agreed with Samuel Pratt and Ebenezer Tinkham Junior, to make up the weir and take the fish both this year and the next year, in the same manner as they used to be taken, and for the same they are to be paid six pence a load in money by those that have the fish, to be paid by the first day of June each year and the weir to be made up by the twelfth day of April each year, and that each man in the town shall have his turn to take one load of fish before any man shall have two loads, and so to keep turns, except when there is a glut of fish that come faster than they are fetched away by those that have not had their turns, in such case any man may take them, but they shall also be counted to him in the next turn; and in taking turns he that first brings his cart to the weir shall have the first turn and that when any man in his turn hath had fish enough for what land he doth improve that then his turn shall cease, and that if any man shall presume to take and carry away fish, more than his turn, as aforesaid, he shall pay a fine of twenty shillings a load; and the town to make choice of and empower Mr. Isaac Howland and Ensign Joseph Vaughan to prosecute any breach of the aforesaid order upon complaint made to them, and they to be paid out of the said fine, for what charge they shall be at, concerning the same, and the rest of said fine shall be turned over by them unto the selectmen for the town's use."

"It is voted that each man that had no fish the last year, shall have their turns to take a load of fish before any that had their turns the last year have any, provided they have their carts ready at the weir to take them when they come down and not else."

"It is also voted that if there be any man in the town that doth not plant any Indian corn, he shall have no turn of fish, and he that plants so little that he needeth not a whole load of fish for it, he shall have no more than for what he doth plant; in which proportion it is to be understood that he shall use but one fish to a hill, and that in all other respects the turns of taking fish shall be as was agreed upon the last year."

"At a town meeting March the 22nd, 1716, the town agreed with Ebenezer Bennett to take the town fish this present year as they use to be taken and he to load the carts and for the same he is to be paid sixteen pence a load by those that carry away the fish, and he is also to take care that there be free passage at the mill dam for the fish to go up the river, and also he is to take care that there be an orderly distribution of the fish that are taken as they come down, according to the rules which have of late years been ordered by the town."

On April 5, 1725, at a town meeting, it was agreed that eight thousand fish should be accounted a load, the number of fish to be estimated by the man who attended the weir.

In 1733, at a town meeting, it was voted that no fish should be taken by a seine.

In 1733 permission was asked to build a dam at Muttock for manufacturing purposes, but strong objection was made on account of the detriment apprehended to the herring fishery, and the petition was not granted.

"At a town meeting Feb. 15, 1742, it was voted and ordered that the slitting mill dam, so called, over Namasket River in said town be opened the ninth day of March inst. so that alewives and other fish shall have a clear and sufficient passage through the dam to pass up said river in the natural ponds to cast their spawn, and that said dam be kept open for 60 days thereafter for the passage of fish," which provision seems to have been observed ever since that time.

In the province laws of 1749 and 1750 an act was passed to prevent the unnecessary destroying of alewives in the town of Middleboro.

"Whereas there are great quantities of the fish called alewives, which pass up the rivers and brooks in the town of Middleborough to cast their spawn; and notwithstanding the penalties annexed to the many good and wholesome laws of this province already made to prevent the destruction of alewives, yet many ill-minded and disorderly persons are not deterred therefrom.

"*Be it therefore enacted by the Lieutenant-Governor, Council and House of Representatives.*

"Sec. 1 provides that whoever shall presume to take any of the said fish in the aforesaid rivers or brooks, or any part thereof, by any ways or means whatever at any other place than at the old Stone Ware, so called, in Namasket River, and may refuse to discover their names, places of abode and occupation, by which means the prosecution of such offenders may be prevented, and the good design of this act be defeated; and there being some passages of said rivers and brooks that are narrower than others and by reason thereof the course of the said fish may be more easily stopped by canoes and other obstructions.

"Sec. 2 and 3 provide for the execution and penalties of this law.

"Sec. 4 provides that when any children or servants shall offend against this act, they shall be punished by whipping, not exceeding 5 stripes, or by being put in the stocks, not exceeding 24 hours, or imprisonment, not exceeding 24 hours, unless the offenders by themselves or parents or masters or others in their behalf shall forthwith pay the forfeits.

"Sec. 5 and 6 provide as to the penalties and punishments connected with the act.

"Sec. 7 provides that this act shall continue in force for the space of three years from its publication and no longer."[1]

The Province laws of 1752 and 1753 provide for a brief extension of the above law.[2]

The town has always received a revenue for the privilege of catching and selling these fish under the rules which they made, at their annual town meeting, from year to year.

The following is among the votes passed: —

"At the town meeting on Oct. 8, 1764, it was voted to sell the privilege of catching the fish at auction to the highest bidder; after the regular business of the meeting, it was adjourned to the house of Ebenezer Sproutt where the fish were sold to Nelson Finney for eighty pounds, he being the highest bidder."

[1] *Province Laws*, vol. iii, pp. 483, 484.   [2] *Ibid.* vol. iii, p. 647.

The rule was made that whoever bought the fish privilege should not pickle for foreign market, and should give sufficient security to the town for the payment of the fish.

Of late the herring have from different causes so decreased in number that the amount received by the town is small, and but few rules and regulations are adopted as compared with former years. At the present day the price paid for the fish privilege per year is only one hundred and twenty to one hundred and forty or fifty dollars.

Undoubtedly, in years gone by, the manufacturing interests of the town suffered in the endeavor to protect these fish, but the last few years would indicate that the time is not far distant when the herring of Nemasket River may become so far extinct as to cease to provoke much attention and action on the part of the town.

INDIAN PATHS

There were seven well-defined Indian paths running through the town. The more important were the upper and lower paths from the wading-place a little below the Star Mills to Plymouth.

The lower path extended from the Star Mills, and passed very near the street from Middleboro to North Carver. The upper path led through the farms of L. B. Pratt and Chester Weston; then following the boundary line of land formerly owned by Mr. Robins and Mr. Weston, striking Wood Street and following the line of Chestnut Street, it passed directly into the woods to P. W. Savery's; passing along and following Wall Street, it followed the highway to North Carver, where it met the lower path. This formed the boundary line between the Five Men's Purchase and Henry Wood's Purchase, and then farther on, between the Five Men's Purchase and the South Purchase, it crossed Mahuchet Brook to North Carver, following the highway to Plymouth.

The Taunton path probably ran along the highway (which was discontinued some fifty years ago), or back of the house of

Dr. G. L. Ellis, to Jose Meadows, then on the easterly side of these meadows to Taunton Street, and followed that street to what was then Taunton village.

The Rochester path probably commenced at the Green, passing through Waupaunucket neighborhood, and following substantially the Marion road.

The Dartmouth path began at Muttock, passing in a southerly direction east of the junction of North and Main streets to the wading-place, then westerly to Main Street, and continued for some distance, following the New Bedford road.

What is known as the Rhode Island road was an old Indian path commencing probably near the wading-place, then by Main Street to the Haskins neighborhood, where it crossed Baiting Brook, continuing on near Myricks Station through Assonet Village, and from there to Mt. Hope.

The Acushnet path followed substantially what is known as the New Bedford road.

The Titicut path commenced at the fording-place a little below Pratt's bridge on the Taunton River, passing Fort Hill not far from the banks of the river, then in an easterly direction a little south of the Congregational Church it entered into what is now Plymouth Street, and following this to the wading-place across the Nemasket River, a little below the Star Mills, it there connected with the paths from that place to Plymouth. This was the path which Winslow and Hopkins followed on their first visit to Massasoit, spending the night at Fort Hill.

There were two other trails leading out of the Titicut path: one to the north, beginning not far from the house of Lysander Richmond, thence a little south of the barn of Seth Alden, continued to Lyon's Neck, and there fording the river, it passed into Bridgewater; the other went from the fording-place a little below Pratt's bridge along substantially what is now Vernon Street across the bridge over Poquoy or Trout Brook.

While there were doubtless other paths running through the

town, these seem to have been best known, and all traces of any others have now been lost. These Indian paths were not wide enough for a carriage-road, but were well defined, having been for generations the accustomed trail of the natives. For many years after the settlement of the town they were often mentioned in the early deeds as boundary lines of land, and upon them were often places of importance.

Aside from the Indian paths, there were several wading-places used by the natives. The most important was that across the Nemasket River near the bridge, a little below the Star Mills. Another wading-place was across the river on the northerly side of what is called Lyon's Neck. On the Taunton River there were several, one a little below Pratt's bridge near Fort Hill, and another just below where the Richmond town brook enters the Taunton River. There was probably another about an eighth of a mile down the river from Pratt's bridge, just beyond the bend near the old shipyard.

ROADS AND HIGHWAYS

Probably the first Indian path to be used as a public highway was the upper path from the wading-place to Plymouth, which followed what is now known as East Main and Plymouth streets. The path to Taunton and Dartmouth or New Bedford was another which early became a public highway.

Whatever records there may have been relating to the laying out of these roads were lost in 1675, and we are unable to give their location except as they followed the Indian paths. After the first incorporation of the town, surveyors were among the officers chosen at the early town meetings. In all of the Old Colony towns, highways were laid out by a number of men, usually called "a jury," chosen for this purpose. That Middleboro men soon recognized the importance of these provisions is seen in an early record. A committee was appointed by the proprietors of the town on the 18th of May, 1675, to settle, among other things, "some course to procure means for building bridges and settling highways," and at a town meeting soon after the return of the early settlers (the record of which is not given) this action was ratified and confirmed, and a committee, consisting of Constant Southworth, Lieutenant Morton, John Tomson, Joseph Warren, and Isaac Howland, was appointed.

The expense of building these highways was met by the labor of the settlers who were immediately benefited by their location, and any persons obstructing them were liable to be fined five pounds. The duties of the surveyor of highways were accurately defined.[1]

As early as 1633 the court had ordered that "at such convenient times as shall seeme meet to the Govr and Council upon three days' warning given all men meet together for the mending of highwaies, with such tooles and instruments as shall be appointed. And for default every person to forfeit three shillings." [2]

Very many of these ancient highways, owing to the changes in occupation, methods of business, and the shifting of the population, have been discontinued, and other roads laid out in their places, so that now it is impossible even to trace them. In many instances they are included in parts of farms and the walls and fences have been taken away; in other instances they have grown up to woods, leaving no clue to what in the early history of the town were well-travelled highways, passing through cultivated farms and near many dwelling-houses.

Soon the Indian paths gave way to the bridle-paths; these, in turn, were widened to the carriage-roads. On the turnpike and principal highways, there was much travel — the stage-

---

[1] "It is enacted by the Court that if an highway bee wanting in any township of this Gou^{r}ment vpon due complaint that then the Gou^r or any of the Assistants Impanell a Jury and vpon oath charge them to lay out such waies both for horse and foot as in Consience they shall find most beneficiall for the Commonwealth, and as little prejudiciall as may bee to the pticulares, and that all old pathes shalbee still alowed except other provision bee orderly made; and that where there are alowed foot pathes over any mans ground which is fenced up; the owners of such fences shall make convenient stiles or Gates." *Plymouth Colony Records*, 1639, p. 112.

[2] *Ibid.* p. 35.

driver being a man of importance as general news-carrier, second only to the landlord of the tavern.

The New Bedford turnpike was chartered about 1805, and laid out in an almost straight line from a point near the present Lakeville town house to Bridgewater village, and thence on through Abington to Weymouth and Boston. Gates and tolls were in use for a few years, but these were soon abandoned and it became a public highway.

In 1846 the opening of the railroad from Boston to Fall River through Middleboro brought about a great change in the business of the town in many ways. It superseded the old line of stage-coaches from Boston to New Bedford. Over this line the merchants of Middleboro were in the habit of driving to Boston with their horses and chaises, usually taking some members of their family, and spending a day or two in the city for the purchase of goods and transaction of business. These journeys were taken two or three times a year, and were events of much importance to the family and neighbors. The railroad also superseded the baggage wagon which transported freight purchased in Boston or New Bedford for the use of the various stores in town. The last baggage wagon to run over this line was owned and driven by Russell Godfrey. This was a large, cumbrous affair, from fifteen to eighteen feet long, covered with a round top canvas, some seven feet in height, and was drawn by three or four horses.

1684

"At a town meeting at John Nelson's house, Sept. 19, 1684, the town has made choice of four men namely, Mr. John Tomson, John Nelson, Isaac Tomson, and John Miller which are empanelled for the laying out of highways to send an answer to Bridgewater men to a letter they sent of a way they have found from their town to Middlebery."

1687

"At this meeting the Towne seeing that of necessity something must be done in order for laying out of high wayes being at some loss in themselves about it in yt their records of them be burnt & that they doe the best they can to renew them againe as may be most beneficial to ye generall & as little preiudicial to any particular as near as we can we have in order thereunto made choice of twelve men for a jury for to be help in this worke & doe prsent them to ye honrd Court for direction &a advice in ye same: ye names of ye men made choice of for a iury ar as followeth.

Mr. John Tomson	John Miller	Ebeneser Tinkcum
Mr. Isaac Howland	John Bennet	Samuell Wood
David Wood	Joseph Vaughan	David Thomas Junir.
Obediah Eddy	Epharim Tinkcum	Nathanill Warren
John Allyn		

"The Jury was approved of by the County Court and Sworne by Justes Morton by order of Court."

1688

May 25, 1688. "The names of the Jury is as followeth, Mr. John Tomson, Isack Howland, Samuell Wood, Ebeneser Tinckom; Ephraim Tinckom; Nathaniell Warren; David Tomas; John Allen; Obediah Edie, Joseph Vaughan; John Miller; have layd out his majesties high ways from Plymouth bounds to Taunton bounds beginning at the aforesaid Plymouth bounds and so along the former road that hath improve to a swamp at the head of raven brook and so along to a red oak tree at the wester most corner of John Hascalls great lot: and so along the north side of William Nelsons fence by the south side of a wallnit tree and so along to the north side of a black oak tree near William Nelson's house and so along to the south side of a white oak tree marked, and so along the aforesaid road to the house formerly the house of Mr. Cooms and so to the south side of a red oak tree marked and so along a range of trees marked, and so along to the aforesaid road, and so along the aforesaid road to Taunton bounds and for parting road it turns out of Taunton road at the going of a little hill at the head of a swamp commonly called John Mortons swamp, and so along the path to the bridge of rooty brook and so along partly by the path and partly by a range of trees marked to Assawamsett neck and so along the path throu the neck to Quiticus."

1689

At a Court held on the 8th of October, 1689, "a petition was presented by Lieut. John Tompson in reference to the want of an highway from Middlebury, Bridgwater, and other places, towards Boston.

"The Court ordered that an highway for that end shall be laid forth and named a jury of sixteen men to have it done. The jury were ordered to meet at the house of said Tompson on the 9th of October. On the 6th of June, 1690, five men were added to the jury, and they were ordered to meet at the house of the said Tompson on the first Tuesday of July, next, to lay out the way. At a session of the Court on the 7th of April, 1691, the following order was passed:

"In pursuance of an order of Court, bearing date the first Tuesday of October, 1689, we, whose names are hereunder written, being impanelled on a jury, & being met together, according to an order of Court, June ye sixth, 1690, and having heard their pleas and vewed the ways according to ye order of sd Court, doe and have agreed and concluded, that the countrey rode, from Middlebury, Bridgwater, and other places, towards Boston, shall and doth begin at ye roads in Middlebury, by the new meeting house in said Middlebury, where we marked a red oak tree, near said meeting house, and on the westerly side of Plimouth road. & from thence said road runeth as y⁰ old way now goeth to Aldens Brooke, where y⁰ bridge now is, and from thence along the old way which lyeth on y⁰ westerly side of the uper meadow to Bear Spring, and so along as ye way now goeth to ye old bridges at Winatuxet River, at or near the bounds betweene y⁰ lands of John Tomson and ye lands of Alexander Standish, having marked severall trees on each side of sd road. & on y⁰ Westerly side of sd river we marked a red oak tree, and from thence y⁰ road runeth to y⁰ road that goeth to Plimouth from Bridgwater, there being many marked trees on sd road, and so it runeth as that way goeth to Bridgwater, by y⁰ house of James Latham, and from thence it runneth to Byrams Plain, as y⁰ way goeth to Waymouth, and from thence as y⁰ way now lyeth on ye westerly side of Andrew Foords house, & so on to y⁰ patent line, where we marked two trees and laid a heap of stones."

Signed by sixteen of the jury named.[1]

1690

In 1690 the town of Bridgewater voted " to build a road from (Sproats) or the meeting-house in Middleboro over Tomson's bridges to the road leading from Bridgewater to Plymouth at Thomas Drews, then following the Bridgewater road by James Lathan's to Bryran's Plain to the road leading to Weymouth, then as the road goes on the westerly side of Andrew Ford's house and so to the patent line."[2]

1693

April 5, 1693, the town voted that they would not mend the road that leads to Mr. Tomson's, and May 29, 1693, it appeared that some action had been taken by the court at Plymouth in reference to a defect in the above highway, and that the town received a warrant from the court to choose an agent to make their return " why they don't mend the way that leads from Mr. Tomson's," and at a town meeting legally warned on the 29th day of May, the town made choice of Joseph Vaughan for an agent to send to the court " to give them the reasons why we do not mend the way that leads to Mr. Tomson's, and to see whether the town can have no redress from the county court either by removing the way or also that the county will help bear the charge of mending of it."

At this meeting the town gave Joseph Vaughan power " to choose a man or two to be helpful to him in that matter if need be and likewise the town promised to bear the charge that shall be about it."

1701

May 20, 1701. " Then was chosen for a jury to lay out the contry road from the meeting house in Midlebourroe to Cipican bounds or town line: Lieut. Tompson the foreman of sd jury : —

[1] *Plymouth Colony Records*, Judicial Acts, 1636–1692, pp. 304, 305, 309, 310.
[2] Mitchell, *History of Bridgewater*, p. 72.

Mr. Isack Howland	Ensign Vaun	Edward Tomas
Ephraim Tinkom	John Cob	Peter Tinkom
Ebeneser Tinkom	James Sole	Samuell Eaton
Thomas Tompson	Abiall Wood	Thomas Nelson "

1702

"At a town meeting July the 2d, 1702, it is voted: In answer to a petition from the neighborhood at Purchade: That there shall be a neighborhood way laid out for said neighborhood unto the Kings highway.

"At a town meeting July the 2d, 1702, eight men were chosen to be added to the former Jury for the laying out of the country rode towards Rochester: the men chosen are Samuel Wood: David Thomas: William Nelson: Jeremiah Thomas: William Thomas: John Fuller: Stephen Barden: Samuel Pratt: and it is also voted that the said Jury shall also lay out the way that is granted for the neighborhood at Pachade."

1705

"At a town meeting May the 24th, 1705, the town made choice of a Jury to joyn with a Jury from Bristol county to lay out a highway from baiting brook towards Freetown; as far as it is needfull to be laid out in the line between Taunton and Midleborough; the men chosen are

John Morton, foreman	Samuel Bowles	Ebenezer Richmond
James Bell	Elkanah Leonard	Ephraim Keen
Samuell Richmond	William Thomas	Electious Renolds
Samuell Pratt	James Reed	Samuel Holmes "

RAILROADS

The story of the steam railroads in Middleboro belongs to the history of the development of the railroads in this part of the state. In March, 1844, a charter was granted to the Old Colony Railroad Corporation for a road from Boston to Plymouth. In 1845 the Old Colony interests were empowered to construct the "Bridgewater Branch" from South Abington to Bridgewater. In the same month the Middleboro Railroad Corporation was chartered to build a road from Bridgewater to a connection with the Fall River Branch, which had been built to Myricks. The incorporators named were Andrew Robeson, Nathan Durfee, Peter H. Peirce, and Philander Washburn. The plan had originally been to go directly from Myricks to Bridgewater, thus leaving the village of the Four Corners at a sidetrack. Through the influence of the Middleboro incorporators a détour was made, and the road brought to the west side of the village as finally located.

The same month another charter was granted to the Randolph and Bridgewater Railroad to run from Bridgewater to a point on the Old Colony at Quincy or Braintree.

In August, 1845, the Middleboro, Fall River Branch, and Randolph and Bridgewater were united under the name of the United Corporation. Peter H. Peirce and Elisha Tucker represented Middleboro on the board of directors. In April, 1846, the United Corporation was authorized to take the name of the Fall River Railroad Company. In March, 1854, the Old Colony and the Fall River were united under the name of the Old Colony and Fall River Railroad Company.

In April, 1846, the Cape Cod Branch Railroad was incorporated to build a road from Middleboro to Sandwich, and on the 29th day of May, 1847, the first passenger train was run to Sandwich. Subsequently the name was changed to the Cape Cod Railroad, and the road was extended to Hyannis, then to Orleans by the Cape Cod Central Railroad, and finally to Provincetown.

In 1848 the Taunton and Middleboro Railroad was chartered, but the stock was not taken up, and the charter was forfeited. In 1853 this was revived under the name of the Middleboro and Taunton Railroad, and was run as a competing road with the Old Colony. Tickets for Boston were sold at the same price as on the Old Colony, although the distance was much greater. The promoters of that road planned to bring their terminal station into the village at a point not far from the Episcopal church, and the land for much of the way was bought and held for many years. But their plans failed to materialize on account of the difficulty in getting permission to cross the Fall River and Cape Cod roads at grade. Later, in the process of consolidation, the Old Colony interests bought up the stock, and the road was merged into the Old Colony system.

The Plympton and Middleboro Railroad Company was incorporated in 1849. The line as surveyed went through Mut-

RAILROAD STATION

tock village near the dam, and entered the Fall River road not far from where the Plymouth and Middleboro road now enters, but that project was only a passing memory.

In 1872 all the roads were consolidated under the name of the Old Colony Railroad Company. In 1892 the Plymouth and Middleboro Railroad was completed and leased to the Old Colony Railroad. The stock of this road was taken mainly by the towns of Plymouth, Middleboro, and Carver, Middleboro taking $20,000. By this time the Old Colony road had absorbed, by lease or purchase, all the roads in this part of the state, and in 1893 it was itself, with all its divisions, absorbed by the New York, New Haven, and Hartford Railroad.

Upon the opening of the Fall River Railroad a station was built at the foot of Station Street. This remained until the year 1890, when the old station was torn down and the present commodious brick structure was erected.

STREET RAILWAYS

There are three electric street railways running through different sections of the town, which have tended to materially increase the value of property along their different routes.

The first road to be built in town was known as the New Bedford, Middleboro, and Brockton Street Railway. This was built in 1898 and 1899. It comes into town at North Middleboro, and runs through Plymouth, Everett, and Center streets to the Four Corners, and from there on South Main Street to the Lakeville line. The stock was soon after bought up by the

Brockton Street Railway, and this, with a number of other roads, was consolidated into the Old Colony Street Railway. By reason of its following the shores of the lakes for so long a distance, it is frequently termed the Lake Shore Route.

The East Taunton Street Railway Company was incorporated June 24, 1898, with a capital of $110,000. It was built in 1899, from Taunton through North Lakeville to Taunton and Center streets in Middleboro.

The Middleboro, Wareham, and Buzzard's Bay Street Railway was built in 1901. It was chartered with a capital stock of $150,000, to run from the Four Corners to Rochester, and through Rochester, Wareham, Onset, and Bourne to Monument Beach. This road was sold under foreclosure, and has been reincorporated as the Taunton and Buzzard's Bay Street Railway.

FIRE DISTRICT

The log houses with thatched roofs and large "catted" chimneys of the first settlers were hardly fireproof, and soon became so dangerous that the towns in the colony suffered much from loss by fire. Laws were passed forbidding the building of these unsafe chimneys; fire wardens were appointed to examine houses, that all precautions might be taken, and householders were obliged to have ladders.[1] Later, most of the householders owned fire buckets made of heavy leather, and marked with the owners' initials for identification after use. In the first organization of a military company under Standish, one portion was to constitute the fire alarm.[2] In Middleboro all of the men were expected to assist. When an

---

[1] "Forasmuch as great losses have heretofore happened by fyer whereby men have had their houses and goods within the same utterly consumed, which might have been prevented in some good measure if Ladders could have beene had neere hand. It is therefore enacted by the Court That every householder within this Colony & Government shall have one sufficient ladder or ladders at least about his house which will reach ye top, upon penalty of every such default to forfaite tenn shillings to be leavyed to the use of the Government." *Laws of Plymouth Colony*, 1636, p. 56.

[2] See chapter on Militia.

alarm of fire[1] was given by shouting or ringing a bell, the neighbors all gathered, buckets in hand; if a man was delayed, he threw his buckets into the street that others might use them. A double line of people was formed from the burning building to the nearest pond or well, and the buckets filled with water were passed from hand to hand up one line while the empty ones came down the other line; boys were usually placed on the latter side, called the "dry lane." When the fire was put out, or as was more usual, had burned itself out, the fire warden took charge of the buckets till they were called for by the owners, who hung them in the entry by their front doors ready for future use.

The first fire engine in the country was a rude affair, made in 1650 by Joseph Jencks for the town of Boston, but in the country villages and towns the primitive buckets and ladders were used till a late date.

It was not until 1852 that the fire district of the town of Middleboro was organized. In order to include a population sufficient to comply with the law in establishing such a district, its boundaries extended considerably beyond the village.[2]

Its first officers were: Chief Engineer, William S. Peirce;

---

[1] As early as 1636 we find in *Laws of Plymouth Colony*, p. 56: "That three pieces shott of distinctly one after another shalbe an allarum. And two peeces to give warneing of some house on fier."

[2] "Commencing at that point on the Boston and New Bedford road near the house of Thomas Doggett where the road to the Alms House leaves said road, thence south thirty-three and one-half degrees east, six hundred and ninety-seven rods by said road to the road leading from the Four Corners to Wareham, near where a school house formerly stood, including the houses of Daniel Macomber, Alms House, Edmund Thompson, Jacob Thomas 2d, and Capt. Abram Bryant, thence north two and one half degrees east, three hundred and eighty-seven rods to the bridge at the foot of long hill near the house of Thomas A. Pratt, not including said house, thence north thirty-two degrees west one hundred and ninety-four rods to the corner of Lorenzo Wood's farm near Elisha Waterman's, thence north twenty-seven degrees west, four hundred and twelve rods, crossing the road in front of Nahum M. Tribou's house, running in the rear of Melzar Tribou's house to the bridge near Thomas Weston's, thence south forty-five degrees west five hundred and sixty-eight rods to an apple tree on the westerly side of Alfred Randall's house, thence south nine degrees east five hundred and forty-six rods to bounds first mentioned."

Assistant Engineers, Sylvanus W. Reed, Andrew M. Eaton, Sylvanus Hinckley, Lemuel G. Peirce ; Prudential Committee, Sylvanus Hinckley, Everett Robinson, Joseph Sampson, Jr. ; Clerk, Jacob B. Shaw.

The fire apparatus consisted of a hand tub, as it was then called, under the name of the Bay State No. 1, and a hook and ladder company. Previous to or at the time of the establishment of the fire department, there was a very small hand tub, capable of being worked by three or four men at the most, which was kept in one of the buildings of the Nemasket Mill Company. On the night of the national election in 1860, when a telegram had announced the certainty of the result, a party of boys, with a desire to celebrate, pulled out the old tub and commenced to parade. Others had built a huge bonfire in the middle of the street at the Four Corners. The tub was drawn near, and a faction in the crowd tipped it over into the fire, where it came to an untimely end.

In 1877 a new ladder truck was purchased, and improved apparatus has since been provided. A house was built on School Street for the department. About 1875 a number of citizens purchased a hand machine named the Young Mechanic No. 6, which was replaced by a steamer in New Bedford ; an independent company was formed, and continued for several years. The district built a house for the company on Oak Street, and in 1882 a chemical engine was added to the apparatus. After building the water works in 1885 with hydrant service, the hand engines were abandoned and sold, and a hose wagon and reels were provided in 1886.

The equipments of the department in its buildings, apparatus, hose, hydrants, and electric fire-alarms are modern, and their usefulness is shown in an emergency.

When Lakeville was set off from Middleboro in 1853, all that portion of the new town which had been included in the district was taken from it. Later, a number of estates at the south end were set off, as well as all that part lying north and east of the Nemasket River. In 1884 the district was incorporated with its then metes and bounds, and authorized to provide a water supply. The pumping-station was on land just outside. A few years later, the pumping-station lot and a large tract of land were re-annexed to the district.

The bounds having become undefined, at the annual meeting in December, 1899, the District by a new survey established the bounds: —

"Beginning at a stone bound on the northerly side of the Nemasket River, a corner of the towns of Middleborough and Lakeville, thence in said town line, north thirty-two degrees forty-six minutes west, nine hundred and forty-eight feet to a stone bound marking an angle in said town line; thence in said town line, north fifty degrees ten minutes west, three thousand four hundred and seventy-two feet to a stone bound on the northerly side line of the land occupied by the New York, New Haven & Hartford Railroad Company, lessees, known as the 'Fall River branch;' thence north two degrees forty-nine minutes west, six thousand eight hundred and six feet to a stone bound on the easterly side of Cross street, the westerly corner of a lot of land owned by George S. Clark and Elmer B. Cole, known as the 'Morton lot;' thence north sixty degrees one minute east, four thousand seven hundred and sixty-six feet to a stone bound on the northeasterly side of Everett street, a short distance northerly from the house owned by Jennie L. Baxter, a corner of lands owned by George R. Sampson and Job Braley; thence in the line between said Sampson and Braley, north eighty-seven degrees thirty minutes east, six hundred and fifty feet to a stone bound; thence in the same course to the centre of the channel of the Nemasket river; thence upstream in the centre of the channel of said river to a point marking its intersection with the centre of the channel of a brook which crosses the northeasterly part of the farm and homestead of George H. Place; thence upstream in the centre of the channel of said brook to a stone bound on the northerly side of East Main street; thence south five degrees fourteen minutes west, six thousand three hundred and eighty-four feet to a stone bound on the northerly corner of the intersection of Wood and Wareham streets; thence south seventy-four degrees twenty-one minutes west, two thousand seven hundred and forty-nine feet to a stone bound on the northwesterly side of Wood street, a corner of lands of Edward S. Hathaway and John W. Tinkham; thence north seventy-one degrees three minutes west, one thousand one hundred and twenty-seven feet to the centre of a gate on the line of the water pipe running from Grove street to the Middleborough almshouse; thence north sixty-two degrees nineteen minutes west, one thousand four hundred and thirty-two feet to a stone bound near the said Nemasket river; thence south seventy-six degrees forty-four minutes west, two thousand three hundred and seventy feet to the stone bound first mentioned. The points of compass given above are magnetic and are twelve degrees eight minutes west of true north."

The District as thus defined contains about three and a quarter square miles.

CHAPTER XXVIII

TOWN OFFICERS, PUBLIC OFFICERS

FROM the earliest settlement of Middleboro to the time of its incorporation in the year 1669, it was a part of Plymouth, and its inhabitants were subject to the jurisdiction of the General Court of the colony. As separate towns were incorporated, the civil affairs, which had been regulated by the court, the governor, and his assistants and deputies, became so numerous that other legislation was necessary to enable the towns to manage in a measure their own affairs, to provide more efficient government, to meet the necessary expenses, and to supply the growing wants of their increasing population.

At the breaking out of King Philip's War the records of the town of Middleboro were burned with all of the houses. We gather, however, from the records of the colony kept at Plymouth, a probably correct list of a few officers of the town prior to the war.

FREEMEN AND TOWN OFFICERS BEFORE 1675

1669. William Hoskins was the first town clerk; John Nelson, constable and surveyor of highways;[1] John Tomson and William Nelson, agents of the town.[2]

1670. Freemen of the town:[3] —

John Morton,	Henry Wood,	Jonathan Dunham.
Francis Combe,	William Nelson, Sr.,	Samuell Eaton.

1671. Gershom Cobb, Constable;[4] Jonathan Dunham, agent to inspect ordinaries, and to prevent the selling of powder to the Indians, and extensive drinking;[5] George Vaughan and John

---

[1] *Plymouth Colony Records*, vol. v, pp. 18, 19.
[2] *Ibid.* vol. v, p. 22.
[3] *Ibid.* vol. v, p. 279.
[4] *Ibid.* vol. v, p. 56.
[5] *Ibid.* vol. v, p. 60.

Morton, agents to view damages done to the Indians by hogs and horses.[1]

1672. John Morton, deputy to the General Court; John Irish, constable; John Miller, Grand Enquest; Isacke Howland, surveyor of highways.[2]

1673. John Morton, deputy to the General Court; Obadiah Eedey, Grand Enquest; John Dunham, constable; Samuell Wood, surveyor of highways.[3]

1674. John Tomson, Jonathan Dunham, Francis Combe, selectmen; John Tomson, deputy; Gershom Cobb, Grand Enquest; Isacke Howland, constable; Samuell Wood, Surveyor of highways.[4]

1675. M^r. Francis Combe, John Tomson, Jonathan Dunham, selectmen; John Tomson, deputy; George Vaughan, constable; John Nelson, Grand Enquest.[5]

At the close of King Philip's War, most of the original settlers returned slowly from Plymouth, and during the years 1676 to 1679 not all of the town offices were filled. They seem to have been so generally engaged in rebuilding their houses and preparing their farms for cultivation that but little, if any, thought was given to the civil affairs of the town. During the unfortunate administration of Governor Andros, in the year 1688, the government of the colony was much disturbed, no courts were held at Plymouth, and owing to the uncertainty of the times and the disturbances on the accession of William and Mary to the throne of England, everything of a political nature in the Massachusetts and Plymouth colonies remained at a standstill, and we find no records of the courts, or of any town officers being elected.

SELECTMEN

Among the officers of the towns in the Old Colony, none were of more importance than the selectmen. This office was filled by the most influential and able men. They were given

[1] *Plymouth Colony Records*, vol. v, p. 62.
[2] *Ibid*. vol. v, pp. 90–93.
[3] *Ibid*. vol. v, pp. 114–115.
[4] *Ibid*. vol. v, pp. 144–146.
[5] *Ibid*. vol. v, pp. 165–166.

large discretion, and until the close of the Revolutionary War, in many ways had the entire management of the civil affairs. Then their duties were curtailed, or given to other officials under different enactments, which accurately determined their power as the growth of the town and the state demanded.

The General Court at Plymouth passed the first statute, creating this office and defining the duties of selectmen, in 1662. Their work was extended in 1666, 1681, and 1683 by further enactments, which provided that every town in the colony should, out of its freemen, choose from three to five selectmen, who should be approved by the court at Plymouth. They were to act as magistrates for the purpose of hearing and determining all matters of dispute among the inhabitants of the town not exceeding forty shillings; they were also to hear and determine differences between the Indians and white inhabitants in reference to damages done by their domestic animals; they had power to summon witnesses and administer oaths; the matters submitted to their determination were to be heard upon competent evidence. Fines were to be imposed upon persons summoned who failed to attend at the time and place appointed for the hearing of these various causes. Their decisions could be appealed from by either party aggrieved, to the next General Court held at Plymouth, provided security was given for the costs which one might incur in prosecuting or defending such suits.

SEAL OF THE TOWN OF MIDDLEBORO

The judiciary powers thus conferred upon the selectmen continued until the uniting of the colonies in 1692, when the new charter from the Crown provided for some changes in the administration of justice, and the judicial functions heretofore performed by the selectmen were transferred to his Majesty's Justice of the Peace, an office of honor and distinction in the colony. The selectmen continued to have the general management of the affairs of the town; they were to encourage education; they were to take notice of all persons desiring a permanent settlement in the town, who came without the approbation of the governor and his assistants, according to the order of court, and it was their duty to notify the governor and council of such. It was also their duty to call to account those who neglected to attend public worship on the Lord's day, and to require satisfactory reasons for their failure to do so, and if any persisted in such neglect, to report their names to the General Court at Plymouth. They had power to provide for the wants of the poor in their respective towns, and such persons as were spendthrifts, or children disobedient to their parents, or persons living in families who were disorderly, or who refused to comply with reasonable requirements, were to be reported to the General Court at Plymouth. The precaution to be observed for a defence against any attack of the Indians, the building and maintaining a fort, and many other duties of a similar nature necessary for the proper protection and government of the town, were left entirely to their discretion.

The following were the selectmen from 1674 to 1900:—

1674. John Tomson, Jonathan Dunham, and Francis Coombs.
1675. John Tomson, Jonathan Dunham, and Francis Coombs.
1680. John Tomson, Francis Coombs, and Samuel Fuller.
1681. John Tomson, Francis Coombs, and John Nelson.
1682. John Tomson, Francis Coombs, and John Nelson.
1683. John Tomson, John Nelson, and Isaac Howland.
1684. John Tomson, Isaac Howland, and Samuel Wood.
1685. John Tomson, John Nelson, and Isaac Howland.
1686. John Tomson, John Nelson, and Isaac Howland.
1687. John Tomson, Isaac Howland, and John Allen.
1688. No record to be found.
1689. Samuel Wood, Joseph Vaughan, and Nathaniel Warren.
1690. Joseph Vaughan, Ebenezer Tinkham, and John Allen.
1691. Joseph Vaughan, Ebenezer Tinkham, and Samuel Wood.
1692. Isaac Howland, Joseph Vaughan, and John Bennett.
1693. Joseph Vaughan, John Bennett, and Samuel Wood.

1694. Joseph Vaughan, Samuel Wood, and Obadiah Eddy.
1695. Ens. Isaac Howland, Joseph Vaughan, and John Bennett.
1696. Isaac Howland, Joseph Vaughan, and Ebenezer Tinkham.
1697. Joseph Vaughan, John Bennett, and Jacob Tomson.
1698. Joseph Vaughan, John Bennett, and Jacob Tomson.
1699. Joseph Vaughan, Samuel Wood, and Jacob Tomson.
1700. Isaac Howland, Ebenezer Tinkham, and Jacob Tomson.
1701. Isaac Howland, Lieut. Jacob Tomson, and Ens. Vaughan.
1702. Isaac Howland, Joseph Vaughan, and John Allen.
1703. Isaac Howland, David Thomas, and Thomas Tomson.
1704. Joseph Vaughan, Thomas Pratt, and Thomas Tomson.
1705. No record.
1706. Ens. Joseph Vaughan, Samuel Wood, and Jacob Tomson.
1707. Ens. Joseph Vaughan, Samuel Wood, and Jacob Tomson.
1708. Lieut. Joseph Vaughan, Samuel Wood, and Jacob Tomson.
1709. Lieut. Joseph Vaughan, Samuel Wood, and Capt. Jacob Tomson.
1710. Lieut. Joseph Vaughan, Ens. Elkanah Leonard, and Rodolphus Elmes.
1711. Samuel Wood, Jacob Tomson, and Elkanah Leonard.
1712. Capt. Jacob Tomson, Lieut. Joseph Vaughan, and Ens. Elkanah Leonard.
1713. Capt. Jacob Tomson, Lieut. Joseph Vaughan, and Ens. Elkanah Leonard.
1714. Capt. Jacob Tomson, Lieut. Joseph Vaughan, and Ens. Elkanah Leonard.
1715. Capt. Jacob Tomson, Peter Bennett, and Rodolphus Elmes.
1716. Capt. Jacob Tomson, Lieut. Joseph Vaughan, and John Bennett, Jr.
1717. Capt. Jacob Tomson, Capt. Joseph Vaughan, and John Bennett, Jr.
1718. Capt. Jacob Tomson, Capt. Joseph Vaughan, and John Bennett.
1719. Jacob Tomson, John Bennett, and Ichabod Southworth.
1720. Capt. Jacob Tomson, Capt. Joseph Vaughan, and John Bennett.
1721. Capt. Jacob Tomson, John Bennett, and Lieut. Ichabod Southworth.
1722. Capt. Jacob Tomson, Capt. Joseph Vaughan, and Lieut. Ichabod Southworth.

1723. Capt. Jacob Tomson, John Bennett, and Deacon Samuel Barrows.
1724. Capt. Jacob Tomson, John Bennett, and Deacon Samuel Barrows.
1725. Capt. Jacob Tomson, Lieut. Nathaniel Southworth, and Deacon Samuel Barrows.
1726. Capt. Jacob Tomson, Deacon Samuel Barrows, and Lieut. Nathaniel Southworth.
1727. Capt. Jacob Tomson, Deacon Samuel Barrows, and Lieut. Nathaniel Southworth.
1728. Deacon Samuel Barrows, Capt. Ichabod Southworth, John Bennett, John Tinkham, and Elkanah Leonard.
1729. Deacon Samuel Barrows, Capt. Ichabod Southworth, John Bennett, Lieut. Nathaniel Southworth, and John Tinkham.
1730. Deacon Samuel Barrows, Capt. Ichabod Southworth, Lieut. Nathaniel Southworth, John Bennett, and John Tinkham.
1731. Deacon Samuel Barrows, Capt. Ichabod Southworth, Lieut. Nathaniel Southworth, John Bennett, and John Tinkham.
1732. Deacon Samuel Barrows, Capt. Ichabod Southworth, John Bennett, John Tinkham, and Thomas Nelson.
1733. Deacon Samuel Barrows, Capt. Ichabod Southworth, John Bennett, Elkanah Leonard, and Jacob Tomson.
1734. Deacon Samuel Barrows, Capt. Ichabod Southworth, John Bennett, Elkanah Leonard, and Jacob Tomson.
1735. Capt. Ichabod Southworth, John Bennett, Jacob Tomson, Elkanah Leonard, and Benjamin White, Esq
1736. John Bennett, Capt. Nathaniel Southworth, Jacob Tomson, Elkanah Leonard, and Benjamin White, Esq.
1737. John Bennett, Nathaniel Southworth, Jacob Tomson, Elkanah Leonard, Esq., Benjamin White, Esq.
1738. John Bennett, Capt. Nathaniel Southworth, Jacob Tomson, Elkanah Leonard, and Benjamin White, Esq.
1739. John Bennett, Capt. Nathaniel Southworth, Jacob Tomson, Elkanah Leonard, Esq., and Benjamin White, Esq.
1740. John Bennett, Capt. Nathaniel Southworth, Jacob Tomson, Elkanah Leonard, Esq., and Benjamin White, Esq.
1741. John Bennett, Capt. Nathaniel Southworth, Jacob Tomson, Elkanah Leonard, Esq., and Benjamin White, Esq.
1742. Capt. Nathaniel Southworth, Jacob Tomson, Benjamin White, Esq., Ens. Jonathan Smith, and Deacon John Hackett.

1743. John Bennett, Capt. Ichabod Southworth, Capt. Nathaniel Southworth, Lieut. Jacob Tomson, and Benjamin White, Esq.
1744. Deacon Samuel Barrows, Capt. Ichabod Southworth, Capt. Nathaniel Southworth, Deacon Samuel Wood, and Capt. Ebenezer Morton.
1745. Capt. Ichabod Southworth, Capt. Nathaniel Southworth, Lieut. Jacob Tomson, Capt. Ebenezer Morton, and Peter Oliver, Esq.
1746. Capt. Ichabod Southworth, Capt. Nathaniel Southworth, Lieut. Jacob Tomson, Capt. Ebenezer Morton, and Peter Oliver, Esq.
1747. John Bennett, Capt. Ichabod Southworth, Capt. Nathaniel Southworth, Lieut. Jacob Tomson, and Capt. Ebenezer Morton.
1748. Capt. Ichabod Southworth, Peter Oliver, Esq., Lieut. Jonathan Smith, Nathaniel Smith, and Deacon Benjamin Tucker.
1749. Capt. Ichabod Southworth, Lieut. Jonathan Smith, Nathaniel Smith, Deacon Benjamin Tucker, and John Weston.
1750. Capt. Ichabod Southworth, Lieut. Jonathan Smith, Nathaniel Smith, Deacon Benjamin Tucker, and John Weston.
1751. Lieut. Jonathan Smith, Capt. Nathaniel Smith, Deacon Benjamin Tucker, Thomas Nelson, Jr., and Elias Miller.
1752. Lieut. Jonathan Smith, Capt. Nathaniel Smith, Deacon Benjamin Tucker, Thomas Nelson, Jr., and Elias Miller.
1753. Lieut. Jonathan Smith, Thomas Nelson, Jr., and Elias Miller.
1754. Lieut. Jonathan Smith, Thomas Nelson, Jr., and Elias Miller.
1755. Elias Miller, Elder Mark Haskell, and Joseph Tinkham.
1756. Elias Miller, Elder Mark Haskell, and Joseph Tinkham.
1757. Elias Miller, Lieut. Thomas Nelson, and Joseph Thompson.
1758. Lieut. Thomas Nelson, John Thompson, Gershom Cobb, David Alden, and Ens. Isaac Peirce.
1759. Lieut. Thomas Nelson, John Thompson, David Alden, John Montgomery, and Henry Thomas.
1760. Lieut. Thomas Nelson, John Montgomery, Henry Thomas, Lieut. Benjamin White, and Ichabod Wood.
1761. Lieut. Thomas Nelson, John Montgomery, Henry Thomas, Lieut. Benjamin White, Ichabod Wood.
1762. Lieut. Benjamin White, Ichabod Wood, Samuel Snow, Capt. Nathaniel Smith, and William Harlow.

1763. Lieut. Thomas Nelson, Lieut. Benjamin White, Ichabod Wood, William Harlow, and Capt. Gideon Southworth.
1764. Lieut. Thomas Nelson, Lieut. Benjamin White, Ichabod Wood, John Thompson, and Gideon Southworth.
1765. Lieut. Thomas Nelson, Lieut. Benjamin White, Ichabod Wood, Capt. Gideon Southworth, and Hon. Peter Oliver.
1766. Capt. Nathaniel Smith, Ichabod Wood, John Montgomery, Capt. Ebenezer Sproutt, and Joshua White.
1767. Capt. Nathaniel Smith, Joshua White, Capt. Ebenezer Sproutt, Nathaniel Wood, and Edward Washburn.
1768. Capt. Ebenezer Sproutt, John Montgomery, Joshua White, Ens. Nathaniel Wood, and Zebulon Leonard.
1769. John Montgomery, Joshua White, Zebulon Leonard, Ens. Nathaniel Wood, and Nathaniel Bumpus.
1770. John Montgomery, Joshua White, Ichabod Wood, Zebulon Leonard, and Capt. Ebenezer Sproutt.
1771. John Montgomery, Ichabod Wood, Zebulon Leonard, Capt. Ebenezer Sproutt, and Capt. Benjamin White.
1772. John Montgomery, Ichabod Wood, Zebulon Leonard, Capt. Ebenezer Sproutt, and Capt. Benjamin White.
1773. Capt. Ebenezer Sproutt, Capt. Benjamin White, Zebulon Leonard, Capt. William Canedy, and Jacob Bennett.
1774. Capt. Ebenezer Sproutt, Capt. Benjamin White, William Harlow, George Leonard, and Nathaniel Sampson.
1775. Maj. Ebenezer Sproutt, Capt. Joshua White, William Harlow, George Leonard, and Nathaniel Sampson.
1776. William Harlow, George Leonard, Nathaniel Sampson, Capt. Nathaniel Wood, and Abner Kingman.
1777. William Harlow, Nathaniel Sampson, Capt. Nathaniel Wood, Lieut. Abner Kingman, and Amos Nelson.
1778. Capt. Nathaniel Wood, Lieut. Abner Kingman, Maj. John Nelson, Deacon Amos Nelson, and Isaac Thompson.
1779. Isaac Thompson, Edmund Wood, Thomas Nelson, John Alden, and Henry Strobridge.
1780. Isaac Thompson, Edmund Wood, Thomas Nelson, John Alden, and Henry Strobridge.
1781. Isaac Thompson, Thomas Nelson, Lieut. John Murdock, Lieut. Ezra Harlow, and Rufus Richmond.
1782. Isaac Thompson, Thomas Nelson, Lieut. John Murdock, Capt. Ezra Harlow, and Rufus Richmond.

1783. Isaac Thompson, Thomas Nelson, Lieut. John Murdock, Rufus Richmond, and Zachariah Weston.
1784. Isaac Thompson, Thomas Nelson, Capt. Ezra Harlow, Rufus Richmond, and Capt. Abner Bourne.
1785. Isaac Thompson, Thomas Nelson, Capt. Ezra Harlow, Rufus Richmond, and Capt. Abner Bourne.
1786. Isaac Thompson, Thomas Nelson, Capt. Ezra Harlow, Rufus Richmond, and Capt. Abner Bourne.
1787. Capt. Ezra Harlow, Joshua White, Esq., Lieut. Peter Hoar, Isaac Soul, and Noah Clark.
1788. Isaac Thompson, Thomas Nelson, Rufus Richmond, Capt. Abner Bourne, and Nehemiah Bennett.
1789. Isaac Thompson, Esq., Thomas Nelson, Rufus Richmond, Capt. Abner Bourne, and Nehemiah Bennett.
1790. Isaac Thompson, Rufus Richmond, Lieut. John Murdock, Nehemiah Bennett, Capt. Perez Churchill, Capt. James Peirce, and Lieut. Robert Strobridge.
1791. Isaac Thompson, Esq., Nehemiah Bennett, David Richmond, Zebulon Leonard, and Hugh Montgomery.
1792. Isaac Thompson, Esq., Nehemiah Bennett, David Richmond, Zebulon Leonard, and Hugh Montgomery.
1793. Isaac Thompson, Nehemiah Bennett, David Richmond, Zebulon Leonard, and Hugh Montgomery.
1794. Hon. Isaac Thompson, Nehemiah Bennett, David Richmond, Zebulon Leonard, and Hugh Montgomery.
1795. Hon. Isaac Thompson, Nehemiah Bennett, Esq., Capt. Peter Hoar, Hugh Montgomery, and Zephaniah Shaw.
1796. Hon. Isaac Thompson, David Richmond, Hugh Montgomery, Capt. Peter Hoar, Capt. John Carver.
1797. Hon. Isaac Thompson, Nehemiah Bennett, Esq., David Richmond, Hugh Montgomery, and Rufus Richmond.
1798. Nehemiah Bennett, Esq., David Richmond, Hugh Montgomery, Rufus Richmond, and Samuel Tucker.
1799. Lieut. John Tinkham, Ens. John Morton, Samuel Tucker, Samuel Pickens, and Zephaniah Shaw.
1800. Lieut. John Tinkham, Capt. John Morton, Samuel Tucker, Samuel Pickens, and Zephaniah Shaw.
1801. Maj. Peter Hoar, Lieut. John Tinkham, Samuel Tucker, Samuel Pickens, and Luke Reed.

1802. Maj. Peter Hoar, Lieut. John Tinkham, Capt. John Morton, Samuel Tucker, and Luke Reed.

1803. Maj. Peter Hoar, Lieut. John Tinkham, Capt. John Morton, Samuel Tucker, and Luke Reed.

1804. Lieut. John Tinkham, Capt. John Morton, Samuel Pickens, Luke Reed, and Elijah Shaw.

1805. Capt. John Morton, Samuel Pickens, Luke Reed, Capt. William Thompson, and Ens. Samuel Cobb.

1806. Capt. John Morton, Samuel Pickens, Luke Reed, Capt. William Thompson, and Ens. Samuel Cobb.

1807. Maj. Peter Hoar, Samuel Pickens, Capt. Calvin Pratt, Joseph Cushman, and Lieut. Seth Miller.

1808. Maj. Peter Hoar, Samuel Pickens, Esq., Capt. Calvin Pratt, Lieut. Joseph Cushman (2d), and Martin Keith.

1809. Maj. Peter Hoar, Samuel Pickens, Esq., Capt. Calvin Pratt, Lieut. Joseph Cushman (2d), and Martin Keith.

1810. Maj. Peter Hoar, Samuel Pickens, Esq., Luke Reed, Lieut. Seth Miller, Jr., and Thomas Weston.

1811. Maj. Peter Hoar, Samuel Pickens, Esq., Capt. Calvin Pratt, Lieut. Seth Miller, Jr., and Thomas Weston.

1812. Peter Hoar, Esq., Samuel Pickens, Esq., Luke Reed, Seth Miller, Jr., Esq., and Thomas Weston, Esq.

1813. Peter Hoar, Esq., Samuel Pickens, Esq., Luke Reed, Seth Miller, Jr., Esq., and Thomas Weston, Esq.

1814. Peter Hoar, Esq., Samuel Pickens, Esq., Thomas Weston, Esq., William Nelson, and Seth Eaton, Jr.

1815. Peter Hoar, Esq., Samuel Pickens, Esq., Thomas Weston, Esq., William Nelson, and Seth Eaton, Jr.

1816. Samuel Pickens, Esq., Thomas Weston, Esq., William Nelson, Seth Eaton, Jr., and Samuel Bates.

1817. Thomas Weston, Esq., William Nelson, Seth Eaton, Jr., Samuel Bates, and Capt. Ebenezer Pickens.

1818. Thomas Weston, Esq., William Nelson, Seth Eaton, Jr., Capt. Ebenezer Pickens, and Capt. Enoch Haskins.

1819. William Nelson, Seth Eaton, Jr., Capt. Enoch Haskins, Capt. Samuel Thompson, and Abner Clark.

1820. Seth Miller, Jr., Esq., Seth Eaton, Jr., Capt. Enoch Haskins, Capt. Samuel Thompson, and Abner Clark.

1821. Seth Miller, Jr., Esq., Seth Eaton, Jr., Capt. Enoch Haskins, Capt. Samuel Thompson, and Abner Clark.

1822. Seth Miller, Jr., Esq., Seth Eaton, Jr., Capt. Enoch Haskins, Capt. Samuel Thompson, and Lieut. Abner Clark.

1823. Seth Miller, Jr., Esq., Seth Eaton, Esq., Capt. Enoch Haskins, Capt. Samuel Thompson, and Abner Clark, Esq.

1824. Seth Miller, Esq., Seth Eaton, Esq., Capt. Enoch Haskins, Capt. Samuel Thompson, and Abner Clark, Esq.

1825. Seth Eaton, Esq., Capt. Enoch Haskins, Capt. Samuel Thompson, Abner Clark, Esq., and Samuel Harlow.

1826. Capt. Enoch Haskins, Capt. Samuel Thompson, Luther Washburn, and Nathan Washburn.

1827. Luther Washburn, Nathan Washburn, Samuel Harlow, Bradford Harlow, and Andrew Haskins.

1828. Luther Washburn, Nathan Washburn, Samuel Harlow, Andrew Haskins, and Reuel Thompson.

1829. Luther Washburn, Nathan Washburn, Andrew Haskins, Reuel Thompson, and Col. Benjamin P. Wood.

1830. Luther Washburn, Nathan Washburn, Andrew Haskins, Reuel Thompson, and Col. Benjamin P. Wood.

1831. Luther Washburn, Seth Eaton, Andrew Haskins, Bradford Harlow, and Col. Benjamin P. Wood.

1832. Seth Eaton, Esq., Andrew Haskins, Bradford Harlow, Col. Benjamin P. Wood, and Ethan Peirce.

1833. Bradford Harlow, Col. Benjamin P. Wood, Andrew Haskins, Capt. Eathan Peirce, and Lieut.-Col. Oliver Eaton.

1834. Bradford Harlow, Capt. Jonathan Cobb, Capt. Ethan Peirce, Capt. Nathaniel Staples, and Gamaliel Rounseville.

1835. Bradford Harlow, Capt. Jonathan Cobb, Luther Washburn, Capt. Nathaniel Staples, and Gamaliel Rounseville.

1836. Bradford Harlow, Capt. Jonathan Cobb, Luther Washburn, Capt. Nathaniel Staples, and Gamaliel Rounseville.

1837. Bradford Harlow, Capt. Jonathan Cobb, Luther Washburn, Capt. Nathaniel Staples, and Gamaliel Rounseville.

1838. Bradford Harlow, Capt. Jonathan Cobb, Gamaliel Rounseville, Zattu Pickens, Jr., and Thomas Doggett.

1839. Bradford Harlow, Gamaliel Rounseville, Zattu Pickens, Jr., Thomas Doggett, and Stillman Benson.

1840. Bradford Harlow, Gamaliel Rounseville, Zattu Pickens, Jr., Thomas Doggett, and Stillman Benson.

1841. Bradford Harlow, Gamaliel Rounseville, Zattu Pickens, Jr., Thomas Doggett, and Stillman Benson.

1842. Bradford Harlow, Gamaliel Rounseville, Zattu Pickens, Jr., Thomas Doggett, and Stillman Benson.
1843. Bradford Harlow, Gamaliel Rounseville, Zattu Pickens, Jr., Thomas Doggett, and Stillman Benson.
1844. Bradford Harlow, Gamaliel Rounseville, Zattu Pickens, Jr., Thomas Doggett, and Stillman Benson.
1845. Thomas Doggett, Stillman Benson, Jirah Winslow, Richard Sampson, and Venus Thompson.
1846. Thomas Doggett, Stillman Benson, Jirah Winslow, Richard Sampson, and Venus Thompson.
1847. Jirah Winslow, Venus Thompson, Ichabod F. Atwood, Williams Eaton, and Nathaniel Sampson.
1848. Ichabod F. Atwood, Williams Eaton, Otis Soule, Nathaniel Sampson, and Job Peirce.
1849. Ichabod F. Atwood, Williams Eaton, Otis Soule, Nathaniel Sampson, and Abiel P. Booth, Esq.
1850. Otis Soule, Zephaniah Shaw, Asa T. Winslow, Ansel Benson, and Apollos Haskins.
1851. Asa T. Winslow, Apollos Haskins, Zephaniah Shaw, Capt. Jonathan Cobb, and Samuel Thompson.
1852. Otis Soule, Apollos Haskins, Capt. Jonathan Cobb, Asa T. Winslow, and Everett Robinson.
1853. Otis Soule, Capt. Jonathan Cobb, Asa T. Winslow, Andrew Haskins, and Everett Robinson.
1854. Stillman Benson, Thomas J. Wood, and Joseph T. Wood.
1855. Joseph T. Wood, Nathaniel Shurtleff, and Lewis Soule.
1856. Col. Benjamin P. Wood, Lewis Soule, and Cornelius B. Wood.
1857. Col. Benjamin P. Wood, Lewis Soule, and Cornelius B. Wood.
1858. Col. Benjamin P. Wood, Lewis Soule, and Cornelius B. Wood.
1859. Col. Benjamin P. Wood, Cornelius B. Wood, and George W. Wood.
1860. Col. Benjamin P. Wood, Cornelius B. Wood, and George W. Wood.
1861. Col. Benjamin P. Wood, Cornelius B. Wood, and George W. Wood.
1862. Col. Benjamin P. Wood, Sidney Tucker, and Ira Smith.
1863. Joseph T. Wood, Ira Smith, and Alpheus K. Bishop.

1864. Joseph T. Wood, Ira Smith, and Alpheus K. Bishop.
1865. Joseph T. Wood, Joshua M. Eddy, and Abishai Miller..
1866. Joseph T. Wood, Joshua M. Eddy, and Abishai T. Clark.
1867. Joseph T. Wood, Joshua M. Eddy, and Thomas Smith.
1868. Joseph T. Wood, Thomas Smith, and Joshua M. Eddy.
1869. Joseph T. Wood, Thomas Smith, and Lewis Leonard.
1870. Joseph T. Wood, Lewis Leonard, and Isaac S. Cushman.
1871. Joseph T. Wood, Lewis Leonard, and Sylvester F. Cobb.
1872. Joseph T. Wood, Lewis Leonard, and Stillman Benson.
1873. Joseph T. Wood, Lewis Leonard, and Stillman Benson.
1874. Joseph T. Wood, Lewis Leonard, and Sylvester F. Cobb.
1875. Joseph T. Wood, Lewis Leonard, and Sylvester F. Cobb.
1876. Albert T. Savery, Alpheus K. Bishop, and Warren H. Southworth.[1]
1877. Joseph T. Wood, Albert T. Savery, and Alpheus K. Bishop.
1878. Joseph T. Wood, Albert T. Savery, and Alpheus K. Bishop.
1879. Joseph T. Wood, Albert T. Savery, and Abishai T. Clark.
1880. Joseph T. Wood, Albert T. Savery, and Nathaniel S. Cushing.
1881. Joseph T. Wood, Albert T. Savery, and Nathaniel S. Cushing.
1882. Joseph T. Wood, Albert T. Savery, and Nathaniel S. Cushing.
1883. Joseph T. Wood, Albert T. Savery, and Nathaniel S. Cushing.
1884. Joseph T. Wood, Albert T. Savery, and Nathaniel S. Cushing.
1885. Joseph T. Wood, Albert T. Savery, and Sylvanus Mendall.
1886. Joseph T. Wood, Albert T. Savery, and Sylvanus Mendall.
1887. Joseph T. Wood, Albert T. Savery, and Sylvanus Mendall.
1888. Joseph T. Wood, Albert T. Savery, and Sylvanus Mendall.
1889. Joseph T. Wood, Albert T. Savery, and Sylvanus Mendall.
1890. Albert T. Savery, Sylvanus Mendall, and Joseph E. Beals.
1891. Albert T. Savery, Jared F. Alden, and Joseph E. Beals.
1892. Albert T. Savery, Jared F. Alden, and Joseph E. Beals.
1893. Albert T. Savery, Jared F. Alden, and Edwin F. Witham.
1894. Albert T. Savery, Chas. W. Kingman, and Edwin F. Witham.
1895. Albert T. Savery, Chas. W. Kingman, and Edwin F. Witham.
1896. Albert T. Savery, Chas. W. Kingman, and Edwin F. Witham.
1897. Albert T. Savery, Chas. W. Kingman, and Edwin F. Witham.
1898. Albert T. Savery, Chas. W. Kingman, and Edwin F. Witham.
1899. Albert T. Savery, Chas. W. Kingman, and Edwin F. Witham.
1900. Albert T. Savery, Chas. W. Kingman, and Edwin F. Witham.

[1] W. H. Southworth was elected, but did not accept, and J. T. Wood was afterwards elected.

TOWN CLERKS

Among the offices which, under the colonial law, each town was obliged to have, was that of town clerk. By the statute of the General Court at Plymouth in 1646, it was enacted that in every town in the colony some one should be appointed as clerk, with the special duty of keeping a register of the marriages, births, and burials, and by a statute of 1671 he was required to publish all contracts of marriage. From the first he kept a record of the election of all officers, and the important votes and acts of the town. In many cases these were quite full and complete. The publishing of intentions of marriage was observed throughout the colony until about the middle of the last century, when it was discontinued by an act of the legislature. These were posted upon a bulletin prepared for the notices in the vestibule of the church.

There is a generally received tradition that William Hoskins [1] (sometimes spelled Haskins, and sometimes spelled Hodskins) was the first town clerk of Middleboro, but this is authenticated by no record. He was chosen by the town May 24, 1681, and according to tradition he had previously served for twelve years. He was one of the proprietors of the Twenty-six Men's Purchase, although at the breaking out of the war he was not in the fort. The rate of compensation for his services was fixed May 24, 1681, when the town agreed that he should receive for keeping their records, a load of fish, taken at the herring-weir and delivered at his house, for each year's services. His successors in this office usually served for a number of years, and their records, beginning with that of 1681, are full and accurate.

The following were town clerks from 1681 to 1900, with the date of election and the period for which they held this office: —

>William Hoskins, May 24, 1681, twelve years.
>John Bennett, March 28, 1693, thirteen years.
>Jacob Tomson, March 14, 1706, thirty years.

[1] See chapter on Early Settlers.

Nathan Bassett, March —, 1736, one year.
Jacob Tomson, March 16, 1737, seven years.
Seth Tinkham, March 14, 1744, one year.
Jacob Tomson, March 5, 1745, three years.
Ebenezer Sproutt, March 28, 1748, seven years.
Joseph Tinkham, March 31, 1755, twelve years.
John Morton, March 23, 1767, eight years.
Abner Barrows, March 13, 1775, six years.
Nathaniel Wilder, March 5, 1781, six years.
Jacob Bennett, March 5, 1787, one year.
Nathaniel Wilder, March 10, 1788, two years.
Cyrus Keith, March 1, 1790, fifteen years.
Sylvanus Tillson, March 11, 1805, seventeen years.
Isaac Stevens, May 8, 1822, eight years.
Reland Tinkham, March 3, 1830, two years.
Foster Tinkham, March 5, 1832, three years.
Allen Shaw, March 9, 1835, eleven years.
Jacob B. Shaw, March 9, 1846, three years.
Everett Robinson, March 5, 1849, two years.
George Pickens, March 10, 1851, four years.
Andrew M. Eaton, March 18, 1855. six years.
Sidney Tucker, March 11, 1861, two years.
John Shaw, Jr., March 9, 1863, one year.
Cornelius B. Wood, March 7, 1864, seventeen years.
Charles T. Thatcher, March —, 1881, to 1894.
Augustus M. Bearse, 1894 to 1898.
Amos H. Eaton, 1898 to the present time.

TOWN TREASURERS

The office of town treasurer was not created until after the union of the two colonies, when by a statute in 1693–94 it was enacted that there should be chosen in each town, at the time and in the same manner as other officers, "a town treasurer, who should have power to receive all debts and dues belonging or owing to such town or to the poor thereof, and to sue for and recover the same by due process of law ; also to pay out such monies according to order from the selectmen or officers of the poor as they shall receive instructions of the town, and such treasurer shall make a true account to the town of such payments and receipts when required."

It is impossible to state when the first town treasurer was chosen under this law. The first to fill this office was Ephraim Tinkham, who served until March 1, 1711. He had been a resident of the town for some time, and probably was duly chosen after the passage of this act, but of this we have no record excepting that he had been town treasurer up to March 1, 1711.

Town treasurers from 1711, with the date of their election and term of service: —

Ephraim Tinkham, from —— to March 1, 1711.
Deacon Jonathan Cobb, March 1, 1711, four years.
John Bennett, Jr., March 7, 1715, seventeen years.
Samuel Tinkham, March 17, 1732, three years.
Simon Lazel, March 17, 1735, one year.
Jacob Thompson, March —, 1736, eight years.
Benjamin Tucker, March 14, 1744, one year.
Jacob Thompson, March 5, 1745, three years.
Elias Miller, March 28, 1748, nine years.
John Thompson, March 14, 1757, ten years.
Captain Ebenezer Sproutt, March 23, 1767, two years.
John Morton, March 27, 1769, six years.
William Bennett, March 13, 1775, four years.
Nathaniel Wilder, March 1, 1779, twenty years.
George Morton, March 11, 1799, six years.
Levi Peirce, March 11, 1805, two years.
Sylvanus Tillson, March 2, 1807, fifteen years.
Levi Tinkham, May 8, 1822, five years.
Isaac Stevens, April 2, 1827, three years.
Reland Tinkham, March 3, 1830, one year.
Foster Tinkham, April 4, 1831, three years.
Allen Shaw, March 11, 1834, twelve years.
Jacob B. Shaw, March 9, 1846, three years.
Everett Robinson, March 5, 1849, two years.
George Pickens, March 10, 1851, four years.
Andrew M. Eaton, March 18, 1855, six years.
Sidney Tucker, March 11, 1861, two years.

John Shaw, Jr., March 9, 1863, one year.
Cornelius B. Wood, March 7, 1864, seventeen years.
Charles T. Thatcher, March —, 1881, to 1894.
Augustus M. Bearse, 1894 to 1898.
Amos H. Eaton, 1898 to the present time.

DEPUTIES

The deputies to the Plymouth Colony Court were very important officials in the Old Colony. As early as 1638, a law was enacted "that every town should make choice of two of their freemen, and the town of Plymouth four, to be the committees or deputies to join with the bench to enact and make all such laws and ordinances as shall be judged to be good and wholesome for the whole." These laws, however, "were to be propounded at one Court and not to be considered until the next Court, and afterwards to be confirmed, and that if any act, confirmed by the bench and committees, which, upon deliberation, shall prove prejudicial, the freemen may, upon the next election, repeal the same and enact others useful for the whole." The expenses of these deputies were to be borne by the town; they were to receive the votes, not only of the freemen, but of such others as had taken the oath of fidelity, masters of families and inhabitants of the towns in which they lived; and in order that the purity of this body might be carefully guarded, it was left for the bench and other members of the court to dismiss such individuals as they deemed improper, and for the town to choose other freemen in their place.

This act was passed in the early days, and the duties of the deputies were afterwards enlarged until they assumed all of the authority belonging to a legislative body acting for the benefit of the colony. In all matters which came before the magistrates they had an equal vote, and it was left with them to propose candidates for freemen. In the early history of Middleboro John Morton was chosen as the first deputy, for the years 1672 and 1673. In 1674 and 1675 John Tomson was the deputy, and there seem to have been no other deputies elected to represent the town until 1680, when John Tomson was reëlected, and served for seven years up to 1686. At the close of Andros's administration Isaac Howland was elected for the years 1689 to 1692, when the Plymouth and Massachusetts colonies were united under the name of the Province of Massachusetts Bay in New England, and from that time the officers who had performed similar service in the Plymouth Colony Court were known as representatives to the Great and General Court.

The representatives from Middleboro to the General Court of the Province of the Massachusetts Bay in New England from 1692 until 1905 were as follows: —

  1692. John Tomson, Isaac Howland.
  1693–1714. No record.
  1715. John Bennett, Jr.
  1716. Capt. Jacob Tomson.
  1717. Malachi Holloway.
  1718. John Bennett.
  1719. Capt. Jacob Tomson.
  1720. Dea. Samuel Barrows.
  1721. John Bennett.
  1722. Lieut. Ichabod Southworth.
  1723. Edward Thomas.
  1724. Nathaniel Southworth.
  1725–28. Lieut. Nathaniel Southworth.
  1729. Samuel Wood.
  1730–31. Samuel Barrows.
  1732. Lieut. Nathaniel Southworth.
  1733–34. Dea. Samuel Barrows.
  1735–37. Elkanah Leonard, Esq.
  1738. John Bennett.
  1739–43. Elkanah Leonard, Esq.
  1744–45. Dea. Samuel Wood.
  1746. Benjamin Tucker.
  1747–48. Samuel Bennett.
  1749. Peter Oliver.
  1750. Voted not to send.

1751. Peter Oliver, Esq.
1752. No record.
1753-54. Capt. Nathaniel Smith.
1755-56. Ebenezer Sproutt.
1757. Capt. Nathaniel Smith.
1758-64. Capt. Ebenezer Sproutt.
1765. Daniel Oliver, Esq.
1766-67. Capt. Ebenezer Sproutt.
1768-69. Capt. Benjamin White.
1770. Capt. Ebenezer Sproutt.
1771-72. Capt. Benjamin White.
1773-74. Mr. Ebenezer Sproutt.
1775. Capt. Joshua White.
1776-77. Benjamin Thomas.
1777. Nathaniel Sampson.
1778. Maj. John Nelson.
1779. Dea. Benjamin Thomas.
1780. Dr. Samuel Clark.
1781-82. Ebenezer Wood.
1782. Isaac Thompson.
1783. Isaac Thompson.
1784. Isaac Thompson, Zebulon Sproat.
1785-86. Isaac Thompson.
1787. Joshua White, Esq., Ebenezer Wood, Perez Thomas, Noah Fearing, Esq.
1788. Benjamin Thomas.
1789. Zebulon Leonard.
1790. Zebulon Leonard, James Sproat.
1791-92. James Sproat, Esq.
1793. Nehemiah Bennett.
1794. James Sproat, Esq.
1795-98. Nathaniel Wilder.
1799. Capt. Nathaniel Wilder.
1800. Nathaniel Wilder.
1801-02. John Tinkham.
1803-04. Lieut. John Tinkham.
1805. Lieut. John Tinkham, John Morton, Levi Peirce, Chillingworth Foster.
1806. Lieut. John Tinkham, Capt. John Morton, Levi Peirce, Dr. Chillingworth Foster.

1807. John Tinkham, Levi Peirce, Maj. Jacob Cushman, Samuel Pickens.
1808. John Tinkham, Esq., Levi Peirce, Maj. Jacob Cushman, Samuel Pickens, Esq.
1809. Maj. Levi Peirce, Samuel Pickens, Esq., Maj. Peter Hoar, Thomas Weston.
1810. Samuel Pickens, Esq., Maj. Peter Hoar, Thomas Weston, Martin Keith, Esq., Hercules Cushman.
1811. Maj. Peter Hoar, Thomas Weston, Esq., Martin Keith, Esq., Hercules Cushman, Esq., Capt. Calvin Pratt.
1812. Thomas Weston, Esq., Martin Keith, Esq., Calvin Pratt, Esq., Maj. Levi Peirce, Rev. Joseph Barker.
1813. Rev. Joseph Barker.
1814-1815. Thomas Weston, Esq.
1816. Samuel Pickens, Esq.
1817-18. Seth Miller, Jr., Esq.
1819. Thomas Weston. Esq.
1820. Had no representative.
1821. Martin Keith, Esq.
1822. Seth Miller, Jr., Esq.
1823-24. Isaac Stevens, Esq.
1825. Seth Eaton, Arad Thompson, Thomas Sturtevant, Esq.
1826. Seth Eaton.
1827. William Nelson, Esq.
1828. Seth Eaton, Esq., William Nelson, Esq., Zachariah Eddy, Esq.
1829. Seth Eaton, Esq., William Nelson, Esq., Zachariah Eddy, Esq., Gen. Ephraim Ward, Oliver Peirce, Esq., John Benson.
1830. Hon. Hercules Cushman.
1831. Hon. Hercules Cushman, Silas Pickens, Ziba Eaton, Andrew Haskins, Samuel Thompson, Esq., Elisha Clarke.
1832. Col. Benj. P. Wood, Reland Tinkham, Esq., Bradford Harlow, Capt. Nathaniel Staples, Luther Washburn, Tisdale Lincoln.
1833. Col. Benj. P. Wood, Bradford Harlow, Luther Washburn, Ephraim Leach, John Perkins, Capt. Ethan Peirce.
1834. Col. Benj. P. Wood, Samuel Thompson, Esq., Ephraim Leach, John Perkins, Capt. Ethan Peirce, Luther Murdock.
1835. Samuel Thompson, Esq., Andrew Haskins, Capt. Ethan Peirce, Ansel Benson.
1836. Andrew Hoskins, Ansel Benson, Capt. Jonathan Cobb, Reuben Hafford, Gamaliel Rounseville, George Atwood.

REPRESENTATIVES

1837. Gen. Ephraim Ward, Andrew Hoskins, Jonathan Cobb, Esq., Reuben Hafford, Gamaliel Rounseville, Lothrop Thomas, George Atwood.
1838. Tisdale Leonard, Eliab Ward, Esq., Stillman Benson.
1839. Tisdale Leonard, Eliab Ward, Esq., Stillman Benson, Zebulon K. Pratt.
1840. Zebulon K. Pratt, Dr. George Sturtevant, Consider Fuller, Thomas Doggett.
1841. Consider Fuller, Thomas Doggett.
1842. Eliab Ward, Esq., Dr. George Sturtevant.
1843-44. Dr. Morrill Robinson, William Shurtleff (2d).
1845-46. Capt. Josiah Tinkham, Asa T. Winslow.
1847. Cephas Shaw, Nahum M. Tribou.
1848. Cephas Shaw, Nahum M. Tribou.
1849. None sent.
1850-52. Joshua Wood, Everett Robinson.
1852. Joseph T. Wood, Eliab Ward.
1853. None sent.
1854. Joseph T. Wood, Richard Sampson.
1855. Col. Nathan King.
1856. Soranus Standish, Jared Pratt (2d).
1857. William H. Wood.
1858. Foster Tinkham.
1859. Everett Robinson.
1860. Andrew M. Eaton.
1861. Francis M. Vaughan.
1862. Andrew J. Pickens.
1863. Everett Robinson.
1864-65. George Soule.
1866-67. Andrew C. Wood.
1868. Levi A. Abbott.
1869. Augustus Pratt.
1870-71. Henry H. Shaw.
1872. Noah C. Perkins.
1873-74. John Shaw.
1875. John B. LeBaron.
1876-77. Isaac Winslow.
1878. James P. Peirce of Lakeville.
1879. Mathew H. Cushing.
1880. James L. Jenney.

1881-82. John C. Sullivan.
1883. Sprague S. Stetson of Lakeville.
1884-85. Albert T. Savery.
1886-87. James H. Harlow.
1888. Sidney T. Nelson of Lakeville.
1889. Jared F. Alden.
1890. Charles W. Turner.
1891. Charles W. Turner.
1892. George L. Soule.
1893. Jabez P. Thompson of Halifax.
1894. George L. Soule.
1895-96. Samuel S. Bourne.
1897-98. David G. Pratt.
1899-1900. William C. Litchfield.
1901. William Perkins, Jr., of Plympton.
1902-03. William A. Andrews.
1904-05. George R. Sampson.

JUSTICES OF THE PEACE

There was no resident of the town who held the commission of a justice of the peace until 1720. From early days to the commencement of the Revolutionary War, this was considered an office of great honor all through the colony; many of the duties of the selectmen were transferred to his Majesty's justices of the peace, who had civil jurisdiction in all matters of debt, trespass, etc., wherein the claim did not involve the title of their lands nor exceed forty shillings in amount. They were bound to keep a regular record of their proceedings, and from time to time their jurisdiction was extended to cover certain criminal offences which might be brought to and passed upon by them, with power to enforce their verdicts as the statutes provided. They held their office for the term of seven years, if during that time they conducted themselves properly in the discharge of said office. Most of the justices so appointed, at the expiration of that time had their commission renewed for a further term of seven years. In addition to the judicial power entrusted to this office, they could administer oaths, take the acknowledgment of deeds, and other legal instruments, and were generally conservators of the peace in the community.

This office in early times was invariably filled by the most prominent men of the towns. The duties continued substantially the same until trial justices were appointed within certain districts, who had exclusive jurisdiction in the trial of civil and criminal causes.

The justices of the peace for the town up to the year 1850 were as follows: —

July 22, 1720, Jacob Tomson
June 22, 1736, Elkanah Leonard
Aug. 18, 1744, Peter Oliver
June 26, 1755, John Fearing
Oct. 31, 1760, Joseph Tinkham
Aug. 28, 1775, Ebenezer Sproutt
Aug. 28, 1775, Joshua White
April 7, 1787, Samuel Clark
April 26, 1787, Isaac Thompson
July 5, 1789, James Sproat
July 18, 1791, John Nelson
Feb. 20, 1795, Nehemiah Bennett
March 2, 1800, Wilkes Wood
May 24, 1800, David Richmond
Feb. 20, 1804, James Washburn
Jan. 23, 1808, Samuel Pickens
Feb. 23, 1808, John Tinkham
March 5, 1808, William Thompson
Feb. 17, 1810, Zachariah Eddy
Sept. 3, 1810, Martin Keith
Feb. 5, 1811, Peter Hoar
Feb. 22, 1811, Thomas Weston
Nov. 14, 1811, Seth Miller, Jr.
Oct. 29, 1811, Hercules Cushman
Jan. 25, 1812, Calvin Pratt
Aug. 3, 1812, William Canedy
June 9, 1813, Jacob Bennett
June 9, 1813, Cyrus Keith
June 9, 1813, Thomas Sturtevant
Oct. 29, 1814, Abiel Washburn
Feb. 16, 1816, William Bourne
June 10, 1817, Charles Hooper
Feb. 3, 1818, Noah Clark
Jan. 23, 1819, Joshua Eddy, Jr.
June 19, 1819, Levi Peirce
Sept. 7, 1821, Amos Washburn
Nov. 21, 1821, Thomas Bennett
Jan. 16, 1822, Ebenezer Pickens
Jan. 23, 1822, Isaac Stevens
Jan. 16, 1823, Abner Clark
Aug. 26, 1823, Abiel P. Boothe
Feb. 17, 1824, William Nelson
Feb. 17, 1824, Oliver Peirce
July 1, 1825, Peter H. Peirce
Feb. 15, 1826, Samuel Thompson
Jan. 2, 1828, Seth Eaton
June 11, 1829, Paul Hathaway
June 9, 1830, Arad Thompson
June 16, 1831, Reland Tinkham
April 24, 1832, Joshua Haskins, Jr.
March 26, 1833, Benjamin P. Wood
March 26, 1833, Bradford Harlow
Aug. 24, 1835, Luther Washburn
March 18, 1836, Jonathan Cobb
Jan. 27, 1837, Abiezer T. Harvey
March 15, 1837, Silas Pickens
March 6, 1838, Eliab Ward
Aug. 24, 1841, Abishai T. Clark

March 31, 1842, Cornelius B. Wood
Dec. 17, 1842, Bela Kingman
Jan. 5, 1843, Nathan King
March 14, 1843, Gamaliel Rounseville
March 14, 1843, George Sturtevant
March 14, 1843, Stillman Benson
Sept. 20, 1843, Tisdale Leonard
Oct. 31, 1843, Andrew Weston
Feb. 3, 1844, William H. Wood
July 1, 1845, James G. Thompson
March 31, 1846, Apollos Haskins
July 7, 1848, Everett Robinson
June 5, 1849, Philander Washburn
Oct. 2, 1849, Ichabod F. Atwood
April 25, 1850, Zebulon Pratt

TRIAL JUSTICE

Ebenezer Pickens

By various legislative enactments the number of trial justices throughout the commonwealth have been much reduced, and their jurisdiction transferred to the various police, district, and municipal courts.

Between the years 1850 and 1868, the office of trial justice for the town was held by Ebenézer Pickens, after which the jurisdiction was enlarged by the creation of a district court under the name of the Fourth Plymouth District Court.

FOURTH PLYMOUTH DISTRICT COURT

This court was established by an act of the legislature in the year 1874, having the usual criminal and civil jurisdiction of the district courts of the commonwealth, embracing the towns of Middleboro, Wareham, Lakeville, Marion, and Mattapoisett, with courts held at Middleboro and Wareham.

JUSTICES

Francis M. Vaughan, appd. 1874, died 1891
George D. Alden, appd. 1892, resigned 1901
Nathan Washburn, appd. 1901

SPECIAL JUSTICES

Andrew L. Tinkham, appd. 1874, died 1887
Lemuel LeB. Holmes, appd. 1874, resigned 1895

Nathan Washburn, appd. 1888, appd. Justice 1901
George W. Stetson, appd. 1895, resigned 1900
Dennis D. Sullivan, appd. 1900
Bert J. Allan, appd. 1901

CLERK

William L. Chipham, of Wareham, 1874 up to the present time

MANDAMUS COUNCILLOR
August 9, 1774, Peter Oliver

The appointment of Peter Oliver and others as Mandamus Councillors was one of the acts of the British Government against what was believed to be the just rights of the colonists as granted by their charter, and which perhaps did much to provoke open resistance to the Crown and led to the ultimate separation of the colonies from the mother country.

In 1774, with the change on the part of the Crown in the appointment of the judges of the courts, the privilege of electing councillors was taken away from the legislature of the province, and their commissions were given directly from the Crown. These mandamus councillors were held in greater odium by the colonists than any other officers appointed by the king. So great was the feeling against them that jurors in many counties refused to serve under judges who were mandamus councillors, or who had received their commission from the governor and these councillors. It was among the first acts of rebellion which soon after led to open rupture at Lexington. It is doubtful whether Judge Oliver ever assumed the duties of this office, but his appointment as the chief justice of the highest court of the province tended greatly to excite the enmity, not only of the people of the town, but throughout the whole province, and his blameless life did not shelter him from bitter opprobrium.

With the evacuation of Boston, in 1776, by the British troops, the office became extinct.

REPRESENTATIVE TO THE NATIONAL CONGRESS

1805–09, Joseph Barker

MEMBERS OF CONVENTION FOR FRAMING A CONSTITUTION OF GOVERNMENT FOR THE STATE OF MASSACHUSETTS BAY

1779, John Miller
1779, Captain William Shaw

MEMBERS OF CONSTITUTIONAL CONVENTION TO ADOPT THE CONSTITUTION OF THE UNITED STATES

1788, Rev. Isaac Backus
1788, Benjamin Thomas
1788, Isaac Thompson
1788, Isaac Soule

MEMBERS OF CONSTITUTIONAL CONVENTIONS

Nov. 15, 1820, Levi Peirce
Nov. 15, 1820, Samuel Pickens
Nov. 15, 1820, Thomas Weston
Nov. 15, 1820, Seth Miller, Jr.
May 4, 1853, William H. Wood
May 4, 1853, Noah C. Perkins

JUDGES OF PROBATE COURT

1821–43, Wilkes Wood
1858–72, Wm. Henry Wood

REGISTER OF THE COURT OF INSOLVENCY

1857–58, Nathan King

This court, in 1858, was abolished, and its duties assumed by the Probate Court, which became a Court of Probate and Insolvency.

REGISTER OF THE COURT OF PROBATE AND INSOLVENCY

1889 to the present time, John C. Sullivan

HIGH SHERIFF

1845–54, Branch Harlow

CLERK OF COUNTY COURTS

1811–13, Hercules Cushman

JUDGE OF THE COURT OF SESSIONS
1828, Thomas Weston

This court was abolished in the year 1828, and a board of County Commissioners was established, having jurisdiction and duties similar to those which had been exercised by the Court of Sessions.

COUNTY COMMISSIONERS

1828–34, Thomas Weston
1847–56, Ebenezer Pickens
1873–82, Joseph T. Wood

PUBLIC OFFICERS
SENATORS

1796–1805, Isaac Thompson
1813–16, Wilkes Wood
1815–17, Thomas Weston
1820–22, William Bourne
1826–28, Peter H. Peirce
1843– Eliab Ward
1848–49, William H. Wood
1849–50, Philander Washburn
1850–53, William H. Wood
1856–57, Nathan King
1867– Everett Robinson
1876– Everett Robinson
1889–90, James H. Harlow
1901–1903, David G. Pratt

MEMBERS OF THE GOVERNOR'S COUNCIL

1759–66, Peter Oliver
1823–27, Thomas Weston
1848–50, William H. Wood
1881–83, Mathew H. Cushing
1896–99, Nathaniel F. Ryder
1906, David G. Pratt

The first Provincial Congress of Massachusetts met at Salem, October 4, 1774; at Concord, October 14; at Cambridge, October 17 and November 23, and prorogued December 10, 1774. Captain Ebenezer Sproutt was a member at that time.

CHAPTER XXIX

CIVIL HISTORY

F the first settlement of the town, no authentic date can be ascertained. The copy of the records of the First Church in 1694 begins with the quotation from Scripture in these words, "Thou shalt remember all the way which the Lord thy God hath led thee these forty years." The early settlers were familiar with the scriptures of the Old Testament, and would hardly have made such a quotation at so solemn a time as the formation of their church had the reference not been true, and as it could only have referred to the time when the town was first occupied by white settlers, it has always been considered that the first settlement was in 1654.

1658

"These may certify all whom it may concerne, that the fourth of March, 1658, that these men whose names are vnderwritten, by the intelligence of an Indian, came to a place a little below Namaskett, where the Indians tooke vp an English man out of the Riuer of Tetacutt, with a blew paire of stockings and a gray listed garter, and likewise p̄te of a lockorum paire of briches with wyer bottons fastened about his wast; but wee found noe blemish about the man that should any way cause his death, but as wee conceiue was drowned accedentally; and finding the man thuse, wee haue buried him, and haue satisfyed the Indians for theire paines.

Samuell Edson	Thomas Haward, Juniʳ
Nathaneell Willis	Wilłam Snow
John Willis	Lawrance Willis
John Vobes	Solomon Lenerson
Arthur Harris	Guydo Bayley
John Haward, Seniʳ	Nathaneell Haward
Marke Laythorpe	John Carew from Bridgwater."[1]

[1] *Plymouth Colony Records*, vol. iii, pp. 159-160.

1661-62

The Twenty-six Men's Purchase was made.

1662

Purchade Purchase was made.

1663

Five Men's Purchase was made.

"This year, there having been a complaint of the inhabitants of the town of Taunton for some years in reference to the bounds of their town, an order was made to establish those bounds."[1]

1664

Little Lotmen's Purchase is recorded.

1665

This year the lands on the westerly side of the Namasket River were apportioned by the General Court among the various owners in the Little Lotmen's Purchase.

1667

"At the Court held on the 2d of July, there was granted Robert Finney 100 acrees of land where m^r Alden and Captaine Southworth hath land att Namassakett River, if it may be had there; if not, then to haue such a portion with Hugh Cole neare Acushenet.[2]

"The bounds of the land of Francis Coombs were laid out lying on the westerly side of Namasket River and was called the 'Black Sachem's' field, abutting upon the river against the stone weir."[3]

1668

In 1668 Governor Thomas Prince and Francis Coombs purchased a tract of land within this territory (known as Prince and Coomb's Purchase).

In June of this year the court ordered Major Winslow, Captain Southworth, and Lieutenant Morton "to lay out this land, as they shall think meet or to settle the whole of it to him if on the site and view thereof, they shall see cause."

1669

From the number of purchases made by order of the court at Plymouth for different settlers during the ten years previ-

---

[1] *Plymouth Colony Records*, vol. iv, p. 45. [2] *Ibid.* vol. iv, p. 160.
[3] *Ibid.* vol. iv, pp. 171, 172.

ous, it is evident that there was a population sufficient for the town to become incorporated, although the number with the names of all who were then inhabitants cannot at present be accurately ascertained. At the court held on the 1st of June, 1669, the town was incorporated by the following order:

"Att this Court, the Court graunted that Namassakett shalbe a township, and to be called by the name of Middleberry, and is bounded with Plymouth bounds on the easterly syde, and with the bounds of Taunton on the westerly syde, and the bounds of Bridgwater on the northerly side or end, and on the southerly side or end to extend six mile from the wadeing place, (and att the end of the said six mile to run east to Plymouth line, and from the said line west to Taunton line; and incase the west line runes to the southward of Taunton line, then to run vntill wee come vp to the southermost p̃te of Taunton bounds, and then square of north to it.) And it is further ordered by the Court, that a competencye of land be prouided and reserued for a minnester within theire township, of such lands as are vnpurchased."[1]

John Nelson was elected constable and surveyor of highways, and William Haskins was probably elected town clerk and served in that capacity for many years, although there is no record of his election until the year 1680. There is no record of any other town officer chosen that year.

1670

On the 29th of May, 1670, Nathaniel Morton, Secretary of the Court at Plymouth, made a transcript of all of the freemen in the colony at that time, and from that record we learn of the freemen in Middleboro.[2]

In this year John Morton, who had formerly resided in Plymouth, bought into the Twenty-six Men's Purchase and took up his residence here, and was then chosen to represent the town in the General Court for the month of June, the first representative sent from Middleboro.

1671

No deputy was sent to the General Court, and the only town officer of whom any record is made is Gershom Cobb, who was chosen constable.

---

[1] *Plymouth Colony Records*, vol. v, pp. 19-20. The addition of the part of the bounds in parentheses was made at the General Court July 7, 1680. *Ibid.* vol. vi, p. 48.

[2] See page 517.

The tax of the colony, exclusive of officers' salaries or wages, for which all the towns were proportionately rated, was £268, but Middleboro was not taxed for the year.

At the General Court held on the 8th of July, the colony was ordered to furnish 102 men to meet a threatened insurrection of the Indians, and Middleboro's quota was two men for this expedition.[1]

"It was alsoe ordered by the Court, that the armes of the Indians of Namassakett and Assowamsett, that were feched in by Major Winslow, and those that were with him, are confiscate and forfeite from the said Indians, for the grounds aboue expressed, they being in complyance with Phillipe in his late plott, and yett would neither by our Gou^{rs} order nor by Phillips desire, bring in theire armes, as was engaged by the treaty; and the said guns are ordered by the Court to the major and his companie, for theire satisfaction in that expedition."[2]

1672

The town was not taxed by the colony.

An island in Quitticus Pond, variously spelled, but in the record called "Quettequas," was let by the colony to a Mr. Palmer to plant and sow.

Elizabeth Howland, the wife of Mr. John Howland, Sr., deceased, came into the court of Plymouth and acknowledged that she freely gave and surrendered all her rights in the lands of her late husband lying at Namasket in the township of Middleboro to Mr. John Gorum of Barnstable.

This year an agreement was made between Mr. Constant Southworth and Philip, the sachem, in reference to the boundary of the land at Assawampsett Pond.

1673

The South Purchase was made. John Morton was chosen deputy for the last time to the General Court this year. The town seems to have chosen no selectmen.

In September there was another court at Plymouth, and a new summons was issued, and Jonathan Dunham was chosen to represent the town, probably on account of the decease of John Morton, the former deputy. The town was not taxed for its proportional part of the expenses of the colony.

As there had been a former grant of certain lands between Assawampsett Pond and the bounds of the town of Dartmouth, the town of Middleboro laid claim to a greater por-

[1] *Plymouth Colony Records*, vol. v, p. 74. [2] *Ibid.* vol. v, pp. 63-64.

tion thereof, and the court ordered "that the town should recover these lands, and that the purchasers thereof have liberty to purchase land elsewhere." [1]

1673

"The Treasurer and Serjeant Tomson are appointed by the Court to make purchase of such lands in the township of Middleberry as the Indians doe or may tender to sell, which may be by them purchased for the vse of the towne, and the propriators of the land in that township, and for the payment of such debts as the Indians owe to any as occation may require, and what lands they purchase; the pay for it to be defrayed by the towne and propriators aforsaid, for the cecuritie of them the said M^r. Constant Southworth and Serjeant Tompson, and in case the said purchassers and propriators doe not make payment of the charge of the purchase within one yeare after the said purchase is made, that then it shalbe in the libertie of the said Treasurer and serjeant to make sale of soe much of the said land as will defray the charge thereof." [2]

1674

The colony tax was £188, 15 shillings, and 10 pence, Middleboro's portion of which was £4, 19 shillings.

"In reference vnto the first propriators of the lands in the Majors Purchase, soe called, which is in the township of Middleberry, between the two pathes, that wheras the record of theire graunte expresseth onely thirty acrees a peece and proportionable comonage, the Court heerby declares, that theire intent was, that all the lands within that tract called the Majors Purchase is settled and doth appertaine vnto them and theire heires and assignes for euer, excepting such smalle p̄sells as haue since bin graunted vnto seuerall p̄sons within said tract, wherof a p̄sell was thirty acrees in the said tracte graunted to John Dunham, Juni^r, as followeth : —

"Thirty acrees of land is graunted by the Court, with the consent and concurrance of such as are the propriators in the said Majors Purchase, vnto John Dunham, Juni^r, being layed out & bounded by Willam Nelson by order from Captaine Southworth, is as followeth, vizs.: it lyeth on the easterensyde of the head of Rauen Brooke, marked with a stake att the northwest corner, and att the northeast corner with a smalle red oake, and on the southeast corner it is bounded with a rocke, and att the southwest corner it is bounded with a smalle red oake." [3]

[1] *Plymouth Colony Records*, vol. v, pp. 132–133.   [2] *Ibid.* vol. v, p. 138.
[3] *Ibid.* vol. v, p. 150.

1675

This was the most eventful year in the history of the colony or of the newly incorporated town of Middleboro. The probable designs of Philip had been previously reported to the government at Plymouth, and his conduct had been viewed with suspicion, although the authorities did not suppose a crisis was so near at hand. The town officers had been elected as usual, John Tomson being deputy; George Vaughan, constable; John Nelson, a member of the grand inquest, with Francis Coombs, John Tomson, and Jonathan Dunham, selectmen, and Obadiah Eedey and John Morton, surveyors of highways. Notwithstanding the excitement in the colony, the town seems to have continued in its ordinary business until after the attack and burning of the town of Swansea on the 24th of June.

In June the court sitting at Plymouth ordered Mr. Constant Southworth and William Peabody "to run the line between Bridgewater and Middleboro. In case the treasurer, Southworth, neglected that, then Nathaniel Thomas, Lieutenant Morton, and John Thomas to supply."

After the attack on Swansea and a burning of a portion of the houses in Middleboro in July, the court at Plymouth evidently thought that there would be a cessation of hostilities and that the Indians would desist from their plan, which gave rise to the passage by the General Court, on the 4th of October, of the following order relating to the resettlement of the towns of Middleboro and Dartmouth, which had suffered so severely by those attacks of the Indians: —

"This Court, takeing into theire serious consideration the tremendus dispensations of God towards the people of Dartmouth, in suffering the barborus heathen to spoile and destroy most of theire habitations, the enimie being greatly advantaged thervnto by theire scattered way of liueing, doe therfore order, that in the rebuilding or resettleing therof, that they soe order it as to liue compact together, att least in each village, as they may be in capassitie both to defend themselves from the assault of an enimie, and the better to attend the publicke worship of God, and minnestry of the word of God, whose carelesnes to obtaine and attend vnto, wee fear, may haue bine a prouocation of God thus to chastise theire contempt of his gospell, which wee earnestly desire the people of that place may seriously consider off, lay to hart, and be humbled for, with a sollisitus indeauor after a reformation therof by a vigorous puting forth to obtaine an able, faithfule dispenser of the word of God amongst them, and to incurrage him therin, the neglect wherof this Court as they must not, and, God willing, they will not pmitt for the future.

"Alsoe this Court doth order, that the people of Middleberry doe attend the like course in theire rebuilding and resettleing, as is ordered for Dartmouth.

"And that none shall for the future erect any house or cottage without speciall lycence giuen him, in any place soe farr remote from the publicke worship of God as that they can not comfortable attend the same."[1]

December 10, 1675, when the forces of Massachusetts Colony which were to serve in King Philip's War were mustered on what was called Dedham Plain to march against the Narragansett fort, a proclamation was made to the soldiers in the name of the governor that if they "made the part of men, took the fort, and drove the enemy out of the Narragansett country that was their great seat, they should have a guarantee of land beside their wages." This promise was not fulfilled until 1734, when, under that guarantee, various lands were awarded, and among others "the soldiers from Middleboro, Daniell Ramsdell, his son being a claimant, Isaac Peirce alive, Ellexander Reynolds (Rynge), and William Hoskins, with others, received lands in the Narragansett township number 4, now in the town of Greenwich, R. I."[2]

Many of the men who served in this war preferred to take their pay in land instead of wages, and a tract of land located at Assawampsett valued at one thousand pounds was so assigned.

1677

Some time in June, 1677, those who had formerly lived in town, together with those who owned land within its borders, to the number of sixty-eight persons met and agreed to resettle the town. They were styled the "proprietors of the town of Middleberry."

"Whereas[3] by the late rebellion of the natives the inhabitants of Middlebery not only lost their habitations with most of their estates and forced to withdraw from them, but also lost their records, whereby great trouble is like to ensue if not finally prevented. Whereas divers of the said inhabitants of the said place are negotiated to return again to endeavor

---

[1] *Plymouth Colony Records*, vol. v, p. 177.
[2] *Soldiers of King Philip's War*, pp. 429 and 463.
[3] Modern spelling has been used in many of the words in these votes.

their resettlement of the Town again, which cannot well be unless some good laws be first made for the resecuring of their records and orderly settleing againe.

"By virtue therefore of a warrant directed unto us the inhabitants and proprietors of the said town from our honored Govr. bearing date the 9th of June 1677 we the said inhabitants and proprietors in obedience thereunto being mett together at Plimouth on Weddenesday the twenty seventh of June aforesaid do unanimously agree by the permission of God and by his gracious assistance to make a beginning again in order unto the repossession of our lands and reeddification of our demolished buildings and habitations which some of us were before the late sad warr in actuall improvement and possession of, and to make such orders and conclusions as may hopefully have a tendency unto the laying a foundation of a towne and pious society in that place.

"therefore we have here drawn up and Inserted an exact list of the names of the proprietors of the township of Middlebery as followeth.

"A List of the names of the Proprietors of the liberties of the township of Middleberry taken att Plimouth att a meeting of the maine or major part of the proprietors the 28th. of June Anno Dom[a]. 1677.

Tho. Prence Esqr.	Francis Combe	2 propriations
Josiah Winslow now Mr. John Brooke	Gabriel Hallowell	1 propriation
Major Bradford now Gydo Baley	Gyles Richard	1 propriation
Edward Gray	John Jordaine	1 propriation
Capt. Perregrine White	Elder Cushman	1 propriation
William Bassett	Anthonio Snow	1 propriation
Nathaniel Warren	John Morton	1 propriation
Mr. John Alden	Plimouth Ministry	1 propriation
—— Sprague now Benjamin Bartlett	Nathaniel Morton	1 propriation
George Partrich	Experience Michell	1 propriation
William Pontus now Thomas Borman	Henery Sampson	1 propriation
	Thomas Little	1 propriation
Samuell Fuller of Plymouth	Thomas Paine	1 propriation
Francis Cooke now Adam Wright and John Tomson junr.	Sergant William Harlow	1 propriation
	Jonathan Dunham	1 propriation
Francis Billington	Sachariah Edey	1 propriation

Edward Bumpas	Lottis Morton now Lotis Ring	1 propriation
Mr. William Brewster now John Turner Senr.	Mr. John Winslow	1 propriation
	John Rogers	1 propriation
John Shaw now Samuell Wood	Elder Chipman	1 propriation
William Hoskins now George Vaughan senr.	Jonathan Sparrow	1 propriation
Resolved White now Isack Howland	John Howland	1 propriation
Moses Simons now John Soule	David Thomas	1 propriation
Andrew Ring	John Miller	1 propriation
William Nelson senr.	John Irish	1 propriation
John Howland now George Danson	John Tomson senr.	1 propriation
George Soule now Francis Walker now John Haskall	For the ministry of Middleberry	1 propriation
William Mullens now John Nelson	David Wood, Joseph Wood, Benjamin Wood	1 propriation
Peter Browne Sergeant Epharim Tinkom	Jonathan Wood Left. Morton	1 propriation
Capt. Mathew Fuller		
Steven Deane now Thomas Doged	Gershom Cobb	1 propriation
Samuell Edey	William Codman	1 propriation
	Nathaniel Southworth	1 propriation "

The condition of the town may be inferred from the fact that no taxes were assessed during these years to support the expenses of the colony.

1678

In October we find the following record of court orders in Plymouth, namely, —

"1678, October. In answare to the petition prefered to the Court by Francis Combe, and likewise the Court being informed that Samuell Fuller is in a likelyhood to be procured to teach the word of God att Middleberry, they doe approue therof; and incase hee be obtained, and be likely to settle amongst them, doe heerby signify, that they will indeauor that the propriators of the lands within that townshipp may be healpfull towards his maintainance." [1]

The General Court at Plymouth estimated the expenses

[1] *Plymouth Colony Records*, vol. v, p. 273.

incurred by the colony in King Philip's War, and Middleboro's proportion was one hundred pounds.[1]

1679

November 21, 1679, the records of the town show that the proprietors of the town appointed John Tomson, Sr., Joseph Warren, and William Crow to "set out and divide the 71 lots of land which were on the East side of the purchase line run by John Tomson and the Indian, Thomas Hunter, and other persons near Titicut, and that these 3 lots Titicut path is through them, 4 poles of land being allowed to them for the path or way that passes through them."

There seems to have been more or less difficulty between the inhabitants of Middleboro and Bridgewater in reference to the location of the boundary line between them, and at the June court, this year, these towns were ordered to send their agents to meet at the next July court, that a settlement might be made. The matter, however, was further adjourned until the September term, when the agents of Bridgewater abruptly went away before the matter was settled. They were then summoned "to the court to be holden at Plymouth the last Tuesday in April, next, to fix a reason for their so acting."

The boundary not then having been settled, the following order was taken at the court of March 1, 1681: —

"The sum of 15 shillings is allowed to the three agents of Middleboro, to be paid them from the town of Bridgewater for their conduct in not attending court."

1680

"November the 6th. At a town meeting at the house of Isack Howland at Middlebery the town voted Mr. John Tomson to join with the Clark of the said town to see that all such writings as are not yet recorded respecting the Towns consarns that they be speedily broat to record."

This year Mr. Isaac Howland was propounded as a freeman.

The court abated forty shillings from the tax which was due to the county from this town the last year.

1681

June 24, 1681. "A full agrement between the Agents of the Towne of Bridgewater and the Agents of the Towne of

---

[1] *Plymouth Colony Records*, vol. v, p. 392.

Middleborough in refference unto ye settlement of the bounde betweene the to foresayd Townes

"Samuell Edson sen: Ensign John Hayward and John Willis sen: being chosen by the Towne of Bridgewater and John Tomson and John Soule chosen by the Towne of Middleborough for the setlment of the bounds betweene the to Towns have agreed as followeth: namely from the center of the Towne of Bridgwater foure miels Est to heap of stones to the North of Satucket ponds neare a foot path as we conceive goes to Mamatakesset wch heap of stones is bounded about wth small marked trees: and from that heap of stones southerly unto Alaxander Standishes land on the same range or line that was formerly run in year 1669 by William Nelson and John Soule for Namaskett and Elder Brett Samuel Edson sen: Ensign Hayward John Willis sen: and John Carver sen: for Bridgwater Leaving Mr. Standishes land only unto the towne of Middleborough and then the great river to be the bounds betwixt Bridgwater and Middleborough untill it come below Titicut and meat with the line betwixt Tanton and Bridgwater and from the fore mentioned heap of stones the line to be runn halfe a point more esterly from the North, then formerly was run into the extent of Bridgwater grant

In witness unto the foresayd premises wee above mentioned have set to our hands

       SAMUELL EDSON
       JOHN HAWARD
       JOHN WILLIS SEN:
       JOHN TOMSON
       JOHN SOULE"

At the July court the following order was passed:—

"This court doth order that Mannamoyett and Middleberry, each of them doe make choise of a fitt man to exercise theire men in armes, and to see theire men well prouided with fixed armes and amunition for their respectiue places and to p̄sent to the next Court for aprobation."

At a town meeting on the 27th of August of this year, among other things Mr. John Tomson was appointed agent of the town to "represent their cause at the next court in the distribution of money arising from Mount Hope which was due to the country that they might have their portion of the same."

At a town meeting on the 6th of December, 1681, at the house of Isaac Howland, the town decided that at all town meetings being legally warned to come together at the house appointed and the time being past that the major part of those that are together have full power to act and yt to stand in full force about matters yt concern ye good and well being of ye town and this to stand as a town order and that all matters debated be carried on in peace and good order, the town hath made choice of three men to be moderators, namely:

Mr. John Tomson, Isaac Howland and William Hoskins for this present year and the town meeting to continue for yt day until these three men dismiss them or some two of them.

"It is agreed upon by the town yt all former neglects in town meetings be passed by to this day as an act of oblivion and not to be called upon but for the time to come whoever he be yt doth not appear being legally warned at the house appointed ye fine to be exacted according to the town order being 2 shillings 6 pence ye $\frac{1}{2}$ to be for ye constable and town clerk and the other half for ye town's use."

1682

No surveyor was elected. John Miller was perhaps chosen deputy for one of the later courts of the year.

The tax was £3 out of £244, the tax of the colony.

1683

April 21, 1683. "At a Town meeting held at Isaack Howland's house The Town hath agreed that their Clarke, William Hoskins shall have a load of fish brought to his field at Lakenham at their own charge, for his services the year past & so yearly as long as he remains their Clarke & to be brought in season."

At a town meeting at the house of Isaac Howland July 20, 1683, "the town hereafter jointly agreed in reference to Goodman Billington being in present want and for his releif they have left it to ye wisdom and discretion of ye selectmen to order ye matter and to take care about it and also to ye disposing of his daughter Dorcas, her land as they shall see cause and what charges shall arise to be defrayed by the town."

July 20, 1683. Town Meeting held at house of Isaack Howland. Town hath also agreed "to build a substantial Ware for the taking of their fish & the men that are to undertake this work is Isaack Howland, John Allyn, David Wood & the Town is to allow them each man 2^s 6^d a day & they are to sett it up at the Bridge or Wading Place & what charges they are out in building this Ware, they are faithfully to give an exact account thereof & they shall be faithfully repaid in silver money or in that which is equivalent thereunto."

August 11, 1683. At this meeting the town made choice of Mr. John Tomson, John Nelson, and Isaac Howland "to agitate and draw up matters concerning the good of the town in order for a proprietors meeting and to act in their behalf as leading men."[1]

1684

At the June session of the court at Plymouth the following order was passed : —

"This Court granted liberty unto Isaac Howland to keep an ordinary at Middleberry and to provide with such necessaries for that purpose as are requisite, as lodgings and victuals for men and fodder for horses; and that he keep good order in his house, that he incur no just blame by his neglect."

William Green was warned out of town by John Tomson and William Nelson, probably in the belief that he might become chargeable to the town.

July 19, 1684. "Town Meeting held at the house of John Nelson. The Town with the Courts approbation have agreed that John Stonewall shall carry a gun so long as he behave himself well & orderly, but if he shall misdemean himself & carry disorderly, the Town shall have liberty from the Court to call his gun in & dispossess him of it."

September 19, 1684. "Town Meeting held at John Nelson's house. The Town do engage John Nelson if he can get either a man or men to sett down a good sufficient herring ware, near about where the Bridge now stands; to pay to him or any man or men that he shall imploy to effect this work 3^d a thousand for the fish, to be satisfied for, as they shall fetch them, in money or halfe a pecke of Indian Corne a thousand & whereas the aforesaid 3^d a thousand is conceived to little to effect this matter, the Town hath agreed to allow 4^d a thousand in silver or in Indian Corne at silver price."

1685

John Howard was warned out of town by the selectmen that he might not be chargeable to the town.

May 22, 1685. "Town Meeting held at house of John Nelson. At this Meeting the Town have agreed with Samuel Wood to satisfy Joel the Indian for killing a wolfe & have

[1] *Bennett Note-Book*, p. 33.

ingaged to repay him again in his money, part of the next rate."

"At a Court of Assistants held at Plymouth the 7th day of July Anno 1685.

"*Whereas* at his Majestics Generall Court held at New Plymouth, the fourth day of June Anº 1685, the said Generall Court did order & impower, the Court of Magistrates, to take notice of & examine such grants of Court, as from time to time, should by any Town-Society or perticular person, be brought before them & to confirm all such grants as they find just, by causing the publick Seal of the Colony to be affixed to such grants or Confirmations.

"And *Whereas* the Generall Court of this Colony in the year one Thousand six Hundred & sixty nine did grant that the Inhabitants of Namaskitt (then so called by the Natives) with such others as they should associate to themselves, should have the Priviledges of a Township, & be called & known by the name of Middlebury, & granted that the said Township should extend unto the borders and limits hereafter expressed: that is to say bounded easterly by the bounds of Plimouth Township & westerly with the bounds of Taunton Township: & northerly with the bounds of Bridgwater Township: and southerly to extend six miles from the wading place, & at the end of the said six miles to run east to Plimouth Line & from the said line to run west to Taunton Line. And in case the said West Line runs to the southward of Taunton Line, then to run untill it comes up with the southermost part of Taunton bounds, & then square off north to it, as the Records of the Court may appear. This Court doth therefore declare by these presents that all the Lands within the bounds & lines above expressed are of & belonging to the Township of Middlebury aforesaid, that is to say to be within the bounds and limits of the said Town. And do further Ratifie & Confirm unto all & every person or persons that are the owners & true Proprietors of any of said Lands, whether inhabiting in said Town or elsewhere, all and singular the Lands within the said Township of Middlebury according as each of the sd Proprietors is respectively interested in the same To have and to Hold the said Lands both Uplands & Meadows & Swamps, Woods & Waters, Trees & Underwoods, Rivers, Brooks & Ponds that are within the said Limits & Bounds, with all other the Rights Priviledges & Appurtenances to the said premises belonging or in any wise appertaining to them the said Proprietors & to every of them according to his & their respective Rights therein according to the true intent and meaning of the said Courts Grants, & his & their respective Heirs & Assignes forever. To be Holden of our Sovereign Lord the King his Heirs & Successors, as of his mannour of East Greenwich in the County of Kent and Realm of England in free and common soccage, — Alwayes yielding & paying to our said Lord the King, his Heirs & successors and to the President of the Honourable Council for New England, all such part of the Gold & Silver Oar, as in & by our Charter or Patent is expressed and reserved.

"In Testimony whereof, this Court by vertue of the power committed to them by the said Generall Court have ordered the publick Seal of this Colony to be affixed to these presents.

"Attest NATH^L CLARK^E Secretary."

"This instrument is recorded in the Book of Evidences & Lands inrolled Date 1681 & in pag 333.

P NATH^L CLARKE Secretary"

1686

In the latter part of this year Sir Edmund Andros arrived at Boston bearing a commission as governor over all the New England colonies. During his administration there was no action taken by the General Court at Plymouth, and the records do not indicate that much was done by the respective towns.

June 18, 1686. "Town Meeting held at the house of John Miller. The Town made choyce of foure men as their agents to treat with Capt. John Williams about his *mill* & also for the fish that they be preserved, yt both may be ordered as may be both for the good of the Town & beneficial to the owner.

"The men chosen as the Town agents are Mr. John Tomson, Isaac Howland, John Nelson, Joseph Warren."

August 30, 1686. "Town Meeting held at house of John Miller. At this meeting the town made choyce & approved of Isaac Howland to keep ye ordinary.

"At this meeting the Town voted & made choyce of Mr. John Tomson & Isaac Howland to agree with Jonathan Washburn or any other to make a pound, whipping post & stocks & what they do agree on in respect of pay the Town agree to make a rate to defray the charge in Corne at money price in three months after the work is done."

RUNNING OF THE TOWN BOUNDS

MIDDLEBORO April 6, 1686.

We John Tomson and John Soul and Isack Howland: being chosen by the Town and proprietors of Middleborough: to settle the bounds of said township: as by the record of sd town bearing date Sept. 12 1683 appeareth: have according to the records of the Court dated June 1669: done the same as followeth: vis: having appointed a certain day for the doing thereof we gave notice to the propriators of the lands adjacent to that side of our town to be present at the doing thereof: and captain Nathaniel Thomas agent of the purchasers of the lands of parts adjacent appeared: and we began at the wading place over Namasket river and measured south six miles: at the extent of which we marked divers trees and saplings all on four sides standing near together — and from thence set east and ran about 50 or 60 rod and came to the river called by the Indians Pookpoawkquachoo river: alias Monhonkenock river: and marked divers trees in that east range on two sides: and one pine tree standing on the east side of the said river: and then went to the aforesaid trees marked on the four sides and set west: and ran about 80 rod and came to the eastermost of Quitequsset ponds: and marked divers trees in said west range to the pond: on two sides: And from thence set over the pond west: and the line took over on the southerly part of two islands in the said pond: and came to the brook which runs out of the westermost of said Quitequesset pond into the said eastermost pond: making there the brook the bounds.

And we the said John Tomson John Soul and Isack Howland set west from the said brook and the line took over the westermost of sd Quitequesset ponds: unto a spruce tree marked on four sides: standing about 60 rod from the sd pond: and from thence ranging west on the southerly side of a high cliff of rock whereon stood the two spruce trees: and from thence ranging west to a red oak tree marked on four sides: standing by the eastermost side of a long pond: called by the Indians Ponaquahot pond: And so crossing the said pond to a heap of stones on a rock by the west side of the said pond: with severall small red oaks marked standing by it: And so ranging west to a great pine tree marked standing on a great rock: And still extending west by a rang of marked trees untill we passed over Assonet river: And on the side of the hill on the west side of the river we pitched a stake: and marked several small saplings by it: which is the extent of our west line: And from the said stake we ran north through a swamp by a rang of marked trees unto Rode Island path and by the path we marked a pine tree: and from thence ranging north unto Tauntons most southerly bounds at Assonet river.

       1 JOHN TOMSON SEENR
       3 JOHN SOUL
       2 ISACK HOWLAND

 Memorand. That I the above named Nathaniel Thomas being then one of the agents of the purchasers of Pocasset lands was present with the above named persons when they ran the abovesaid six miles & when they ran from the extent thereof west so furr as the said Pocasset purchasers lands there joyned to the said Middleborough Township as witness my hand
          NATH^{LL} THOMAS.

1687

"The town being met together, at the house of John Miller do ioyntly agree by their vote to accept of John Bennett as a townsman and have the privileges of the same."

1688

The following named inhabitants of the town in the year 1688 took the oath of freemen: "Mr. John Tomson, Isaac Howland, Nathaniel Warren, David Tommas, Jr., Obediah Edy, Samuel Wood, Ebenezer Tinkham, Joseph Vaughan, John Tomson, Jr., John Allyn, David Wood, John Haskell;" and the following took the oath of fidelity: "John Bennet, Jonathan Morse, Jeremya Tommas, Benjamin Wood, William Nelson, John Fuller, William Tommas, James Wood, Samuel Eaton, John Cobb, John Howard, Philip Bumpas, Jonathan Baker."

1690

 The population of the town in 1690, as near as can be estimated, was about two hundred.
 The court at Plymouth, in July, ordered that "Middleboro should make choice of a fit man to examine their men in arms, and to see that they are provided with fixed arms and ammunition for their respective plans, and to be presented to the court for approbation."
 "Out of the tax of 245 pounds to be raised by the colony, Middleberry's portion for this year was 3 pounds."

1693

The town passed the following vote June 22: —

"Our town being met together do agree not to choose a representative because we are few in number and not well able to bear the charge and the law do excuse as we conceive, being low in our estates.

By order of the Town,
JOHN BENNETT, Clerk."

1694

July 30, 1694. "Town meeting held at Town House in Middlebery. We, the inhabitants of said Town being greived that Capt. Williams of Scituate, now deceased, should upon his will goe to plant an Indian in the heart and midst of our Town, we fearing what damages & trouble may follow, have chosen & desired Joseph Vaughan & Samuel Wood to use & lawful means to prevent the same."

October 9, 1694. "At a town meeting Mr. John Tomson was made choice of to go to Boston to endeavor to get our money which we, being over rated, paid; and the town agrees to give him 3^s p^r day for his charges, but if he gets the money then we agree to give him more."

1695

June 11, 1695. . . . "At the same meeting the town jointly agreed together by their vote to accept of Eleazer Lewis, John Gibbs, William Thomas, Edward Thomas and John Bennet Jr. as townsmen and to have the privileges of the same."

July 30, 1695. . . . "At the same meeting the town jointly agreed to accept of Jacob Tomson as a townsman and to have the privileges of the same."

"Memorander that the Agents of Plymouth Middlebury & Rochester being impowered by their above sd Towneships did meet at Mr. Howlands house in Middleburry on the 23 instant and on the 24 of said month by mutual consent all went to the head south bounds of sd Towne being 6 miles from ye ware & so found being measured by Capt. Nath^{ll} Thomas of Marshfield Agent for Pochasset & accompanied with Midleberry Agents from which south or head Bounds all the Agents of the 3 Townes above sd mutually agreed to run the East line as begun by Capt. Nath^{ll} Thomas &c and proceeded east by divers stations till they came on the 25 instant near ye south meadow River where they marked a small pine tree on 4 sides for a Boundary between the 3 Towns above sd two biger pine trees on each side thereof & both marked with M: P: R whence ye line runs between Plymouth & Middleberry about one rod on ye easten side of William Ellis his new house n & by w. on the 26 instant beginning at the corner Boundary marked M: P: R: the Line runs between Plymouth & Middleberry n: & by w to 2 red oakes both marked and the one with M: P whence tho not on ye same yet on a straight line ye course is to the Bridge on south meadow River in the roade from Rochester to Plymouth. And from sd Bridge the River to be the bounds up stream unto the Lower part of the body of meadow there below the double brooks. And thence on the westerly side of said meadow with convenience of upland for fencing to the place where Plymouth Towne line shall come from Mahutchit tree to the meadow

"The above sd Agreement is on ye daye above written saned: & confirmed by us underwritten: [This date is September 26, 1695]

Agents of Plymouth { John Bradford
John Waterman
John Murdo

Agents of Midlebury { John Soule
Isaac Howland
Jacob Tomson in behalf of his father

Agents of Rochester { Ichabod Wisewall
Joseph Dotey
Aaron Barlowe"

"At this proprietors meeting held at the house of Mr Howland this 12th day of November 1695 John Richmond was chosen Moderator: John Sole and Joseph Vaughan chosen to regulate the meeting: finding many strong Indians living on Assawamset neck without our leave; we have made choice of Joseph Vaughan and Jacob Tomson of Middlebery to treate with them for so doeing and for those Indians that have a right, to show their title for the same: and that such as can show a right title should not be molested: and such as cannot show an honest title to warn them of sd land: or if they will live peaceably they may let it to them on reasonable terms for one year and so from yeare to yeare till such time the proprietors shall see reason for the contrary and that the above named town men shall have power to chuse a counsell to be with them when they treate the Indians if they shall see cause.

"This is voted by the proprietors at theire meeting held this 12th Novembr 1695."

CIVIL HISTORY

"At a meeting of the proprietors held at the house of Isack Howlands this 12 of November 1695 it was voated and agreed that all the house keepters and all the male persons at 21 yeares and upwards that have been brought up in the town and have theire residence now in the town shall be accounted Inhabitants in this case with the proprietors in this purchase purchased by Capt Church and Mr John Tomson."

"A List of the names of the Inhabitants and Proprietors of the township of Middlebery taken this 12th. day of November 1695 is as followeth:

Leiut. John Tomson	John Eddie	William Harlow
Ensign Isack Howland	Samuell Eddie	Francis Walker
John Allen	William Tomas	Plymouth Ministry
Joseph Vaughan	Thomas Nelson	Jonathan Sparrow
Samuell Wood	Joseph Barden	Nathaniell Southworth
Ephram Tincom	George Vaughan	William Cadman
Ebenezer Tincom	William Ellis	
John Bennet Seenr.	Isack Fuller	
John Miller Seenr.	Ephraim Morton	
Abiall Wood	Joseph Bumpas jr.	
Edward Tomas	Governer Prince	
John Cob	Maj. Winslow now Joseph Warren	
John Holms	Samuell Swift	Robert Sprout paid
Daniell Vaughan	John Alden	3 shillings in money to
John Tomson junr.	Ichabod Bartlett	Arthur Howland for
Jacob Tomson	John Wadsworth	the defraying his part
James Soule	John Churchill	in the laying out of
Obediah Eddie	Benjamine Nye	that purchas which
Peter Tincom	William King	was purchased by
Jonathan Morse seenr.	Thomas Fance	Capt. Church paid the
John Hascall seenr.	John Doged	1st. of January 1696
William Nelson	Abraham Jackson	
David Tomas	Experience Michell in behalf	Phillip Dillino
Jeremiah Tomas	Nathaniell Morton	John Rogers deceast
James Wood	Joseph Richmond	
Jonathan Cob	Benjamine Warren	Ebenezer Edie paid
Eleazer Lewis	Thomas Morton	his fathers pur-
Joseph Bumpas Seenr	Middlebery Ministry	chase money to
Isack Billington	Adam Right	Arthur Howland
John Fuller	John Soule seenr	this 17th May 1698
John Guibs	Jonathan Dunham	
Richard Warren	Zachariah Eddie	

Stephen Barden
John Hayward
Samuell Eaton
James Reed
David Wood
John Barden
Abraham Barden
Samuell Pratt
Thomas Tomson
Peter Tomson
John Miller junr
John Bennet junr
Peter Bennet
John Soule junr.
William Hascall
Jonathan Morse junr.

John Howland now
  Samuell Richmond
George Morton
John Jones
Edward Gray
Paragrim White
William Brewster
Matthew Fuller
Francis Combs
Grabrill Followell
Anthony Snow
Elder Chipman
John Morton
Henry Samson
Thomas Little
David Alden

Jonathan Dunham have paid his purchase money to Arthur Howland this 15 May 1698."

November 14, 1695. "At a Town Meeting held this day John Haskit was denied by the proprietors and inhabitants of our Town any residence within our Town as an inhabitant amongst us & he have been warned out several times as the law directs."

"At a town meeting held at the town house in Middleboro this 12th. of Dec., 1695, Jonathan Cobb and John Bennett Sr. were chosen to treat with Mr. Cushman and to take his answer whether he will be our teacher or not, and if he declines to come to be our teacher then to take his proposition and terms on which he declines to come."

1696

May 20, 1696. "At the town meeting held at the Meetinghouse, it was then voted thus: All those that are willing that a petition shall be drawn up to be sent to the Great Court at Boston in order for the procuring of help of the proprietors that live out of the town for the carrying on of the work of the ministry amongst us, let them manifest it by lifting up their hands. This is clearly voted."

1698

April 11, 1698. . . . "At the same meeting Lieutenant Jacob Thompson and Joseph Vaughan are chosen and empowered to buy plank in redyness for the building of the meeting house and to pay for sd plank of that money which they take for the land which is assigned towards the building of said meeting house."

1700

Know all men by these presents that whereas wee Isral Chittington Josiah Edson and William Bassett having been nominated and chosen by Capt. James Warren, Insign John Waterman and Mr. William Shirtliff agents of the town of Plymouth of the one party and Lieut. Jacob Tomson Mr. John Sole, and Mr. Joseph Vaughan agents for the Town of Middleborough of the other party, as a comitty run the line fix and settle the bounds and dividing line between the sd Towns of Plymouth and Middleborough part of the way between sd Towns as pr bounds enterchangeably given between the 3d partys dated the 14th instant may more fully appeare Wee the sd comitty have therefore run the sd line fixed and settled the sd bounds as followeth that is to say beginning att a great white oake tree marked on foure sides standing neere the place called Mahutchett on the southerly side of an old pauth by a swamp and thence running south a little easterly by marked range trees unto a great swamp pine or spruce tree marked on foure sides standing by the edge of a piece of fresh meadow neere the bever dam brook, and from that spruce tree running westerly on a straight line to the mouth of the brooke called Springie brook where it runs into Rockey meadow broke and thence unto a marked maple tree standing on the westerly side of sd Rockey meadow brooke and thence on a straight line to a pine tree marked on foure sides a little above the sd maple tree, and thence by marked range trees on the westerly side of the meadow down to a marked pine tree standing on the west side of a cart path neere the great body of meadow, and thence running partly by the east pauth on the westerly side of it and partly by marked trees untill it come to a pine tree standing above a rockey point runing down into the meadow, being marked on foure sides, and thence runing nere east northeast down to a greate pine tree marked on foure sides standing on the sd point and so on the sd streight line down to the river having had due regard to include ye meadows formerly granted to sd Town of Plymouth with conveniencys of upland for fencing of sd meadows acording to Court grant

In Witness whereof we have here unto sett our hands this 15th day of May 1700.

ISRAELL CHITTENDEN
JOSIAH EDSON
WM. BASSETT

To all people to whom these presents shall come greeting &c: whereas there has been some contest continuously and debate between the town of Plymouth and the Town of Midlebery about and concerning the dividing line between the said Towns that is to say from a white oak tree standing at or near the place called Mahuchet formerly setled by the Court of Plymouth: unto the lower part of the body of the meadow called the south meadow where it was on the 26th: of September 1695 agreed upon by the agents for the towns of Plimouth Rochester and Middlebery: now Know yee that wee James Warren: William Shurtliff and John Waterman: of and agents for the said town of Plimouth and wee Jacob Tomson John Soul and Joseph Vaughan agents for said town of Middleberry have as agents aforesaid mutually elected and chosen Capt. Israel Chitington Capt. Josiah Edson and Capt. William Bessit as a committee to settle and determine the said dividing line between said towns of Plimouth and Midlebery and the Court records and any former agreement made between the said Towns or their agents to be as a rule or direction for the said commite to ground their actions upon: and we the said agents before named do firmly bind and oblige ourselves together with the sd towns of Plimouth and Midlebery each unto the other: in the full sum of one hundred pounds in currant mony of New England: that the said towns shall stand to and abide by such a line or bounds as shall be run and stated by them the sd Israel Chitington Josiah Edson and William Bassit and the two of them: their said setlement being given unto of them: any time on or before the first day of date hereof In witness whereof th presents have to two Instruments of the tennour of these their hands and seals this 14th day of May 1700

JAMES WARREN (Seal)

In presence of

BETTY W WATERMAN   WILLIAM SHURTLEF (Seal)
  her   mark

ANNA A RANSOM

NEHEMIAH ʔ BASSIT   JOHN WATERMAN (Seal)
   his   mark

May 20, 1700. "Being a town meeting it was voted by the inhabitants that 40 shillings shall be raised on the town to be expended on the raising of the meeting house for the refreshment of such as shall be at the raising. It is likewise agreed on and carried by the vote of the inhabitants of the town that the meeting house shall be raised on that piece of land that lies between the two roads, that is to say, on the Northerly side of the County Road that leads to Plymouth and on the Southeast side of the road that leads to Bridgewater."

1701

August 5, 1701. "At a town meeting of the inhabitants of Midleberry Aug. 5, 1701, the meeting house was exposed to seale at an outcry and Patiance Hascall, the wife of John Hascall, bid five pounds, 2 shillings money to be paid to the selectmen within 3 months and the meeting house to be removed some time between this and winter."

1702

February 15, 1702. "At a Town Meeting held this day, it is voted that whereas the Town have formerly agreed with Edward Thomas concerning the raising of the Bridge & Causey near his house that it should be raised 3 foot and that the said Edward Thomas should make & maintain the Causey & the Town the Bridge, which accordingly hath been raised near the heights of aforesaid, wherefore the Town doth now agree with said Edward Thomas that he shall keep the Causey in repair & the Town the Bridge, the length that the Bridge now is & when the Bridge shall have need to be repaired again it shall be Made as high as the Causey then is."

1705

"At a town meeting Dec. 10, 1705, the town voted that the Indians shall have 10 shillings for the lumber that was cut on their land for the building of our meeting house to be paid out of the next town rate."

1706

March 29, 1706. "The Town voted that each housekeeper in the Town shall sometime before the middle of June next bring or send in unto Peter Bennet six blackbirds heads upon the penalty of two shillings, that is to say four pence for each head that shall not so be brought in and whoever shall bring or send unto said Peter Bennet more than the aforesaid six heads shall be paid after the rate of twelve pence for six blackbirds heads, & the said Peter Bennet is hereby ordered to receive the said heads & keep an account of the same, & that one Crow's head shall be accepted instead of three blackbirds heads."

June 12, 1706. "Town voted that there shall be no ware nor dam set across Namasket River between the Town Ware, that is now to be set up by the Town & the mouth of Assawampsett Pond.

"Also voted that there shall be a rate of 10 pounds levied on the inhabitants of the Town for the procuring a supply of the Town stock of Ammunition."

1707

June 3, 1707. "Town agreed with Ebenezer Tinkham, Jonathan Cob & Jeremiah Thomas to provide for the Ministers & Messengers that are sent for to sit in Council the next week, & the Town vote to pay unto them after the rate of ten pence a meal each for their diet in money, to be paid by a Town rate by the last of July next & the Town voted that those that provide for them either rum or wine, shall be paid in money for the same in said rate & that those who pasture their horses shall be allowed six pence for 24 hours for the same in money in said rate & said rate to be made by the Selectmen."

1708

The petition of Ephraim Little for himself and the other proprietors of the town, to the General Court of the state or province, May 26, 1708, sets forth that the general Court in 1703 appointed "a committee to hear the claims of sundry Indians to land on Nantucket, Martha's Vineyard, Assawamset, Titticut &c^a. which committee, having notified the English & Indians concerned and heard the please & allegations on both sides, made their Report the said yeare, to this Court: the fourth paragraph whereof to Assawomset Neck, in Middleberry aforesd. and contains as follows vixt. Concerning the Claim of Betty Sassamon to Assawomset Neck & other lands thereabouts, we find that the Will presented to us, which she saith was made by Pamattaqeasson dec^d: is not truly translated, as having the original to compare with the copy; and also by the comparison of Capt. Howdee one of the witnesses present that the said Will was written many years since the said " Mattaqeason's death; as also that the English do not molest the sd Betty from the quiet enjoyment of the 27 acres of land that was her father's John Sassamon's, neither do they molest her nor the heires of said Feelix from the enjoyment of the fifty eight acres formerly possessed by sd Feelix on Assawomset neck," — which report had lain before the court ever since the beginning of 1704, without being passed upon.

"In the House of Representatives, June 24th. Read 25th Read & Ordered That the praier of this petition be granted saving to the Indians the 27 acres & the 58 acres, as reserved in the Report," which was finally concurred in October 27.

Rev. Thomas Palmer brought several actions against the town for recovering his salary during the years 1708–09.

1717

During the winter of this year occurred the great snowstorm so often mentioned by older inhabitants of the town. It commenced on Sunday, and continued until the next Wednesday night. The snow fell at an average depth of seven feet, and drifted to the depth of twelve feet. The lower windows of houses were covered, and so great was the weight of snow that supports had to be placed in many houses under the roofs in garrets to prevent their falling in. Paths were dug under the snow from houses to barns, and snow was melted for cattle to drink. In some instances trees were so buried that men walked to their neighbors' on snowshoes, going over orchards. When the snow melted, it caused great freshets, destroying many dams and mills throughout the colony.

1718

At a town meeting February 17, 1718, the town voted "to make choice of Jeremiah Thomas to be their agent to go to Freetown and to treat with Mr. Craghdad and the scholar that is with him in order to procure the said scholar to come to us and to be with us about six weeks upon trial in order that his settling with us as school master if we can agree upon terms and our said agent to agree with him upon terms for the aforesaid six weeks."

At a town meeting November 26, 1718, the town voted that "the gallery in the meeting-house shall be taken down on the Northerly side of the house 30 feet in length and that the pulpit shall be got home to the wall on that side of the house, and that the selectmen should agree with the carpenter in the town's behalf concerning the difference that there may be in the charge by reason of the taking down the gallery from what it would have been in the former way proposed."

The town at a town meeting this year passed several votes in reference to allowing persons to build pews in the meeting-house.

1721

May 26, 1721. "Town voted for the ensuing year there shall be liberty for swine to go at large being ringed & yoked according as the law directs & that the Field drivers be understood to be the proper officers to take care of the just observation of the law in that case provided."

1722

April 17, 1722. "Town agreed with Thomas Nelson that he should take his fish at the ware that now is at Assawampsett Brook & load the carts, for 12 pence a load."

1723

At the town meeting March 10, 1723, "the town voted that the hind seat below in the meeting house and the hind seat in each of the men's galleries shall be for the boys to sit in and that Andrew Mansfield and Joseph Bale, two of the tithing men and Daniel Wood shall be empowered to have inspection over the boys to prevent their playing at meeting."

1724

At the town meeting February 17, 1724, "the town being informed that several of the neighbors are about to set a wear over Namasket River at Pochade Neck, the town voted their disapprobation of their proceedings therein and voted to leave it to the selectmen of the town to take due care to prevent the said wear from being built."

1726

September 13, 1726. "Voted that Zacheus, the Indian shall have 8 shillings for killing a wild cat in the Town."

In 1726 so severe a sickness prevailed in town that more than four hundred and fifty persons were ill at one time for several months, and the number of well were not sufficient to attend to the necessities of the sick and the funeral services of those who had died; no business could be transacted; but little grain was sown or corn planted, and there were not enough well men in town to harvest the scanty crops. The selectmen petitioned the General Court for relief, and the court the next session remitted the whole amount of the town tax.

1728

At a town meeting May 7, 1728, "the town voted to take their part of the 60,000 pounds bills of public credit sent to them according to the act of the General Assembly and also voted to make choice of Deacon Samuel Barrows, Lieutenant Nathaniel Southworth and Ensign Elkanah Leonard for their trustees to demand and receive the same of the province treasurer and to let it out in the town upon good personal security at 6% per annum and that no one person shall take out above 20 pounds nor under 10 pounds, the personal security to be a good surety or sureties, the principal and surety or sureties to be bound jointly and severally in the discretion of the trustees, etc."

At the same town meeting it was voted "that Lieut. Nathaniel Southworth and Mr. John Bennet and Ensign Elkanah Leonard be a committee to provide for the town 1 drum, 4 halberds, 1 flight of colors at as reasonable rate as they can, and the town to bear the charge thereof, the money to be raised at the next town rate."

1729-30

At a town meeting March 10, 1729-30, the town voted "to raise money for the enabling Francis Wilks and Jonathan Belcher Esquires, to wait on the affairs of the province at the court of Great Britain and also to raise said money by way of subscription and whereas it is expected that said money will be returned to the town out of the province treasury wherefore the town voted that in case the money is not paid to the town or particular persons who subscribed the money out of the province treasury that in one year and that in case thereof the town voted to pay unto the particular persons their respective sums which they subscribed, the same to be made at the town rate."

March 10, 1729-30, "an account of the money raised for the enabling Francis Wilks and Jonathan Belcher Esquires to wait on the affairs of this province at the court of Great Britain as followeth, that is, to pay money let to the town by the particular persons hereinafter named: —

    Lieutenant Nathaniel Southworth 2 pounds
    John Tinkham 2 pounds
    Deacon Samuel Barrows 2 pounds
    Jacob Thompson 2 pounds
    Samuel Wood 1 pound 10 shillings
    Thomas Thompson Sr. 2 pounds
    Mr. Samuel Palmer 10 shillings
    Mr. John Bennet 1 pound
    Shubel Tinkham 1 pound
    Joel Ellis 1 pound

Jonathan Smith 15 shillings
Capt. Peter Bennet 1 pound
Capt. Vaughan 10 shillings
Benjamin White 1 pound
Ephraim Thompson 10 shillings.
Ensign Jacob Vaughan 15 shillings
Francis Miller 1 pound
John Cobb 10 shillings
Mr. Experience Sprout 1 pound
John Thompson 1 pound
Barnabas Thompson 1 pound

"And on May 13, 1730, the above parties acknowledged that they had received in full of Mr. Samuel Wood each of us his money that he raised for the use of Squire Belcher and Mr. Wilks and do aquit and discherge him, the said Samuel Wood and the town for the same as witness our hands."

1731

At a town meeting September 15, 1731, "the town voted that they are humbly of the opinion that it is a duty incumbent on the honorable house of representatives to take care to maintain their just and valuable privileges respecting the supplying the treasury and that no money ought to be issued out of the treasury without any inquiry of the house for what ends and use it is issued and that it is necessary for their consent and allowance thereto as well as of the other privileges of the legislative power to which is a privilege the house of representatives have enjoyed as an undoubted right under this present constitution."

December 13, 1731. "Town voted that they will make their cartways about 8 inches wider than they now are, by setting their cart wheels so much further at a distance, provided that the Towns of Bridgewater & Plimpton fall in with us & do the same sometime before the last day of April next."

1735

At the Town meeting December 8, 1735, Mr. Elkanah Leonard was chosen agent to appear in the town at the town's behalf at the next general session of the peace to be holden at Plymouth to answer the town's presentment for being destitute of a Grammar School Master three months in the summer past.

" We Thomas Nelson and Thomas Peirce of Middleboro are

appointed by the Church of Swansea to take and give in a list to the assessors of each precinct of Middleboro of the names of all those called Ana-Baptists that we believe are conscientious of their opinion and we desire they may have the benefit of the law in that case made and provided." The list is as follows: —

Benjamin Booth, Sr., Thomas Nelson, Sr., Thomas Peirce, Sr., Joshua Howland, Thomas Nelson, Jr., Thomas Peirce, Jr., William Nelson, Jr., John Howland, Foxel Nelson.

1738

MIDDLEBORO Sept. 22, 1738.

We whose names are hereunto subscribed hombly showeth to the assessors of the westerly precinct in Middleboro who acknowledge that we are of the Baptist opinion and who frequent their meetings at all hours and have done for the support and willing so to do if occasion should serve and further do desire to be excused from paying minister's rates as the law directs.

ISAAC REYNOLDS.	EBENEZER PEIRCE.
EPHRAIM REYNOLDS.	ISAAC PEIRCE JR.
ELECTIUS REYNOLDS.	ELISHA PEIRCE.
AMBROSE BRAYLEY.	TIMOTHY ROGERS.
CALEB PEIRCE.	WM. HOLLOWAY.

and we do also inform you that each of the persons above mentioned do frequently and usually attend our meetings for the worship of God on the Lord's Day and we claim are conscientious of the Baptist opinion from under our hands.

THOMAS NELSON, THOMAS PRINCE chosen by the Baptist Church of Swansea.

1740

September 29, 1740. "Town voted that the selectmen shall provide at the Town's cost, for a Town stock, two barrels of powder, & shot in proportion to it, & that the Selectmen draw money out of the Town Treasury to pay for same."

1746

January 6, 1746. "This day being appointed for electing guardians to the Indians in their several plantations, the two houses proceeded to the said choice. And the following persons were duly chosen by the major vote of the Council and House of Representatives: [1] —

[1] *Province Laws*, vol. iii, p. 341.

"For Plymouth, Pembroke and Middleboro, John Cushing and James Warren Esq., and Capt. Josiah Edson, Jr."

"At a town meeting held at M. old meeting house July 21, 1746, Capt. Nathl. Southworth was chosen Moderator of said meeting. And then the town by vote chose capt. Nathl Southworth, capt. Ebenr Morton, John Miller, Mr. John Bennet, and Jacob Tomson a committee to view the Iron Ore in Assawamset pond near Robert Richmond's and to lease out or sell the same to the best advantage they can for the use of the town ; and if they lease it, not to exceed the time of fifteen years : Mr. Jonathan King of Taunton to have the preference in case he will give as much for the same as any other person."

1747

Town meeting held February 15, 1747. "Voted to proceed to choose a Committee of three Men to take care of all the Ore in Assawampsett Pond to the directions the Town shall now & from time to time give them.

"Committee : Isaac Sampson, Joseph Padock, Capt. Ichabod Southworth.

"Voted at same meeting that the above Committee shall dig & sell 50 tons of said Ore to the best advantage they can & render an account to the Town at the next Town Meeting after such Ore is dug & sold, the product thereof to be paid into the Town. Voted that the above Committee shall have the oversight of all the Ore in Assawampsett Pond, with full power to prosecute all & every person that shall dig or carry off any of the above Ore without their order until said Committee shall have other instructions from this Town of Middleboro."

1756

March 22, 1756. "Voted that there should be no Alewives taken at Assawampsett Brook (so called) this spring, saving at the Highway near Mr. Samuel Thrasher's & then only Tuesdays, Wednesdays & Thursdays in each week & no longer."

1775

"Town Meeting held at the Easterly Precinct Meetinghouse in Middleborough on Monday, the 22nd. of October last, at said meeting, the Town then made choice of us, the subscribers to provide a place to keep the Town stock of ammunition in and accordingly we have agreed with Mr. Samuel

Tinkham Jun. to keep it in his Corn house, which he will do provided the Town will pay him four shillings as long as the Town shall see cause."

1777-78

This year the smallpox, one of the most dreaded diseases known to the country, was prevalent in Middleboro. A large number of inhabitants between the ages of sixteen and sixty were in the war, and it was with difficulty that persons could be found to take proper care of those who were sick. As soon as any one was known or suspected to have this disease, he was at once removed to one of the pest-houses in town. One of them was located in the Soule neighborhood, in the house now standing near Brook Street; at the time it was owned by Seth Eddy, a brother of Captain Joshua Eddy. Rev. Sylvanus Conant and eight of his parishioners were taken here and died. Another of these houses was on a cross-road which led from Plymouth Street near to the residence of the late Nahum M. Tribou across to Precinct Street, not far from the late residence of Mr. Foley. It was situated on the westerly side of this road about halfway between Plymouth and Precinct streets, and known as the Baxter Place. But one person died here, and was buried not far from the house. The place where the house stood is now grown up to woods. The other pest-house was located in the Leonard house, still standing, on Vernon Street, in Titicut. A number died here, and were buried by the side of the wall near this house.

This disease was so dreaded that no one would take care of the patients, except those who had previously had it. This involved great inconvenience in obtaining what was needed. A certain part of the day some one from the pest-house would walk to within hailing distance of passers-by, call out their necessities, then return to the house. The person accosted would bring the articles wanted and leave them at a proper distance from the house, to be taken as soon as he retired. Often the fires in these houses would go out, and the inmates would call for live coals, which were brought in the same way, and thus the fires could be rekindled. At this time vaccination was not generally approved, and there was great terror lest this disease should become more general. The matter came before the town at various times, and the following votes were passed : —

"Town Meeting held March 9 - 1778. Voted not to allow an anoculation of the small pox to be set up in any house or houses in this Town.

" Voted that the infected persons of this Town that have the small pox remain where they are under the inspection of the Selectmen.

" Voted that the Selectmen of the town shall inquire into the conduct of those persons that have set up an anoculation of small pox in this town & proceed with them according to law.

" Voted that no persons shall presume to go to the houses that are infected with the small pox, without a permit from the selectmen of this Town.

" Voted to choose a committee of five men for inspection."

" Adj. meeting held March 11–1778.

" Voted to choose a Committee of nine men to make report to the town relative to the small pox."

" Report of the Above Committee: In consideration that the season of the year is now opening and a formidable preparation is now making by the invatorite forces of this land & at present it being very uncertain where the seat of war will be this present year, therefore it is in our opinion that all proper measures should be taken to prevent the spreading of the small pox in this place and we forthermore report that all those persons who have or shall for the future presume to anoculate with the small pox shall be prosecuted according to law & that the selectmen shall immediately take all possible measures to prevent the spreading of the small pox and also that all the good people of this Town that are friends to their Country exert themselves to their utmost to secure the Town from the small pox."

" Town Meeting held June 2, 1778. Report of Committee to draw plan for Town to admit of an Anoculation : —

" To admit of one anoculation hospital in some convenient place in easterly part of Town and also another anoculating hospital in westerly part of Town.

" That the Doctors & undertakers or managers shall be laid under good & sufficient bonds to see that there are good regulations kept up in said hospitals.

" That no person shall pass the operation of the small pox by anoculation in either of said hospitals only by leave from the Doctors & managers of said hospitals and to give good and sufficient bonds that they will obey all rules and regulations accepted in said hospitals.

" That there shall at all times be kept sufficient room for any that may be taken with small pox the natural way, and that all taken with small pox the natural way in this Town shall be received into the nearest of said hospitals, and be well provided for and taken good care of by the Doctors and undertakers of said hospital.

" That all persons or any clothing or any other thing directed to said hospital by the selectmen to be cleansed shall be renovated and sufficiently cleansed.

" That all the cost arising shall be paid by those having the small pox if they are able, but the cost of any taken the natural way if unable to pay the cost, then for the town to pay their cost.

" Town Voted at said meeting :

" That the selectmen have the whole power in providing the said hospitals and the time how long said anoculation shall continue."

Joshua White and Solomon Reade, March 18, 1778, petitioned the General Court for leave to erect a hospital at some convenient place in Titicut, "where persons may receive the Smallpox in the easiest manner which would save persons and their families great expense with going a great distance for inoculation."

1779

"Jan. 29, 1779, Committee chosen at a previous meeting regarding plans & best place to erect a work house, reported as follows : —

"'To take the house now owned by the Town standing on Mr. Jonathan Wood's land & move it & set it on the south easterly corner of the home farm of Israel Wood, near the land lately owned by Judge Oliver, to be under the inspection of & regulated by the selectmen agreeable to the law of this state.

Signed JOHN ALDEN ICHABOD WOOD }
GEORGE LEONARD JAMES SMITH } Committee'
HENRY PEIRCE }

"Town voted to accept the above report & chose David Vaughan Nathan Eddy & Ezra Harlow as a Committee to remove, set up & finish the house.

" Also voted to take a lease of Mr. Israel Wood for 30 yrs. for the work-house to stand on his land; said 'Wood' promised the Town that so long as he received no damage by the house standing on his land, he would exact no cost."

May 17, 1779. "Voted to repair the House owned by the Town that stood on the land of Jonathan Wood for a workhouse where it now stands."

1786–87

During the troubles arising from the depreciated currency, which in other parts of the state led to Shays's Rebellion, there was no open revolt in Middleboro, and the only action taken by the town was the passing of the following votes after much discussion in town meeting and elsewhere : —

At a Town Meeting holding at Middleborough Jan ye 2d 1786 for the Purpose of Instructing their Deputy at the Grate and General Court Respecting the   a bank of paper money.

To MR. ISAAC TOMSON SR.

It cannot be that you are unacquainted with the Grate Scarsety of money which is utterly Inadequate to the Requission of authority made on us and answering the Purpose of a medium of Trade — you have Doutless bin Informed of the

Imprisonment of one our Collector and Should the Execution now in the hands of the officers be Leveld Grat Numbers of that Class of Men Would find themselves in the Same Predicament With a Possabelaty of Prevension.

Not to mention the Numberles Actions Daly Commensing in our Courts that the unhappy Defendant have it not in their Power Barely to pay the Cost which will Ruine

We your Constituants therefore[1]
Duty to Give you our Direction and you to obay them
We Do Sr Injoin it on you that you Do to of your ability
by Every Possable argument bring forward of a bank
of paper money on the following establishment. . . .

that it be made a Legal Tender in all Payments Throughout this State.

Whatever and that the Tender on Said money be not Taken of on any Pretenc without Previously Obtaining the Consent of the People at Large.

that the money So Do not Exceed the Sum of thirteen Hundred thousand pounds and that it Makes it way into Circulation by Dischargeing the Most Pressing Demands on the State with the Changes of Government and those Publick Cecurities that are on Intrest and Demandable there by Stoping their Intrest and affording an amediate Releas to the Distrest.

that this States Treasurer be Directed to give it the Preference of to Gold or Silver in all and throughout this Commonwealth.

that Said money Continue in Circulation the Irim of Nine years and to be Redeemed annually by applying to that Purpose all Duties Customs and

& what Said Duties &c Doth not Redeem the Remainder to be on the & Estate of this Commonwealth in the then Currant money of Said State.

their may be Sum of the that may Subject themselves to the Lost of their Property When rendered we Request their may be a Limited Time for Such to Demand and Receive their Money which if Neglected the Debtor to be Intitled to the Money and have a right of action against the Creditor for his Security and Cost.

Sr we Plainly forsee their will be Grat Opposition in the Esstablishment of a Paper Currency by Wealthy and Overbaring Setts of men who can build up their fortens on the Ruens of their Country in its Present Distrest Situation than with a Lively Medium of Trade & we Sr Injoin it in you that this be made known to the Court that they may be made acquainted with our Distresses and that all Execution be Susspended untill a Medium in trade be Substituted.

To THE GENTLEMEN Representatives of the Town of Middleborough.

GENTLEMEN as we have Chosen you to Represent us att the Great and General Court who are to meet at Boston on the last wenday of This Instant May and Then from time to time to Do the benefits of this Common Wealth for the Ensuing year.

[1] The original, from which this is copied, is so worn as to be illegible in places.

Special Trust and Confidence in your Loyalty, faithfullness Wisdom and zeal for the Good of this Common Wealth We Recommend the following Instructions for the General Rule of your Conduct. We think the Great Distress and Difficulty of the Present Unhappy Ciuation and Disturbences of this Distress: Commonwealth in General and of the western Countys In Particular is for want of some medium of trade we therefore expect you will use your Endeavors to Provide These for and an act of Indemnity for all These Pittyfull Peopil who Have Been Led a Stray from Good order so far as is Consistent with the Safety of this Common wealth Even those who are att Present Condemned to Death from the highest to the Lowest and That the Troops in that part of this Common Wealth may be Call^d Without loss of time this we give as our Possivitive Instructions. We think that a medium of trade is necessary in a Common Wealth as blood is in the veans of the Hemain Body We Instruct you to use your Influences to have a Bank of Paper money made to Redeem the publick Securities that the Interest May Stop and if a Sufficiency of paper for a medium Sho^d fall Short of Redeeming the whol of the publick Security Lett the Remainder thereof be Sav^d as other monies are we know of Nothing that will Substitute in the Lew of Silver and gold beter than paper.

We Insist at all Events that the Sender act be Continued with the Inlargement that the Same Committy that prize the Estate Sho^d also say what part of it shall be Sett of to the Creditor.

We think the Constitution might be amended and we wo^d that the minds of the Common Wealth might be known and if the two thirds a Grea uppon an amendment we might be in a way to accomplish it.

We think that a Small tax to be paid in flaxseed & in the Contry towns and in fish and oil in the Seeports towns Might answer Sum valuable purpus in the Lew of hard money.

That you use your Influence to have the Cost Removed out of Boston as we think the members will be more attentive and Constant in the Publick business.

We wish that this State might be Divided in three parts the old Colleny of Plymouth in one and Boston in one and the Province of Main in one and Each to have three Parts of the Lands and all other Priviledgies.

We Recomend that a Duty may be Laid upon all Superflueitys as far as may be for the We Sopose that a Small Duty uppon Commissions of honner and Profit might answer a Good Purpus.

That there have been Divers poor familys that have had but one Cow and that has ben taken for Rates where by the Poor wido and others have been Put to Extrem Poverty and wholly Dependent on the Neighbours &c. that you wod use your Influence that Something may be Done to Refeive Such Porpous That the Constables and Collectors for there tax Sho^d not be oblig^d Suddenly to Drive to Extremity for Gathering the &c Last.

1793

July 11, 1793. "*Voted* that Capt William Pratt & Capt. Polycarpus Edson remove the whole of the dam or incumbrance put in by them into the River at Titiquot Falls, within three weeks from the passing of this vote."

1794

November 3, 1794. "*Voted* that the selectmen request the several ministers in said Town of Middleborough to call a contribution for the late sufferers by fire in the Town of Boston, said contribution to take place on the evening of Thanksgiving Day."

1801

May 13, 1801. "*Voted* that the Representative to the General Court be instructed to oppose the petition of William Rotch & others respecting the cutting of a navigable canal from the Tide waters of Aquishnet River in New Bedford into the Long Pond in Freetown & from thence into the great Assawampsett Pond in Middleborough — Vote — yeas 214; nays 160."

1803

"Town Meeting held Mar. 7, 1803.

"*Voted*, to accept the Report of the Committee chosen by the Town to draw up a plan for the sale of the Poor.

"*Voted*, to sell the said Poor at auction this day in Town meeting agreeably to said report & the Selectmen appointed Capt. William Thomson, Vendue Master; Capt. James Pierce, being the lowest bidder, bought the support of the Poor for one year for $769."

1804

"Town Meeting held May 9, 1804.

"*Voted*, that the Selectmen be instructed to post up as the law directs, any person belonging to said Town, who shall be found tippling & spending their time & property in stores &c, in order as far as possible to prevent the unnecessary practice of tippling."

1805

"Town Meeting held April 1, 1805.

"*Voted* that the poor man that keeps but one cow, have liberty to let it run on the highways & commons the present year."

1807

"Town Meeting held Apr. 13, 1807.

"*Voted* to allow for a man 10¢, a yoke of oxen 10¢ per hour for all the work done on the highways & bridges before the first day of July next, & all the work done on the highways after that period to be allowed 7¢ per hour & a yoke of oxen 7¢ by the hour & for a horse, cart & plough, to be left to the discretion of the assessors to fix the price per day or hour as they shall think proper."

1839

This year sixty-four of the farmers of the town were paid bounties for raising wheat. The bounty was two dollars for every fifteen bushels, with five cents a bushel for every additional one. There were thirteen hundred and thirty bushels, upon which bounty was paid to the amount of one hundred and forty-six dollars and fifty-seven cents. The largest amount raised by any one person was Peter H. Peirce, fifty-six bushels; the next, Lorenzo Wood, thirty-nine bushels.

CHAPTER XXX

EARLY PURCHASES FROM THE INDIANS

AS the population of the colony increased, settlements were at first confined to the coast in Duxbury, Marshfield, and along the shores of Cape Cod. It was not long before the enterprising men foresaw the growing needs of the population and began to buy lands, usually in large tracts in the outlying district. Not a few of them had made purchases which now include whole townships. In order carefully to protect the interest of the Indians and to see that no undue advantage was taken of them, as early as 1643 the General Court at Plymouth forbade the purchasing or hiring of any land from the Indians without consent of the magistrates of the colony, under a penalty of five pounds for every acre so purchased or rented.[1]

Such was the fairness of the pilgrims of Plymouth and their immediate descendants that no portion of the land in the Old Colony was ever acquired from the Indians without their receiving its full value.

---

[1] *Plymouth Colony Laws*, 1643, p. 74. " Whereas it is holden very unlawfull and of dangerous consequence and it hath beene the constant custome from our first beginning That no person or persons have or ever did purchase rent or hire any lands herbage wood or tymber of the Natives but by the Majestrates consent, It is therefore enacted by the Court that if any person or persons as hereafter purchase rent or hyre any lands herbage wood or tymber of any of the Natives in any place within this Governt without the consent and assent of this Court every such person or persons shall forfait five pounds for every acree which shalbe so purchased hyred rented and taken and for wood and tymber to pay five times the value thereof to be levyed to the Colonies use."

Ibid. p. 129. In 1660, " In reference unto the law prohibiting buying or hiering land of the Indians directly or indirectly bearing date 1643 the Court interpretts those words alsoe to comprehend under the same penaltie; a prohibition of any mans receiving any lands under pretence of any gift from the Indians without the approbation of the Court." And in the edition of the *General Laws* published in 1672, the same provision is inserted.

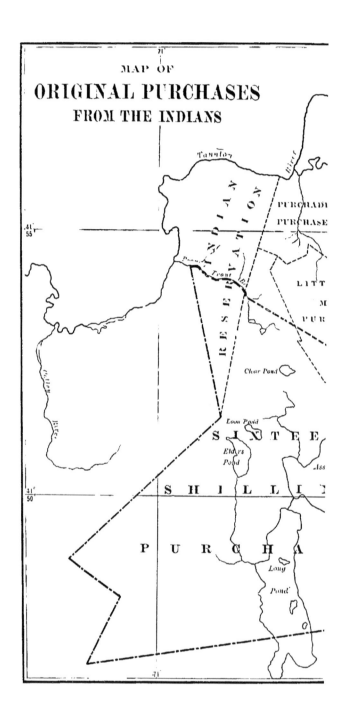

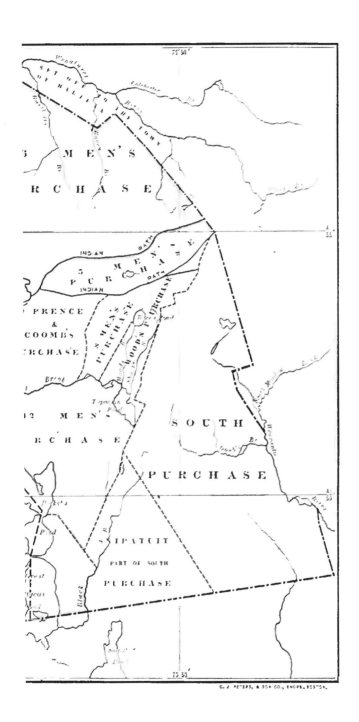

EARLY PURCHASES FROM THE INDIANS

While many of the towns in the present county of Plymouth were covered by grants, Middleboro was purchased from the Indians by some one or more persons appointed by the General Court as agents for those who desired to become owners.[1] The first purchase was made in 1662, and in the next twenty years the greater portion of the town had been bought, excepting small tracts around the great ponds and the Titicut reservation, which the Indians retained.

The purchases were carefully recorded, most of them having been preserved in their original form and deposited for safe-keeping in the town clerk's office.

The boundary lines of many of these purchases and their subsequent divisions into lots were usually marked by oak or

THE OLD OAK TREE
(This marks the easterly boundary of the Indian Reservation in Titicut)

pine trees. Most of these trees have long since disappeared, and there is at present but one known to exist and positively identified, which marked the easterly border of the Indian reservation in Titicut. This tree is probably more than three hundred years old, and is located on the brow of the hill on

[1] Baylies, *New Plymouth*, p. 310.

the south side of Center Street, thirty rods west of Pleasant Street. Near it was the house of one of the three Indians who gave their land to Titicut parish.

TWENTY-SIX MEN'S PURCHASE

On March 7, 1661, Captain Thomas Southworth of Plymouth, in behalf of the court for the jurisdiction of Plymouth, bought of Josiah Wampatuck, Indian sagamore, for seventy pounds, land which has always been known as the Twenty-six Men's Purchase. It was confirmed by order of the court the June following, 1662–63, and again in September, 1680.

To all people to whom these presents shall Come Josias Wampatucke Indian Sagamore sendeth Greet &c

Know yee that I the said Josias Wampatucke for and in Consideration of the full Sume of three Star (?) and ten pounds for which I have Received a bill of Edward Gray of Plymouth in New England in America Planter; have freely and absolutely bargained allianated and sold, enfeofed and Confirmed; and by these presents doe bargaine sell enfeof and Confirme unto Captaine Thomas Southworth of Plymouth aforsaid in the behalfe of the Court for the Jurisdiction of Plymouth in New England; a Tract of land bounded as followeth viz: from William hopkins his house at Lakenham alonge the old Indian path; to the wading place at Namassakett River, Namly all that land that lyeth bounded on the south side by the said path and on the west side by Namassaket River and on the East side by the brooke at Tepikamicut; on the north side and end by Wimabusksett Brooke and the River that goes to Taunton; That is to say all the land within the said bounds; with all and singular the woods waters Rivers meddows and all other appurtenances privilidges and ennuities in and within and upon the said land soe bounded as aforsaid with libertie to make use of the alewives with libertie for Cattle alsoe to pasture freely on the southerly side of the afors^d path excepting the Indian field by Namassaket River; To have and to hold all the said tract of land bounded as aforsaid with all and Singulare the privilidges and appurtenances belonging thereunto or to any p^t or p^{r}cell therof; unto the said Captaine Thomas Southworth and Court of New Plymouth his and theire heires and assignes forever, from mee the said Josias Wampatucke and my heires. To him the said Capt. Thomas Southworth and Court of New Plymouth his and theire heires and assignes forever; To bee holden as of his Majties manor of Wast greenwich in the County of Kent in free and Comon Tenage and not in Capite nor by Knights service; by the Rents and services therof and therby due and of Right accustomed warranting the sale therof and every pte. and p^{r}cell therof and all and singulare the appurtenances belonging therunto against all p^{r}sons whatsoever that Shall att any time lay or make any claime Right or Interest in the said premises or any p^t or p^{r}cell thereof; Reserving libertie for hunting within the said lands in any way; excepting by seting of Trapps wherby theire Cattle may be Indangered; which together with un Necesary and un Reasonable dividing of theire Cattle thereon; I doe heerby engage not to doe, also for the use of some few trees either Cedar or Spruce; if occasion Shall Require; as alsoe that the Indians Shall have libertie to gather flaggs on the said ground; if they shall see cause or have occasion; All the said lands with theire said appurtenances excepting those particulars last excepted and expressed; I the said Josias Wampatucke doe by these presents fully freely and absulutely with all my Right, title and Interest; make over sell and confirme unto the said Captaine Thomas Southworth and Court of New Plymouth to his and theire heires and assignes forever as above expressed warranting the sale of the said premises and all theire appurtenances against all pr̄sons whatsoever as above expressed. Moreover I the said Josias Wampatucke doe by these presents give libertie for the said Captaine Southworth or Court of New Plymouth to enrowle these presents or to Cause them to bee Recorded or enrowled in the court records of Plymouth aforsaid according to the usuall manor of Recording or enrowling evidences in such cases provided. In Witnes wherof I the said Josias Wampatucke have sett to my hand and seale this seaventh day of March Anno. dom : one Thousand six hundred sixty and one 1661.

Signed Sealled and delivered   The mark ✣
   in the presence of   Josias
Nathaniel Morton   Wampatucke
Joseph Bradford   and his seale
The × marke of Paxquimanekett
The × marke of George Manakes

After this land was surveyed, it was apportioned among the proprietors for whom it had been purchased.[1]

The following is a list of the original purchasers:[2] —

John Adams	Samuel Eddy
William Bassett	Lieut. Matthew Fuller
Francis Billington	Samuel Fuller
Thomas Bordman	Edward Gray
William Brewster	William Hodskins
Peter Brown	John Howland
Edward Bumpus	William Mullins
Francis Cook	William Nelson
Philip Delano	George Partridge
Thomas Dotey	William (Pontus) ?

[1] *Plymouth Registry of Deeds*, Book II, Pt. II, p. 109.

[2] *New England Historical and Genealogical Register*, vol. iii, p. 334. This is probably correct, although some records give other names in a few instances. It is impossible to give a more exact list, as accounts vary. See *History of the First Church of Middleboro*, p. 123.

Andrew Ring   George Soule
John Shaw   Francis Sprague
Moses Simmons   Resolved White

JOHN ADAMS was the son of John Adams, a passenger in the Fortune, who came to Plymouth in 1621, and settled in that part of Marshfield called Green Harbor. He was one of the Purchade purchasers, but neither he nor his descendants lived in town.

WILLIAM BASSETT was probably a son of William, who came over in the Fortune. The first William lived in Plymouth, Duxbury, and in West Bridgewater. He was an extensive land-owner at the time of his death (1667). His son settled in Sandwich.[1]

FRANCIS BILLINGTON. See chapter on Early Settlers.

THOMAS BORDMAN, sometimes spelled Burman, at one time lived in Lynn, and in 1637 moved to Sandwich. He was one of the owners in the Sixteen Shilling and the Purchade Purchases. He probably disposed of his allotment in this tract before the resettlement of the town.

WILLIAM BREWSTER was the son of Jonathan Brewster, and grandson of Elder Brewster of the Mayflower. He lived upon land of his grandfather in Duxbury, and was also one of the proprietors of the Purchade Purchase.[2]

PETER BROWN. But little is recorded concerning him. He may have been a son of the Peter Brown who was a passenger in the Mayflower. In addition to his interest in this purchase, he had originally one of the lots in the Purchade territory.

EDWARD BUMPUS. See chapter on Early Settlers.

[1] See Mitchell's *History of Bridgewater*, p. 111; *New England Historical and Genealogical Register*, vol. iii, p. 334.
[2] Winsor, *History of Duxbury*, p. 236.

FRANCIS COOK was a passenger in the Mayflower,[1] and one of the proprietors of the Purchade Purchase. He died in 1663, aged about eighty-one. Neither he nor his descendants ever lived in town. The whole or a portion of this tract of land was conveyed to Adam Wright and John Tomson before the general meeting of the "Liberties of Middleberry" in 1677.

PHILIP DELANO was of French origin, and his name originally was spelled De la Noye, from which the modern name of Delano is derived. He was born in 1602, was with the pilgrims at Leyden as a young lad, and came to this country in the Fortune at the age of nineteen years. He settled in Duxbury, and was admitted as a freeman in 1632. He was one of the original proprietors of Bridgewater, and of the Purchade and South Purchases. He married Hester Dewsbury in 1634, and for his second wife Mary, daughter of James Glass, in 1657. He died in 1681, aged seventy-nine years. Neither he nor his descendants ever lived in town.[2]

THOMAS DOTEY or DOTED was a son of Edward Dotey, who came over in the Mayflower. His father fought the first duel in New England, with Edward Leister, at Plymouth, June 18, 1621.

SAMUEL EDDY was born in England in 1608. He was a son of Rev. William Eddy of England, a non-conformist minister. He came to this country with his brother John, who sailed from Buxted, England, August 10, 1630, and arrived in Plymouth in the ship Handmaid, October 29, 1630. Governor Winthrop says that this vessel had sixty passengers and lost one, and he further says that "one of the Eddy's told me he had many letters in the ship for me." On November 7, 1637, he had three acres of land in Plymouth set off to him, and in 1641 had six acres of land and thirty acres of meadow land set off to him. He bought a house of Experience Mitchell at Spring Hill, at

---

[1] Goodwin, *Pilgrim Republic*, p. 474.
[2] Winsor, *History of Duxbury*, p. 251.

the end of Main Street, Plymouth, May 9, 1634. He owned land in other places than Middleboro and Plymouth. He spent a portion of the latter part of his life in Middleboro, and died in Swansea. He was enrolled as a person capable of bearing arms in Plymouth in 1643, and a freeman in 1658.

On the 3d of June, 1662, Samuel Eddy with others petitioned to the court at Plymouth for right to be granted them as being the first-born children of this government, and that the right purchased by Major Winslow and Captain Southworth should be assigned to them. He died in 1688, aged seventy-seven years.[1]

MATTHEW FULLER was a son of Edward Fuller, but his parents died soon after their arrival at Plymouth, and little is known of his early history. He was the earliest regular physician in Barnstable, where he settled in 1652. He probably came over to Plymouth in 1640, and was admitted as a freeman in 1653. In 1673 he was appointed surgeon-general of the troops of the colony, and served as a captain of the Plymouth forces in King Philip's War. He died at Barnstable in 1678.[2]

SAMUEL FULLER. See chapter on Early Settlers.

EDWARD GRAY was a merchant and ship-owner in Plymouth, and lived not far from the Kingston line. He came to Plymouth with his brother Thomas in 1643, and was a large owner of land at Rocky Nook. In 1678 he hired of the colony Clark's Island for seven years, with liberty to "keep ten neat cattle free of rent," but the people of Plymouth were to have liberty to bring wood for fencing and firing from the island. He died at Plymouth in 1681, and his grave is marked by a stone, one of the oldest upon Burial Hill. Neither he nor his descendants ever lived in town. He was an extensive owner of real estate in different parts of the colony, and was also one of those interested in the Purchade, Sixteen Shilling, Little Lotmen's, and

[1] *Eddy Family*, p. 102.
[2] Savage, *Genealogical Dictionary*, vol. ii, p. 217.

South Purchases. At the time of his death he was the richest man in the colony.

WILLIAM HODSKINS or HOSKINS. See chapter on Early Settlers.

JOHN HOWLAND was one of the passengers in the Mayflower. He married Elizabeth Tilley, a daughter of John Tilley, of the Mayflower. The Plymouth Colony Records speak of him as a "godly man, an ancient professor in the ways of Christ, and an instrument of good in his place." He was the last male survivor of those who came in the Mayflower, who remained in Plymouth. He died March 5, 1673, at the age of eighty. He was one of the persons for whose benefit the Sixteen Shilling and the Purchade Purchases were made. He probably sold that portion of his land included in the Twenty-six Men's Purchase before the breaking out of King Philip's War.[1] He left four sons; Isaac lived in Middleboro.

WILLIAM MULLINS was probably the son William, one of the signers of the civil compact in the cabin of the Mayflower, and his name is among the original Purchade purchasers. Neither he nor his descendants ever lived in town.

WILLIAM NELSON. See chapter on Early Settlers.

GEORGE PARTRIDGE came to the colony in 1636. He always resided in Duxbury, and was admitted as a freeman from that town in 1646. He was one of the original purchasers of much of the territory of Bridgewater, and one of the proprietors of the Purchade and Sixteen Shilling Purchases. Neither he nor his descendants ever lived in town. He died about 1695.

Of WILLIAM PONTUS but little is known; a man of that name died at Plymouth February 9, 1652, leaving two daughters.

[1] Goodwin, *Pilgrim Republic*, p. 507.

There was a William in "Namasakeesett" in 1663, and this is probably the man who bears that name in the original Twenty-six Men's Purchase, in the Purchade, and in the Sixteen Shilling Purchase. His interest in these had been conveyed before the meeting of the proprietors of the "Liberties of Middleberry," in 1677.[1]

ANDREW RING. See chapter on Early Settlers.

JOHN SHAW. See chapter on Early Settlers.

MOSES SIMMONS, originally spelled Symonson,[2] came to Plymouth in the ship Fortune in 1621. Governor Winslow says of him: "He was a child of one that was in communion with the Dutch Church at Leyden; is admitted into church fellowship in New England and his children also to baptism as well as our own." He was one of the first settlers in Duxbury, an original proprietor in Bridgewater, and one of the Purchade purchasers, but he never lived here. His name is, however, on the list of those in the garrison, but he was probably with other land-owners at this outpost at the time and sought refuge there.

His sons were Moses, who settled in Duxbury and died in 1689, and Thomas, who settled in Scituate.

GEORGE SOULE was the thirty-fifth signer of the compact in the Mayflower, and a member of Governor Winslow's family. He married Mary Becket. In 1637 he volunteered in the Pequot War, but was not called into service. He was the owner of land in Plymouth, but before 1645 he sold that and moved to Duxbury. He was one of the deputies from that town to the General Court in Plymouth, and one of the original proprietors of the Sixteen Shilling and Purchade Purchases, and of the territory of

[1] Winsor, *History of Duxbury*, p. 293.
[2] *New England Historical and Genealogical Register*, vol. iii, p. 335.

Bridgewater. He died in 1680, a "very aged man." He never lived in Middleboro, but soon after its resettlement his descendants became residents of the town. The name was early spelled Sole, Soul, and Soule.[1]

FRANCIS SPRAGUE came to Plymouth in the ship Anne in 1623, and settled in Duxbury. He was a man of note in the early history of that town, an original proprietor of Bridgewater, and conveyed his estate in the Twenty-six Men's Purchase, before King Philip's War, to Benjamin Bartlett. He was one of the original owners in the Purchade Purchase.[2]

RESOLVED WHITE was the oldest son of William White, the eleventh signer of the civil compact in the cabin of the Mayflower, who died in the terrible winter of 1621. He lived in Marshfield, and his allotment was conveyed to Isaac Howland before 1677.

CONSTANT and THOMAS SOUTHWORTH, the purchasers of this land, were very important men in Plymouth Colony, and their names often appear in the various purchases of land made *Constant Southworth* of the Indians in Middleboro.
Their father, Edward, married Alice Carpenter; the sons, Constant and Thomas, were born in Leyden, Holland. Upon the death of their father Mrs. Southworth sailed for Plymouth, and later became the wife of Governor Bradford. Constant came to Plymouth in 1628, and Thomas soon after.

Constant moved from Plymouth and settled in Duxbury about the year 1637. He was admitted a freeman that same year. He was in the Pequot War, and represented Duxbury as deputy for seventeen years. He was treasurer of the colony from 1659 to 1678, and also served as an assistant; he was in King Philip's War as Commissary-General. He was one of the

---

[1] Goodwin, *Pilgrim Republic*, p. 475; *New England Historical and Genealogical Register*, vol. iii, p. 335.
[2] Mitchell, *History of Bridgewater*, p. 306.

grantees in behalf of the court in the Great Men's Purchase, and treasurer in behalf of the colony of a purchase made from Philip, March 4, 1669, of a tract at the Nemasket Pond, and of the Sixteen Shilling Purchase with John Tomson. He died in 1679. His daughter Alice married Colonel Benjamin Church. In his will, he gave his daughter Elizabeth "my next best bed and furniture, with my wife's best bed provided she do not marry William Fobes; but if she do then to have five shillings." The bed was considered worth thirty times as much as the five shillings, but it was the old story, and " Elizabeth chose to have five shillings with William to two beds without him."

Thomas Southworth, upon the death of Elder Brewster, was elected ruling elder in the church at Plymouth, but through the influence of his stepfather, Governor Bradford, he declined that office. He was an assistant to the governor in 1652, and continued in the government of the colony until his death in 1669. He was one of the commissioners of the United Colonies in 1659, and was appointed governor of the colonies' territory on the Kennebec River in 1664. He was known as Captain Thomas Southworth, and the "New England Memorial" .thus speaks of him: "This year 1669 was rendered sorrowful and remarkable by the death of Captain Thomas Southworth, who full of faith and comfort expired at Plymouth December 8, being fifty-three years old, after he had served God in his generation faithfully both in public and private station." He was the grantee for the owners of the Twenty-six Men's Purchase in behalf of the court for the jurisdiction of Plymouth, and of the Little Lotmen's Purchase, with his brother Constant.

In the History of the First Church we find Nathaniel Southworth and John Alden mentioned in the list of purchasers.

LIEUTENANT NATHANIEL SOUTHWORTH was the second son of Constant Southworth. He was born at Plymouth in 1648, married January 10, 1672, a daughter of Edward Gray of

Plymouth, and died January 14, 1711. He always resided in Plymouth, and was prominent in affairs of that town.[1]

JOHN ALDEN was the youngest of the pilgrims of Plymouth who took a prominent part in the government of the colony. He was born in 1599, and died in 1687. His biography is too well known to receive an extended notice. He became a proprietor of the Twenty-six Men's Purchase before King Philip's War, and was one of the original proprietors of the town of Bridgewater. There is a tradition, not substantiated, that for a little time he was a resident of Middleboro.[2]

Soon after this purchase was made, many of the original proprietors transferred their shares, and at the commencement of King Philip's War, in 1675, the owners are mentioned as in the fort.[3]

A LIST OF PROPRIETORS IN 1690

1. ffrancis Sprague, now in possession of Benj. Bartlett's son
2. John Adams   "   "   "   " Jabez Warren — since of John Wadsworth
3. George Partrage   "   "   "   " John Wadsworth and James Partrage
4. ffrancis Cook   "   "   "   " Lieut. Thompson and Adam Wright
5. Thomas Bordman   "   "   "   " Benjamin Nye
6. William Pontus   "   "   "   " William and John Churchill
7. Samuel ffuler
8. Edward Bumpus   "   "   "   " Joseph Bumpus
9. Francis Billenton "   "   "   " Isaac Billenton
10. William Brewster "   "   "   " Solliman hewit
11. John Shaw   "   "   "   " Samuel Wood
12. Edward Gray   "   "   "   " Ephraim Tinkham
13. Edward Gray   "   "   "   " Ebenezer Tinkham
14. Resolved White   "   "   "   " Isaac Howland
15. William Hodgkins "   "   "   " Joseph Vahan
16. Andrew Ring   "   "   "   " William and Eliazer Ring
17. Moses Simmons   "   "   "   " John Soule

[1] Winsor, *History of Duxbury*, p. 314.
[2] Goodwin, *Pilgrim Republic*, p. 566; Winsor, *History of Duxbury*, p. 213.
[3] See chapter on Early Settlers.

18. William Nelson, now in possession of John Bennett
19. John Howland   "   "   "   " Thomas and Joseph Faunce
20. Georg Sole
21. Philip Dellano Sr.
22. William Mullens   "   "   "   " William Nelson and John Cobb jr.
23. peter Brown   "   "   "   " Peter Tinkham
24. Samuel Eady   "   "   "   " Obadiah Eddy
25. Lefton ffuller
26. William Twining   "   "   "   " John and Samuel Doggett

March 5, 1690. "At a meeting of the proprietors above named on the 5th of March, 1690, at the house of Jacob Howland in Middleboro, all did agree upon the several lying lots . . . as hereinafter recorded."

A new survey of the Twenty-six Men's Purchase was made March 3, 1695, and Jacob Tomson was appointed surveyor.

WILLIAM TWINING'S name does not appear on the earlier lists. He was a son of William Twining of Eastham, born in England. He married Elizabeth, daughter of Stephen Dean, and had four children. "He was living in 1695." [1]

PURCHADE PURCHASE [2]

The second or Pachade Purchase was made July 9, 1662, in accordance with the following order of court passed June 4, 1661: —

"Libertie is granted unto Major Josiah Winslow and others the first born children of the jurisdiction of New Plymouth in reference unto an order or grant of the Court bearing date 1633 to purchase certain parcells of land for their accomodation ; viz. a parcell next to the Massachusetts' bounds, and another parcell between Namassakett and Bridgewater, and to make report thereof unto the Court that all such may be accomodated as aforesaid."

In reference to this purchase it was subsequently arranged by the court June 4, 1669, that the first mentioned tract should belong to those eight who had their allotments upon Pochade

[1] Savage, *Genealogical Dictionary*, vol. iv, p. 353.
[2] This is often spelled Pochade, Pachade, Pachaeg, Puchade.

neck and to their heirs; and the second to not only those eight, but to those also who had their allotments on the east side of Nemasket River in Captain Southworth's purchase.

Know all men by these presents that I Josias Wampetuck Sachem have and by these presents doe bargaine sell allien and dispose of; in the behalf of myself and such other Indians as are Interested therein; a Certaine nocke of Land Comonly Called Pachaeg pond lying and being between Namassakett River and a certain Brook that falleth into Titicutt River; namely the most westerly of the three Smale brooks that doe fall into the said River and bounded on the south by Certaine Swamps and low valleys that goe from the said Namassakett River on the east unto the above said brook with all the woods waters meddows and all priviledges and appurtenances therunto appertaining and belonging unto Major Josias Winslow for himself and other English; and alsoe all the meddows lying on the westward syde of said Namassakett River, as high as the wadeing place att the Taunton path and all such meddows as lye upon any the three brookes abovementioned though without the Crosse exit that bounds the Nocke for and in consideration of twenty one Pounds of him in hand Received, and doe herby fully and absolutely Resigne and give up unto the said Josias Winslow pteners and to theire heires executors and assignes forever all and singulare the above mentioned lands woods waters meddows etc: with all privilidges and appurtenances by them to be held possessed and enjoyed forever; and alsoe I the said Josias have as freely and absolutely sold unto the said Josias Winslow; one other Tract of land and meddowes bounded by the lands of Plymouth and Duxburrow on the one syde and of Bridgwater on the other Syde; and extending North and south from the land formerly purchased by Captaine Thomas Southworth unto the Great pond of Mattakeesett provided it enclude not the Thousand acres given to my sonne and Gorg Wampey about those ponds; and I doe by these presents Resigne up unto the said Josias Winslow his heires executors and assignes forever; all and singulare the lands above mensioned by him and them to be held possessed and enjoyed forever; In witness wherof I have herunto sett my hand and seale this ninth day of July 1662.

Signed sealed and delivered
in the presence of
   the mark O of Edward Gray
   mark A of George Wampey
   mark X of John Wampenes [1]

The mark of Josias ✝
Wampatucke
And a seale

The lands abovemensioned sold by Josias Wampetuck to mee and to my pteners although Included in one deed are to be understood to be two definite purchases; the former belonging unto those eight persons that had theire allotments upon Pochaeg necke and to theire heires forever; and the latter Tract mensioned lying between the bounds of Plymouth duxburrow and Bridgwater;

[1] *Plymouth Registry of Deeds*, Book III, p. 138.

and extending northward towards Mattakeeseet great ponds; are belonging unto all the first propriators of Namassakett plantation on both sydes of the River; viz. unto the eight shares upon Pachaeg and unto those that had theire allotments on the Easterly side of Namassakett upon the Purchase made by Captaine Southworth. In witness wherof I have hereunto sett my hand.

Josias Winslow.

This was done in the Court held att Plymouth the 4th. of June 1669.

Upon the preceding purchases, the following orders of court were adopted June 3, 1662: —

"in reference to a petition profered to the Court by sundry of the freemen, and in reference unto a graunt made to some to looke out accomodations of land as being the first borne children of this government, and for the disposing of two small tracts of land lately purchased, the one by Major Winslow and the other by captaine Southworth, the Court having viewed the small lists of the names of those that desired to be accomodated therein, have settled it upon these whose names follow: —

Mr. Prince	Mr. Howland [1]
Mr. Bradford	Francis Cooke [1]
Major Winslow	Lieutenant Matthew Fuller [1]
Mr. Aldin [1]	Lieutenant White
William Mullins [1]	William Pontus [1]
Mr. Brewster [1]	Steven Dean
Phillip Delanoy [1]	Andrew Ringe [2]
Mr. John Winslow	Francis Billington [2]
John Adams [1]	Moses Simonson [1]
Peter Browne [1]	Resolved White [1]
John Chace	William Bassett [1]
Anthony Annable for his daughter	Edward Bumpus [2]
Hannah Bumpus	Samuel Eddy [1]
Francis Sprague [1]	William Hoskins [2]
Gorg Soule [1]	Gorg Partrig [1]
Nathaniel Warren	William Nelson by right of his wife [2]
Samuel Fuller jun. of Plymouth [2]	

"Edward Gray to have a double share to be laid forth together." [1]

[1] See sketches of owners in Twenty-six Men's Purchase.
[2] See chapter containing sketches of the lives of the early settlers.

A large majority of the men for whose behalf this purchase was made were among the first settlers, or owners of the other purchases.

The following is an account of the lives of the remaining purchasers : —

ANTHONY ANNABEL came in the Ann, in 1623, with his wife Jane and two children. In 1634 he moved to Scituate, where he was one of the founders of the town. In 1636 he was one of eight men, together with the Governor and Council, to prepare a system of laws for the colony.[1] In 1645 he married Ann Clark. After moving to Barnstable, in 1640, he took a prominent part in all town matters, although unable to write his name, "and with the exception of Gov. Hinckley no Barnstable man was oftener employed in the transaction of public business." He never received the title of Mr., but was known as Goodman. He died in 1674.[2]

HANNAH BUMPUS was probably the wife of Edward Bumpus.

CAPTAIN BRADFORD was known in the latter part of his life as Major William Bradford. He was born at Plymouth, in 1624, and always resided there, one of her most honored citizens. Next to Standish, he was probably the principal military man of the colony. He was first made captain, and in King Philip's War held the rank of major. He was one of the owners of the Little Lotmen's Purchase, but never lived in town. He served as deputy assistant from Plymouth for twenty-four years, and for the last ten years of the colony's existence was deputy governor, excepting the three years of Andros's administration. From 1695 to 1702 he was the judge of probate.

Captain Bradford is buried on Burial Hill at Plymouth, and the ancient tombstone bears this inscription : —

[1] Goodwin, *Pilgrim Republic*, p. 401.
[2] *Barnstable Families*, pp. 13, 14.

HERE LYES Y^E BODY OF
Y^E HONOURABLE MAJOR
WILLIAM BRADFORD
WHO EXPIRED FEB^R Y^E 20
170¾ AGED 79 YEARS

He lived long but stil was dojng good
& in his countres service lost much blood
After a life well spent hes now at rest
His very name and memory is blest.

In his will he mentions giving to his son John "my father's manuscript, namely, a narrative of the beginning of New Plymouth." This history, after having been taken by the English from the Old South Church in Boston, in the time of the Revolution, and carried to England, was lost to the American people for many years. It was accidentally discovered by Rev. Thomas Barry, the author of the history of Massachusetts, and through the efforts of Senator Hoar and our minister to England, Mr. Bayard, has been recovered, and is now deposited in the library of the State House in Boston. In his will giving certain lands to his children, they were enjoined to sell the land they received "to none that do not bear the name of Bradford and be not descended from him."[1]

JOHN CHASE, STEVEN DEAN. We have found no mention of the lives of these men.

THOMAS PRENCE. At the time of the Purchade Purchase, Thomas Prence was Governor of Plymouth Colony. He was elected in 1635, again in 1638 and 1658, and continued in that office until the year 1673, when he died, aged seventy-two. He married Patience Brewster, in 1624. He had held many prominent offices in the colony. It was during his administration that the Quakers and Roger Williams were banished for their interference with the political affairs of the colony.[2]

[1] Winsor, *History of Duxbury*, p. 231 ; Goodwin, *Pilgrim Republic*, p. 466.
[2] Savage, *Genealogical Dictionary*, p. 477.

PEREGRINE WHITE, the son of William White of the Mayflower, was the first child born in Plymouth Colony. In 1646 he married Sarah Bassett, and died in 1704, at the age of eighty-four years. He moved to Marshfield with his step-father in 1632. In 1636 he was in the Pequot War, and in 1642 was an ensign in the train band of Captain Myles Standish, and later acquired the title of captain. His life is too well known to require an extended notice. Neither he nor his descendants occupied any portion of the Purchade or Little Lotmen's Purchases. By his will, dated July 14, 1704, he gave one half of his land in Middleboro to his son Daniel, and the other half to his two sons, Jonathan and Peregrine.[1]

NATHANIEL WARREN, the son of Richard Warren, for whom Warrentown was named, was a passenger in the Mayflower. He was born in Plymouth in 1624, and was an extensive landowner there and in other parts of the colony, and was one of the proprietors of the Sixteen Shilling Purchase. He was a member of the Plymouth militia in 1643, one of the selectmen in 1667, the year of his death, and had been a representative to the General Court for seven years. In the apportionment of the Purchade Purchase, he was assigned to lot number five, and bought John Adams's share in the Twenty-six Men's Purchase.

JOSIAH WINSLOW, whose name appears as Major Winslow, was the first of the Purchade purchasers, also one of the Sixteen Shilling proprietors. He was the son of Governor Edward Winslow, born in 1628, and seems to have inherited many of his father's characteristics as one of the most prominent and honored men of the colony. He began his public life soon after he was of age, as a deputy from Marshfield. At the age of thirty he began a term of sixteen years as governor's assistant, and then was governor of the colony, until his death in 1680. In the Narragansett War, he was a general of the united forces of the colonies. He was for many years a resident of Marshfield, and his house, where Alexander was taken sick,

[1] *White Family.*

is still standing.[1] He had command of the military company in Marshfield in 1652, and in 1658 was appointed major, afterwards commander, of the military forces of the united colonies raised in King Philip's War.

Acting under authority of the court at Plymouth, he made this purchase, and with Edward Gray the Twelve Men's Purchase, for the benefit of those who afterwards received a title in these second tracts of land.

John Winslow, one of the proprietors of the Purchade Purchase, was a brother of Edward Winslow, and arrived at Plymouth in 1621, in the Fortune. He married Mary Chilton, who is said to have been the first woman who came on shore from the Mayflower. He early moved to Boston, where he died in 1674.

MAJOR'S OR FIVE MEN'S PURCHASE

Other purchases in town were made from Tispequin. The first of these was the Major's or Five Men's Purchase, so called, and made July 13, 1663, Tispequin conveying to Major Josiah Winslow of Marshfield a narrow tract on the east side of Nemasket River lying between the upper and lower Indian paths to Plymouth, and extending to the Carver line.

Twenty acres of this tract having been before given to an Indian named Acomowett, he by his own deed conveyed it to the same purchasers.

> Know all men by these presents that I Tuspequin alias ye Black Sachem of Namasket out of my good affection and singular respect unto Major Josias Winslow of Marshfield Have given unto him the sd Major Winslow A certain Tract or parcell of land lying and being on ye easterly side of Namasket River & is next adjoining unto ye lands formerly bought by Capt. Southworth & is particularly bounded by ye said Namasket River on ye west and by ye cart path from ye said Namasket unto Tippecannicut on ye north and by another path called ye new path on ye south side and so unto a little brook called Manyhootset near Tippecannicut. All which lands bounded as above sd with all and singular ye woods waters swamps meadows & all benefits Privileges & Immunities there unto appertaining I ye above said sachem do by these presents give grant

[1] See chapter on Indians.

FIVE MEN'S PURCHASE

and bequeath unto my above said friend Major Winslow. To have and to hold to him and to his heirs for ever. And I do also acknowledge that I have received from him gratitudes in lieu of it to my content. And I shall warrant him quit possession thereof against all other claymers In witness whereof I have hereunto set my hand this 13th. of July 1663:

Witness

   The mark × of Peter Indian   The ⟨ ⟩ Mark of
   The mark × of Joseph Indian   Tispequin.

"The Names of such as are graunted Land in that Tract of Land comonly called the Majors Purchase, whoe are to haue thirty Acrees appcccc out of the best of it, and Comoning proportionable.

  Willam Clarke, of Duxburrow . . . . . one share [1]
  Jonathan Dunham . . . . one share [1]
  Benjamine Eaton . . . . one share
  Joseph Dunham . . . . one share
  Thomas Savory for his children . . . one share

"It was ordered likewise by the Court, that wheras the lott of Mr. Howland and the lott of Willam Nelson, with two others, which are judged very meane, that they bee alowed twelue acrees apeece att the heads of theire said lotts."

WILLIAM CLARK. See chapter on Early Settlers.

JOHN or JONATHAN DUNHAM. See chapter on Early Settlers.

JOSEPH DUNHAM was the son of John. In 1657 he married Mercy, daughter of Nathaniel Morton, and as a second wife, in 1669, Esther Wormall.

BENJAMIN EATON was the second son of Francis Eaton, born about the year 1627. He was in the family of the widow Bridget Fuller for some fourteen years, and while living with her attended school for two years. He was in Duxbury in 1648, and in Plymouth in 1650, but never lived in Middleboro.

THOMAS SAVORY is first mentioned in the records of the town as one of the company appointed in 1634 to remove trespassers on the property of the Plymouth Colony on the

[1] See chapter containing sketches of the lives of the early settlers.

Kennebec River. Here he narrowly escaped being shot by the trespasser Hocking while executing a command of Captain John Howland. This is characterized in Bradford's journal as "one of the saddest things which befel them since they come." In 1652 he was an under marshal of the court, and in 1655 he received one share of the Major's Purchase. In 1670 he was dismissed from his office of under marshal for negligence, but was soon reinstated. He died in 1674. His son Thomas was killed in King Philip's War, March 27, 1676, while serving in Captain Peirce's Company at Pawtucket.[1]

GREAT MEN'S PURCHASE

November 13, 1663. This purchase of land was made from Tispequin by Thomas Prence, John Winslow, Jr., Constant Southworth, and William Bassett, Jr.

"The tract lies principally on the north of the River on the west side of the brook which is the western bound of Pachade neck and runs upon the south side of Titacutt river until the river winds about to the north and there it crosses and runs, at a breadth of half a mile from the river, down from the bite of the river up it to the mouth of Winnetuxet.

"This tract the court disposed of to the propriators of Pachage Neck together with Kenelme Winslow and Josiah W. in right of their brother Gilbert W."

LITTLE LOTMEN'S PURCHASE [2]

The next purchase was made from Wampatuck August 16, 1664, by Thomas Prence, Captain William Bradford, and Edward Gray.

Be it known unto all men by these presents that I Josiah Wampatuck Sachem and Watchtameske Squa Sachem of Namasket have freely bargained and really sold all our lands at Namasket. That is to say, on the western side of the said

---

[1] Savery's *Families*, pp. 19-25; *New England Historical and Genealogical Register*, vol. ix, p. 80.

[2] Perhaps properly called Little Allotment Purchase.

Namasket river, from Pochauge neck to Mashucket brook all along by the side of the said river and westward up to the meadows sold formerly to the Major, belonging to Pochauge neck, with all and singular the privileges thereof as woods, swamps, grounds, herbage &c. unto Mr. Thomas Prence, Capt. William Bradford, and Edward Gray of Plymouth. To them their heirs or assigns. To have and to hold forever for a valuable consideration in hand paid. Only reserving to ourselves eight acres to be set out by Edward Gray upon some convenient place upon the river where they shall desire, and ten acres upon the hill where James and Thomas the Indians now plant, as also a little hill reserved for a burying place for the Indians with liberty of firewood from the commons and free liberty for fishing for bass and eels, together with the English, and free liberty and access to the river for herrings for their use in the season thereof. These things excepted we acknowledge ourselves to be fully satisfied for the said tract of land above said and do warrant the sale thereof against all other demands of any other Indians whatever. In witness whereof we have set to our hands and seals this sixteenth of August Annus Domini 1664.

Signed and sealed in the presence of us   his
   Indian Sachem Tispaquine   Josias ╈O Wampatuck (SS
           his Ɛ\ mark   mark   his
   John Taber his Ƴ mark   Wachtamaske ⟊   (SS
                                                 mark
   The "burying hill"

"The Names of those that haue Lands graunted vnto them by the Court, vizs, the Land which is purchased on the westerly Side of Namasskett Riuer, which is to bee equally deuided amongst them, and being soe deuided, is conceiued it will amount vnto thirty Acrees a Share of good Land, as alsoe Comoning adjoyning therevnto proportionable.

"Imp^rmes, to the towne of Plymouth for a minnester,
                                                                         one share
To Namasskett for a minnester, ... one share
To the Elder Cushman for his children, . . . one share
To Henery Sampson for his children, . . . one share
To Experience Michell for his children, . . . one share
[1] To Edward Gray ten acrees, to lye in a square
To Gabriell Fallowell, ... one share
[1] To Captaine Bradford, ... one share
[1] To James Cole, Seni^r, ... one share
To Gyles Rickard, Seni^r, ... one share
To Mr. Josepth Bradford, ... one share
To Anthony Snow, ... one share
To Nathaniell Morton, ... one share

[1] See chapter on Early Settlers, or other purchases.

[1] To John Morton, ... one share
To Ephraim Morton, ... one share
[1] To Edward Dotey, ... one share
To Gorge Bonum, ... one share
To Willam Harlow, ... one share
[1] To John Wood, ... one share
[1] To Henery Wood, ... one share
[1] To John Dunham, Juni^r, ... one share
To Samuell Dunham, ... one share
To Josepth Warren, ... one share
To John Jourdaine, ... one share
In all 24 shares.

"It was ordered by the Court, that the charge of the purchase of the said land shalbee equally bourne by all those which haue lands there, euery one a like proportion; and that none shall posesse aboue two shares of that land either of the ptenors or any other; and that if any one shalbee found to posesse aboue two shares thereof, it shalbee forfeit to the countrey." [2]

GEORGE BONUM or BONEHAM in 1644 married for his second wife, Sarah Morton, a daughter of George Morton. He built a house at Plymouth in 1678, which is still standing, known as the Leach house. He always resided in Plymouth, and died April 28, 1704, aged eighty-six.[3]

JOSEPH BRADFORD, the son of Governor Bradford by his second wife, Alice Southworth, was born in 1630. In 1664 he married Jael, daughter of Peter Hobart.

THOMAS CUSHMAN, familiarly known as Elder Thomas Cushman, arrived at Plymouth in the ship Fortune in 1621, with his father, Robert Cushman. He was at that time fourteen years of age. Five years after the death of Elder Brewster, he was appointed ruling elder of the church at Plymouth (1649).

[1] See chapter on Early Settlers, or other purchases.
[2] *Plymouth Colony Records*, vol. iv, p. 94.
[3] Savage. *Genealogical Dictionary*, vol. i, p. 210.

He was the owner with Thomas Prince and others of a tract of land in Rehoboth. He died December 10, 1691, in the eighty-fourth year of his age. In his will, he gives to his son, Isaac Cushman, "one-half of my land at Namasket Pond in the township of Middleborough as also ye one-half of my right in the Sixteen Shilling Purchase so called in township above sd." He also gave to his son, Elkanah Cushman, by his will, "one-half of my land lying at Namasket Pond as also ye one-half of the Sixteen Shilling Purchase as above expressed also one-third of my meadow at Wintuxet." He was also one of the owners of the South Purchase.

SAMUEL DUNHAM was the son of John or Jonathan Dunham, who married the widow of William Falloway in 1649.[1]

GABRIELL FALLOWELL came to Plymouth from Boston in 1639, and was admitted a freeman September 1, 1640. He was a proprietor in the Sixteen Shilling Purchase and of the "Liberties of Middleberry," and there is a tradition that he was a resident of the town before King Philip's War. Savage in his Genealogical Dictionary says: "We only know of him that he died Dec. 28, 1667, aged 83." He probably had a son William, who married Martha Beal, daughter of one of the first settlers of Hingham, and who was the father of John Fallowell, who married Sarah Wood in 1669.[2]

WILLIAM HARLOW, known as Sergeant William Harlow, is first mentioned as of Lynn in 1637; and later of Sandwich and Plymouth. He was born probably in England in 1624, and his stay in Sandwich and Lynn must have been short. He lived in Plymouth, where certain land had been granted, and in 1654 he was admitted as a freeman. In 1673 and 1675 he was a deputy from Plymouth to the General Court, and was selectman for fifteen years between 1669 and 1691. He was a cooper by trade, and died August 26, 1691, aged sixty-seven.

---

[1] Davis, *Ancient Landmarks of Plymouth*, p. 98.
[2] Savage, vol. ii, p. 138; Davis, *Ancient Landmarks of Plymouth*, p. 105.

He never was a resident upon the portion of the Little Lotmen's Purchase assigned to him, or of the South Purchase.[1]

JOHN JORDAN or JORDANE was one of the proprietors of the "Liberties of Middleberry" in 1677, and had a son in 1650, called Barack Jordan. He was an owner in the Sixteen Shilling Purchase.

EXPERIENCE MITCHELL came from Leyden with the pilgrims in the ship Anne in 1623; in 1645 he moved to Duxbury, and in the latter part of his life to Bridgewater, of which he was one of the original proprietors, and where he died in 1689, aged ninety years. He was one of the original proprietors of the South Purchase. He married for his first wife Jane, daughter of Francis Cook of the Mayflower.[2]

EPHRAIM MORTON was the sixth son of George Morton, and a brother of Nathaniel Morton, the secretary of Plymouth Colony. He was born on the ship Anne in 1623, on her voyage to Plymouth. He married Ann Cooper in 1644, and Mary Harlow in 1692. He became a freeman in 1648, and was a representative to the General Court for twenty-eight years from 1657. He was one of the first representatives to the Massachusetts General Court after the union of the colonies. In 1683 he was chosen a magistrate of the colony, and at the time of his death he was a justice of the court of common pleas. He was a member of the council of war in Plymouth, and served during King Philip's War. He never occupied any portion of this or the Sixteen Shilling Purchase. He died September 7, 1693.

NATHANIEL MORTON, the eldest son of George Morton, was born at Leyden, Holland, in 1613, and accompanied his parents to Plymouth in 1623. He was made a freeman in 1635, and

---

[1] *New England Historical and Genealogical Register*, vol. xiv, p. 227.
[2] Winsor, *History of Duxbury*, p. 282; Mitchell, *History of Bridgewater*, p. 241; *Mayflower Descendants*, vol. i, 1899, pp. 97, 98.

in 1645 was chosen secretary of the colony, which office he held until his death in 1685; most of the records of the colony were made by him. He was the author of the "New England Memorial," a record of prominent events within his personal knowledge, and of many works of interest relating to the early history of Plymouth Colony. He died June 29, 1685. He was never a settler upon any portion of the Little Lotmen's Purchase, or of the South Purchase, of which he was a proprietor. In 1635 he married Lydia Cooper, and in 1674 Mrs. Hannah Templar.[1]

GILES RICKARD was a resident of Plymouth and a freeman in 1637. He married Judith ——, and for a second wife, Joan Tilson. He died in 1684, aged eighty-seven years. He had a son Giles, who married, October 31, 1651, Hannah Dunham, perhaps a daughter of John Dunham. He was one of the owners of the Sixteen Shilling Purchase, and his name is among the proprietors of the "Liberties of Middleberry" in 1677. In October, 1671, he was fined by the Court ten shillings for selling "syder" to the Indians.[2]

HENRY SAMSON or SAMPSON was one of the early settlers of Duxbury, and his name occurs in the list of men between sixteen and sixty, capable of bearing arms, reported to the court on the 2d of October, 1643. He was a constable in 1661, and a freeman in 1670. He was one of the original proprietors of the town of Bridgewater, but never lived upon the lot assigned him in this purchase. In 1666 he married Ann Plummer, and in 1667 was allowed by the General Court to select land for himself. He was an owner in the South Purchase. He died December 24, 1684, leaving a large family.[3]

ANTHONY SNOW was in Plymouth in 1638. He married Abigail, the youngest daughter of Richard Warren. He early removed from Plymouth, and settled at Green Harbor, Marsh-

---

[1] *Morton Memoranda.*   [2] Savage, *Genealogical Dictionary.* vol. iii, p. 527.
[3] Winsor, *History of Duxbury*, p. 300.

field. He often represented the town in the General Court of the colony, and was a man of considerable influence. Cedar Grove Cemetery, near the present meeting-house, was his gift to Marshfield a little before his death. His descendants lived in Middleboro at Muttock, in the north corner of "Great Gate," where in changing the street, a few years ago, the workmen came upon the site of the house.

WOOD'S PURCHASE

Wood's Purchase was made August 9, 1667, by Henry Wood[1] of Plymouth, from Tispequin, with the consent of his wife Anny, for the consideration of four pounds. He sold also by the same deed six acres of meadow on the south side of the path from Nemasket to Agawam (Wareham).

This Writing witnesseth that I Tuspaquin otherwise called ye Black Sachem with the full consent of my wife Anny for and in consideration of ye sum of four pounds to me in hand paid by Henry Wood of Plymouth do by these presents sell and make over all my right and title to a parcell of land lying on the east side of Namaskett River to ye Southward of ye Upper Way to Namaskett being bounded on ye one end by ye pond called ye Black Sachems pond ye Indian name being Wampaucutt, on ye other end by a little pond called Asnemscussett, on ye one side bounded from ye corner of that pond called Asnemscussett and twenty pole from it, and so upon a direct line to a place of the Brook that comes out of that pond called before Wampaucutt, to that part of ye brook that is stony like to a fall called Sawcomet, on ye other side bounded with a swamp or swamps. The swamps being included in ye sale. With all priviledges belonging thereunto; With free liberty for his cattel to feed in ye places adjacent without being molested. Together with a parcell of meadow land being six acres lying on ye south side of the path goith from Namaskett to Agawam. To have & to hold all ye said land & meadow land with all priviledges & appurtenances belonging thereunto: do sell from me & my heirs to him ye said Henry Wood he his heirs & assigns forever. To have & to hold all ye above land to him ye said Henry Wood and his heirs forever. The said Tuspaquin Reserving liberty to get cedar bark in ye swamp above expressed: All ye above land expressed with all priviledges belonging thereunto I the sd Tuspaquin do warrant ye sale of these lands above expressed, from any other claim or right or title thereunto. In Witness hereunto I have set to my hand this present ninth of August 1667.

In ye Presence of
John Morton
Thomas Southworth

The mark of ϛ Tuspaquin
The mark of Ƶ his wife Anny

[1] For sketch of life of Henry Wood, see chapter on Early Settlers.

The next purchase was made July 7, 1669, from Tispequin and his son William, a sachem, by Experience Mitchell, Henry Sampson, Thomas Little, and Thomas Paine.

To all to whome these presents shall come, Wee Tispiquin alius Blacke Sachem and William Sonne of the sd Tispiquin, Indian Sachems sendeth greeting Know yee that wee Tispiquin alius Blacke Sachem and William Sonne of the sd Tispiquin; for and In concideration of the sume of tenne pounds St£ to us in hand payd; by; Experience Mitchell, Henry Sampson of Duxborough; Thomas Little of Marshfield and Thomas Paine of Eastham wherewith we doe acknowlidge our selves Jointly & Severally, payd and fully Sattisfide, and thereof and of every part and parcell thereof doe Acquit, Exonerate, and Discharge the Afforesaid Experience Mitchell, Henry Sampson, Thomas Little and Thomas Paine, Their and Every of their Heirs Executors and Administrators and every of them forever have Bargained; and sold, alienated, Enfeoffed and Confirmed and by these Presents doe bargaine, sell; Alienate, Enfeofe and Confirme, from us the Afforesaid Tispiquine and William and our heirs unto the Afforesaid Experience Mitchell, Henry Sampson, Thomas Little, and Thomas Paine, theire heires and Assignes for ever All that our tract or parcell of Land that Lyeth on the westward side of a Tract of land Purchased by Mr. John Alden and others from the Sachem Josias Wampetucke wch Lyeth nere Assawampsett Ponds; wch Aforesd Tract now sold by these p&sents is one halfe mile in Bredth, and is in Length from the Aforesd Ponds to Dartmouth Path where ye sd Path Crosses the westward side Line of the Aforesaid Land of Mr. Alden and others and from the said Dartmouth Path into the woods ye said Land Purchased by these presents is to extend in Length one mile and one halfe mile; ye Aforesd halfe mile in bredth is to be measured according to ye Square according to ye westward side line of the Aforesaid Mr. Aldens Land with all and Singular the Appurtenances and Priviledges thereunto belonging: And all our right Title and Interest of and into the Aforesaid Premises and Every part and Parcell thereof: To have and to hold all that our said Tract or parcell of Land being one halfe mile in Bredth and in length one mile and halfe mile from ye-sd dartmouth path into the woods and from ye said path to Extend home to the Aforesaid pond wch pond is to be the bounds of one end of the sd land with all and singular the Appurtenances and Priviledges thereunto belonging and all our right Title and Interest of and into the Aforesaid premises and Every part and parcell thereof, unto the Aforesaid Experience Mitchell, Henry Sampson, Thomas Little & Thomas Paine ther Heires and Assignes forever With Warranties Against all people whatsoever for ever by these presents; To Claime any Right, Title or Interest of or into the Aforesaid Premises with ther Appurtenances or any part or parcell thereof; And wee the said Tispiquin, alius Black Sachem and William doe by these presents Authorise the said Experience Mitchell Henry Sampson Thomas Little & Thomas Paine either by themselves or ther Attorney to record and Enrolle these presents or cause them to be recorded and Enrolled before the Governoȓ of Newplymouth or some one of his Assistantce for the time being According to the usuall mannor of Recording and Enrolling

Deeds and Evidence in ye Kings Maties Court of Newplymouth aforesd In wittnes whereof we the Aforesaid Tispiquin and William have hereunto set to our hands and Seales this seventh day of July one thousand six hundred sixty and nine

Signed Sealed and Delivered
in pṛsents of

Willyam Nickerson   The mark ⸜ of Tispiquin   LS
                    Mark of
Wᵐ Crowe   The ⸝ Samuel

        Henry ye Indian   The Mark of ⚑ William   LS
The Mark ◯ of   his sonne
Danniell ye Indian

        The Mark ⸙ of old
        Harry ye Indian
           This deed was acknowledg this 7th of July
           1669: before mee
                John Alden Asist
Ye words in breadth betwixt ye twelfe and
thirteenth Line ; and land betwixt the
thirteenth & fourteenth Line before
the sealing and delivery hereof [1]

TWELVE MEN'S PURCHASE

June 30, 1672, Tispequin and Mantomapact, alias William, his son, in consequence and in consideration of a debt of the latter to Major Winslow for the amount of ten pounds, eight shillings, conveyed to Edward Gray and Major Winslow a tract on the east side of Assawampsett Pond, since known as the Twelve Men's Purchase. It was a triangular piece of land, extending upon the northern side at a distance of about three miles, and upon the easterly and westerly sides at a distance of about four miles.[2]

---

[1] From the original in the late Earl Alden's possession. The acknowledgment in bluer and paler ink, and is between the signatures of the witnesses and the Tispequins Deed very fairly and plainly written by the witness Nickerson. Seals cut out and lapped over. A stamp on the wax. Well preserved every way.

[2] Tispequin to Edward Gray and Major Winslow, *Plymouth Registry of Deeds*, Book III, p. 238.

To all people to whom these presents shall come Tispaquin the Black Sachem of Namaskett and Wantowapatt (?) allias William (his sonne) sendeth greet, and further know yee That we the said Tispaquin and William have Given Granted bargained sold allianed enfeofed and Confirmed and by these presents doe give Grant bargaine sell alien enfeofe and Confirm from us and our heires unto Mr. Edward Gray and Major Josias Winslow and theire heires forever a Certaine Tract or Prcell of land settuate lying and being on the Easterly Syde of Anowamsett (?) pond, and is bounded as followeth, viz. beginning att that place of the said pond wher Namaskett River floweth out of the pond, and so Ranging southward the pond being the easterly bounds on till it comes to a Pynne tree marked standing neare the pond syde and so by a Range of Pyne Trees Runing to the Southward still, untill it Comes againe to touch upon another Corner of the pond, and then againe bounded by the pond on to a little brooke that floweth out of it, and Runs toward the east; and soe to a great Cedar Swamp being the southeast boundary; and from the said swamp is bounded on the easterly end or syde by a brooke that floweth out the said Cedar Swamp, and Runs Northeasterly toward a pond comonly called Tispaquin's pond, and soe home to the lands formerly sold to henery Wood; and from Tispaquin's pond by a brook Called the fall (?) brooke; that Comes out of the saide pond, and falleth into Namaskett River, and soe up the said River to the first mentioned boundary upon Namaskett pond, only it must be understood that one hundred acres more or less as bounded; which was formerly sold to Mr. Thomas Prence; and lyeth on the southerly syde of the above mentioned fall brooke, although Comprehended within the above written bounds, is not hereby sold nor by us disposed unto the abovesaid Winslow and Gray, but all the Rest of the lands contained within the above mentioned bounds, wee the said Tispaquin and William doe herby fully freely clearly and absolutely sell and passe over from us and our heires unto them the said Major Winslow and Edward Gray and theire heires forever; Together with all the woods, waters and all other benefitts emolluments and privilidges therunto appertaining to them the said Winslow and Gray and theire heires from the day of the sale herof for ever, to be held possessed and enjoyed in the most free and ample tenor that lands by us sold can be holden in; for the valluable consideration of twenty seven pounds of Good and Currant pay to us in hand alreddy payed, and of which sume and of every pt and prcell therof, wee doe herby fully and Clearly acquitt exonerate and discharge them the abovesaid Winslow and Gray and theire heires forever, and for this wee the abovesaid Tispaquin and William doe Covenant to and with the said Buyers that wee att this day and untill the ensealing and delivery hereof, the true and Right proprietors of the above mensioned Lands; and that wee will warrant and defend them now and att all times against any that shall or may claim from by or under us, and to doe and performe any further acte that may by them be Required according to law, for the clere making and the firme settling of the premises unto them; In witness whereof wee have herunto sett our hands and seales this thirtieth day of June, Anno. Dom. one thousand six hundred seventy and two.

Signed sealled and delivered   Tispaquin ✕ his mark and (seal)
in presence of John Thomas   The ✕ mark of
and Elizabeth Pelham.   William or Wantomapatt and (seale)

This deed of sale was acknowledged by Tispaquin and William his son this third day of July in open Court before mee

Thomas Prence Govr.

Major Winslow was allowed to make this purchase by the court in the May preceding, on his complaining to that body of the Indian's neglect or refusal to pay him his debt. In allowing this grant, the court directed that from this land the proprietors should pay all of the indebtedness of the Indians, and this was done before the close of the year. This is a circumstance which should acquit our pilgrim fathers of fraud and injustice towards the natives in the purchase of lands. The names of those to whom the Indians owed money were: George Vaughan, Jonathan Dunham, John Nelson, Edward Gray, John Wood, Gershom Cobb, and John Dunham, Jr.

LOTS

	First Draught	Second Draught
Abraham Jackson	1	19
John Dunham [1]	2	18
Benjamin Warren	3	16
Benjamin Warren	4	24
Thomas Morton	5	14
George Morton	6	17
John Cob [1]	7	23
Mrs. Clark for her children	8	15
John Bennet [2]	9	21
Mrs. Doritie Clark for Samuell	10	22
John Morton [1]	11	00
Nathaniell Morton [1]	12	20
John Morton [1]	13	00

THOMAS FAUNCE,[1] the clerk who kept the records of these proprietors, was a son of John Faunce, who came over in the Anne in 1623. He succeeded Elder Cushman in 1699, and was the last ruling elder of the church at Plymouth. He was town clerk of Plymouth for more than thirty-five years, and died in 1745, in his ninety-ninth year. It is from him that

---

[1] See chapter containing sketches of the lives of the early settlers and early purchasers.

[2] See chapter containing an account of The Green.

much of the early history of the pilgrims has been derived, particularly our knowledge of the genuineness of the rock at Plymouth.[1]

Proprietors of the Twelve Men's Purchase, an account of whose lives has not previously been given: —

MRS. CLARK. We find nothing relating to her.

ABRAHAM JACKSON, an apprentice of Secretary Morton, was always a resident of Plymouth. He married Remember, a daughter of Nathaniel Morton, in 1657, and died October 4, 1714. He was also a proprietor in the South Purchase.[2]

GEORGE MORTON, a grandson of the first George Morton who came into the colony, was known as Deacon George Morton. He was born in 1645, and died October 7, 1693. His father was Lieutenant Ephraim Morton.

THOMAS MORTON. We find no record relating to him.

BENJAMIN WARREN. We find no one of this name of age at the time of this purchase.

SOUTH PURCHASE

July 23, 1673, Tispequin and his son sold for fifteen pounds to Benjamin Church of Duxbury and John Tomson of Barnstable, for the inhabitants of Middleborough, an extensive tract conveying a part of what is now Rochester and Wareham and Carver as well as Middleboro, and known as the South Purchase. It contained all the unpurchased lands on the east and north bounds. By a subsequent adjustment of these bounds, the purchase extended on the south only to the southern boundary line of the town.

---

[1] Goodwin, *Pilgrim Republic*, p. 469.
[2] Savage, *Genealogical Dictionary*, vol. ii, p. 527.

Know all men by these pr̃esnts that one Tispaquin allies the black Sachem of Namassekett and William his sonn, doe acknowledge for and in consideration of the sume of fifteen pounds to us in hand paid by Benjamin Church of the Towne of Duxburrow in the Jurisdiction of Plymouth in New England in America housecarpenter and John Tomson of the Towne of Barnstable in ye Jurisdiction aforesaid housecarpenter and in ye behalfe of all & singular the Inhabitants and proprietors of ye lands in & within ye Township of Middleberry in ye Jurisdiction aforesaid where with we ye said Tuspaquin ye black Sachem & William his son doe acknowledge orselves fully satisfied contented and paid, and thereof & of every pr̃t and pr̃cell thereof doe exonerate acquitt and discharge them ye said Benjamin Church & John Tomson & all and singular ye Inhabitants & proprietors of ye lands in ye Township of Middleberry aforesaid them and every of them their and every of their heirs executors & administrators for ever. That we have freely & absolutely bargained allienated & sold enfeofed & confirmed & by these pr̃esents doe freely and absolutely bargaine alienate sell enfeofe & confirme from us ye said Tuspaquin & William his son, & our heirs, to them ye said Benjamin Church & John Tomson for & in ye behalfe of all & singular ye Inhabitants & proprietors of ye Towne of Middleberry aforesaid & their & every of their heires & assignes for ever, A certaine Tract of land lying at & near ye Township of Middleberry aforesaid bounded westerly by a River caled Monhiggin which runneth into a pond called Quitquassett ponds & so ye westerly side of a Cedar swamp & so ranging to a pond called Tuspaquins & along to ye lands of henery Wood & a Cedar swamp & so along to an old Indian path to a place called Pochaboquitt with all ye vacant land between Tuspaqins ponds & ye said Pochaboquitt Northerly it is bounded by ye said Indian path to Mahudsett River & from ye sd Mahudsett River to a swamp purchased by William Bassett & so to a River that runneth out of Swanhold unto a place called Tusconnanset, Easterly it is bounded with ye South meadow River, so caled, & so along by the said river to a place caled by the Indians Massapanoh, & ye Southerly bounds is from ye said Massapanoh ranging to a pond caled Sniptuet to ye easterly side of an Indian field taking in a fresh meadow & so over ye pond to a little Iland & so to a Rivers mouth caled Tuppatwett which runneth into ye pond caled Quittuwashett & along ye ponds side to ye fore named River caled Monheggen Containing within ye said purchase all ye unpurchased lands lying on ye easterly & northerly boundes aforesaid; To have and to hold all ye said tract of land bounded as aforesaid with all & singular ye appurtenances & priviledges belonging thereunto or to any pr̃te or pr̃cell thereof, from us the said Tuspaquin and William his son & our heires to them ye said Benjamin Church & John Tomson, and in ye behalfe & to ye use of all & singular ye Inhabitants and proprietors of ye lands in ye Township of Middleborough to them and every of them & every of their heires and assigns for ever. The sd Tract of land bounded as aforesaid with all & singular ye woods waters meadows & meadow lands herediments profitts priviledges enrollments belonging thereunto or to any pr̃te or pr̃cell thereof with all our Right title and Interest of & into ye same or any part or pr̃cell thereof To belong & appurtaine unto ye only proper use & behoofe, of them ye sd Benjamin Church & John Tomson for and in ye behalfe & to ye use of ye Inhabitants & proprietors of ye lands in ye Township of Middleberry aforesaid. To them & every of them their & every of their heires & assignes forever free & clear & clearly acquitted of &

1673]   SOUTH PURCHASE   615

from all other & former gifts grants bargains sales Ingagements & Intanglements whatsoever had made suffered comitted or done, or by us or either of our knowledge privity or procurement and to be holden of his Matie, Charles ye second King of England, etc: his manor of East Greenwich in ye County of Kent in ye realm of England in free & common soccage & not in capite nor by Knights service nor by ye rents & services thereof & thereby due & of right accustomed with warrantie against all persons that by our right or title of or into ye same or any p^rte or p^rcell thereof, granting libertie unto ye said Benjamin Church & John Tomson for & in ye behalfe of ye Inhabitants & proprietors of ye lands of ye Towne of Middlebury aforesaid or either of them either by themselves or their Attorney to record & Inrole these presents or to cause them to be recorded or enrolled in his Maties Court of Records, for ye true performance of ye premises Wee ye said Tuspaquin ye sachem of Namaskett commonly caled & Knowne by ye black Sachem & William his son doe hereby binde o^rselves o^r heires executors & Administrators by these presents In witness whereof we ye said Tuspaquin & William his son have hereunto subscribed o^r hands & affixed o^r seals this twenty third day of July one thousand six hundred seventy & three 1673.

Signed sealed & delivered   The ◯ mark of Tuspaquin (S
in ye presence of   the Black Sachem
  John Cotton
  John Cushen   The ⚭ mark of William (S
  The mark ⚹ of Sam Harry   son to ye Black Sachem
  The mark ℞ of Joseph of Namassakett

                Tuspaquin ye black sachem & William
                his son acknowledged this deed July 22,
                1673: before Josiah Winslow
                                  Governor

It is doubtful who were the original parties for whom this South Purchase was made. They were to pay the expenses of the purchase, and have the territory apportioned among themselves. For some reason, they did not pay or settle for the same, and John Tomson and Benjamin Church were allowed to take about one third of the southern portion of this land as their own, which was afterwards known as the Snipetuit Purchase, and the remainder was laid out as the South Purchase.

November 1, 1673, William, Wetispaquin, Assaweta, Tobyas, and Beevatt Indians,—for 10 lb. sold to John Tomson, Joseph Lathrop and Barnabas Laythrop, all of Barnstable,—a tract bounded northerly by Quetaquash pond, easterly by Quetaquash river and Snipetuet pond; and from the easternmost end and southermost side of a little neck of land by the said Snipetuit pond, and so from the easternmost side of a little pond on a straight line from thence to Dartmouth path 100 rods; southerly from Dartmouth new bound tree, and so all along by Dartmouth path until within sight of Quatequash pond; and from the path upon a straight line to the southermost end of the pond and by the pond.

(Wit. John Bryant, Nathl Thomas;) Old Tispaquin alias the Black Sachem and Daniel Pachange the same day gave up their right in the above sd deed. Actcewamequa resigned his June 25, 1674.

July 13, 1685. This court allow & confirme all the lands contained in the above mentioned deed unto the 'bove mentioned Mr. Barnabas Laythrop, capt. Joseph Laythrop and John Thompson according to ye order of the General Court to hold to them the said Barnabas Laythrop, Joseph Laythrop, John Thompson their heirs & assigns for ever.

Attest Nathl Clarke Secretary
of the jurisdiction of New Plymouth.

The following were the names of the proprietors of this purchase, found in the earliest list recorded: —

"A list of the proprietors of the South purchase taken at the proprietors meeting at the house of Isaac Howland in Middleborough on Tuesday the 17 day of May 1698 and at said meeting upon the drawing of the Lots: the Lots fell as they are here in Respectively afixed to each proprietors name

Experience Michill [1]	18 : 14	Edward Gray [1]	131 : 63
Phillip Dillinoc [1]	146 : 145	Peregrine White [1]	48 : 41
Nathaniel Morton [1]	7 : 83	Sollomon Huet	135 : 136
John Rogers deceast	203 : 169	Mathew Fuller [1]	191 : 181
Benjamin Warren [1]	140 : 147	Francis Combs [2]	185 : 186
Thomas Morton [1]	17 : 115	Gabrill Followell [1]	74 : 38
Midlebery Ministry	55 : 26	Anthony Snow [1]	20 : 149
Adam Wright [2]	52 : 107	Elder Chusman [1]	133 : 134
John Soule seen [3]	174 : 163	John Morton [2]	204 : 158
Jonathan Dunham [2]	1 : 111	Henry Sampson [1]	200 : 155
Zechry Edie [2]	128 : 196	David Alden	141 : 156
Samuell Richman	89 : 104	William Harlow [1]	70 : 27
George Morton [1]	3 : 80	Francis Walker and John Hascall jur [2]	93 : 102
John Jones [1]	121 : 143		
Plymouth Ministry	95 : 180	John Winslow [1]	14 : 152
Jonathan Sparrow	68 : 132	Abraham Jackson [1]	193 : 215
Nathaniel Loweth	50 : 31	Spare Lot	205 : 46
William Cadman	2 : 113	is given to John Bennet theire clerk in way [4] of gratification of his service in the office of his clerkship "	
Liut Isack Little	99 : 171		
Edward Gray [1]	34 : 161		
John Dunham [2]	97 : 159		

[1] See other purchases.
[2] See sketches of the lives of the early settlers.
[3] See chapter on Soule Neighborhood.
[4] See chapter containing an account of the Green.

DAVID ALDEN, one of the proprietors of the South Purchase, was the son of John Alden of the Mayflower. He resided in Duxbury, was a man of influence in town and colony, and often employed in public matters. He died in 1719, aged ninety-three, when his estate in Middleboro, probably that portion which had been assigned to him in the South Purchase, May 20, 1719, was appraised. He married Mary, a daughter of Constant Southworth.[1]

WILLIAM CADMAN of Portsmouth, R. I., held many public offices. In 1669 land at Middleboro was conveyed to him by James Cole of Plymouth. This was afterward sold by his grandson to Seth Howland, in 1708.[2]

SOLOMON HUET may have been the son of Thomas Huet, who settled in Hingham. In 1715 Solomon Huet of Marshfield bequeathed land in Middleboro to his son John.

ISAAC LITTLE, the son of Thomas Little, was born at Plymouth in 1646. He was chosen lieutenant of the Plymouth County militia, July 7, 1681, and was one of a Council of War of the colony, August 14, 1689. He died in 1712. He and his brother Ephraim became residents of the town soon after its resettlement. In 1706 they kept an ordinary in what was afterwards known as the Sproat Tavern.

NATHANIEL LOWETH. We have been unable to find any facts concerning him.

SAMUEL RICHMOND, the son of John Richmond, was born in Taunton, September 23, 1668. His father was a large owner of land, and was one of the distributors of the Irish Charity in 1677, to distressed sufferers from King Philip's War. He took part in many matters of public interest in Taunton, and was the ancestor of many of that name in Middleboro. He

---

[1] Winsor, *History of Duxbury*, p. 214.
[2] *Plymouth Colony Deeds*, vol. vii, p. 251.

was probably the purchaser of the lot standing in the name of his son Samuel. As this purchase was made from the Indians June 30, 1672, his son Samuel was only four years old, and the entry upon the records is either a mistake, or else was entered subsequently, after the death of his father.[1]

JOHN ROGERS is named as "John Rogers deceased" in the list of proprietors of this purchase. He was probably the son of John Rogers, who was one of the early settlers of Duxbury, having bought land in 1634. He died in 1660. John, Jr., who was also a native of Duxbury, married Elizabeth Pabodie in 1666, and died in 1696.

JONATHAN SPARROW, son of Richard, was constable of Eastham in 1656, and took the freeman's oath in 1667; in 1662 he was appointed by the court one of a committee to take an inventory of the "liquors, gunpowder, shot and lead that is brought into this government;" in 1665 he was engaged as a schoolmaster. He was a deacon of the church. He was one of the selectmen of Eastham for ten years, deputy many years to the colony court, and representative to the Massachusetts General Court at Boston after the union of the colonies. In 1689 he was commissioned one of the justices of the Association Court. In 1675 he was in the Narragansett fight as first lieutenant of the second company of Plymouth, and in the French and Indian War, in 1690, he was appointed captain of the militia of Eastham.[2]

SIXTEEN SHILLING PURCHASE

May 14, 1675, land was bought for £33 by Constant Southworth and John Tomson, of Watispaquin (Tispequin) Sr., and William Tispaquin, "Indian sachems now dwelling within the township of Middleborough three tracts of land, called the

---

[1] *Genealogy of the Richmond Family*, p. 3.
[2] *History and Genealogy of the Bangs Family*, p. 20.

'Sixteen Shilling Purchase.'" This was by far the largest purchase, embracing what is now Lakeville.

May 14, 1675 Wituspequin alias the Black Sachem, and William alias Will Tispequin bind and make oath to Constant Southworth and John Tomson and the rest of the proprietors of Middleboro all Assawampsett Neck or Necks and places adjacent as security for the peaceable enjoyment of those tracts lately bought by a deed of this date.

Know all men by these presents that wee Witispican sinr and William Tispican iur: indian shachims now dwelling within the township of Middilbury in the iuzidickon of New Plimonth in New England in America: have for the iust some of thirty and three pounds starling: in hand paid before the insealing herof: by Constant Southworth and John Tomson of the same colliny or iuridicktion afore said: which said some wee doe acknowledge our selves fully satisfied contented and payd: and thereof: and of every part thereof: doe exonerate aquite and discharge the said Constant Southworth and John Tomson: them there airs exsecutors and administrators forever: have freely fully absolutly bargained and sould infefed and confirmed: and by these presents doe bargaine sell infeefe and confirme from us and our aires (or any "other Indians now belonging or withing this iuridicktion as above said:) to them the said Constant Southworth John Tomson and the rest of thes parnors or propriators whose names are inroulled or recorded in the Records of the towne booke of Midd:bury" as is above expressed to whom it properly belongs unto: to them and every of them ther airs and every of ther airs for ever: all those trakts of lands boutte uplands and medowlands lying and beeing within the compus of these bounds herin exspressed: as namely one trackt or parsell of land lying on the south-southwest: and westerly side or parts of sertaine ponds as namely one is commonly called by the name of Ninipoket the other gos by the name of quitticus pond: the ponds being the bounds on the one sid and end: and we are to close home unto a purchase of land made by Tresurer Southworth and now belongs unto Elder Thomas Chushman's and some of the Littills: ther southerly bounds is our northerly: and from thire bounds by ther pond: upon the same point of compus as ther land runs wee are to extende three miles into the woods: and att the end of the three miles: then to rune or range away southerly till it meets with tow reed oke trees marked: the one is marked on foure sids the other on tow sids: they stand about a rode from eche other and on a littill knowle between tow swamps the one swamp runs away westerly the other northerly: and then from the aforesaid reed oke trees on a strait line through a sedar swampe till wee meete with tow white oke trees marked on foure sids ech of them and standing about three or foure roods asunder from ech other the one of them havth a heape of stones about him: and from these aforesaid white oks on a strait line southerly till wee meete with Dartmouth westerly line: and then to rune esterly as Dartmouth line runs till wee come to the path that gos from Middilebury unto Dartmouth wher stands by the path side a tree marked and is Dartmouth head bounds: and soe from the aforesaid tree notherly till wee clos with quitticus ponds: and soe to close home to those lands purchased by John Tomson and the Lathrops: a second trackt of land is neck of land commonly cald by the name of Wappond: and is bounded on the northerly sid with Assawamset pond and on the westerly sid or end with a pond comonly cald Poksha: and on the easterly sid or end with a tract of land comonely cald by gray's purchase and is to run as that purchase runs till it meets with the abovesaid Assawamset pond: a third trakt of land is lying betwene the aforesaid Grais purchase: and a trake of land sould by Tispaquin to his father in law an indian cald by the name of John Taswood: and is bounded on the one side by the above said purchas of Edward Gray where runs a littill brooke: that parts that purchas and this of ours: the brook is cald by the name of pocaset: and runs into Poksha pond and from the head of that brooke or swampe on a strait line esterly till it meets with a great scraged rock and from tha rocke on a strait line till it meets with the river caled Sucktteqesite: which River parts this land and the lands purchased by John Tomson and Bin Church: and soe as the River runs till it meets with a white oke tree marked on tow sids and stands by the River: and from the said white oke tree marked on a strait line till it meets with a great rocke clift in thre: and soe from this rock till it meets with some marked trees standing by a swamp sid: and from them unto the pond called qsastenaqut: and allsoe a sedar swampe lying at the head of stony brooke or fall River: and is compased aboute with the lands purchased by John Tomson and Bin Church on the one sid or end and the lands of hiniry Woods on the other sid or end: and the lands of Govr Prince on the one end and a pond at the other end: wee say all these trakts of land with the sedar swampe thus described and bounded with all woods waters and libirtys of fishing fowling with whatever apurtenances privildges Imunitys thereunto belonging or any ways therunto apertaining: To have and to hould all thse abovesaid trakts of land unto them the above said Constant Southworth John Tomson and the rest of the proprietors to them and every of them thire airs and evry of ther airs forever: we say unto the proper use and behofe of Constant Southworth John Tomson and the rest of the proprietors to them ther airs and asigns forever: waringting the sale of hereof and of every part and parsall herof and titill or titills herof against all people whatsoever from by or under us the said Wetispican sir and William Tispican iur wee our airs and every of our airs forever: claiming any right titill whatsoe ever into any parte or parsall of any of the lands above exspressed and bounded: wee say to have and to hold all thes abovesaid lands soe bounded be it more or les with all and singgelar the prividges and apurtences therunto belonging or therunto apertaining: quit and clerly aquitted and discharged of and from all other former gifts grants Bargains sals morgages Lesses Charges and all other incumbrances whatsoe ever: To be howld according to the manor of est   in the county of Kent in fre and common sockkage and not in cappite nor by knits servis: the rents and servi's: the rents and servises thereof due and of Right acustomed: as allsoe it shall be lafull for the abovesaid Constant Southworth John Tomson or any of the proprietors to inrole or cause thes presents to be recorded or inroled in the records of Newplimouth according to the usshuall maner of recording of evidences of land: In witnes herof wee have herunto set to our hands and efixed our seals the ‡fourtinth day‡ of May one thousand sixe hundred seventy and five : 1675

Signed sealed in the presents of us

| Nicholas Byram | The mark of ⁊ David | The mark ⌐ | The marke of ◊ wetispican |
| Samuell Edson | alius Jokome | Pipiurphum alius Joseph | The mark W T of Wille Tispican |

This deed was acknowledged by old Tuspaquine and his sone William Tuspaquine to be theire free act and Deed so acknowledged the date abovesaid

Pr me Will Bradford Assistant.

The following are the original proprietors of the Sixteen Shilling Purchase, with the lots that were respectively assigned to them November 21, 1679: —

1. Joseph Warren [1]
2. George Partridge [1]
3. John Howland [1]
4. Adam Wright and John Tomson [1]
5. Joseph Vaughan [1]
6. Guido Bayley, (now Samuel Eaton) [1]
7. Thomas Dogget
8. Lettice Morton [2]
9. John Winslow [1]
10. Isaac Little [1]
11. Edward Gray [1]
12. Middleboro Ministrey
13. William Pontus [1]
14. Peregrine White [1]
15. John Alden [1]
16. Samuel Wood [1]
17. William Bassit [1]
18. Gershom Cob [1]
19. Andrew Ring [1]
20. Plymouth Ministry
21. Jonathan Donham [1]
22. John Jones [1]
23. Benjamin Bartlett
24. John Wood of Plymouth [1]
25. Serjant William Harlow [1]
26. Giles Rickard, senior [1]
27. William Cadman [1]
28. David Wood,[1] Joseph Wood,[1] Benjamin Wood
29. Nathanel Warren [1]
30. John Nelson [1]
31. John Morton [1]
32. Frances Walker and John Hascol, — A lot formerly belonging to Ephraim Little, now Thomas Palmer [1]
33. William Nelson, Jr.[1]
34. William Bradford, Jr.
35. Frances Coombs [1]
36. Josiah Winslow, Esq. [1]
37. Phillip and Thomas Delano
38. Robert Sproat and Caleb Samson
39. Frances Billington [1]
40. Samuel Fuller [1]
41. Jonathan Wood [1]
42. David Thomas, senior [1]
43. Nathanel Morton [1]
44. Experience Mitchell [1]
45. Edward Gray [1]
46. Anthony Snow [1]
47. Elder Chipman

[1] See chapter on Early Settlers, or other purchases.
[2] She was the wife of John Morton.

48. John Irish [1]
49. Thomas Prence, Esq.
50. Thomas Pain
51. Zachariah Eddy [1]
52. Nathanel Southworth [1]
53. John Turner, senior
54. Isaac Howland [1]
55. Ephraim Tinkham, senior [1]
56. John Miller [1]
57. Isaac Cushman and Elkanah Cushman
58. Matthew Fuller [1]
59. John Rogers, senior [1]
60. Joseph Bumpas [1]
61. John Jordan [1]
62. John Eddy
63. John Tomson, senior [1]
64. Lieut. Ephraim Morton [1]
65. John Soule [1]
66. Frances Coombs [1]
67. George Danson [1]
68. Thomas Bordman [1]
69. Samuel Little
70. Gabril Fallowell [1]
71. John Sparrow [1]

The proprietors of the Sixteen Shilling Purchase were numerous. Many of them were proprietors of the "Liberties of Middleberry" in 1677, and owners in the other purchases which made up the original town. The following are brief sketches of the lives of those not before mentioned: —

BENJAMIN BARTLETT was a son of Robert Bartlett. He married Sarah Brewster in 1656, and in 1678, Cecilia ——. His home was in Duxbury, where he was regarded as one of the wealthy men, at his death in 1691 leaving property to the amount of nearly four hundred pounds.[2]

ELDER JOHN CHIPMAN, the son of Thomas Chipman, was born in Dorsesthire, England, about 1621. He came to this country with his cousin, Richard Derby, in May, 1637, and landed in Plymouth. In 1646 he married Hope, a daughter of John Howland; in 1649 he was a freeman of Barnstable, and was the last ruling elder of that church. He was one of the committee appointed by the court in Plymouth, June, 1659, to attend the meetings of the Quakers, "to endeavor to reduce them from the error of their wayes." They recommended the repeal of the laws of the colony against Quakers, but their report did not meet with the

---

[1] See chapter on Early Settlers, or other purchases.
[2] Winsor, *Duxbury*, p. 225.

approval of the court. While living in Barnstable, he filled many of the offices of the town, but in 1684, after his second marriage, he moved to Sandwich, where he died April 7, 1708.[1]

ISAAC and ELKANAH CUSHMAN were sons of Elder Thomas Cushman, and each received under the will of their father one half of lot 57 in the Sixteen Shilling Purchase. Isaac Cushman was a clergyman, born February 8, 1647; he married Mary Rickard about 1675. He was one of the selectmen of the town of Plymouth in 1685, 1690, and 1691; he was one of the deputies to the General Court at Plymouth, and was reëlected in 1692 to the first General Court at the union of the provinces. Before the settlement of Mr. Fuller, he was called to the church in Middleboro, but declined; after Mr. Fuller's death, he again received a call to be a pastor here, but at the same time the church in Plympton called him, and for thirty-seven years he acted as minister there, until his death, October 21, 1732.

Elkanah Cushman was born June 1, 1651, and lived in Plympton, where he was the deacon of the church about nine years. He represented the town at the General Court, and held the office of ensign in the military company of that town. He died the 4th of September, 1727.[2]

THOMAS DELANO, the second son of Philip Delano, was one of the earliest settlers of Duxbury, where he always lived. He married for his first wife Mary, a daughter of John Alden.[3]

THOMAS DOGGETT, a prominent citizen of Marshfield, was born in England in 1607, and arrived at Boston or Salem in May, 1637, in the Mary Ann. He first settled in Concord, where his wife died in 1642. He then moved to

---

[1] *Barnstable Families*, vol. i, pp. 155, 159.
[2] *Cushman Genealogy*, pp. 101-124.
[3] Savage, *Genealogical Dictionary* vol. ii, p. 34.

Weymouth, and finally settled in Marshfield, where he was an extensive land-owner. He died in Marshfield, August 18, 1692. His descendants in the middle and latter part of the eighteenth century were quite numerous in Middleboro, among whom were Jabez and Simeon Doggett, who served in the French and Indian War, the latter being one of the loyalists of the Revolution. Thomas Doggett gave to his son Samuel by deed "one-half of all my land in Middleboro." The Thomas Dogget who moved from Marshfield to Middleboro in 1741 was in 1732 a part owner of a sloop, called Middleboro.[1]

JOHN EDDY, a son of Samuel Eddy, was born December 25, 1637. In 1660 he was a blacksmith in Plymouth, and in 1689 was one of the proprietors of Taunton, where he lived for awhile. In 1711 he resided in Tisbury, where he held public office until his death, in 1715. During King Philip's War he had a personal encounter with the Indians, and after killing one of them, he made his escape to the house. He never occupied the lot assigned him in the Sixteen Shilling Purchase, and was not a resident of Middleboro.[2]

SAMUEL LITTLE, son of Thomas Little, was born in 1656, and in 1682 married Sarah Gray. He was one of the family mentioned above who kept the Sproat Tavern.

THOMAS PAINE settled in Eastham, but at what date is not known. He married Mary, daughter of Nicholas Snow. In 1653 he was constable of Eastham; in 1655 was one of the nineteen mentioned as townsmen of Eastham, and in 1658 was propounded at the colony court at Plymouth as a freeman. As one of the original purchasers of the Sixteen Shilling Purchase, he was assigned lot 50. He also purchased of Tispequin, the Black Sachem, and his son William, for ten pounds sterling, land adjoining John Alden's tract at Assawampsett Pond, and later owned land in Truro. In 1671 he represented Eastham at the colony court, and was a deputy for seven years.

[1] *Doggett Genealogy*, pp. 325, 341.   [2] *Eddy Family*, p. 103.

He moved from Eastham to Boston previous to 1695, but died at Eastham, August 16, 1706.[1]

CALEB SAMPSON was a son of Henry Sampson, one of the first settlers of Duxbury, an account of whose life has been previously given. He was a resident of Duxbury, and married Mercy, a daughter of Alexander Standish.[2]

ROBERT SPROAT was in Scituate in 1660, but later became a resident of Middleboro, where he died in 1712. He married Elizabeth, a daughter of Henry Sampson of Duxbury, and had several children. From him Colonel Ebenezer Sprout of Revolutionary fame descended. He left land at "Edy's Pond" to three daughters, and two lots in South Purchase to two others. He died in the Canada expedition in 1690, under Sir William Phipps, at the taking of Port Royal and the attempt upon Quebec.[3]

JOHN TURNER was the eldest son of Humphrey Turner, who arrived at Plymouth in 1628, and resided there probably until 1634, when he moved to Scituate, where he was one of the founders of the church. He married Mary Brewster, and in 1683 was still living.

BENJAMIN WOOD was the son of Henry Wood.[4] On his father's death he, with Joseph and David, chose John Morton, Sr., to be their guardian. He was drafted into his Majesty's service in the expedition to Canada in 1690. On his way to Plymouth, July 19, 1690, in presence of John Tomson and John Allen, he made what is known as a noncupative will, as follows : "Being drafted upon his Majesty's service against Canada as he was on his way going to Plymouth on the 19th. day of July, 1690, did desire us whose names are under written to take knowledge of it if it should so please God that he should not return again that his brother James should have

---

[1] *Paine Genealogy*, pp. 12-15.   [2] Winsor, *History of Duxbury*, p. 300.
[3] Deane's *History of Scituate*, pp. 131 and 340.   [4] *Eddy-Note Book*.

his estate." He probably died in the service, as his will was probated in Plymouth December 5, 1690. In his will he is called Benjamin Wood, alias Atwood.

As a boy he lived with his brothers Joseph and Samuel in Middleboro before the breaking out of King Philip's War, and was among those who returned upon the resettlement of the town.

EIGHT MEN'S PURCHASE

This purchase included about nine hundred acres, and adjoined the Wood's Purchase; its greatest width is about three hundred rods from the Wood's Purchase.

Whereas there was a meeting of the proprietors of a certain purchase of land lying within the township of Middleborough and is bounded northerly by the Indian path that goes from the wading place towards Lakenham: westerly it is bounded by Governour Prences Purchase: and southerly and easterly it is bounded by Henry Woods Purchase: said meeting was held at the house of Mr. Isaac Howland in Middleborough: June the : 3d : 1696 : At said meeting it is agreed by the said proprietors that the bounds should be renewed between the said purchase: and the other purchases adjacent And whereas there is eight shares in said purchase it is agreed that there should be fifty acres laid out to each share or more at the discretion of the layers out: and to be laid out for Quantity according to the Quality : The men appointed to do said work are : Jacob Tomson : David Thomas : James Wood : George Shaw : and John Hascol Junior : and said proprietors have agreed that the charge of doing said work shall be equally defrayed amongst them : it was also agreed that when said work is done : that there should be a meeting of said proprietors warned for the drawing of the lots and defraying the charg : David Thomas and John Hascol Junior are apointed to warn said meeting. In witness whereof we the aforesaid proprietors have hereunto set our hands this third day of June one thousand six hundred ninety six.

    George Shaw: for Daniel Done
    John Irish for himself and John Simmons
    David Thomas
    John Hascal Junr for himself
    & Francis Walker & John Blackwell
    James Wood

The next year a meeting of the proprietors was held at the house of David Thomas, April 24, 1697, when a report was made of the laying out of the land included in this purchase, and the proprietors drew the lots of the first division in said purchase as follows : —

>   First lot . . . . John Simmons
>   Second lot . . . . Daniel Done
>   Third lot . . . . John Blackwell
>   Fourth lot . . . . Francis Walker
>   Fifth lot . . . . David Thomas
>   Sixth lot . . . . James Wood
>   Seventh lot . . . . John Irish
>   Eighth lot . . . . John Hascol Jr.

Nothing definite is known concerning the owners of the first three lots. The others have been mentioned before.

Other purchases of small tracts of land lying between the ones mentioned above were made at different times. Some of these are the following : —

Tispequin sold two small tracts of land for £2 5s. to James Cole and John Rickard. One was at Tippicunnicut, beginning at a brook called Cadohunset, bounded on the south by a swamp, on the north by a meadow compassing it, and so along Tippecunnicut brook; the other was on the west side of Tippecunnicut brook, on the south side of the old Nemasket path, up to Mahuchet, and so running southward to the south end of the pond. The time of this sale is not specified.[1]

JAMES COLE was in Plymouth in 1633, and was the first occupant of the hill where the early pilgrims were buried. He kept an inn from 1638 to 1660, and was living in 1688, "very aged." He had a son James, who was called Junior in 1643, and was enrolled among those able to bear arms. It is doubtful whether it is the father or son who is referred to in the purchase. He probably moved early to Kennebec.

[1] *Eddy Note-Book.*

JOHN RICKARD, son of Giles, married Esther Barnes in 1651, and had several children.

June 21, 1666, Wampatuck sold for £20 a tract called Sammauchamoi, bounded north by the former purchase, south by Nemasket (Assawampsett) pond, southwest by a little brook which lies southwest of Rootey brook, and so northward to the pond which is the bound of the former purchase : excepting one hundred acres of upland reserved for his loving friend John Winslow, Jr., to be laid out from Nemasket River to a pond lying by Taunton path; and also one fourth of the meadow lying upon Rootey brook.

1668, October 29. "Whereas a former graunt hath bine made by the court unto Experience Michell, Henery Sampson, Benjamin Church and Thomas Little to look out for land for thire accomodation; and that since the said graunt they have sought out a prsell of land for that end lying at Namassakett pond these are to be a memorandum that none shall Interfere soe as to deprive them of the said land untill the Court have taken course for the purchase of it and settling such a proportion thereof to the said prsons as shall be by the Court thought meet;

"The Court have graunted libertie unto the Govr Mr Thomas Prence to exchange fifty acres of land adjoining to his land on the south side of the brooke that falls out of Tuspaquins pond:

"Likewise that in case it may be purchased that a competencye of Land be graunted and Reserved thereabouts or neare unto it for the use of the ministry att Namassakett."

1668. "Thomas Prence and Francis Coombe, by order of the General Court of New Plymouth, purchased a large tract in Middleborough at Namassaket."

It was subsequently ordered by the court that the remainder not disposed of — the commonage and profits — "should belong to Prence and Combe until otherwise disposed of by the court; and the charges of the purchase to be paid by such as it was disposed of unto." An "ancient bound" of this Purchase to the east stood about one hundred and ninety rods north of the southerly range of the Eight Men's Purchase.

1669. "March 4, Phillip, alias Metacom, sachem of Pocanokett and Tispequin alias the Black Sachem, in consideration of thirteen pounds sterling paid by Mr. Constant Southworth, treasurer, in behalf of the colony, sell a tract at Namassakett pond (Nesamamset) bounded on the south-east with the lands of Thomas Little & Experience Mitchells & others and to extend along the said pond for the breadth of it three quarters of a mile upon a line including all the land home to the pond — and to run from sd pond a mile for the length of it up into the woods," etc.

"Wit. — Benj. Church, Nathl. Morton, Thomas the Interpreter," and "William the Black Sachems son."

On the same page of the records are the two following entries: —

"In reference unto a former grant of accommodations of land under Mr. Thomas Cushman The Court doth grant and confirme unto him the one half of the last purchase of land made by the Treasurer of Philip sachem of Pocanokett: viz: the one half of that tract of land purchased by Mr. Constant Southworth Treasurer lying and being at Assowamsett ponds on the easterly syde of the said ponds: The other half belonging unto Thomas Little: Likewise the Court have granted unto the said Thomas Cushman that in case any meddow can be found to be neare or convenient unto the aforesaid land that he shall have a convenient proportion thereof.

"Likewise Mr. Constant Southworth is appointed by the Court to sett the bounds of the said Tract of land and Mr. William Crow and Mr. Edward Gray are appointed by the Court to make a division thereof between the said Thomas Cushman & Thomas Little."

June 10, 1670, Tispequin with his son William sold to Edward Gray, who purchased as usual in behalf of the colony, all their meadow in or near Middleboro on the west side of a tract belonging to John Alden and Constant Southworth, between Assawampsett Pond and Taunton path (which runs upon what is now the Assonet road, from the Four Corners). They sold also a small lot of meadow on the other, the north side of Taunton path, near or next to one of the three other parcels which was that formerly sold to Major Winslow and the other proprietors of Purchade. The deed was witnessed by Annie, the wife of Tispequin.

The Titicut Purchase was made April 20, 1675, from Owen, alias Thomas Hanter, and Popennohoc, alias Peter. Consideration, twelve pounds. They sold a tract from Pachusett brook on the east, where it runs into Titicut or Great River, to the lands before purchased; and from the mouth of the brook westward, butting upon the river, one mile, till it meets with certain trees by the side of the river, and thence to the Taunton bounds at the highway to Taunton and Rhode Island, where a brook runs through it.

"At a Court at Plymouth the 4th of July 1673; Liberty is granted unto Benjamin Church to purches a certaine parsell of land and swamp of Tispequin the Black Sachim and William his sonne for the inhabitants and proprietors of the town of Middleborrow: and that the said Inhabitants and proprietors have Liberty untill the last of November next to make payment to him or his order of what he shall disburse for the said lands for the purchas thereof: and in case they shall neglect to make payment thereof by the time perfixed that then the said land is to be his: vera copia as apears of records in Plymouth book of acts and passages of Court the day & year above written. Examined March the 18:1694/5.

SAM^L SPRAGUE
Keeper of Records."

1677. "Att this Court it was agreed by and between Mr. Constant Southworth and Philip the Sachem in reference to the land att Assowampsett pond that whereas the land purchased of the said sachem there was formerly to go three quarters of a mile broad and to goe over Wachamotussett brook; it is now bounded by the said brook below; and soe to goe up by a pond; and what is wanting below by reason the breadth is cutt short; by the said brook. it is to make up above."

"On the 6th. day of Nov., 1690, Felix, an Indian of Assawampsett, conveyed in consideration of 4 pounds, to John Tomson Sr., of Middleboro, and Capt. Nath. Thomas, of Mansfield, the following described parcel of upland, being a part of Felix land at Assawampsett Neck out of the head, so called, of the land which he then owned. This tract of land was bounded at the Northerly corner with a heap of stones on the East side of a great stump; and thence ranging Southwest half a point Southerly 90 rods to a heap of stones; thence ranging Southeast, half a point Easterly 59 rods to a heap of stones between 2 saplins, and from these ranging Northeasterly 90 rods to a heap of stones; and from thence ranging Northwesterly, half a point Westerly 59 rods to a heap of stones first mentioned."

CHAPTER XXXI

FRATERNAL ORGANIZATIONS

FOR many years there have been in Middleboro various organizations having the general object of rendering assistance when needed, and of giving mutual and social benefit to the personal welfare of their respective members. They are for the most part in a prosperous condition. A detailed account of its history, object of its work, with a list of officers and members, can be readily obtained from each society.

The first Masonic organization in Middleboro was Social Harmony Lodge, formed in 1823. In 1828, by vote of the members, it moved to Wareham, holding meetings there for a few years. At this time the opposition to Masonry became so strong throughout the country that this, with most other societies, was abandoned, and was not revived until the year 1856, when Benjamin Leonard of Middleboro and Thomas Savery of Wareham met at the latter place and organized a society under the old charter, taking the name of the Mayflower Lodge. Two hundred and sixty-six persons had been admitted to membership in 1903.

Assawampsett Division, No. 34, Sons of Temperance, was organized May 12, 1858. About the year 1867 women were admitted to full membership, new interest was aroused, and the division became the largest one in the state, and held that distinction for some time. Later the interest declined again, and at the end of its forty-seventh year it had less than thirty members.

E. W. Peirce Encampment, Post 8, Grand Army of the Republic, is the oldest in Plymouth County. It was organized by Austin S. Cushman in 1867, and was named for General Ebenezer W. Peirce of Freetown, Mass. From the beginning to the present time, there have been three hundred and one members, but at present the membership has been reduced by death to one hundred and twenty.

In connection with the E. W. Peirce Encampment, Post 8, G. A. R., is the Woman's Relief Corps, which was organized January 20, 1885, with forty charter members.

The Union Veteran's Union, Stephen Thomas Command, No. 23, with twenty-four charter members, was organized June 23, 1896.

The Sons of Veterans, T. B. Griffith Camp, No. 22, Division of Massachusetts, was organized November 10, 1887, with thirty-three charter members.

At one time there was a society in connection with this post, called the Ladies' Aid Society, but this has gone out of existence.

The Nemasket Tribe I. O. R. M. of Middleboro was instituted June 25, 1889, with thirty-two charter members. The membership at the present time is one hundred and seventy-three.

The Middleboro Lodge, No. 665, of the Knights of Honor was instituted June 11, 1877, with but three charter members; its present membership is between sixty and seventy.

American Legion of Honor, Old Colony Council, No. 1152, was established in Middleboro August 9, 1883, with thirty-six charter members, but its present membership seems to be reduced to about ten.

Lenhart Lodge, No. 102, A. O. U. W., was formed August 14, 1889. It has, at present, a membership of about one hundred.

Middleboro Lodge, No. 135, I. O. O. F., was organized May 14, 1884, and has, at present, a membership of one hundred and seventy-nine.

Colfax Encampment, No. 64, I. O. O. F., was instituted April 17, 1888, with thirteen charter members. It has, at present, a membership of one hundred and four.

Assawampsett Lodge, No. 6995, I. O. O. F., M. U., was formed May 24, 1890, with a charter membership of twenty-three, and has now grown to a membership of one hundred and fifty.

The Nemasket Grange, No. 158, was formed on the 9th of February, 1888, largely through the influence of the late Elbridge Cushman of Lakeville, to advance the interest of agriculture throughout the county. It has, at present, a membership of ninety-two persons.

Progress Assembly, No. 202, R. S. G. F., was organized October 9, 1888, with thirty-four charter members. This went into a receiver's hands in December, 1905.

Tispequin Council, No. 23, Jr. O. U. A. M., was organized June 26, 1890, with twenty-three charter members. There are now about fifty members.

The Citizen's Aid Society was organized September 28, 1893. It has a membership of forty-eight.

Arbutus Lodge, No. 123, K. of P., was instituted November 17, 1895. It has a membership of fifty-eight.

Knights of Columbus was organized, in Middleboro, April 29, 1897. It has a membership of fifty.

The Business Men's Club is one of the active organizations, combining business and social elements, with a membership of more than one hundred.

The Cabot Club was organized by the women of Middleboro March 4, 1897. The present membership is over one hundred.

CHAPTER XXXII

CEMETERIES

THE Nemasket Hill Cemetery, beautifully situated on a high bank on the Nemasket River, is the oldest in town. It was set apart by the proprietors of the Twenty-six Men's Purchase in 1662, and was used by the early settlers as their only burial-place for more than two generations. It was formerly known as the Old Burial Hill, or simply The Hill. The oldest stone is that of Elizabeth Vaughan, who died June 24, 1693, aged sixty-two years. It was not until the latter part of the seventeenth century that inscribed stones giving the name, birth, and death of the deceased were used to any great extent in any of the burial grounds of the Old Colony. The graves were usually marked, if marked at all, by ordinary stones set at the head and foot of the grave. Here most of the early settlers were buried, although the graves of John Tomson and Samuel Fuller are the only ones now known. It was incorporated by a special act of the legislature March 24, 1885, as the Nemasket Hill Cemetery Association. At the time of the Twenty-six Men's Purchase, it was controlled by them, and afterwards by their descendants, who had here the rights of burial until the time of its incorporation.

The Parish Burial Ground at the Green, containing about two acres of land, was conveyed to about fifty persons as proprietors by James Soule in a deed dated March 30, 1717.[1] Many prominent in the history of the town are here buried; among them Peter Thacher, Jacob Tomson, and Isaac Howland. It is probably the largest burial ground, there being ten hundred and seventy-four memorial stones now standing. Adjoining this cemetery upon the northerly side are the tombs

---

[1] See chapter containing an account of The Green.

ENTRANCE TO HILL CEMETERY

of Zachariah Eddy, Esq., and Thomas Weston, and on the easterly side is the family tomb of Rev. Peter Thacher.

Titicut Cemetery was set apart from land given by the Indian James Thomas in 1750. Some years ago it was enlarged by a gift of land from David G. Pratt. It is controlled by a board of trustees connected with the Titicut parish. A monument has been erected to commemorate the gift, which bears also the names of the three Indians who conveyed land for the Titicut church.

Warrentown Cemetery, one of the oldest in town, is situated on the westerly side of Summer Street, between the houses formerly occupied by Mr. George Hartwell and Solomon Beals. The land was probably given by Daniel Warren in the early part of the eighteenth century. There have been but few recent interments. The oldest grave in this cemetery now marked is that of Elizabeth Lewes, widow of James Lewes, who died in March, 1744, in her ninetieth year.

The Alden Cemetery, situated on Plymouth Street between Purchade and North Middleboro, was probably an old Indian burial ground, and many Indian remains have been there found. It was considerably enlarged in the early part of the last century by a gift from Obadiah Sampson, and has recently been extended by the purchase of other adjoining land. At present it is controlled by a board of trustees. The first burial was that of Hepzibah Allen, who died November 28, 1728. In this, as in the other old burial grounds, there are no stones or monuments to mark the place of those interred before this date.

The cemetery at South Middleboro near the Methodist Church was given by Consider Benson and others in 1768, and since that time has been twice enlarged by the purchase of adjoining land. It was incorporated a few years since, and is now managed by a board of trustees. The oldest burial is that of Joseph Harris, who died November 21, 1771, aged fifty-nine years and six months.

The Central Cemetery is located on the northerly side of Center Street opposite Nevertouch Pond. In the early part of the last century the land was owned by Mr. James A. Leonard, who consented to its use as a burial-place, and afterwards, on August 18, 1842, and in 1858, by two deeds conveyed the land to the Central Baptist Society of Middleboro. It consists of about one and a half acres of land. The oldest stone in this cemetery is that of Bathsheba, wife of Hercules Richmond, who died October 24, 1819.

Rock Cemetery, situated west of the church, was used prior to 1795. It is controlled by the deacons of the Baptist Church and the Baptist Society. The oldest burial is that of Eunice, daughter of Nathaniel and Hannah Barrows, who died August 22, 1791, aged twenty-two years.

There are other cemeteries at Rock, first used in the early part of the last century, one adjoining the old training-green, another lying on the east side of the church, the Ewer Cemetery on the south of the church, and Hope Rest Cemetery.

The Wood Cemetery, known as the Thomas Wood Cemetery, was a family burial ground at the corner of Grove and Wood streets. It has been in disuse for almost a hundred years, and trees and bushes have now so grown over the entire lot that it is difficult to distinguish it in passing by. The oldest interment here was that of Abner, son of Joshua and Hannah Waterman, who died July 18, 1796, in his twenty-second year.

CEMETERIES

Thomastown Cemetery is a well-kept burial-place on Purchase Street, and consists of about two acres of land controlled by the Ladies' Sewing Circle of that neighborhood. The first burial here was that of Ruth Shaw, who died May 21, 1811, in her twenty-first year.

Waupaunucket Cemetery is situated on both sides of Vaughan Street, and has been used for more than fifty years.

St. Mary's Catholic Cemetery, on Wood Street, consists of eight acres of land, purchased and dedicated in May, 1891.

Poorhouse Cemetery is a small lot on the east side of the railroad track near Wood Street bridge and the town farm, used only as a pauper burying-ground, and containing about thirty graves with rough stones but no inscriptions. It was first used about 1831.

Tispequin Street Cemetery, near Fall Brook, is small and well kept. The oldest inscription is that of Zilpah, wife of Nathaniel Atwood, who died August 28, 1838, aged fifty-six years.

In addition to the above-named cemeteries, there are the Leonard Cemetery, on Taunton Street near the Lakeville line; the Gammons Cemetery on Sachem Street near Fall Brook; the Eaton Cemetery on Taunton Street between Center and Cross streets; the Drake Cemetery on Pleasant Street, North Middleboro; the Benson Cemetery, South Middleboro, which has not been used for more than one hundred years; and the Old Smallpox Cemetery, now overgrown with pine wood and underbrush, at the corner of Brook and Soule streets, near the Plympton line.

GRAVESTONE OF
REV. SAMUEL FULLER

CATALOGUE

OF THE

MEMBERS OF THE FIRST CHURCH

MIDDLEBOROUGH, MASS.

> The saints on earth, and all the dead,
> But one communion make;
> All join in Christ, their living head,
> And of his grace partake.

Reprinted from the History of the First Church, published 1854

INDEX TO THE NAMES OF MEMBERS

ALDEN
  32 John
  33 Hannah
 222 David
 223 Judith
 334 Noah
 401 Solomon
 427 John
 617 Elijah
 618 Mary
 619 Elihu

ALLEN
  65 Mary
  76 Nathaniel
 305 Mary
 326 David

AMES
 301 Elizabeth

ANTONY
 315 Else

ATWOOD
 720 John
 721 Rhoda
 840 Francis
 841 Shadrach
 962 Mary R.
1004 Joanna

BARDEN
  20 Deborah
  85 Abigail
  88 Stephen sr.
 170 Abraham sr.
 181 Mary
 203 Elizabeth
 204 Esther
 229 Abraham jr.

BARKER
 545 Joseph, Rev.
 579 Eunice
 714 William
 760 Anna
 788 Elizabeth

BARROWS
  30 Mercy
  59 Samuel
 132 Samuel jr.
 133 Susanna
 208 Coombs

BARROWS
 248 Fear
 274 Ruth
 552 Ruth
 914 Freeman

BASSETT
 125 Nathan
 294 Nathan
 302 Thankful

BATES
  86 Joseph sr.
 144 Joanna
 310 Joseph jr.
 474 Mary
 677 Susanna
 678 Joseph

BENNET
   3 John
   4 Deborah
 147 Samuel sr.
 179 Nehemiah
 180 Mercy
 207 Mary
 215 Eleanor
 216 Ruth jr.
 221 Ruth sr.
 273 Thankful
 538 Bachelor
 763 Mercy
 775 Mercy
 780 Jacob 2d
 794 Rebecca

BENSON
 477 Samuel

BENT
 671 Experience

BILLINGTON
  14 Isaac
 186 Mary
 499 Ichabod
 518 Elenor

BOOTH
 472 Priscilla

BOURNE
 563 Abner
 568 Mary
 575 Abigail

BOURNE
 587 Newcomb
 588 Abigail
 607 Lydia
 755 Abigail
 765 Joseph
 766 Sophia
 815 Louisa
 895 Lucy

BRAND
1044 Joanna

BRANNACK
 520 Consider

BRIGGS
 490 John
 491 Remember
 522 Ebenezer
 523 Abigail
 708 George
 709 Patience
1034 Mary

BROWN
 561 Elizabeth

BRYANT
 540 Margaret
 580 Hannah
 636 Jesse
 637 Mercy
 816 Hillyard

BUMP
 596 Mercy

BUMPAS
  18 Weibra
 111 Mary
 405 Nathaniel

BURGESS
 287 Jacob
 782 Temperance
1041 Cornelius
1042 Melissa

BUSS
 842 Martin
 843 Eliza

CALIMINCO, 463

CANEDY
 189 Anibal
 432 Elizabeth

CARVER
 611 Josiah
 612 Jerusha

CARY
 536 Ichabod
 537 Hannah

CASWELL
  56 Mary
 171 Daniel
 192 Mary
 277 Else
 899 Polly W.

CAVENDER
 126 Ann
 266 John

CHAMBERLAIN
 844 Joseph

CHAMMUCK
 383 Martha

CLAPP
 138 Ezra
 139 Waitstill
 362 Elijah
 375 Hope
 437 Manasseh

CLARKE
  77 Nathan
 807 Josiah
 808 Mary
 809 Deborah P.
 845 Elizabeth
1015 Zilpha

CLEAVES
  51 Eleanor

COADE
 774 Hannah

COBB
  17 John
  22 Jonathan
  23 Hope

[1695-1846]   MEMBERS OF THE FIRST CHURCH   641

COBB
57 Rachel
70 Lydia
119 Joanna
219 Thankful
236 Ebenezer
237 Lydia
272 Gershom
419 John jr.
421 John sr.
422 Mary
434 Patience
436 Hope
455 Meletiah
469 Ebenezer
470 Mary
518 Abijah
525 Mercy
628 Ebenezer
629 Lydia
644 Binney
645 Azubah
684 Mary
707 Jacob
754 Priscilla
846 Otis T.
847 Adeline
903 Olive T.

COLE
473 Thomas

COLWELL
966 Mary Ann

CONANT
101 Elizabeth
468 Sylvanus, Rev.
492 Abigail

CORNISH
593 William

COX
307 Hannah
398 John sr.
410 John jr.
430 Hannah
431 Mary

CROCKER
290 Lydia

CROSSMAN
209 Barnabas
253 Hannah

CURTIS
759 Sally

CUSHMAN
368 William
369 Susanna
445 Ichabod
497 Deborah

CUSHMAN
548 Susanna
565 Mercy
741 Sylvia
930 Susanna
1012 Adoniram J.
1013 Ann S.

CUTBART
16 Samuel

DARLING
42 Joanna
149 Thomas
265 Rebecca
365 John
423 Elizabeth
715 Daniel
716 Polly
848 Alanson
849 Hannah H.
850 Aurilla

DEAN
964 Eliab
986 Lydia
987 Lois

DELANO
89 David sr.
168 Meribah
169 Ann
438 David jr.

DOANE
1031 Calvin

DOGGETT
803 Eliphalet

DOTY
615 Isaac

DREW
78 John
99 Sarah
173 Elizabeth

DUNHAM
162 Ephraim
211 Lemuel
260 Elizabeth
288 Joshua
289 Keturah
404 Ephraim
433 Mercy
983 Henry

EARLE
1021 Halford
1022 Elizabeth

EASTMAN
932 Mary Jane

EATON
15 Samuel
226 Francis
886 William, Rev.
890 Lydia

EDDY
60 Melatiah
61 Samuel
100 Abigail
234 Jabez sr.
243 Samuel jr.
244 Lydia
263 Jedidah
341 Zachariah
342 Mercy
450 Jabez jr.
451 Patience
516 Nathan
535 Samuel
543 Susanna
633 Joshua
634 Lydia
603 Seth
606 Jerusha
601 Silvanus
682 Nathaniel
683 Lydia
718 Zechariah
719 Sarah
761 Anna
797 Abby
851 Thalia
852 Anne Juliet
868 Lydia
915 Betsey
916 Betsey M.
944 Joshua
955 Jane Ellen
967 Charles E.
968 Eliza
969 Susan M.
970 Ann Elizabeth
988 Charlotte E.
1009 Lucy Ann
1010 Mary Jane

EDSON
853 Charlotte

ELLIS
190 Elizabeth
384 Elizabeth jr.
623 Lucia
677 Deborah
680 Southworth
971 Susanna M.
984 Lucia C.

ELMES
172 Sarah
524 Elkanah
792 Leonard
804 Eliphalet jr.

ELMES
817 Eliphalet sr.
818 Chloe
854 Lavinia
855 Louisa

FAUNCE
476 Abigail

FELIX
324 Thomas jr.

FINNEY
240 Ebenezer
246 Jane
354 Nelson
586 Sarah
609 Martha
657 Margaret
819 Jane

FOLEY
1035 James

FREEMAN
486 Bethiah
676 John
820 Hannah
856 Mercy
893 Mary
972 Jane

FULLER
1 Samuel, Rev.
2 Elizabeth
28 John sr.
29 Mercy
41 Mary
91 Isaac
94 Ebenezer
95 Elizabeth
97 Hannah
103 Elizabeth
146 Silence
151 Lydia
155 Mercy
156 John
247 Jabez
276 Mary
304 Timothy
370 Mary
647 Betty
673 Lucy
674 Sally
685 Sophia
799 Sylvia
857 Lauretta Ann
878 Jabez
879 Sally
881 Susan B.

GIBBS
167 Elizabeth

GISBY
773 William
928 Thomas

GODDARD
1045 Almira

GRIFFETH
251 Elizabeth
283 Mary

GUMEE
220 Sarah

HACKET
48 Elizabeth
150 Lydia

HALL
453 Mercy

HARLOW
632 Betsey
767 Mercy
769 Hepzibah
936 David
989 Stephen jr.
990 Jonathan
991 Sarah
992 Betsey B.
993 Mary L.
1029 Bethiah O.

HARRINGTON
956 Lucy

HARRIS
420 Seth

HASKELL
49 Mary
594 Abigail
598 Zebulon

HASKINS
973 Jerusha

HATHAWAY
331 Mary

HAYFORD
225 Mary
239 Benjamin sr.

HILL
945 Harriet

HITCHCOCK
1038 Henry D.
1039 Olivia

HOLMES
625 Thankful
858 Rufus
859 George L.

HOLMES
860 Eunice

HOWLAND
382 Joseph

HUBBARD
728 Serena

JACKSON
278 Joanna
335 John jr.
462 Sarah
909 Sarah

JENNY 416

KIDDER
687 Sally

KING
79 Ichabod
83 Judith
279 Mary
787 Mercy
925 Nathan

KNOWLTON
185 Martha
188 Thomas
388 Prudence

LAWRENCE
965 Sarah

LAZELL
312 Joshua

LEACH
316 Abiel
361 Susanna
435 Sarah
504 John
505 Betty
517 Phebe
704 Susanna

LEONARD
66 Charity
443 Margery
446 John sr.
603 Lucy
686 Betsey
888 Elizabeth
951 Sally

LEWIS
26 Elizabeth
34 Mary
285 Shubael
286 Hazadiah
381 Elizabeth

LING
658 Jane

LITTLEJOHN
805 Deliverance
821 Miriam
861 Hannah

LOVELL
31 Mary
367 John jr.
408 Lydia
413 Thankful
449 Joseph
758 Jerusha

LUCAS
599 Elijah
600 Sarah
822 Job

LYON
201 Samuel
202 Joanna
228 Bethiah
293 William
329 Jedediah
389 Martha
390 Sarah
391 Phebe
589 Mary

MACHAAN
152 Patience

McDOWALL
641 John

MANSFIELD
109 Andrew
110 Sarah

MARGARET 36

MAXFIELD
521 Catherine

MILLER
157 Lydia
264 Waitstill
409 John jr.
560 Sarah
882 Susanna

MORSE
5 Jonathan
6 Mary
50 Mary jr.
284 Martha
498 Desire
549 Isaac
574 Thankful
626 Desire
712 Sage

MORSE
889 Lucy W.
891 Ruth
1016 Marston S.

MORTON
80 Hannah
127 Mercy
495 Ichabod
496 Deborah
662 Daniel O.
789 Hepzibah
862 Lendall P.
904 Eliza S.
910 Hannah D.

MUXHAM
533 Edmund

NICHOLS
974 Lucia Maria

NORCUTT
622 Mary
905 Mary

NYE
73 Elizabeth

OLIVER
528 Peter jr.
531 Sarah

ORCUTT
975 Harriett

ORRINGTON
954 Mary Ann

OSGOOD
942 Adeline H.

PADDOCK
210 Ichabod
261 Joanna
699 Lydia
798 Julia

PAINE
791 Emerson, Rev.

PALMER
21 Thomas, Rev.
142 Samuel
158 Elizabeth
184 Elizabeth jr.
296 Job

PARKER
461 Joseph

PARLOW
153 Hannah
448 Hannah

PERKINS
749 Lothrop
750 Mercy
790 John
863 Nathan jr.
1023 Eunice
1043 Ann

PEGGY 303

PERU 444

PICKENS
896 Ebenezer
897 Mary B.
943 Caroline M.
1033 Abigail S.

PIERCE
642 Experience

POMROY
475 Hannah
485 Francis jr.

POOL
906 Samuel
907 Lydia

PORTER
620 Mercy
729 Sybil
776 Sarah

POWERS
500 Stephen
501 Lydia

PRATT
27 Thomas
191 Hannah
200 Phebe
227 Jane
270 John
394 Eleazer sr.
396 Joanna
406 Samuel 3d
407 Hannah sr.
440 Samuel jr.
441 Jerusha
466 Elizabeth
604 Sarah
610 Margaret
621 Benaiah
624 Lucy
646 Benjamin
772 Thomas
823 Lydia
824 Phebe
864 Olive
963 Betsey
976 William
1024 Benjamin F.
1025 Abby B.

PRATT
1026 Mahala S.
1032 Thomas A.

PRINCE
117 Nathan
120 Samuel
121 Mercy
128 Mercy
129 Alice

PRINCE 314

PURRINGTON
256 Hezekiah
257 Mercy
507 Mercy

PUTNAM
939 Israel W. Rev.
941 Julia Ann
1006 Harriot O.
1036 William F.

RANSOM
130 Sarah

RAYMOND
52 ———
87 James
104 John sr.
187 Elizabeth
213 John jr.
254 Mercy
255 Alice
291 Christiana
325 Barnabas
330 Patience
373 Elizabeth jr.
393 Ebenezer
457 Thomas
458 Mary
459 Amos
460 Peter

REDDING
62 Ebenezer
123 Mercy
245 Bennet
353 Deborah
426 John
439 William
467 Thomas
478 Joanna
494 Thankful
508 Sarah jr.
513 Fear
597 Luther

REED
937 Ruth

RICHMOND
58 Ebenezer

RICKARD
205 Elkanah
233 Bethiah
374 Japheth

RIDER
756 Jael

RIPLEY
576 Tilson
688 Hezekiah
689 Priscilla

ROBBINS
1030 Consider

ROGERS
108 Sarah

ROUNSEVILLE
931 Freelove G.

SAMBO 415

SAMPSON
67 Samuel
193 Obadiah
206 Mary
224 Bethiah
562 Thankful
732 Samuel
733 Lydia

SAVERY
479 Mary
667 Daniel
668 Huldah

SEARS
333 David
399 Phebe
703 Abiah

SHAW
483 Elkanah
527 Elizabeth
529 Thomas
530 Mary
557 William
558 Lydia
572 James
573 Lois
648 Isaac
651 Samuel
654 Mark

SHORT
197 Luke sr.

SIMMONS
447 Martha

SMITH
63 Jonathan
90 Abigail

SMITH
154 Sarah
161 James
309 Rachel
313 Deborah
318 Jonathan jr.
360 Samuel
392 Sarah
417 Experience
564 Susanna
679 Levi
690 James
691 Patience
865 Lydia
977 Mahala

SNOW
317 Jonathan

SOULE
55 Martha
442 John jr.
464 Rebecca
465 Rachel
471 Esther
554 Sarah
555 Lydia
664 James 2d
710 John
711 Joanna
866 James
867 Ruth
952 Irene
978 Isaac 3d
979 Priscilla
980 Rebecca
1011 Alfred B.

SOUTHWORTH
69 Esther
135 Nathaniel
137 Jael
308 Rebecca

SPARROW
643 Rhoda
734 Josiah
735 Minerva
825 Bathsheba

SPROAT
136 Experience
143 Abigail
292 James
323 Ebenezer
793 James
827 Lucy
868 Thomas
883 Mary

STANDISH
194 Ichabod
198 Phebe
740 Irene
826 Josiah O.

STANDISH
900 Jane

STAPLES
929 Simeon

STROWBRIDGE
106 William
107 Margaret

STURTEVANT
195 Moses
196 Elizabeth
627 Sarah
731 Abigail
764 Priscilla
779 Eunice
795 Fanny

SWIFT
786 Lucy
828 Joseph jr.
829 Mercy
830 Lucy jr.

THACHER
35 Peter, Rev.
47 Mary
183 Mary
262 Peter jr.
275 Samuel
299 Thomas
306 John
352 Susanna
451 Oxenbridge

THAYER
321 Abigail

THOMAS
43 Mary
44 David
45 Susanna
64 Lydia
81 Jeremiah sr.
96 Elizabeth
98 Mary
103 Elizabeth jr.
115 Hannah
163 Miriam
218 Susanna
238 Henry
249 Abigail
250 Anna
258 Noah
271 Abigail
281 Mary
282 Mary
293 Israel
322 Mary
328 Benoni
350 Eleazer
385 Phebe
386 Sarah
387 Abigail
402 Sarah

THOMAS
403 Asa
424 William
425 Benjamin
452 Barzillai
484 Elizabeth
506 Elizabeth
509 Lucy
510 Lemuel
532 Keziah
544 Daniel
546 David
547 Churchill
550 Deborah
556 Mercy
566 Thankful
602 Abigail
608 Nathan sr.
638 Zilpah
649 Perez
650 Sarah
669 Zenas
670 Mary
692 William
700 Edward
701 Lydia
702 Betsey
736 Jacob
737 Lucy
738 Hope
743 Silvanus
744 Susanna
785 Serena
869 Daniel
884 Silas
885 Eleazer
887 Azel
892 Phebe
894 Betsey
917 Hannah
918 Seneca
919 Hope
920 Eunice
921 Anna
922 Lucia Ann
923 Winslow
924 Huldah
957 Lothrop jr.
958 Louisa F.
959 Saba S.
960 Mary Ann
961 Mary H.
1017 Phebe

THOMPSON
9 Jacob
10 Abigail
134 Mary
159 Mary
235 Thomas sr.
268 Caleb
269 Abigail
376 John
418 Lydia
569 Caleb jr.

THOMPSON
570 Mary
581 William
582 Deborah
583 Isaac
584 Lucy
585 Freelove
640 Otis
655 Weltha
656 Lydia
705 Reuel
706 Nathaniel
722 Lydia
723 Lucy
724 Mary
725 Irene
730 Ezra
770 Arad
871 Marietta T.
872 Cordelia
926 Charles F.
927 Florantha
935 Cephas
981 Anna T.
994 Venus
995 Jane
996 Benjamin
1007 Sarah T.
1027 Mary H.

TILSON
480 Ann
515 Silence
652 Calvin
653 Joanna
693 Calvin jr.
739 Hannah
796 Joanna
873 Judith

TINKHAM
11 Ebenezer
12 Elizabeth
19 Hester
24 Patience
25 Priscilla
37 Mary
40 Ephraim jr.
46 Ephraim sr.
72 Joanna
74 Mary
93 Isaac sr.
112 Hannah
145 Mary
148 Seth
214 Abijah
267 Mary
336 Peter sr.
337 Samuel 3d
338 Susanna
345 Joseph
346 John jr.
347 Hannah
348 Priscilla
349 Patience

TINKHAM
357 Martha
358 Agnes
359 Esther
397 Hannah
428 Ebenezer
482 Isaac
519 Hannah
526 Sarah
551 Chloe
577 Lucy
578 Ruth
592 Jeremiah
595 Hannah
601 Mary
614 Elizabeth
631 Sarah
660 Squire
661 Anna
663 Silas
771 John
781 Orin
806 Susanna
831 Elizabeth
901 Barbara
933 Betsey
938 Harvey
985 Jane
997 Oliver G.

TISDALE
605 Jacob
694 Hannah

TORRY
590 Samuel
591 Mary
717 Lydia

TOTMAN
502 Experience

TRIBOU
695 Bathsheba

TUCKER
164 Benjamin
165 Sarah
327 Woodward
489 Sarah jr.
541 Benjamin jr.
635 Samuel
746 Jedidah
757 Hannah
912 Susanna
933 Mandana

TUPPER
176 Ichabod
259 Thomas
411 Rebecca

TURNER
456 Elizabeth
616 Priscilla

MEMBERS OF THE FIRST CHURCH [1695-1846]

VALLER
606 Mercy

VAUGHAN
38 Joseph
39 Joanna sr.
92 Deborah
113 John
114 Jerusha
131 Joanna
166 Faithful
230 Desire
241 Hinksman
297 Jabez
310 John jr.
320 Jerusha jr.
351 Elisha
363 Daniel
364 Joseph
371 Joanna
372 Sarah
395 Mercy
503 Abraham
567 Lucy

VINICA
998 Rachel
999 Dorlisca N.
1000 Lydia

WARREN
174 Samuel
175 Eleanor
182 Priscilla
343 Benjamin
344 Jedidah
511 Joseph
512 Mercy
659 Keziah
696 John
832 James
833 Margaret
908 Betsey
1019 George

WASHBURN
539 Huldah
559 Azel

WASHBURN
810 Abiel
811 Elizabeth
812 Abigail
813 Caroline
814 Louisa Jane
946 Elizabeth H.
982 Eunice

WESTON
231 Edmund sr.
232 Susanna
300 Elizabeth
493 Hannah
571 Priscilla
613 Isaiah
745 Priscilla jr.
762 John
777 Hannah
778 Salome
834 Thomas
835 Abigail
836 Abigail jr.
837 Bethania
838 Lavinia
839 Thomas jr.

WHITE
160 Benjamin sr.
199 Ann

WILBUR
1018 Perry A.

WILDER
639 Ebenezer
726 Mary
727 Mary
753 Susanna
875 James D.
1001 Bathsheba L.

WILLIAMS
339 John
340 Elizabeth
481 Thomas
770 Jabez

WILLIAMSON
412 Fear

WILLIS
487 Ebenezer
488 Mary
802 Ebenezer
876 Jane
940 Sabina

WING
874 Betsey L.
880 Lura
902 Lauretta

WINSLOW
53 Nathaniel
54 Elizabeth
366 Susanna

WOOD
7 Abiel
8 Abijah
13 Samuel
68 Ephraim
71 Rebecca
75 James
82 Samuel jr.
84 Experience
102 Sarah
116 Elnathan
118 Patience
122 Mercy
124 Elizabeth
140 Timothy
141 Mary
177 David
178 Joanna
212 Thomas
217 Jemima
242 Sarah
252 Hannah
280 Sarah
295 John jr.
311 Ephraim jr.
332 Bathsheba
355 Ephraim

WOOD
356 Edmund
377 Joanna
378 Nathaniel
379 Ichabod
380 Patience
400 Samuel
414 Lydia
429 Lydia
542 Elizabeth
553 Rebecca
672 Sarah
697 Lydia
698 Lucy
713 Maria
742 Abigail
747 Israel
748 Ichabod
751 Elizabeth sr.
752 Theodate
768 Betsey
783 Ichabod 2d
784 Mary
800 Elizabeth jr.
801 Horatio G.
877 Lydia
911 Lucy C.
934 Matilda
947 Wilkes
948 Charles W.
949 Emily Louisa
950 Mary T.
953 William H.
1002 Abigail T.
1003 Mercy L.
1005 Mary C.
1008 Alfred jr.
1014 Abiel
1020 Mary
1028 Eleanor B.
1037 Phebe H.

WRIGHT
534 Cuffee
630 Anna

WRIGHTINGTON
1040 Hope

EXPLANATORY NOTICE

THE Descriptive Catalogue contains the names of all persons who have been or are members of the First Church in Middleboro', including the successive pastors, so far as records and other documents which the committee have been able to examine will show.

The *half-way covenant*, which was in practice from the earliest records until about 1760, has in some cases made it difficult to determine the question of full membership. The existing church records do not give the admissions of all, as is evident from other proceedings of the church; and the absence of all records (except the Fuller copy of the organization), until 1708, makes it almost certain that a portion of the admissions of that period of thirteen years have not been ascertained. Much care has been taken to enrol none but members in full communion; and the committee are not sure but a few others, excluded for want of fuller evidence, were not also members.

It will be seen that the Catalogue is columnar in three respects, namely : — the regular numbering of the whole church; the dates of admission; and the names of the members, followed by a particular notice of each; — the whole occupying but one line when practicable. The order of the particular notices is as follows : —

1. A reference to ancestry or kindred, or both, by abbreviations and the regular numbers if in the church, or by the christian name if not.
2. Reference to the wife or wives by their regular numbers *in parenthesis*, if members, or by their whole original name, if not.
3. The year of marriage.
4. Time of death and the age.

This order varies only in the case of married women, where the name of the husband, or reference to his number, is placed next after her name, and the reference to kindred after her original surname. In a few instances, where nothing else is known of a member, one or more of their children has been entered in the line. Members whose time of admission is unknown have been inserted near the time when they were found to have been such.

The fourteen members, from Nos. 21 to 34 inclusive, were probably nearly all admitted during the time of which there are no records.

The double dating of the years before Sept. 1752, is made to agree with New Style, but the day of the month conforms to the records. To bring these to New Style, add ten days to dates prior to the year 1700, and eleven days to dates occurring between 1700 and Sept. 2, 1752, when the New Style was first established in England.

ABBREVIATIONS

MONTHS

Ja.	Ap.	Jy.	Oc.
Fe.	Ma.	Au.	No.
Mh.	Ju.	Se.	De.

KINDRED

fa.	.	.	.	.	father
gr. fa.	.	.	.	.	grandfather
gr. gr. fa.	.	.	.	great grandfather
mo.	.	.	.	.	mother
br.	.	.	.	.	brother
sis.	.	.	.	.	sister
s.	.	.	.	.	son
dau.	.	.	.	.	daughter
chi.	.	.	.	child or children
h.	.	.	.	.	husband
w.	.	.	.	.	wife
wid.	.	.	.	.	widow
m.	.	.	.	.	married
sr.	.	.	.	.	senior
jr.	.	.	.	.	junior

COUNTRIES

| *Eng.* | . | . | . | . | England |
| *Ir.* | . | . | . | Ireland or Irish |

TOWNS

Barnst.	.	.	.	Barnstable
Bridg'r.	.	.	.	Bridgewater
Carv.	.	.	.	. Carver
Hal'x.	.	.	.	. Halifax
Plym.	.	.	.	. Plymouth
Plymt.	.	.	.	. Plymton
Sandw.	.	.	.	. Sandwich

| *Scitu.* | . | . | . | . | Scituate |
| *War'm.* | . | . | . | . Wareham |

CHURCHES

C. C. C. Central Congregational Church of Middleboro'
N. P. . North Parish, Middleboro'
W. P. . West Parish, Middleboro'

MISCELLANEOUS

abt.	.	.	.	.	about
æ.	.	.	.	.	age [1]
Afr.	.	.	.	.	African
bap.	.	.	.	.	baptised
bef.	.	.	.	.	before
b.	.	.	.	.	born
chh.	.	.	.	.	church
d.	.	.	.	.	died
dis.	.	dismissed to another church
dea.	.	.	.	.	deacon
ex.	.	.	.	.	excluded
fr.	.	.	.	.	from
Ind.	.	.	.	.	Indian
o.	.	original or maiden name
p.	.	.	.	.	page
re.	removed from town, and no record of dismission
re. in, resides in the town or State specified
re-ad.	readmitted to this church after dismission to another
Rev.	.	.	.	.	Reverend
M. F.	.	.	.	the May-Flower
unc.	.	.	.	.	uncertain
unm.	.	.	.	.	unmarried

Figures in parentheses *thus* (2) refer to the regular number of the husband or wife; when separated by a comma *thus* (2, 12) they indicate successive husbands or wives, and refer to them. Figures not in parentheses, and preceded by abbreviations, refer to the ancestors or kindred indicated, thus *fa.* 20 shows the father may be found at No. 20. Remarks or references in brackets apply to the person preceding, and who is not a member of this church.

The names of members admitted by letters of recommendation from other churches are followed, without the comma, by *fr.* and the name of the town or place. Names of churches are not usually given.

[1] When either *th., st.,* or *d.* follows the figures for the age, the person is supposed to have attained to within six months of the age stated; without these additions, the exact age may exceed the figures six months.

DESCRIPTIVE CATALOGUE

FROM THE ORGANIZATION IN 1695 TO 1846 [1]

A careful attention to the Explanatory Notice, p. 647, and to the table of abbreviations, including the note respecting *th. st.* and *d.* on the opposite page, will facilitate the understanding of this catalogue.

1694

1	de. 26, o.s.	REV. SAMUEL FULLER fr. Plym., ord. 1st Pastor, (2) d. Au. 17, 1695, æ. 71st.
2		Elizabeth Fuller, (1) o. Brewster, d. at Plymt. No. 4, 1713. "The aged relict of Rev. Samuel."
3		John Bennet sr., (4) Dea. 1695, d. Mh. 21, 1718, æ. 76. s. of Peter, of Bristol Eng., arr. in Va. 1665; *here*, 1692.
4		Deborah Bennet, (3) o. Grover, m. in Beverley, 1671, came here in 1692, d. Mh. 22, 1718, æ. 70.
5		Jonathan Morse, (6?) d. Jy. 9, 1709, æ. 70th.
6		Mary Morse, (5), chi. 50.
7		Abiel Wood, s. of Henry, fr. Eng., (8) d. oc. 10, 1719, æ. 61st.
8		Abijah Wood, (7) o. Bowen, m. 1683, d. Ma. 21, 1746, æ. 83d.
9		Jacob Tomson, s. Jn. [fr. Eng. 1623], (10) d. Se. 1, '26, æ. 64.
10		Abigail Tomson, (9) m. 1693, o. Wadsworth, dau. John and Abigail, d. Ja. 15, 1745, æ. 74.
11		*Ebenezer Tinkham sr.*, s. of Eph'm, fr. Eng., (12) m. bef. 1679, Dea. 1695, d. Ap. 8, 1718, æ. 73d.
12		Elizabeth Tinkham, (11), o. Liscom, d. Ap. 8, 1718, æ. 64.
13		Samuel Wood sr., br. 7, (71) d. Fe. 3. 1718, æ. 70th.
14		Isaac Billington, d. De. 11, 1709, æ. 66th.
15		Samuel Eaton; 4 chi. b. fr. 1695, d. Mh. 18, 1724, æ. 61st.
16		Samuel Cutbart, d. Ap. 17, 1699, æ. 42.
17		John Cobb jr., (57), d. Oct. 8, 1727, æ. 68th.
18		Weibrah Bumpas, w. Joseph bef. 1670, d. Dec. 27, 1711.
19		Hester Tinkham, (46), o. Wright? d. Ma. 28, 1717, æ. 68th.
20		Deborah Barden, wid. of William Barden.

(Left margin bracket: These first twenty persons were organized as the First Church of Christ in Middleboro', Dec. 26, 1694. (O. S.))

[1] So many of the early settlers worshipped with, or were connected with, the First Church, this descriptive catalogue of its members is here inserted by permission of the Church as a valuable addition to the history and genealogy of many families now or formerly residents of the town.

21		REV. THOMAS PALMER, 2d Pastôr, (158) m. bef. 1699, chi. 142, 184, 296, d. Ju. 17, 1743, æ. 78th.
22		{ Jonathan Cobb, (23), *Dea.* d. Aug. 15, 1728, æ. abt. 68.
23		{ Hope Cobb, (22), d. Jy. 26, 1728, æ. abt. 76.
24		Patience Tinkham, w. Eben'r, jr., m. '03, o. Pratt, d. bef. Ju. 5, '20.
25		Priscilla Tinkham, w. Shubael, m. 1718, o. Childs, chi. 345, 348. d. Jy. 11, 1739, æ. 45th.
26		Elizabeth Lewis, wid. of James, d. Mh. 1744, æ. 90th.
27		Thomas Pratt, chi. Abigail, b. 1701, Hepzibah, b. 1705.
28		{ John Fuller sr, fa. 1, br. 91, (29), chi. 94. d. abt. 1710, æ. 42.
29		{ Mercy Fuller, (28) m. 1686? o. Nelson, 2d m. Wm. Eaton.
30		Mercy Barrows, (59), o. Coombs, sis. 157, d. Mh. 4, 1718, æ. 44.
31		Mary Lovell, w. of John bef. 1702, chi. 367, 413, 449.
32		{ John Alden, s. of Joseph & gr. s. of John of the M. F., (33) m. bef. 1702, d. Se. 29, 1730, æ. 56th.
33		{ Hannah Alden, (32) o. White, dau. Eben'r of Weymouth, d. Oct. 5, 1732, æ. 52d.
34		Mary Lewis, w. of Eliezer, chi. Keziah bap. 1713.

These fourteen persons, being found to have been members, by the existing records, doubtless admitted bef. 1708.

1709.
35	Nov. 2.	REV. PETER THACHER Jr., 3d Pastor, (47), chi. 183, 262, 275, 299, 306, 352, 454, d. Ap. 22, 1744, æ. 56th.

1710.
36	Ja. 22.	Margaret, (Afr.) servant of Jn. Alden, 32.
37	Ma. 7.	Mary Tinkham.
38	" 9.	{ Joseph Vaughan, s. of Geo. fr. Eng.,? (39) m. 1680, 2d m. 1720, to Mercy Fuller, wid. of Jabez, o. Wood, d. Mh. 2, '34, æ. 81st.
39	Au. 20.	{ Joanna Vaughan sr., (38), br. 44, d. Ap. 11, 1718, æ. 61st.
40	" 20.	Ephraim Tinkham jr., fa. 46, br. 93, (447), m. 1708, d. Jy. 11, 1713, æ. 31st.
41	" 20.	Mary Fuller, (91), m. bef. 1710, o. Eddy, br. 61.
42	" 20.	Joanna Darling, w. Thomas sr., chi. Thomas b. 1704.
43	" 20.	Mary Thomas, w. Jona., m. 1703, o. Steward; 4 chi. bap.
44	" 27.	David Thomas, "abt. 60 yrs. old," s. David, sis. 39, 1st w. Abigail bef. 1669, (96).
45	Se. 9.	Susanna Thomas, w. Wm. 2d., m. bef. 1711.
46	Oc. 28.	Ephraim Tinkham sr., (19) m. 1678? d. Oc. 13, 1714, æ. 66th.

1712.
47	Dc. 7.	Mary Thacher, (35), o. Prince, fa. 120, d. Oc. 1, '71, æ. 84.

1713.
48	Fe. 15.	Elizabeth Hacket, w. John bef. 1712, [*Dea.* at W. P.] dis. 1726 to W. P., d. Apr. 17, 1728, æ. 42.
49	unc.	Mary Haskell, w. John Jr., m. 1699, o. Squier, dis. 1727, to Killingly, Ct.
50	"	Mary Morse, mo. 6, m. Francis Moro, 1723.

MEMBERS OF THE FIRST CHURCH

1713.
51 unc. Eleanor Cleaves. A gr. chi. bap. 1721, bro't by her.
52 " Mrs. Raymond, styled "goodwife" in 1709, and with No's. 50, 51 and 6, " yielded grievances."
53 Mh. 15. { Nathaniel Winslow fr. Rochester, (54).
54 " 15. { Elizabeth Winslow fr. Rochester, (53).
55 Au. 4. Martha Soul, w. Jn. m. '01, o. Tinkham, d. Fe. 16, '58, æ. 80.
56 Oc. 11. Mary Caswell fr. Taunton.

1714.
57 Mh. 28. Rachel Cobb, (17), m. 1688, o. Soul, d. Se. 18, 1727, æ. 65th.

1715.
58 Fe. 13. Ebenezer Richmond, m. bef. 1701, Re. to W. P.
59 " 20. *Samuel Barrows*, (30), 1st m. bef. 1702; 2d w. Joanna, *Dea.* 1725, d. De. 30, 1755, æ. 83d.
60 Ma. 20. { Melatiah Eddy, (61) m. 1703, o. Pratt, d. 1769, æ. 92.
61 Ju. 12. { Samuel Eddy sr., s. of Obadiah, sis. 41, (60), d. 1752, æ. 77.
62 Jy. 10. Ebenezer Redding, (123, 131), d. May 5, 1751, æ. ab't 72.
63 " 17. Jonathan Smith, m. Susanna Thomas 1713, (154), chi. 318, 360, d. Se. 6, 1767, æ. 79th.
64 " 17. Lydia Thomas, (81) m. 1684, o. Howland, dau. Isaac, sis. 595, d. Jy. 6, 1717, æ. 52d. *1st burial in The Green Cemetery.*
65 Au. — Mary Allen, (76) m. bef. 1708 in Bridgewater.
66 " — Charity Leonard, wid.; m. J. Perkins of Norwich 1722.
67 " — Samuel Sampson, d. Sep. 10, 1744, æ. 75th. [w. Mercy, o. Eddy, br. 61, d. 1743, æ. 77th.]
68 " 22. *Ephraim Wood*, fa. 13, br. 82, m. Susanna bef. 1710, (2d w. 118), *Dea.* 1725, d. Jy. 9, 1744, æ. 65th.
69 Oc. — Esther Southworth, w. of Ichabod bef. 1713. [*he* d. Se. 13, 1757, æ. 79th.]
70 " — Lydia Cobb.

1716.
71 Ma. 27. Rebecca Wood, (13) m. bef. 1679, d. Fe. 10, 1718, æ. 67th.
72 Au. — Joanna Tinkham, wid. Jeremiah Jr. bef. 1711, [his fa. 11.] 2d. m. 1720.
73 " 26. Elizabeth Nye, w. Ichabod bef. 1713; chi. Sam'l b. 1715.
74 Oc. 7. Mary Tinkham; m. Henry Wood 1717; chi. Moses, &c.
75 Nov. 4. James Wood, br? 7, (84?); chi. bap., Benj., Barna., Abel, Ich.
76 " 25. Nathaniel Allen, s. of Sam'l of Bridg'r, (65), 1st w. Bethiah Conant, m. 1696; chi. 228, 305, 326.
77 " 25. Nathan Clark, m. Jemima ——; chi. Ichabod b. 1716.
78 Dec. 2. John Drew sr., (99); dis. 1734 to Hal'x.
79 " — Ichabod King fr. Scitu., 2d m. 1716, (83), 1st w. Hannah, [d. 1716, æ. 36 yrs.] dis. 1733 to Rochester.

1717.
80 Jan. 2. Hannah Morton, dau. Jn., sis. 131, 134, (125?).

1718.
81 Ma. 4. Jeremiah Thomas sr., (64, 98), d. Fe. 2, 1736, æ. 77th.
82 " 4. *Samuel Wood Jr.*, fa. 13, br. 68, (124, 242), *Dea.* 1737, b. 1684, d. bef. 1754.
83 June 1. Judith King, (79), wid. Gibbs bef., dis. 1733 to Rochester.
84 Jy. 20. Experience Wood, (75?) o. Fuller, fa. 1, brs. 28, 91.
85 Au. 10. Abigail Barden, (88), chi. Sarah b. 1695, Abigail, &c.
86 " 10. Joseph Bates, (144, 474), 2d m. 1743, d. Au. 31, 1778, æ. 86th.
87 " 10. James Raymond, m. Mercy Tinkham 1716, 2d w. (187), dis. 1753, with w. and dau. 373, to Pomfret, Conn.

1719.
88 Mh. 19. Stephen Barden sr., (85), chi. Wm. b. 1697, &c. (ex. 1727.)
89 June 9. David Delano sr., m. 1706 Elizabeth Eddy.
90 No. 15. Abigail Smith, m. Eb. Dunham '19, dis. bef. 1731 to Plym.

1720.
91 Mh. 6. Isaac Fuller, fa. 1, (41), chi. Isaac b. 1712, d. 1727, æ. abt. 50.
92 Dec. 4. Deborah Vaughan, (297), m. 1711, o. Bennet, fa. 3, br. 147, d. Ap. 26, 1761, æ. 79th.

1721.
93 Mh. 12. Isaac Tinkham sr., fa. 46, br. 40, 595, (214), dis. 1734 to Hal'x; *Deacon in Hal'x*, d. Ap. 7, 1750, æ. 65th.
94 " 12. Ebenezer Fuller, fa. 28, br. 156, sis. 151, (95), m. bef. 1716. he & w. dis. '34 to Hal'x., d. '85? æ. 98th.
95 " 12. Elizabeth Fuller, (94), o. Short, b. 1693 in Weymouth, dau of Luke jr., gr. fa. 197.
96 " 12. Elizabeth Thomas sr. fr. Plymt. (44), m. 1718, o. Canedy.
97 Ma. 14. Hannah Fuller, (156), o. Thomas, dis. 1734 to Halifax.
98 " 14. Mary Thomas fr. Taunton, (81) m. 1720, bef., wid. Durfee, d. Nov. 15, 1749, æ. 85th.
99 Oc. 15. Sarah Drew, (78), chi. Abigail b. 1721, dis. 1734 to Hal'x.

1722.
100 Mh. 11. Abigail Eddy, w. Benj'n, [br. 61, 234] m. bef. 1717; 2d m. 1747 to Elisha Hayward. 3d m. 1752 (161).
101 Apr. 8. Elizabeth Conant, w. Josiah, m. 1701, o. Washburn.
102 " 16. Sarah Wood, w. John sr., chi. Stephen b. 1712, David, &c.
103 " 29. Elizabeth Fuller, gr. fa. or fa. 1, m. John Eaton 1729, dis. 1731 to Kingston.
104 " 29. John Raymond sr., "in 74th yr."; d. Ju. 5, 1725, æ. 77th.
105 Ju. 14. Elizabeth Thomas, fa. 81, sis. 219, 242, m. John Tomson '23; dis. 1734 to Hal'x, d. Aug. 1776, æ. 86th.
106 Sept. 9. William Strowbridge fr. Donaugh Ir. (107), Re. 1725 to W. P., d. No. 14, 1777, æ. 87.
107 " 9. Margaret Strowbridge fr. Donaugh Ir., (106), dis. 1726 to W. P., d. De. 8, 1776, æ. 83.
108 Oc. 17. Sarah Rogers; probably m. Samuel Ford in Marshfield.

1723.
109 July 1. (Andrew Mansfield fr. 1st ch. in Lynn, (110).
110 " 1. (Sarah Mansfield fr. 1st ch. in Lynn, (109).
111 " 1. Mary Bumpas, w. Joseph, [b. 1674] m. bef. 1713. [fa. d. 1705.]
112 " 1. Hannah Tinkham fr. Scitu., (176), d. Ap. 13, 1771, æ. 91st.
113 " 1. (John Vaughan, fa. 38, (114), m. 1718, d. Ma. 8, 1770, æ. 78th.
114 " 1. (Jerusha Vaughan, (113), o. Wood, fa. 7, b. 1695, d., æ. 90?
115 " 21. Hannah Thomas, m. 1721, o. Turner, chi., 2 s., 7 dau.
116 De. 15. Elnathan Wood, fa. 7, m. Mary Billington 1712, 2d. w. 1735 (380), d. Ap. 20, 1752, æ. 66.

1724.
117 Mh. — NATHAN PRINCE, fa. 120, sis. 128, d. Jy. 25, '48, æ. 50.
118 May 3. Patience Wood, (68), m. bef. 1724, chi. 332, & Manassah.
119 Ju. 30. Joanna Cobb, "on her bed at her house," (421), m. bef. 1714, o. Thomas, dau. Wm. sr., d. No. 11, 1724, æ. 32d.
120 Oc. 25. (Samuel Prince Esq. fr. Sandwich, (2d w. 121), d. Jy. 3, 1728, æ. 80.
121 " 25.) Mercy Prince fr. Sandw. (120), dau. Gov. Hinckley, m. bef. 1687, d. Ap. 25, 1736, æ. 73, chi. 47, 117, 128, 129.
122 No. 8. Mercy Wood, w. of Abiel Jr., o. Hacket, m. 1718.
123 " 29. Mercy Redding, (62) m. 1706, o. Miller, d. Mh. 31, '28, æ. 43d.

1725.
124 Ma. 30. Elizabeth Wood, (82) m. bef. 1717, chi. Joshua, Ann, &c.
125 Jy. 4. Nathan Bassett fr. Sand'h, (80?); *Dea.* in Mr. Weld's chh.
126 " 29. Ann Cavender, (266) m. bef. 1731, chi. Catharine, b. 1731.
127 " 29. Mercy Morton, (ad. 58), m. bef. 1722, o. Foster, d. Ap. 4, 1782, æ. 84th.
128 Se. 5. Mercy Prince, fa. 120, sis. 47, 129, d. Au. 9, 1748, æ. 48th.
129 " 5. Alice Prince, fa. 120, sis. 128, m. Samuel Gray of Harwich, d. July 4, 1733, æ. 31st.
130 " 5. Sarah Ransom, w. Robert; chi. Wm., Robert, & c. bap. '29.
131 Oc. 3. Joanna Vaughan, wid. Elisha, o. Morton, sis. 80. 2d m. (62).

1726.
132 Ma. 1. (Samuel Barrows Jr., fa. 59, br. 208, (133). He & w. dis. 1740 to Killingly Ct.; 6 sons and 2 daughters.
133 " 1. (Susannah Barrows, (132), chi. fr. 1724, Sarah, Geo., Sam. &c.
134 Jy. 17. Mary Tomson, (235), m. 1715, o. Morton, dau. John, sis. 80, dis. 1734 to Hal'x, d. Mh. 20, 1781, æ. 91st.
135 No. 27. Nathaniel Southworth, (137), m. bef. 1710, d. Ap. 8, 1757, æ. 72.

1727.
136 Jan. 8. Experience Sproat, "wid. of Lt. Ebenezer who with her was propounded in July last." [He d. Sep. 28, 1726, æ. 52d.] "I was, (says Mr. Thacher,) by an illness of 11 weeks, disenabled to proceed with them." Her 2d m. 1731 to Francis Miller, d. Nov. 19, 1758, æ. 74th.

1727.

137	Ja.	22.	Jael Southworth, (135), o. Bennet, d. No. 9, 1745, æ. 67th.
138	"	22.	⎰ Ezra Clap fr. Milton, (139), d. Se. 20, 1761, æ. 68th.
139	"	22.	⎱ Waitstill Clap fr. Milton, (138), o. Tucker, d. Jy. 31,'68, æ. 73d.
140	Jy.	30.	⎰ Timothy Wood, fa. 7, (141). Both dis. 1734 to Hal'x. d. Au. 22, 1756, æ. 63.
141	"	30.	⎱ Mary Wood, (140) m. bef. 1726, d. May 12, 1756, æ.
142	De.	—	SAMUEL PALMER, fa. 21, mo. 158, sis. 184, br. 296, dis. 1731 as *Pastor* at Falmouth, Mass.
143	"	—	Abigail Sproat, mo.? 136, m. Rev. John Wadsworth, of Canterbury, Ct., 1729, d. 1778, æ. 71.

1728.

144	Ja.	28.	Joanna Bates, (86) m. '17, o. Tinkham, d. Ju. 28, 1738, æ. 42d.
145	"	28.	Mary Tinkham, (148) m. bef. 1726, d. Ju. 16, 1745, æ. 43d.
146	"	28.	Silence Fuller, w. of Samuel, m. 1726, o. Short, b. 1704, dau. of Luke jr., gr. fa. 197.
147	Mh.	10.	Samuel Bennet sr., fa. 3, sis. 92, (221) chi. Samuel, b. 1710.
148	"	10.	Seth Tinkham, s. Peter & Mercy, (145), d. Fe. 9, 1751, æ. 47th.
149	"	10.	Thomas Darling, mo. 42, br. 365, (265), d. No. 2, 1792, æ. 88th.
150	"	10.	Lydia Hackett, w. Geo. m. 1724, o. Thomas, b. 1694. fa. 81.
151	"	10.	Lydia Fuller, fa. 28, (226) m. 1733.
152	"	17.	Patience Machaan, wid. of Duncan, dau. 291, bap.
153	"	24.	Hannah Parlow, wid. of Thomas, m. 1722, o. King.; 2d m. 1740 (161), d. Ap. 5, 1750, æ. 48.
154	Ma.	12.	Sarah Smith, (63) m. '25, o. Churchill, d. Ju. 5, 1744, æ. 48.
155	"	12.	Mercy Fuller, m. —— Ford, "dis. 1761 to chh. in Paquague."
156	June	6.	John Fuller, fa. 28, (97, 244), 1st m. 1719, dis. 1734 to Hal'x. d. 1766, æ. 74.
157	Jy.	14.	Lydia Miller, w. John, m. 1702, o. Coombs, dau. Francis, [who d. 1683] d. Mh. 6, 1735, æ. 56th.
158	"	14.	Elizabeth Palmer, (21) d. Ap. 17, 1740, æ. 64th.
159	Oc.	13.	Mary Tomson, fa. 9, br. 268, sis. 180, m. Reuben Tomson, dis. 1734 to Hal'x. d. Jy. 19, 1769, æ. 58.
160	No.	17.	Benjamin White sr. Esq., (199), d. De. 10, 1750, æ. 67th.
161	"	17.	James Smith, (153) 2d m. '52 (100), d. Se. 9, '63, æ. 72 d.

1729.

162	Mh.	24.	Ephraim Dunham, m. Annas Smith 1725, s. Jona. b. 1726.
163	"	24.	Miriam Thomas, w. Jer'h, jr., o. Thomas, d. Ja. 10, '68, æ. 73d.
164	"	24.	⎰ *Benjamin Tucker*, (165) *Dea.* 1745, d. Jy. 9, '81, æ. 76th.
165	"	24.	⎱ Sarah Tucker, (164) o. Woodward, d. Mh. 13, '79, æ. 67th.
166	Apr.	6.	Faithful Vaughan, m. 1720? d. Ap. 5, '53, æ. 66th.
167	"	6.	Elizabeth Gibbs. chi. Jabez, bap.
168	"	6.	Meriba Delano, b. 1709, dau. Nathan, m. C. Dexter, 1731.
169	"	6.	Ann Delano, sis. 168 probably.
170	"	20.	Abraham Barden sr., (181), chi. 229, Joseph, Isaac.
171	"	20.	Daniel Caswell, (192), chi. Mary, Deborah, Jael; bap.

	1729.	
172	Apr. 27.	Sarah Elmes, w. Ignatius, m. 1728, o. Bennet, dau. Eben'r. gr. fa. 3, d. Jy. 1789, æ. 82.
173	" 27.	Elizabeth Drew, dis. 1734 to Hal'x., d. No. 14, 1779.
174	July 6.	{ Samuel Warren, (175) m. 1704, chi. 182, Samuel, James.
175	" 6.	{ Eleanor Warren, (174), o. Billington, chi. Nathan, &c.
176	" 6.	Ichabod Tupper, (112?) m. 1729.
177	" 6.	{ David Wood, s. David, (178) m. 1720, d. Jy. 29, '38, æ. 50.
178	" 6.	{ Joanna Wood, (177) o. Tilson, chi. Edmund, David, &c.
179	" 6.	{ Nehemiah Bennet, s. John jr., gr. fa. 3, (180) m. 1721, d. Au. 15, 1769, æ. 74th.
180	" 6.	{ Mercy Bennet, (179) o. Tomson, fa. 9, d. Se. 4, 1799, æ. 99 yrs. 10 mo. 11 days.
181	Au. 10.	Mary Barden, (170) m. bef. 1698, chi. Mary, 203, Sarah.
182	" 10.	Priscilla Warren, b. De. 12, 1704, fa. 174, br. 343, 511.
183	" 10.	Mary Thacher, b. 1711, fa. 35, m. Rev. Nathan Stone, 1751, dis. 1753 to Southboro'.
	1730.	
184	Ja. 18.	Elizabeth Palmer, b. 1704, fa. 21, m. Eben'r Cheney, d. bef. 1780. Their dau. *Mary* m. Jn. Morey & d. *here*, 1821.
185	" 18.	Martha Knowlton, (188), 1st chi. at Ipswich, b. 1712.
186	" 18.	Mary Billington, w. Isaac, [His fa. 14.] m. 1730, o. Dunham, d. Ju. 24, 1777, æ. 72d.
187	Jy. 19.	Elizabeth Raymond, (87) bef. 1724, dis. 1753 to Ct.
188	" 19.	Thomas Knowlton, (185) d. Ju. 22, 1755, æ. 69th.
189	Aug. 7.	Anibal Canedy, chi. Hopestill & Sarah bap.; 2d m. bef. 1739 to —— Paine.
190	No. 22.	Elizabeth Ellis, m. 1715? d. Ap. 3, 1753, æ. 66th
	1731.	
191	Ma. 23.	Hannah Pratt jr., w. Eleazer jr., o. Short, dau. Luke jr., gr. fa. 197, d. Se. 4, 1793, æ. 82.
192	Ju. 20.	Mary Caswell, (171) m. bef. 1732.
193	" 20.	Obadiah Sampson fr. Marshfield, fa. 67, (206), chi. fr. 1737.
194	Aug. 8.	Ichabod Standish, (198), dis. 1734 to Hal'x, d. Fe. 29, 1772.
195	" 8.	{ Moses Sturtevant fr. Plymt., (196), s. Consider, b. 1733.
196	" 8.	{ Elizabeth Sturtevant fr. Plymt., (195) s. Jos. b. 1734.
197	Se. 23.	Luke Short sr., chi. Luke, *here*. d. 1746, æ. 116.
198	Oc. 10.	Phebe Standish fr. Plymt., (194) m. 1719, o. King, dis. 1734 to Hal'x.
199	" 10.	Ann White, (160), m. bef. 1727, d. Se. 13, 1778, æ. 81st.
200	" 10.	Phebe Pratt, w. Benaiah bef. 1737, d. Mh. 5, 1800, æ. 88.
	1732.	
201	Ja. 23.	{ Samuel Lyon, (202), chi. 329, d. Fe. 22, 1756, æ. 76th.
202	" 23.	{ Joanna Lyon, (201), o. Bates? No chi. recorded *here*.
203	Apr. 1.	Elizabeth Barden, mo. 181, *b*. Oc. 1, 1702, *m*. Sampson?

1733.
204 Mh. 19. Esther Barden, (229), m. '26, o. Sampson, fa. 67, dis. '37.
205 Ap. 29. Elkanah Rickard, 1st w. Ketura bef. 1730; chi. Nath'l, '30, Elkanah 1732, (2d w. 233), re. to Bridgewater.
206 " 29. Mary Sampson, (193) m. 1731, o. Soul, d. 1743.
207 " 29. Mary Bennet, w. Isaac, m. 1732, o. Drew; 4 sons & 2 daus.
208 unc. Coombs Barrows, fa. 59, m. '29 & '32, d. No. 30, '75, æ. 71st.
209 " Barnabas Crossman, (253) m. bef. 1729; 5 sons & 2 daus.; d. Oc. 1, 1744, æ. 44th.
210 " Ichabod Paddock, (261), m. bef. '23, d. Au. 26, '50, æ. 64th.
211 " Lemuel Donham, (260), m. 1735; 6 sons & 3 dau's.
212 " Thomas Wood, fa. 7, m. Hannah Alden, 1729. [Her fa. 32.] d. Ja. 27, 1745, æ. 42d.
213 " John Raymond jr., fa. 104, 1st. m. bef. 1703, 2d m. 1726.
214 " Abijah Tinkham, (93), o. Wood, fa. 7, dis. 1734 to Hal'x. d. De. 25, 1777, æ. 88th.
215 July 1. Eleanor Bennet, b. 1711, fa. 147, sis. 216, m. Z. Whitman, of Bridg'r, 1733, d. No. 10, 1777, æ. 66.
216 " 1. Ruth Bennet jr., b. 1714, fa. 147, m. Jona Snow, 1746.
217 " 1. Jemima Wood, b. 1712, fa. 116, br. 355, sis. 263, 414.
218 " 1. Susanna Thomas.
219 " 1. Thankful Cobb, w. James, m. 1718, o. Thomas, fa. 81, sis. 242, 105, d. Ap. 17, 1743, æ. 48th.
220 " 1. Sarah Gumee; or Gurnee; perhaps Gurney.
221 Aug. 5. Ruth Bennet sr., (147) m. bef. 1710, o. Perry; chi. 215, 216.
222 " 5. ⎰ David Alden, fa. 32, (223) m. bef. 1728, d. Au. 24, 1763, æ. 61.
223 " 5. ⎱ Judith Alden, (222) o. Paddleford, d. 1802, æ. 94th.
224 " 5. Bethiah Sampson, m. 1727, o. Clark.
225 " 5. Mary Hayford, (239) m. bef. 1728.
226 Se. 30. Francis Eaton, m. 1727, 2d w. (151).

1734.
227 Mh. 17. Jane Pratt
228 Ap. 28. Bethiah Lyon, w. Eleazer, m. 1732, o. Allen, b. 1708, fa. 76.
229 Ju. 10. Abraham Barden jr., b. 1698, (204), 1st m. Priscilla Alden 1722, dis. to Stafford, Ct. 1737.
230 Au. 11. Desire Vaughan, (241) m. bef. 1733, d. Se. 10, '84, æ. 89th.
231 " 11. ⎰ Edmund Weston sr. fr. Plymt., (232, 300), d. Ap. 29, '73, æ. 76.
232 " 11. ⎱ Susanna Weston fr. Plymt., (231) m. bef. 1723, o. Jackson, d. No. 4, 1734, æ. 28th.
233 Se. 29. Bethiah Rickard, (205) m. 1733, o. Conant, dau. Nath'l.
234 " 29. Jabez Eddy sr. fr. Carv.,[1] br. 61, chi. 450, Moses 263. "dis. Se. 6. 1749 to unite with members of Rev. Mr. Shaw's chh. at Titicut."
235 Oc. 10. Thomas Tomson sr., s. John fr. Eng., br. 9, (134), dis. '34 to Hal'x. d. Oc. 26, 1742, æ. 78.

[1] Then and until 1792 called "The second Church in Plympton."

	1734.	
236	Oc. 10.	{ Ebenezer Cobb, (237), dis. 1734 to Hal'x.
237	" 10.	{ Lydia Cobb, (236), m. bef. 1731, dis. 1734 to Hal'x.
238	" 10.	Henry Thomas, m. Ruth Nelson 1726, chi. 452.
239	" 10.	Benjamin Heyford Sr., (225), sons Benjamin, John, Jacob.
240	Nov. 3.	Ebenezer Finnea fr. Norton, (246), *Dea.* 1737, d. Sept. 21, 1745, æ. 47th.
241	" 21.	Hinksman Vaughan, b. 1708, mo. 131, (230). 3 sisters b. July 1, 1711; also 3 sons b. June 1, 1735.
	1735.	
242	Ap. 20.	Sarah Wood, (82) m. '30, 1st h. Isaac Howland, o. Thomas, sis. 105, 219, d. Ap. 3, 1756, æ. 68.
243	Ju. 12.	{ Samuel Eddy jr., fa. 61, (244) m. '33, d. '46, æ. 36.
244	" 12.	{ Lydia Eddy, (243) o. Alden, fa. 32, br. 334, 223, sis. 271, (2d h. 156,) d. Mh. 1, 1803, æ. 92.
245	" 12.	Bennet Redding (439) m. 1734, o. Eddy, fa. 61, br. 243, 341, sis. 412, d. Jy. 15, 1797; æ. 83?
246	Se. 28.	Jane Finnea fr. Norton, (240); chi. 354, Lewis, &c.
	1736.	
247	Ja. 11.	Jabez Fuller, b. 1717, s. Jona. m. Hannah Pratt 1744, gr. fa. 1; Re. to Medfield; himself & 3 chi. Tho., Jabez & Jona., Physicians.
248	Ap. 11.	Fear Barrows, m. '36, o. Thomas, d. No. 2, '61, æ. 40th.
249	Ju. 13.	Abigail Thomas, w. Edward jr., m. 1720, o. Parlow, d. Oct. 13, 1756, æ. 62d.
250	" 13.	Anna Thomas, w. Eben'r, m. 1731, o. Ransom, d. 1763, æ. 52d.
251	" 13.	Elizabeth Griffith, w. Jesse, m. 1723, o. Bent; dis. 1742 to Plymt., d. 1743, æ. 37?
252	July —	Hannah Wood, 2d. w. John sr., m. 1731, o. Chiles.
253	" —	Hannah Crossman, (209) m. bef. 1729.
254	" —	Mercy Raymond, (393) m. bef. 1732.
255	" —	Alice Raymond, (325) m. 1729, o. Bent, dau. Experience?
256	" —	{ Hezekiah Purrington, (257); chi. Joshua, Sam'l, Jn.
257	" —	{ Mercy Purrington, (256) m. 1735, o. Bates, b. '19, fa. 86.
258	" —	Noah Thomas, s. Edw'd sr., br. 608, (281) d. De. 20, '58, æ. 49.
259	Se. —	Thomas Tupper, (411) m. 1735, re. to Munson, Ms. 1797?
260	" —	Elizabeth Donham, (211), o. Tinkham, br. 337, sis. 357, 433, d. æ. 63.
261	Oc. 21.	Joanna Paddock, (210), o. Faunce, d. May 4, 1758, æ. 68.
	1737.	
262	Ap. 24.	PETER THACHER Jr., fa. 35, dis. 1748 to Attleboro, Pastor there; m. 1749 Bethiah Carpenter, d. Se. 13, 1785, æ. 70th.
263	Jy. 17.	Jedidah Eddy, w. Moses [fa. 234], m. 1735, o. Wood, fa. 116, d. Mh. 9, 1788, æ. 73.

658   HISTORY OF THE TOWN OF MIDDLEBORO   [1695-1846]

1737.
264 Se. 24. Waitstill Miller, (409), o. Clap, d. Au. 27, 1754, æ. 38th.
265 No. 6. Rebecca Darling, (149) m. bef. 1725.
1738.
266 Ap. 16. John Cavender, (126); dau. Catherine b. 1731.
267 Oc. 12. Mary Tinkham.
1739.
268 Fe. 17. { Caleb Tomson, fa. 9, (269), d. Ja. 10, 1787, æ. 75.
269 " 17. { Abigail Tomson, (268) m. bef. 1737, o. Crossman, d. No. 23, 1791, æ. 77th.
270 Ma. 13. John Pratt, s. Sam'l, m. H. Turner, 1725, 2d. w. 1729, (466?)
271 " 13. Abigail Thomas, w. Nathan (608) m. 1735, o. Alden, fa. 32, d. Ja. 1744, æ. 29.
272 Jy. 1. *Gershom Cobb*, b. 1714, fa. 421, br. 419, sis. 377, (455) *Dea.* 1745, Re., & d. in old age, in Hardwick, Mass.
273 " 1. Thankful Bennet, m. 1724, 2d. m. Seth Samson 1758, o. Sproat.
274 " 1. Ruth Barrows, w. Sylvanus bef. 1738 at Barnst., dis. to " Wendham," 1755.
275 " 1. Samuel Thacher fr. Plym., fa. 35, m. Debo'h Bennet 1747, 2d. w. Sarah bef. 1759, 3d. m. 1779 Catherine Stephens, d. Mh. 21, 1795, æ. 78th.
276 Au. 19. Mary Fuller.
277 Se. 16. Else Caswell, m. Benj'n. Heyford? 1752.
278 Oc. 14. Joanna Jackson, (335) m. 1735, o. Bates, b. 1718, fa. 86.
279 " 28. Mary King, m. 1732, o. Green, dis. 1747 to Turkey, N. J.
1740.
280 Mh. 11. Sarah Wood, (295) m. bef. 1739, dis. 1744 to Berkley.
281 Ju. 15. Mary Thomas, (258) m. 1733, o. Alden, fa. 32, br. 222, 334, 427, sis. 271, 244, d. Au. 1, 1787, æ. 75th.
282 " 15. Mary Thomas, (424) m. bef. 1733, d. Au. 4, 1768, æ. 58th.
1741.
283 Ma. 7. Mary Griffeth fr. Rochester.
284 " 7. Martha Morse fr. Carver, w. Jona. d. 1805, æ. 95.
285 " 10. { Shubael Lewis fr. Carv. (286); chi. Samuel b. 1739, &c.
286 " 10. { Hazadiah Lewis fr. Carv. (285), o. Eddy, b. 1712, fa. 234.
287 " 10. Jacob Burges fr. Yarmouth 2d. chh., m. bef. 1741.
288 Ju. 21. { Joshua Donham fr. Carv. (289.)
289 " 21. { Keturah Donham fr. Sandw., (288) m. 1740, o. Barlow.
290 " 21. Lydia Crocker fr. Carv., w. Theopholus bef. 1731.
291 Au. 2. Christiana Raymond fr. Bridg'r., (460), o. Machaan, mo. 152.
292 " 16. JAMES SPROAT, mo. 136, br. 323, Pastor d. 1793, æ. 71.
293 Dec. 6. William Lyon, (389); s. Elisha b. 1744, Daniel b. 1761.
294 " 6. Nathan Bassett Jr., fa. 125, 1st. w. bef. 1730, 2d. w. (302.)
295 " 6. John Wood Jr., b. 1716, (280), dis. 1744 to Berkley.
296 " 6. Job Palmer, fa. 21, br. 142, sis. 184, d. Ja. 1, 1746, æ. 26th.

	1742.		
297	Jan.	3.	Jabez Vaughan, fa. 38, br. 113, (92) d. Ap. 13, 1773, æ. 91st.
298	"	3.	Israel Thomas, mo. 402, sis. 119, (391), d. Ju. 29, 1778, æ. 65.
299	"	3.	Thomas Thatcher, fa. 35, unm., d. De. 10, 1744, æ. 24th.
300	"	3.	Elizabeth Weston, (231) m. 1735, o. Smith?
301	"	3.	Elizabeth Ames, wid. of Seth, 2d. m. 1742 (312), o. Prince dau. of John, gr. fa. 120, d. 1753.
302	"	3.	Thankful Basset, (294) 2d. w. bef. 1740.
303	"	3.	Peggy, (Ind.) m. Tom (Afr.) 1741, servants of E. Leonard.
304	"	10.	Timothy Fuller, b. 1721, br. 247, dis. 1766 to Attleboro'.
305	"	10.	Mary Allen, b. Mch. 4, 1715, fa. 76, br. 326.
306	"	10.	John Thacher, b. Ap. 27, 1723, fa. 35, brs. 262, 275, 299.
307	"	10.	Hannah Cox, (398) m. 1721, o. Smith, d. De. 18, 1777, æ. 78?
308	"	10.	Rebecca Southworth, m. 1741, o. Ellis, mo. 190, br. John 384, d. Ju. 19, 1781, æ. 60th.
309	"	16.	Rachel Smith, (360) m. 1738, o. Cobb, mo. 219, sis. 379, d. Mh. 2, 1767, æ. 47.
310	"	24.	Joseph Bates Jr., b. 1722, fa. 86, sis. 257, 278, m. Eunice Tinkham 1749, dis. 1787 to Hartland, Vt.
311	"	24.	Ephraim Wood Jr., fa. 68, br. 400, sis. 332, m. Mary Lazell 1742, 2d. w. (442) m. 1752, d. De. 14, 1781, æ. 66th.
312	"	24.	Joshua Lazell, (301), s. Prince b. 1745, dau's Elizabeth and Mary; d. in Bridg'r, 1749.
313	"	24.	Deborah Smith, o. Barden, d. Ja. 9, 1801, æ. 93d.
314	"	24.	Prince, (Afr.), (416) m. 1747, serv't of Eben'r Morton.
315	"	24.	Else Antony, (Ind.) d. about 1790.
316	"	24.	Abiel Leach fr. Hal'x, (435) m. bef. 1739, d. Oc. 2, 1787, æ. 87th.
317	"	24.	Jonathan Snow fr. Bridg'r, m. Sarah Soul 1728, 2d. m. 1746 to Ruth Bennet; gr. fa. of Aaron, d. 1783, æ. 81.
318	Fe.	14.	Jonathan Smith Jr., b. Fe. 14, 1716, (417) m. 1737, fa. 63, br. 360, dis. 1753 to Boulton.
319	"	14.	John Vaughan Jr., b. Ap. 5, 1720, fa. 113, br. 364, 351, sis. 320, 478, 395, 405.
320	"	14.	Jerusha Vaughan, fa. 113, (346) m. 1743, d. No. 25, 1787, æ. 66.
321	"	14.	Abigail Thayer, b. 1718, dau. of Isaac, m. L. Kitts, 1754.
322	"	14.	Mary Thomas, m. James Willis 1759.
323	"	14.	Ebenezer Sproat, mo. 136, br. 292, (332), d. Ja. 23, 1786, æ. 69th.
324	"	14.	Thomas Felix Jr., (Indian.)
325	"	14.	Barnabas Raymond, b. Ma. 21, 1710, fa. 213, br. 393, (255).
326	"	14.	David Allen, b. 1713, fa. 76, sis. 305, m. Fear —— bef. 1745, [who d. 1753, æ. 53d.]
327	Mh.	7.	Woodward Tucker, "aged 9 yrs." fa. 164, br. 541, 635, sis. 489, m. Mercy Tinkham 1756, d. Ap. 12, 1761, æ. 28th.
328	"	7.	Benoni Thomas, unm. d. about 1750?
329	"	7.	Jedediah Lyon, fa. 201, (589) m. 1743, d. Fe. 9, 1807, æ. 86th.
330	"	7.	Patience Raymond, b. No. 11, 1724, fa. 87.

1742.

331	Mh. 7.	Mary Hathaway, dis. 1745 to Berkley.
332	" 7.	Bathsheba Wood, fa. 68, (323) m. 1749, d. Ju. 28, 1798, æ. 74.
333	" 7.	David Sears, (399, 347) m. 1734 & 1781, chi. Zebedee, &c.
334	" 7.	NOAH ALDEN, fa. 32, br. 222, 427, (371); dis. 1749 to Stafford, Pastor at Bellingham, d. 1797, æ. 71st.
335	" 7.	John Jackson Jr., (278) Re. to St. of Maine, d. 1811, æ. 95.
336	" 7.	Peter Tinkham sr., mo. 24, gr. fa. 11, m. 1730, d. Oc. 10, 1745, æ. 36.
337	" 7.	Samuel Tinkham 3d., gr. gr. fa. 46 sis. 357, 260, 433, (436) m. Patience Simmons 1760, d. Mh. 28, 1796, æ. 72.
338	" 7.	Susanna Tinkham, mo. 595, br. 346, sis. 359, 347, m. Jas. Cobb 1749, d. Ju. 21, 1813, æ. 88.
339	" 7.	John Williams. No early records of this name.
340	" 14.	Elizabeth Williams, m. Jabez Eaton 1759?
341	" 14.	{ Zachariah Eddy, fa. 61, br. 243, (342) d. De. 6, 1777, æ. 66.
342	" 14.	{ Mercy Eddy, (341) m. 1737, o. Morton, mo. 127, d. Au. 25, 1802, æ. 80.
343	" 14.	{ Benjamin Warren, fa. 174, (344) m. '41, d. Ja. 1802, æ. 81.
344	" 14.	{ Jedidah Warren, (343) o. Tupper, d. Oc. 20, 1807, æ. 83d.
345	" 14.	Joseph Tinkham, mo. 25, (358) m. 1740, d. Ap. 28, 1767, æ. 45.
346	" 14.	John Tinkham Jr., mo. 595, (320) d. Au. 22, 1793, æ. 74.
347	" 14.	Hannah Tinkham Jr., mo. 595, br. 346, sis. 338, (364, 333), 1st m. 1742, 2d. m., 3d. m. 1781, d. Ap. 14, 1802, æ. 79.
348	" 14.	Priscilla Tinkham, mo. 25, br. 345, (419, 368) m. 1743, 1751, d. Ap. 5, 1769, æ. 43d.
349	" 14.	Patience Tinkham, (356) m. 1744, d. Ap. 9, 1791, æ. 74th.
350	" 14.	Eleazer Thomas, mo. 45, br. 425, 424, m. Mary Shaw Jr., 1746, d. Se. 23, 1808, æ. 83.
351	" 14.	Elisha Vaughan, fa. 113, br. 364, (359) m. 1746, b. De. 1723.
352	" 14.	Susanna Thacher, b. 1719, fa. 35, br. 262, 275, 299, 306, sis. 183, m. Samuel Tucker of Milton, 1742.
353	" 14.	Deborah Redding, b. 1722, fa. 62, br. 426, 439, 467, sis. 410.
354	" 14.	Nelson Finney, fa. 240? m. Martha Simmons 1749, Rosamond Thomas 1755; d. Ju. 22, 1781, æ. 53d.
355	" 28.	Ephraim Wood, fa. 116, (448) m. 1743, d. No. 8, 1783, æ. 68.
356	" 28.	Edmund Wood, fa. 177, (349) m. 1744, d. De. 29, 1805, æ. 84.
357	" 28.	Martha Tinkham, br. 337, (378) m. 1742, d. Mh. 20, 1744, æ. 24th.
358	" 28.	Agnes Tinkham, b. 1721, mo. 72, br. 428, (345, 477) m. 1740, 1769; a 3d. m? o. Mackfun, alias Maxwell.
359	" 28.	Esther Tinkham, b. 1721, mo. 595, br. 346, sis. 338, (351).
360	" 28.	Samuel Smith, fa. 63, br. 318, (309), d. De. 16, 1781, æ. 67.
361	" 28.	Susanna Leach, æ. 9 yrs. fa. 316, d. Mh. 22, 1751, æ. 18.
362	" 28.	Elijah Clap, fa. 138? br. 437? (375) m. 1741, d. 1790.
363	" 28.	Daniel Vaughan, fa. 297, sis. 371, (372), d. Ja. 8, 1812, æ. 99¼.

	1742.	
364	Mh. 28.	Joseph Vaughan, fa. 113, br. 319, (347) m. 1742, b. Ja. 26, 1719, d. abt. 1746.
365	" 28.	John Darling, mo. 42, br. 149? (423) m. 1721; had 8 ss. & 5 daus.
366	" 28.	Susanna Winslow, wid. James m. 1732, 2d. m. 1744, to Jesse Bryant, o. Conant, mo. 101, sis. 422, d. Ap. 17, 1801, æ. 90th.
367	" 28.	John Lovell Jr., b. 1702, mo. 31, br. 449, (408) m. bef. 1729.
368	" 28.	⎰ William Cushman, (369, 348) m. '35, '51, d. Au. 27, 1768, æ. 53d.
369	Ap. 11.	⎱ Susanna Cushman, (368) o. Sampson, d. Se. 13, 1749, æ. 33.
370	" 11.	Mary Fuller, dau. Jonathan and Elinor, b. 1725, br. 247.
371	" 11.	Joanna Vaughan, fa. 113, br. 319, 351, 364, sis. 320, 395, (334) m. 1744, b. 1725, dis. 1749 to Stafford.
372	" 11.	Sarah Vaughan, (363) m. 1735, o. Cushman, d. Fe. 1, 1791.
373	" 11.	Elizabeth Raymond Jr., b. 1728, fa. 87, sis. 330, m. 1745 Silas Rickard, dis. 1749, to Pomfret, Ct.
374	" 11.	Japheth Rickard, m. Martha bef. '55, re. d. No. 25, 1798.
375	" 11.	Hope Clap, (362) o. Thomas, dis. 1792 to Brookfield.
376	" 11.	John Tomson, s. of Shubael, (418)? d. Ju. 22, 1766, æ. 49.
377	" 11.	Joanna Wood, (400) m. 1737, o. Cobb, b. 1715, fa. 421, br. 272, 419, Re. to Hadley, Mass. and died in old age.
378	" 11.	Nathaniel Wood, fa. 82, br. 379, (357), 2d. m. 1744 Mary Winslow, dis. 1783 to Woodstock, Vt., d. 1803, æ. 78.
379	" 15.	Ichabod Wood, fa. 82, br. 378, m. 1743 Thankful Cobb, mo. 219, 2d. m. 1777 Priscilla Thomas, mo. 250, d. Au. 8, 1787, æ. 68.
380	" 15.	Patience Wood (116) m. 1735; 1st. h. Ichabod Cushman sr., d. Se. 8, 1755, æ. 65th.
381	" 15.	Elizabeth Lewis, wid. (prob.) of Jas. m. 1716, o. Parlow.
382	Ma. —	Joseph Howland.
383	" —	Martha Chummuck, (Afr.) chi. James bap'd. (415) m. 1748.
384	" —	Elizabeth Ellis Jr., w. John, o. Coomer, 8 chi. b. fr. 1742, to 1759, d. Mh. 3, 1781, æ. 60th.
385	" —	Phebe Thomas, w. Jabez, bef. 1737, d. Fe. 12, 1772, æ. 58.
386	" —	Sarah Thomas, w. Eph'm. bef. 1740, d. Fe. 20, 1810, æ. 89th.
387	" —	Abigail Thomas, prob. w. Nath'l. sr., m. bef. 1722.
388	" —	Prudence Knowlton, w. John, m. 1742, o. Thomas, b. 1722, mo. 387.
389	" —	Martha Lyon, (293) m. 1740, o. Knowlton, b. 1718, fa. 188.
390	" —	Sarah Lyon, br. 293? sis. 391?
391	" —	Phebe Lyon, (298) m. 1742, br. 293? d. Ma. 27, 1795, æ. 72d.
392	" —	Sarah Smith, fa. 63, (467?) m. 1747, d. De. 8, 1777, æ. 50th.
393	" —	Ebenezer Raymond, b. 1703, fa. 213, (254) m. bef. 1732.
394	" —	Eleazer Pratt Sr., (407) chi. Eleazer b. 1705.
395	" —	Mercy Vaughan, b. 1727, fa. 113, m. Jos. Barden Jr. 1747.

	1742.		
396	Ma.	27.	Joanna Pratt, wid.
397	"	—	Hannah Tinkham, (428) m. bef. 1739, o. Shaw, d. Sc. 5, 1794. æ. 79th.
398	"	27.	John Cox Sr., (307) m. 1721, d. Ju. 5, 1761, æ. 66th.
399	"	27.	Phebe Sears, (333) m. bef. 1734, d. Oc. 9, 1779, æ. 67th.
400	"	27.	Samuel Wood, fa. 68, br. 311, sis. 332, (377) m. 1737, d. Jy. 12, 1750, æ. 37.
401	"	27.	Solomon Alden, b. 1728, fa. 222, d. abt. 1813, æ. 84?
402	"	27.	Sarah Thomas, 2d. w. and wid. of Wm. sr., m. 1705, o. Barden, d. Ma. 9, 1745, æ. 62d.
403	"	27.	Asa Thomas, b. 1721, mo. 249, brs. Hushai, Zadock, &c.
404	Ju.	13.	Ephraim Donham Jr., fa. 162, (433) m. 1741, d. abt. 1750.
405	"	20.	Nathaniel Bumpas, b. 1717, mo. 111, m. Abiah Vaughan [her fa. 113] 1752.
406	"	20.	Samuel Pratt 3d. m. Wilberce Bumpas 1741, (ex. 1783.)
407	"	20.	Hannah Pratt Sr., (394.)
408	"	20.	Lydia Lovell, (367) m. bef. 1729, chi. Peter, James, &c.
409	"	20.	John Miller Jr., (264) m. 1732. d. Ma. 27, 1759, æ. 47th.
410	"	20.	John Cox Jr., m. Lydia Redding '46, d. Jy. 6, 1770, æ. 47th.
411	"	20.	Rebecca Tupper, (259) m. 1735, o. Bumpas, b. 1713, mo. 111.
412	Jy.	4.	Fear Williamson, w. Geo. Jr., m. '38, o. Eddy, fa. 61, Re. to N. J.
413	"	4.	Thankful Lovell, bap. 1723, mo. 31, br. 367.
414	"	4.	Lydia Wood, b. 1722, fa. 116? m. Benj'n. Shelley? 1745.
415	"	4.	Sambo, (Afr.), (383) m. 1748, serv't. of the Pastor.
416	"	4.	Jenny, (Afr.), (314) m. 1747, serv't. of Peter Bennet.
417	"	4.	Experience Smith, (318) m. 1737, o. Cushman.
418	"	4.	Lydia Tomson, (376?) m. bef. 1742, d. Ja. 28, 1761, æ. 39th.
419	"	4.	John Cobb Jr., br. 272, sis. 377, (348) d. Ju. 22, 1750, æ. 28.
420	"	4.	Seth Harris, m. Abiah Alden, dau. Samuel, dis. 1759 to Bridg'r., d. in Abington, 1797, æ. 74?
421	"	7.	{ John Cobb Sr., fa. 17, br. 219, sis. 447, (119, 422) m. bef. 1714, and 1725, d. Jy. 6, 1750, æ. 61.
422	"	7.	{ Mary Cobb, (421), o. Conant, mo. 101, d. Au. 16, 1795, æ. 92d.
423	"	7.	Elizabeth Darling, (365) o. Bennett, d. Ja. 22, 1774, æ. 73.
424	Au.	19.	William Thomas Jr., mo. 45, br. 425, (282) d. Ju. 7, '64, æ. 53d.
425	"	19.	*Benjamin Thomas* fr. Carv., mo. 45, br. 424, 350, (484), *Dea.* 1776, d. Ja. 18, 1800, æ. 78.
426	"	19.	John Redding, fa. 62, br. 439, 467, sis. 353, m. Sarah —— bef. 1748, d. Au. 14, 1750, æ. 31st.
427	"	19.	John Alden, fa. 32, br. 222, 334, m. Lydia, bef. 1740, m. Rebecca Weston 1750, d. Mh. 27, 1821, æ. 102.
428	"	19.	Ebenezer Tinkham, mo. 72, (397) d. No. 17, 1801, æ. 87th.

1742.
429 Au. 19. Lydia Wood, m. 1728, o. Lovell, d. Oc. 3, 1789, æ. 83.
430 " 19. Hannah Cox, fa. 398, br. 410, sis. 431, 506, m. Benj. Philips, 1749, dis. 1776 to Ashfield.
431 " 19. Mary Cox, b. 1725, fa. 398, m. Joseph Thomas 1746.
432 " 19. Elizabeth Canada, m. '27, o. Eaton, b. 1701, fa. 15.
433 " 19. Mercy Dunham, (404), 2d. m. to Joseph Besse 1756, o. Tinkham, dau. Samuel Jr., br. 337, d. Fe. 16, 1811, æ. 85th.
434 " 19. Patience Cobb, m. Wm. Winslow, '47, dis. 1784 to War'm.
435 " 19. Sarah Leach fr. Bridg'r., (316), d. Ma. 21, 1795, æ. 87th.
436 Oc. 8. Hope Cobb, fa. 272, (337) m. 1745, d. Ju. 3, 1760, æ. 33d.
437 " 8. Manasseh Clap, br. 362, m. Rebecca Cushman 1744, d. Mh. 17, 1757, æ. 32d.
438 " 8. David Delano Jr., fa. 89, m. Deborah Holmes 1745.
439 " 16. William Redding, fa. 62, br. 426, (245), d. Oc. 6, 1791, æ. 85.
440 De. 5. ⎧ Samuel Pratt Jr., b. Ma. 15, 1697, (441, 604), 2d. m. 1751.
441 " 5. ⎩ Jerusha Pratt, (440) m. bef. 1726, d. bef. 1751.
442 " 5. John Soul Jr., mo. 55, sis. 465, 471, m. Mary Leach 1750, [2d. h. (311)] d. Fe. 19, 1751, æ. 46th.
443 " 5. Margery Leonard, m. Eben'r. Briggs of Taunton, '46.
444 " 5. Peru, (African).
445 unc. Ichabod Cushman, mo. 380, sis. 589? m. Patience McFunn, alias Maxwell 1751, d. 1768, æ. 52.
446 " John Leonard Sr., m. Abigail —— bef. 1735, d. abt. 1775.
1743.
447 Mh. 13. Martha Simmons, w. Aaron m. 1716, (1st. h. 40) o. Cobb, fa. 17, br. 421, d. Au. 8, 1775, æ. 84.
448 " 13. Hannah Parlow, b. 1725, mo. 153, (355) m. 1743.
449 " 13. Joseph Lovell, mo. 31, m. Patience Barrows 1751? d. Fe. 11, 1796, æ. 79.
450 " 13. ⎧ Jabez Eddy Jr. fr. Carv., b. Ap. 14, 1700, fa. 234, (451).
451 " 13. ⎩ Patience Eddy fr. Carv., (450) o. Pratt.
452 Ma. 5. Barzillai Thomas, fa. 238, (506) m. 1757, only chi., Barzillai, d. No. 5, 1813, æ. 82.
453 " 5. Mercy Hall, dis. 1750 to Raynham.
454 " 5. Oxenbridge Thacher, b. July 11, 1725, fa. 35, removed.
455 Ju. 16. Meletiah Cobb, (272) m. 1727, o. Smith, b. 1705, dau. J'n. sr. & Mary; re. to Hardwick. Both d. in old age.
456 " 16. Elizabeth Turner, w. Japheth, m. 1725, o. Morse.
457 Jy. 28. ⎧ Thomas Raymond Sr., (458).
458 " 28. ⎩ Mary Raymond, (457) m. bef. 1708; 9 sons & 4 dau's.
459 " 28. Amos Raymond, b. 1710, fa. 457, m. Susanna bef. 1733, 6 chi.; re. to Martha's Vineyard.
460 Se. 8. Peter Raymond, b. 1718, fa. 87, (291) m. 1739.
461 " 8. Joseph Parker. He was here in 1749.

	1743.		
462	Se.	8.	Sarah Jackson, br. 335, m. Jacob Green 1746; 5 s., 3 dau's.
463	"	8.	Calliminco, (Afr.,) m. Anna; serv't of the Pastor.
	1744.		
464	Fe.	5.	Rebecca Soul, mo. 55, d. Ja. 24, 1759, æ. 46; or dau. James and Lydia, d. Ju. 22, 1747, æ. 47.
465	"	5.	Rachel Soul, mo. 55, m. Eb. Vaughan '44, d. Se. 4, 1778, æ. 59.
466	"	5.	Elizabeth Pratt, wid. (270?) m. bef. 1729.
467	"	5.	Thomas Redding, b. 1727, fa. 62, (392), dis. 1784 to Keene.
	1745.		
468	Mh. 28.		REV. SYLVANUS CONANT fr.? 4th Pastor, (3d. w. 492), d. De. 8, 1777, æ. 58th. Tradition says, 1st. w. Bethan? of Boston; 2d. w. Williams of Roxbury.
	1746.		
469	Mh.	2.	{ Ebenezer Cobb fr. Falmouth, (470).
470	"	2.	{ Mary Cobb fr. Falmouth, (469).
471	Ju. 22.		Esther Soul fr. Hal'x., br. 442, unm., d. Ma. 15, 1793, æ. 86.
	1747.		
472	Au. 16.		Priscilla Booth, w. John sr., bef. 1721, s. John &c.
	1748.		
473	Fe. 14.		Thomas Cole Sr., d. Ma. 16, 1759, æ. 57th, s. Thomas &c.
474	De. 25.		Mary Bates fr. Barnst., (86), o. Blossom, d. De. 30, 1750, æ. 42.
475	" 25.		Hannah Pumroy fr. Hal'x., br. 485, m. Jn. Eddy 1760; 2d. m. to Jn. Bradford 1765, d. in old age.
	1749.		
476	Ja. 15.		Abigail Faunce fr. Bridg'r., w. James m. 1747, 2d. m. Jn. Jacobs 1766, o. Rickard, d. Mh. 29, 1777, æ. 54th.
	1750.		
477	Ju.	3.	Samuel Benson fr. War'm., m. Keziah bef. '30, 2d. m. '69 (358).
478	Se.	2.	Joanna Redding, w. Moses m. 1745, o. Vaughan, fa. 297, br. 363, d. Ap. 1805, æ. 85½.
479	No. 18.		Mary Savery, w. Thomas m. 1738, o. Williams, dis. 1758 to Andover, Ct.
	1751.		
480	Mh. 24.		Ann Tilson fr. Barnst., w. John gr., s. 652, o. Hamblin, resided in Carver, and d. in old age.
481	Oc.	6.	Thomas Williams.
	1754.		
482	Mh. 31.		Isaac Tinkham fr. Hal'x., fa. 93, (519) d. Oc. 28, 1779, æ. 59.
	1755.		
483	Au. 24.		Elkanah Shaw, s. of George, (527), d. De. 31, 1805, æ. 81.
	1756.		
484	Ap. 11.		Elizabeth Thomas fr. Carv., (425) m. bef. 1743, o. Churchill, sis. 629, d. De. 26, 1804, æ. 80th.

	1757.	
485	Jy. 3.	Francis Pumroy Jr., m. Sarah Nye of Plymt. 1763, sis. 475, chi., Dr. John d. in Vt., 1844 æ. 80; Hannah b. 1766.
486	Oc. 16.	Bethiah Freeman fr. Sandw., w. Josiah bef. 1725, o. Hall, dau. of Elisha, d. Mh. 4, 1812, æ. 90th.
	1758.	
487	Ju. 25.	⎧ Ebenezer Willis Sr., (488) m. 1753, re. to Hardwick.
488	" 25.	⎩ Mary Willis, (487) o. Jackson, dis. to Hardwick, 1801.
489	" 25.	Sarah Tucker, fa. 164, br. 327, unm. d. Ap. 11, 1773, æ. 42.
490	Au. 13.	⎧ John Briggs fr. Hal'x., (491), m. Ab. Morse 1763, d. 1810? æ. 99.
491	" 13.	⎩ Remember Briggs fr. Hal'x., (490) m. 1740, b. 1719, fa. 213.
492	" 13.	Abigail Conant fr. Norwich, (468) o. Huntington, dau. Col. Hezekiah of Ct. d. Ja. 3, 1759, æ. 28.
493	Oc. 1.	Hannah Weston.
	1759.	
494	Au. 12.	Thankful Redding, fa. 439, unm. d. Ja. 11, 1810, æ. 74.
	1760.	
495	Ma. 11.	⎧ *Ichabod Morton* (496), *Dea*. 1782, d. Ma. 16, 1809, æ. 85th.
496	" 11.	⎩ Deborah Morton, mo. 127, (495) m. '49, d. No. 17, 1789, æ. 59.
497	Jy. 20.	Deborah Cushman, wid. John Jr., m 1746, b. 1729, fa. 325.
	1761.	
498	Ju. 14.	Desire Morse, mo. 284, sis. 574, bap. 1743.
	1762.	
499	Ap. 4.	Ichabod Billington, b. 1737, mo. 186, m. Bette Peck, 1758.
500	July 4.	⎧ Stephen Powers, (501) re. to Vt. ⎧ chi., Susanna, Mary, John, and Stephen, *father of the Sculptor*.
501	" 4.	⎩ Lydia Powers (500), o. Drew. ⎩
502	Oc. 3.	Experience Totman, w. Samuel? chi. Samuel, bap.
	1763.	
503	Mh. 27.	Abraham Vaughan, fa. 241, m. Ann Russell 1764, d. Se. 14, 1811, æ. 76. A *tri-birth* with Eben'r. & Elisha, b. 1735.
504	Ju. 19.	⎧ John Leach, (505) m. 1759, 2d. m. 1785 Rebecca Sturtevant, d. No. 9, 1822, æ. 85, (ex. 1803.)
505	" 19.	⎩ Betty Leach, (504), o. Vaughan, fa. 363, d. Ap. 21, '73, æ. 36.
506	Jy. 10.	Elizabeth Thomas, (452) m. 1757, o. Cox, fa. 398, br. 410, sis. 430, 431, d. 1814, æ. 82.
507	" 10.	Mercy Purrington, b. 1737, fa. 256, br. Joshua, Jn. &c.
508	Aug. 7.	Sarah Redding Jr., "age 10 yrs," fa. 467, m. Jas. Tinkham 1770 [his fa. 592], d. Ap. 2, 1774, æ. 22d.
509	" 28.	Lucy Thomas, w. Hushai m. 1756, o. Vaughan, dau. of David, d. Oc. 31, 1822, æ. 84.
510	Oc. 30.	Lemuel Thomas, mo. 163, m. 1750 Mehitable Weston, d. Ja. 26, 1776, æ. 53d.
511	" 30.	⎧ Joseph Warren, b. 1715, fa. 174, (512) m. bef. 1757.
512	" 30.	⎩ Mercy Warren, (511). Both dis. 1771 to Ashfield.

1763.
513 De. 25. Fear Redding, fa. 439, m. Nehemiah Holmes 1771, dis. 1773 to Plymt. d. here Mh. 6, 1816, æ. 69.

1764.
514 Ap. 22. Elenor Billington, w. Nath'l. m. 1756, o. Warren, dis. 1789 to Ashfield.
515 " 22. Silence Tilson, w. Timo. o. Whitting; chi. Timothy bap.

1765.
516 Ja. —Nathan Eddy, fa. 243, m. Eunice Sampson 1757, [sis. 538], d. in N. Y. State, 1813, æ. 80.
517 Au. 18. Phebe Leach, wid. of Samuel m. 1750, o. Rickard, 2d. m. 1766 to Joshua Willis.
518 Se. 29. Abijah Cobb, w. Nathan m. 1753, o. Tinkham, fa. 93, br. 482, d. Fe. 5, 1776, æ. 48th.

1766.
519 Mh. 20. Hannah Tinkham, (482) m. bef. 1754, o. Robbins, mo. ad. 35, d. Ja. 11, 1780, æ. 51st.
520 Ju. 8. Consider Brannack, m. Desire Simmons, [b. 1744, dau. of David sr.] 1764, re. to Vt. 1789.
521 Au. 17. Catharine Maxfield fr. Carv., wid., d. after 1790? in old age.

1767.
522 Ju. 17. { Ebenezer Briggs fr. Hal'x. (523), d. Fe. 18, 1795, æ. 68th.
523 " 17. { Abigail Briggs fr. Hal'x, (522) o. Bryant, d. 1808, æ. 88.
524 No. 1. Elkanah Elmes, b. '29, mo. 172, m. Sarah Lazell '50. (Ex. 1803.)

1768.
525 Ap. 3. Mercy Cobb fr. Barnst., wid. of Silvanus of Barnst., chi. 628, 644, d. Mh. 4, 1781, æ. 75th.

1770.
526 Ja. 14. Sarah Tinkham, wid. Eph'm. m. bef. 1758, o. Standish, 2d. m. Adam Wright of Plymt.
527 Se. 2. Elizabeth Shaw, (483) m. bef. '50, d. Au. 19, 1786, æ. 61st.

1771.
528 Ja. 13. Peter Oliver Jr., son of Judge O., (531) chi. Margaret H. b. 1771, Thomas H. b. 1772, Peter b. 1774; Re. 1775, d. in Eng. in 1822, æ. 81.
529 " 20. { Thomas Shaw, (530) m. bef. '71, d. in the army, 1778, æ. 40.
530 " 20. { Mary Shaw, (529) o. Atwood, d. Ja. 10, 1808, æ. 71st.
531 Fe. 24. Sarah Oliver, (528) o. Hutchinson, dau. Gov. H., Re. 1775.
532 Ju. —Keziah Thomas, w. Jedediah Jr., m. 1749, o. Churchill, sis. 484, 629, d. Ju. 21, 1800, æ. 67th.

1773.
533 Fe. 24. Edmund Maxham, m. Rebecca Faunce 1771, 3 sons b.
534 Mh. 28. Cuffee Wright, (Afr.), (630), d. Fe. 22, 1796, æ. 44th.
535 Au. 8. Samuel Eddy, fa. 243, br. 516, m. Re. to N. Y. State, d. 1821, æ. 79th.

MEMBERS OF THE FIRST CHURCH

1773.
536 Se. 18. ⎰ Ichabod Carey fr. Bridg'r., (537), Re. to Chesterfield?
537 " 18. ⎱ Hannah Carey fr. Bridg'r., (536), m. 1741, o. Gannett?
538 " 26. Bachelor Bennet, m. Mary Sampson 1764, Re. to Vt.

1774.
539 Au. 7. Huldah Washburn, w. Jonah m. 1756, o. Sears, b. Au. 10, 1737, fa. 333, dis. 1787 to Randolph, Vt.

1776.
540 Ju. 30. Margaret Bryant, w. Micah m. '70, o. Paddock; Re. to St. Me.
541 Se. 8. Benjamin Tucker Jr., b. 1738, fa. 164, m. Mary Thomas 1760, dis. 1786 to Randolph, Vt., d. æ. 77?
542 Oc. 6. Elizabeth Wood, w. Nathan m. 1757, o. Shaw; Re. to Vt.

1777.
543 Ap. 16. Susanna Eddy, fa. 243, br. 535, unm. d. Jy. 29, '17, æ. 81st.

1780.
544 Jy. 30. Daniel Thomas, fa. 258, m. Thankful —— bef. 1778, 2d. m. Mary Jakok bef. 1781, d. Ma. 14, 1789, æ. 46th.

1781.
545 De. 5. REV. JOSEPH BARKER, 5th Pastor, (579, 760), s. of Joseph, of Branford, Ct. b. Oc. 19, 1751, chi. 714, 788, d. Jy. 25, 1815, æ. 64th.
546 Au. 21. David Thomas, b. 1742, fa. 424, br. 743, m. Deborah Howland 1764, 2d. m. Mary Thomas, wid. (544), dis. 1793 to Woodstock, Vt.
547 " 21. Churchill Thomas, mo. 532, m. Hannah Cushman, dau. Joseph, d. De. 31, 1809, æ. 48.
548 " 21. Susanna Cushman, w. Zenas, o. Wild, d. Mh. 18, 1830, æ. 86.

1782.
549 Ap. 28. Isaac Morse, s. Jonathan Jr., mo. 284, gr. gr. fa. 5, m. Jemima Pratt bef. 1769, d. Se. 22, 1832, æ. 91st.
550 " 28. Deborah Thomas, w. Joseph Jr., m. 1770, o. Thomas, b. 1736, mo. 386; Re. to Vt.
551 " 28. Chloe Tinkham, w. James m. 1777, o. Rickard, dau. Sam'l. sr. and Sarah, d. De. 29, 1822, æ. 68.
552 " 28. Ruth Barrows, mo. 274, m. James McFarland 1793, d. Fe. 20. 1808, æ. 51.
553 Ju. 2. Rebecca Wood, w. Lemuel m. 1765, o. Tupper, b. 1743, fa. 259; Re. to N. Y. State.
554 " 30. Sarah Soule, wid. Wm. m. 1762, o. Briggs, br. 490, 522, 2d. m. to Timothy Cobb, d. No. 4, 1820, æ. 80th.
555 " 30. Lydia Soule, b. 1763, mo. 554, m. Alvin Robinson 1792, dis. 1803 to Sumner, Me.
556 Jy. 7. Mercy Thomas, w. John m. 1752, o. Shaw, sis. 645; dis. 1803 to Woodstock, Vt., wid.

1782.
557 Jy. 7. { William Shaw, (558), br. 572, d. Mh. 7, 1807, æ. 68.
558 "   7. { Lydia Shaw, (557), o. Soule, dau. Jacob sr., d. Ju. 10, 1826, æ. 84.
559 " 21. Azel Washburn, b. 1764, mo. 539, dis. 1789 to Royalton, Vt., d. 1841, æ. 77.
560 No. 17. Sarah Miller, wid. of Elias m. 1732, o. Holmes, d. Se. 28, 1800, æ. 89th.
561 " 17. Elizabeth Brown fr. Eastham, w. Thomas, Re. to Vt. St.
562 " 17. Thankful Sampson fr. Eastham, w. Israel, m. 1780, o. Martin, d. Se. 24, 1831, æ. 82.
563 De. 1. *Abner Bourne*, mo. 575, br. 587, (568), m. bef. 1770, *Dea.* 1796, d. Ma. 25, 1806, æ. 59th.

1783.
564 Ja. 5. Susannah Smith Jr., fa. 360, (747), d. Ju. 24, 1824, æ. 72.
565 " 26. Mercy Cushman, w. Noah, m. 1769, o. Soule, dau. Jabez, d. Mh. 24, 1788, æ. 40th.
566 Jy. 27. Thankful Thomas, mo. ad. 85, (648) m. bef. 1792, d. Fe. 27, 1847, æ. 95th.
567 Au. 3. Lucy Vaughan fr. Bridg'r., w. Eben'r., o. Pratt, d. Ja. 1, 1822, æ. 74?
568 " 10. Mary Bourne, (563) o. Torry, d. Ma. 9, 1837, æ. 88th.

1784.
569 Ja. 18. { Caleb Thompson Jr., fa. 268, (570); He and w. dis. 1810 to Windsor, Vt., d. Fe. 9, 1821, æ. 68.
570 " 18. { Mary Thompson, (569), o. Perkins, dau. of Eben'r., sis. 711, d. De. 9, 1816, æ. 60.
571 " 18. Priscilla Weston, (762) m. 1776, o. Sturtevant dau. Dr. Josiah of Hal'x., chi. 777, d. Mh. 16, 1834, æ. 83d.
572 Fe. 22. { James Shaw fr. Duxbury, (573), br. 557; He and w. dis. 1791 to Bakertown, Pa.
573 " 22. { Lois Shaw fr. Duxb'y, (572) m. 1749, o. Thomas.
574 Ma. 16. Thankful Morse, b. 1745, mo. 284; Re., m. —— Gannet?
575 Au. 29. Abigail Bourne fr. Pembroke, wid. Eben'r. o. Newcomb, d. De. 10, 1821, æ. 98th.

1785.
576 Ma. 22. Tilson Ripley, "on a bed of sickness," w. Rebecca, 9 chi. b. fr. 1749, to '67, d. Ju. 16, 1785, æ. 67th.
577 Au. 21. Lucy Tinkham, fa. 428, gr. mo. 72, gr. gr. fa. 11, m. Issachar Fuller 1785. Her memory of early families and facts was remarkable. D. Ap. 30, 1847, æ. 95.
578 " 28. Ruth Tinkham, fa. 428, sis. 577, unm., d. Oc. 9, 1805, æ. 51.
579 Oc. 16. Eunice Barker fr. Longmeadow, (545) m. 1785, o. Stebbins, dau. Wm. and Eunice, d. Oc. 6, 1809, æ. 49th.
580 " 30. Hannah Bryant, w. Nehemiah, m. 1757, o. Totman, d. Fe. 16, 1814, æ. 83d.

MEMBERS OF THE FIRST CHURCH

1786.
581 Ja. 22. ⎧ Wm. Thompson, fa. 268, (582) m. '70, d. Mh. 14, 1816, æ. 69.
582 " 22. ⎨ Deborah Thompson, (581) o. Sturtevant, dau. Lemuel of Hal'x., sis. 584, d. De. 25, 1842, æ. 96th.
583 Ma. 14. ⎧ Isaac Thompson, fa. 376, sis. 744, (584) m. 1775, d. De. 21, 1819, æ. 74th.
584 " 14. ⎨ Lucy Thompson, (583) o. Sturtevant, d. No. 6, '34, æ. 81st.
585 Jy. 2. Freelove Thompson, w. Jacob m. 1761, o. Finney, dau. of Pelatiah, d. No. 7, 1826, æ. 87th.
586 " 9. Sarah Phinney, wid. John, 2d. m. 1799 to Ezra Holmes, o. Thompson, b. 1762, dau Nathan, dis. 1808 to Norton.

1787.
587 Ap. 8. ⎧ Newcomb Bourne fr. Hal'x., mo. 575, br. ⎫
  563, (588.)   ⎬ dis. 1802 to
588 " 8. ⎨ Abigail Bourne, (587) o. Cushman.   ⎭ Springfield, Vt.
589 Au. 12. Mary Lyon, (329) m. 1743, o. Cushman, d. Ju. 8, 1796, æ. 73d.
590 Se. 2. ⎧ Samuel Torry sr., b. 1753, s. of Wm. (591); 8 chi. bef. 1793.
591 " 2. ⎨ Mary Torry, (590), o. Finney, b. 1757, fa. 354, Re. West.
592 " 23. Jeremiah Tinkham, mo. 72, gr. fa. 11, m. Naomi Warren 1740, d. Ju. 7, 1790, æ. 76.
593 No. 4. William Cornish sr., sis. 677, m. Mercy Swift bef. 1786, 2d. w. Mehitable Bates, d. Fe. 24, 1836, æ. 79th.

1788.
594 Jy. 20. Abigail Haskell, (598) o. Tabor, d. Jy. 26, 1811, æ. 54.
595 No. 6. Hannah Tinkham, wid. John sr., m. 1716, o. Howland, dau. of Isaac, and gr. gr. dau. of John of the M. F., sis. 64? d. Mh. 25, 1792, æ. 97.
596 De. 7. Mercy Bump, w. Joseph m. 1775, o. Barden, sis. 666, d. Ju. 5, 1811, æ. 57th.

1789.
597 Ja. 25. Luther Redding, b. 1748, mo. 478, m.; Re. to Taunton & d.
598 Mh. 15. Zebulon Haskell, (594) m. bef. 1785, d. Oc. 27, 1820.
599 Ap. 5. ⎧ Elijah Lucas, (600), Re. to Freetown, d. Ju. 8, 1806.
600 " 5. ⎨ Sarah Lucas, (599) m. abt. 1780, o. Shaw, fa. 529, br. 651.
601 Jy. 19. Mary Tinkham, w. Peter Jr., [fa. 336,] m. 1764, o. Thompson, fa. 268, br. 581, d. Ma. 30, 1815, æ. 70th.
602 Au. 2. Abigail Thomas, w. Israel, o. Finney, fa. 354, sis. 609, d. Fe. 6. 1829, æ 77th.
603 " 23. Lucy Leonard, w. Henry, 1st. m. 1762 to Samuel Turner, 3d. m. to Mr. Doty, o. Pratt, mo. 191, d. May — 1835, æ. 93d.

1790.
604 Oc. 3. Sarah Pratt, (440) o. Fuller, mo. 146, d. No. 1794, æ. 64?

1791.
605 Ju. 26. Jacob Tisdell, (694), dis. 1795 to N. P., d. in N. Y. City.
606 Au. 14. Mercy Valler fr. Carv., w. Silas, Re. to Freetown.

1791.
607 Oc. 9. Lydia Bourne, w. Eben'r. m. 1788, o. Leach, b. 1766, dau. of Abiel Jr., gr. fa. 316. Re. to Milton.
1792.
608 Ap. 1. Nathan Thomas sr., b. 1707, s. of Edward sr., br. 258, (271) 2d. m. 1751 to Abigail Sturtevant, d. in old age.
609 Se. 30. Martha Finney, fa. 354, sis. 602, unm d. Mh. 11, 1833, æ. 69.
1793.
610 Ma. 26. Margaret Pratt, br. 772, unm. d. Se. 8, 1800, æ. 42d.
611 Oc. 6. ⎧ Josiah Carver fr. War'm., (612), d. Ap. 5, 1799, æ. 74.
612 " 6. ⎨ Jerusha Carver fr. War'm., (611), 1st m. 1744 to Edw'd Sparrow, o. Bradford, dau. Wm. & Elizabeth of Plym., d. Apr. 23, 1820, æ. 97.
1794.
613 Ja. 19. ISAIAH WESTON, b. 1770, s. Zach'h, dis. 1794 to N. Bedford, m. Sarah Dean of Raynham d.
614 Fe. 2. Elizabeth Tinkham, w. Cyrus, m. 1788, o. Turner, b. 1764, mo. 603, sis. 716, d. at Colraine, abt. 1843.
615 " 2. Isaac Doty, m. ——— Nimlet '89, dis. '03 to Brookfield, Vt.
616 " 9. Priscilla Turner, w. David, m. '86, o. Pratt; Re. to Me.
617 Mh. 2. ⎧ Elijah Alden, fa. 427, (618) m. 1779, d. Ju. 26, '26, æ. 72.
618 " 2. ⎩ Mary Alden, (617) o. Alden, fa. 401? d. Se. 22, 1839, æ. 84th.
619 " 2. Elihu Alden, b. 1775, fa. 427, dis. 1818 to Dixmont, Me.
620 " 2. Mercy Porter, w. Jonathan, m. 1761, o. Redding, fa. 439, sis. 513, 494, d. Jy. 22, 1833, æ. 93.
621 " 9. Benaiah Pratt, s. of Paul, gr. mo. 407, m. Louisa Warren 1792, Re. to Me., a 2nd. & 3d. m.
622 Au. 24. Mary Norcutt, w. Eph'm. m. 1782, o. Kitts, mo. 321, d. Fe. 3, 1842, æ. 83d.
623 No. 2. Lucia Ellis, wid. of Matthias, m. 1743, o. Bennet, mo. 273, d. Oc. 3, 1804, æ. 79.
624 " 2. Lucy Pratt, dau. Eben'r., br. 772, unm. d. Au. 19, 1844, æ. 80.
625 " 23. Thankful Holmes, w. Ezra, o. Clark, d. Apr. 2, '99, æ. 50th.
1795.
626 Ap. 29. Desire Morse, fa. 549, dis. 1819 to Hal'x., (re-ad. 1833.)
627 Au. 23. Sarah Sturtevant, w. Dr. Thomas m. 1777, o. Soule, dau. Zach'h & Sarah, d. Mh. 11, 1839, æ. 83.
628 No. 15. ⎧ Ebenezer Cobb, mo. 525, br. 644, (629), d. Au. 22, 1811, æ. 80.
629 " 15. ⎩ Lydia Cobb, (628), m. '54, o. Churchill, d. Ja. 10, 1822, æ. 80.
1796.
630 Ju. 5. Anna Wright, (Afr.), (534), 2d. m. to Swansey Hart, d.
631 Au. 14. Sarah Tinkham, wid. of Amos, [mo. 595], m. 1752, o. Tinkham, dau. Peter, gr. mo. 24, d. Fe. 13, 1820, æ. 85th.
1797.
632 Mh. 26. Betsey Harlow fr. Plym., w. Jonathan sr., o. Blackmar, dau. of John & Mercy, d. Se. 9, 1833, æ. 87th.

MEMBERS OF THE FIRST CHURCH

	1797.		
633	Ap.	9.	⎰ *Joshua Eddy*, fa. 341, br. 665, sis. 673, 856, (634) *Dea.* 1806, d. Ma. 1, 1833, æ. 85.
634	"	9.	⎱ Lydia Eddy, (633), o. Paddock, dau. Zachariah, gr. fa. 210, d. Fe. 13, 1838, æ. 82.
635	Ma.	21.	Samuel Tucker, fa. 164, (757), d. Oc. 29, 1820, æ. 75th.
636	"	21.	⎰ Jesse Bryant, mo. 366, (637), d. Oc. 26, 1828, æ. 82.
637	"	21.	⎱ Mercy Bryant, (636), o. Shaw, d. Ja. — 1819, æ. 73.
	1798.		
638	Au.	5.	Zilpah Thomas, w. Jeremiah Jr. m. 1786, o. Wood, dau. of Amos, sis. 794, d. Mh. 15, 1825, æ. 61.
	1799.		
639	Ap.	7.	Ebenezer Wilder fr. Chelsea, s. of Nathan'l, sis. 727, (726) m. 1800, d. Se. 21, 1848, æ. 76th.
640	Ma.	12.	OTIS THOMPSON, fa. 706, sis. 684; Pastor in Rehoboth, 1st. w. Rachael Chandler [d. 1827, æ. 48th.]; a 2nd. m.; Re. in Abington.
641	De.	29.	John McDowall fr. Scotland Eu.; s. bap.; Re. to St. of Me.?
	1800.		
642	Ma.	18.	Experience Peirce, dau. Wm., unm. d. Jy. 14, 1845, æ. 70?
643	Ju.	29.	Rhoda Sparrow fr. War'm; w. of Edward, [his mo. 612] m. 1765, o. Bump, dau. Phillip, d. Ja. 10, 1816, æ. 68th.
644	Au.	24.	⎰ Binney Cobb, mo. 525, br. 628, (645) ⎰ Re. to
645	"	24.	⎱ Azubah Cobb, (644) m. 1762, o. Shaw, sis. 556, ⎱ Woods'k Vt.
	1801.		
646	Ju.	20.	Benjamin Pratt, s. Noah of Plymt., sis. 713, m. Jemima Bryant 1785, d. Oc. 18, 1838, æ. 75th.
647	Au.	16.	Betty Fuller, w. John, o. Smith, dau. of John, gr. fa. 63, 164, chi. 685, 799, 1050, d. Se. 23, 1832, æ. 75th.
	1802.		
648	Ju.	13.	Isaac Shaw, (566), chi. 1079, d. Fe. 2, 1824, æ. 75th.
649	"	13.	⎰ *Perez Thomas*, fa. 425, (650), *Dea.* 1803, d. Ju. 21, 1828, æ. 77.
650	"	13.	⎱ Sarah Thomas, (649) m. 1774, o. Wood, fa. 378, d. Apr. 3, 1829, æ. 76th.
	1803.		
651	Ap.	24.	Samuel Shaw, fa. 529, m. Lydia Cobb 1791, [fa. 628.]
652	Ma.	22.	⎰ *Calvin Tilson*, s. of Isaiah, gr. mo. 480, (653, 882), 2d. m.
	1804.		1824, *Dea.* 1819. d. Jy. 3, 1852, æ. 83d.
653	Ap.	8.	⎱ Joanna Tilson, (652), o. Cobb, dau. Wm., d. Oc. 16, 1822, æ. 56.
	1805.		
654	Ma.	19.	Mark Shaw, fa. 483, m. Elizabeth Sampson 1785, [gr. fa. 193, br. 732, 2nd. h. (664)], d. Se. 5, 1806, æ. 47.
	1806.		
655	Ju.	8.	Weltha Thompson, w. Thomas, o. Whitmore, sis. of Rev. Benj'n., d. Apr. 16, 1848, æ. 76.

	1806.	
656	Au. 10.	Lydia Thompson, w. Solomon, m. '86, o. Murdock, dau. Jn.
657	Se. 1.	Margaret Finney, w. Lewis, o. Barden, d. Se. 11, '29, æ. 55.
658	" 1.	Jane Ling, w. Sylvanus, m. 1796, o. Cushman, b. 1776, mo. 701, dis. 1839 to Lisbon Me. & Re. there.
659	" 9.	Keziah Warren, w. Nathan m. 1786, o. Weston, 2d. m. to Wm. White, d. Au. 17, 1830, æ. 66th.
	1807.	
660	Ju. 28.	⎧ Squire Tinkham, mo. 631, sis. 672, (661), m. 1797, Both dis. 1823 to Hartland Vt. d. Oc. 17, 1851, æ. 79.
661	" 28.	⎩ Anna Tinkham, (660) o. Wood, fa. 747, d. Se. 1849, æ. 76th.
662	" 28.	Daniel Oliver Morton, fa. Livy, br. 862, sis. 910, d. Mh. 25, 1852, æ. 62.
663	Jy. 12.	Silas Tinkham, s. Samuel, br. 526, gr. fa. 46? m. Lydia Smith [wid. of Jabez, o. Savery, br. 667], d. Ja. 22, 1816, æ. 77th.
664	" 12.	James Soule 2d., mo. 554, m. Eunice Thompson, dau. of Eben'r; 2d. m. 1813, (654), d. Fe. 2, 1845, æ. 83.
665	" 12.	⎧ Seth Eddy, fa. 341, br. 633, (666), d. Au. 17, 1837, æ. 83.
666	" 12.	⎪ Jerusha Eddy, (665), o. Barden, sis. 596, d. Oc. 29, '35, æ. 76.
667	" 12.	⎪ Daniel Savery, sis. 663, gr. gr. mo. 43, (668) m. 1794, d. Se. 21, 1836, æ. 72.
668	" 12.	⎨ Huldah Savery, (667) o. Soule, mo. 554, br. 664, d. Oc. 17, 1853, æ. 78.
669	" 12.	⎪ Zenas Thomas, fa. 425, br. 649, (670), d. Ma. 12, 1821, æ. 59.
670	" 12.	⎩ Mary Thomas, (669) m. 1783, o. Vaughan, dau. of Jesse, gr. fa. 319, d. Fe. 24, 1828, æ. 64.
671	" 12.	Experience Bent, s. John, m. Salome Cushing of Hal'x, d. Jy. 13, 1849, æ. 85th. (ex. 1826.)
672	" 12.	Sarah Wood, (748) o. Tinkham, mo. 631, d. Se. 20, 1846, æ. 89.
673	" 12.	Lucy Fuller, wid. of Dr. Jonathan, m. 1775, o. Eddy, fa. 341, dis. 1834, to Fairhaven. (Re-ad. 1839.)
674	" 12.	Sally Fuller, mo. 673, m. —— Jenny, dis. 1829 to Fairhaven and Re. there.
675	" 12.	Deborah Ellis, (680) m. 1792, o. Hall, dau. Jabez and Deborah, d. Se. 6, 1826, æ. 59th.
676	" 12.	*John Freeman*, s. of Elisha, (893), *Dea.* 1833, dis. 1846 to Carver, d. Fe. 10, 1847, æ. 60th.
677	" 12.	Susanna Bates, w. Thomas, [fa. 86], o. Cornish, br. 593, d. Ju. 13, 1823, æ. 69.
678	" 12.	Joseph Bates, mo. 677, unm. d. Ju. 19, 1846, æ. 62d.
679	" 26.	Levi Smith, s. Israel, gr. mo. 313, m. Charity Bryant.
680	Au. 23.	Southworth Ellis sr., s. of Thomas & Ruth, gr. mo. 190, (675, 971), d. Dec. 15, 1840, æ. 72d.
681	" 23.	Sylvanus Eddy, s. of Sam'l. gr. fa. 341, m. —— Fuller, dau. Sam'l of Hal'x., d. 1852 in Vt.

1807.

682 Au. 23. Nathaniel Eddy, fa. 633, br. 718, 944, sis. 683, (761, 797), Dea. 1852.
683 " 23. Lydia Eddy Jr., fa. 633, br. 718, 944, m. Barzillai Crane 1810, dis. 1811 to Berkley, d. Fe. 10, 1842, æ. 55th.
684 " 23. Mary Cobb, w. Crocker, o. Thompson, fa. 706, br. 640.
685 " 23. Sophia Fuller, mo. 647, sis. 799, (696) m. 1813.
686 " 23. Betsey Leonard, w. Nathan'l. m. 1788, o. Bryant, fa. 636, d.
687 " 23. Sally Kidder, w. Nathan, o. Chaddick of Sandw., Re. to Foxboro', d. Fe. 28, 1840, æ. 61.
688 " 23. ⎧ Hezekiah Ripley, (689), Both dis. '09 to Middlebury Vt.
689 " 23. ⎩ Priscilla Ripley, (688) m. '92, o. Wood, b. '76, dau. Eph'm.
690 " 23. ⎧ James Smith, mo. 313, (691), m. 1766, d. Se. 29, 1815. æ. 78th.
691 " 23. ⎩ Patience Smith, (690), o. Wood, fa. 356, d. Ma. 12, 1822, æ. 76.
692 " 23. William Thomas, fa. 649; Re. to St. of Me. m. d. 1821, æ. 34.
693 " 23. Calvin Tilson Jr., fa. 652, unm. d. Ju. 19, 1817, æ. 24th.
694 " 23. Hannah Tisdale, (605) o. Shaw, dau. Elijah sr., sis. 740, dis. 1826 to N. Y. City.
695 " 23. Bathsheba Tribou, w. Melzar, m. 1789, o. Thomas, dau. David and Rebecca, d. Fe. 13, 1837, æ. 71st.
696 " 23. John Warren, mo. 659, br. 832, (685) m. 1813, chi. 1019.
697 " 23. Lydia Wood, w. Jacob, m. 1784, o. Miller, dau. John & Zilpha, sis. 735, d. Fe. 13, 1849, æ. 83d.
698 Se. 13. Lucy Wood, w. Abner Jr. m. 1797, o. Thompson, fa. 581, br. 770, sis. 725, dis. 1831 to No. Rochester.
699 " 27. Lydia Paddock, w. John, [gr. fa. 210], o. Cushing, dau. Col. Cushing, d. Ma. 30, 1826, æ. 60.
700 Oc. 11. ⎧ Edward Thomas, mo. 509, (701), d. Ja. 16, 1844, æ. 85th.
701 " 11. ⎨ Lydia Thomas, (700), 1st. m. 1774? to Sam'l Cushman, dau. ⎩ 658, o. Gano, dau. Jas? d. Ju. 8, 1839, æ. 87th.
702 " 11. Betsey Thomas, w. Daniel m. 1793, o. Alden, fa. 427, dis. 1847 to C. C. C., d. Au. 26, 1849, æ. 76½.
703 " 11. Abiah Sears, w. of Leonard, 1st h. Sebra Simmons, o. Leonard, dau. Joseph, d. 1828, æ. ab't 55.
704 " 11. Susanna Leach, w. Joseph, o. Sturtevant of Hal'x.
705 " 11. Reuel Thompson, s. Francis, m. Thankful Wood 1802, [d. 1843, æ. 66th, fa. 747], d. Oc. 3, 1851, æ. 75th.
706 No. 29. Nathaniel Thompson, fa. 268, 569, m. Hannah Thomas 1775, dis. 1819 to Rehoboth, d. Ja. 31, 1833, æ. 82½.
707 " 29. Jacob Cobb, b. 1782, s. of James, gr. fa. 628, m. Patience Barrows 1804, Re. in Hartford Me.
708 " 29. ⎧ George Briggs, s. of Eben'r, gr. fa. 522, (709), He. & W. dis. ⎨ 1818 to Hartford & Sumner Me.
709 " 29. ⎩ Patience Briggs, (708), 1st. h. —— Holmes, o. Clarke.

1807.
710 No. 29. John Soule, s. of James, (711), d. Ja. 29, 1815, æ. 66.
711 " 29. Joanna Soule, (710), o. Perkins, dau. of Eben'r, sis. 570, 2d. m. Nathan Alden of Bridg'r, 1818.
712 " 29. Sage Morse, w. Wm., o. Staples, d. May 21, 1834, æ. 89.
713 " 29. Maria Wood, w. Joshua, 1st. h. Hacket, o. Pratt, br. 646.
1808.
714 Fe. 21. William Barker, fa. 545, unm. d. No. 9, 1809, æ. 22.
715 Mh. 13. Daniel Darling, s. of Benj., gr. fa. 149, (716) d. No. 14, '14, æ. 42.
716 " 13. Polly Darling, (715) m. 1795, o. Turner, mo. 603, sis. 614, chi. 848, 849, 850, d. Ju. 17, 1843, æ. 69.
717 " 13. Lydia Torry, w. Caleb, m. 1789, o. Darling, b. 1771, br. 715, (ex. 1824.) d. Ja. 5, 1848, æ. 77th.
718 " 13. Zechariah Eddy, fa. 633, br. 682, 944, sis. 683, (719.)
719 " 13. Sarah Eddy, (718), o. Edson, sis. 853, gr. gr. fa. 226, & gr. gr. gr. fa. 32, d. Se. 7, 1850, æ. 69th.
720 " 20. John Atwood, (721), d. Ju. 17, 1839, æ. 63.
721 " 20. Rhoda Atwood, (720), o. Johnson, d. Oc. 11, 1814, æ. 39.
722 Ap. 3. Lydia Thompson, fa. 583, br. 730, dis. to Plymt.
723 " 3. Lucy Thompson, fa. 583, (935), m. 1819, d. Oc. 13, 1852. æ. 66.
724 " 3. Mary Thompson, fa. 583, m. Dr. R. Capen, Re. in Boston.
725 " 3. Irene Thompson, fa. 581, br. 870, 935, m. Daniel Warren.
726 " 3. Mary Wilder, (639), o. Bump, mo. 596, d. Mh. 30, 1848, æ. 71.
727 " 3. Mary Wilder, br. 639, m. Henry Holmes 1813, dis. 1815 to Alfred Me. d. there No. 14, 1847, æ. 63d.
728 " 3. Serena Hubbard, w. Ahira, o. Tucker, mo. 746, dis. 1810 to Windsor, Vt. (Re-ad. 1824.)
729 " 3. Sybil Porter, dau. of Isaac of Hal'x, m. —— Noyes, dis. 1838 to Plainfield.
730 Ma. 15. Ezra Thompson, fa. 583, sis. 722, m. Cynthia Gifford, Re. in New Bedford.
731 " 15. Abigail Sturtevant, mo. 627, d. De. 30, 1834, æ. 51st.
732 Au. 14. Samuel Sampson, s. John, gr. fa 193, sis. 654, (733), Dea. 1826, d. Jy. 30, 1850, æ. 86.
733 " 14. Lydia Sampson, (732), o. Holmes, d. Se. 13, 1828, æ. 57th.
734 Se. 11. Josiah Sparrow, mo. 643, (735) m. 1800, dis. 1827 to Rochester, 2d. m. wid. Clarissa Hayward, 3d m. wid. Alice Cushing, d. Ja. 25, 1851, æ. 76.
735 " 11. Minerva Sparrow, (734) o. Miller, sis. 697, d. Au. 15, 1839, æ. 60.
736 " 11. Jacob Thomas, s. of Jeremiah, br. 884, (737) m. 1799, 2d. w. Cynthia Thomas, [fa. 743]. d. Mh. 22, 1851, æ. 77.
737 " 11. Lucy Thomas, (736) o. Thomas, mo. 550, d. Jy. 10, 1815, æ. 40th.

	1808.	
738	Se. 11.	Hope Thomas, b. 1787, mo. 550, sis. 737, Re. to Hartford Me. m. Phillip Ellis, d. before 1840.
739	" 11.	Hannah Tilson, w. Sylvanus, o. Southworth, mo. 308, gr. fa. 135, d. No. 30, 1821, æ. 66.
740	Oc. 16.	Irene Standish, w. Jonathan, o. Shaw, sis. 694, br. Elijah sr., d. Fe. 28, 1822, æ. 44.
741	" 23.	Sylvia Cushman, w. Jacob, m. 1796, o. Thompson, fa. 569, sis. 742, dis. 1829 to Bristol R. I., d. Oc. 13, 1845, æ. 67.
742	" 23.	Abigail Wood, w. Nelson, [br 782, gr. mo. 429,] o. Thompson, fa. 569, sis. 741, d. Mh. 31, 1843, æ. 60.
	1809.	
743	Ap. 9.	⎧ Sylvanus Thomas, fa. 424, (744), d. Au. 30, 1814, æ. 74.
744	" 9.	⎨ Susanna Thomas, (743) m. 1761, o. Thompson, br. 583, d. Se. 4, 1822, æ. 79.
745	Ju. 4.	Priscilla Weston Jr., fa. 762, sis. 777, 778, m. Joseph Tinkham, dis. 1850 to Hali'x.
746	Jy. 23.	Jedidah Tucker, wid. of Nathaniel, [fa. 164] m. 1767, o. Warren, fa. 343, chi. 728, d. Mh. 25, 1819, æ. 71.
747	Oc. 22.	Israel Wood, fa. 379, m. Priscilla Vaughan, 1772, [d. 1808, æ. 59th. fa. 351], 2d. m. 1810 (564), d. Ma. 12th, 1829, æ. 85th.
748	" 22.	Ichabod Wood, fa. 379, (672) m. '75, d. De. 30, 1825, æ. 74½.
749	" 22.	⎧ Lothrop Perkins, br. 790, (750), dis. 1831 to N. Rochester; a 2d. m.
750	" 22.	⎨ Mercy Perkins, (749), o. Cushman, mo. 565, d. Ap. 30, 1815, æ. 34.
751	" 22.	Elizabeth Wood, w. Gorham, m. 1799, o. Sparrow, mo. 643, sis. 882, 758, br. 734, dis. 1847, to C. C. C.
752	" 22.	Theodate Wood, br. 947, (792), d. Jy. 31, 1828, æ. 49.
753	" 22.	Susanna Wilder, w. Benaiah, [he d. Ma. 15, 1818, æ. 43, br. 639], o. Bryant, fa. 636, d. Ja. 1, 1818, æ. 39?
754	" 22.	Priscilla Cobb, b. 1770, mo. 338, unm., d. in Vt. 1851.
	1810.	
755	Fe. 25.	Abigail Bourne, w. Abner, o. Williams of Taunton? d. Ju. 15, 1845, æ. 64.
756	Ap. 8.	Jael Rider, w. Jesse m. 1804, o. Elmes, b. 1772, dau. John, gr. mo. 172, dis. 1825 to Plym., d.
757	Jy. 8.	Hannah Tucker, (635), o. Dunbar, d. No. 1, 1838, æ. 83.
758	" 8.	Jerusha Lovell, w. Joseph m. 1783, o. Sparrow, mo. 643, sis. 751, 882, br. 734, 2d. m. (771), d. Au. 6, 1843, æ. 77.
759	" 15.	Sally Curtis fr. Plym., w. David, o. Clarke.
760	Oc. 14.	Anna Barker fr. Branford Ct., (545), 1st. h. Rev. Jason Atwater, 2d. h. Rev. Lynde Huntington, o. Williams, dau. of Rev. Warham, dis. 1816 to Branford.

1811.
761 De. 22. Anna Eddy fr. Plainfield Ct., (682), o. Andros, dau. of Dea. Abel of P., sis. 797, d. Jy. 13, 1812, æ. 28.
1812.
762 Se. 6. John Weston, s. John & Content, m. Elizabeth Leonard 1757, 2d. m. 1776 (571), d. No. 15, 1815, æ. 82.
1813.
763 Jy. 4. Mercy Bennet, wid. John, m. 1791, o. Morton, dau. Seth, gr. mo. 127, d. Mh. 2, 1826, æ. 57.
764 " 4. Priscilla Sturtevant, mo. 627, m. Robert Blair '13. [d.]
765 Au. 15. ⎧ Joseph Bourne, fa. 563, (766), He & w. dis. 1816 to N. Bedford, d. there Ju. 17, 1829, æ. 41st.
766 " 15. ⎨ Sophia Bourne fr. Fairhaven, (765), o. Bates, dau. Dea. Joseph of F., Re. in Newton Ms.
767 Se. 26. Mercy Harlow, mo. 632, sis. 768, d. Mh. 30, '54, æ. 84th.
768 " 26. Betsey Wood, w. Eliab m. 1808, [he d. Oc. 12, 1852, æ. 71st., fa. 747], o. Harlow, mo. 632, sis. 737.
769 " 26. Hepzibah Harlow fr. Sandw., w. Samuel, o. Burgess; Re.
770 " 26. Jabez Williams, (785) m. 1815, (ex. 1827)., Re. to Penn.
771 No. 14. John Tinkham, fa. 346, m. Mary Wood 1778, 2d m. Lydia Wood, wid. of Thomas 1810, 3d. m. (758), d. Ap. 5, 1829, æ. 75.
772 " 14. Thomas Pratt, b. 1775, s. of Eben'r, sis. 610, 624, (823).
773 " 14. William Gisby, s. of Edw'd. br. 928, gr. gr. mo. 172, m. Ruth T. Bennett [dau. of Thomas & Ruth.]
774 " 14. Hannah Coade, dau. of Joseph & Sarah of Plymouth, dis. 1837 to Dunkirk N. Y. (Re-ad. 1840).
775 De. 19. Mercy Bennet, w. Jacob, m. 1780, o. Porter, mo. 620, sis. 825, d. Jy. 6, 1847, æ. 85.
776 " 19 Sarah Porter, dau. Zacha'h., gr. mo. 620, Re., m. Dr. —— Brown of Pa.; now a wid.
777 " 19. Hannah Weston, fa. 762, sis. 745, unm., d. Ja. 6. 1840, æ. 49.
778 " 19. Salome Weston, fa. 762, mo. 571, sis. 745, 777, (802).
779 " 19. Eunice Sturtevant, mo. 627, unm., d. Ma. 14, 1815, æ. 22.
1814.
780 Ja. 2. Jacob Bennet 2d., s. Eben'r. Livy, (794), d. Au. 20, '50, æ. 76.
781 " 23. Orin Tinkham, fa. 771, m. Achsa Townsend, Re. in Me.
782 " 23. Temperance Burgess, m. Levi Wood 1814, [s. of Levi, gr. mo. 429], dis. 1837 to Fall River.
783 " 23. Ichabod Wood 2d., fa. 747, sis. 661; Re. to Ind. m. bef. 1823, Left 4 chi.; d. Oc. 31, 1830, æ. 42.
784 Ap. 10. Mary Wood, (801), o. Weston, dau. Abner and Huldah, gr. mo. 539, gr. gr. fa. 231, d. Se. 30, 1827, æ. 40.
785 " 10. Serena Thomas, dau. Seth, sis. 738, (770), m. 1815, dis. 1833 to Pittsburg Pa.

1814.
786. Ap. 10. Lucy Swift, w. Joseph sr., o. Cornish, fa. 593, sis. 985.
787. No. 20. Mercy King, dau. John & Elizabeth, gr. mo. 384, m. Josephus Bump 1814, d. Se. 19, 1818, æ. 29?
788. " 27. Elizabeth Barker, fa. 545, mo. 579, br. 714, dis. 1827 to Freetown; d. in Chicago, Ill. Ap. 5, 1854, æ. 63d.

1815.
789. Ma. 21. Hepzibah Morton fr. Salsbury Vt., dau. Seth jr., gr. gr. mo. 127, sis. 1061, dis. 1840 to N. Bedford, d. Ma. 16, 1848? æ. 50?
790. Se. 17. John Perkins, br. 749, m. Sarah Snow, 2 m. (1043), dis. 1825 to N. Rochester. (Re-ad. 1845).

1816.
791. Fe. 14. REV. EMERSON PAINE, 6th Pastor, m. Lydia Pendleton, Re. 1822, d. Ap. 26, 1851, æ. 65.
792. Oc. 6. Leonard Elmes fr. Abbeville S. C., fa. 817, (752), (ex. 1827), Re. in Dighton, 2d. m. —— Stephens.
793. No. 17. *James Sproat*, s. Robert jr., gr. gr. fa. 135, (827) m. 1800, *Dea.* 1833, d. Ap. 15, 1837, æ. 63d.

1819.
794. Ap. 4. Rebecca Bennet, (780) m. 1802, o. Wood, dau. Amos, sis. 638, dis. 1828 to No. Rochester, d. Ma. 24, 1846, æ. 67th.
795. Ma. 16. Fanny D. Sturtevant, mo. 627, unm., d. De. 22, 1845, æ. 48.
796. " 16. Joanna Tilson, fa. 652, mo. 653, br. 693, sis. 873.
797. Ju. 27. Abby Eddy, (682), o. Andros, sis. 761, d. Oc. 28, 1848, æ. 55th.
798. " 27. Julia Paddock, mo. 699, unm., d. Ju. 6, 1849, æ. 50th.
799. " 27. Sylvea Fuller, mo. 647, sis. 685.
800. " 27. Elizabeth Wood, mo. 751, m. Collester Wood [d. 1850].
801. Au. 15. *Horatio G. Wood*, s. of Eben'r., br. 947, sis. 752, gr. mo. 429, (784, 836), *Dea.* 1842, dis. 1847 to C. C. C. with 32 others.
802. " 15. Ebenezer Willis, sis. 876, (778), d. Ja. 20, 1840, æ. 49.
803. " 15. Eliphalet Doggett, s. of Mark, m. Sybil Peabody, dis. 1828 to E. Brid'r., 2d. m. —— Keith, Re. in N. Bedford
804. Oc. — Eliphalet Elmes Jr., fa. 817, (854), Re. in Taunton.

1820.
805. Ja. 11. Deliverance Littlejohn, w. Wm. m. '94, o. Muxham, dau. Jn., Admitted at her house, d. Ja. 11, 1820, æ. 51st.

1823.
806. Se. — Susanna Tinkham, fa. 663, Admitted at her house, unm., d. De. 30, 1823, æ.
807. Oc. 19. Josiah Clarke, m. Hannah Harlow, d. Ma. 3, 1839, æ. 95.
808. " 19. Mary Clarke, mo. 845, sis. 809, m. Edward Stetson 1827, dis. 1828 to N. Bedford, d. Oc. 13, 1836, æ. 37th.
809. " 19. Deborah P. Clarke, mo. 845, sis. 808, gr. fa. 807, m. Geo. Thompson 1826, [his fa. 583], d. Mh. 23, 1853, æ. 55.

1823.

810 Oc. 19. ⎧ Abiel Washburn, s. Edward, (811), d. Ju. 17, 1843, æ. 80½.
811 " 19. ⎨ Elizabeth Washburn, (810) m. 1788, o. Pierce, dau. Job, sis.
         ⎩   895, d. Mh. 23, 1850, æ. 84.
812 " 19. Abigail Washburn, fa. 810, dis. 1851 to C. C. C.
813 " 19. Caroline Washburn, fa. 810, m. Rev. Francis Horton, dis. 1833 to Brookfield Ms., d. at W. Cambr'ge Sc. 20, 1849, æ. 42¼.
814 " 19. Louisa Jane Washburn, fa. 810, m. Rev. Elam Smalley, dis. 1832 to Franklin Ms., Re. in Worcester, Ms.
815 " 19. Louisa Bourne, mo. 895, sis. 870, m. Alexander Wood 1824, [fa. 748], Re. in Hanover, Ms.
816 " 19. HILLIARD BRYANT, s. of Seth, gr. mo. 673, dis. 1827 to Amherst Ms.
817 " 19. ⎧ Eliphalet Elmes sr., fa. 524, (818), d. Au. 4, '30, æ. 77th.
818 " 19. ⎩ Chloe Elmes, (817) m. '77, o. Leonard, d. Jy. 5, '43, æ. 86th.
819 " 19. Jane Finney, mo. 657, m. Eber Beal, d. Jy. 7, 1825, æ. 26th.
820 " 19. Hannah Freeman, mo. 856, unm., d. Se. 22, 1842, æ. 59.
821 " 19. Miriam Littlejohn, mo. 805, sis. 861, gr. gr. mo. 163.
822 " 19. Job Lucas, s. of Samuel, m. Mary Morse.
823 " 19. Lydia Pratt, (772), o. Macomber, dau. Simeon, sis. 854.
824 " 19. Phebe Pratt, w. Zerubbabel, o. Stone, d. Mh. 4, '45, æ. 49.
825 " 19. Bathsheba Sparrow, w. Edward, [d. No. 18, '53, æ. 86th,] m. 1798, o. Porter, mo. 620, sis. 775, d. Mh. 27, 1853, æ. 80th.
826 " 19. Josiah O. Standish, s. Joshua sr., Re., m., Re. in Plymouth.
827 " 19. Lucy Sproat, (703) o. Clarke, dau. Dr. Joseph & Rebecca, [sis. 544] gr. gr. mo. 127, d. De. 7, 1849, æ. 69.
828 " 19. Joseph Swift jr., mo. 786, unm., d. Oc. 9, 1829, æ. 20.
829 " 19. Mercy Swift, mo. 786, m. Ich. Shurtliff, dis. '43 to Carv.
830 " 19. Lucy Swift jr., mo. 786, m. W. Taylor of Pembroke, Re.
831 " 19. Elizabeth Tinkham, fa. 663, unm., d. Mh. 28, 1846, æ. 74.
832 " 19. ⎧ James Warren, br. 696, (833), He & W. dis. '47 to C. C. C.
833 " 19. ⎩ Margaret Warren, (832) o. Finney, mo. 657, sis. 819.
834 " 19. ⎧ Thomas Weston sr., s. Edmund jr., gr. fa. 231, (835), d. Ja. 17, 1834, æ. 64.
835 " 19. ⎩ Abigail Weston, (834), o. Doggett, d. Au. 11, 1830, æ. 55.
836 " 19. Abigail Weston Jr., fa. 834, (801) m. 1830, dis. 1847 to C. C. C., d. Ja. 7, 1854, æ. 53d.
837 " 19. Bethania Weston, fa. 834, m. Earl Sproat, [fa. 868].
838 " 19. Lavinia Weston, fa. 834, m. Reland Tinkham [d. Ma. 2, '54, æ. 56.]; his and her gr. gr. mo. 595; d. Oc. 15, 1849, æ. 41st.
839 " 19. Thomas Weston Jr., fa. 834, gr. gr. fa. 231, (851).
840 No. 23. Francis Atwood, s. Wm., m. Elizabeth Ward, dau. Benj'n., 2d. m. Abigail Shurtliff, d. Ja. 22, 1853, æ. 79.
841 " 23. Shadrach Atwood, fa. 840, Re., m., Re. in Franklin, Ms.
842 " 23. ⎧ Martin Buss, (843), Re.
843 " 23. ⎩ Eliza Buss, (842), Re.

| 1823. |

844 No. 23. Joseph Chamberlain, d. in Plymt. Oc. 6, 1825.
845 " 23. Elizabeth Clarke, w. Joseph, m. 1791, o. Morton, dau. of John, gr. mo. 127, d. Mh. 19, 1840, æ. 70.
846 " 23. Otis T. Cobb, mo. 684, dis. 1834 to Amherst, Ms., m. Maria Cady, dau. of Squire of Ct. Re. in Plainfield, Ct.
847 " 23. Adaline Cobb, mo. 684, br. 846, m. Heman Cobb, dis. 1840 to Plym. Re-ad. 1853.
848 " 23. Alanson Darling, fa. 715, sis. 849, 850, (857).
849 " 23. Hannah H. Darling, fa. 715, m. —— Spaulding, dis. 1837 to Lempster, N. H.
850 " 23. Aurilla Darling, fa. 715, m. Hiram Fletcher, dis. 1832 to Lempster, N. H.
851 " 23. Thalia Eddy, fa. 944, br. 967, sis. 955, 968, 969, (839).
852 " 23. Ann Juliett Eddy, fa. 718, sis. 988, m. Samuel Barrett, dis. 1833, to Cambridge, Re. in Newton, Ms.
853 " 23. Charlotte Edson, sis. 719, Re. in Titicut.
854 " 23. Lavinia Elmes, (804), o. Macomber, sis. 823, d. Oc. 29? 1836, æ. 29?
855 " 23. Louisa Elmes, fa. 817, m. Samuel G. Drake of Boston.
856 " 23. Mercy Freeman, w. Elisha, o. Eddy, fa. 341, d. Au. 19, 1828, æ. 82.
857 " 23. Lauretta Ann Fuller, gr. mo. 647, (848).
858 " 23. Rufus Holmes, s. of Zaccheus, (861) dis. 1828 to War'm., d. Mh. 20, 1839, æ. 35.
859 " 23. George L. Holmes, mo. 860, Re., m., Re. in Tenn.
860 " 23. Eunice Holmes, w. Peleg, o. Wood, dis. 1840 to N. Bridg'r.
861 " 23. Hannah Littlejohn, mo. 805, (858), dis. 1828 to War'm.
862 " 23. Lendall P. Morton, br. 662, (904), d. Ja. 11, 1843, æ. 46th.
863 " 23. Nathan Perkins Jr., gr. gr. mo. 172, (1023) 2d. m. Mrs. Sias, o. Dean, dis. 1847 to C. C. C.
864 " 23. Olive Pratt, fa. 772, br. 1032, m. Darius Wentworth, dis. 1835 to Bridg'r. He d., she Re. there.
865 " 23. Lydia Smith, dau. Jabez, gr. gr. fa. 161.
866 " 23. James Soule 4th, aged 12 yrs., s. Wm., gr. fa. 664.
867 " 23. Ruth Soule, w. Isaac o. Fuller, d. Se. 30, 1849, æ. 69th.
868 " 23. Thomas Sproat, fa. 323, (883) d. Fe. 3, 1833, æ. 75.
869 " 23. Daniel Thomas, mo. 702, m. Phebe Thomas, '25, Re. in Pa.
870 " 23. Arad Thompson, fa. 581, br. 935, sis. 698, 725, m. Mercy Bourne, [her mo. 895, sis. 815], d. Ap. 22, 1843, æ. 56.
871 " 23. Marietta T. Thompson, fa. 935, br. 926, sis. 872, 927.
872 " 23. Cordelia Thompson, fa. 935, sis. 871, m. Benj'n. Bryant, Re. in Philadelphia.
873 " 23. Judith Tilson, fa. 652, br. 693, unm. d. Ja. 22, 1836, æ. 30½.
874 " 23. Betsey L. Wing, mo. 880, m. Elii. Burgess, dis. '47 to C. C. C.

| 1823.
875 No. 23. James D. Wilder, æ. 15th year, fa. 639, (1001), dis. 1847 to
C. C. C.; *Dea.* there, d. Fe. 7, 1854, æ. 45th.
876 " 23. Jane Willis, dau. Eben'r and Joanna of Bridgewater, br. 802.
877 " 23. Lydia Wood, dau. Timothy, br. 1014, gr. gr. mo. 429, gr. gr. gr. fa. 135, m. Caleb Bassett, Re. in W. P.
| 1824.
878 Ja. 7. (Jabez Fuller fr. Wrentham, mo. 673, sis. 674, (879), he and W. dis. 1826 to Berkley. They Re. in Ver.
879 " 7. (Sally Fuller fr. Plymt., (878), o. Churchill.
880 " 7. Lura Wing fr. War'm., wid. of Ansel, o. Leonard, dau. of Archippus, gr. mo. 338, d. De. 15, 1851, æ. 71.
881 Ap. 4. Susan B. Fuller fr. Plainfield Ct., w. Zachariah, [his mo. 673, br. 878], o. Barstow, d. in Plainfield, Ct.
(728) " 4. Serena Hubbard fr. Windsor, Vt. o. Tucker, gr. fa. 164, dis. 1838 to Chicago, Ill. and Re. there; wid. of Ahira.
882 " 4. Susanna Miller, wid. John [d. Jy. 16, '18, æ. 47th,] m. '92, (652), o. Sparrow b. 1772, mo. 643, br. 734, sis. 751.
883 " 4. Mary Sproat, (868), o. Briggs, d. Sep. 3, 1834, æ. 73.
884 " 4. Silas Thomas, s. of Jer'h, gr. mo. 387, 484, br. 736, m. Mary Shurtliff, d. Au. 10, 1834, æ. 69th.
885 " 4. Eleazer Thomas, s. of Eleazer, gr. fa. 350, (920).
886 Mh. 10. REV. WILLIAM EATON fr. Fitchburg, 7th Pastor, (890), dis. 1834, d. April 15, 1840, æ. 56.
887 Jy. 4. Azel Thomas, mo. 892, sis. 894, gr. gr. fa. 428, 298, m. Harriet Thompson 1837, d. Mh. 31, 1844, æ. 47th.
| 1825.
888 Se. 9. Elizabeth Leonard fr. Plym., w. of Eph'm., 1st h. Geo. Churchill, o. Harlow, dau. of Seth and Sarah *Warren*,[4] *Dea. Nath'l*,[3] *Benj'n*,[2] *Richard* of the M. F., d. De. 28, 1846, æ. 78.
889 " 9. Lucy W. Morse fr. Nor. Bridg'r., dau. of Sam'l, br. 1016, gr. fa. 549, m. Edw'd. Adams.
| 1826.
890 Ja. 22. Lydia Eaton fr. Fitchburg, (886), o. Sanford, dis. 1834, d. in Worcester Ms., Mh. 25, 1850, æ. 55.
891 Jy. 2. Ruth Morse, w. of Levi, o. Savery, dis. 1839 to Carv.
892 Se. 21. Phebe Thomas, w. Azel, m. 1796, o. Ellis, dau. of Geo., gr. mo. 623, d. in the St. of Me. Feb. 3, 1851, æ. 76.
| 1827.
893 De. 2. Mary Freeman, (676), o. Cole, dau. of Job, sis. 917, dis. 1846, to Carv., d. Ju. 13, 1852, æ. 65th.
| 1829.
894 Jy. 5. Betsey Thomas, mo. 892, m. Sam'l Ellis, dis. '33 to War'm.
895 Se. 27. Lucy Bourne, w. Wm., o. Pierce, dau. Job, dis. '48 to C. C. C.

1695-1846] MEMBERS OF THE FIRST CHURCH 681

1829.
896 Se. 27. ⎧ Ebenezer Pickens, son of Sam'l, (897), he and w. dis. '47 to C. C. C.
897 " 27. ⎩ Mary B. Pickens, (896,) o. Thompson, dau. Benj'n. sis. 931, 947, gr. fa. 563.
898 " 27. Lydia M. Eddy, (944), o. Morton, dau. Joshua, sis. 971.
899 " 27. Polly W. Caswell, w. Eleazer, o. Cobb, dau. of Lemuel, gr. gr. fa. 363.
900 " 27. Jane Standish, w. John, o. Churchill dau. Elias; Re.
901 " 27. Barbara Tinkham, dau. Eben'r. gr. fa. 592.
902 " 27. Lauretta Wing, mo. 880, m. Wm. T. Estes, dis. 1843, to Taunton, d. in Sandwich, De. 24, 1852, æ. 43.
903 No. 8. Olive T. Cobb, dau. Levi, gr. fa. 628, gr. mo. 550, m. Philander Hacket, d. Au. 12, 1850, æ. 40.
904 " 8. Eliza S. Morton, (862), m. 1824, o. Hacket, dau. George, sis. 924, br. 903, d. Ja. 12, 1843, æ. 38.
905 " 8. Mary Norcutt, mo. 622, m. Dan'l Dunham, dis. '47 to C. C. C.
906 " 8. ⎧ Samuel Pool, (907); they Re. in South Abington.
907 " 8. ⎩ Lydia Pool, (906), o. Cox.
908 " 8. Betsey Warren, w. Galen, [he d. Ju. 19, 1853, æ. 55; br. 696], o. Tribou, mo. 695, gr. gr. fa. 298.

1830.
909 Ja. 20. Sarah Jackson fr. Windsor Vt., dau. of Joseph sr., gr. fa. 335, dis. 1847 to C. C. C.
910 Ap. 2. Hannah D. Morton fr. Shoreham Vt., fa. Livy, br. 662, 862, m. Horatio N. Wilbur, d. Jy. 26, 1846, æ. 37th.
911 Au. 1. Lucy C. Wood fr. Scitu., (947,) m. '27 1st. m. —— Cushing, o. Nichols, dis. 1847 to C. C. C., d. Se. 26, 1848, æ. 61st.
912 De. 5. Susanna Tucker, w. Daniel [fa. 327], o. Thompson, dau. Nathan, gr. mo. ad. 64, 16 chi. fr. '83, d. Fe. 25, '50, æ. 86th.
913 " 5. Mandana Tucker, mo. 912.

1831.
914 Ju. 5. Freeman Barrows, mo. 971, dis. 1832 to N. Bedford, Re. in Mo.; m.
915 " 5. Betsey Eddy, w. Eben'r, [fa. 633], o. Stetson, dau. Caleb,
916 " 5. Betsey M. Eddy, mo. 915, gr. fa. 633, m. Amasa Thompson [gr. gr. gr. fa. 9], d. No. 17, 1851, æ. 38.
917 " 5. Hannah Thomas, wid. of Ezra, [gr. fa. 425], o. Cole, dau. of Job, sis. 893, d. Jy. 5? 1853, æ. 63.
918 " 5. ⎧ *Seneca Thomas*, fa. 649, br. 923, sis. 921, (919) *Dea.*, 1852.
919 " 5. ⎩ Hope Thomas, (918), o. Faunce, dau. Ansel, gr. mo. 433.
920 " 5. Eunice Thomas, (885), o. Shurtliff, dau. Gideon.
921 " 5. Anna Thomas, w. Andrew, [d. 1853, æ. 75th. mo. 550], o. Thomas, fa. 649, br. 918, d. Ap. 12, 1833, æ. 49.
922 " 5. Lucia Ann Thomas, fa. 885, unm., d. No. 30, 1836, æ. 20.
923 " 5. Winslow Thomas, fa. 649, br. 918, m. Charity Thomas, [dau. of Isaiah], d. No. 14, 1843, æ. 52.

1831.
924 Ju. 5. Huldah Thomas, w. of Benj'n, o. Hacket, dau. of Geo. sis. 904, d. Se. 25, 1852, æ. 60th.
925 " 5. Nathan King, m. Ellen Thompson, dis. 1847 to C. C. C.
926 " 5. Charles F. Thompson, fa. 935, sis. 927, d. Se. 3, '39, æ. 23.
927 " 5. Florantha Thompson, fa. 935, br. 926, sis. 871, 872, m. Granville T. Sproat, dis. '39 to La Pointe, L. S.
928 Au. 7. Thomas Gisby, br. 773, m. Mehetabel Daniels.
929 " 7. Simeon Staples, s. of Eben'r of Taunton, m. Lydia Sampson, [her. fa. 732], d. Ja. 17, 1833, æ. 37½.
930 " 7. Susanna Cushman, w. Adoniram, o. Bump, mo. 596.
931 " 7. Freelove G. Rounseville, w. Gamaliel, o. Thompson dau. of Benj'n, sis. 897, gr. mo. 585, dis. 1847 to C. C. C.
932 " 7. Mary Jane Eastman fr. Brunswick Me., m. Rev. Sam'l Utley, dis. 1838 to So. New Marlboro'.
933 " 7. Betsey Tinkham fr. Wrentham, w. of Geo. W., o. Cole.
934 " 7. Matilda Wood, (1014), o. Thompson, dau. of Samuel and Clara, br. 916; dis. 1852 to C. C. C.

1832.
935 Ap. 1. Cephas Thompson, fa. 581, m. Olivia Leonard, (2d. w. 723).
936 Oc. 17. David Harlow fr. Brookfield, s. Jesse, m. —— Finney, Re. in Plymouth.

1833.
(626) Ma. 5. Desire Morse from Halif'x., unm., d. De. 29, 1851, æ. 80.
937 Ju. 2. Ruth Reed, w. Sam'l., o. Sampson, dau. Icho. dis. '47 to C. C. C.
938 " 2. Harvey Tinkham, s. of Hazael, gr. gr. fa. 148, (985); 2d. m. —— Ramsdell.

1835.
939 Oc. 28. REV. ISRAEL W. PUTNAM fr. Portsmouth, N. H., 8th Pastor, s. of Eleazer of Danvers, 1st m. Harriot Osgood, 2nd. m. (941), chi. 1006, 1036.

1836.
940 Ja. 3. Sabina Willis fr. Hal'x., w. Martin, o. Thompson, dau. Isaac sr., br. 981, gr. gr. gr. fa. 9, dis. 1849 to Hal'x.
941 Mh. 6. Julia Ann Putnam fr. Portsm'h. N. H., (939), o. Osgood, dau. of Sam'l and Maria of N. Y., 1st. h. S. Osgood jr., chi. 942.
942 " 6. Adeline H. Osgood fr. Portsmouth N. H., mo. 941, m. Wm. C. Eddy, [s. of Wm. S., gr. fa. 633.]
943 No. 6. Caroline M. Pickens, fa. 896, mo. 897, dis. '47 to C. C. C., m. John McCloud.

1837.
944 Mh. 5. Joshua Eddy, fa. 633, br. 682, 718, sis. 683, (898).
945 " 5. Harriet Hill, came fr. and returned to Boston.
946 " 5. Elizabeth H. Washburn, w. Philander, o. Homes, dau. of Henry and Dorcas of Boston, dis. 1847 to C. C. C.

1837.
947 Ma. 7. Wilkes Wood, s. Eben'r., br. 801, m. Betsey Tinkham 1798, [gr. fa. ·345]; 2d. w. Betsey Thompson, 3d. w. (911), d. Oc. 1, 1843, æ. 73.
948 " 7. CHARLES W. WOOD, fa. 947, dis. 1839 to Ashby, m. Eliza Ann Bigelow, 2d. m. Catharine Lemist, o. Clarke.
949 " 7. Emily Louisa Wood, fa. 947, br. 948, 953, sis. 950, 951, dis. 1847, to C. C. C.
950 " 7. Mary T. Wood, fa. 947, m. Russell L. Hathaway; Re. in Ind.
951 " 7. Sally Leonard, w. Jas., o. Wood, fa. 947, d. Ja. 1846, æ. 43d.
952 Ju. 2. Irene Soule, w. Otis, o. Cushman, dau. Jacob, of Plymt.
953 Se. 3. William Henry Wood, fa. 947, br. 948, sis. 949, 950.
1838.
954 Jy. 1. Mary Ann Orrington, came from and returned to Boston.
955 Se. 2. Jane Ellen Eddy, fa. 944, br. 967, sis. 851, 969, m. Timothy Cobb, dis. 1842 to Carv., Re. in Fall River.
956 " 2. Lucy Harrington, w. Isaac, o. Raymond, dau. Joshua.
957 " 2. { Lothrop Thomas Jr., gr. gr. fa. 350, (958).
958 " 2. { Louisa Faunce Thomas, (957), o. Thomas, fa. 918.
959 " 2. Saba S. Thomas, fa. 885, unm., d. De. 18, 1845, æ. 25.
960 " 2. Mary Ann Thomas, mo. 921, m. Soranus Wrightington.
961 " 2. Mary H. Thomas, w. Albert, o. Churchill, dau. Edmund.
962 No. 4. Mary Reed Atwood, w. Daniel, o. Whitmarsh, dau. Wm.
1839.
963 Ja. 4. Betsey L. Pratt fr. Bridgewater, w. Simeon o. Leach, dau. of Levi, of Bridg'r, d. Ap. 19, 1839, æ. 27.
(673) Jy. 6. Lucy Fuller from Fairhaven, d. Se. 13, 1839, æ. 81½.
1840.
964 Jy. 5. Eliab Dean, s. of Seth of Raynham, (986), chi. 987.
(774) " 5. Hannah Coade fr. Dunkirk N. Y.
965 " 5. Sarah Lawrence, w. Dan'l, o. Custens, dau. of Thomas.
966 Se. 6. Mary Ann Colwell, dau. Eben'r., m. Eben'r. Fuller, Hal'x.
967 " 6. Charles E. Eddy fr. N. Bedford, fa. 944, dis. 1847 to Providence, m. Elizabeth Simmons of Prov.
968 " 6. Eliza Eddy, fa. 944, mo. 898, br. 967, sis. 851, 955, 969.
969 " 6. Susan M. Eddy, fa. 944, mo. 898, br. 967, sis. 851, 968, 955.
970 " 6. Ann Elizabeth Eddy, fa. 682, mo. 797, sis. 1010, (976), dis. 1844 to Baltimore, Md.
971 " 6. Susanna M. Ellis, (680), 1st h. Freeman Barrows, o. Morton, sis. 898, s. 914, dis. 1844 to N. Bedford.
972 " 6. Jane Freeman, gr. mo. 856, (997), Re. in No. Bridgewater.
973 " 6. Jerusha Haskins, w. Job, o. Raymond.
974 " 6. Lucia Maria Nichols, w. James G., o. Cole, dau. Lemuel, gr. fa. 665.
975 " 6. Harriet Orcutt, w. Alpheus, o. Soule, mo. 867; Re. in W. P.

1840.
976 Se. 6. William Pratt, s. of Simeon, (970), dis. '42 to Balt. Md.
977 " 6. Mahala Smith, w. Earl, 1st h. Alfred Soule, o. Shaw, fa. 654, dis. 1845 to Manchester N. H.
978 " 6. Isaac Soule, 3d, mo. 867, m. Polly Fuller, dau. of Sam'l.
979 " 6. Priscilla Soule. mo. 867, m. S. M. Stephens, Re. in Boston.
980 " 6. Rebecca Soule, mo. 867, br. 978, sis. 975, 979.
981 " 6. Anna T. Thompson, fa. 705, br. 996, gr. fa. 747, m. Isaac Thompson Jr., d. in Hal'x. Ma. 11, 1852, æ. 38th.
982 " 6. Eunice Washburn, w. Lewis, o. Leonard, dau. Jonathan.
983 No. 1. Henry Dunham fr. Carv., s. of Israel of Carv., m. Louisa Jane Pratt, [fa. 772, sis. 864]; dis. 1850 to C. C. C.
984 " 1. Lucia C. Ellis, w. Southworth Jr., o. Thomas, dau. Noah, gr. fa. 350.
985 " 1. Jane Tinkham, (938), o. Cornish, fa. 593, d. Se. 16, '48 æ. '54.
1841.
986 Ja. 4. Lydia Dean, (964), o. Paddleford, dau. Solomon.
987 " 4. Lois Dean, fa. 964, mo. 986.
988 " 4. Charlotte Elizabeth Eddy, fa. 718, sis. 852, m. Rev. F. G. Pratt Pastor Winthrop Church, So. Malden.
989 " 4. Stephen Harlow Jr., gr. mo. 632, br. 990, sis. 991, (1029).
990 " 4. Jonathan E. Harlow, s. Stephen sr., br. 989, Physician in Hingham. m.
991 " 4. Sarah Harlow, br. 989, sis. 992, m. John A. Williams.
992 " 4. Betsey B. Harlow, br. 989, sis. 993, m. John M. Soule.
993 " 4. Mary L. Harlow, gr. mo. 632, sis. 992, 991, br. 989, 990.
994 " 4. ⎰ Venus Thompson, mo. 655, gr. gr. mo. 372, (995).
995 " 4. ⎱ Jane Thompson, (994), o. Southworth, dau. Seth and Hope.
996 " 4. Benjamin F. Thompson, fa. 705, sis. 981, m. Sarah A. Wood, [dau. David, gr. gr. fa. 356, d. Ja. 10, 1854, æ. 35].
997 " 4. Oliver G. Tinkham, fa. 938, (972), Re. in N. Bridg'r.
998 " 4. Rachel Vineca, w. David, o. Vaughan, mo. 567.
999 " 4. Dorlisca N. Vineca, mo. 998, m. Francis Thompson.
1000 " 4. Lydia Vineca, mo. 998, m. Martin Wood of Hal'x.
1001 " 4. Bathsheba L. Wilder, (875), o. Murdock, dis. '47 to C. C. C.
1002 " 4. Abigail T. Wood, mo. 742, sis. 1003, gr. fa. 569.
1003 Ma. 7. Mercy L. Wood, mo. 768, gr. fa. 747.
1004 " 7. Joanna Atwood, w. of Jacob, o. Wood, mo. 742, sis. 1002.
1005 " 7. Mary C. Wood, w. of Eliab Jr., o. Freeman, fa. 676, mo. 893.
1006 Se. 12. Harriet O. Putnam, fa. 939, br. 1036, m. Charles F. Pierce, [s. Peter H., gr. fa. 868].
1007 " 12. Sarah T. Thompson, w. of Reuel Jr. [fa. 705], o. Wood, dau. Alfred sr. and Rhoda, br. 1008. gr. mo. 672, 643.
1008 " 12. *Alfred Wood* Jr. fr. Woodstock Ct., sis. 1007, Dea. '52.
1009 No. 7. Lucy Ann Eddy, dau. Wm. S., gr. fa. 633 m. Dr. Geo. King.

	1841.		
1010	No.	7.	Mary Jane Eddy, fa. 682, sis. 970, m. Charles F. Thayer; Re. in Ogdensburg, N. Y.
1011	"	7.	Alfred B. Soule, mo. 977, gr. fa. 664, 654, dis. 1845 to Manchester, N. H.
	1842.		
1012	Ja.	2.	⎧ Adoniram J. Cushman, 930, (1013), dis. 1847 to C. C. C.
1013	"	2.	⎨ Ann S. Cushman, (1012), o. Reed, dau. of Dean H., dis. ⎩ '47 to C. C. C.
1014	"	2.	Abiel Wood, s. of Timothy, sis 877, (934), dis. '52 to C. C. C.
1015	Ju.	26.	Zilpha m. Clarke, w. Joseph 3d., o. Miller, dau. of John, mo. 882, 1847 to C. C. C.
1016	"	26.	Marston S. Morse, s. Sam'l, sis. 889, gr. fa. 549.
1017	"	26.	Phebe Thomas, wid. of Israel, o. Thompson, dau. of Dan'l.
1018	"	26.	Perry A. Wilbur, s. Jas., m. Betsey B. Wilder, dis. '49 C. C. C.
1019	"	26.	George Warren, fa. 696, mo. 685, unm. d. Ap. 21, 1848, æ. 29.
1020	"	26.	Mary Wood, w. Thomas J., o. Tinkham, dau. Levi, gr. fa. 346.
1021	Se.	4.	⎧ Halford Earle fr. Brunswick Me., s. Frederic, (1022), he and W. dis. 1847 to E. Thomaston Me.
1022	"	4.	⎩ Elizabeth Earle fr. N. Bedf'd., o. Barker, dau. Joshua.
1023		4.	Eunice Perkins, (863), o. Bisbee, dau. of Joseph, gr. gr. gr. fa. 68, d. Se. 16, 1844, æ. 40.
1024	"	4.	⎧ Benj. F. Pratt, s. Benj. Jr., gr. fa. 646, (1025), Re. to Plymo.; 2d. m. Brayley, d. Ja. 21, 1853, æ. 34th.
1025	"	4.	⎨ Abby B. Pratt, (1024), o. Morse, br. 1016, d. Jy. 14, '44, ⎩ æ. 25.
1026	"	4.	Mahala S. Pratt, gr. fa. 646, br. 1024, m. Sam'l Morse Jr.
1027	"	4.	Mary H. Thompson fr. Plymt., w. Edw'd, o. Bryant, du. of Micah.
1028	"	4.	Eleanor B. Wood, mo. 751, sis. 800, dis. 1847 to C. C. C.
1029	"	4.	Bethiah O. Harlow fr. E. Bridg'r, (989), o. Keith, dau. Geo.
	1843.		
1030	Ja.	1.	Consider Robbins fr. Carv., s. of Consider, m. Martha Richardson, dis. 1847 to C. C. C.
1031	Ma.	7.	Calvin Doane, m. Huldah Willis, [mo. 940], Re.
1032	"	7.	Thomas A. Pratt, fa. 772, sis. 864, m. Ruth C. Bradford.
1033	Ju.	2.	Abigail S. Pickens fr. Rochester, w. of Andrew J., o. Snow, dau. Linus of Rochester, dis. 1847 to C. C. C.
	1844.		
1034	Ja.	7.	Mary Briggs fr. W. P., w. of Eben'r Jr., o. Dean, dau. Rev. Joshua Dean, d. No. 1, 1846, æ. 28.
1035	"	7.	James Foley, s. Laurens and Catharine of Ireland, m. Sylvia Standish, wid. Jn. C., o. Perkins, dau. Gideon.
1036	"	7.	William F. Putnam, fa. 939, sis. 1006, dis. '49 to Brooklyn N. Y., d. in Middleboro', Feb. 11, 1853, æ. 25.
1037	Ma.	5.	Phebe H. Wood fr. Pawtucket, w. of Ansel, o. Hamilton.

	1844.		
1038	Jy.	7.	⎧ Dr. Henry D. Hitchcock fr. Westminster Vt., s. David, (1039), d. by R. R. disaster, Feb. 23, 1847, æ. 27½.
1039	"	7.	⎨ Olivia Hitchcock fr. Westminster Vt., (1038), o. Arnold, dau. Rev. Seth S., dis. '47 to C. C. C.; a 2d. m. in Vt.
1040	"	7.	Hope Wrightington, dau. of David, dis. 1847 to C. C. C., unm., d. Ja. 4, 1850, æ. 43d.
1041	No.	3.	⎧ Dea. Cornelius S. Burgess fr. New Bedf'd, dis. '47 to C. C. C.
1042	"	3.	⎩ Melissa Burgess fr. N. B., (1041), o. Cobb, dau. Nehemiah.
	1845.		
(790)	Ja.	5.	⎧ Dr. John Perkins fr. No. Roch'r, (1043), dis. '47 to C. C. C.
1043	"	5.	⎨ Ann S. Perkins fr. N. Y. city, (790), o. Nelson, dau. of Dr. Thomas [a native of Middleboro'], dis. '47 to C. C. C.
1044	Ma.	4.	Joanna Brand fr. N. P., (Ind.) unm. d. Jy. 31, 1851, æ. 82?
	1846.		
1045	Se.	6.	Almira Goddard fr. Roxbury, w. John H., o. Porter, dau. Aaron and Pauline, dis. 1847 to C. C. C.

INDEX

INDEX

ABBOTT, Rev. Levi A., 485.
Abbott, Rev. Samuel, 481; ministry of, 472.
Abercrombie's brigade, 178.
Abiel, Nehemiah, pastor of Indian church, 20.
Abington, 123, 269, 411.
Academies: New England academies, 249, 250; Pierce Academy, 251–257; Titicut Academy, 258–263.
Acadia, capture of, 89; expedition to, 94.
Acadians, 99, 100; bill for their support, 100.
Acomowett, 600.
Actions against town, 569.
Acushnet, 84, 545.
Acushnet Path, description of, 504.
Adams, John, 196, 585, 593, 596; life of, 586.
Adams, Rev. John Q., 487.
Advent Church, 494.
Agents of town, 225, 226, 553, 554, 558, 559, 561, 562, 565, 572.
Ahanton, John, conveyance of land to Titicut Parish, 20.
Alarm list, 196, 197, 202, 203.
Alarms, 74, 314; Rhode Island, 125.
Alden, Albert, 293, 498; life of, 294; portrait of, 294.
Alden, Andrew, 297.
Alden, Arthur B., 293, 300.
Alden, Arthur H., 297.
Alden, C. H., 411.
Alden, Charles F., 300.
Alden, David, 464, 564, 616; life of, 617.
Alden, Elijah, life of, 395.
Alden, Frederick L., 297.
Alden, George D., 227.
Alden, John, 35, 394, 446, 545, 551, 563, 577, 592, 596, 621, 629; autograph of, 593; life of, 394–395, 593; portrait of, 395; slave of, 105.
Alden, Corp. John, 198.
Alden, John F., 390.
Alden, Capt. Rufus, 202.
Alden, Samuel, 463.
Alden, Rev. W. H. H., 414.
Alden Cemetery, history of, 635–636.

Aldrich, Daniel, 155.
Aldrich, Rev. Jonathan, 485.
Alewives, 499, 502.
Alexander, 7–9; embarkation of, 8; picture of Alexander about to embark on the river, 8; sickness and death of, 8, 9; visit to Marshfield and Plymouth, 8.
Alexandria, 176, 187.
Alger, Roland F., 258.
Algonquin tribes, 304.
Allan, Bert J., 227.
Allen, B. J., 262.
Allen, Rev. Charles W., 480.
Allen, Rev. Ephraim W., 466.
Allen, Hepzibah, 636.
Allen, or Allyn, John, 89, 254, 555, 560, 563.
Allen, Capt. Nehemiah, 200.
Almanacs, 343.
America, 209, 213.
American Congress, 168.
American inventions, 206.
American Legion of Honor, history of, 632.
American navy, 157.
American states, 196.
Ammunition, 196, 568, 574.
Amusements of the 18th century, 217, 218.
Anabaptists, 573.
Anchor Works, 382.
Andem, Rev. James, ministry of, 474.
Andirons, 348.
Andrew, Gov. John A., 169, 176.
Andrews, Henry, 28.
Andros, Sir Edmund, 558.
Angier, Oakes, 227.
Annabel, Anthony, 596; life of, 597.
Antietam, battle of, 173, 178, 179.
Apothecary shops, 291.
Apples, uses of, in 18th century, 208, 212, 216.
Appomattox Court House, 171, 185.
Archives of State House, 166.
Arms, orders to exercise men in and to provide, 554, 560.
Army of the Potomac, 178, 179, 180, 185, 187.

Arrowfield Church, 184; battle of, 187.
Arrows, 193.
Articles of submission to King James signed by Chickataubut, 10.
Artillery in local militia, major of battalion of, 205.
Artillery in War of 1812, number of, 159.
Artillery in War of the Rebellion, 172, 180.
Ashley, Capt. Silas P., 201.
Assawampsett, xvii, 2, 17, 18, 270, 440, 475, 547, 550, 568, 630.
Assawampsett Brook, 570, 574.
Assawampsett Neck, 83, 226, 562, 568, 630.
Assawampsett Pond, 1, 2, 304, 419, 428, 434, 481, 547, 568, 574, 580, 628–630; canal on, 427; discovery of iron ore in, 426; history of, 423, 424; Indian legend concerning, 424–426; tradition concerning, 427; view of, 72.
Assawampsett post-office, 270.
Assaweta, deed of, 515, 516.
Assessors, 573, 581.
Atlanta, 170.
Attorneys and barristers, distinction between, 226–227.
Attorneys, duties of, in 18th century, 226, 227; province law concerning, 226.
Atwood, Capt. and Lieut.-Col. Daniel, 202, 204.
Atwood, Harvey N., 271.
Atwood, Capt. Ichabod F., 202.
Atwood, Nathaniel, 637.
Atwood, Lieut. Pelham, 162.
Atwood, Reuel, 394.
Atwood, Zilpah, 637.
Austrian musket, 172.
Averill, Rev. Alexander M., 485.

Backus, Rev. Isaac, 20, 221, 401, 406, 421, 463, 464, 470, 542; autograph of, 471; house of; 406; inscription on gravestone of, 471, 472; life of, 402, 405; ministry of, 470, 471; portrait of, 470.
Backus, Joseph A., 406.
Backus Historical Society, 406.
Backus House, picture of attic in, 221.
Bags made and used in 18th century, 215.
Baiting Brook, xx, 28.
Baker, Jonathan, 560.
Baker, Dr. Joseph C., 244.
Bale, Joseph, 570.
Ball, Rev. Mr., 479.
Baltimore, 176.
Baltimore Cross Roads, 187.
Banks, General, 173, 178.
Banks, 299–302; Middleboro National, 299–301; Middleboro Savings, 301; Middleboro Loan and Fund Association, 301; Middleboro Coöperative, 301–302; picture of bank block, 292, site of bank block in 1875, 292.
Baptist churches, 469–485; First (Titicut), 469–474, picture of, 470; Second (Lakeville), 474–477; Third (Rock), 477–480, picture of, 478; Fourth (Pond) (United Brethren), 480–482; Central, 482–485, pictures of, 253, 255, 483; church in Swansea, 573.
Baptist Education Fund, trustees of, 253.
Barbour, Rev. Joseph, 480.
Barden, Abraham, 564.
Barden, John, 564.
Barden, John, Jr., 288.
Barden, Joseph, 563.
Barden, Mercy, 486.
Barden, Patience, 483.
Barden, Stephen, 564.
Barden, William, life of, 302.
Barden Hills, 302.
Barden House, picture of the old, 302.
Bareneed, Shute, and Littleworth farms, 28.
Barker, John, 302.
Barker, Rev. Joseph, 459, 542; life of, 316–317; ministry of, 454–455.
Barns, description of, used in 18th century, 207.
Barnstable, 302, 547, 613.
Barrels, 212.
Barricades, 197.
Barristers, duties of, in 18th century, 226–227.
Barrows, Abner, diary of, 95–98, 116.
Barrows, Capt. Abner, Jr., 200.
Barrows, Clement, 304.
Barrows, Rev. Elijah W., 486.
Barrows, Eunice, 636.
Barrows, Corp. George W., 175.
Barrows, Hannah, 636.
Barrows, Rev. Homer, ministry of, 461.
Barrows, Horatio, 296, 498; portrait of, 296.
Barrows, Capt. Jacob T., 202.
Barrows, Capt. John, 200.
Barrows, Nathaniel, 636.

INDEX 691

Barrows, Samuel, 34, 35, 78, 198, 277, 446, 448, 571; autograph of, 36; life of, 35-36.
Barrows, Capt. Sylvanus, 202.
Barrows, Thomas, 276; picture of house of, 277.
Barrows house, picture of the old, 277.
Barstow, Elmer W., 262.
Bartlett, Benjamin, 225, 621; life of, 622.
Bartlett, Ichabod, 563.
Bartlett Brook, 386, 387.
Bassett, William, 551, 585, 596, 621; life of, 586.
Bassett, William, Jr., 602.
Batchelder's Creek, 184.
Baton Rouge, 173.
Battell, Rev. A. E., 480.
Battelle, Hezekiah, Jr., 254.
Bayberry, 211.
Bayley, Guido, 621.
Bayonets, 196.
Beals, Eber, 392, 397.
Beals, Joseph E., 265, 302.
Beals, Sergt. Solomon F., 181, 186.
Bear Spring, 387.
Bearse, Augustus M., 270.
Beaver Dam, 334.
Beaver Dam Swamp, 387.
Bed coverlids, 215.
Bedrooms, 210-211.
Beech Woods, 422, 437, 467, 475, 480.
Beech Woods Church, history of, 467, 475.
Beecher, Rev. George Fletcher, 474.
Beevatt, deed of, 615-616.
Belcher, Jonathan, 571, 572.
Belgium, 167.
Bell, Rev. J. S., 489.
Bennett, Jabez, xxii.
Bennett, Jacob, 287.
Bennett, or Bennet, John, 60, 246, 305, 445, 560, 561, 563, 564, 571, 574, 594, 612, 616; autograph of, 317; life of, 317-318.
Bennett, or Bennet, John, Jr., 561, 564.
Bennett, Mercy, 34, 446; life of, 318.
Bennett, Nehemiah, 318, 496; autograph of, 318.
Bennett, Peter (of England), 317.
Bennett, Peter, 564, 567.
Bennett, Capt. Peter, 306, 572; life of, 305.
Bennett, Capt. and Major Thomas, 201, 205, 317.
Bennett Mills, 287.
Bennington, battle of, 125.

Benson, Lieut. Consider, 128, 138, 636.
Benson, John S., 270.
Benson, Lieut. Joshua, Jr., 119.
Benson, Stillman, 339; portrait of, 340.
Benson Cemetery, 637.
Benson Lumber Mill, 340.
Benthuysen, Sergt. T. P., 190.
Bentley, Rev. William, 253.
Bermuda Landing, 187.
Betty's Neck, 13, 303, 428; tradition concerning, 427.
Bigelow, Rev. John F., D.D., 485.
Billington, Francis, 34, 35, 551, 555, 585, 586, 593, 596, 621; life of, 64-65.
Billington, Isaac, 563, 593; life of, 65.
Billington Sea, description of, 64; discoverer of, 64; picture of, 64.
Bills of Continental money, value of, 224.
Binney, Rev. Amos, 487.
Bisbee, Joseph H., 378.
Black sachem's field, 545.
Blackbirds, 567.
Blacksmith shops: Eddyville, 347; Green, 328; Muttock, 378; Purchade, 397; Soule Neighborhood, 351; Warrentown, 394.
Blackwell, John, 626, 627.
Blake, Barton F., 258.
Blanket, 196.
Blast furnaces, 209, 298, 305, 339, 360, 377, 378, 412.
Bliss, Rev. Thomas E., 466.
Blount's Creek, 172.
Boarding-school for boys, 263.
Bodfish, Rev. Asa N., 487.
Bodkin, 209.
Bog ore in ponds, 307, 426-427.
Bonum, or Boneham, George, 604; autograph of, 604; life of, 604.
Book of Evidences and Lands, 558.
Booth, Benjamin, Sr., 573.
Boots and shoes, manufacture of, 295, 296-298; methods of, 294-295.
Bordman, or Burman, Thomas, 585, 593, 622; life of, 586.
Boston, 124, 139, 171, 178, 220, 268, 413, 434, 561, 580.
Boston Common, 169, 213.
Boston Harbor, 171.
Boucher, Rev. Oliver, 494.
Boundaries of town, xviii-xx, 28; agreement as to, 561, 562; Bridgewater, 549, 553-554; incorporation, 546, 557-558; Plymouth, 565, 566; running of, 559-560; Taunton, 546.
Bounty paid for linen, 213.

Bourne, Capt. Abner, 136, 200, 203, 278, 288; house of, 278.
Bourne, Richard, 19.
Bourne, S. S., 302.
Bourne, Capt. and Major William, 201, 205, 254, 288, 380; life of, 289.
Bourne house, picture of the old, 278.
Bowdoin, Gov. James, life of, 374-376; portrait of, 375.
Bowen, Rev. William H., 485.
Box factories at Eddyville, 347.
Box-board mills, xxi; at Soule Neighborhood, 351; at South Middleboro, 339; at Waterville, 349.
Braddock, General, 92.
Bradford, Col. Gamaliel, 139.
Bradford, Joseph, 603; life of, 604.
Bradford, Gov. William, 8, 193.
Bradford, Capt. and Major William, 195, 551, 596, 602, 603; life of, 597-598; inscription on tombstone, 598.
Bradford, William, Jr., 621.
Bragg, Rev. Jesse K., ministry of, 461.
Braley, Job, 408.
Brandywine, battle of, 125.
Brass, 209.
Brayley, Ambrose, 573.
Brayton, George, 288.
Bread, preparation and kinds of, used in 18th century, 216.
Brett, Elder Pliny, 489.
Brewster, William, 552, 564, 585, 593, 596; life of, 586.
Bricklayers, 302.
Bricks, manufacture of, at Purchade, 396; at Soule Neighborhood, 351.
Bridges, price paid for labor on, 581.
Bridgewater, xviii, 53, 80, 84, 123, 227, 269, 392, 398, 401, 433, 437, 462, 504, 509, 549, 553, 554, 567, 572.
Bridgewater Path, description of, 504.
Bridle-paths, 506.
Briggs, Ensign Abiatha, 163.
Briggs, Rev. Avery, 254; ministry of, 473.
Briggs, Capt. Ebenezer, Jr., 201.
Briggs, Elder Ebenezer, 291, 481-482, 483; portrait of, 481.
Briggs, Capt. Elisha, 201.
Briggs, Levi, 254.
Briggs, Malborne, life of, 437.
Briggs, Lieut. William S., 173.
Briggs house, 277.
British fleet in Revolution, appearance and withdrawal of, 136.
British forces, 125; at Newport, 134.
British navy, 157.
British officers, actions of, 392-393.

Broadaxes, 207.
Brooms in 18th century, 217.
Brown, Corp. Charles I., 182, 186.
Brown, Rev. Frederic C., 491.
Brown, Joseph, 288.
Brown, Peter, 54, 359, 552, 585, 594, 596; life of, 586.
Brown, Samuel P., 267.
Brown, Rev. Theophilus, 486, 487, 489.
Brown, Rev. Thomas G., 487.
Brown, William L., 290.
Brown bread, 209.
Brush, 196.
Bryant, Dr., 239.
Bryant, Capt. Arad, 202.
Bryant, Caleb, 114.
Bryant, Ira, 317.
Bryant, Isaac, 347.
Bryant, Corp. and Capt. James W., 172, 188.
Bryant, Jesse, 373, 376.
Bryant, Corp. William F., 188.
Bryant, Rev. William M., 486.
Bugles, 197.
Bull Run, battle of, 170, 176; second battle of, 170, 177, 179, 185.
Bullard, N. Josephine, 266.
Bullets, 196.
Bump, Clark, 154.
Bump, Bumpus, or Bumpas, Edward, 34, 35, 552, 585, 586, 593, 596; descendants of, 393; life of, 36-37.
Bump, James, 197.
Bump, James S., 394.
Bump, or Bumpus, John, 34; life of, 37.
Bump, Bumpus, or Bumpas, Joseph, 34, 359, 393, 563, 593, 622; autograph of, 37; life of, 37.
Bump, Josiah C., 433.
Bump, Lavinia (Mrs. Tom Thumb), 394; residence of, 394.
Bump, Capt. Nathaniel, life of, 393, 394.
Bump, William E., 394.
Bump Neighborhood, 165.
Bumpas, Joseph, Jr., 563.
Bumpus, Hannah, 596, 597.
Bumpus, or Bumpas, Philip, 225, 560.
Bunker Hill, battle of, 115.
Burdan's sharpshooters, 179.
Burgess, Betsey T., 468.
Burgess, Cornelius, 468.
Burgess, Corp. F. O., 188.
Burgess, Rev. I. J., 480.
Burgess, Melissa, 468.
Burgoyne, Gen., 125, 131, 139.
Burial customs of the 18th century, 220-221.

INDEX

Burke, Rev. John B., 485.
Burnside, Gen., 178, 179, 184.
Business, changes in, xxi.
Business Men's Club, 633.
Butler, Gen. B. F., 185.
Byram, Rev. Mr., 462.

Cabot Club, 633.
Caches, 4.
Cadman, or Codman, William, 552, 563, 616, 621; life of, 617.
Cadohunset Brook, 627.
Calhoun, J. C., 168.
Calico, 215.
Callihan, Corp. Jeremiah, 190.
Cambric, 212.
Camp, Abram, 454-455.
Camp Joe Hooker, 172, 173.
Camp Jourdan, 172.
Campbell, Onesimus, 463.
Canada, 157.
Canals, 360, 127, 580.
Candles, 211, 212, 217.
Candlesticks, 211.
Canedy, Alexander, 99; life of, 435-436.
Canedy, Capt. William, 90, 91, 116, 155, 200, 435, 496.
Canedy Family (Lakeville), tradition concerning, 434-435.
Canedy's Corner, 475.
Cann, Rev. Frank S., 474.
Cannon and cannon-balls, manufacture of (Titicut), 407.
Canonicus, revolt of, 193.
Canteen, 196.
Cape Cod, 21, 582.
Cape Cod Railroad, 304.
Capen, Sergt. R. S., 190.
Capen, Sergt. Major Robert S., 190.
Card-playing in 18th century, 217.
Carle, Sergt. William H., 181.
Carpenter, Rev. George, 480.
Carpenter shops, at Purchade, 397.
Carpets of the 18th century, 214-215.
Carriage roads, 506.
Carroll, Rev. J. S., 487.
Carrollton, 173.
Carter, Richard, 397.
Cartways, 572.
Cart-wheels, 207.
Carver, 477, 613.
Carver, Capt. Josiah, 203.
Cary, Col. Simeon, 122.
Case, Edward, 28.
Catalogue of members of First Church, 639-686; index of, 640-644.

Cathcart, Rev. Samuel M., 469.
Catlett's Station, 177.
Cavalry, in local militia, 201, 205; in Rebellion, 189-191; in War of 1812, 159.
Cemeteries, 334, 383, 634-637.
Central Baptist Church, 482-485, 636; pictures of, 253, 255, 483.
Central Congregational Church, 467-469; chapel built, 467; picture of, 468.
Central Methodist Church, 486-488; picture of, 488.
Centreville, 178.
Chaddock, Rev. Calvin, 466.
Chadwick, Rev. M. S., 486.
Chamberlain, Dr. William, 244.
Chancellorsville, battle of, 170, 176, 177, 178, 180, 185, 189.
Chapin, Dr., 244.
Chapman, Rev. Calvin, ministry of, 462.
Character of early settlers, 29, 32, 33.
Charles, David, 407.
Charles River, 10.
Charleston harbor, 187.
Chase, John, 596, 598.
Chesapeake Bay, 158.
Chesemuttock (an Indian), 355.
Chickahominy, 179.
Chickamauga, battle of, 170.
Chickataubut, 10, 399; deed of, 399.
Chimneys, 208.
Chipman, Elder John, 552, 564, 621; autograph of, 622; life of, 622, 623.
Choules, John O., 254.
Christian Church (Lakeville), 486.
Christmas, 209.
Church, Capt. Benjamin, 81, 89, 428, 563, 613, 615, 628, 629, 630; autograph of, 81; campaign of, 81-86.
Church, Richard, 55.
Church councils, provisions to pay for expenses of, 568.
Churches, 439-494; Advent, 494; Baptist, 469-485; Christian, 486; Congregationalist, 439-469; Episcopal, 492; Methodist, 486-489; Roman Catholic, 493-494; Unitarian, 490-491; United Brethren, 480; Universalist, 490.
Churches, see Ecclesiastical History; act concerning, 439; first built in Plymouth, 55; First Church, 309-317, 354, 439-459; Halifax, 354, 462; Indian, 17-20, 400, 401, 440; North Rochester, 466.
Churchill, Asaph, 247, 376.

Churchill, John, 563, 593.
Churchill, Capt. Perez, 134, 138, 201.
Churchill, William, 593.
Cider, 212, 216.
Citizen's Aid Society, 633.
"City, The," 396.
Civil history (1654–1839), 544–581.
Civil War, 168.
Clapp, Ebenezer, 448.
Clapp, Edward, 448.
Clarinets, 197.
Clark, Major, 348.
Clark, Abishai T., life of, 304.
Clark, Amos, 410.
Clark, Augusta, 486.
Clark, Corp. Darius B., 182.
Clark, Mrs. Doritie, 612, 613.
Clark, Lieut. Ezra, 137.
Clark, Harrison, 348.
Clark, Capt. Horatio G., 201.
Clark, James M., 270.
Clark, Dr. Joseph, 239, 277, 496, 497; life of, 276.
Clark, Joseph, Jr., 277.
Clark, Robert, 410.
Clark, Dr. Samuel, 239, 278; life of, 275; picture of house of, 275.
Clark, Samuel, 612.
Clark, Susan S., 486.
Clark, Thomas, 275.
Clark, Thurston, 54.
Clark, or Clarke, William, 34, 601; life of, 38.
Clark, Mrs. Zilpha M., 469.
Clark House, description of, 275; picture of the Dr., 275.
Clark's Island, 275.
Clarke, Nathaniel, 558.
Clarke, Mrs. Rebecca Scollay, 218, 276.
Clear Pond, 419.
Clerks, Town, 530–531.
Clocks, manufacture of, 411.
Coat of arms, king's, 272.
Cobb, Andrew B., 270.
Cobb, Ebenezer, 462.
Cobb, Gershom, 34, 449, 517, 518, 546, 552, 612, 621; life of, 38; death of, 75.
Cobb, or Cob, John, 34, 35, 560, 563, 572, 612; autograph of, 65; life of, 65.
Cobb, John, Jr., 594.
Cobb, Capt. Jonathan, 202.
Cobb, or Cob, Jonathan, 563, 564, 568.
Cobb, Lydia, 462.
Cobb, Lieut. Sylvanus, 128.
Cobb, Capt. Sylvester F., 202.

Coffins, how made, 220.
Colby, Harrison Gray Otis, life of, 414.
Colby, Rev. Philip, 270, 407, 414; ministry of, 465.
Cold Harbor, battle of, 170, 177, 184, 185, 187, 189.
Cole, Andrew, 482.
Cole, Lieut. Archipus, 121.
Cole, Hugh, 545.
Cole, James, Sr., 603, 627; life of, 627.
Cole, Capt. Nathaniel, 200.
Colonial laws, 196, 495, 530.
Commissioners, 60.
Committee of Correspondence, 109; letters of clerk of, 111–114; members of, 110.
Committee of Inspection, 155.
Committee of Safety, 155.
Committee to look into sale of Indian lands at Muttock appointed, 356; report of, 358–359.
Compromise of 1850, 168.
Comstock, Dr. William W., life of, 243; portrait of, 243.
Conant, Rev. Sylvanus, 313, 350, 459; autograph of, 314; death of, 575; house of, 315; inscription on gravestone of, 316; life of, 314, 315; ministry of, 447–449.
Confectionery, 198.
Confiscation of Indian arms, 547.
Congregational churches: Central, 467–469, picture of, 468; First, see First Church; Halifax, 462; Independent, 467; Lakeville, 460–462; North Rochester, 466; Separatist, 467; Titicut, 462–466, pictures of, 415, 466.
Conlin, Rev. ——, 493.
Connecticut, 89, 136.
Constables of town from 1669, 517, 518, 546, 549.
Constitutional Conventions, members of, 542.
Continental Congress, 114, 221, 223; act of, 196, 223.
Continental money, depreciation of, 464.
Cook, Francis, 551, 585, 593, 596; life of, 587.
Cookies, 217.
Coombs, Combe, or Combs, Francis, 34, 35, 39, 76, 287, 306, 517, 518, 545, 549, 551, 552, 564, 621, 622, 628; life of, 38–40.
Coombs, Rev. Henry C., 474, 480; life of, 281; portrait of, 281.
Coombs, Rev. Isaac W., 474.

INDEX

Coombs, James M., 267.
Coombs, Mrs. Mary, 39.
Coombs, Rev. Simeon, 253; ministry of, 476-477.
Coombs Tavern, 39.
Copeland, Dr. George W., 300.
Copeland, Marcus M., 268.
Corbitant, attack upon Squanto and Hobomok, 24; chief of Pocassets, 24.
Core Creek, 172.
Corn, xxi, 26, 31, 89, 501, 556; how planted by Indians, 4; used for ballots in voting, 31; legend of, 3-4.
Corn gardens, 3.
Cotley, Shute, and Littleworth farm, 28.
Cotton, Rev. John, 18, 354, 462.
Cotton-batting mills, 430.
Cotton-gin, 206.
Cotton mills, xxi, 430.
County commissioners, established 1828, 543; list of, 543.
County courts, clerk of, 542.
Court End, 272, 278.
Court of Assistants, 557.
Court of Insolvency, Register of, 542.
Court of Probate and Insolvency, Register of, 542.
Court of Sessions, judge of, 543.
Covington, Thomas, 250, 388.
Crafts, Rev. Thomas, ministry of, 461.
Cranberry bogs at Rocky Meadow, 335.
Crandon, Benjamin, 267.
Crandon, Rev. Philip, 487, 489.
Cranes, 208.
"Crater, battle of the," 189.
Cressey, Rev. ——, 492.
Crocheting, 215.
Crocker, Rev. E. R., 490.
Crossman, Alpha, 378.
Crowe, or Crow, William, 54, 60, 553, 629.
Crown Point, 99, 115.
Crows, 567.
Cudworth house, history of, 436, 437; picture of, 436.
Culver, Rev. David, 487.
Cummings, Dr. C. S., 244.
Cups, description of, 209.
Currency, issued during the Revolution, 221, 222, 223; depreciation of, 222, 223, 464, 577; value of Continental, 224; votes relating to, 577-579.
Cushing, Matthew H., 300, 301.
Cushing, Rev. Perez Lincoln, 263.

Cushman, Mr., 564.
Cushman, Adoniram J., 468.
Cushman, Mrs. Ann S., 469.
Cushman, Rev. Bartlett, 486.
Cushman, Clarence L., 271.
Cushman, Elkanah, 622; life of, 623.
Cushman, Herbert L., 271.
Cushman, Hercules, 227, 254, 457, 542; life of, 232, 233.
Cushman, Isaac, 622; life of, 623; autograph of, 623.
Cushman, Senior Major Jacob, 205.
Cushman, Capt. Joseph, 162.
Cushman, Elder Thomas, 304, 551, 603, 616, 629; life of, 604-605.
Cushman, Zenas, 457.

Daland, Rev. George, 480.
Dams, 35, 288, 305, 359, 360, 378, 407, 408, 433, 499, 501, 568, 580.
Dancing, attitude towards, in 18th century, 217.
Danforth, Rev. Samuel, 18.
Danson, or Dawson, George, 34, 386, 622; life of, 40; manner of death of, 57, 75.
Danson Brook, 40, 75, 386; view of, 79.
Darling, Ens. Benjamin, 118.
Darling, Corp. Thomas, 198.
Darling, Thomas, 388.
Dartmouth, 80, 428, 547, 549, 550.
Dartmouth Path, description of the, 504.
David, Stephen, conveyance of land to Titicut Parish, 20.
Davis, Corp. Nehemiah D., 182.
Davis, Rev. William F., 488.
DeNormandie, Rev. C. Y., 490.
Dean, Corp. Alexis C., 184.
Dean, John, 28.
Dean, Steven, 596, 598.
Dean, W. H., 297.
Dean, Walter, 28.
Deane, Benjamin, 461.
Deane, Corp. David W., 189.
Deane, Steven, 552.
Declaration of Independence, signing of, 124.
Dedham Plain, 550.
Deeds, early, 311, 312, 400; rights reserved to take ore, 307.
Deeds, Indian, 357-358, 399, 584-585, 595-596, 600-601, 602-603, 608, 609-610, 611-612, 614-616, 619-621.
Delano, or Dillino, Philip, 563, 585, 594, 596, 616, 621; life of, 587.
Delano, Thomas, 225, 621; life of, 623.

Delaware River, 125.
Democrats, 160.
Dentistry, early methods of, 238.
Deputies to General Court, none sent, 1671, 546; 1673, 547; 1675, 549; 1682, 555.
Deputies to Plymouth Colony Court, 533-534; duties, expenses, and choice of, 533; duties enlarged, 533; list of, 533-534.
Dermer, Capt. Thomas, 21.
Detroit, surrender of, 157.
Diaries of, Abner Barrows, 95-98; Mr. ——Bennett, 466; Peter Oliver, Jr., 148-150; Miss Rebecca Scollay, 272.
Dickey, Rev. R. B., ministry of, 480.
Dickinson, Rev. William C., 469.
Dike, Col. Nicholas, 123.
Dilley, Miss Anna, 247.
Dining-room, 210.
Dishes, used by early settlers, 30-32; used in 18th century, 209.
District schools, 248; description of, 247-249.
Doane, George E., 300, 301.
Dodd, Rev. Stephen G., 469.
Doggett, or Doged, John, 225, 563, 594; life of, 153-154.
Doggett, Samuel, 594.
Doggett, Simeon, 430, 497; life of, 153; picture of house of, 153.
Doggett, Rev. Simeon, 153.
Doggett, Rev. Thomas, 153.
Doggett, Thomas, 621; autograph of, 623; life of, 623-624.
Doggett, William E., 153, 378.
Doggett House, picture of, 153.
Done, Daniel, 626, 627.
Dorchester, 268.
Dorrance, F. B., 275.
Dotey, Edward, 604; life of, 587.
Dotey, Thomas, 585; life of, 587.
Drake, Dr. Ebenezer W., life of, 242; portrait of, 242.
Drake, Rev. Ellis R., 469.
Drake Cemetery, 637.
Dred Scott Decision, 168.
Dress, of early settlers, 218-219; of 18th century, 215, 216, 218-221, 367, 375.
Drew, Major Benjamin, Jr., 204, 267.
Drew, Elizabeth, 462.
Drew, John, Jr., 462.
Drew, Sarah, 462.
Drewry's Bluff, 184, 187.
Driggs, Capt. Leonard, 382.
Drummond, Gov., letter from Isaac Winslow to, 435.

Drums, 197, 571.
Drunkenness, how regarded, 319; law passed in regard to, 319.
Dudley, Gov., 11.
Dunbar, Daniel, life of, 146.
Dunbar, Jesse, life of, 146-147.
Dunham, Calvin, work of, 216.
Dunham, or Donham, John or Jonathan, 34, 517, 518, 547, 549, 551, 563, 564, 601, 612, 616, 621; life of, 41.
Dunham, or Donham, John or Jonathan, Jr., 548, 604, 612; life of, 41-42.
Dunham, Joseph, life of, 601.
Dunham, Josiah, 392.
Dunham, Mrs. Mary, 469.
Dunham, Samuel, 604; life of, 605.
Dunham Pond, 419.
Dunlap, Timothy L., 288.
Durfee, Nathan, 510.
Dutch ovens, 209.
Duxbury, 8, 146, 159, 582, 601, 613.
Dwellings, enclosure of, 194; protection against fire of, 194.
Dwight, President Timothy, tables of longevity, xxii-xxiii.
Dyer, Rev. Nathan Tirrell, 459.

Early purchases from the Indians, 548, 582-630; boundary lines how marked, 583; date of first, 583; Eight Men's Purchase, 626, 627; fairness of pilgrims in, 582; Great Men's Purchase, 602; Little Lotmen's Purchase, 602-608; Major or Five Men's Purchase, 600-602; map of, 582; Middleboro, purchase of, 583; minor purchases, 627-630; old oak tree, 583, 584, picture of, 583; Purchade Purchase, 594-600; Sixteen Shilling Purchase, 618-626; South Purchase, 613-618; Twelve Men's Purchase, 610-613; Twenty-six Men's Purchase, 584-594; Wood's Purchase, 608-610.
Early settlers, 1, 2, 15, 21, 28, 29; before King Philip's War, 29-67; character of, xxi; first, 54; from Plymouth, xx-xxi; hardships of, 32, 33; lists of, 34, 35; lives of, 35-67; religion of, 439.
East Freetown, 467.
East Middleboro, 267, 270.
East Middleboro post-office, 270, 348.
Eastern Bay State Regiment, 185.
Eaton, Amos H., 263.
Eaton, Andrew M., 515.
Eaton, Benjamin, life of, 601.
Eaton, Francis, 394.

INDEX   697

Eaton, Lieut.-Col. Oliver, 205; life of, 413; portrait of, 413.
Eaton, Samuel, 34, 35, 225, 517, 560, 564, 621; life of, 42-43.
Eaton, Corp. Samuel, 198.
Eaton, Solomon, 413; portrait of, 412.
Eaton, Solomon K., 413, 498.
Eaton, Rev. William, 317; ministry of, 156-157.
Eaton, Williams, 412.
Eaton Cemetery, 637.
Eaton Family School, 263.
Eaton's Inn, S., 268, 412, 413.
Ecclesiastical history, 439-494.
Eddy, Sergt. Albert, 190.
Eddy, Andros, 343.
Eddy, Anna C., 270.
Eddy, Rev. Clarence, 466.
Eddy, or Edie, Ebenezer, 346, 563.
Eddy, Jabez, petition of, xviii.
Eddy, John, 346; almanacs of, 343; life of, 343-344, 624; printing-office of, 343.
Eddy, Capt. Joshua, 139, 321, 335, 346, 347, 348, 376, 388, 496, 497, 575; life of, 344-346; portrait of, 344.
Eddy, Joshua M., 270, 347, 349.
Eddy, Morton, 346.
Eddy, Nathaniel, 270, 346, 348, 349.
Eddy, Eddie, Edy, or Eedey, Obadiah, 34, 35, 343, 518, 549, 560, 563, 594; life of, 44.
Eddy, Eady, Eddie, or Edey, Samuel, 344, 347, 359, 448, 552, 563, 585, 594, 596, 624; autograph of, 343; life of wife of, 342; life of, 342-343, 587-588; residence of, 347.
Eddy, Sergt. Samuel, 198.
Eddy, Samuel, Jr., 343, 347; life of, 347.
Eddy, Seth, 575.
Eddy, W. Osgood, 299.
Eddy, William C., 344, 349.
Eddy, William S., 346, 348, 349; portrait of, 349.
Eddy, Eddie, Edey, or Edie, Zachariah, 34, 54, 147, 227, 254, 315, 321, 343, 346, 551, 563, 616, 622, 635; letter from, 404-405; life of, 43, 230-232; office of, 347; portrait of, 232; residence of, 346.
Eddy's furnace, description of, 348-349.
Eddyville, 247, 270, 342-348.
Edson, Abiezer, 464.
Edson, Capt. Charles F., 180.
Edson, Capt. Josiah, Jr., 574.

Education, 245-263; methods of early settlers, 32.
Edwards, Rev. Henry L., 466.
Eight Men's Purchase, 626-627, 628; description of, 626; proprietors of, 627; vote in regard to, 626.
Elder's Pond, 419, 422; description of, 429.
Eldridge, Dr. Benjamin, 244.
Electric light plants, 290.
Eliot, Rev. John, labors of, 16, 17, 19.
Ellis, Dr. George L., 244, 296.
Ellis, Joel, 571.
Ellis, Col. Southworth, 457.
Ellis, Thomas, 114.
Ellis, Capt. William, 347.
Ellis, William, 562, 563.
Elmes, Ens. Ignatious, 94.
Emery, Rev. Samuel Hopkins, 405, 466, 470.
England, 146, 148, 154, 155, 195, 212, 320.
Episcopal Church, 492; picture of, 492.
Essay and Literary Journal, 267.
Everett, Rev. Thomas J., 488.
Ewer Cemetery, 636.
Ewer, Rev. Ebenezer, 487.

Fairbanks, Rev. George G., 485.
Fair Haven, 135, 160, 161.
Fair Oaks, 177.
Fall Brook, 303, 305, 308, 460, 637; business at, xxi.
Fall Brook Furnace, 305.
Fallowell, or Followell, Gabriel, 564, 603, 616, 622; life of, 605.
Farm implements, 206-207.
Farnsworth, Rev. B. F., 254.
Farragut, Admiral, 170, 174.
Farwell, Frank S., 288.
Faunce, Joseph, 594.
Faunce, or Fance, Thomas, 563, 594; life of, 612-613.
Fay, Lucien D., 258.
Fearing, Senior Major Israel, 128; letter of, 129-130.
Feather-beds, 211.
Felix, 420, 427, 568, 630.
Felix, Thomas, pastor of Indian church, 20.
Fidelity, oath of, 33; list of men, 560.
Fifes, 197.
Fines, relating to, blackbirds' and crows' heads, 567; church, not attending, 59; herring privileges, 501, 502; highways, repairing, 506; Indian lands, 582; sabbath-breaking, 40, 342;

town meetings, not attending, 496, 519, 555; war, refusing to go to, 89, 350.
Finney, Corp. Albert F., 188.
Finney, Ebenezer, 446.
Finney, Ens. Nelson, 92.
Finney, Robert, 545.
Fire district, 513-516; bounds of present, 516; incorporation of, 515; organization and officers of, 514, 515.
Fire engines, apparatus, 515; first, 514.
Firearms, 193, 194, 195, 196.
Fire-frames, manufacture of, 407.
Fireplaces, 208, 397.
Fires, early methods of fighting, 514; military companies to assist at, 513; protection against, 194, 513.
First Baptist Church (Titicut), 469-474; pictures of, 470, 473.
First Brigade, 173, 176, 179, 184, 185, 189.
First Cadet Corps, 196.
First Church, xvii, 18, 34, 35, 130, 197, 220, 379, 439, 460, 462, 467, 468, 477, 544, 592; first meeting-house, 441, 445; original parish of, 309; picture of pulpit, 456; pictures of, 311, 457; polity of, 442, 443, present meeting-house, 312, 456, 457; records of, 441-442; second meeting-house, 311, 445-446, 449; third meeting-house, 450-454; used as town house, 495-496.
First Provincial Congress of Mass., 543.
Fisher, Rev. Ward, 480.
Fisheries, herring, 498-503.
Fitch, Lieut. J. Arthur, 187, 188.
Fitz, Harvey, 254.
Fitz, Rev. Hervey, life and ministry of, 484; portrait of, 484.
Fitz-John Porter's Division, 184.
Five Men's Purchase. See Major's or Five Men's Purchase.
Flags, 571.
Flails, 207, 216.
Flax, preparation and use of, 212-213.
Flaxseed, 213.
Fleeces, preparation of, in 18th century, 214.
Flintlock muskets, 195.
Flints, 196.
Fobes, Mr., 464.
Fobes, Abigail, 463.
Fobes, Abigail, Jr., 463.
Fobes, Esther, 463.
Fobes, Joshua, 20.
Food of early settlers, 30-32.
Foot companies, 195.
Forbes, Rev. Dr., 228.

Forbes, Rev. Isaac B., 489.
Forges, 288, 417, 433, 437.
Forks, 209.
Fort Bisland, 173.
Fort Donelson, 170.
Fort Duquesne, defeat and recapture of, 92.
Fort Edwards, 99.
Fort Harrison, 187.
Fort Henry, 98, 170.
Fort Sumter, 168.
Fort Totten, 172.
Fort Wagner, 187.
Fort Warren, 176, 178, 185.
Fort William Henry, 95.
Fortress Monroe, 171.
Forts, 593; abandonment of, 78; burning of, 80; description of, 74, 277; location of, 74; men in, 34, 593-594.
Foshay, Rev. J. H., 485.
Foster, General, 184.
Foster, Mr., 247.
Foster, Capt. Richard B., 201.
Foundries, 360; at Titicut, 407.
Four Corners, xxi, xxii, 13, 103, 252, 254, 267, 272-302, 380, 390, 411, 429, 430, 467; view of, in 1832, xx; views of, 297, 300; views of, in 1850, 298; views of, at present time, 299.
Four Mile line, 462.
Fourth Baptist Church (Lakeville), United Brethren, 426, 427, 480-482; called Pond Church, 480; organization of church of United Brethren, 481.
Fourth Plymouth District Court, 540-541; clerk of, 541; establishment and jurisdiction of, 540; justice of, 540-541.
France, 336-339.
France (in Europe), 336.
Franklin, Colonel, 176.
Franklin, Benjamin, 217, 321, 322, 376.
Franklin stove, 217.
Fraternal organizations, 631-633.
Fredericksburg, 178, 185, 187.
Freeman, Capt. Morton, 202.
Freemen of town, 33, 533, 553; lists of, 34, 517, 546, 560.
Freetown, xx, 130, 145, 428, 580.
Free-Will Baptist Church (Lakeville), 475.
French, 193, 336.
French and Indian Wars, 88-99; diary concerning, 95-98; place of enlistment, 320; soldiers in, 90-93, 94-95, 99; tax for, 89.

INDEX

French neutrals, 99–100; bills for their support, 100; number in Middleboro, 99, 100.
Fryer, Dr. Winsor F., 244.
Fugitive Slave Law, 168.
Fuller, Lieut., 594.
Fuller, Ebenezer, 462.
Fuller, Elizabeth, 462
Fuller, Hannah, 462.
Fuller, Isaac, 50, 563.
Fuller, Dr. Isaac, 354, 446; life of, 238–239.
Fuller, Major Isaac, 205.
Fuller, Capt. John, 373.
Fuller, John, 462, 560, 563.
Fuller, Capt. and Lieut. Matthew, 552, 564, 585, 596, 616, 622; life of, 588.
Fuller, Rev. Samuel, 32, 34, 35, 44, 76, 220, 495, 496, 551, 552, 585, 588, 593, 596, 621, 634; autograph of, 309; call to Middleboro, 440–441; gravestone of, 637; inscription on gravestone of, 310; life of, 309–310; ministry of, 443.
Fuller, Seth, 410.
Fuller, Mrs. Seth, 466.
Fulling-mills, xxi, 407.
Funeral customs of the 18th century, 220.
Furnace, the, 348.
Furnaces, blast, xxi, 209, 298, 305, 339, 360, 378, 412; picture of site of old Fall Brook, 305.

Gage, Gen., 109.
Gaines's Mills, 179.
Gainesville, 187.
Gammon, Sergt. George N., 185.
Gammons, Alanson, 486.
Gammons, E. H., 270.
Gammons, Rev. John G., 489.
Gammons, Rev. Roland, 487.
Gammons Cemetery, 637.
Gardner, Sir Christopher, life of, 26, 27.
Garrison houses, 277, 328, 431; description of, 58, 277.
Gay, Corp. Erastus E., 175.
General Assembly, 570.
General Court Acts relating to, arms, Indian, 547; arms, providing, 554, 560; boundaries of town, 549, 553, 557–558; churches, organization of, 439; Coombs, Francis, 40; dancing, 42, 43; drunkenness, 310; flax and linen, 213; French and Indian Wars, 88; guns, carrying to church, 75; highways, 506, 508, 509; houses remote from public worship, 550; incorporation of town, 546, 557–558; Indian lands, 356, 358, 548, 582, 630; Indian reservation, guarding of, 400; Indians, men for expedition against, 547; land at Assawampsett Pond, 630; land purchases, 548, 628, 630; lands, disposition of, etc., Thomas Cushman et als., 629; Little Lotmen's Purchase, 545, 603, 604; lottery for rebuilding Titicut Bridge, 408–409; Major's Purchase, 548, 601; military companies, 194; ministry, support of, 552; Old and New Lights, 448; ordinaries, 60; Purchade Purchase, 594–596; Ransome, Lemuel, 155; rebuilding town, 58; resettling town, 549, 550; Revolution, expenses of, 130–131; Sassamon, John, 420; schools, 245; selectmen, 519; town clerks, 530; town deputies, 533; town treasurers, 531; Twelve Men's Purchase, 612; Twenty-six Men's Purchase, 584; Vaughan, George, 60; woolen and silk garments, 218.
General Court of the Province of Mass. Bay in New England, representatives to, 534–538.
George III, 106, 145, 322.
Georgia, 170.
Germantown, battle of, 125.
Gettysburg, battle of, 170, 177, 178, 180, 185.
Ghent, 167.
Gibbs, or Guibs, John, 561, 563.
Gilbert, John, Sr., 28.
Gill, Rev. Jason, 487.
Gilman, Dr., 244.
Gingerbread, 217; sugar, 198.
Goddard, Mrs. Almira, 469.
Godfrey, Rufus, 268.
Goldsboro, 184.
Goodwin, Mrs., 410, 413.
Goodwin, Charles, 410.
Goodwin, Gen. Nathaniel, 159, 165.
Gorges, Sir Ferdinando, expedition of, 21.
Gorum, John, 547.
Gosport Navy Yard, 171, 178.
Gould, Linus A., 258.
Grand Army of the Republic, 192; history of, 631–632.
Grand Inquest, members of, 549.
Grand Jury, action of, for not employing a schoolmaster, 246.
Grant, Rev. George A., 488.

Grant, Rev. Henry M., 469.
Grant, Gen. U. S., 171, 180.
Gravestones, 220.
Gray, Edward, 47, 54, 67, 551, 564, 585, 593, 596, 602, 603, 610, 612, 616, 621, 629; life of, 588–589.
Great Awakening, the, 446, 462, 463.
Great Britain, 157, 158, 167.
Great Cedar Swamp, 386.
Great Court at Boston, 564.
Great Men's Purchase, 602; date of, 602; description of, 602; disposition by court and purchasers of, 602.
Great Quittacus Pond, 263, 303, 339, 419; description of, 429.
Green, the, 309–328, 346, 381, 634; parish set off, xviii.
Green, Dr. Charles, 257.
Green, William, 556.
Gridirons, 209.
Grinnell, Charles E., 380.
Grist-mills, xxi, 289, 290, 305, 306, 378, 390, 407.
Grover's Brigade, 178.
Gun shops, 407.
Guns, 75, 212; description of, used in 1675, 76–77; permission to carry, 556.
Gurnet, 159.
Gurney, Rev. David, autograph of, 465; house of, 406; life of, 406; ministry of, 465.
Gye, George, 155–156.

Hackett, John, 460.
Halberds, 195, 571; picture of, 58.
Hale, Rev. William Bayard, 492.
Halifax, xvii, 8, 55, 59, 145, 343, 351–354, 490; church at, history of, 462; date of incorporation of, 462.
Hall, Dr. Edward I., 244.
Hall, Rev. Silas, 474; ministry of, 472, 473.
Hallowell, Gabriel, 551.
Hamilton Crossing, 187.
Hammer shops, 391.
Hammond, George A., 297.
Hanaford, Rev. Howard Alcott, 459.
Hancock, Gen., 177.
Hancock, John, 114, 155.
Hand Rock, description of, 77; picture of, 77.
Hand-looms, 214, 308; picture of, 214.
Hanover Court House, 179.
Harlow, Major Branch, 205, 542; life of, 286–287; portrait of, 286.
Harlow, Capt. Ezra, 200, 203.
Harlow, James H., 301.

Harlow, Capt. Joseph S., 169, 172.
Harlow, Sergt. Josiah, 124.
Harlow, Rev. Lemuel, 487.
Harlow, Thomas S., 394.
Harlow, Sergt. W. H., 188.
Harlow, Sergt. William, 551, 563, 604, 614, 621; life of, 605–606.
Harrington, Herbert A., 297, 300.
Harris, Joseph, 636.
Harrison, Sergt. Edgar, 181.
Hartford, 167.
Hartford Convention, 167.
Hartland, Vt., 305.
Hartwell, Capt. George, 391, 635.
Harvey, Joseph, 463.
Harvey, Joseph, Jr., 463.
Haskell, Lieut. Elisha, 135.
Haskell, or Hascall, John, 34, 350, 560, 563, 567, 621; life of, 44–45.
Haskell, Hascall, Hascol, or Hascal, John, Jr., 616, 626, 627.
Haskell, Sergt. John T., 181, 186.
Haskell, or Hascall, Patience, 567.
Haskell, or Hascall, William, 564.
Huskins, Capt. Enoch, 200.
Haskins Neighborhood, 373, 412.
Haskit, John, 564.
Hat factory at Waterville, 349.
Hats, manufacture of (Four Corners), 291–292.
Hatcher's Run, 185.
Hathaway, Dr. Joseph, 415.
Hathaway, Paul, 415.
Hathaway, Savory C., 297.
Haversack, 196.
Hayne, Mr., 168.
Hayward, John, 564.
Heath, Gen., 136.
Heffords, Mr., work of, 411.
Heintzelman's corps, 178.
Hemphill, Rev. Joseph, 490.
Herring, 359, 570; agents appointed, 500; Assawampsett Brook, 574; Indian uses of, 498; number first allowed each inhabitant, 500; payment of town clerk's salary, 530, 555; picture of stick of, 500; present attitude of town as to, 503; protection by town of, 499, 500, 502; revenue received by town from sale of, 502; rule as to fish privilege, 503; votes relating to, 500–502, 558.
Herring fisheries, 498–503.
Hicks, Rev. Daniel, 486.
Hidden, Rev. Ephraim M., 459.
Higgins, Rev. O. R., 489.
High school, 249–252; appropriations

INDEX   701

for, 251; erection of building of, 251; law for establishment of, 249–250; picture of, 252; principals of, 251–252; report of committee on, 250, 251.
Highways, 505–510.
Hill, Rev. Alfred S., 474.
Hill, Rev. E. S., 480.
Hinckley, Gov., 19, 195.
Hinckley, Rev. Charles N., 489.
Hinckley, Sylvanus, 515.
Hinds, Capt. Abanoam, 201.
Hinds, Rev. Ebenezer, 93, 467, 475; life and ministry of, 476; portrait of, 476.
Hines, Anna, 483.
Hitchcock, Dr. Henry D., life of, 241.
Hitchcock, Mrs. Olivia A., 469.
Hoar, Col. Jonathan, 99.
Hoar, Lieut., Capt., Major, and Senior Major Peter, 133, 137, 200, 205, 481; life of, 429–430; residence of, 429.
Hoar, Capt. and Lieut. Samuel, 127, 132, 201.
Hoar, Samuel, 460.
Hobomok, 24.
Hodges, Corp. Francis M., 188.
Hodgson, Dr. Thomas S., 244.
Holbrook, Rev. ——, 480.
Holidays, 197.
Holland, 15, 107.
Hollow-ware, 305, 339, 348, 407.
Holloway, William, 573.
Holmes, Deacon ———, 411.
Holmes, Dr. Daniel S., 244.
Holmes, or Holms, John, 34, 35, 225, 563; life of, 65.
Holmes, John, Jr., life of, 65.
Holmes, Joseph, 352.
Holmes, Prudence, 483.
Holmes, Sergt.-Major R. H., 180.
Homespun goods, 213–214.
Hooker, Gen., 170, 176, 178.
Hooper, Mr., 339, 410.
Hooper, James, 463.
Hooper, William, 463.
Hope Rest Cemetery, 636.
Hopkins, Stephen, 22, 398.
Horses, xxi, 568, 581.
Horton, Rev. J. W., 480.
Hoskins, Haskins, or Hodskins, William, 34, 54, 460, 517, 546, 550, 552, 555, 585, 589, 593, 596; life and work of, 45–46, 530.
House of Representatives, 572; members of, 534–538; orders of, 569, 573–574.
House-cleaning in 18th century, 217–218.
Houses, xxi, 584; destroyed in King Philip's War, 56, 78, 80, 549; not to be erected remote from public worship, 550.
Houses, description of, after King Philip's War, 208–211, 389; after resettlement of town, 277; new garrison house, 58, 277; of early settlers, 30; used by people of 18th century, 207.
Hovey, James, 227.
Howard, John, 556, 560.
Howes, Corp. Charles A., 182.
Howland, Arthur, 563, 564.
Howland, Elizabeth, 547.
Howland, Isaac, 34, 35, 76, 77, 84, 195, 225, 305, 495, 506, 518, 552, 553, 554, 555, 556, 558, 559, 560, 561, 562, 563, 616, 622, 626, 634; autograph of, 46; life of, 46.
Howland, Jacob, 594.
Howland, John, 305, 547, 552, 564, 573, 585, 594, 596, 621; autograph of, 589; life of, 589.
Howland, Joshua, 573.
Howland, Sergt. Seth, 198.
Hubbard, Harry, 378.
Hubbard, Rev. William, ministry of, 479.
Hubs, manufacture of, at Titicut, 412.
Hudson, 139.
Huet, or Hewit, Solomon, 593, 616; life of, 617.
Hull, Rev. John, 487.
Hunt, Rev. Asa, 477; ministry of, 479.
Hunt, Rev. E. A., 489.
Hunt, Rev. George W., 488.
Hunter, Thomas, 553.
Husking-bees of 18th century, 217.
Hutchinson, Gov., 109; slave of, 105.
Hutchinson, Elisha, letter from Peter Oliver, Jr., to, 151; letter from Thomas Hutchinson, Jr., to, 152.
Hutchinson, Rev. Joseph, 474.
Hutchinson, Thomas, Jr., letter to Elisha Hutchinson, 152.
Hyde, Rev. Edward L., 488.

Implements of warfare used in King Philip's War, 76–77.
Implements used in 18th century, 206, 207.
Imported goods, attitude of women before Revolution towards, 213–214.
Incorporation of town, date of, 1, 517; order for, 546.
Independent Congregationalist Church, 467.

Indian Bend, 173.
Indian fort, 398; picture of site of old, 398.
Indian graves found, 317.
Indian legends concerning, Assawampsett Pond, 424–426; corn, 3–4; lying, 5–6.
Indian monument, picture of, 14.
Indian Paths, 29, 503–505, 506, 600.
Indian relics found, 307, 317.
Indian reservation, xx, 28; description of, 399–400; easterly boundary of, 583–584.
Indian wading-places, 74, 505.
Indian weirs, 359, 399, 499.
Indians, 1–14, 29, 56, 66–99, 193, 307, 355, 400, 401, 544, 547, 548, 553, 562, 567, 635; attack on town by, 36; churches of, 16–20, 440; customs of, 2–5; debts of, 612; extinction of, 14, 307, 400, 419; fishing privileges of, 498–499; guardians for, 573–574; lands of, 356–359, 401, 419, 562; last, 14; pastors, 18, 20; petitions concerning lands of, 568, 569; petitions of, 355, 356; picture of utensils of, 87; protection of rights of, 582; purchases from, 582–630; settlements, 1–2, 355, 401, 419; tribes, 2, 304; warfare of, 68–99.
Indians, Praying, 15–20.
Indigo, preparation and uses of, in 18th century, 214.
Infantry, in local militia, 202–205; in Rebellion, 171–189; in Revolution, 125–144; in War of 1812, 159, 161–165.
Ingals, Earl, 262.
Inhabitants of town, as freemen, 34, 517, 560; at resettlement, 551–552; before 1675, 33, 34, 35; before settlement, 29; in 1695, 563–564; purchases for, 582–630.
Inn, S. Eaton's, 412; description of, 413.
Inn-keepers, 413; to locate near meeting-house, 319; to clear their houses during church service, 319.
Inscriptions on gravestones of Backus, Rev. Isaac, 471–472; Bradford, Major William, 598; Conant, Rev. Sylvanus, 316; Dunham, John or Jonathan, Jr., 42; Fuller, Rev. Samuel, 310; Leonard, Capt. Zadock, 414; Miller, Francis, 47; Nelson, William and Ruth, 66; Palmer, Rev. Thomas, 328; Tomson, John, 58.
Insurrection of Indians, men furnished to meet, 547.

Introduction, xvii–xxiii.
Irish, John, 34, 518, 552, 622, 626, 627; life of, 47.
Iron, 208, 212, 221, 224, 348, 377.
Iron industry, 308, 377.
Iron ore, 348, 574; discovered in ponds, 426–427, 428.
Iron works at Titicut, 407, 408, 417, 418.
Island Number Ten, 170.
Islands: in Assawampsett Pond, 424; in Long Pond, 428; in Quittacus Pond let to plant and sow, 547.
Isle of Grand Menan, 154.

Jack-knives, 206, 216.
Jackson, Abraham, 563, 612, 616; life of, 613.
Jackson, C. S., 262.
Jackson, Dr. C. S., 244.
Jackson, Major Harry, 205.
Jackson, Miss Sarah, 469.
Jackson, Stonewall, 170.
Jacksonville, 187.
Jacobs, Col., 135.
Jenks, Elisha T., 299.
Jenks, Prof. J. W. P., 13, 251, 252, 254, 494; life and work of, 255–257; portrait of, 256.
Jenney, Rev. C. E., 489.
Jewelry worn in 18th century, 219, 220.
Job, Rev. Herbert Keightley, 466.
Joel (an Indian), 556.
John Brown Raid, 168.
Johnson, Sergt. George N., 182.
Johnson, Isaac, 394.
Johnson, Rev. M. F., 485.
Johnson, Rev. Oscar E., 488.
Jones, Rev. Ebenezer, 477; ministry of, 478–479.
Jones, Sergt. George W., 182.
Jones, John, 564, 616, 621.
Jones County, 172.
Jordan, Jordaine, Jordane, or Jourdaine, John, 551, 604, 622; life of, 606.
Justices of the peace, 519, 538–540; duties of position, 538–539; term of office, 538; list up to 1850, 539–540.

Kansas, 168.
Keith, Cyrus, 270.
Keith, Ephraim, 464.
Keith, James, 464.
Keith, Jared, 411.
Keith, N. Williams, 411.
Keith, Nahum, 410, 411, 412.

INDEX 703

Keith, Percy W., 270.
Keith, Samuel, 464.
Kelly, Rev. Jeremiah, ministry of, 473.
Kendall, Rev. Ezra, 471; ministry of, 472.
Kennebec River, 21.
Kent, Rev. Asa, 486, 487.
Kerr, Rev. Archibald, 480.
Ketchum, Rev. Charles J., 492.
Kettles used in 18th century, 208, 209, 211.
Kimball, Rev. Isaac, 254; ministry of, 479.
King, Asa, 482.
King, Dr. George, life of, 241.
King, Corp. James W., 182.
King, Sergt. John W., Jr., 182.
King, Lieut.-Col. and Col. Nathan, 204, 205, 301, 469, 542; life of, 295-296; portrait of, 295.
King, William, 563.
King, William A., 292.
King George, 431.
King Louis, 99.
King Philip, 9, 12, 16, 195, 274, 355, 547, 549, 628, 629, 630; capture of, 84, 85; character of, 68, 69; death of, 85; number of his tribe, 68; territory ruled by, 9, 419-420.
King Philip's Lookout, 73, 420; picture of, 73.
King Philip's War, 68-87, 88, 89, 208, 273, 274, 400, 420, 550; attack, 68, 549; cause of, 9, 68, 72; equipment of companies for, 76, 77, 195; expenses of, 552, 553; first Indian shot, 77; houses burned in, 57, 78, 80, 549; records of, destroyed, 517, 550; warriors in, 71.
King William's War, 88-89.
Kingman, C. W., 296, 301.
Kingman, Calvin D., 265, 296, 297, 300, 301.
Kingman, Hosea, 410.
Kingman, P. E., 296.
Kingsbury, Rev. A. W., 488.
Kingsbury, Rev. Josiah Weare, 459.
Kingston, 146, 159, 352.
Kinston, 172, 184.
Kitchen utensils used in 18th century, 208-209.
Kitchens, description of, 18th century, 208-210.
Knight, Dr. E. C., 244.
Knights of Columbus, history of, 633.
Knights of Honor, history of, 632.
Knights of Pythias, history of, 633.

Knitting, 215.
Knives of the 18th century, 206, 208, 209, 216.
Kuchamakin, 11.

Labor, prices paid by town for, 581.
Ladies' Aid Society, 632.
La Hogue, 160.
Laidlaw, Rev. Gilbert W., 492.
Lake, Arthur, 258.
Lake, Rev. E. H., 490.
Lake Champlain, 158.
Lake Erie, 158.
Lake Ontario, 158.
Lakenham, 61, 555.
Lakeville, 14, 172, 173, 198, 251, 269, 270, 303, 309, 317, 399, 412, 419-438, 474, 515, 540, 619, 637; changes in population, xxii; date of incorporation, 419; history of churches in, 460-462, 474-177, 480-482, 486; land in, xvii, xviii, xx; lands productive, xxi; map of ponds at, 419; men in secret expedition to R. I. in the Revolution from, 132; picture of town house in, 434; soldiers in Revolution, 132, 135, 153.
Land, grants of, 583; claim laid by town to certain, 547-548; to Cushman, Thomas et als., 629; to Finney, Robert, 545; to soldiers of King Philip's War, 550.
Latten-ware, 209.
Laurel Hill, 180.
Lawsuits: against George Vaughan, 59; against William Shurtleff, 59-60; action for felling timber, 226; action in regard to title to Assawampsett Neck, 225-226; action of trespass, 225; trial of cases, 226, 227.
Lawrence, H. B., 262.
Lawrence, Rev. John B., 469, 474.
Laws concerning, alewives, 502; attorneys, 226; fire, 513; letters, carrying, 268; non-intercourse, 157; settlers, early, 33.
Lawyers, 225-237.
Lazelle, Col., 165.
Leach, Mr., 392.
Leach, Andrew, 376-377.
Leach, Daniel, 464.
Leach, Ephraim, 463.
Leach, George M., 347.
Leach, Ruth, 463.
Leach, Sarah, 463.
Leather, 216, 218.
LeBaron, C., 270.

LeBaron, E. Leonard, 298.
LeBaron, Eugene P., 298, 491.
LeBaron, Frederick N., 298.
LeBaron, J. Baylies, 298.
LeBaron, John B., 298.
LeBaron, Joseph, 159.
Lebaron, Dr. Francis, life of, 336-337.
Lebaron, James, 336; life of, 337-338.
Lebaron, Capt. Joseph, 338.
Lee, General, 170, 171, 180.
Legislature, acts of the, authorizing towns to transport scholars to save expense, 249; banishment of tories and confiscation of their estates, 376; for establishment of a high school, 249-250; to fix standard prices of labor, goods, etc., 222-223.
Leonard, A. H., 296, 301.
Leonard, Archippus, 396.
Leonard, Benjamin, 288.
Leonard, C. H., 297.
Leonard, C. M., 296, 300.
Leonard, Charles E., 296.
Leonard, Daniel, 414; life of, 146.
Leonard, Major and Ens. Elkanah, 154, 204, 227, 438, 571, 572; autograph of, 228; house of, 138; life of, 228-229; slave of, 105.
Leonard, Ephraim, 288.
Leonard, George, 254, 288, 577.
Leonard, James A., 254, 296, 636.
Leonard, John, 461.
Leonard, Jonathan, 413.
Leonard, Capt. Joseph, 200.
Leonard, Molly, 483.
Leonard, Capt. Nehemiah, 202.
Leonard, Capt. Seth, 396.
Leonard, Major Thomas, 437.
Leonard, Prof. Willard T., 257.
Leonard, Capt. Zadock, 414; inscription on gravestone of, 414.
Leonard Cemetery, 637.
Letters: Adams, John, 196; Clarke, Mrs. Rebecca Scollay, 218; Eddy, Hon. Zachariah, 404-405; Fearing, Major, to Col. Ebenezer Sproat, 129-130; Hutchinson, Thomas, Jr., to Elisha Hutchinson, 152; Lincoln, Col. Benjamin, to Capt. Nathaniel Wilder, 163-164; Oliver, Peter, 361; Oliver, Peter, Jr., 150-151, 152; Oliver, Peter, Jr., to Elisha Hutchinson, 151, 152; Pratt, Enoch, to stockholders of Titicut Academy, 259, 261; Town to representatives of General Court, 578-579; Sproat, James, to Col. John Nelson, 421-422; Tomson, John, to Governor Winslow, 7-9; town to Isaac Tomson, 577-578; Winslow, Gov., to Capt. Benjamin Church, 81; Winslow, Isaac, to Gov. Drummond, 435.
Letters, description of early, 269; early methods of sending and delivering, 268; law as to carrying of, 268; rates of postage on, 269.
Lewes, Elizabeth, 635.
Lewes, James, 635.
Lewis, Eleazer, 246, 561, 563.
Lewis, Rev. Fred R., 491.
Lewis Island, 428.
Lexington Alarm, 117.
Lexington, battle of, 109, 114, 156, 392.
"Liberties of Middleberry," proprietors of, 33, 622; list of, 551-552.
Liberty pole, the, 320.
Librarians, 266.
Libraries, 263-266; Philological, 263; Middleboro Social, 263-264; Middleboro Public, 264-266.
Licenses, conditions upon which granted, 319; first granted, 60; to keep an ordinary, 39, 556.
Lighting, method used for, in houses of 18th century, 211-212.
Lightwood, Mr., 297.
Lincoln, President Abraham, 168, 191.
Lincoln, Col. Benjamin, letter to Capt. Nathaniel Wilder, 163-164.
Linen, 30, 214, 308; bounty paid for, 213.
Liquor, uses of, at funerals, 220; by laymen and clergy, 319.
Liquors, used by early settlers, 31.
Litch, Rev. Josiah, 487.
Litchfield, Rev. William C., 491.
Little, Rev. E. G., 466.
Little, Ephraim, 568, 621.
Little, Lieut. Isaac, 616, 621; life of, 617.
Little, Samuel, 622; life of, 624.
Little, Thomas, 551, 564, 609, 628, 629.
Little Lotmen's Purchase, 355; dates when recorded and apportioned, 545; dates when made, 602; deed of, 602-603; names of grantees, 603-604; order of court as to payment of, 603; sketch of lives of purchasers of, 604-608.
Little Quittacus Pond, 419.
Little Round Top, 180.
Littleworth farm, 28.
Livermore, Rev. S. T., 474.
Livesey, Rev. J., 489.
Local militia, 193-205; alarm list, 196; age of men in, 196; annual muster, 198; before the Revolution, 196;

INDEX 705

companies, 194–196; drills of, 193–194; equipment of, 195, 196, 197; first muster in New England, 194; first regiment, 195; influence of, 193, 205; laws in regard to, 194, 196, 205; letter of John Adams in regard to, 196; list of men in the Revolution, 117–119; list of officers, 198–205; record of first company in Middleboro, 198–199; reorganization of, 197; train bands, 196; training greens, 197; village protected by, 193–194.
Long, Ex-Gov. John D., 192.
Long Island, battle of, 125.
Long Point Road, 429.
Long Pond, 419, 580; description of, 428–429.
Lookout Mountain, battle of, 170.
Looms, hand. 214, 308; picture of family loom of the 18th century, 214.
Loon Pond, 419.
"Lord's Prayer," 325; acrostic on the, 326–327.
Loring, Lieut. Southworth, 172, 188.
Lottery, for rebuilding Titicut bridge, 408–409; for support of minister, 465.
Louisburg, siege and capture of, 91; thanksgiving day appointed for, 91.
Love, Hannah, 315.
Lovell, Rev. Shubael, ministry of, 472–473.
Lower Dam mills, 287.
Lower Factory mills, 287.
Lower Green, 311, 317, 318.
Lower Path, 600; description of, 503.
Loweth, Nathaniel, 616, 617.
Lowlands, the, 388–390.
Loyalists, 145-156; attitude toward, 146–152, 156; banishment of, 145, 146, 147; lives of, 147–155; number in Massachusetts, 145.
Lucas, Thacher B., 270.
Luge-poles, 208.
Lumber-mills, at Eddyville, 347; at France, 339; at South Middleboro, 340; at Warrentown, 390; at Waterville, 349.
Lunt, Dr., 239.

MacIlwain, Rev. George E., 491.
Macomber, Rev. George, 487.
Macomber, Corp. Isaac E., 175.
Macomber, John, 461.
Macomber, Lieut. Joseph, 118.
Macreading, Rev. Charles A., 487.
Mad Mare's Neck, 303–304.

Mahuchet Pond, description of, 335.
Mahutchet (an Indian chief), 334.
Mahutchet (Rocky Meadow), 334, 565, 566, 627.
Maine, xxii, 89.
Major's or Five Men's Purchase, 600–602; boundaries of, 548, 600; commissioners to establish bounds, 60; date when made, 545, 600; deed of, 600–601; division of, 548; lives of purchasers of, 601–602; purchasers of, 601.
Malvern Hill, 177, 178.
Manassas, 185; battle of, 178.
Mandamus councillor, 541; appointment of, and effect on colonists, 541.
Manner of living of early settlers, 30–31.
Manomet, 26.
Mansfield, Andrew, 570.
"Mansion house," 328, 448; description of the, 313.
Mantomapact, 610; deed of, 611–612.
Maps: of early purchases of land from Indians, 582; of Middleboro in 1831, xvii; of Middleboro in 1853, vii; of Middleboro in 1855, 1; of proposed division of the town of Middleboro to form a new town with a portion of Taunton, xix; of Judge Oliver's estate and works, 365.
Marion, 540.
Marks, J., killed by Indians, 78.
Marriage intentions to be published, 530.
Marsh, Rev. Proctor, 487.
Marshfield, 122, 145, 147, 168, 561, 582, 600.
Marston, S. W., 263.
Martha's Vineyard, 568.
Martindale's Brigade, 184.
Mason, Albert, 437.
Mason, Chief Justice Albert, life of, 437–438.
Mason, Albert T., 437.
Masonic organization, history of, 631.
Massachusetts, 1, 9, 165, 218, 412, 419; army, 130; call for militia in Revolution, 136; men required and furnished in French and Indian Wars, number of, 89, 91; opinion concerning War of 1812, 157; preparation for War of the Rebellion, 169; ravages of coast in War of 1812, 158; regiments in War of the Rebellion, 171, 184; sends first troops in War of the Rebellion, 169; sheep, number in 1664 in, 214.

INDEX

Massachusetts Bay, 21, 26, 27, 145.
Massasoit, 1, 7, 12, 16, 22, 23, 24, 25, 26, 355, 398, 498.
Matches, use and cost of friction, in 18th century, 212.
Matchlock muskets, 195.
Mattapoisett, 355, 540.
Mattashinnay, 73; execution of, 74.
Maxim, Carlton W., 299.
Maxim, Corp. Elbridge A., 173.
Mayflower, the, 350; picture of, 42.
McBurney, Rev. Samuel, 488.
McClellan, Gen. George B., 178, 179.
McClellan, Isaac, 348.
McCully, 2d Lieut. Andrew, 135.
McCully family (Lakeville), tradition concerning, 434-435.
McCumber family (Lakeville), tradition concerning, 434-435.
McDougall, Rev. C. H., 490.
McDowell's army, 176.
McFarlin, Sergt. H. L., 188.
McLearn, Rev. Alexander, 474.
Mead, Rev. James, 467; work of, 475.
Medberry, Rev. Nicholas, ministry of, 483.
Medicines, 238.
Meerneed, Shute, and Littleworth farms, 28.
Meeting-House Swamp, 387.
Meeting-house at Rock, 334.
Meeting-houses: building pews in, 569; changes in, 569; location of first one, 309, 310-311; provision for erection of, 495; sale at auction of, 311, 567; seats in, 570; used for town business, 495; vote to pay Indians for lumber for, 567; votes to erect, 564, 566-567.
Mendall, Corp. Sylvanus, 175.
Merrill, Rev. J. W., 480.
Merrimac, 170.
Messenger, Rev. E. C., ministry of, 480.
Methodist Episcopal churches: Fall Brook, 486-487, picture of, 303; Four Corners, 487-488, picture of, 488; South Middleboro, 488-489, 636, picture of, 489.
Middleboro, attitude of, towards loyalists, 147-152; banks in, 299-302; boundaries of, xviii, xx, 557, 562; cemeteries, 634-637; cider, 216; civil history (1658-1839), 544-581; destroyed in King Philip's War, 68, 81, 517; division of, proposed, xviii, xix; early purchases from the Indians in, 582-630; education, 245-263; extent of, xvii; fire district, 513-516; flax in, 212-213; fraternal organizations, 631-633; French and Indian Wars, men required for, from, 89; health of, xxii; herring fisheries, 498-503; high school in, 249-252; in the Revolution, 106-144; in the War of 1812, 157-167; in the War of the Rebellion, 168-192; incorporation of, 1, 517, 546; Indian paths, 503-505; Indians, number in, 29; King Philip's War, expenses of, 552-553; known as Middleberry, 29; lawyers, 225-237; libraries, 263-266; men before 1675 in, 33-35, 517-518; men from, xxii; name, origin of, xvii; newspapers, 267, 268; part of Plymouth, xvii, 29, 517; physicians, 238-244; population of, xxiii, 560; postmasters, 229, 270-271; post-offices, 269-271; prices fixed in, 222-223; public officers, 534-543; purchase of, 583; railroads in, 510-512; removal of men from, xxii; removal of men to, 83; resettlement of, 58, 518, 549, 550, 551; roads and highways, 505-510; schoolhouses, 247; schools, 245-263; seal of, 519; settlement, probable date of first, 29, 544; sheep-raising in, 214; social events in 18th century, 217-218; street railways in, 512, 513; town meetings, 495-498; town officers, 517-543, 549; town records burned, 33, 517, 550.
Middleboro Canal Company, 427.
Middleboro Coöperative Bank, 301-302.
Middleboro Loan and Fund Association, history of, 301.
Middleboro ministry, 552, 563, 616, 621.
Middleboro National Bank, 299-301.
Middleboro Savings Bank, 301.
Military drill, 193, 197; annual muster of regiments in, 198; at the Green, 197, 320; first account of, 193.
Militia, Middleboro men in local, 198-205; reorganization of local, 197; state, 196; to constitute part of fire alarm, 513.
Militia in the War of 1812: call for, 158; list of soldiers in, 161-165; of Plymouth Colony, 159.
Militia in the War of the Rebellion: call for, 169; number in Second Regiment, 171.
Militia in the Revolution, 116; local, 117-119, 134-138.

INDEX   707

Militia laws, 194, 205.
Miller, Abishai, 306; life of, 306-307; portrait of, 306.
Miller, Lieut. Alden, 163.
Miller, Capt., Major, Col., and Brigadier-Gen. Darius, 202, 203, 204, 205, 306.
Miller, Elias, 288.
Miller, Francis, 34, 35, 305, 572; life of, 47-48.
Miller, John, 34, 225, 305, 306, 518, 542, 552, 555, 558, 560, 563, 574, 622; life of, 47-48.
Miller, Capt. John, 201.
Miller, John, Jr., 564; autograph of, 48; life of, 48.
Miller, Seth, 306, 308.
Miller, Seth, Jr., 542.
Miller, Thankful, 483.
Miller family, 303, 305, 306.
Miller farm, 305, 307; picture of the old Miller house, 307.
Mills, at Lakeville, 430; at Titicut, 418.
Mills, box-board, cotton, cotton-batting, fulling, grist, lumber, saw, slitting, xxi.
Milne, Rev. Alexander, ministry of, 480.
Mine, discovery of iron (Lakeville), 426-427.
Mine Run campaign, 177.
Ministry, support of, 465; court action in regard to, 552; town action in regard to, 564; Middleboro, 552, 563, 616, 621; Nemasket, 603, 628; Plymouth, 551, 603, 616, 621.
Minor, Rev. Uriah, 489.
Minute men, 196.
Minute men in the Revolution, number of, 114; list of, 119-122.
Missionary Ridge, battle of. 170.
Mitchell, Michell, or Michill, Experience, 551, 563, 603, 609, 616, 621, 628; life of, 660.
Mitchell, Moses C., 262.
Mitchell, Nahum, 376.
Mitchell, Capt. and Sergt. Oreb F., 172, 188.
Mitchell, William R., 300.
Mobile, 170.
Money, 222-224, 577-579; scarcity of, in 18th century, 221.
Monitor, 170.
Monmouth, battle of, 125.
Montcalm, General, 92.
Montgomery, Hugh, 436.

Montgomery, John, 429; slave of, 105.
Montgomery family (Lakeville), tradition concerning, 434-435; land of, 436.
Morey house, description of, 328.
Morse, Jonathan, 560, 563.
Morse, Jonathan, Jr., 564.
Morse, Capt. Levi, 202.
Morton, Lieut., 506, 545, 549, 552.
Morton, Madam, 247, 446; slaves of, 103-104; life of, 274.
Morton, Capt. Ebenezer, 200, 274, 275, 574.
Morton, Ephraim, 563, 604, 622; life of, 606.
Morton, George, 564, 612, 616; life of, 613.
Morton, John, 34, 35, 60, 76, 246, 274, 277, 517, 518, 546, 547, 549, 551, 564, 604, 612, 616, 621; autographs of, 48, 354; life of, 48-49, 354.
Morton, Capt. John, 200.
Morton, John, Jr., 34, 49, 274; autograph of, 49; life of, 49-50.
Morton, John Q., 271.
Morton, Lettice, 48, 621.
Morton, Levi P., 392.
Morton, Livy, 392.
Morton, Lottis, 552.
Morton, Gov. Marcus, 49, 247, 429.
Morton, Marcus, Jr., 49.
Morton, Nathaniel, 9, 247, 546, 551, 563, 603, 612, 616, 621, 629; life of, 48, 606-607.
Morton, Sarah (widow), 496.
Morton, Seth, 275.
Morton, Thomas, 563, 612, 613, 616.
Morton family, 274; slave of, 104.
Morton house, the, 49, 208, 272; description of, 273-275; picture of, 273; tradition concerning, 274.
Morton town, 272-276; houses in, 272-276.
Mount Carmel, 349.
Mount Hope, capture of King Philip at, 85.
Mullein Hill meeting-house, 486.
Mullins, or Mullens, William, 552, 585, 594, 596; life of, 589.
Murdock, Calvin, 396.
Murdock, Lieut. John, 126, 136.
Murdock, Levi, 396.
Murdock, Lieut. Luther, 164.
Murphy, Rev. ———, 494.
Muskets, 144, 194, 195.
Muster, expense of annual, 198.
Muttock (or Chesemuttock), xxi, 1, 2,

3, 147, 197, 210, 247, 248, 273, 274, 307, 355-385, 430, 501.
Muttock Hill, 6, 13, 355, 377, 381.

Nail-rods, 362.
Nails, manufacture of cut, at Titicut, 418; hammered, at Muttock, 377-378.
Namascheuks, settlement of, 398.
Nantucket, 568.
Napoleon, 157.
Narragansett, 26, 45, 550.
Narragansetts, 8, 24, 71, 550; surrender of, 82-83; Canonicus, 193.
National Congress, representative to, 542.
Neighborliness, 319.
Nelson, Abiel, 486.
Nelson, Ebenezer, 431.
Nelson, Rev. Ebenezer: life and ministry of, 484-485; portrait of, 485.
Nelson, Foxel, 573.
Nelson, Mrs. Hope, life of, 420-421.
Nelson, John, 34, 62, 225, 305, 317, 420, 517, 518, 546, 549, 556, 558, 612, 621; life of, 50.
Nelson, Capt., Major, and Col. John, 128, 198, 204, 205, 496; life of, 421-422; letter from James Sproat to, 421-422.
Nelson, John H., 430.
Nelson, Nancy, 287.
Nelson, Ruth, 66; inscription on gravestone of, 66.
Nelson, Samuel, 436.
Nelson, Rev. Samuel, ministry of, 479.
Nelson, Stephen, extract from diary of, 427.
Nelson, Sydney T., 420.
Nelson, Thomas, 66. 474-475, 563, 570, 572, 573; life of, 420, 421; autograph of, 420; life of wife of, 420-421.
Nelson, Thomas, Jr., 573.
Nelson, William, 34, 35, 60, 431, 437, 517, 548, 552, 556, 560, 563, 585, 589, 594, 596, 601; life of, 50-51.
Nelson, William, Jr., 34, 573, 621; inscription on gravestone of, 66; life of, 66.
Nelson's Island, 428.
Nemasket, 17, 18, 21, 24, 26, 83, 440, 498, 500, 547, 608, 628.
Nemasket Gazette, 267.
Nemasket Grange, history of, 633.
Nemasket Hill Cemetery, 220; history and description of, 383, 634; picture of entrance to Hill Cemetery, 635.
Nemasket Indians, 1, 2, 18, 307, 547; burial place of, 6, 13, 355.
Nemasket, ministry at, 603, 628.
Nemasket Path, 627.
Nemasket Pond, 628.
Nemasket River, 1-2, 74, 288, 304, 305, 427, 499, 502, 503, 545, 568, 570, 595, 600, 603, 628.
Nepeof, assistant of Corbitant, 25.
Nevertouch Pond, 636.
New Bedford, 2, 135, 139, 160, 268, 269, 288, 303, 320, 348, 410, 413, 428, 430, 434, 580.
New Bedford stage, 413, 428, 434; route of, 269.
New Bedford turnpike, 412-413, 434, 507.
New Brunswick, 146, 154.
New England, 158, 159, 166, 167, 212, 319, 430.
New England academies, 249, 250.
New England Guards, 185.
New England rum, 207.
New Jersey, 348.
"New Lights," 274, 401, 463, 474, 477; history of, 448-449.
New Orleans, battle of, 167, 170, 173.
New Plymouth, 24, 628.
New Works, 500.
New York, 166, 268.
Newbern, 172, 184.
Newcomb's Tavern, 268.
Newell, Rev. F. C., 487.
Newport, 134.
Newspapers, 266-268; Essay and Literary Journal, 267; first in town, 267; Middleboro Gazette, 267; Middleboro Gazette and Old Colony Advertiser, 267; Middleboro News, 268; Nemasket Gazette, 267; Old Colony Democrat, 267; scarcity of, 268, 319; taverns used as, 266; The Boston News-Letter, 266-267; Wareham Times, 267.
Niles, Rev. Asa, ministry of, 473.
Nimrod, the, 159, 161.
Norcutt, Ephraim, 382.
Norcutt, Mrs. Mary, 370, 382; description given of Oliver Hall by, 371-373.
North Middleboro, 635, 637.
North Middleboro post-office, 270.
North Rochester Parish, 466.
Nova Scotia, 99, 146.
Nye, Benjamin, 563, 593.

Oak Grove, 177. 178.
Oak trees: as boundary lines, 583-584; picture of, 583.
Ober, Dr. Charles S., 251-252.
Occupations, of early settlers, 29, 30; of men, 206-217; of women, 212-215, 216.
Odd Fellows, history of, 632, 633.
Officers, public, 534-543.
Officers, town, 517, 543; before 1675, 517-518.
Officers of court in the 18th century, 226.
Old Colony Democrat, 267.
Old English or Indian Church, history of, 401, 402.
"Old Lights," 401, 477; history of, 448-449.
Oliver, Andrew, 274, 359, 373.
Oliver, Daniel, 359, 373; instructions to, 106-107; life of, 147-148.
Oliver, Judge Peter, 247, 321, 376, 378, 382, 453; autograph of, 363; book-plate of, 366; diary of, 368-370; estate, description of, 367-368; lands of, 383-385; letters of, 361; life of, 147, 359-361, 368-369; plan of estate and works of, 365; Oliver Hall, description of, 362-367, 370-373; portrait of, 363; slaves of, 104.
Oliver, Dr. Peter, Jr., 147, 148, 275, 373, 376, 377; diary of, 148-150; letters of, 150-152; life of, 148, 239; residence of, 374; slaves of, 105, 374; stairs in house of, 373; wedding, description of, 367.
Oliver, Madam Phœbe, life of, 274, 373.
Oliver, William, 373.
Oliver Hall, 104, 217, 218, 274, 275, 313, 320, 431, 453; burning of, 370; description of, given by Mrs. Mary Norcutt, 370-373; description of, 362-367; picture of backpiece in fireplace at, 384.
Oliver's furnace, 360, 378, 396; plan of, 365.
Oliver's slitting-mill, tradition concerning, 361-362; plan of, 365.
Oliver's Walk, 3, 355, 366; picture of, 360.
Oliver's works, 360-362, 378, 381, 382; plan of, 365.
Olustee Station, 187.
O'Neil, Rev. J. H., 494.
Onslow County, 172.
Orchards, 51.
Ordinances, regarding Indians, 41.

Ordinaries: authorized, 319; licenses to keep, 39, 60. 556.
Ordway, Rev. Otis Osgood, 474.
Orr, Col. Hector, 165.
Osborne, Lieut. Selleck, 160.
Otis, James, 106.
Ovens, description of, 208-209.
Owen (an Indian), 629.
Oxen, xxi. 206, 216, 581.

Pachade (Pochade or Pachage) Neck, 570, 594, 602.
Pachusett Brook, 629.
Packard, Rev. Charles, 466.
Packard, Rev. Elijah, 449.
Packard, Rev. William, 487.
Paddock, John, 217.
Paddock, or Padock, Joseph, 574.
Pails, description of, 209.
Paine, Rev. Emerson, ministry of, 455, 456.
Paine, or Pain, Thomas, 551, 609, 622; life of, 624-625.
Palmer, Samuel, 571.
Palmer, Rev. Thomas, 569, 621; inscription on gravestone of, 328; life of, 239, 328; ministry of, 443-445; autograph of, 443.
Pamantaquash (the pond sachem), 9, 419-420; will of, 9-10.
Pamattaqueasson, 568.
Pamunkey River, 180.
Paris, treaty of peace, 139.
Parishes, division of town into two, 447, 460, 462; first, extent of, 309, 448, 459; Halifax, 447, 462; North Rochester, 466; petition for setting off North Middleboro and Bridgewater as a separate, xviii; suit brought against, 445; Titicut, 401, 462.
Parish Burial Ground (Green), 328; description of, 634-635; names of purchasers, 311-312.
Parris, Capt. Sylvanus, 201.
Parsonages at the Green, description of the first one, 313.
Partridge, Partrage, or Partrich, George, 551, 585, 593, 596, 621; life of, 589.
Partridge, or Partrage, James, 593.
Patchwork of the 18th century, 215.
Paths, Indian, 29, 503-505, 600; description of, 503-505.
Patterson, Rev. S. T., 487.
Patuckson, 73.
Patuxet, 21.
Paun, Dr Amos B., 244.
Pawtucket fight, 51, 80.

710　　　　　　　　INDEX

Peabody, E. H., 262.
Peabody, William, 549.
Peace Session, agent to, 572.
Peddlers in 18th century, 216.
Peels, 209.
Peirce, Capt. Abiel, 93, 99, 118, 124; life of, 93, 94, 341.
Peirce, Caleb, 573.
Peirce, Charles F., 272, 278.
Peirce, Major, Lieut.-Col., and Gen. Ebenezer W., 204, 267.
Peirce, Ebenezer, 573.
Peirce, Elisha, 573.
Peirce, Capt. Elkanah, 201.
Peirce, Capt. Ethan, 201.
Peirce, Rev. George, 486.
Peirce, Capt. and Lieut. Henry, 130, 133, 137, 201, 203.
Peirce, Henry, 577.
Peirce, Isaac, Sr., 550; life of, 422.
Peirce, Isaac, Jr., 573; slave of, 105.
Peirce, Corp. and Capt. James, 124, 201.
Peirce, James E., 492.
Peirce, Capt. Job, 127, 132, 201, 282, 496; house of, 423; life of, 422, 423; slaves of, 105.
Peirce, Lieut. John, 94.
Peirce, Lemuel G., 515.
Peirce, Major and Senior Major Levi, 160, 205, 252, 254, 270, 289, 291, 380, 427, 429, 430, 482, 483, 542; life of, 282–283; portrait of, 283.
Peirce, Capt., Major, Lieut.-Col., and Col. Peter H., 13, 74, 164, 200, 205, 254, 283, 288, 289, 305, 493, 510, 511, 581; home of, 285; life of, 283–285; portrait of, 285, store of, 286.
Peirce, Sally, 483.
Peirce, Thomas, 572, 573.
Peirce, Thomas, Jr., 573.
Peirce, Thomas S., 285; bequests of, 265; portrait of, 265.
Peirce, William R., 265.
Peirce, William S., 484, 514.
Peirce Academy, 251, 252–257, 482; students, 252; erection and struggle to maintain, 252–255; cost of, 253, 255; incorporated, 254; trustees, 254; principals, 254, 257; buildings, 252, 255, 256; pictures of, 253, 255, 284.
Peirce Block, picture of, 293; site of, in 1875, 293.
Pembroke, 574.
Peninsular campaign, 176.
Penniman, Josiah F., 297.

Penniman, William O., 297.
Pennsylvania, 91.
Pepperrell, William, 91.
Pequot War, 64, 71.
Pequots, 71.
Perkins, Sergt. A. M., 188.
Perkins, Abraham, 416.
Perkins, Mrs. Ann S., 468.
Perkins, D. Sumner, 410.
Perkins, Lieut-Col. and Col. Edward G., 204, 205.
Perkins, Elijah E., 410, 416, 466; portrait of, 410.
Perkins, Mrs. Elijah E., 466.
Perkins, Isaac, 464.
Perkins, Isaac E., 406.
Perkins, Jacob, 416.
Perkins, Dr. John, 244.
Perkins, John, 468.
Perkins, Nathan, 486.
Perkins, Nathan, Jr., 468.
Perkins, Noah C., 301, 542; life of, 296–297.
Perry, Commodore, 158.
Perry, Rev. Philander, 480.
Pesthouses, 413, 575.
Petersburg, 171, 187; siege of, 170, 178, 180, 187, 189.
Petitions to General Court: by Indians to sell land, 355–358; to build a slitting-mill, 359; to incorporate Titicut, 401; to establish Titicut as separate precinct, 401; in regard to claim of Betty Sassamon, 568, 569; for relief on account of sickness, 570.
Pews, picture of olden time square, 494.
Pewter, 209.
Philadelphia, 114.
Phillips, Capt. Dexter, 202.
Philological Society, 263.
Phinney, Elmer E., 297.
Phinney, Joseph, 463.
Physicians, 238–244.
Pickens, Mrs. Abigail S., 468.
Pickens, Albert G., 273.
Pickens, Capt. Andrew J., 202, 292.
Pickens, Miss Caroline M., 468.
Pickens, Ebenezer, 201, 468, 540, 543; life of, 281, 282; portrait of, 282.
Pickens, George, Jr., 270.
Pickens, Capt. James, 201.
Pickens, James M., 292, 457.
Pickens, Mrs. Mary B., 468.
Pickens, Samuel, 281, 542.
Pickens, Stephen B., 295.
Pickens, Thomas, 460.

Pickens family (Lakeville), 436; tradition concerning, 434-435.
Pierce, Capt. James, 580.
Pierce, 2d Lieut. Job, 122.
Pierson, Rev. Mr., 487.
Pies, 209.
Pig iron, payments made in 18th century in, 221, 224.
Pikes, 195.
Pilgrims, 1, 193, 209, 318, 582.
Pine lumber, 339.
Pine woods, 340.
Pioneers, 197.
Pittsburg landing, 170.
Plague, 1.
Platters, 209.
Ploughs, 206, 216; introduction of first iron, 412; picture of wooden, 67.
Plymouth, xvii, xx, 1, 8, 9, 11, 24, 26, 29, 30, 55, 57, 80, 83, 87, 88, 89, 145, 146, 159, 164, 168, 193, 195, 268, 318, 320, 398, 561, 562, 565, 566, 567, 572, 574, 582, 584, 603, 608, 621, 630.
Plymouth Colony, 15, 16, 218, 221, 355.
Plymouth Colony Court, 533, 534.
Plymouth Colony militia, 195.
Plymouth County, 583; militia of, 159.
Plymouth Court records, 342.
Plymouth laws, 194.
Plymouth ministry, 551, 563, 603, 616, 621.
Plympton, 57, 391, 572, 637.
Pocasset, 80, 561.
Pocasset Swamp, 69.
Pocksha Pond, 303, 419.
Pokanoket, 21, 628, 629.
Pokanokets, 1, 9.
Pokeberry, 214.
Pollocksville, 172.
Pometicon, 7.
Pond Meeting-house, 18, 426, 427, 482, 483; history of, 480-482.
Pondsbrook, Shute, and Littleworth farms, 28.
Pontus, William, 551, 585, 593, 596, 621; life of, 589-590.
Poole, Miss Elizabeth, settlement in 1637 at Titicut, 28.
Poole, Sir William, 28.
Poor, vote to sell at auction, 580.
Poor Richard's Almanac, 321.
Poorhouse Cemetery, history of, 637.
Pope's army, Gen., 178.
Popennohoc (an Indian), 629.
Poplar Spring Church, 189.
Population: changes in, xxi, xxii; increase of, 582; of colony, 29; of town, xxiii, 33.
Poquoy Brook, xx, 28.
Porridge, Indian, 31.
Port Hudson, 170, 173.
Port Royal, capture of, 89.
Porter, Gen., 179.
Porter, Fitz-John, 184.
Porter, James, 305.
Porter, Zachariah, 305.
Porter's Division, 179.
Postal rates, 269.
Postal surveyor, first, 268.
Postmasters, 270-271; first one, 229, 270; Assawampsett office, 270; East Middleboro office, 270; Middleboro office, 229, 270; North Middleboro office, 270; South Middleboro office, 270; Rock office, 271.
Post-offices, 268-271; first post-office, 269; Assawampsett, 270; East Middleboro, 270; North Middleboro, 270; South Middleboro, 270; Rock, 271.
Potomac, army of the, 178-180, 185, 187.
Potter, A. K., Jr., 252.
Pound, 558.
Powder, 196, 212, 573.
Powderhorn, picture of, 144.
Powers, Hiram, 348.
Powers, Dr. Stephen, xiv, 348; life of, 240; slave of, 105.
Pratt, Albert, 407.
Pratt, Corp. Albert H., 182.
Pratt, Alton G., 411.
Pratt, Augustus, 262.
Pratt, Capt. Benjamin, 92, 98, 153, 411, 414.
Pratt, Christopher, 417.
Pratt, David G., 301; gift of, 635.
Pratt, Enoch, 258, 411; gifts of, 262, 265, 490; letters from, 259-261; portrait of, 259.
Pratt, Rev. Francis Greenleaf, 348.
Pratt, George G., 262.
Pratt, Capt. Greenleaf, 164, 166.
Pratt, Herbert A., 411.
Pratt, Isaac, 270, 410, 416; life of, 417-418; portrait of, 416.
Pratt, Jared, 270, 410, 418; life of, 416-417; portrait of, 416.
Pratt, Lucy H., 270.
Pratt, Nathan F. C., 262.
Pratt, Nathan W., 270.
Pratt, Otis, 412.
Pratt, Phineas, life of, 52.
Pratt, Samuel, 34, 35, 564; autograph of, 51; death of, 80; life of, 51-52.

Pratt, Rev. Stillman, 267.
Pratt, William, 270.
Pratt, Capt. William, 413, 414.
Pratt, Zebulon, 258, 262, 498.
Pratt Free School, 258-263, 416; picture of, 260.
Pratt's Bridge, 8, 407-408, 411; wading-place at, 28, 504, 505; weir at, 8.
Praying Indians, 15-20, 401; churches of, 18, 355, 400.
Preble's Farm, battle of, 185.
Precinct Church, The, 437, 574.
Precincts, east and west, 460, 462.
Prentice, Rev. Dwight W., 466.
Prescriptions, 238.
Price, Rev. John W., 489.
Prices: fixed by selectmen, 222-223; of food in French and Indian Wars, 89; paid for labor on highways and bridges, 581.
Priming-wire, 196.
Prince, Gen., 172.
Prince, Nathan, 446; life of, 313.
Prince, Samuel, 227, 313, 446; autograph of, 227; life of, 227-228.
Prince, Thomas, 91, 228, 573.
Prince, or Prence, Gov. Thomas, 545, 551, 563, 596, 602, 622, 628; autograph of, 598; life of, 598.
Prince and Coomb's Purchase, 626; date of, 545; description of, 628.
Princeton, battle of, 125.
Printing-offices at Eddyville, 343.
Prizes given for spinning and weaving in 18th century, 213.
Probate Court, judges of, 542.
Proclamation of Emancipation, 170.
Progress Assembly, R. S. G. F., history of, 633.
Proprietors of the liberties of Middleboro, 33, 622; list of, 551-552.
Proprietors of the town of Middleberry, 550, 553, 559, 563-564, 630; list of, 563-564; to pay debts of Indians, 612.
Proprietors' Meetings, votes of, 562, 563, 564; in regard to inhabitants of town, 563; to divide land, 553; to treat with Indians, 562.
Provincial Congress of Mass., First, dates, meeting-places, and members of, 543.
Public Library, 264-266; picture of, 264.
"Publick Occurrences," 266.
Public officers, 534-543; clerk of County Courts, 542; County commissioners, 543; deputies and representatives, 534-538; judge of Court of Sessions, 543; judges of Probate Court, 542; justices of the peace, 538-541; Mandamus Councillor, 541; members of Constitutional Conventions, 542; members of First Provincial Congress of Mass., 543; members of Governor's Council, 543; Register of Court of Insolvency, 542; Register of Court of Probate and Insolvency, 542; Representative to Congress, 542; Senators, 543; Sheriff, High, 542; sheriffs, deputy, 287.
Pumpkins, 208.
Punkapoags, 71.
Purchade, 394-397, 490, 635.
Purchade Brook, 462.
Purchade Meadows, 394.
Purchade Purchase, 594-600, 629; date when made, 545, 594; deed, 595-596; orders of court, 594-595, 596; lives of purchasers of, 597-600; purchasers of, 596.
Purchases from the Indians: early, 582-630; men appointed to make, 548; map of early, 582.
Purdy, Rev. C. A., 489.
Purses of beads used in 18th century, 215.
Putnam, Rev. Israel W., D. D., life and ministry of, 458-459; portrait of, 458.

Quebec, 268; battle of, 94; death of Generals Wolfe and Montcalm, 92; expedition against, 89; fall of, 92; soldiers of Middleboro in, 89-94.
Quilting-frames, 215.
Quilting-parties of 18th century, 215, 217.
Quincy, 268.
Quincy granite, 192.

Railroads, 510-512; Bridgewater branch, 510; Cape Cod Branch R. R., 511; charter of Old Colony R. R. Corp., 510; Middleboro R. R. Corp., 510; Old Colony R. R. Co., 512; Plymouth and Middleboro R. R. Co., 511-512; Taunton and Middleboro R. R., 511; station built and rebuilt, 512; picture of railroad station, 512.
Railways, street, 512-513.
Ramrods, 196.
Ramsdell, Daniel, 550.
Ramsey, Rev. William M., 491.

Randall, Abraham G., 254.
Ransome, Lemuel, 153, 430; life of, 154-155; picture of house of, 153.
Ransome house, picture of, 153.
Rattlesnake's skin, 193.
Rawson, Rev. Grindal, 18.
Raymond, John, 80; life of, 335.
Raymond Neighborhood, 335.
Raynham, xx, 10. 482.
Raynor, Rev. B. F., 489.
Reade, Solomon, 577.
Reading, Sarah, 315.
Rebellion, War of the, 168-192, 397.
Red Men, history of, 632.
Red River, 174.
Redding, Mr., 414.
Reed, Capt. Apollos, 201.
Reed, Hannah, work of, 216-217.
Reed, James, 460, 564.
Reed, Levi, 14.
Reed, Mrs. Ruth, 468.
Reed, Rev. Solomon, ministry of, 464-465.
Reed, Sylvanus W., 515.
Reformed Methodist Church, 488.
Refreshments: at musters, 198; at raising of houses in 18th century, 207; at raising of meeting-house, 566, 567.
Regiments in War of the Rebellion: number from Mass., 169; Infantry regiments: Second, 171; Third, 171-173; Fourth, 173-176; Ninth, 176; Eleventh, 176-178; Twelfth, 178; Sixteenth, 178-179; Eighteenth, 179-183; Nineteenth, 183; Twentieth, 183-184; Twenty-second, 184; Twenty-third, 184-185; Twenty-fourth, 185; Twenty-eighth, 185; Thirtieth, 185; Thirty-second, 185-186; Fortieth, 187-188; Third Veteran, 188; Fifty-eighth, 188-189; Fifty-ninth, 189; Cavalry Regiments, 189-191.
Relics of Indians, 307.
Religion: in 18th century, 319; of early settlers, 32, 439.
Representative to National Congress, 542.
Representatives to General Court, 561; instructions to, 107, 580; letter in re-depreciation of currency to, 578-579.
Representatives to the General Court of the Province of Mass. Bay in N. E.: list of representatives. 534-538; uniting of Plymouth and Mass. colonies to form court, 534.

Resettlement and settlement of town, 27, 29, 544, 549, 550-552, 582.
Revolution, the, 106-144; action of Middleboro, 106-109; attitude of Middleboro, 115-116; condition of nation at close of, 139; correspondence at time of, 109-115, 129-130; currency during, 221-222; petition against tax, 130-131; soldiers in, 116-128, 130, 132-142; votes of town, 109, 110, 115-116, 142-144.
Reynolds, Alexander, 550.
Reynolds, Electious, 460, 573.
Reynolds, Ephraim, 573.
Reynolds, Isaac, 573.
Rhode Island, 9, 80, 125, 130, 131, 132, 133, 139, 630; alarms, 125.
Rhode Island Road, the, 430; description of, 504.
Richardson, Rev. Samuel, 474.
Richmond, Mr., exhuming of, 400; life of, 400.
Richmond, Bathsheba, 636.
Richmond, David, 496.
Richmond. E. W., 297.
Richmond, Ebenezer, 460.
Richmond, Edward, 460.
Richmond, Hercules, 636.
Richmond, Jonathan, 400.
Richmond, John, 562.
Richmond, Capt. Joseph, 497.
Richmond, Joseph, 563.
Richmond, Lysander, 397.
Richmond, Robert. 574.
Richmond, or Richman, Samuel, 564, 616; life of, 617-618.
Richmond, Seth, 461.
Richmond, Stephen, life of, 155.
Richmond, Lieut. Sylvester, 92.
Richmond, 171, 187, 188.
Richmond Farm, Elisha. 397.
Rickard, or Richard, Giles, Sr., 551, 603, 621; life of. 607.
Rickard, John, 627; life of, 628.
Ring, or Ringe, Andrew, 34, 552, 586, 590, 593, 596, 621; life of, 52-53.
Ring, Eleazer, 593.
Ring, William, 593.
Riordan, Rev. D. C., 494.
Ritchie, John, 382.
Ritchie House: picture of, 382; tradition concerning, 382.
Roach. Nicholas, 466; life of, 436.
Roads and highways, 505-510; court orders, 506, 508, 509; first public, 505; prices for labor on, 581; laying out and repairing of, 506-510.

Roanoke Island, 184.
Robbins, Consider, 468.
Roberts, Rev. Mr., 263.
Roberts, A. J., 263.
Roberts, Thomas, 247.
Roberts' Tavern, 429.
Robeson, Andrew, 510.
Robin's Hill, 334.
Robinson, Everett, 227, 301, 515; life of, 236-237; portrait of, 236.
Robinson, Dr. Morrill, 262, 270, 400; life of, 241, 414-415; portrait of, 241.
Rochester, xviii, 145, 201, 429, 434, 477, 561, 562, 566, 613.
Rochester Path, description of the, 504.
Rock, 197, 251, 334, 467, 477; view of the, 334.
Rock Cemetery, 334; history of, 636.
Rock Meeting-house (Rock), 334, 483.
Rock post-office, 271.
Rocky Meadow, 334.
Rocky Meadow Pond, 334-335.
Rocroft, 21.
Rogers, Sergt. Andrew P., 190.
Rogers, John, 552, 563, 616, 622; life of, 618.
Rogers, Timothy, 573.
Roman Catholic Church, 493-494; picture of, 493.
Rootey Brook, 628.
Rotch, William, 580.
Rounseville, Mrs. Freelove P., 469.
Rounseville, Gamaliel, 430; life of, 377.
Rounseville, Capt. Levi, 130.
Rowlandson, Mary, 355.
Roxbury, 122.
Ruberg, Rev. George L., 474.
Ruggles, Rev. Benjamin, life and ministry of, 460.
Rum, 198, 207, 568.
Running of town bounds, 559-560.
Russell, Rev. P. R., 480.
Ryder, Rev. Freeman, 487.
Ryder, Rev. W. Clarkson, 467

Salem, 218, 335.
Sammauchamoi, description of, 628.
Samplers, 215.
Sampson, Capt. Abiel M., 201.
Sampson, or Samson, Caleb, 621; life of, 625.
Sampson, Deborah, 478; home of, 331; life of, 213, 329-333; portrait of, 330.
Sampson, Capt. Elias, 201.
Sampson, Elias, Jr., 270.
Sampson, George R., 301, 306.
Sampson, H. LeBaron, 262.
Sampson, or Samson, Henry, 551, 564, 603, 609, 616, 628; life of, 607.
Sampson, Isaac, 574.
Sampson, Jonathan, Jr., 330.
Sampson, Capt. and Major Joseph, Jr., 202, 204, 295, 515.
Sampson, Obadiah, gift of, 635.
Sampson, Samuel, life of, 395-396.
Sampson, Walter, 252.
Sampson's Cove, 427.
Sampson's Tavern, 268, 269; history of, 427-428; picture of, 428.
Sassamon, Betty, 427; claim of, 568.
Sassamon, John, 13, 68, 71, 427, 568; death of, 72-73; facsimile of letter of, 72; lands of, 420; life of, 17, 71-72.
Savery, Albert T., 349.
Savory, Nathan, 486.
Savory, Thomas, autograph of, 602; life of, 601-602.
Sawin, Rev. Theophilus Parsons, 459.
Sawmills, xxi, 290, 306, 335, 352, 378, 387-388, 390, 407, 437.
Sawyer, Rev. Rufus M., 459.
Sayer, Rev. Benjamin L., 489.
Scholars, punishment of, in early times, 248.
School District No. 19, 394.
School districts, 245-247, 249; in Lakeville, 437; number of, 247.
School-teachers, 246-248, 250, 251, 252, 564, 569, 572.
Schoolhouses, 247; Bell, 437; description of oldest, 247; old red schoolhouse, 376.
Schools, 245-263; academies, 250-262; boarding, 263; early teachers of, 246, 247; grammar, 245; high, 249-252; summer, 247, 248; winter, 247, 248.
Scituate, 80, 86, 159.
Scollay, John, 276.
Scollay, Miss Rebecca, 276; extract from diary of, 272.
Scott, Rev. Elias C., 487.
Scythes, 207.
Sears, 2d Lieut. David, 92.
Sears, Nathaniel, 270.
Second Baptist Church, Lakeville, 474-477.
Selectmen, 518-529, 538, 547, 549, 567, 568, 569, 570, 573, 580; acts of, 222-223; list of, 520-529; powers and duties of, 518-520.
Senators, list of, 543.
Separatist Church at Beech Woods, 467, 475.
Settlement and resettlement of town:

INDEX   715

court order for, 549-550; first settlement, 582; list of proprietors, 550-552; probable date of, 27, 29, 544.
Settlers, early, xx, xxi, 439, 440; before King Philip's War, 29-67.
Seven Days' Fight, 179.
Seventy kettles, 211.
Shaw, Capt. Abraham, 201, 203.
Shaw, Allen, 13, 270, 291.
Shaw, 1st Sergt. Asa, 173.
Shaw, Ensign Calvin, 161.
Shaw, Corp. Dennis, 175.
Shaw, E. G., 413.
Shaw, Corp. Eben A., 173.
Shaw, Capt. Gaius, 163.
Shaw, Ensign and 2d Lieut. George, 133, 138.
Shaw, George, 626.
Shaw, Jacob B., 270, 291, 301, 515.
Shaw, Capt. James, 201, 203.
Shaw, John, 34, 35, 254, 258, 291, 552, 586, 590, 593; life of, 53.
Shaw, Rev. John, ministry of, 461.
Shaw, Sergt. Orlando H., 175.
Shaw, Ruth, 637.
Shaw, Samuel, 297.
Shaw, Capt. William, 119, 200, 203, 542.
Shaw, Corp. William B., 182.
Shays's Rebellion, 577.
Sheedy, Rev. P. J., 494.
Sheep-raising, 214.
Shenandoah Valley, 170.
Shepard, Benjamin, Jr., 287.
Shepard, Sarah W., 287.
Shepherdstown, 179.
Sheridan, Gen., 185.
Sheridan's raid, 170.
Sheriff, high, 542.
Sheriffs, deputy, 287.
Sherman, Gen., 170.
Sherman, Capt. David, 201.
Sherman, Rev. Isaac, 489.
Sherman, Dr. J. H., 244.
Sherman, Joseph, Esq., 341.
Sherman, Nathaniel B., 290.
Shingle mills: at South Middleboro, 339; at Soule Neighborhood, 351; at Warrentown, 390.
Shingles, 208.
Ships, built, xxi; at Lowlands, 388; at Titicut, 411-412, picture of site of shipyard, 411; at Woodward's Bridge, 388; picture of shipyard from Woodward's Bridge, 388.
Shirley, General, 91, 99.

Shockley's Hill, 420, 481.
Shoe shops: Eddyville, 347; Four Corners, 294-298; Purchade, 397; Titicut, 410-411.
Shoemakers of 18th century, 216.
Shoes, in 18th century, 216, 219.
Short, Luke, 446; life of, 327.
Shot, 573.
Shovel manufactories, xxi, 197; at Four Corners, 288; at Muttock, 378; at Warrentown, 391; at Waterville, 349.
Shovels, 206; "Peel" or "Slice," 209.
Shurtleff, Dr. James F., 244.
Shurtleff, Elder William, 475, 486; ministry of, 477.
Shurtliff, Corp. Gideon, 173.
Shute farm, 28.
Sickness in town, severe (1726), 570.
Signal Hill, 188.
Silk, 215, 218, 219.
Silver, 209.
Simmons, David, 449.
Simmons, John, 626, 627.
Simmons, or Simonson, Moses, 35, 586, 593, 596; life of, 590.
Simonds, Ben, 14; inscription on gravestone of, 14.
Simons, John, 20.
Simons, Moses, 552.
Simpson, Rev. Douglass Hazard, 474.
Singing-schools of 18th century, 217.
Sitting-rooms, 210.
Sixteen Shilling Purchase, 303, 618-626; date of, 618, 619; deed of, 619-621; list of proprietors of, 621-622; lives of proprietors of, 622-626.
Skillets, 209.
Slave question, 168-169.
Slavery, 168, 170.
Slaves, 101-105; anecdotes of, 101-104; disappearance of, 105; number of, 101.
Sleds, 206, 216.
Slitting-mills, xxi; at Muttock, 350, 373, 377, 378; tradition concerning, 361-362.
Smallpox, 341, 413, 575-576; pesthouses, 413, 575; petition for hospital in Titicut, 577; treatment of, 575; votes, 576.
Smallpox Cemetery, Old, 637.
Smith, Dr. A. Vincent, 244.
Smith, Bethia, 315.
Smith, Chandler R., 270.
Smith, Corp. Charles H., 182, 186.
Smith, Capt. Daniel, 201, 270.

716 INDEX

Smith, Dr. Henry Sutton Burgess, life of, 242–243.
Smith, Israel, 271.
Smith, Lieut. James, 125.
Smith, James. 577.
Smith, Capt. John, 21, 201.
Smith, John, 270, 315.
Smith, Jonathan, 572.
Smith, Joseph, 315.
Smith, Ens. Joseph (2d), 117.
Smith, 1st Lieut. and Sergt. Josiah, 118, 127, 132; life of, 338–339.
Smith, Capt. Nathaniel, 116, 200.
Smith, Widow Rhoda, 315.
Smith, Samuel, life of, 340–341.
Smith, Corp. Vanzandt E., 184.
Smith, William, 475.
Snaphances, 195.
Snipetuit Purchase, 303, 615.
Snow, Aaron, 397.
Snow, Anthony, 551, 564, 603, 616. 621; life of, 607–608.
Snow, Dr. George Walter: life of, 244; portrait of, 244.
Snow, Capt. Jabez, 99.
Snow, James, 397.
Snow, Rev. Joseph, 463.
Snow, Loum, 288.
Snow, Loum, Jr., 288.
Snow. Rev. S. P., 489.
Snow, T. Newton, 258.
Snow, Venus, 394.
Snowstorm of 1717, 569.
Soap-making in 18th century, 212, 217.
Social customs of the 18th century, 206–224.
Social events of 18th century, 217–218.
Soldiers in local militia, 198–205.
Soldiers in the French and Indian Wars, 89, 90–95, 99; Capt. Canedy's companies, 90–91; Capt. Pratt's company, 92–93; Capt. Snow's company, 99; Capt. Thacher's company, 94–95.
Soldiers in the Revolution, 116–117; Local militia: First Company of, 117–118; Second Company of, 118–119; Minute men: First Company of, 119–120; Second Company of, 120–121; Third Company of, 121–122; Capt. Wood's Company, 122–123; Capt. Peirce's company, 124; Infantry: First Company of 125–126; Third Company of, 126–127; Fourth Company of, 127–128; Fifth Company of, 128; Capt. Rounseville's Company, 130; Capt. Peirce's Company, 132; Capt. Tupper's Company, 132–133; Capt. Peirce's Company, 133–134; Capt. Churchill's Company, 134; Capt. Washburn's Company, 135; Col. Jacobs's Regiment, 135–136; Second Company, 136; Third Company, 136–137; Fourth Company, 137–138; Fifth Company, 138; Capt. Eddy's Company, 139–142.
Soldiers in the War of 1812, 158–160; 163, 164; Capt. Cushman's Company, 162; Capt. Peirce's Company, 164–165; Capt. Shaw's Company, 163; Capt. Wilder's Company, 161–162.
Soldires in War of the Rebellion, 169–170; Infantry: Second Regiment of, 171; Third Regiment of, 171; Company B, 172; Third Regiment of, 172–173; Fourth Regiment of, 173–176; Ninth Regiment of, 176; Eleventh Regiment of, 176–178; Twelfth Regiment of, 178; Sixteenth Regiment of, 178–179; Eighteenth Regiment of, 179–183; Nineteenth Regiment of, 183; Twentieth Regiment of, 183–184; Twenty-second Regiment of, 184; Twenty-third Regiment of, 184–185; Twenty-fourth Regiment of, 185; Twenty-eighth Regiment of, 185; Thirtieth Regiment of, 185; Thirty-second Regiment of, 185–186; Fortieth Regiment of, 187–188; Fifty-eighth Regiment of, 188–189; Fifty-ninth Regiment of 189; Cavalry Regiments, 189–191.
Soldiers' monument, 192; picture of, 191.
Sons of Liberty, 107.
Sons of Temperance, history of, 631.
Sons of Veterans, history of, 632.
Soule, E. T., 377.
Soule, or Sole, George, 35, 350, 487, 552, 586, 594, 596; life of, 590–591; autograph of, 590.
Soule, Isaac, 350, 542; life of, 351.
Soule, Sergt. J. Horace, 175.
Soule, Jabez, 56–57.
Soule, James, 89, 197, 311, 312, 351, 563, 634; life of, 350.
Soule, Sole, or Soul, John, 225, 312, 350, 351, 554, 559, 560, 562, 563, 565, 566, 593, 616, 622; life of, 350; autograph of, 350.
Soule, John, Jr., 564.
Soule, Otis, 315.
Soule, Sergt. Preston, 183.
Soule, Rufus A., 297.
Soule, William, 351.

INDEX

Soule Neighborhood, 350-351, 575.
South, 168.
South Middleboro, 270, 339-341, 477, 637.
South Middleboro Cemetery, history of, 636.
South Middleboro post-office, 270.
South Purchase, 613-618; meeting of proprietors of, 225-226; date of, 547, 613; deeds of, 614-616; payment for, 615; purchasers of, 616; lives of purchasers of, 617-618.
Southworth, Capt., 545, 548, 595.
Southworth, Capt. Constant, 506, 548, 549, 602, 618, 628, 629, 630; life of, 591, 592; autograph of, 591.
Southworth, Lieut.-Col. Ellis, Jr., 205.
Southworth, Capt. Gideon, 200.
Southworth, Capt. Ichabod, 200, 574.
Southworth, Capt. and Lieut. Nathaniel, 35, 76, 200, 563, 571, 574, 622; life of, 592-593.
Southworth, Capt. Seth, 202.
Southworth, Capt. Thomas, 584; life of, 591-592; autograph of, 592.
Southworth, W. H., 302.
Sparrow, Major, Lieut.-Col., and Col. Edward, 204, 205.
Sparrow, Edward, Jr., 288.
Sparrow, H. P., 301.
Sparrow, James, 459.
Sparrow, John or Jonathan, 552, 563, 616, 622; life of, 618.
Spencer, Gen., 131, 132.
Spinning, 213, 214, 216; prizes given in 18th century for, 213.
Spinning-wheels, 212.
Spooner, Benjamin, Jr., 422.
Spooner, Ebenezer, 274, 276, 373.
Spooner Hill, 276.
Spoons, description of, 209.
Spottsylvania, battle of, 170, 177, 178, 180, 185.
Sprague, Francis, 586, 593, 596; life of, 591.
Spray, Samuel, 9.
Sproat, Capt. Earl, 383.
Sproat, or Sproutt, Major and Col. Ebenezer, 116, 128, 200, 204, 312, 320, 543; autograph of, 322; letter to, 129-130; life of, 322-325; portrait of, 323.
Sproat, Ebenezer, life of, 322.
Sproat, Granville T., 267, 371.
Sproat, Hannah, 432.
Sproat, James, 254, 277, 288, 431, 460; letter to Capt. John Nelson, 421-422.
Sproat, or Sprout, Capt. Robert, 200, 431, 563, 621; life of, 625.
Sproat, Thomas, 325.
Sproat, Zebedee, 431; tradition concerning, 432.
Sproat house, the, 105, 373-374; picture of, 374; picture of stairs in, 373.
Sproat Tavern, 268, 320, 325, 454; description and history of, 318-322; people who gathered at, 320-322; picture of, 319; picture of sign on, 321.
Sprout, Experience, 572.
Spruce Meeting-house, 477.
Squanto (or Tisquantum), 21, 22, 24, 25, 26, 193, 398.
Squawbetty, 72.
St. Augustine, 268.
St. George's River, attack on fort, 90; result of attack, 90.
St. Mary's Catholic Cemetery, 404; history of, 637.
Stage-coach, uses and routes of, 268-269, 319-320, 413, 428, 434, 506.
Stamp Act, 106; copy of stamp under, 106.
Standford, Ens. Robert, 90.
Standish, Rev. Edmund A., 487.
Standish, Ichabod, 462.
Standish, Capt. Miles, 24, 31, 193, 194.
Standish, Phœbe, 462.
Staples, George, 461.
Star Mills, 277, 503; history of, 287-288.
State militia, 196.
Stearns, Rev. George Warren, 459.
Stetson, George W., 227.
Stetson, Capt. Peleg, 433.
Stetson, Sprague S., 431; life of, 433; portrait of, 433.
Stevens, Capt. Isaac, 202, 227, 254; life of, 233.
Stillwater, battle of, 125.
Stillwater furnace, 339.
Stocks, 558.
Stoddard, Rev. Isaac, 487.
Stokes, Rev. Charles, 489.
Stone, Rev. Harvey M., 469.
Stonewall, John, 556.
Stony Point, battle of, 125.
Stores: at Eddyville, 345, 347; at Fall Brook, 308; at Four Corners, 273, 291; at Lakeville, 429, 430; at Muttock, 376, 377, 378; at Rock, 334; at South Middleboro, 339; at Titicut, 410; at Waterville, 349; scarcity of, in 18th century, 216.

718 INDEX

Straw hats, method of manufacturing, 291-292.
Street Railways, 512-513; East Taunton, 513; Middleboro, Wareham, and Buzzard's Bay, 513; New Bedford, Middleboro, and Brockton, 512-513; Old Colony, 513.
Strobridge, Capt. John, 201.
Strobridge, William, 422, 436, 460.
Strobridge Family (Lakeville), tradition concerning, 434-435; land of, 436.
Strong, John, 28.
Sturtevant, Dr. George, 325; life of, 239.
Sturtevant, Isaac, 58.
Sturtevant, Moses, 359; picture of plough owned by, 67.
Sturtevant, Gov. Peter, 388.
Sturtevant, Dr. Thomas, 238, 327; life of, 239, 325.
Sturtevant, Thomas, 378; life of, 325; acrostic on Lord's Prayer, 326-327.
Sturtevant farm, 325.
Sturtevant house, 311, picture of, 315.
Submission men, 157.
Sullivan, Gen., 132.
Sullivan, Dennis D., 227.
Sullivan, John C., 227, 542.
Superb, the, 159.
Surveyors of Highways, 1675, 549; 1682, 555.
Swamps: Beaver Dam. 387; Great Cedar, 386; Meeting-House, 387; Pocasset, 69; White Oak Island, 387, 388.
Swansea, 16, 43, 75, 80, 549, 573.
Sweet, Sergt. Sargeant S., 175.
Swett, Rev. C. D., 480.
Swift, Samuel, 563.
Swine, vote concerning, 570.
Sylvester, H. H., 268.
Sylvester, Harriet B., 300.
Symons, Rev. T. M., 480.

Tack Factory, the (Lakeville), 437-438.
Tacks, manufacture of, in Lakeville, 437; in Waterville, 349.
Tailors of 18th century, 216.
Tallow, 211.
Tamplin, Rev. William, 487.
Tandy, Rev. Lorenzo, 474.
Tanneries: at Soule Neighborhood, 351; at Lakeville, 430.
Taunton, xvii, xviii, 10, 62, 69, 80, 145, 309, 320, 399, 460, 493, 545, 546, 630.
Taunton Academy, 153.
Taunton Path, the, 628, 629; description of, 503-504.
Taunton River, xx, xxi, 2, 22, 27, 80, 398, 399.
Taverns, xxi, 268, 269; Briggs's, 277; Coombs's, 39; Eaton's, 413; licenses, 39, 60, 319, 556; Roberts', 420; Sampson's, 427-428; Sproat, 318-322; in Titicut, 413; Weston, 392-393; Wood's, 272.
Taxes: abatement of, 553; levied on inhabitants, 568; not assessed, 547, 552; paid to colony, 548, 555, 560; remitted by colony, 570; vote to get rebate, 561.
Tea party, the Boston, vote concerning, 109.
Texas, 174.
Thacher, Rev. Peter, 440, 477, 634, 635; slaves of, 101-103; life of, 313; ministry of, 446-447; autograph of, 313.
Thanksgiving, 209.
Thanksgiving Day, 580.
Thatcher, Adelaide K., 266.
Thatcher, Allen C., 291; life of, 289-290.
Thatcher, Charles M., 266.
Thatcher, Rev. Isaiah C., ministry of, 469; portrait of, 469.
Thatcher, Madam Mary, 313, 447; slave of, 105.
Thatcher, Capt. Samuel, 92, 94.
The Boston News-Letter, description of, 266-267.
Third Baptist Church (South Middleboro), 488, 489.
Third Calvinistic Baptist Church, 477-480; picture of, 478.
Third Veteran Regiment, 188.
Thomas, the Interpreter, 629.
Thomas, Capt., 179.
Thomas, Mrs., 225, 359.
Thomas. A. A., 300.
Thomas, Capt. Albert, 202.
Thomas, Amos, 291.
Thomas, Barzillai, 446.
Thomas, (Deacon) Benjamin, 115, 446, 449, 496, 542; life of, 329.
Thomas, Mrs. Betsey, 469.
Thomas, or Tomas, David, xxii, 34, 35, 329, 552, 563, 621, 626, 627; life of, 53; autograph of, 53.
Thomas, or Tommas, David, Jr., 34, 560, life of, 53-54.
Thomas, or Tomas, Edward, 225, 387, 561, 563, 567.
Thomas, Corp. Francis S., 175.

Thomas, Sergt. George B., 182.
Thomas, Corp. Harrison O., 182.
Thomas, Hushai, tradition concerning, 361-362.
Thomas, Deacon Ira, 291.
Thomas, Ira M., 291.
Thomas, Rev. J. S., 489.
Thomas, Capt. Jabez, 200.
Thomas, Capt. Jacob, 202.
Thomas, James (an Indian), 20, 635.
Thomas, Tomas, or Tommas, Sergt. Jeremiah, 198, 560, 563, 568, 569.
Thomas, John, 549.
Thomas, Capt. and Lieut.-Col. Lothrop, 202, 204.
Thomas, Capt. Lothrop S., 202.
Thomas, Lydia, 312.
Thomas, Martha, 486.
Thomas, Capt. Nathaniel, 549, 559, 560, 561, 630.
Thomas, Perez, 82.
Thomas, Capt. Robert M., 202.
Thomas, Lieut.-Col. S., 180.
Thomas, Samuel (an Indian), 356; deed of, 357-358.
Thomas, Capt. Seneca, 175.
Thomas, Capt., Major, and Col. Stephen, 202, 204.
Thomas, Major William, 205.
Thomas, Tomas, or Tommas, William, 225, 560, 561, 563.
Thomastown, 53, 82, 329-333, 335.
Thomastown Cemetery, description of, 637.
Thompson, Lieut., 593.
Thompson, Capt. Amasa J., 202.
Thompson, Dr. Arad, 254, 390; life of, 240; portrait of, 240.
Thompson, Barnabas, 572.
Thompson, Cephas, 389, 415, 452; life of, 389-390; portrait of, 389.
Thompson, Cephas G., 390.
Thompson, Elizabeth, 462.
Thompson, Ephraim, 572.
Thompson, George, life of, 387; house of, 387.
Thompson, Isaac, Esq., 496, 542.
Thompson, Jacob, 571. See Tomson.
Thompson, Jerome B., 390.
Thompson, John, 572.
Thompson, Marietta T., 390.
Thompson, Mary, Sr., 462.
Thompson, Mary, 462.
Thompson, Reuel, 386.
Thompson, Thomas, 462, 571.
Thompson, Venus, 386.
Thompson, Ens. William, 119.

Thompson Road, 386-388.
Thomson, Caleb, 388.
Thomson, Isaac, life of, 386-387; portrait of, 386.
Thomson, Jacob, 387, 388.
Thomson, Capt. William, 580; life of, 388-389.
Thousand Acre Lot, the, 303.
Thrasher, John, 460.
Three Mile Run, the, 187.
Threshing, 216.
Ticonderoga, 99, 115.
Tillson, Granville E., 300.
Tillson, Capt. Sylvanus, 200.
Tilson, Deacon, 327.
Tilson, Ichabod, 349.
Tilton, T. W., 262.
Timber lands, 352.
Tin, 209.
Tinckom, Corp. John, 198.
Tinder-box, description of, 211.
Tingley, Rev. James W., 474.
Tinkham, Abigail, 462.
Tinkham, Andrew L., 270.
Tinkham, 1st Sergt. C. G., 178.
Tinkham, Lieut. Cornelius, 120.
Tinkham, Dennis, 475.
Tinkham, or Tincom, Ebenezer, 34, 445, 560, 563, 568, 593; life of, 55; autograph of, 445.
Tinkham, Tincom, or Tinkom, Ephraim, 34, 35, 76, 359, 552, 563, 593, 622; life of, 54-55; tradition concerning, 54.
Tinkham, Ephraim, Jr., 34; life of, 55.
Tinkham, Isaac, 388, 462.
Tinkham, John, 288, 387, 388, 571.
Tinkham, Capt. Joseph, 200.
Tinkham, Capt. Josiah, 202.
Tinkham, Ens. and Capt. Orrin, 164, 200.
Tinkham, or Tincom, Peter, 563, 594.
Tinkham, Priscilla, 483.
Tinkham, Samuel, 298.
Tinkham, Seth, 448.
Tinkham, Shubael, 359, 571.
Tinkham, Wallace, 267.
Tippicunnicut, 627.
Tippicunnicut Brook, 627.
Tippling, 580.
Tirrell, Rev. Eben. 488.
Tispequin (the black sachem), 9, 10, 73, 81, 83, 86, 307, 602, 610, 613, 627, 628, 629, 630; deeds of, 600, 601, 608-612, 614-616, 619-621; life of, 12-13.
Tispequin Council, O. U. A. M., history of, 633.

720 INDEX

Tispequin Pond, 305, 628; description of, 307.
Tispequin Street Cemetery, history of, 637.
Tisquantum. See Squanto.
Tithing-men, 570.
Titicut, xviii, xxi, 2, 11, 17, 18, 20, 22, 80, 270, 355, 398-418, 440, 469, 498, 499, 553, 568, 575, 577, 583, 584; extent of, 462; made a precinct, 401, 462; settlement at, 28; weir, 28, 409.
Titicut Academy, 258-262; gifts to, 261, 262; incorporation of, 258; teachers, 258, 262; trustee of, 262.
Titicut Bridge, 407, 408-410; lottery for rebuilding, 408-409; rebuilt, 410.
Titicut Cemetery, history of, 635.
Titicut Church, 462-466; description of first meeting-house, 463; description of second meeting-house, 465; first members of, 463; Indian gift of land, 462; lottery to support minister, 465; pictures of, 415, 466; tax, 463.
Titicut Falls, 580.
Titicut Indians, 20, 399, 462, 584.
Titicut Parish, 401, 462, 463, 465, 584, 635.
Titicut Path, the, 8, 553; description of, 504.
Titicut Purchase, 28, 629-630; consideration and date, 629; description of, 629-630.
Titicut River, 602, 629.
Tiverton, 131.
Tobacco, how regarded by early settlers, 319.
Tobey, Charles H., 288.
Tobey, Rev. Leonard, 254.
Tobias, 73-74; deed of, 615-616.
Toll rates, 413.
Toll-gates, 412, 434, 507.
Tolls, 434, 507.
Tomahawks, 70.
Tomblen, Rev. Charles L., 466.
Tompkins, Rev. Lemuel, 487.
Tomson, Sergt., 548.
Tomson, Isaac, letter to, 577-578.
Tomson, or Tompson, Capt. and Lieut. Jacob, 35, 198, 199, 225, 353, 561, 562, 563, 564, 565, 566, 574, 594, 626, 634; autograph of, 352; life of, 352-354; map drawn by, xvii.
Tomson, John, 34, 35, 60, 76, 89, 220, 350, 353, 386, 388, 506, 517, 518, 549, 552, 553, 554, 555, 556, 558, 559, 560, 561, 563, 613, 615, 618, 621, 622, 630, 634; autograph of, 55; inscription on gravestone of, 52; life of, 55-59; picture of gun of, 76; picture of pistol of, 354.
Tomson, John, Jr., 34, 551, 563; autograph of, 59; life of, 59.
Tomson, Peter, 564.
Tomson, Thomas, 89, 564; life of, 354.
Tories, 122, 145-156; banishment of, 376.
Towle, Rev. E. D., 488.
Town clerks, 530-531, 546, 553, 583; duties of, 530; list of, 530-531; salary, how paid, 555; tradition concerning first, 530.
Town hall, new, 265, 498; building committee, 498; cost, 498; date, 498; picture of, frontispiece.
Town house, old, 495-498; committee to build, 496, 497; erection of, 406, 497; law concerning, 495; location of, 496, 497; meeting-houses used for, 495; picture of, 497; plan of, 496-497.
Town meetings, 495-498; abandoned and reëstablished, 495; fine for not attending, 496; votes of, 106, 107-108, 109, 110-111, 115, 142-144, 156, 159, 246, 250, 251, 264, 310, 311, 351-352, 381-382, 392, 495-497, 500-502, 507-510, 553, 554, 555, 556-558, 560, 561, 563, 564, 566-571, 576, 577, 580, 581; where held, 495, 496.
Town officers, 517-533; clerks, town, 530-531; selectmen, 518-529; treasurers, town, 531-533.
Town officers before 1675, list of, 517-518; vacancies in, 518.
Town records, 311; burned, 33, 517, 550; perfecting of, 553.
Town treasurers, 531-533; duties of, 531-532; list of, 532-533.
Townsend, Ens. Abram, 120.
Townsman, men accepted as, 560, 561; men denied as, 564.
Traditions concerning, Betty's Neck, 427; Lakeville families, 434-435; Mad Mare's Neck, 303; Morton, John, Jr., 49; Morton house, 274; Nelson, Mrs. Hope, and an Indian, 421; Ritchie house, 382; settlers, first, 54; slitting-mill at Muttock, 361-362; Sproat, Zebedee, 432; town clerk, first, 530.
Train bands, 195-197; captains of, 202, 203.
Training day, 197, 320.
Training-greens: at the Green, 197, 311,

INDEX 721

320; at Muttock, 197; at Rock, 334,
636; at Warrentown, 394.
Trasher, Samuel, 574.
Travel: early mode of, 32; mode of, in
18th century, 216.
Treasurers, town, 531-533.
Treat, Rev. Mr., 18.
Trees, oak and pine, 583.
Trenchers, 206.
Trenton, battle of, 125.
Trial justice, 540.
Tribou, Isaac, xxii.
Tribou, Melzar, 397.
Tribou, Nahum M., 397, 575.
Tribou, Nahum M., Jr., 397.
Trout Brook, xx.
Tucker, Benjamin, life of, 449.
Tucker, Corp. David A., 175.
Tucker, Major Elisha, 254, 289, 483, 511; life of, 290; portrait of, 290.
Tucker, George Fox, 227.
Tucker, Rev. J. Foster, 491.
Tucker, Sally B., 483.
Tucker, Sidney, 270.
Tupper, Ichabod: autograph of, 124; life of, 124.
Tupper, 1st Lieut. Joseph, 122.
Tupper, Capt. and Lieut.-Col. William, 124, 126, 132, 200, 204; autograph of, 376; life of, 376.
Turner, Rev. Benjamin Francis, 474.
Turner, Rev. Caleb, ministry of, 461.
Turner, Charles W., 270.
Turner, John, Sr., 622; life of, 625.
Turner, Joseph L., 271.
Turnpike, the, 410, 411, 413, 429; description of, 412-413, 433-434, 507.
Twelve Men's Purchase, 303, 610-613; date and consideration of, 610; deed of, 611-612; lives of purchasers of, 612-613; order of court to pay Indian debts, 612; purchasers of, 612.
Twenty-six Men's Purchase, 27, 225, 546, 584-594, 634; agreement of proprietors in 1690, 594; date, 545, 584; deed of, 584-585; lives of proprietors of, 586-593, 594; proprietors of, 585-586, 593-594; new survey made, 594.
Twining, William, 594; life of, 594.
Tyler, Rev. George, 486.

Union Veterans' Union, history of, 632.
Unitarian Society, First, 490, 491; picture of meeting-house of, 491.
United Brethren, 480-481.
United States, 167.

United Workmen, history of, 632.
Universalist Society, 490; organization of, 490; united with Unitarians, 490.
Upper Factory, The, 288-292.
Upper Four Corners, 198, 429-430.
Upper Green, the, 312, 317.
Upper Path, the, 503, 600; description of, 505.
Upper and Lower Works, 291.
Utensils, used by early settlers, 30-31; used in 18th century, 208-209.

Valley Forge, sufferings of army at, 125.
Vaughan, Capt., 572.
Vaughan, Daniel, 563.
Vaughan, Capt. David, 203.
Vaughan, Ens. Ebenezer, 162.
Vaughan, Elizabeth, 634.
Vaughan, Francis M., 227; life of, 237.
Vaughan, or Vaughn, George, 34, 35, 64, 304, 517, 518, 549, 563, 612; autograph of, 59; life of, 59-60.
Vaughan, Capt. George, 200, 291.
Vaughan, Ens. Jacob, 572.
Vaughan, Ens. Jesse, 572.
Vaughan, or Vahan, Joseph, 34, 560, 561, 562, 563, 564, 565, 566, 593, 621; autograph of, 60; life of, 60-61.
Vaughan, Capt. Joseph, 199.
Vaughan's Bridge, 427.
Vehicles used in 18th century, 216.
Vermont, xxii, 305, 335, 392.
Vicksburg, battle of, 170.
Virginia, 187.

Wachamotussett Brook, 630.
Wade, Capt. Amos, 121.
Wading-places, 505, 555; at Pratt's Bridge, 28, 504, 505; at Star Mills, 499, 505; on Taunton River, 505.
Wadsworth, John, 563, 593.
Walker, Francis, 34, 350, 563, 616, 621, 626, 627; life of, 61.
Walker, George A., 297.
Wallen, Frank, 341.
Walnut Plain (Waupaunucket) 304.
Wampatuck, Josiah, 584, 602, 628; deeds of, 399, 584-585, 595-596, 602-603; life of, 11-12.
Wamsutta, 7, 355.
Wanno, Isaac, 407.
War, French and Indian, 88-99, 320.
War, King Philip's, 68, 87.
War, King William's, 88-89.
War of 1812, 157-167, 306, 430; call for soldiers, 158; companies, 160-

166; equipment and discipline, 157; list of soldiers, 161–165; result of, 158, 167; votes of town, 159.
War of the Rebellion, 168-192, 397; call for volunteers, 169-170; causes, 168; companies in, 171-191; expense of, 191; number from Middleboro in, 191–192; soldiers in, 171–191.
War of the Revolution, 106-144.
Ward, Lieut.-Col., Col., and Brigadier-Gen. Eliab, 203, 204, 227; life of, 233-234; portrait of, 234.
Ward, Capt., Major, Lieut.-Col., Col., and Brigadier-Gen. Ephraim, 164, 165, 166, 200, 203, 204, 205, 430, 431, 437; life of, 432; home of, 431.
Ward, Capt. and Major George, 202, 204.
Ward, George, 295; life of, 432–433; portrait of, 432.
Ward house, the, 430, 437; description and history of, 431-433; picture of, 431.
Wardrop, Col., 171.
Wareham, 123, 159, 201, 477, 540. 608, 613.
Wareham Times, 267.
Warming-pans, 211.
Warren, Benjamin, 563, 612, 613.
Warren, Benjamin F., 391.
Warren, Daniel, 635.
Warren, Corp. Henry M., 182.
Warren, Jabez, 34, 35, 390, 593; life of, 66.
Warren, James, 468.
Warren, John, 390, 391, 394; house of, 391.
Warren, Joseph, 34, 506, 553, 558, 563, 604, 621; life of, 66–67.
Warren, Mrs. Margaret, 468.
Warren, Minnie, 394.
Warren, Nathan, life of, 391.
Warren, Nathaniel, 226, 551, 560, 596, 621, life of, 599.
Warren, Richard, 563.
Warren, Capt. Sylvanus, life of, 391.
Warrentown, 390–394.
Warrentown Cemetery, history of, 635.
Washburn, Major, Lieut.-Col., Col., and Brigadier-General Abiel, 203, 204, 205, 254, 288, 377, 378, 379, 427; life of, 380–381; residence of, 381.
Washburn, Capt. and Lieut. Amos, 117, 135, 201.
Washburn, B. Sumner, 295.
Washburn, Mrs. Elizabeth H., 469.
Washburn, Rev. George, D. D., 291.
Washburn, Israel, 463.
Washburn, Rev. Israel, 487.
Washburn, James, 227, 270; life of, 229, 430; house of, 430.
Washburn, 1st Lieut. Jonah, 125.
Washburn, Jonathan, 558.
Washburn, Jonathan T., 490.
Washburn, Leah, 463.
Washburn, Lieut. Linus, 161.
Washburn, Nathan, 227.
Washburn, Nehemiah, 462.
Washburn, Peter, 290.
Washburn, Hon. Philander, 378, 381, 510; life of, 291.
Washburn, Major Philo, 205.
Washburn house, picture of the, 430.
Washing, when and how done, 212.
Washington, 176, 185, 189.
Washington, Gen. George, 115, 125, 146.
Waste, Richard, 460.
Waterman, Abner, 636.
Waterman, Edward H., 394.
Waterman, Hannah, 636.
Waterman, Joshua, 636.
Waterville, xxi, 307, 335, 348–349.
Watson, Col., slave of, 104.
Waupaunucket (or Wappanucket), 304–305; known as Walnut Plain, 304.
Waupaunucket Cemetery, history of, 637.
Weapons, used by first military company, 195.
Weaving, 214; prizes given in 18th century for, 213.
Webster, Daniel. 168, 206.
Webster, Col. Fletcher, 178.
Webster Regiment, 178.
Weeks, Rev. William M., 480.
Weirs, herring, 500, 502: Indian, 2, 28, 359, 498, 499; view of herring-weir, Muttock, 499; votes concerning, 555–556, 568, 570.
Weld, Rev. Thomas, 466; ministry of, 447–449.
Weld, W. F. H., 270.
Wells, Dr. William K., 244.
West Middleboro post-office, 270.
Westgate, Abner L., 487.
Weston, Abner, 376, 391.
Weston, Rev. David, D. D., life of, 414.
Weston, Sergt. Davis S., 175.
Weston, Edmund, 390, 391–392, 448.
Weston, Ellis, 13.
Weston, Henry, life of, 383.
Weston, 2d Lieut. James, 134, 136.

INDEX 723

Weston, John, 110, 111, 391; house of, 391.
Weston, Louis, 378.
Weston, Judge Thomas, 153, 254, 370, 374, 377, 378, 379, 391, 427, 542, 543, 635; life of, 380; portrait of, 380.
Weston, Major, Lieut.-Col., and Col. Thomas, 180, 202, 204, 205, 287, 377, 380, 391, 392; life of, 393; portrait of, 392.
Weston, Zachariah, 254.
Weston Tavern, 268, 392–393; picture of old, 393.
Wetispequin, deed of, 615–616.
Wettamoo, 355.
Weweantitt River, 336.
Weymouth, 268.
Wheat, bounties paid for raising, 581.
Wheeler, Rev. Charles, 254.
Wheelwright shops, 394, 397.
Wheelwrights of 18th century, 217.
Whidden, Rev. Samuel, 487.
Whipping-post, 558.
Whitaker, Ens. Stephen, 91.
White, Capt. Benjamin, 116.
White, Benjamin, 359, 572.
White, Lieut.-Col. Ebenezer, 128.
White, J. A., 299.
White, Joshua, 577.
White, Capt. and Lieut. Peregrine, 51, 551, 564, 596, 616, 621; life of, 599.
White, Resolved, 552, 586, 593, 596; life of, 591.
White, Solomon, 270, 416.
White, Solomon, Jr., 416.
White, Sergt. William E., 188.
White House Landing, 179, 187.
White Oak Island, 387, 388.
White Plains, battle of, 125.
Whitehall, engagement at, 172.
Wicket, Feb, life of, 307.
Wigwams, 3, 355; description of, 2.
Wilbur, Dr. A. C., 244.
Wilbur, Major and Col. Elnathan W., 204.
Wilbur, Horatio N., 397.
Wilbur, Corp. Sidney B., 188.
Wilbur, Simeon D., 270.
Wildcats, 570.
Wilde, William H., 297.
Wilder, Mrs. Bathsheba, 468.
Wilder, Benaiah, 382.
Wilder, Benjamin, 267.
Wilder, Ebenezer, 382–383.
Wilder, James D., 468.
Wilder, Capt. Nathaniel, 61, 200, 203.
Wilder, Capt. Nathaniel, Jr., 161, 163, 200; letter to, 163–164.
Wilder, Rev. Otis, 487.
Wilderness, battle of the, 170, 177, 178, 185.
Wilks, Francis, 571, 572.
Willard, Rev. Elijah, 487.
Willett, Capt. Thomas, 43.
Williams, Rev. Elmer S., 485.
Williams, Capt. John, 558.
Williams, Roger, 31.
Williamsburg, 176, 187.
Willis, Nathan E., 258.
Willoughby, J. H., 251.
Wills, Zephaniah, 464.
Wilson, Abraham, 288.
Wilson, Hon. Henry, 184.
Winchester, Rev. George H., Sr., 487.
Winchester, Rev. George H., Jr., 487.
Wine, 568.
Winnetuxet River, xviii, 44, 602.
Winslow, Gen., 93, 99.
Winslow, Gov., 15, 22, 26, 398.
Winslow, Deborah, 486.
Winslow, Edward (Governor), 99, 376, 398, 486.
Winslow, Gilbert W., 602.
Winslow, John, 552, 596, 616, 621; life of, 600.
Winslow, John, Jr., 602, 628.
Winslow, Major Josiah, 545, 551, 563, 594, 596, 610, 611, 621, 629; life of, 599–600.
Winslow, Josiah W., 602.
Winslow, Josias, 226.
Winslow, Kenelme, 602.
Winslow, Pelham, 227.
Winthrop, Gov., 209.
Winthrop, John, Jr., expedition up Taunton River in 1636, 27; letter to his father, 27–28.
Witherbee, Alanson, 287.
Wolfe, Gen., death of, 92, 94.
Wolftrap Hill, 350.
Woman's Relief Corps, history of, 634.
Wood, Capt. Abiel, 202.
Wood, Deacon Abiel, 103, 247.
Wood, Abiel, 563.
Wood, Mrs. Abigail W., 468.
Wood, Andrew M., 301.
Wood, Benjamin, 89, 552, 560, 621; life of, 625–626.
Wood, Lieut.-Col. Benjamin P., 205; life of, 304–305; portrait of, 304.
Wood, Caleb, xxii.
Wood, Rev. Charles W., life of, 280–281; portrait of, 280.

Wood, Cornelius B., 301, 355.
Wood, Cyrus, slave of, 103.
Wood, Daniel, 570.
Wood, 1st Lieut. Daniel F., 175.
Wood, David, 34, 552, 555, 560, 564, 621; life of, 67.
Wood, Miss Eleanor B., 469.
Wood, Eleazer, xxii.
Wood, Mrs. Elizabeth, 469.
Wood, Miss Emily T., 468.
Wood, Ephraim, 246, 307, 446; life of, 63.
Wood, Sergt. Frederick E., 175.
Wood, George W., 410.
Wood, Henry, 34, 35, 76, 359, 387, 517, 604, 608, 626; life of, 61-62; tradition concerning, 54.
Wood, Horatio G., 287, 427, 457, 468; life of, 285-286.
Wood, Ichabod, 577.
Wood, Capt. Isaac, 120.
Wood, Israel, 577.
Wood, Rev. J. A., 489.
Wood, Rev. J. E., 480.
Wood, James, 225, 560, 563, 626, 627.
Wood, John or Jonathan, 34, 552, 577, 604, 612, 621; life of, 62.
Wood, Joseph, 34, 552, 621; life of, 63.
Wood, (Deacon) Joseph T., 484, 543; life of, 279-280; portrait of, 279.
Wood, Ens. Lemuel, 121.
Wood, Capt. Lemuel, 203.
Wood, Levi, 272.
Wood, Lorenzo, 54, 267, 499, 581.
Wood, Mary, 462.
Wood, Capt. Nathaniel, 116, 117, 122, 200.
Wood, Nathaniel, xxii.
Wood, Samuel, 34, 60, 62, 446, 518, 556, 560, 561, 563, 571, 572, 593, 621; autograph of, 63; life of, 63.
Wood, Samuel, Jr., autograph of, 63; life of, 63.
Wood, Silas, 272, 273, 288; picture of house of, 272.
Wood, Timothy, 462.
Wood, Judge Wilkes, 227, 254, 277, 278-279, 288, 542; life of, 229-230; portrait of, 230; picture of office of, 237; picture of house of, 278.
Wood, William H., 227, 265, 542; life of, 234-236; portrait of, 235.
Wood, William W., 313.
Wood, Capt. Zenas, 339.
Wood, 206, 209.
Wood Cemetery, history of the, 636.
Wood's Pond, 307.
Wood's Purchase, 63, 608-610, 626; date and consideration of, 608; deeds of, 608, 609-610.
Wood's Tavern, 272.
Woodbridge, Rev. Richard G., 469.
Woods, Jonathan, 463.
Woodstock, Vt., removal of families to, xxii.
Woodward's Bridge, 388.
Wool, preparation, spinning and uses of, in 18th century, 213, 214.
Wool goods, 213, 214, 218, 308.
Workhouses, 577.
Worm, 196.
Worsted, 213.
Wright, or Right, Adam, 34, 225, 563, 593, 616, 621; life of, 63, 64.
Wright, Lieut. Benjamin, 90.
Writhington, Miss Hope, 469.

Yarn, 214.
Yellow fever, 184.
Yokes, 206.
York, England, xvii.
Yorktown: victory at, in Revolution, 139; siege of, in Rebellion, 171, 176.
Young Ladies' School, 263.
Young Men's Christian Association, 264, 494.

Zacheus, the Indian, 570.

The Riverside Press
Electrotyped and printed by H. O. Houghton & Co.
Cambridge, Mass., U. S. A.

LIBRARY OF CONGRESS

0 014 078 799 1

CPSIA information can be obtained
at www.ICGtesting.com
Printed in the USA
BVHW042045240222
629779BV00015B/194